ROTHMANS ENCYCLOPAEDIA OF WORLD FOOTBALL

ROTHMANS ENCYCLOPAEDIA OF WORLD FOOTBALL

EDITED BY JACK ROLLIN

WH SMITH
EXCLUSIVE
· BOOKS ·

A QUEEN ANNE PRESS BOOK

First published in Great Britain in 1990 by
Queen Anne Press, a division of
Macdonald & Co (Publishers) Ltd
Orbit House
1 New Fetter Lane
London EC4A 1AR

This edition first published exclusively for W. H. Smith Ltd by Queen Anne Press
A member of Maxwell Macmillan Pergamon Publishing Corporation

ISBN 0-356-18918-X

Typeset by MS Filmsetting Limited, Frome
Printed and bound in Great Britain by Butler & Tanner Ltd, Frome

Contents

Origins

Propelling an object, preferably round, or at least resembling a spherical shape, using a foot is such a basic instinct that it is not surprising that claims for the discovery of the game can go back for centuries. Indeed, the most likely source of anything that could be loosely connected with football probably dates back to China around 200 BC or perhaps even earlier. There, a game known as *tsu chu* has been thoroughly researched by Professor H.A. Giles, classical and antiquarian writer and Professor of Chinese at Cambridge University. He discovered that a leather ball was used and there was some evidence to imply that emphasis was placed on dribbling. The Japanese game of *kemari*, which was played c.600 BC, has also been suggested as a forerunner.

The handling code, which developed as rugby football, can find its formative years in the Greek *episkyros* and the Roman *harpastum*. They have been more closely associated with rugby, rather than soccer, simply because carrying the ball was a feature of both games. Similarly, the medieval mob football, which often surrounded Shrovetide games played in many parts of the country, also involved handling the ball in moving it across the countryside.

There were a number of attempts to ban these wideranging pursuits, notably in the first instance by Edward II in 1314. But the peasants and labourers carried on with them in some form or other until the practice virtually died out in the 18th century.

It was only in the early years of the 19th century that the beginnings of a more organised and acceptable form of the game developed in the public schools and then the universities. Indeed, it was at Cambridge where the earliest attempts to adopt a uniform code of rules were made in 1848. Oxford, not to be outdone, subsequently led the way on the field. In all, they appeared in six FA Cup semi-finals, four finals and even won the trophy once in 1874.

It was also at Oxford that the term 'soccer' is said to have arisen from the habit prevalent at the University of adding 'er' to certain words like togs (toggers), swots or mugs (swotters or muggers). Towards the end of the 19th century the game was always referred to as Association Football, to differentiate it from rugby football. At Oxford they took the 'soc' out of 'Association' and then turned this into 'soccer'. The creation of the word is often attributed to one of Oxford's most famous internationals, Charles Wreford Brown. When asked one day whether he was going to play rugger, he replied: 'No – soccer.'

The Harrow School football team ready for action in the 1860s. Clearly, the game was very different then!

Milestones

1848 The first rules drawn up at Cambridge University.

1855 Sheffield, the oldest soccer club still in existence, founded.

1862 Notts County, the oldest Football League club, was said to have been founded. It has since been discovered that the club was put on a firm basis from 1864 only.

1863 Football Association formed in London on 26 October.

1865 Tape stretched across the goals 8ft (2.4m) from the ground.

1866 Offside rule altered to allow a player to be onside when three of opposing team are nearer their own goalline. Fair catch rule omitted.

1867 Queen's Park, the oldest Scottish club, founded.

1869 Kick-out rule altered and goal kicks introduced.

1871 FA Cup introduced. Goalkeepers first mentioned in Laws.

1872 First official international between England and Scotland in Glasgow; result: 0–0. The Wanderers win the FA Cup final. Corner kick introduced.

1873 Scottish FA formed and the start of the Scottish Cup.

1874 Oxford and Cambridge meet for the first time. Umpires first mentioned in Laws. Shinguards introduced.

1875 The crossbar replaces tape on the goalposts.

1876 FA of Wales formed. First international between Scotland and Wales.

1877 The London Association and the Sheffield Association agree to use the same rules. A player may be charged by an opponent if he is facing his own goal. Welsh Cup introduced.

1878 Referees use a whistle for the first time.

1879 First international between England and Wales. Cliftonville, the oldest Irish club, founded.

1880 Irish FA formed and the start of the Irish Cup.

1882 Ireland's first internationals with Wales and England. International Football Association Board set up. Two-handed throw-in introduced; handling rule of 1881 rescinded.

1883 First international between Scotland and Ireland. The first British International Championship.

1885 Professionalism legalised in England. Arbroath beat Bon Accord 36–0 in Scottish Cup, a record score for an official first-class match.

1886 International caps first awarded.

1887 Record FA Cup score: Preston North End 26, Hyde United 0.

1888 Football League formed.

William McGregor from Aston Villa, founder of the Football League.

Aston Villa clinch the double in the Cup final of 1897 at Crystal Palace against Everton.

1889 Preston North End achieve the League and FA Cup 'double'.

1890 Scottish League formed. Irish League formed. Goal nets invented.

1891 Referees and linesmen replace umpires. Penalty kick introduced.

1892 Division Two of the Football League formed. Penalty-taker must not play the ball twice; extra time allowed for taking a penalty. Goal nets used in the FA Cup final for the first time. Inter-League matches started.

1893 Scotland adopts professionalism.

1894 Division Two of the Scottish League formed. First FA Amateur Cup final. Referee given complete control of the game; unnecessary for players in future to appeal to him for a decision. Goalkeeper can be charged only when playing the ball or obstructing an opponent.

1895 FA Cup stolen from a Birmingham shop window; it was never recovered. Goalposts and crossbars must not exceed 5in (127mm) in width. Player taking throw-in must stand on touchline.

1897 Aston Villa win both the League and the FA Cup. The Corinthians tour South America. The word 'intentional' introduced into the Law on handling.

1898 Players' Union first formed.

1899 Promotion and relegation between divisions first used in the Football League, replacing Test Matches.

1901 Maximum wage rule brought in. Tottenham Hotspur become first London-based professional club to win the FA Cup and the last non-League side to do so, as members of the Southern League. First six-figure attendance: 110,802 at FA Cup final.

1902 Terracing collapses during the Scotland v England match at Ibrox Park, killing 25. Welsh League formed.

1904 FIFA formed in Paris on 21 May with seven members.

1905 England joins FIFA. First £1,000 transfer: Alf Common, Sunderland to Middlesbrough. First international in South America: Argentina v Uruguay.

1907 Amateur FA formed. Players' Union reformed.

1908 England play in Vienna, their first international against a foreign side. The first official Olympic soccer tournament in London, won by the United Kingdom. Transfer fee limit fixed at £350, then scrapped. FA Charity Shield started.

1910 Scotland, Wales and Ireland join FIFA.

1912 Goalkeeper not permitted to handle ball outside his own penalty area.

1913 Defending players not to approach within 10 yards of the ball at a free kick.

1914 Defending players not to approach within 10 yards of ball at corner kick.

1916 Entertainment tax introduced. South American Championship first held.

1920 Division Three (Southern Section) of the Football League formed. Players cannot be offside at a throw-in.

1921 Division Three (Northern Section) formed.

1922 Promotion and relegation introduced in the Scottish League.

1923 First FA Cup final at Wembley; Bolton beat West Ham before a crowd of 126,047, though many more thousands gain admittance without paying. Football pools introduced.

1924 First international at Wembley: England v Scotland. A goal may be scored direct from a corner kick.

1925 Offside Law changed to require two instead of three defenders between attacker and goal. Player taking throw-in must have both feet on touchline.

1926 Huddersfield Town achieve the first hat-trick of League Championships.

1927 Cardiff City take the FA Cup out of England for the first time; it is the first final to be broadcast on the radio. Earlier Arsenal v Sheffield United had been the first League game covered by the wireless.

1928 British Associations leave FIFA over broken-time payments to amateurs. First £10,000 transfer: David Jack, Bolton to Arsenal. Dixie Dean scores 60 goals for Everton in Division One, a Football League record.

1929 England lose 4–3 to Spain in Madrid, their first defeat on the Continent. Goalkeeper compelled to stand still on his goalline at penalty kick.

1930 Uruguay win the first World Cup in Montevideo, Uruguay. Frederick Wall, Secretary of the FA, knighted.

1931 Scotland lose 5–0 to Austria in Vienna, their first defeat on the Continent. Goalkeeper permitted to carry ball four steps instead of two. Instead of free kick after a foul throw-in, the ball reverts to opposing side.

1933 Numbers worn for the first time in the FA Cup final, but from 1–22.

1934 Stanley Rous becomes FA Secretary.

1935 Arsenal equal Huddersfield's hat-trick of League Championships. Experiments carried out for two referees in one match.

1936 Dixie Dean overhauls Steve Bloomer's 352 League goals. Joe Payne scores 10 goals for Luton against Bristol Rovers. Defending players not permitted to tap the ball into goalkeeper's hands from a goal kick.

1937 A record crowd of 149,547 watch the Scotland v England international at Hampden Park. Defending players not permitted to tap the ball into goalkeeper's hands from free kick inside penalty area. Weight of ball increased from 13–15oz (368–425g) to 14–16oz (397–454g). Arc of circle 10yd (9m) radius from penalty spot to be drawn outside penalty area.

1938 Laws of the Game redrafted by Stanley Rous. Jimmy McGrory retires after scoring 550 goals in first-class football in Scotland.

1939 First six-figure attendance for a League match: Rangers v Celtic 118,567. Compulsory numbering of players in Football League.

1946 British Associations rejoin FIFA. Burnden

Uruguay score in their 4–2 victory over Argentina in the first World Cup final in front of a delighted home crowd of approximately 90,000.

Hungary celebrate a goal on the way to their historic 6–3 victory over England at Wembley in 1953.

Park tragedy: 33 killed and over 400 injured during an FA Cup tie between Bolton and Stoke.

1949 England are beaten 2–0 by the Republic of Ireland at Goodison Park, first home defeat against a team outside British Championship. Stanley Rous knighted. Rangers win the first 'treble': Scottish League, Scottish Cup and League Cup. Superga air disaster near Turin, killing all on board including Italian champions Torino.

1950 England suffer humiliating defeat at the hands of the USA in the World Cup. Scotland's unbeaten home record against foreign opposition ends in defeat by Austria. Record crowd 203,500 for the last game in the World Cup tournament in Rio between Uruguay and Brazil.

1951 Obstruction included as an offence punishable by indirect free kick. White ball officially recognised. Studs must project $\frac{3}{4}$in (19mm) instead of $\frac{1}{2}$in (13mm) under football boots.

1952 Newcastle United retain the FA Cup, the first club to do so in the 20th century.

1953 England lose their unbeaten home record against Continental opposition, 6–3 to Hungary at Wembley.

1954 England suffer their heaviest defeat, beaten 7–1 by Hungary in Budapest.

1955 European Cup of the Champions and Inter-Cities Fairs Cup started.

1956 Real Madrid win the European Cup. First floodlit League match in England: Portsmouth v Newcastle United.

1957 Entertainment tax withdrawn.

1958 Munich air disaster: eight Manchester United players killed. Division Four created in Football League from regional Divisions Three.

1959 Football League establish fixtures copyright; pools must pay for use.

1960 USSR win first European Nations Cup in Paris. Real Madrid win European Cup for fifth consecutive time.

1961 Sir Stanley Rous becomes President of FIFA. Tottenham Hotspur win the League and Cup, the first 'double' of the 20th century. The Professional Footballers' Association succeed in achieving the abolition of the maximum wage. First British player to earn £100 a week: Johnny Haynes (Fulham). First £100,000 British transfer: Denis Law, Manchester City to Torino. Fiorentina win the first European Cup-Winners' Cup.

Denis Law shows why he twice broke the transfer record as he moves past Bobby Moore.

1962 Law makes it back, this time to Manchester United for £115,000, record fee for a British club.

1963 The Football League's retain and transfer system declared illegal in High Court test case. Tottenham Hotspur win the European Cup-Winners' Cup, the first British success in Europe. Season extended to May because of severe weather; pools panel instituted.

1964 More than 300 killed and 500 injured after rioting during an Olympic qualifying game in Lima between Peru and Argentina. First televised 'Match of the Day' on BBC2: Liverpool v Arsenal.

1965 Stanley Matthews becomes the first footballer to be knighted, in his farewell season. Arthur Rowley retires having scored 434 Football League goals, a record. The Football League agree to substitutes for one injured player per team. Ten players jailed and banned for life by the FA for match-fixing.

1966 England win the eighth World Cup at Wembley. The League allows substitutes for any reason.

1967 Alf Ramsey, England's team manager, knighted. Celtic become the first Scottish club to win the European Cup.

1968 Manchester United win the European Cup; manager Matt Busby knighted. Leeds United become the first British club to win the Fairs Cup.

1970 Brazil win the ninth World Cup in Mexico and the Jules Rimet Trophy outright after their third such success.

1971 Ibrox Park disaster: 66 killed at Rangers v Celtic match. Arsenal achieve the League and Cup 'double'.

1973 Johan Cruyff becomes the first £1 million transfer, moving from Ajax to Barcelona for £922,300. Football League introduce three up and three down promotion/relegation between top three divisions and four up and down between bottom two divisions.

1974 Joao Havelange of Brazil replaces Sir Stanley Rous as President of FIFA. League football played on a Sunday for the first time in industrial and fuel restriction crisis. FA Amateur Cup ended.

1975 Leeds United banned from competing in Europe for two seasons in the next four, after fans riot in the European Cup final in Paris. Scottish Premier Division introduced.

1976 The Football League abandon 'goal average', introducing 'goal difference'.

1977 Liverpool achieve their tenth League title and win the European Cup as well. Kevin Keegan transferred from Liverpool to Hamburg for £500,000, the highest fee involving a British club.

1978 Freedom of contract for players accepted by Football League, who also introduce Transfer Tribunal.

1979 Trevor Francis, transferred from Birmingham City to Nottingham Forest for £1 million, breaks the record for a single transfer involving British clubs and is the first to move for a seven-figure fee.

1981 Tottenham Hotspur win the 100th FA Cup. Liverpool win the European Cup for the third time. Football League award three points for a win instead of two. First artificial pitch for a Football League club installed at Queen's Park Rangers.

1982 League Cup is sponsored by the Milk Marketing Board as the Milk Cup.

Ricky Villa scores the first goal in the replayed 100th FA Cup final, sending Spurs on their way to a 3–2 triumph.

1983 Football League sponsored for the first time by Canon, Japanese camera and business equipment manufacturers, in three-year deal. League clubs vote to keep their home match receipts.

1984 British International Championship ends. FA National School opens at Lilleshall. Britain's highest score this century: Stirling 20, Selkirk 0 in Scottish Cup.

1985 Valley Parade tragedy: 56 killed and more than 200 injured in a fire. First £1 million receipts from match in Britain at FA Cup final; Kevin Moran (Manchester United) becomes the first player sent off in the fixture. Celtic win 100th Scottish Cup final. Rioting Liverpool supporters at European Cup final at the Heysel Stadium, Brussels cause 39 deaths (31 of them Italian) and 437 injuries before match with Juventus. English clubs banned from European competition. Charlton Athletic move to Selhurst Park to share Crystal Palace's ground.

1986 Football League clubs agree to reduce First Division to 20 by 1988 with no overall loss of membership. Juventus agree to pay Liverpool £3.2 million for Ian Rush with effect from 1987, record fee for British player. Death of Sir Stanley Rous at 91. Two substitutes allowed in FA Cup and Littlewoods-sponsored League Cup matches. Luton ban away supporters. Bristol Rovers share Bath City's ground, Twerton Park. Football League sponsored by *Today* newspaper. Football League voting majority for rule changes reduced from $\frac{3}{4}$ to $\frac{2}{3}$. Two-season Football League TV deal at £6.2 million. Clyde move in with Partick Thistle at Firhill Park.

1987 *Today* drop their Football League sponsorship, but are replaced by Barclays Bank. First Division reduced to 21 clubs. Two substitutes approved by Football League. Red and yellow disciplinary cards reintroduced after six years.

1988 B & Q replace Fine Fare, sponsors of the Scottish League for the past three years. Football League's First Division reduced to 20 clubs. New TV deal provides £44 million over four years for the Football League from ITV, £30 million over five years from BBC/BSB for FA Cup.

1989 Hillsborough disaster: 95 killed at FA Cup semi-final between Liverpool and Nottingham Forest. Arsenal win closest League Championship race by scoring more goals than Liverpool, their last match opponents and victims; both teams had identical points and goal difference.

1990 Swindon Town, demoted from First to Third Division following irregular payments, allowed to stay in Division Two after appealing to the FA. Players level no longer to be given offside. England fourth in the World Cup. Rumbelows sponsor the League Cup for £5 million over four years. Chester City share Macclesfield's ground. Manchester United and Aston Villa allowed back into European competition.

English Clubs

Aldershot

Address: Recreation Ground, High Street, Aldershot GU11 1TW
Record Crowd: 19,138 v Carlisle U, FA Cup 4th round replay, 28 January 1970
Stadium Capacity: 12,000
Year Formed: 1926
Colours: Red shirts with blue trim, blue shorts, red socks with blue trim
Joined League: 1932 Elected to Division 3 (South)
Honours Highest Placing: 8th, Division 3, 1973–74.

Have twice achieved promotion from the Fourth Division in 1973 and 1987. In their first season in Division Three (South) they reached the fifth round of the FA Cup and again in 1978–79 when involved in a replayed tie.

Arsenal

Address: Arsenal Stadium, Highbury, London N5 1BU
Record Crowd: 73,295 v Sunderland, Division 1, 9 March 1935
Stadium Capacity: 47,193
Year Formed: 1886
Colours: Red shirts with white sleeves, white shorts, red socks with white trim
Joined League: 1893 Elected to Division 2
Honours: Division 1 Champions: 1930–31, 1932–33, 1933–34, 1934–35, 1937–38, 1947–48, 1952–53, 1970–71, 1988–89. FA Cup winners: 1930, 1936, 1950, 1971, 1979. League Cup winners: 1987. European Fairs Cup winners: 1970.

Enjoyed their most successful period during the 1930s when they won five First Division titles and the FA Cup twice. The appointment of Herbert Chapman as manager in 1925 transformed them, though he died in 1934 and was unable to see his work completed. In 1970–71 they achieved the League and Cup double, while their ninth Championship came after a dramatic last match in 1988–89. They won 2–0 at Liverpool to wrest the title by the closest of margins: more goals scored after both teams had finished with the same points and goal difference.

The dynamic and prolific Ted Drake inspired Arsenal towards three titles in the 1930s.

Aston Villa

Address: Villa Park, Trinity Road, Birmingham B6 6HE
Record Crowd: 76,588 v Derby Co, FA Cup 6th round, 2 March 1946
Stadium Capacity: 42,039
Year Formed: 1874
Colours: Claret and blue shirts, white shorts, blue socks
Joined League: 1888 Founder members of the Football League
Honours: Division 1 Champions: 1893–94, 1895–96, 1896–97, 1898–99, 1899–1900, 1909–10, 1980–81. Division 2 Champions: 1937–38, 1959–60. Division 3 Champions: 1971–72. FA Cup winners: 1887, 1895, 1897, 1905, 1913, 1920, 1957 (Seven wins – a record held with Tottenham H and Manchester U). League Cup winners: 1961, 1975, 1977. European Cup winners: 1982. European Super Cup winners: 1983.

Were the second club to perform the League and Cup double in 1896–97. Of their seven Championships and seven FA Cup successes, all but one of each were achieved before 1921. Although most of their Football League career has been spent in the First and Second Divisions, they had two seasons in Division Three from 1970 to 1972. Their finest achievement in Europe was to win the European Champion Clubs Cup in 1981–82.

Barnsley

Address: Oakwell Ground, Grove Street, Barnsley S71 1ET
Record Crowd: 40,255 v Stoke C, FA Cup 5th round, 15 February 1936
Stadium Capacity: 30,099
Year Formed: 1887
Colours: All red
Joined League: 1898 Elected to Division 2
Honours: Division 3 (North) Champions: 1933–34, 1938–39, 1954–55. FA Cup winners: 1912.

Did not lose their Second Division status until 1932, but had their most prominent period in the years before the First World War. They finished third in 1914–15 after winning the FA Cup three seasons earlier. In 1921–22 they were again third in the League. Since the middle 1930s Barnsley have appeared in both lower divisions, including two spells in Division Four, but have remained in Division Two since 1981.

Birmingham City

Address: St Andrews, Birmingham B9 4NH
Record Crowd: 66,844 v Everton, FA Cup 5th round, 11 February 1939
Stadium Capacity: 27,689
Year Formed: 1875
Colours: Royal blue shirts with white trim, white shorts, blue socks with white trim
Joined League: 1892 Elected to Division 2
Honours: Division 2 Champions: 1892–93, 1920–21, 1947–48, 1954–55. League Cup winners: 1963.

Before 1989, the club had never played in the Third Division; their existence had been confined to Divisions One and Two. Had an uninterrupted spell of 18 years in the First Division from 1921

The Villa squad of 1981 celebrates the club's first Championship success in over 70 years. Next season, they went one better and took the European Cup.

until relegated in 1939. They won the League Cup in 1963 and have twice finished as runners-up in the FA Cup as well as the Fairs Cup.

Blackburn Rovers

Address: Ewood Park, Blackburn BB2 4JF
Record Crowd: 61,783 v Bolton W, FA Cup 6th round, 2 March 1929
Stadium Capacity: 17,819
Year Formed: 1875
Colours: Blue and white halved shirts, white shorts, blue socks with red and white trim
Joined League: 1888 Founder members of the Football League
Honours: Division 1 Champions: 1911–12, 1913–14. Division 2 Champions: 1938–39. Division 3 Champions: 1974–75. FA Cup winners: 1884, 1885, 1886, 1890, 1891, 1928. Full Members' Cup winners: 1987.

Their six FA Cup wins include three in succession from 1884–1886, though the last was in 1928. After being one of the founder members of the League in 1888, they stayed in the First Division until 1936, but have since spent spells in all three of the top divisions. Their two Championships came in the years before the First World War.

Stanley Matthews holds the FA Cup with pride – it remains Blackpool's only major trophy.

Blackpool

Address: Bloomfield Road Ground, Blackpool, FY1 6JJ
Record Crowd: 39,118 v Manchester U, Division 1, 19 April 1952
Stadium Capacity: 9,760
Year Formed: 1887
Colours: All tangerine with white trim
Joined League: 1896 Elected to Division 2
Honours: Division 2 Champions: 1929–30. FA Cup winners: 1953. Anglo-Italian Cup winners: 1971.

Survived a season out of the Second Division, when not re-elected in 1899, to climb into the First Division by 1930. They come closest to a Championship success in 1955–56 when they finished as runners-up on goal average, 11 points behind the Champions. After losing twice in the final of the FA Cup, they won it at the third attempt in 1953. But, since losing their First Division status in 1971, have had spells in both Third and Fourth Divisions.

Bolton Wanderers

Address: Burnden Park, Bolton BL3 2QR
Record Crowd: 69,912 v Manchester C, FA Cup 5th round, 18 February 1933
Stadium Capacity: 25,000
Year Formed: 1874
Colours: White shirts, navy blue shorts, white socks
Joined League: 1888 Founder members of the Football League
Honours: Division 2 Champions: 1908–09, 1977–78. Division 3 Champions: 1972–73. FA Cup winners: 1923, 1926, 1929, 1958. Associate Members' Cup winners: 1989.

Have spent 60 seasons in the First Division, longer than any other club which has not won the Championship. On three occasions they have finished third, but have fared better in the FA Cup with four victories, three of them in the 1920s. Did not drop into Division Three until 1971 but also had one season in the Fourth Division.

AFC Bournemouth

Address: Dean Court Ground, Bournemouth BH7 7AF
Record Crowd: 28,799 v Manchester U, FA Cup 6th round, 2 March 1957
Stadium Capacity: 11,375
Year Formed: 1899
Colours: All red with white trim
Joined League: 1923 Elected to Division 3 (South)
Honours: Division 3 Champions: 1986–87. Associate Members' Cup winners: 1984.

Elected to the Third Division (South) in 1923, they remained a Third Division club for a record number of years, until falling briefly into Division Four in 1970. Fought their way into the Second Division by 1987, but were relegated in 1990. In 1956–57 reached the sixth round of the FA Cup.

Bradford City

Address: Valley Parade Ground, Bradford BD8 7DY
Record Crowd: 39,146 v Burnley, FA Cup 4th round, 11 March 1911
Stadium Capacity: 14,814
Year Formed: 1903
Colours: Claret and amber striped shirts, black shorts, claret socks
Joined League: 1903 Elected to Division 2
Honours: Division 2 Champions: 1907–08. Division 3 Champions: 1984–85. Division 3 (North) Champions: 1928–29. FA Cup winners: 1911 (first holders of the current trophy).

They became the first holders of the present FA

Cup trophy in 1911, which was also their best season in the League as they finished fifth in the First Division. Lost their status in the top echelon in 1922 and have subsequently sampled fare in all three other divisions.

Brentford

Address: Griffin Park, Braemar Road, Brentford, Middlesex TW8 0NT
Record Crowd: 39,626 v Preston NE, FA Cup 6th round, 5 March 1938
Stadium Capacity: 10,850
Year Formed: 1889
Colours: Red and white striped shirts, black shorts, red socks with white trim
Joined League: 1920 Founder members of Division 3
Honours: Division 2 Champions: 1934–35. Division 3 (South) Champions: 1932–33. Division 4 Champions: 1962–63.

Won promotion from the Third Division (South) to the First Division in three years during the 1930s, but were relegated in 1947 and have had to be content with life in the lower three divisions since then. On four occasions they have reached the sixth round of the FA Cup.

Brighton & Hove Albion

Address: Goldstone Ground, Old Shoreham Road, Hove, West Sussex BN3 7DE
Record Crowd: 36,747 v Fulham, Division 2, 27 December 1958
Stadium Capacity: 18,493
Year Formed: 1900
Colours: Blue and white striped shirts, blue shorts and socks
Joined League: 1920 Founder members of Division 3
Honours: Division 3 (South) Champions: 1957–58. Division 4 Champions: 1964–65.

Their most rewarding period came from 1979 when they achieved promotion to the First Division from Division Three, having had two seasons in the Fourth Division from 1963–65. Their four years in the top flight were difficult ones and 16th place in 1979–80 was the highest they achieved. In 1982–83 they were runners-up in the FA Cup.

Bristol City

Address: Ashton Gate, Bristol BS3 2EJ
Record Crowd: 43,335 v Preston NE, FA Cup 5th round, 16 February 1935
Stadium Capacity: 25,271
Year Formed: 1894
Colours: Red shirts, white shorts, red socks
Joined League: 1901 Elected to Division 2
Honours: Division 2 Champions: 1905–06. Division 3 (South) Champions: 1922–23, 1926–27, 1954–55. Welsh Cup winners: 1934. Anglo-Scottish Cup winners: 1978. Associate Members' Cup winners: 1986.

Runners-up in the First Division in 1906–07, their sixth season in the League and only their first in the top bracket, they lost their position before the First World War and did not regain it until 1976. Relegation in 1980 sent them plummeting to Division Four in successive seasons. Were FA Cup runners-up in 1909.

Bristol Rovers

Address: Twerton Park, Bath, Avon BA2 1DB
Record Crowd: 38,472 v Preston NE, FA Cup 4th round, 30 January 1960
Stadium Capacity: 9,813
Year Formed: 1883
Colours: Blue and white quartered shirts, white shorts, blue socks
Joined League: 1920 Founder members of Division 3
Honours: Division 3 Champions: 1989–90. Division 3 (South) Champions: 1952–53.

One of the original members of the Third Division, they won promotion to Division Two in 1953 and remained there for nine years. A further spell of seven years followed up to 1981. Their highest placing was sixth, achieved on two occasions, and they have never played in Division Four. Have twice reached the sixth round of the FA Cup.

Burnley

Address: Turf Moor, Burnley BB10 4BX
Record Crowd: 54,775 v Huddersfield T, FA Cup 3rd round, 23 February 1924
Stadium Capacity: 25,000
Year Formed: 1882

Colours: Claret shirts with light blue sleeves, white shorts and socks
Joined League: 1888 Founder members of the Football League
Honours: Division 1 Champions: 1920–21, 1959–60. Division 2 Champions: 1897–98, 1972–73. Division 3 Champions: 1981–82. FA Cup winners: 1914. Anglo-Scottish Cup winners: 1979.

Spent two periods in the Second Division before winning the First Division Championship for the first time in 1920–21, though in 1913–14 they had won the FA Cup. They had another spell out of the top division before winning their second Championship honour in 1959–60. Their first taste of Fourth Division football came in 1985.

Bury

Address: Gigg Lane, Bury BL9 9HR
Record Crowd: 35,000 v Bolton W, FA Cup 3rd round, 9 January 1960
Stadium Capacity: 8,500
Year Formed: 1885
Colours: White shirts, navy blue shorts and socks
Joined League: 1894 Elected to Division 2
Honours: Division 2 Champions: 1894–95. Division 3 Champions: 1960–61. FA Cup winners: 1900, 1903.

They made their name at the turn of the century by winning the FA Cup on two occasions in 1900 and 1903. During this time they had a long spell in the First Division, but it was in their second period that they finished as high as fourth in 1925–26. In 1971 they fell into Division Four for the first time.

Cambridge United

Address: Abbey Stadium, Newmarket Road, Cambridge CB5 8LL
Record Crowd: 14,000 v Chelsea, friendly, 1 May 1970
Stadium Capacity: 10,218
Year Formed: 1919
Colours: Black and amber striped shirts, black shorts and socks
Joined League: 1970 Elected to Division 4
Honours: Division 4 Champions: 1976–77.

Elected to the Fourth Division in 1970, they achieved promotion to Division Three in three seasons, only to fall back immediately. But they fought their way into Division Two by 1978 and remained there for six years. In 1990 they reached the FA Cup sixth round for the first time.

Cardiff City

Address: Ninian Park, Cardiff CF1 8SX
Record Crowd: 57,893 v Arsenal, Division 1, 22 April 1953
Stadium Capacity: 19,300

The Cardiff team of 1927 display the FA Cup during its only venture out of England.

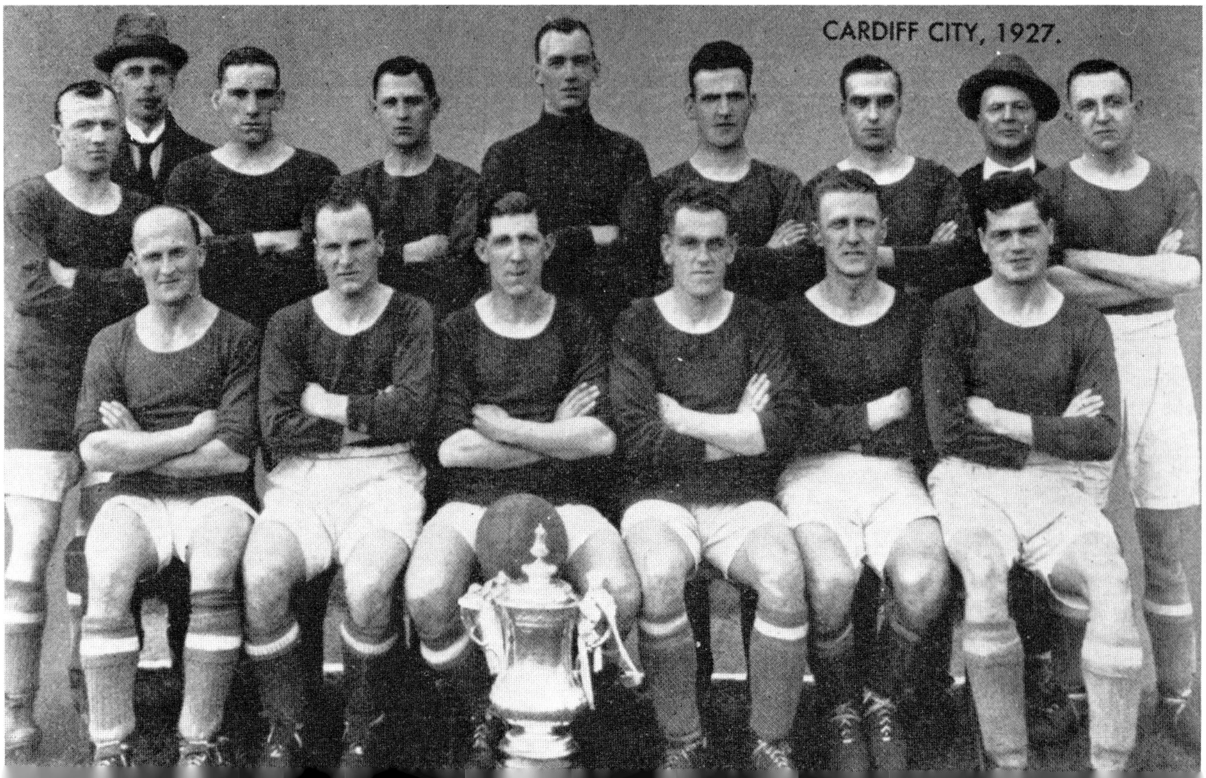

Year Formed: 1899
Colours: Royal blue shirts and socks, white shorts
Joined League: 1920 Elected to Division 2
Honours: Division 3 (South) Champions: 1946–47. FA Cup winners: 1927. Welsh Cup winners: 1912, 1920, 1922, 1923, 1927, 1928, 1930, 1956, 1959, 1964, 1965, 1967, 1968, 1969, 1970, 1971, 1973, 1974, 1976, 1988.

Following a purple patch in the 1920s, when they failed to win the League Championship on goal average in 1923–24 and took the FA Cup out of England for the first and only time in 1926–27, they crashed to the bottom of the Third Division (South) and were forced to seek re-election in 1934. But they did return to the First Division for five years from 1952 to 1957.

Carlisle United

Address: Brunton Park, Carlisle CA1 1LL
Record Crowd: 27,500 v Birmingham C, FA Cup 3rd round, 5 January 1957 and v Middlesbrough, FA Cup 5th round, 7 February 1970
Stadium Capacity: 16,267
Year Formed: 1903
Colours: Blue shirts and socks, white shorts
Joined League: 1928 Elected to Division 3 (North)
Honours: Division 3 Champions: 1964–65.

After 30 years became one of the clubs demoted to Division Four in 1958. Had one brief spell in Division Three then made a successful effort to reach the First Division by 1974 only to be immediately relegated. In the same season they reached the sixth round of the FA Cup.

Charlton Athletic

Address: Selhurst Park, London SE25 6PH
Record Crowd: 75,031 v Aston Villa, FA Cup 5th round, 12 February 1938 (at The Valley)
Stadium Capacity: 30,484
Year Formed: 1905
Colours: Red shirts, white shorts and socks
Joined League: 1921 Elected to Division 3 (South)
Honours: Division 3 (South) Champions: 1928–29, 1934–35. FA Cup winners: 1947.

After one abortive spell in the Second Division, they made a spectacular return and went straight up into Division One in 1936. Finished runners-up the following season. Relegated in 1957, they had two more periods in Division Three before regaining First Division status in 1986 until 1990. In 1946–47 they won the FA Cup.

Chelsea

Address: Stamford Bridge, London SW6 1HS
Record Crowd: 82,905 v Arsenal, Division 1, 12 October 1935
Stadium Capacity: 36,364
Year Formed: 1905
Colours: All royal blue
Joined League: 1905 Elected to Division 2
Honours: Division 1 Champions: 1954–55. Division 2 Champions: 1983–84, 1988–89. FA Cup winners: 1970. League Cup winners: 1965. Full Members' Cup winners: 1986, 1990. European Cup-Winners' Cup winners: 1971.

Can claim a broad sweep of at least one major honour in leading competitions. Became First Division Champions in 1954–55, won the League Cup 10 years later, the FA Cup in 1970 and the European Cup-Winners' Cup the following year. Have still played more seasons in the First Division than in Division Two.

Chester City

Address: The Stadium, Sealand Road, Chester CH1 4LW
Ground: Moss Rose Ground, Macclesfield
Record Crowd: 20,500 v Chelsea, FA Cup 3rd round replay, 16 January 1952 (at Chester)
Stadium Capacity: 10,000
Year Formed: 1884
Colours: Royal blue shirts and socks, white shorts
Joined League: 1931 Elected to Division 3 (North)
Honours Highest Placing: 5th, Division 3, 1977–78. Welsh Cup winners: 1908, 1933, 1947.

Had to wait longer than any other club in either of the two sections of the old Third Division before achieving promotion, following the drop into Division Four on its foundation in 1958. Finally moved up in 1975. Coupled this success with an appearance in the League Cup semi-final. Have twice reached the fifth round of the FA Cup.

Chesterfield

Address: Recreation Ground, Chesterfield S40 4SX
Record Crowd: 30,968 v Newcastle U, Division 2, 7 April 1939
Stadium Capacity: 11,638
Year Formed: 1866
Colours: Royal blue shirts, white shorts and socks
Joined League: 1899 Elected to Division 2
Honours: Division 3 (North) Champions: 1930–31, 1935–36. Division 4 Champions: 1969–70, 1984–85. Anglo-Scottish Cup winners: 1981.

Lost their League status when not re-elected in 1909 and had to wait until the formation of the Third Division after the First World War to return. Have subsequently had two spells in the Second Division. Best in the FA Cup: three times in the fifth round.

Coventry City

Address: Highfield Road Stadium, King Richard Street, Coventry CV2 4FW
Record Crowd: 51,455 v Wolverhampton W, Division 2, 29 April 1967
Stadium Capacity: 26,218
Year Formed: 1883
Colours: All sky blue
Joined League: 1919 Elected to Division 2
Honours: Division 2 Champions: 1966–67. Division 3 Champions: 1963–64. Division 3 (South) Champions: 1935–36. FA Cup winners: 1987.

Achieved their first major honour in 104 years of existence when they won the FA Cup in 1986–87. Have also played in all four present divisions of the Football League and both sections of the old regional Third Division. Highest placing in the First Division was sixth in 1969–70.

Crewe Alexandra

Address: Football Ground, Gresty Road, Crewe CW2 6EB
Record Crowd: 20,000 v Tottenham H, FA Cup 4th round, 30 January 1960
Stadium Capacity: 7,200
Year Formed: 1877
Colours: Red shirts, white shorts, red socks
Joined League: 1892 Founder members of Division 2
Honours Highest Placing: 10th, Division 2, 1892–93.

Spent four seasons in the Second Division before failing to gain re-election in 1896. Came back when the Third Division was created after the First World War. Reached the semi-final of the FA Cup in 1888 before the start of the Football League.

Crystal Palace

Address: Selhurst Park, London SE25 6PU
Record Crowd: 51,482 v Burnley, Division 2, 11 May 1979
Stadium Capacity: 31,439
Year Formed: 1905
Colours: Red and blue striped shirts, red shorts and socks
Joined League: 1920 Founder members of Division 3
Honours: Division 2 Champions: 1978–79. Division 3 Champions: 1920–21.

Founder members of the Third Division they won immediate promotion as Champions. Have had three separate spells in the First Division and their highest placing came in 1979–80 when they were 13th. Reached the final of the FA Cup for the first time in 1990.

Darlington

Address: Feethams Ground, Darlington DL1 5JB
Record Crowd: 21,023 v Bolton W, League Cup 3rd round, 14 November 1960
Stadium Capacity: 10,932
Year Formed: 1883
Colours: All white
Joined League: Founder members of Division 3 (North)
Honours: Division 3 (North) Champions: 1924–25.

Enjoyed two seasons in the Second Division during the 1920s and have reached the fifth round of both the FA Cup and League Cup. Regained a place in the League in 1990 after a season in the GM Vauxhall Conference. Highest placing: 15th in Division Two in 1925–26.

Derby's Dave Mackay, Footballer of the Year in 1968–69, challenges George Best for the ball.

Derby County

Address: Baseball Ground, Shaftesbury Crescent, Derby DE3 8NB
Record Crowd: 41,826 v Tottenham H, Division 1, 20 September 1969
Stadium Capacity: 24,000
Year Formed: 1884
Colours: White shirts, black shorts and socks
Joined League: 1888 Founder members of the Football League
Honours: Division 1 Champions: 1971–72, 1974–75. Division 2 Champions: 1911–12, 1914–15, 1968–69, 1986–87. Division 3 (North) Champions: 1956–57. FA Cup winners: 1946.

Founder members of the League, they had to wait until the 1970s before winning the Championship on two occasions. At one time they slipped into the Third Division (North) for two seasons in the middle 1950s, after a chequered career between the top two divisions. Again relegated to Division Three in 1984, they returned to the First Division by 1987 after spending two seasons in Division Three. FA Cup winners in 1946.

Doncaster Rovers

Address: Belle Vue Ground, Doncaster DN4 5HT
Record Crowd: 37,149 v Hull C, Division 3 (North), 2 October 1948
Stadium Capacity: 7,759
Year Formed: 1879
Colours: White shirts and socks with red trim, red shorts
Joined League: 1901 Elected to Division 2
Honours: Division 3 (North) Champions: 1934–35, 1946–47, 1949–50. Division 4 Champions: 1965–66, 1968–69.

Were twice voted out of the Second Division in the early 1900s before finally returning to the Third Division (North) in 1923. Have had three spells in the Second Division, the last ending in 1958. Reached the fifth round of the FA Cup four times in the 1950s.

Everton

Address: Goodison Park, Liverpool L4 4EL
Record Crowd: 78,299 v Liverpool, Division 1, 18 September 1948
Stadium Capacity: 41,366
Year Formed: 1878
Colours: Royal blue shirts and socks, white shorts
Joined League: 1888 Founder members of the Football League

Everton's Peter Reid in a midfield tussle with Steve McMahon in 1986–87.

Honours: Division 1 Champions: 1890–91, 1914–15, 1927–28, 1931–32, 1938–39, 1962–63, 1969–70, 1984–85, 1986–87. Division 2 Champions: 1930–31. FA Cup winners: 1906, 1933, 1966, 1984. European Cup-Winners' Cup winners: 1985.

Have had more seasons in the First Division than any other club. One of the founder members, they have spent only four terms in the Second Division, one in the 1930–31 season, the others in the mid-1950s. Have won the First Division Championship on nine occasions, the FA Cup four times and the Cup-Winners' Cup once in 1985. They have a record of 22 appearances in FA Cup semi-finals.

Exeter City

Address: St James Park, Exeter EX4 6PX
Record Crowd: 20,984 v Sunderland, FA Cup 6th round replay, 4 March 1931
Stadium Capacity: 9,260
Year Formed: 1904
Colours: Red and white striped shirts, black shorts and socks
Joined League: 1920 Elected to Division 3
Honours: Division 4 Champions: 1989–90.

Entered the Third Division upon its creation but had fallen into the Fourth Division on the formation of that division in 1958. Have had three separate spells in the Third Division since then, their highest placing being eighth in 1979–80. Appeared in a sixth round FA Cup replay in 1931.

Fulham

Address: Craven Cottage, Stevenage Road, Fulham, London SW6 6HH
Record Crowd: 49,335 v Millwall, Division 2, 8 October 1938
Stadium Capacity: 18,304
Year Formed: 1879
Colours: White shirts and socks, black shorts
Joined League: 1907 Elected to Division 2
Honours: Division 2 Champions: 1948–49. Division 3 (South) Champions: 1931–32.

Elected to the Second Division in 1907 they made slow progress, but survived a drop into the Third Division (South) and reached the First Division in 1949. Relegated after three years, they contrived a return, staying for nine years from 1959. Had their best season when finishing 10th. Were FA Cup runners-up in 1974–75.

Gillingham

Address: Priestfield Stadium, Gillingham ME7 4DD
Record Crowd: 23,002 v QPR, FA Cup 3rd round, 10 January 1948
Stadium Capacity: 19,581
Year Formed: 1893
Colours: Royal blue shirts, white shorts and socks
Joined League: 1920 Founder members of Division 3
Honours: Division 4 Champions: 1963–64.

Failed to gain re-election to the Third Division (South) in 1938 but regained their status on the expansion of the division in 1950. Have moved between the two lower divisions since then, with a best season position of fourth achieved twice in Division Three in 1978–79 and 1984–85. Reached FA Cup fifth round in 1969–70.

Grimsby Town

Address: Blundell Park, Cleethorpes, South Humberside DN35 7PY
Record Crowd: 31,651 v Wolverhampton W, FA Cup 5th round, 20 February 1937
Stadium Capacity: 18,496
Year Formed: 1878
Colours: Black and white striped shirts, black shorts, white socks
Joined League: 1892 Founder members of Division 2
Honours: Division 2 Champions: 1900–01, 1933–34. Division 3 Champions: 1979–80. Division 3 (North) Champions: 1925–26, 1955–56. Division 4 Champions: 1971–72. League Group Cup winners: 1982.

Failed to gain re-election in 1910 for one season having been in the First Division briefly from 1901–03. Had two further periods in the top echelon and have had 23 switches of division involving all four in the League since 1892. FA Cup semi-finalists in 1936 and 1939.

Herbert Chapman (standing, left) with his Huddersfield team of 1924–25. He made them the best side in the land.

Halifax Town

Address: Shay Ground, Halifax HX1 2YS
Record Crowd: 36,885 v Tottenham H, FA Cup 5th round, 14 February 1953
Stadium Capacity: 5,656
Year Formed: 1911
Colours: Blue and white striped shirts, white shorts, blue socks
Joined League: 1921 Founder members of Division 3 (North)
Honours Highest Placing: 3rd, Division 3, 1970–71.

Managed to finish seventh, high enough to stay in the Third Division under the lower divisions rearrangement in 1958, but were relegated to the Fourth Division in 1963. Promoted again in 1969 they had seven more seasons in Division Three. Reached the FA Cup fifth round twice.

Hartlepool United

Address: The Victoria Ground, Clarence Road, Hartlepool TS24 8BZ
Record Crowd: 17,426 v Manchester U, FA Cup 3rd round, 5 January 1957
Stadium Capacity: 9,675
Year Formed: 1908
Colours: All blue
Joined League: 1921 Founder members of Division 3 (North)
Honours Highest Placing: 22nd, Division 3, 1968–69.

Apart from a brief season in the Third Division in 1968–69, they have spent their career in the Fourth Division since it was formed. Had been founder members of the Third Division (North) and were runners-up in it in 1956–57.

Hereford United

Address: Edgar Street, Hereford HR4 9JU
Record Crowd: 18,114 v Sheffield W, FA Cup 3rd round, 4 January 1958
Stadium Capacity: 13,777
Year Formed: 1924
Colours: White shirts and socks with black trim, black shorts
Joined League: 1972 Elected to Division 4
Honours: Division 3 Champions: 1975–76. Welsh Cup winners: 1990.

Won immediate promotion to the Third Division in 1973 after being elected to Division Four. Reached the Second Division in 1976 but were relegated after a season. Fell into Division Four in 1978. Never past the fourth round of the FA Cup.

Huddersfield Town

Address: Leeds Road, Huddersfield HF1 6PE

Record Crowd: 67,037 v Arsenal, FA Cup 6th round, 27 February 1932
Stadium Capacity: 32,000
Year Formed: 1908
Colours: Blue and white striped shirts, white shorts and socks
Joined League: 1910 Elected to Division 2
Honours: Division 1 Champions: 1923–24, 1924–25, 1925–26. Division 2 Champions: 1969–70. Division 4 Champions: 1979–80. FA Cup winners: 1922.

Herbert Chapman's managership of the club produced three successive First Division Championships from 1923 to 1926, by which time the maestro had moved to Arsenal. They had previously won the FA Cup in 1922. But in the 1970s they slumped from the First to the Fourth Division in three years after several spells in Division Two.

Hull City

Address: Boothferry Park, Hull HU4 6EU
Record Crowd: 55,019 v Manchester U, FA Cup 6th round, 26 February 1949
Stadium Capacity: 17,932
Year Formed: 1904
Colours: Amber shirts and socks with black and red trim, black shorts
Joined League: 1905 Elected to Division 2
Honours: Division 3 Champions: 1965–66. Division 3 (North) Champions: 1932–33, 1948–49.

Though relegated to the Third Division (North) in 1930 they also reached the semi-final of the FA Cup the same year. Have had varying spells in each of the lower three divisions since then. Highest Second Division placing: third in 1909–10.

Ipswich Town

Address: Portman Road, Ipswich IP1 2DA
Record Crowd: 38,010 v Leeds U, FA Cup 6th round, 8 March 1975
Stadium Capacity: 31,100
Year Formed: 1878
Colours: Blue shirts with white trim, white shorts, blue socks
Joined League: 1938 Elected to Division 3 (South)
Honours: Division 1 Champions: 1961–62. Division 2 Champions: 1960–61, 1967–68.

Mick Mills, who made more appearances for Ipswich than anyone else, beats Jan Peters in the UEFA Cup final of 1981.

Division 3 (South) Champions: 1953–54, 1956–57. FA Cup winners: 1978. UEFA Cup winners: 1981.

Despite having spent little more than 50 years in the League, they can claim to have won the First Division Championship, the FA Cup and the UEFA Cup each on one occasion. They have also twice reached the semi-final of the League Cup. Provided England with two managers: Alf Ramsey and Bobby Robson.

Leeds United

Address: Elland Road, Leeds LS11 0ES
Record Crowd: 57,892 v Sunderland, FA Cup 5th round replay, 15 March 1967
Stadium Capacity: 33,235
Year Formed: 1904 as Leeds City. Reconstituted as Leeds United in 1919 after Leeds City had been disbanded by order of the FA
Colours: All white
Joined League: 1920 Elected to Division 2
Honours: Division 1 Champions: 1968–69, 1973–74. Division 2 Champions: 1923–24, 1963–64, 1989–90. FA Cup winners: 1972. League Cup winners: 1968. European Fairs Cup winners: 1968, 1971.

Enjoyed a period of dominance in the 1960s and early 1970s under the influence of manager Don Revie. Although they won the First Division on two occasions, they were runners-up five times. They also won the FA Cup in 1972, the League Cup in 1968 as well as the Fairs Cup in 1968 and 1971. Were also runners-up in other European competitions on three occasions.

Leicester City

Address: City Stadium, Filbert Street, Leicester LE2 4FL
Record Crowd: 47,298 v Tottenham H, FA Cup 5th round, 18 February 1928
Stadium Capacity: 26,770
Year Formed: 1884
Colours: Blue shirts, white shorts and socks
Joined League: 1894 Elected to Division 2
Honours: Division 2 Champions: 1924–25, 1936–37, 1953–54, 1956–57, 1970–71, 1979–80. League Cup winners: 1964.

Despite successfully remaining Full Members of the League since being elected to the Second Division, they have moved up and down between the top two divisions at regular intervals. However, in their second-longest spell of 10 years in Division One they were runners-up in 1928–29. Four times beaten finalists in the FA Cup, Leicester did win the League Cup in 1964.

Leyton Orient

Address: Leyton Stadium, Brisbane Road, Leyton, London E10 5NE
Record Crowd: 34,345 v West Ham U, FA Cup 4th round, 25 January 1964
Stadium Capacity: 18,869
Year Formed: 1881
Colours: Red shirts and socks with white trim, white shorts
Joined League: 1905 Elected to Division 2
Honours: Division 3 Champions: 1969–70. Division 3 (South) Champions: 1955–56.

Promoted to the First Division for one season in 1962–63. They reached the FA Cup semi-final in 1978. Have also enjoyed several spells in the Second Division and did not drop into Division Four for the first time until 1985.

Johnny Giles was a key figure in Don Revie's Leeds side, controlling the midfield.

Lincoln City

Address: Sincil Bank, Lincoln NL5 8LD
Record Crowd: 23,196 v Derby Co, League Cup 4th round replay, 15 November 1967
Stadium Capacity: 10,369
Year Formed: 1883
Colours: Red and white striped shirts, black shorts, red socks
Joined League: 1892 Founder members of Division 2
Honours: Division 3 (North) Champions: 1931–32, 1947–48, 1951–52. Division 4 Champions: 1975–76.

Can claim to have been rejected by the League on three occasions through not being re-elected and once demoted to the GM Vauxhall Conference in 1987. Bounced back on every occasion. Four periods in the Second Division with a highest placing fifth in 1901–02, when they also equalled their best FA Cup run to the equivalent of the present fifth round.

Liverpool

Address: Anfield Road, Liverpool L4 0TH
Record Crowd: 61,905 v Wolverhampton W, FA Cup 4th round, 2 February 1952
Stadium Capacity: 39,772
Year Formed: 1892
Colours: All red
Joined League: 1893 Elected to Division 2
Honours: Division 1 Champions: 1900–01, 1905–06, 1921–22, 1922–23, 1946–47, 1963–64, 1965–66, 1972–73, 1975–76, 1976–77, 1978–79, 1979–80, 1981–82, 1982–83, 1983–84, 1985–86, 1987–88, 1989–90 (the record – 18 titles). Division 2 Champions: 1893–94, 1895–96, 1904–05, 1961–62. FA Cup winners: 1965, 1974, 1986, 1989. League Cup winners: 1981, 1982, 1983, 1984. League Super Cup winners: 1986. European Cup winners: 1977, 1978, 1981, 1984. UEFA Cup winners: 1973, 1976. European Super Cup winners: 1977.

Had enjoyed many successes before Bill Shankly was appointed manager in 1959, but established themselves as the leading club in the League during the next 30 years with a succession of outstanding managers and players, and a system that produced many trophies. Bob Paisley succeeded Shankly in 1974 and, during his nine-year reign, they won 20 major prizes: six League titles, three European Cups, three League Cups, one UEFA Cup, a Super Cup and six Charity Shields. By winning the First Division in 1976–77 they set up a record 10 Championships and took their total to 18 in 1989–90. Overall they have won four FA Cups, another four in both the League Cup and European Cup as well as two UEFA Cups.

Two of Liverpool's stars of the 1970s, Keegan and Hughes, celebrate winning the FA Cup in 1974.

Luton Town

Address: Kenilworth Road Stadium, Luton. Postal address: 1 Maple Road, Luton LU4 8AW
Record Crowd: 30,069 v Blackpool, FA Cup 6th round replay, 4 March 1959
Stadium Capacity: 13,023
Year Formed: 1885
Colours: White shirts and socks with navy blue and orange trim, navy blue shorts
Joined League: 1897 Elected to Division 2
Honours: Division 2 Champions: 1981–82. Division 3 (South) Champions: 1936–37. Division 4 Champions: 1967–68. League Cup winners: 1988.

Winning the League Cup in 1987–88 represented their first major honour in their 103-year history. Became runners-up the following season, 30 years after finishing as beaten finalists in the FA Cup. Failed re-election at the turn of the century but returned in the Third Division (South). Highest League placing: seventh in Division One, 1986–87.

Maidstone United

Address: Watling Street, Dartford, Kent DA2 6EN
Record Crowd: 10,591 v Charlton A, FA Cup Jan 1979 (at Maidstone)
Stadium Capacity: 5,250
Year Formed: 1897
Colours: Amber shirts, black shorts and socks
Joined League: Promoted to Division 4 1989
Honours Highest Placing: 5th, Division 4 1989–90

Promoted to the Fourth Division from the GM Vauxhall Conference in 1989 they had a successful first season in the League.

Manchester City

Address: Maine Road, Moss Side, Manchester M14 7WN

Francis Lee was Manchester City's leading striker between 1967 and 1974, their most successful period.

Record Crowd: 84,569 v Stoke C, FA Cup 6th round, 3 March 1934 (British record for games played outside London or Glasgow)
Stadium Capacity: 46,000
Year Formed: 1887
Colours: Sky blue shirts, white shorts, navy blue socks
Joined League: 1892 Founder members of Division 2 (as Ardwick FC)
Honours: Division 1 Champions: 1936–37, 1967–68. Division 2 Champions: 1898–99, 1902–03, 1909–10, 1927–28, 1946–47, 1965–66. FA Cup winners: 1904, 1934, 1956, 1969. League Cup winners: 1970, 1976. European Cup-Winners' Cup winners: 1970.

Have achieved a widespread sprinkling of honours, including two First Division titles, four FA Cup wins, two in the League Cup and one European Cup-Winners' Cup success. Longest period in the First Division was between 1966 and 1983, but rarely kept in Division Two for longer than two seasons.

Manchester United

Address: Old Trafford, Manchester M16 0RA
Record Crowd: 70,504 v Aston Villa, Division 1, 27 December 1920. Stadium record: 76,962, Wolverhampton W v Grimsby T, FA Cup semi-final, 25 March 1939
Stadium Capacity: 50,726
Year Formed: 1878
Colours: Red shirts, white shorts, black socks with red and white trim
Joined League: 1892 Elected to Division 1 (as Newton Heath)
Honours: Division 1 Champions: 1907–08, 1910–11, 1951–52, 1955–56, 1956–57, 1964–65, 1966–67. Division 2 Champions: 1935–36, 1974–75. FA Cup winners: 1909, 1948, 1963, 1977, 1983, 1985, 1990 (Seven wins – a record held jointly with Aston V and Tottenham H). European Cup winners: 1968.

Enjoyed considerable popularity at home and abroad under the guidance of Matt Busby after the Second World War, heightened by the Munich air disaster in 1958. Have achieved seven First Division titles, seven FA Cup wins and reached a peak when winning the European Cup in 1968. But their last Championship success was gained in 1967. Have spent only two seasons in the Second Division since 1937 and in five years of European Cup competition never failed to reach at least the semi-final.

Bobby Charlton personified Manchester United in the Busby era. He made 606 League appearances for the club.

Mansfield Town

Address: Field Mill Ground, Quarry Lane, Mansfield NG18 5DA
Record Crowd: 24,467 v Nottingham F, FA Cup 3rd round, 10 January 1953
Stadium Capacity: 10,468
Year Formed: 1910
Colours: All amber with blue trim
Joined League: 1931 Elected to Division 3 (South)
Honours: Division 3 Champions: 1976–77. Division 4 Champions 1974–75. Associate Members' Cup winners: 1987.

Their geographical position in the Midlands had them switching between both regional sections of the old Third Division. Elected to the Southern section, they did not find themselves relegated to Division Four until 1960 and had one season in Division Two during 1977–78. Reached the sixth round of the FA Cup in 1968–69.

Middlesbrough

Address: Ayresome Park, Middlesbrough, Cleveland TS1 4PB
Record Crowd: 53,596 v Newcastle U, Division 1, 27 December 1949
Stadium Capacity: 30,000
Year Formed: 1876
Colours: Red shirts and socks with white trim, white shorts
Joined League: 1899 Elected to Division 2
Honours: Division 2 Champions: 1926–27, 1928–29, 1973–74. Anglo-Scottish Cup winners: 1976.

Had twice won the Amateur Cup in 1895 and 1898 before entering the Second Division in 1899. Have had several lengthy periods in the First Division, their best season being 1913–14 when they finished third. Six times reached the sixth round of the FA Cup and were League Cup semi-finalists in 1975–76.

Millwall

Address: The Den, Cold Blow Lane, London SE14 5RH
Record Crowd: 48,672 v Leicester C, FA Cup 5th round, 20 February 1937
Stadium Capacity: 19,000
Year Formed: 1885
Colours: Blue shirts and socks, white shorts
Joined League: 1920 Founder members of Division 3
Honours: Division 2 Champions 1987–88. Division 3 (South) Champions: 1927–28, 1937–38. Division 4 Champions: 1961–62. Football League Trophy winners: 1983.

Promoted to the First Division for the first time in 1988, they even topped the table for a week in October. In 1937 they became the first Third Division side to reach the semi-final of the FA Cup, but had twice previously reached this stage while still outside the League.

Newcastle United

Address: St James' Park, Newcastle-upon-Tyne NE1 4ST
Record Crowd: 68,386 v Chelsea, Division 1, 3 September 1930
Stadium Capacity: 33,530
Year Formed: 1881
Colours: Black and white striped shirts, black shorts and socks
Joined League: 1893 Elected to Division 2
Honours: Division 1 Champions: 1904–05, 1906–07, 1908–09, 1926–27. Division 2

Jackie Milburn (right) after winning the FA Cup in 1955. He is still revered on Tyneside.

Champions: 1964–65. FA Cup winners: 1910, 1924, 1932, 1951, 1952, 1955. European Fairs Cup winners: 1969. Anglo-Italian Cup winners: 1973.

Won three of their four First Division Championships in the 1900s, the last back in 1926–27. Have had six FA Cup wins including three in the 1950s. Also won the Fairs Cup in 1968–69. Originally elected to the Second Division in 1893, they won promotion five years later and have had some lengthy spells in Division One since then.

Northampton Town

Address: County Ground, Abington Avenue, Northampton NN1 4PS
Record Crowd: 24,523 v Fulham, Division 1, 23 April 1966
Stadium Capacity: 11,907
Year Formed: 1897
Colours: Claret shirts with white sleeves, white shorts, claret socks
Joined League: 1920 Founder members of Division 3
Honours: Division 3 Champions: 1962–63. Division 4 Champions: 1986–87.

The 1960s were the most eventful period in the club's history: they moved from Division Four to Division One in four years and came down again in three. Three times reached the fifth round of the FA Cup and were original members of the Third Division.

Norwich City

Address: Carrow Road, Norwich NR1 1JE
Record Crowd: 43,984 v Leicester C, FA Cup 6th round, 30 March 1963
Stadium Capacity: 24,284
Year Formed: 1902
Colours: Yellow shirts and socks, green shorts
Joined League: 1920 Founder members of Division 3
Honours: Division 2 Champions: 1971–72, 1985–86. Division 3 (South) Champions: 1933–34. League Cup winners: 1962, 1985.

Promoted to Division Two for the first time in 1934. Relegated before the War, they returned in 1960 and entered the First Division in 1972. Have since spent just three separate seasons in the Second Division. Highest First Division placing: fourth in 1988–89. Twice FA Cup semi-finalists and twice winners of the League Cup.

Nottingham Forest

Address: City Ground, Nottingham NG2 5FJ
Record Crowd: 49,946 v Manchester U, Division 1, 28 October 1967
Stadium Capacity: 31,920
Year Formed: 1865
Colours: Red shirts and socks, white shorts
Joined League: 1892 Elected to Division 1
Honours: Division 1 Champions: 1977–78. Division 2 Champions: 1906–07, 1921–22. Division 3 (South) Champions: 1950–51. FA Cup winners: 1898, 1959. League Cup winners: 1978, 1979, 1989, 1990. European Cup winners: 1979, 1980. European Super Cup winners: 1980. Anglo-Scottish Cup winners: 1977. Full Members' Cup winners: 1989.

Apart from two seasons in Division Three (South) between 1949 and 1951, have been in the top two divisions since their election to the First Division. Started their most settled period at the forefront in 1977, winning the First Division title in the first season. Also added four League Cup trophies and two European Cup successes. Had in 1898 and 1959 also taken the FA Cup. Their recent triumphs have been under the managership of Brian Clough, appointed in 1975.

Brian Clough, Forest's controversial and highly successful manager, after winning the League Cup for the first time in 1978.

John Chiedozie, the record transfer for the oldest League club in England.

Notts County

Address: County Ground, Meadow Lane, Nottingham NG2 3HJ
Record Crowd: 47,310 v York C, FA Cup 6th round, 12 March 1955
Stadium Capacity: 21,097
Year Formed: 1862 (The oldest club in the Football League) and on a firm basis from 1864
Colours: Black and white striped shirts, black shorts and socks
Joined League: 1888 Founder members of the Football League
Honours: Division 2 Champions: 1896–97, 1913–14, 1922–23. Division 3 (South) Champions: 1930–31, 1949–50. Division 4 Champions: 1970–71. FA Cup winners: 1894.

One of the founders of the League they were relegated to the Second Division in 1893 only to win the FA Cup that season. Have subsequently experienced periods in all other divisions and played more League games than any other club. Highest placing: third in the First Division 1890–91 and 1900–01.

Oldham Athletic

Address: Boundary Park, Oldham OL1 2PA
Record Crowd: 47,671 v Sheffield W, FA Cup 4th round, 25 January 1930
Stadium Capacity: 19,432
Year Formed: 1895
Colours: All blue
Joined League: 1907 Elected to Division 2
Honours: Division 3 Champions: 1973–74. Division 3 (North) Champions: 1952–53.

Had their most successful time during their one period in the First Division from 1910 to 1923. Were runners-up in 1914–15, needing only two more points to have won the Championship. In 1913 they had reached the semi-finals of the FA Cup. Have remained in the Second Division in their current spell since 1974. Littlewoods Cup finalists in 1990.

Oxford United

Address: Manor Ground, Headington, Oxford OX3 7RS
Record Crowd: 22,730 v Preston NE, FA Cup 6th round, 29 February 1964
Stadium Capacity: 11,117
Year Formed: 1893
Colours: Gold shirts with navy blue sleeves, navy blue shorts and socks
Joined League: 1962 Elected to Division 4
Honours: Division 2 Champions: 1984–85. Division 3 Champions: 1967–68, 1983–84. League Cup winners: 1986.

Elected to the Fourth Division, they set a record in their second season in 1963–64 for a club in the division, by reaching the sixth round of the FA Cup. Won promotion to the Third Division the following season and had only one other spell in the division after reaching Division Two in 1968. Spent three years in the First Division from 1985–88. League Cup winners 1986.

Peterborough United

Address: London Road Ground, Peterborough PE2 8AL
Record Crowd: 30,096 v Swansea T, FA Cup 5th round, 20 February 1965
Stadium Capacity: 16,414
Year Formed: 1934
Colours: Blue shirts and socks, white shorts
Joined League: 1960 Elected to Division 4
Honours: Division 4 Champions: 1960–61, 1973–74.

Had a highly successful first season in Division Four during 1960–61 to win promotion. Lost their Third Division status in 1968 but returned in 1974. Twelve years in Division Four during their present period. Reached the sixth round of the FA Cup in 1965 and were League Cup semi-finalists in 1966.

Plymouth Argyle

Address: Home Park, Plymouth PL2 3DQ
Record Crowd: 43,596 v Aston Villa, Division 2, 10 October 1936
Stadium Capacity: 26,000
Year Formed: 1886
Colours: Green shirts, black shorts, white socks
Joined League: 1920 Founder members of Division 3
Honours: Division 3 Champions: 1958–59. Division 3 (South) Champions: 1929–30, 1951–52.

Created an unusual record in their days in Division Three (South) by finishing runners-up in six consecutive seasons before gaining promotion three seasons later in 1929–30. Became semi-finalists in the League Cup in 1965 and again in 1974. Also reached the same stage of the FA Cup in 1984.

Portsmouth

Address: Fratton Park, Frogmore Road, Portsmouth PO4 8RA
Record Crowd: 51,385 v Derby Co, FA Cup 6th round, 26 February 1949
Stadium Capacity: 23,000
Year Formed: 1898
Colours: Royal blue shirts, white shorts, red socks
Joined League: 1920 Founder members of Division 3
Honours: Division 1 Champions: 1948–49, 1949–50. Division 3 Champions: 1961–62, 1982–83. Division 3 (South) Champions: 1923–24. FA Cup winners: 1939.

They won a place in the First Division by 1927 and entered their most rewarding years. Won the FA Cup in 1939 having twice been runners-up and after the War achieved the First Division title in successive seasons 1948–49 and 1949–50. Have played in all four divisions.

Port Vale

Address: Vale Park, Hamil Road, Burslem, Stoke-on-Trent ST6 1AW
Record Crowd: 50,000 v Aston Villa, FA Cup 5th round, 20 February 1960
Stadium Capacity: 20,950
Year Formed: 1876
Colours: White shirts and socks, black shorts
Joined League: 1892 Founder members of Division 2
Honours: Division 3 (North) Champions: 1929–30, 1953–54. Division 4 Champions: 1958–59.

Had a chequered career in the League at first: failing re-election, returning, resigning then finally taking over the fixtures of Leeds City in 1919. Played in both sections of the Third Division and Division Four. Fifth in Division Two in 1930–31. Won promotion again to the Second Division in 1954 and reached the FA Cup semi-final the same year.

Preston North End

Address: Deepdale, Preston PR1 6RU
Record Crowd: 42,684 v Arsenal, Division 1, 23 April 1938
Stadium Capacity: 15,000
Year Formed: 1881
Colours: All white
Joined League: 1888 Founder members of the Football League
Honours: Division 1 Champions: 1888–89, 1889–90. Division 2 Champions: 1903–04, 1912–13, 1950–51. Division 3 Champions: 1970–71. FA Cup winners: 1889, 1938.

The Preston North End side that won the first League Championship in 1889.

Won the League and Cup double in the first season of the Football League in 1888–89 and retained their Championship title the following season. Won the FA Cup for a second time in 1938. Suffered ups and downs in subsequent years and have had several periods in Division Three and one in the Fourth Division.

Queen's Park Rangers

Address: South Africa Road, London W12 7PA
Record Crowd: 35,353 v Leeds U, Division 1, 27 April 1974
Stadium Capacity: 23,480
Year Formed: c.1885
Colours: Blue and white hooped shirts, white shorts and socks
Joined League: 1920 Founder members of Division 3
Honours: Division 2 Champions: 1982–83. Division 3 Champions: 1966–67. Division 3 (South) Champions: 1947–48. League Cup winners: 1967.

Had one promotion success in 1948 before a more impressive move from Division Three to Division One in successive seasons to 1968. Relegated immediately, they have had two subsequent periods in the First Division and were runners-up in 1975–76. FA Cup runners-up in 1982 and League Cup winners in 1967.

Reading

Address: Elm Park, Norfolk Road, Reading RG3 2EF
Record Crowd: 33,042 v Brentford, FA Cup 5th round, 19 February 1927
Stadium Capacity: 12,500
Year Formed: 1871
Colours: Sky blue shirts and shorts, navy blue socks
Joined League: 1920 Founder members of Division 3
Honours: Division 3 Champions: 1985–86. Division 3 (South) Champions: 1925–26. Division 4 Champions: 1978–79. Full Members' Cup winners: 1988.

Won promotion from the Third Division (South) in 1926 and the following year reached the FA Cup semi-final. However, their highest placing in the Second Division was achieved in 1986–87 when they were 13th. This was during their second spell in the division.

Rochdale

Address: Spotland, Willbutts Lane, Rochdale OL11 5DS
Record Crowd: 24,231 v Notts Co, FA Cup 2nd round, 10 December 1949
Stadium Capacity: 10,250
Year Formed: 1907
Colours: All royal blue
Joined League: 1921 Elected to Division 3 (North)
Honours Highest Placing: 9th, Division 3, 1969–70.

Entered the League when the North section of the Third Division was formed in 1921. Had one season in the re-structured version of the division in 1958–59 but only one other period in Division Three since then. Never higher than ninth in the division, but runners-up in the 1962 League Cup, a record for a Fourth Division club.

Rotherham United

Address: Millmoor Ground, Rotherham S60 1HR
Record Crowd: 25,000 v Sheffield U, Division 2, 13 December 1952 and v Sheffield W, Division 2, 26 January 1952
Stadium Capacity: 15,736

Year Formed: 1884
Colours: Red shirts, white shorts and socks
Joined League: 1919 Elected to Division 2
Honours: Division 3 Champions: 1980–81. Division 3 (North) Champions: 1950–51. Division 4 Champions: 1988–89.

Entered as Rotherham County in 1919 and amalgamated with Rotherham Town in 1925, a League club in the 1890s. Came close to promotion to the First Division in 1954–55 finishing on equal points with the Champions and runners-up, but third on inferior goal average. Twice reached the FA Cup fifth round and League Cup runners-up in 1961.

Scarborough

Address: The Athletic Ground, Seamer Road, Scarborough YO12 4HF
Record Crowd: 11,130 v Luton T, FA Cup 3rd round, 8 January 1938
Stadium Capacity: 7,600
Year Formed: 1879
Colours: All red
Joined League: Promoted to Division 4 1987
Honours Highest Placing: 5th, Division 4 1988–89.

Promoted to the Fourth Division in 1987, they finished fifth in the table in their second season. Have four times reached the third round of the FA Cup.

Scunthorpe United

Address: Glanford Park, Doncaster Road, Scunthorpe, South Humberside
Record Crowd: 23,935 v Portsmouth, FA Cup 4th round, 30 January 1954 (at The Old Showground)
Stadium Capacity: 10,300
Year Formed: 1899
Colours: All claret and blue
Joined League: 1950 Elected to Division 3 (North)
Honours: Division 3 (North) Champions: 1957–58.

Came into the Third Division (North) on the expansion of the League and won promotion to the Second Division in 1958. Highest placing: fourth in 1961–62. Have moved between the lowest two divisions since 1964. Twice reached the fifth round of the FA Cup.

Sheffield United

Address: Bramall Lane, Sheffield S2 4SU
Record Crowd: 68,287 v Leeds U, FA Cup 5th round, 15 February 1936
Stadium Capacity: 35,618
Year Formed: 1889
Colours: Red and white striped shirts, black shorts, red socks
Joined League: 1892 Elected to Division 2
Honours: Division 1 Champions: 1897–98. Division 2 Champions: 1952–53. Division 4 Champions: 1981–82. FA Cup winners: 1899, 1902, 1915, 1925.

Elected to the Second Division, they won promotion in their first season and became First Division Champions in 1897–98. Had switched between the top two divisions at varying intervals until relegated to Division Three for the first time in 1979. Two years later they were in Division Four. FA Cup winners on four occasions.

Sheffield Wednesday

Address: Hillsborough, Sheffield S6 1SW
Record Crowd: 72,841 v Manchester C, FA Cup 5th round, 17 February 1934
Stadium Capacity: 38,780
Year Formed: 1867

Varadi beats Chelsea's Joey Jones in 1984. His goals helped Wednesday to promotion that year.

Colours: Blue and white striped shirts, black shorts, white socks
Joined League: 1892 Elected to Division 1
Honours: Division 1 Champions: 1902–03, 1903–04, 1928–29, 1929–30. Division 2 Champions: 1899–1900, 1925–26, 1951–52, 1955–56, 1958–59. FA Cup winners: 1896, 1907, 1935.

Four times First Division Champions, the last in 1930. Have won the FA Cup on three occasions but not since 1935. In the 1950s changed between Division Two and the First Division seven times. Also had five years in Division Three from 1975 to 1980. Returned to the First Division in 1984, but relegated in 1990.

Shrewsbury Town

Address: Gay Meadow, Shrewsbury SY2 6AB
Record Crowd: 18,917 v Walsall, Division 3, 26 April 1961
Stadium Capacity: 15,000
Year Formed: 1886
Colours: White shirts and socks, blue shorts
Joined League: 1950 Elected to Division 3 (North)
Honours: Division 3 Champions: 1978–79. Welsh Cup winners: 1891, 1938, 1977, 1979, 1984, 1985.

Elected to the Third Division (North) on League expansion but dropped for one season to Division Four on its formation in 1958. Had 10 years in the Second Division from 1979, following another single term in Division Four in 1974–75. Twice in the FA Cup sixth round and League Cup semi-finalists in 1961.

Southampton

Address: The Dell, Milton Road, Southampton SO9 4XX
Record Crowd: 31,044 v Manchester U, Division 1, 8 October 1969
Stadium Capacity: 21,900
Year Formed: 1885
Colours: Red and white striped shirts, black shorts, white socks
Joined League: 1920 Founder members of Division 3
Honours: Division 3 Champions: 1959–60. Division 3 (South) Champions: 1921–22. FA Cup winners: 1976.

One of the most consistent teams in the First Division since 1978, they were runners-up in 1984. Had won the FA Cup in 1976 and were runners-up in the League Cup in 1979. Began in Division Three in 1920 and had one previous period in the First Division from 1966 to 1974. Twice beaten finalists in the FA Cup at the turn of the century.

Southend United

Address: Roots Hall Ground, Victoria Avenue, Southend-on-Sea SS2 6NQ
Record Crowd: 31,090 v Liverpool, FA Cup 3rd round, 10 January 1979
Stadium Capacity: 11,053
Year Formed: 1906
Colours: Blue shirts and socks, yellow shorts
Joined League: 1920 Founder members of Division 3
Honours: Division 4 Champions 1980–81.

One of the original members of the Third Division, they twice finished third in the division before reorganisation in 1958 kept them in it. Since then have been relegated five times to the Fourth Division. Three times reached the fifth round of the FA Cup.

Stockport County

Address: Edgeley Park, Hardcastle Road, Stockport, Cheshire SK3 9DD
Record Crowd: 27,833 v Liverpool, FA Cup 5th round, 11 February 1950
Stadium Capacity: 8,520
Year Formed: 1883
Colours: White shirts and socks, royal blue shorts
Joined League: 1900 Elected to Division 2
Honours: Division 3 (North) Champions: 1921–22, 1936–37. Division 4 Champions: 1966–67.

Survived one season out of the League in the 1900s and had two later spells in Division Two. Their highest placing came in 1905–06 when they finished 10th, the first season after re-election. Twice reached the fifth round of the FA Cup.

Stoke City

Address: Victoria Ground, Stoke-on-Trent ST4 4EG

The Sunderland team that collected the League title in 1895.

Record Crowd: 51,380 v Arsenal, Division 1, 29 March 1937
Stadium Capacity: 35,812
Year Formed: 1863, on a firm basis from 1868
Colours: Red and white striped shirts, white shorts and socks
Joined League: 1888 Founder members of the Football League
Honours: Division 2 Champions: 1932–33, 1962–63. Division 3 (North) Champions: 1926–27. League Cup winners: 1972.

The former Stoke club briefly failed to be re-elected then resigned. Returned under its present title in 1919 and apart from one season in the Third Division (North) in the 1920s remained in Divisions One or Two until 1990. Highest placing: fourth in the First Division on two occasions. Three times FA Cup semi-finalists and League Cup winners 1972.

Sunderland

Address: Roker Park Ground, Sunderland SR6 9SW
Record Crowd: 75,118 v Derby Co, FA Cup 6th round replay, 8 March 1933
Stadium Capacity: 31,887
Year Formed: 1879
Colours: Red and white striped shirts, black shorts, white socks
Joined League: 1890 Elected to Division 1
Honours: Division 1 Champions: 1891–92, 1892–93, 1894–95, 1901–02, 1912–13, 1935–36. Division 2 Champions: 1975–76. Division 3 Champions: 1987–88. FA Cup winners: 1937, 1973.

Enjoyed 68 years association with the First Division until relegated in 1958. Had several ups and downs between the top two divisions until relegated to the Third Division for the first time in 1987. Six times First Division Champions, twice FA Cup winners, and League Cup runners-up once. Three Division One titles achieved in the 1890s.

Swansea City

Address: Vetch Field, Swansea SA1 3SU

Record Crowd: 32,796 v Arsenal, FA Cup 4th round, 17 February 1968
Stadium Capacity: 16,098
Year Formed: 1912
Colours: White shirts and shorts, black socks
Joined League: 1920 Founder members of Division 3
Honours: Division 3 (South) Champions: 1924–25, 1948–49. Welsh Cup winners: 1913, 1932, 1950, 1961, 1966, 1981, 1982, 1983, 1989.

Highest placing in the League was sixth in the First Division in 1981–82, their first in the top flight. Had originally been members of the Third Division, but have had four periods in the Second Division. Quickly relegated from Division One to Division Four from 1983 to 1986. Twice FA Cup semi-finalists.

Swindon Town

Address: County Ground, Swindon, Wiltshire SN1 2ED
Record Crowd: 32,000 v Arsenal, FA Cup 3rd round, 15 January 1972
Stadium Capacity: 16,153
Year Formed: c.1881
Colours: All red
Joined League: 1920 Founder members of Division 3
Honours: Division 4 Champions: 1985–86. League Cup winners: 1969. Anglo-Italian Cup winners: 1970.

Won promotion from the Third Division for the first time in 1963 and have twice repeated the process. Highest placing: fourth in the Second Division in 1989–90. Had twice been FA Cup semi-finalists in 1910 and 1912 before entering the League in the Third Division on its formation. League Cup winners 1969. Won promotion to Division One in 1990, but the League ordered them back down owing to financial irregularities.

Torquay United

Address: Plainmoor Ground, Torquay, Devon TQ1 3PS
Record Crowd: 21,908 v Huddersfield T, FA Cup 4th round, 29 January 1955
Stadium Capacity: 5,539
Year Formed: 1898
Colours: All white with blue and yellow trim
Joined League: 1927 Elected to Division 3 (South)
Honours Highest Placing: 4th, Division 3, 1967–68.

Entered the Third Division (South) in 1927 but became Fourth Division members upon reorganisation in 1958. Have had two subsequent spells in Division Three. Reached the fourth round of the FA Cup on five occasions.

Tottenham Hotspur

Address: 748 High Road, London N17 0AP
Record Crowd: 75,038 v Sunderland, FA Cup 6th round, 5 March 1938
Stadium Capacity: 29,700
Year Formed: 1882
Colours: White shirts and socks, navy blue shorts
Joined League: 1908 Elected to Division 2

Danny Blanchflower and Bobby Smith parade the FA Cup in Spurs' double-winning year of 1961.

Honours: Division 1 Champions: 1950–51, 1960–61. Division 2 Champions: 1919–20, 1949–50. FA Cup winners: 1901 (as a Southern League club), 1921, 1961, 1962, 1967, 1981, 1982 (Seven wins – a record held jointly with Manchester United and Aston Villa). League Cup winners: 1971, 1973. European Cup-Winners' Cup winners: 1963. UEFA Cup winners: 1972, 1984.

The last non-League club to win the FA Cup in 1901, they hold the joint record of seven wins in the competition and did not lose in the final until 1987. Twice First Division Champions in 1951 and 1961. League Cup winners on two occasions. Achieved European Cup-Winners' Cup success in 1963 and have twice won the UEFA Cup in 1972 and 1984. Five periods in the First Division, the last beginning in 1978.

Tranmere Rovers

Address: Prenton Park, Prenton Road West, Birkenhead L42 9PN
Record Crowd: 24,424 v Stoke C, FA Cup 4th round, 5 February 1972
Stadium Capacity: 14,200
Year Formed: 1883
Colours: All white
Joined League: 1921 Founder members of Division 3 (North)
Honours: Division 3 (North) Champions: 1937–38. Welsh Cup winners: 1935. Associate Members' Cup winners: 1990.

Spent one season in Division Two in 1938–39, but have since shifted between the Third and Fourth Divisions. Three separate periods in the Fourth Division, the longest from 1979 to 1989. Reached the fifth round of the FA Cup in 1967–68.

Walsall

Address: Bescot Stadium, Walsall WS1 4SA
Record Crowd: 25,453 v Newcastle U, Division 2, 29 August 1961 (at Fellows Park)
Stadium Capacity: 15,250
Year Formed: 1888
Colours: Red shirts, white shorts and socks
Joined League: 1892 Elected to Division 2
Honours: Division 4 Champions: 1959–60.

Elected to the Second Division in 1892, they twice failed re-election and had to wait 20 years before returning as members of the Third Division (North) in 1921. Later played in the South section and dropped into the Fourth Division in 1958. Have since had two spells in Division Two. Three times in the FA Cup fifth round and 1984 League Cup semi-finalists.

Watford

Address: Vicarage Road Stadium, Watford WD1 8ER
Record Crowd: 34,099 v Manchester U, FA Cup 4th round, 3 February 1969
Stadium Capacity: 23,000
Year Formed: 1891
Colours: Yellow shirts with black and red trim, black shorts, red socks
Joined League: 1920 Founder members of Division 3
Honours: Division 3 Champions: 1968–69. Division 4 Champions: 1977–78.

Dropped into the Fourth Division on reorganisation in 1958 having been original members of Division Three. Reached Division Two for the first time in 1969 and again in 1979 before attaining First Division status in 1982 which they held for six years. FA Cup runners-up in 1984 a year after finishing second in the League Championship. League Cup semi-finalists 1979.

West Bromwich Albion

Address: The Hawthorns, West Bromwich B71 4LF
Record Crowd: 64,815 v Arsenal, FA Cup 6th round, 6 March 1937
Stadium Capacity: 33,565
Year Formed: 1879
Colours: Navy blue and white striped shirts, navy blue shorts, white socks
Joined League: 1888 Founder members of the Football League
Honours: Division 1 Champions: 1919–20. Division 2 Champions: 1901–02, 1910–11. FA Cup winners: 1888, 1892, 1931, 1954, 1968. League Cup winners: 1966.

Founder members of the League, they have remained in either of the top two divisions as Full Members ever since. First Division Champions in

1920, they have won the FA Cup five times, including the season before the League was formed. Also won the League Cup in 1966. Had an uninterrupted run in Division One from 1949 to 1973.

West Ham United

Address: Boleyn Ground, Green Street, Upton Park, London E13 9AZ
Record Crowd: 42,322 v Tottenham H, Division 1, 17 October 1970
Stadium Capacity: 35,510
Year Formed: 1895

Trevor Brooking celebrates scoring the winner in West Ham's 1980 FA Cup triumph.

Colours: Claret shirts with blue trim, white shorts and socks
Joined League: 1919 Elected to Division 2
Honours: Division 2 Champions: 1957–58, 1980–81. FA Cup winners: 1964, 1975, 1980. European Cup-Winners' Cup winners: 1965.

Won promotion four years after entering the League. Had a lengthy spell in the Second Division either side of the War, before 20 years in Division One from 1958. Highest placing: third in the First Division in 1985–86. Three times FA Cup winners and twice runners-up in the League Cup. Won the European Cup-Winners' Cup in 1965.

Wigan Athletic

Address: Springfield Park, Wigan WN6 7BA
Record Crowd: 27,500 v Hereford U, FA Cup 2nd round, 12 December 1953
Stadium Capacity: 11,434
Year Formed: 1932
Colours: Royal blue shirts and shorts, white socks
Joined League: 1978 Elected to Division 4
Honours: Associate Members' Cup winners: 1985.

Elected to the Fourth Division in 1978, they were promoted to Division Three in 1982. Have twice reached the fourth round of the FA Cup in 1980 and 1986.

Wimbledon

Address: Plough Lane Ground, Durnsford Road, Wimbledon, London SW19 8HG
Record Crowd: 18,000 v HMS Victory, FA Amateur Cup 3rd round, 1934–35
Stadium Capacity: 13,806
Year Formed: 1889
Colours: All royal blue with yellow trim
Joined League: 1977 Elected to Division 4
Honours: Division 4 Champions: 1982–83. FA Cup winners: 1988.

Despite reaching the Third Division after two seasons in Division Four, following their election in 1977, suffered two bouts of relegation before gaining First Division status in three years, 1983–86. Won the FA Cup in 1988. Highest placing: sixth in Division One 1986–87.

Wolverhampton Wanderers

Address: Molineux Grounds, Wolverhampton WV1 4QR
Record Crowd: 61,315 v Liverpool, FA Cup 5th round, 11 February 1939
Stadium Capacity: 25,000
Year Formed: 1877 or 1879
Colours: Old gold shirts and socks, black shorts
Joined League: 1888 Founder members of the Football League
Honours: Division 1 Champions: 1953–54, 1957–58, 1958–59. Division 2 Champions: 1931–32, 1976–77. Division 3 Champions: 1988–89. Division 3 (North) Champions: 1923–24. Division 4 Champions: 1987–88. FA Cup winners: 1893, 1908, 1949, 1960. League Cup winners: 1974, 1980. Associate Members' Cup winners: 1988.

Derek Dougan scored 93 goals for Wolves in his seven-year career with the club 1967–74.

Enjoyed their most successful period in the 1950s when they won the First Division title three times. Only club to win championship of all four divisions. FA Cup winners on four occasions, they also achieved the League Cup twice. Their worst spell came in 1984–86 when they dropped from the First to the Fourth Division.

Wrexham

Address: Racecourse Ground, Mold Road, Wrexham LL1 2AN
Record Crowd: 34,445 v Manchester U, FA Cup 4th round, 26 January 1957
Stadium Capacity: 20,000
Year Formed: 1873
Colours: Red shirts and socks with white trim, white shorts
Joined League: 1921 Founder members of Division 3 (North)
Honours: Division 3 Champions: 1977–78. Welsh Cup winners: 1878, 1883, 1893, 1897, 1903, 1905, 1909, 1910, 1911, 1914, 1915, 1921, 1924, 1925, 1931, 1957, 1958, 1960, 1972, 1975, 1978, 1986.

Original members of the Third Division (North), they enjoyed their best spell from 1978 when they had four years in the Second Division. During this period they finished 15th in 1978–79. Twice reached the sixth round of the FA Cup in the 1970s.

York City

Address: Bootham Crescent, York YO3 7AQ
Record Crowd: 28,123 v Huddersfield T, FA Cup 6th round, 5 March 1938
Stadium Capacity: 14,109
Year Formed: 1922
Colours: Red shirts, navy blue shorts, white socks
Joined League: 1929 Elected to Division 3 (North)
Honours: Division 4 Champions: 1983–84.

As members of the Third Division (North) they reached the FA Cup semi-final in 1955. Had two seasons in Division Two during the 1970s and finished 15th in 1974–75. They have had five periods in Division Four.

Scottish Clubs

Aberdeen

Address: Pittodrie Stadium, Aberdeen AB2 1QH
Record Crowd: 45,061 v Hearts, Scottish Cup 4th round, 13 March 1954
Stadium Capacity: 22,568
Year Formed: 1903
Colours: All red
Joined League: 1904
Honours: Division 1 Champions: 1954–55. Premier Division Champions: 1979–80, 1983–84, 1984–85. Scottish Cup winners: 1947, 1970, 1982, 1983, 1984, 1986, 1990. Scottish League Cup winners: 1955–56, 1976–77, 1985–86, 1989–90. European Cup-Winners' Cup winners: 1983. Drybrough Cup winners: 1971, 1980.

Have had more than 80 years in the top division, but had to wait until the 1980s before breaking into the Celtic-Rangers stranglehold on the Championship and Scottish Cup. Promoted after their first season in the Second Division, achieved their initial honour in the Scottish Cup in 1947.

Willie Miller takes the trophy on a lap of honour after Aberdeen won the European Cup-Winners' Cup in 1983.

Airdrieonians

Address: Broomfield Park, Gartlea Road, Airdrie ML6 9JL
Record Crowd: 24,000 v Hearts, Scottish Cup 4th round, 8 March 1952
Stadium Capacity: 11,830
Year Formed: 1878
Colours: White shirts and shorts, red socks
Joined League: 1894
Honours: Division 2 Champions: 1902–03, 1954–55, 1973–74. Scottish Cup winners: 1924.

Finished runners-up in the First Division four seasons in succession from 1922–23 to 1925–26 and also won the Scottish Cup during this period. Have had several spells in the Second Division but won promotion to the Premier Division in 1980, staying for two seasons.

Albion Rovers

Address: Cliftonhill Stadium, Main Street, Coatbridge ML5 9XX
Record Crowd: 27,381 v Rangers, Scottish Cup 2nd round, 8 February 1936
Stadium Capacity: 878
Year Formed: 1882
Colours: Yellow shirts and socks, red shorts
Joined League: 1903
Honours: Division 2 Champions: 1933–34. Second Division Champions: 1988–89.

Entered the Second Division originally and gained a place in the enlarged First Division after the First World War. After being relegated in 1923, won the Second Division title by one point in 1933–34. Scottish Cup runners-up in 1920.

Alloa

Address: Recreation Park, Clackmannan Road, Alloa FK10 1RR
Record Crowd: 13,000 v Dunfermline Ath, Scottish Cup 3rd round replay, 26 February 1939
Stadium Capacity: 3,100
Year Formed: 1883

Colours: Gold shirts and socks, black shorts
Joined League: 1921
Honours: Division 2 Champions: 1921–22.

A highly successful first season brought them promotion and a place in Division One. Have four times finished runners-up in the new-style Second Division since the reorganisation in 1975.

Arbroath

Address: Gayfield Park, Arbroath DD11 1QB
Record Crowd: 13,510 v Rangers, Scottish Cup 3rd round, 23 February 1952
Stadium Capacity: 10,000
Year Formed: 1878
Colours: Maroon shirts and socks, white shorts
Joined League: 1921
Honours: Division 2 Runners-up: 1934–35, 1958–59, 1967–68, 1971–72.

Gained fame in pre-Scottish League days by winning a Scottish Cup tie 36–0 against Bon Accord in 1885. Had four different periods in the old First Division but have spent over 10 years in the Second Division since their last spell.

Ayr United

Address: Somerset Park, Tryfield Place, Ayr KA8 9NB
Record Crowd: 25,225 v Rangers, Division 1, 13 September 1969
Stadium Capacity: 18,500
Year Formed: 1910
Colours: White shirts and socks, black shorts
Joined League: 1897
Honours: Division 2 Champions: 1911–12, 1912–13, 1927–28, 1936–37, 1958–59, 1965–66. Second Division Champions: 1987–88.

Have experienced varying fortunes in the League since joining the Second Division. Their longest period in the First Division came from 1928–36 but they also spent three seasons in the Premier Division on its formation.

Berwick Rangers

Address: Shielfield Park, Tweedmouth, Berwick-upon-Tweed, TD15 2EF
Record Crowd: 13,365 v Rangers, Scottish Cup 1st round, 28 January 1967
Stadium Capacity: 10,673
Year Formed: 1881
Colours: All black
Joined League: 1955
Honours: Second Division Champions: 1978–79.

The only English-based club in the Scottish League, they have spent all but two seasons of their existence in the competition as members of the Second Division. Won the championship of the division in 1978–79 by two points.

Brechin City

Address: Glebe Park, Brechin, Angus DD9 6BJ
Record Crowd: 8,122 v Aberdeen, Scottish Cup 3rd round, 3 February 1973
Stadium Capacity: 3,491
Year Formed: 1906
Colours: All red
Joined League: 1929
Honours: Second Division Champions: 1982–83, 1989–90. Division C Champions: 1953–54.

Had 10 years in the Second Division up to the Second World War but found themselves out of the League after post-War reorganisation. Came through via the old C Division and returned in 1954. In 1983 won a place in the First Division for the first time.

Celtic

Address: Celtic Park, 95 Kerrydale Street, Glasgow G40 3RE
Record Crowd: 92,000 v Rangers, Division 1, 1 January 1938
Stadium Capacity: 60,800
Year Formed: 1888
Colours: Green and white hooped shirts, white shorts and socks
Joined League: 1890 Founder members of Division 1
Honours: Division 1 Champions: 1892–93, 1893–94, 1895–96, 1897–98, 1904–05, 1905–06, 1906–07, 1907–08, 1908–09, 1909–10, 1913–14, 1914–15, 1915–16, 1916–17, 1918–19, 1921–22, 1925–26, 1935–36, 1937–38, 1953–54, 1965–66, 1966–67, 1967–68, 1968–69, 1969–70, 1970–71, 1971–72, 1972–73, 1973–74. Premier Division

A fine, attacking full back, Danny McGrain made over 600 appearances for Celtic.

Champions: 1976–77, 1978–79, 1980–81, 1981–82, 1985–86, 1987–88. Scottish Cup winners: 1892, 1899, 1900, 1904, 1907, 1908, 1911, 1912, 1914, 1923, 1925, 1927, 1931, 1933, 1937, 1951, 1954, 1965, 1967, 1969, 1971, 1972, 1974, 1975, 1977, 1980, 1985, 1988, 1989. Scottish League Cup winners: 1956–57, 1957–58, 1965–66, 1966–67, 1967–68, 1968–69, 1969–70, 1974–75, 1982–83. European Cup winners: 1967.

Have enjoyed an uninterrupted century of association with the First Division and then the Premier Division to become the second most successful club in the country's history. Between 1965–66 and 1973–74 achieved a record nine consecutive titles under the managership of Jock Stein. The club also became the first in Britain to win the European Cup. Still lead in the number of Scottish Cup trophies.

Clyde

Address: Firhill Park, 90 Firhill Road, Glasgow G20 7AL
Record Crowd: 52,000 v Rangers, Division 1, 21 November 1908
Stadium Capacity: 20,600
Year Formed: 1878
Colours: White shirts and socks, black shorts
Joined League: 1891
Honours: Division 2 Champions: 1904–05, 1951–52, 1956–57, 1961–62, 1972–73. Second Division Champions: 1977–78, 1981–82. Scottish Cup winners: 1939, 1955, 1958.

Won their initial Second Division title in the year before there was automatic promotion. Enjoyed several other championship successes in the division in the 1950s and were able to record their second and third Scottish Cup wins in the same era.

Clydebank

Address: Kilbowie Park, Arran Place, Clydebank G81 2PB
Record Crowd: 14,900 v Hibernian, Scottish Cup 1st round, 10 February 1965
Stadium Capacity: 9,900
Year Formed: 1965
Colours: All white
Joined League: 1966
Honours: Second Division Champions: 1975–76.

Became the first Scottish club to win promotion to the Premier Division in successive seasons from the Second Division but stayed just one season in the upper bracket during 1977–78. Had two more campaigns in the Premier from 1985–87.

Cowdenbeath

Address: Central Park, Cowdenbeath KY4 9EY
Record Crowd: 25,586 v Rangers, Scottish League Cup quarter-final, 21 September 1949
Stadium Capacity: 7,250
Year Formed: 1881
Colours: Royal blue shirts and socks, white shorts
Joined League: 1905
Honours: Division 2 Champions: 1913–14, 1914–15, 1938–39.

Suffered badly during their three championship seasons in Division Two. During the first two title runs, automatic promotion had not been brought in and their last before the Second World War came to a halt when reorganisation left them back in the lower division.

Dumbarton

Address: Boghead Park, Miller Street, Dumbarton G82 2JA
Record Crowd: 18,000 v Raith R, Scottish Cup quarter-final, 2 March 1957
Stadium Capacity: 10,700
Year Formed: 1872
Colours: Gold shirts, black shorts, gold and black socks
Joined League: 1890 Founder members of Division 1
Honours: Division 1 Champions: 1890–91 (Shared with Rangers), 1891–92. Division 2 Champions: 1910–11, 1971–72. Scottish Cup winners: 1883.

Had the distinction of sharing the first Championship with Rangers and finishing two points ahead of Celtic the following season to take it for their own. Have had one season in the Premier Division during 1984–85, but their only Scottish Cup success came last century, when they were also runners-up on five other occasions.

Dundee

Address: Dens Park, Sandeman Street, Dundee DD3 7JY
Record Crowd: 43,024 v Rangers, Scottish Cup 2nd round, 7 February 1953
Stadium Capacity: 22,381
Year Formed: 1893
Colours: Dark blue shirts with red and white trim, white shorts, red socks
Joined League: 1893
Honours: Division 1 Champions: 1961–62. First Division Champions: 1978–79. Division 2 Champions: 1946–47. Scottish Cup winners: 1910. Scottish League Cup winners: 1951–52, 1952–53, 1973–74.

Have not been in the Second Division since winning the championship in 1946–47, but have had to struggle to keep a place in the Premier Division. In 1989–90 they were in their third spell at the top, but were relegated. Have achieved several cup honours in both competitions.

Dundee United

Address: Tannadice Park, Tannadice Street, Dundee DD3 7JW

Paul Hegarty, a stalwart in defence for Dundee United throughout the 1980s.

Record Crowd: 28,000 v Barcelona, Fairs Cup 2nd round, 16 November 1966
Stadium Capacity: 22,310
Year Formed: 1909
Colours: Tangerine shirts and socks, black shorts
Joined League: 1910
Honours: Premier Division Champions: 1982–83. Division 2 Champions: 1924–25, 1928–29. Scottish League Cup winners: 1979–80, 1980–81.

One of the founder members of the Premier Division in 1975, they have since established themselves. Also finished as runners-up in the UEFA Cup in 1986–87 and had reached the semi-final of the European Cup three seasons earlier. Manager Jim McLean, appointed in 1971, has led them to their success.

Dunfermline Athletic

Address: East End Park, Halbeath Road, Dunfermline KY12 7RB
Record Crowd: 27,816 v Celtic, Division 1, 30 April 1968
Stadium Capacity: 27,500
Year Formed: 1885
Colours: Black and white striped shirts, black shorts and socks
Joined League: 1912
Honours: First Division Champions: 1988–89. Division 2 Champions: 1925–26. Second Division Champions: 1985–86. Scottish Cup winners: 1961, 1968.

The 1980s provided the club with various changes involving all three divisions. Between 1985 and 1987 they reached the Premier Division in successive seasons, but were immediately relegated. Bounced back at the first attempt. Had some Scottish Cup success in the 1960s and were semi-finalists in the Cup-Winners' Cup in 1968–69.

East Fife

Address: Bayview Park, Methil, Fife KY8 3AG
Record Crowd: 22,515 v Raith R, Division 1, 2 January 1950
Stadium Capacity: 14,200
Year Formed: 1903
Colours: Black and gold striped shirts, black shorts and socks with gold and white trim
Joined League: 1921
Honours: Division 2 Champions: 1947–48. Scottish Cup winners: 1938. Scottish League Cup winners: 1947–48, 1949–50, 1953–54.

Can claim to be the only Second Division team to win the Scottish Cup and the League Cup. Had only a few seasons in three separate periods in the old-style First Division and have yet to play in the Premier Division.

East Stirlingshire

Address: Firs Park, Firs Street, Falkirk FK2 7AY
Record Crowd: 11,500 v Hibernian, Scottish Cup 2nd round, 10 February 1969
Stadium Capacity: 6,000
Year Formed: 1881
Colours: White shirts, black shorts and socks
Joined League: 1900
Honours: Division 2 Champions: 1931–32.

Have had breaks in their membership of the League, including one when combined with Clydebank in 1964–65. Won promotion to the First Division in 1931–32 but stayed just one season in the top bracket and did the same in 1963–64.

Falkirk

Address: Brockville Park, Hope Street, Falkirk FK1 5AX
Record Crowd: 23,100 v Celtic, Scottish Cup 3rd round, 21 February 1953
Stadium Capacity: 18,000
Year Formed: 1876
Colours: Dark blue shirts with white trim, white shorts, red socks
Joined League: 1902
Honours: Division 2 Champions: 1935–36, 1969–70, 1974–75. Second Division Champions: 1979–80. Scottish Cup winners: 1913, 1957.

Despite two seasons in the Premier Division between 1986 and 1988, they have also had spells in the Second Division. But in the years before the First World War they were twice runners-up to Celtic in the First Division in 1907–08 and 1909–10.

Forfar Athletic

Address: Station Park, Carseview Road, Forfar DD8 3BT
Record Crowd: 10,780 v Rangers, Scottish Cup 2nd round, 2 February 1970
Stadium Capacity: 8,732
Year Formed: 1885
Colours: Sky blue shirts and socks, white shorts
Joined League: 1921
Honours: Second Division Champions: 1983–84. Division C Champions: 1948–49.

Re-entered the League from the old C Division, having lost their status in post-War reorganisation. Also had a break for one season in 1925–26. Scottish Cup semi-finalists in 1982 and in the last four of the League Cup in 1978.

Brian Whittaker was part of the Hearts side that regularly challenged for honours in the late 1980s.

Hamilton Academical

Address: Douglas Park, Douglas Park Lane, Hamilton ML3 0DF
Record Crowd: 28,690 v Hearts, Scottish Cup 3rd round, 3 March 1937
Stadium Capacity: 14,505
Year Formed: 1875
Colours: Red and white hooped shirts, white shorts and socks
Joined League: 1897
Honours: First Division Champions: 1985–86, 1987–88. Division 2 Champions: 1903–04.

Came into the League on the demise of Renton, then gained promotion to the First Division and had a lengthy period in it until relegated in 1947. Have had two seasons in the Premier Division but went back down again on each occasion. Twice runners-up in the Scottish Cup in 1911 and 1935.

Heart of Midlothian

Address: Tynecastle Park, Gorgie Road, Edinburgh EH11 2NL
Record Crowd: 53,496 v Rangers, Scottish Cup 3rd round, 13 February 1932
Stadium Capacity: 29,000
Year Formed: 1874
Colours: Maroon shirts and socks, white shorts
Joined League: 1890 Founder members of Division 1
Honours: Division 1 Champions: 1894–95, 1896–97, 1957–58, 1959–60. First Division Champions: 1979–80. Scottish Cup winners: 1891, 1896, 1901, 1906, 1956. Scottish League Cup winners: 1954–55, 1958–59, 1959–60, 1962–63.

Returned to the Premier Division in 1983 and have had only four seasons out of the top echelon since coming into the League. Enjoyed 87 years there before suffering relegation for the first time in 1977. Have achieved honours in the Championship and both cup competitions. Their last First Division title was 30 years ago.

Hibernian

Address: Easter Road Stadium, Albion Road, Edinburgh EH7 5QG
Record Crowd: 65,860 v Hearts, Division 1, 2 January 1950
Stadium Capacity: 23,353
Year Formed: 1875

Gordon Rae on the ball for Hibernian.

Colours: Green shirts with white sleeves, white shorts and socks
Joined League: 1893
Honours: Division 1 Champions: 1902–03, 1947–48, 1950–51, 1951–52. First Division Champions: 1980–81. Division 2 Champions: 1893–94, 1894–95, 1932–33. Scottish Cup winners: 1887, 1902. Scottish League Cup winners: 1972–73.

Gained a place in the First Division after two seasons in the League, but apart from two terms (1931–33 and 1980–81) have remained in the leading division. Their best period was in the years after the Second World War and in 1950–51 they finished 10 points ahead of Rangers in the Championship. First Scottish club to play in Europe.

Kilmarnock

Address: Rugby Park, Kilmarnock KA1 2DP
Record Crowd: 34,246 v Rangers, Scottish League Cup, August 1963
Stadium Capacity: 17,528
Year Formed: 1869
Colours: Blue and white hooped shirts, blue shorts and socks
Joined League: 1895
Honours: Division 1 Champions: 1964–65. Division 2 Champions: 1897–98, 1898–99. Scottish Cup winners: 1920, 1929.

Succeeded in gaining a place in Division One after twice winning the Second Division title in the years before the turn of the century. Kept their position until 1947. Despite having three short spells in the Premier Division were relegated to the Second Division for the first time under the new structure in 1989, but came back.

Meadowbank Thistle

Address: Meadowbank Stadium, London Road, Edinburgh EH7 6AE
Record Crowd: 4,000 v Albion R, Scottish League Cup 1st round, 9 September 1974
Stadium Capacity: 16,500
Year Formed: 1943
Colours: Amber shirts and socks with black trim, black shorts
Joined League: 1974
Honours: Second Division Champions: 1986–87

Elected to the League when reorganisation was about to take place and, apart from a few years struggling at the foot of the Second Division, have improved their status. Were unlucky not to gain a place in the Premier Division in 1988 after finishing runners-up. Only one team was promoted.

Montrose

Address: Links Park, Wellington Street, Montrose DD10 8QD
Record Crowd: 8,983 v Dundee, Scottish Cup 3rd round, 17 March 1973
Stadium Capacity: 6,500
Year Formed: 1879
Colours: Blue shirts, white shorts, red socks
Joined League: 1929
Honours: Second Division Champions: 1984–85.

Had 10 pre-War years in the Second Division, but found no place after post-War reorganisation. Came back in 1955 and in the first season of the three-division arrangement finished third in the First Division.

Morton

Address: Cappielow Park, Sinclair Street, Greenock PA15 2TY
Record Crowd: 23,500 v Rangers, Scottish Cup 3rd round, 21 February 1953
Stadium Capacity: 16,000
Year Formed: 1874
Colours: Blue and white hooped shirts, white shorts, blue socks
Joined League: 1893
Honours: First Division Champions: 1977–78, 1983–84, 1986–87. Division 2 Champions: 1949–50, 1963–64, 1966–67. Scottish Cup winners: 1922.

Their longest period in the First Division was between 1900 and 1927. Won their Scottish Cup honour during this time. Also had five years in the Premier Division from 1978–83 followed by two more isolated seasons.

Motherwell

Address: Fir Park, Motherwell ML1 2QN
Record Crowd: 35,632 v Rangers, Scottish Cup 4th round replay, 12 March 1952

Stadium Capacity: 23,500
Year Formed: 1886
Colours: Amber shirts with claret trim, claret shorts, amber socks
Joined League: 1893
Honours: Division 1 Champions: 1931–32. First Division Champions: 1981–82, 1984–85. Division 2 Champions: 1953–54, 1968–69. Scottish Cup winners: 1952. Scottish League Cup winners: 1950–51.

Between 1904 and 1948 they were the only team to win the First Division Championship other than Rangers or Celtic. Were runners-up four times during the same period. Have had several seasons in different spells in the Premier Division.

Partick Thistle

Address: Firhill Park, 90 Firhill Road, Glasgow G20 7AL
Record Crowd: 49,838 v Rangers, Division 1, 18 February 1922
Stadium Capacity: 20,600
Year Formed: 1876
Colours: Amber shirts with red sleeves, red shorts and socks
Joined League: 1893
Honours: First Division Champions: 1975–76. Division 2 Champions: 1896–97, 1899–1900, 1970–71. Scottish Cup winners: 1921. Scottish League Cup winners: 1971–72.

Had an uninterrupted 68 years between 1902 and 1970 in the First Division, but since reorganisation have remained in Division One except for six years in the Premier Division. Have won both of the cup competitions once.

Queen of the South

Address: Palmerston Park, Terregles Street, Dumfries DG2 9BA
Record Crowd: 24,500 v Hearts, Scottish Cup 3rd round, 23 February 1952
Stadium Capacity: 13,000
Year Formed: 1919
Colours: Royal blue shirts and socks, white shorts
Joined League: 1925
Honours: Division 2 Champions: 1950–51.

Their most successful period came immediately before and just after the Second World War in the First Division. Even won the championship of the Second Division the season after relegation. Have shuttled between the lower two divisions since reorganisation.

Queen's Park

Address: Hampden Park, Mount Florida, Glasgow G42 9BA
Record Crowd: 95,772 v Rangers, Scottish Cup 1st round, 18 January 1930. Stadium record: 149,547 Scotland v England, 17 April 1937.
Stadium Capacity: 74,730
Year Formed: 1867
Colours: White and black hooped shirts and socks, white shorts
Joined League: 1900
Honours: Division 2 Champions: 1922–23, 1955–56. Second Division Champions: 1980–81. Scottish Cup winners: 1874, 1875, 1876, 1880, 1881, 1882, 1884, 1886, 1890, 1893.

The only amateur club in the Scottish League, whose major achievements were made in the years before they entered the competition. Also reached the FA Cup final twice in the 1880s. In the Scottish Cup they won 28 consecutive ties from the start of 1879–80 to the last eight teams in 1882–83.

Raith Rovers

Address: Stark's Park, Pratt Street, Kirkcaldy KY1 1SA
Record Crowd: 31,306 v Hearts, Scottish Cup 2nd round, 7 February 1953
Stadium Capacity: 9,500
Year Formed: 1883
Colours: Navy blue shirts with white sleeves, white shorts, red socks
Joined League: 1902
Honours: Division 2 Champions: 1907–08, 1909–10 (shared with Leith), 1937–38, 1948–49.

In 1949 they began their most rewarding period in the League as Second Division champions and League Cup runners-up. Remained in the First Division until 1963, but have switched between the two lower divisions since reorganisation.

Appointed player/manager in 1986, Graeme Souness has restored Rangers' position as the leading Scottish club.

Rangers

Address: Ibrox Stadium, Glasgow G51 2XD
Record Crowd: 118,567 v Celtic, Division 1, 2 January 1939
Stadium Capacity: 44,500
Year Formed: 1873
Colours: Royal blue shirts, white shorts, red socks
Joined League: 1890 Founder members of Division 1
Honours: Division 1 Champions: 1890–91 (shared with Dumbarton), 1898–99, 1899–1900, 1900–01, 1901–02, 1910–11, 1911–12, 1912–13, 1917–18, 1919–20, 1920–21, 1922–23, 1923–24, 1924–25, 1926–27, 1927–28, 1928–29, 1929–30, 1930–31, 1932–33, 1933–34, 1934–35, 1936–37, 1938–39, 1946–47, 1948–49, 1949–50, 1952–53, 1955–56, 1956–57, 1958–59, 1960–61, 1962–63, 1963–64, 1974–75. Premier Division Champions: 1975–76, 1977–78, 1986–87, 1988–89, 1989–90. Scottish Cup winners: 1894, 1897, 1898, 1903, 1928, 1930, 1932, 1934, 1935, 1936, 1948, 1949, 1950, 1953, 1960, 1962, 1963, 1964, 1966, 1973, 1976, 1978, 1979, 1981. Scottish League Cup winners: 1946–47, 1948–49, 1960–61, 1961–62, 1963–64, 1964–65, 1970–71, 1975–76, 1977–78, 1978–79, 1981–82, 1983–84, 1984–85, 1986–87, 1987–88, 1988–89. European Cup-Winners' Cup winners: 1971–72.

The most successful team in Scottish League history and leading in the League Cup. Just behind Celtic in Scottish Cup honours. Under the managership of Willy Struth, who led them between August 1920 and April 1953, they won 15 Championships, 10 Scottish Cups and two League Cup trophies. Won the European Cup-Winners' Cup in 1972. Despite a slow start to chasing Premier Division honours, they have responded impressively in recent years.

St Johnstone

Address: McDiarmid Park, Crieff Road, Perth PH1 2SJ
Record Crowd: 29,972 v Dundee, Scottish Cup 2nd round, 10 February 1952
Stadium Capacity: 10,169
Year Formed: 1884
Colours: All royal blue
Joined League: 1911
Honours: First Division Champions: 1982–83, 1989–90. Division 2 Champions: 1923–24, 1959–60, 1962–63.

Their outstanding period was short but productive in the 1930s. Won promotion for the third time in 1932 as runners-up on goal average. Finished fifth in the First Division the following season and were Scottish Cup semi-finalists in 1933–34. Two separate seasons in the Premier Division before 1990.

St Mirren

Address: St Mirren Park, Love Street, Paisley PA3 2EJ
Record Crowd: 47,438 v Celtic, Scottish Cup 4th round, 7 March 1925
Stadium Capacity: 25,344
Year Formed: 1877
Colours: Black and white striped shirts, black shorts and socks
Joined League: 1890 Founder members of Division 1
Honours: First Division Champions: 1976–77. Division 2 Champions: 1967–68. Scottish Cup winners: 1926, 1959, 1987.

Before the 1970s had spent only two isolated seasons in the Second Division. After gaining a berth in the Premier Division in 1977 have remained in the top flight. Twice Scottish Cup winners and three times beaten finalists, as well as once League Cup runners-up.

Stenhousemuir

Address: Ochilview Park, Gladstone Road, Stenhousemuir FK5 5QL
Record Crowd: 12,500 v East Fife, Scottish Cup 4th round, 11 March 1950
Stadium Capacity: 4,000
Year Formed: 1884
Colours: Maroon shirts and socks, white shorts
Joined League: 1921
Honours: Scottish Cup semi-finalists 1902–03.

Have the unenviable record of remaining in the Second Division longer than any other club. Have had continuous association with the division since being elected to the competition. Third on two occasions: 1958–59 and 1960–61.

Stirling Albion

Address: Annfield Park, St Ninian's Road, Stirling FK8 2HE
Record Crowd: 26,400 v Celtic, Scottish Cup 4th round, 14 March 1959
Stadium Capacity: 4,000
Year Formed: 1945
Colours: Red shirts with white sleeves, white shorts and socks
Joined League: 1947
Honours: Division 2 Champions: 1952–53, 1957–58, 1960–61, 1964–65. Second Division Champions: 1976–77. Division C Champions 1946–47.

Won the C Division in only their second season of existence and entered the League in 1947. Had 10 changes of division in the next 15 years. Have never reached the Premier Division. First Scottish League club to use an artificial pitch.

Stranraer

Address: Stair Park, London Road, Stranraer DG9 8BS
Record Crowd: 6,500 v Rangers, Scottish Cup 1st round, 24 January 1948
Stadium Capacity: 4,000
Year Formed: 1870
Colours: All royal blue
Joined League: 1955
Honours Highest Placing: 4th, Division 2, 1960–61, 1976–77.

Have yet to finish higher than fourth in the Second Division, having achieved this position in 1960–61 and again in 1976–77. One of the oldest surviving clubs in Scotland.

Foreign Clubs

Ajax

Address: De Meer, Middenweg 401, Amsterdam
Stadium Capacity: 27,000
Year Formed: 1900
Colours: Red and white shirts, white shorts, red and white socks
Honours: League Champions: 1918, 1919, 1931, 1932, 1934, 1937, 1939, 1947, 1957, 1960, 1966, 1967, 1968, 1970, 1972, 1973, 1977, 1979, 1980, 1982, 1983, 1985, 1990. Cup winners: 1917, 1943, 1961, 1967, 1970, 1971, 1972, 1979, 1983, 1986, 1987. European Cup: 1971, 1972, 1973. European Cup-Winners' Cup winners: 1987. Super Cup winners: 1972, 1973. World Club Champions: 1972.

Ajax goalkeeper Heinz Stuy saves, despite the strong challenge of the Juventus forwards, during the European Cup final of 1973.

Named after the Greek god, they are the most successful club in the Netherlands. They owed their early achievements to British-born Jack Reynolds who took control in 1915 and guided them to five titles in the 1930s. Later Ajax became the first Dutch club to appear in the European Cup final and epitomised the concept of 'total' football.

RSC Anderlecht

Address: Vanden Stock Stadium, Brussels
Stadium Capacity: 32,900
Year Formed: 1908
Colours: All white with violet trim
Honours: League Champions: 1947, 1949, 1950, 1951, 1954, 1955, 1956, 1959, 1962, 1964, 1965, 1966, 1967, 1968, 1972, 1974, 1981, 1985, 1986, 1987. Cup winners: 1965, 1972, 1973, 1975, 1976, 1988, 1989. European Cup-Winners' Cup winners: 1976, 1978. UEFA Cup winners: 1983. Super Cup winners: 1976, 1978.

Did not establish themselves until after the Second World War, having spent many years in the shadow of neighbours Union St Gilloise. Their outstanding manager was Pierre Sinibaldi who from 1960–65 built a team which dominated domestic football. They have had five titles in a row and two hat-tricks.

Athletic Bilbao

Address: Estadio San Mames, Bilbao
Stadium Capacity: 46,500
Year Formed: 1898
Colours: Red and white striped shirts, black shorts and socks
Honours: League Champions: 1930, 1931, 1934, 1936, 1943, 1956, 1983, 1984. Cup winners: 1903,

1904, 1910, 1911, 1914, 1915, 1916, 1921, 1923, 1930, 1931, 1932, 1933, 1943, 1944, 1945, 1950, 1955, 1956, 1958, 1969, 1973, 1984.

Won Spain's first cup trophy in 1903 and are still the most successful in the knockout competition, with 23 successes. The oldest club in the country whose policy of using only Basque players still brought them trophies. Reverted to their English-style name in recognition of their early years when Spanish students were taught to play in England.

Atletico Madrid

Address: Estadio Vicente Calderon, Madrid
Stadium Capacity: 70,000
Year Formed: 1901
Colours: Red and white striped shirts, blue shorts, red socks, white trim
Honours: League Champions: 1940, 1941, 1950, 1951, 1966, 1970, 1973, 1977. Cup winners: 1960, 1961, 1965, 1972, 1976, 1985. European Cup-Winners' Cup winners: 1962. World Club Champions: 1974.

Forever in the shadow of Real, they came close to dislodging their illustrious rivals in the 1958–59 European Cup semi-final and became the first Spanish club to win the European Cup-Winners' Cup. Combined for a time with the Air Force team Atletico Avacione after the civil war.

FK Austria

Address: Hohe, Vienna
Stadium Capacity: 12,000
Year Formed: 1911
Colours: Violet shirts, white shorts, violet socks
Honours: League Champions: 1924, 1926, 1949, 1950, 1953, 1961, 1962, 1963, 1969, 1970, 1976, 1978, 1979, 1980, 1981, 1984, 1985, 1986. Cup winners: 1921, 1924, 1925, 1926, 1933, 1935, 1936, 1948, 1949, 1960, 1962, 1963, 1967, 1971, 1974, 1977, 1980, 1982, 1986, 1990.

The second most successful club in Austria, they can trace their origins to the Vienna Cricket and Football Club formed in the 1890s when there was a sizeable British colony in Vienna. Adopted their present name in the 1920s. Were runners-up in the European Cup-Winners' Cup in 1978.

Spanish international Carrasco played in both of Barcelona's successful Cup-Winners' Cup sides in 1979 and 1982.

Barcelona

Address: Nou Camp, Barcelona
Stadium Capacity: 115,000
Year Formed: 1899
Colours: Red and blue striped shirts, navy blue shorts, blue socks, red trim
Honours: League Champions: 1929, 1945, 1948, 1949, 1952, 1953, 1959, 1960, 1974, 1985. Cup winners: 1910, 1912, 1913, 1920, 1922, 1925, 1926, 1928, 1942, 1951, 1952, 1953, 1957, 1959, 1963, 1968, 1971, 1978, 1981, 1983, 1988, 1990. European Cup-Winners' Cup winners: 1979, 1982, 1989. Fairs Cup winners: 1958, 1960, 1966. Super Cup winners: 1989.

Despite massive support and resources they have been unable to dominate Real Madrid in the League or Athletic Bilbao in the Cup. Formed by a Swiss called Hans Gamper, they played their first match against a team of British sailors. Overcame post-civil war prejudice to enjoy a measure of success in the 1940s and 1950s. They have won seven European trophies in all.

The Bayern Munich side of 1976 lines up behind three European Cups, having won the trophy three times in succession.

Bayern Munich

Address: Olympiastadion, Munich
Stadium Capacity: 73,132
Year Formed: 1900
Colours: All red
Honours: League Champions: 1932, 1969, 1972, 1973, 1974, 1980, 1981, 1985, 1986, 1987, 1989, 1990. Cup winners: 1957, 1966, 1967, 1969, 1971, 1982, 1984, 1986. European Cup winners: 1974, 1975, 1976. European Cup-Winners' Cup winners: 1967. World Club Champions: 1976.

Struggled insignificantly in their early years and apart from one isolated championship and a cup success, made no impression on the scene until the 1960s. Were not even in the Bundesliga when it was formed in 1963 but once promoted soon dominated West German football. Had a hat-trick of European Cup wins and have rarely been out of contention for honours at home, winning six championships in the 1980s.

Benfica

Address: Estadio da Luz, Lisbon
Stadium Capacity: 120,000
Year Formed: 1904
Colours: Red shirts, white shorts, red socks
Honours: League Champions: 1930, 1931, 1935, 1942, 1943, 1945, 1950, 1955, 1957, 1960, 1961, 1963, 1964, 1965, 1967, 1968, 1969, 1971, 1972, 1973, 1975, 1976, 1977, 1981, 1983, 1984, 1987, 1989. Cup winners: 1930, 1931, 1935, 1940, 1943, 1944, 1949, 1951, 1952, 1953, 1955, 1957, 1959, 1962, 1964, 1969, 1970, 1972, 1980, 1981, 1983, 1985, 1986, 1987. European Cup winners: 1961, 1962.

Threatened to assume the mantle of Real Madrid in the European Cup in the 1960s but did not quite sustain their international challenge. Have been the most successful club in Portugal with as many titles as their nearest rivals between them. Their founder and inspiration was Cosme Damiao, who had been taught the game by British residents.

Boca Juniors

Address: Estadio Bombonera, Buenos Aires
Stadium Capacity: 58,570
Year Formed: 1905
Colours: Dark blue shirts, yellow hoop, dark blue shorts and socks
Honours: League Champions: 1919, 1920, 1923, 1926, 1930, 1931, 1934, 1935, 1940, 1943, 1944, 1954, 1962, 1964, 1965, 1976, 1981. South

American Cup winners: 1977, 1978. World Club Champions: 1977.

The most popular club in Argentina and the winners of the first professional championship in 1931. One of the few South American clubs who took a serious interest in the Copa Libertadores when it was being organised. Their rivals for popularity are River Plate.

Bologna

Address: Renato Dell'Ara Stadio, Bologna
Stadium Capacity: 40,782
Year Formed: 1909
Colours: Red and blue striped shirts, blue shorts, blue socks, red trim
Honours: League Champions: 1925, 1929, 1936, 1937, 1939, 1941, 1964. Cup winners: 1970, 1974.

After half a dozen seasons in the Second Division, returned to the upper bracket in 1988. Held sway in the 1930s but arguably their finest achievement came in the 1964 championship-winning success when they defeated Internazionale 2–0 in a play-off in Rome.

Bordeaux

Address: Parc de Lescure, Bordeaux
Stadium Capacity: 50,000
Year Formed: 1898
Colours: Marine blue shirts, white shorts, blue socks
Honours: League Champions: 1950, 1984, 1985, 1987. Cup winners: 1941, 1986, 1987.

Turned professional in 1937 but did not succeed in gaining a Second Division place until 1938–39. Established themselves in the 1980s and in 1986–87 achieved a league and cup double and also reached the semi-finals of the European Cup-Winners' Cup. Had been European Cup semi-finalists in 1985.

Borussia Dortmund

Address: Westfalenstadion, Dortmund
Stadium Capacity: 53,870
Year Formed: 1909
Colours: Yellow shirts, dark brown shorts, yellow socks

Eusebio, Benfica's dazzling forward of the 1960s, scored twice in his club's 1962 European Cup triumph.

Honours: League Champions: 1956, 1957, 1963. Cup winners: 1965, 1989. European Cup-Winners' Cup winners: 1966.

For a period of 10 years from the mid-1950s they dominated West German football and reached their zenith in the 1966 European Cup-Winners' Cup final when they defeated Liverpool 2–1 in extra time. Suffered relegation from the Bundesliga for a time in the early 1970s.

Borussia Moenchengladbach

Address: Bokelberg Stadion, Moenchengladbach
Stadium Capacity: 34,500
Year Formed: 1900
Colours: White shirts, green and blue trim, white shorts and socks
Honours: League Champions: 1970, 1971, 1975, 1976, 1977. Cup winners: 1960, 1973. UEFA Cup winners: 1975, 1979.

Rivalled Bayern Munich in the 1970s as West Germany's top team. Runners-up to Liverpool in the 1973 UEFA Cup and again in the 1977 European Cup, they had two successes in the UEFA Cup and were beaten finalists in 1980.

Botafogo

Address: Estadio General Severiano, Rio de Janeiro
Stadium Capacity: 23,000
Year Formed: 1904
Colours: Black and white striped shirts, black shorts and socks
Honours: League Champions: 1910, 1930, 1932, 1933, 1934, 1935, 1948, 1957, 1961, 1962, 1967, 1968.

One of the founder members of the Rio Metropolitan League championship, they enjoyed their chief success in the 1960s and became one of the most fashionable clubs in the country following amalgamation in 1942. Then the Botafogo club combined with the Club de Regatas.

Club Brugge

Address: Olympiastadion, Brugge
Stadium Capacity: 30,378
Year Formed: 1891
Colours: Light and dark blue shirts, light blue shorts, light and dark blue socks
Honours: League Champions: 1920, 1973, 1976, 1977, 1978, 1980, 1988, 1990. Cup winners: 1968, 1970, 1977, 1986.

Only became a force to be reckoned with in the 1970s and twice in three seasons found themselves narrowly beaten by Liverpool in European finals. Having lost in the 1976 UEFA Cup, they failed again at Wembley in the 1978 European Cup.

Colo Colo

Address: Estadio Colo Colo, Santiago
Stadium Capacity: 10,000
Year Formed: 1925
Colours: White shirts, black shorts, white socks
Honours: League Champions: 1937, 1939, 1941, 1944, 1947, 1953, 1956, 1960, 1963, 1970, 1972, 1979, 1981, 1983, 1986, 1989.

Formed by breakaway members of Magallanes in 1925; the club name is a Chilean expression for wildcat. In the 1940s became a prime mover towards a South American Cup idea. The most successful Chilean club.

IFC Cologne

Address: Mungersdorfer Stadion, Cologne
Stadium Capacity: 60,398
Year Formed: 1901 (re-formed 1948)
Colours: All white
Honours: League Champions: 1962, 1964, 1978.

The influential manager Rinus Michels despairs as Cologne go out of the UEFA Cup in 1981 against Ipswich.

Cup winners: 1968, 1977, 1978, 1983.

Won the first Bundesliga title in 1964 having been right behind the concept of a national league for many years. Twice semi-finalists in the European Cup and the European Cup-Winners' Cup, they were beaten finalists in the UEFA Cup in 1986.

Corinthians

Address: Parque Sao Jorge, Sao Paulo
Stadium Capacity: 30,000
Year Formed: 1910
Colours: White shirts, black shorts, white socks
Honours: League Champions: 1914, 1916, 1922, 1923, 1924, 1928, 1929, 1930, 1937, 1938, 1939, 1941, 1951, 1952, 1954, 1977, 1979, 1982, 1983, 1988.

Founded by a handful of Brazilians after the English club Corinthians had toured the country. The most popular club in Brazil next to Flamengo, despite lack of honours in more recent years.

Cruzeiro

Address: Estadio Magalhaes Pinto, Belo Horizonte
Stadium Capacity: 110,000
Year Formed: 1921
Colours: Blue shirts, white shorts and socks
Honours: League Champions: 1940, 1943, 1944, 1945, 1959, 1960, 1961, 1965, 1966, 1967, 1968, 1969, 1972, 1973, 1974, 1975, 1977, 1984, 1987. South American Cup winners: 1976.

In the mid-1970s Cruzeiro enjoyed a run of success in the South American Cup and gave provincial clubs in Brazil considerable encouragement. The club was originally called Palestra Italia but changed during the Second World War.

CSKA Sofia

Address: Narodna Armia, Sofia
Stadium Capacity: 35,000
Year Formed: 1948
Colours: Red shirts, white shorts, red socks
Honours: League Champions: 1948, 1951, 1952, 1954, 1955, 1956, 1957, 1958, 1959, 1960, 1961, 1962, 1966, 1969, 1971, 1972, 1973, 1975, 1976, 1980, 1981, 1982, 1983, 1987, 1989, 1990. Soviet Army Cup winners: 1951, 1954, 1955, 1960, 1961, 1965, 1969, 1972, 1973, 1974, 1985, 1986, 1989, 1990. Cup winners: 1981, 1983, 1987, 1988, 1989.

The club of the Bulgarian army, they have undergone several name changes since their formation. The club was re-formed in 1985 after the incidents in the Bulgarian Cup final and re-named Sredets, before reverting to CSKA Sofia in 1989.

Dinamo Bucharest

Address: Dinamo Stadion, Bucharest
Stadium Capacity: 18,000
Year Formed: 1948
Colours: White shirts, red shorts, white socks
Honours: League Champions: 1955, 1962, 1963, 1964, 1965, 1971, 1973, 1975, 1977, 1982, 1983, 1984, 1990. Cup winners: 1959, 1964, 1968, 1982, 1984, 1986, 1990.

The club of the Securitatea (secret police), they threatened to change their name after the Rumanian revolution in 1989. Reached the semi-final of the European Cup in 1984. Scored a club record 107 goals in 1987–88, but still finished runners-up to their rivals Steaua.

Dukla Prague

Address: Juliska Stadion, Prague
Stadium Capacity: 28,000
Year Formed: 1948
Colours: Yellow shirts, dark red trim, yellow shorts, yellow socks, dark red trim
Honours: League Champions: 1953, 1956, 1958, 1961, 1962, 1963, 1964, 1966, 1977, 1979, 1982. Cup winners: 1961, 1965, 1966, 1969, 1981, 1983, 1985, 1990.

The club of the Czech army, it is named after the village in the Carpathians where the Czechs fought heroically against the Nazis. Achieved considerable success in the 1960s, winning the league and cup double in 1961 in the first year of the knockout trophy.

Dynamo Berlin

Address: Friedrich-Ludwig-Jahn Sportpark, Berlin
Stadium Capacity: 20,000
Year Formed: 1949
Colours: Red and white shirts, white shorts, red socks
Honours: League Champions: 1979, 1980, 1981, 1982, 1983, 1984, 1985, 1986, 1987, 1988. Cup winners: 1959, 1988, 1989.

Created a record in Europe by winning 10 successive championship titles. The club of the East German secret police, it has never been popular with the general public despite its achievements. Changed its name FC Berlin in 1990 to improve the image under the country's changing regime.

Dynamo Kiev

Address: Republic Stadion, Kiev
Stadium Capacity: 100,169
Year Formed: 1927
Colours: All white with blue trim
Honours: League Champions: 1961, 1966, 1967, 1968, 1971, 1974, 1975, 1977, 1980, 1981, 1985, 1986. Cup winners: 1954, 1964, 1966, 1974, 1978, 1982, 1985, 1987, 1989. European Cup-Winners' Cup winners: 1975, 1986. Super Cup winners: 1975.

Finally broke the Moscow domination of the Soviet championship in the 1960s and established a fine reputation. With a large following at home they became formidable opponents. Have formed the nucleus of the national team and thus attracted the better players.

Dynamo Moscow

Address: Dynamo Stadion, Moscow
Stadium Capacity: 50,475
Year Formed: 1923
Colours: All white
Honours: League Champions: 1936 (spring), 1937, 1940, 1945, 1949, 1954, 1955, 1957, 1959, 1963, 1976 (autumn). Cup winners: 1937, 1953, 1967, 1970, 1977, 1984.

The club owes its origins in the 1880s to English mill owners Clement and Harry Charnock. Made a short but memorable tour of British clubs in 1945 then disappeared from outside contact along with their fellow countrymen. Reached the European Cup-Winners' Cup final in 1972, losing to Rangers, but have achieved little since then.

Oleg Blokhin, European Player of the Year in 1975, scored in both of Dynamo Kiev's Cup-Winners' Cup successes.

Eintracht Frankfurt

Address: Waldstadion, Frankfurt
Stadium Capacity: 61,146
Year Formed: 1899
Colours: Red and black diagonal striped shirts, black shorts and socks
Honours: League Champions: 1959. Cup winners: 1974, 1975, 1981, 1988. UEFA Cup winners: 1980.

Despite playing a secondary role to Real Madrid in the unforgettable 1960 European Cup final, they entered into the attacking spirit of the match after one of their most successful seasons. Reached the semi-final of the Cup-Winners' Cup in 1976.

Fenerbahce

Address: Fenerbahce, Istanbul
Stadium Capacity: 32,500
Year Formed: 1907
Colours: Blue and yellow striped shirts, white shorts and socks
Honours: League Champions: 1959, 1962, 1964, 1965, 1968, 1970, 1974, 1975, 1978, 1983, 1985, 1989. Cup winners: 1968, 1974, 1979, 1983.

Had an impressive championship-winning season in 1988–89, scoring 100 goals and losing just once in the league. It made up for a disappointing previous season in which they were eighth. Turkey's most successful club.

Ferencvaros

Address: Ulloi ut Stadion, Budapest
Stadium Capacity: 27,136
Year Formed: 1899
Colours: Green and white striped shirts, white shorts and socks
Honours: League Champions: 1903, 1905, 1907, 1909, 1910, 1911, 1912, 1913, 1926, 1927, 1928, 1932, 1934, 1938, 1940, 1941, 1949, 1963, 1964, 1967, 1968, 1976, 1981. Cup winners: 1913, 1922, 1927, 1928, 1933, 1935, 1942, 1943, 1944, 1958, 1972, 1974, 1976, 1978. Fairs Cup winners: 1965.

Have won more honours than any other Hungarian club and were the first to have success in Europe. They also reached the European Fairs Cup final in 1968, losing to Leeds United. Have had several changes of name but retain their popularity, nicknamed 'Fradi'.

Johan Cruyff in action for Feyenoord late in his career. But he originally made his name at Ajax.

Feyenoord

Address: Feyenoord, Olympiaweg, Rotterdam
Stadium Capacity: 56,128
Year Formed: 1908
Colours: Red and white shirts, black shorts and socks
Honours: League Champions: 1924, 1928, 1936, 1938, 1940, 1961, 1962, 1965, 1969, 1971, 1974, 1984. Cup winners: 1930, 1935, 1965, 1969, 1980, 1984. European Cup winners: 1970. UEFA Cup winners: 1974. World Club Champions: 1970.

Initially financed by the mining millionaire C.R.J. Kieboom, they did not win a title until 1924. Again, after adopting professionalism when it became legal in 1953, they had to wait until 1961 for another milestone. First Dutch club to win the European Cup.

Fiorentina

Address: Stadio Comunale, Florence
Stadium Capacity: 49,033
Year Formed: 1926
Colours: All violet
Honours: League Champions: 1956, 1969. Cup winners: 1940, 1961, 1966, 1975. European Cup-Winners' Cup winners: 1961.

Had to wait 30 years for their first championship but did so in impressive fashion, losing only their last game when the title was already secured. Reached the final of the European Cup the following season and were finalists in the first two European Cup-Winners' Cup competitions.

Flamengo

Address: Estadio da Gavea, Rio de Janeiro
Stadium Capacity: 8,000 (top games at Maracana 160,000)
Year Formed: 1895
Colours: Red and black hooped shirts, white shorts, red and black socks
Honours: League Champions: 1914, 1915, 1920, 1925, 1927, 1939, 1942, 1943, 1944, 1953, 1954, 1955, 1963, 1965, 1972, 1974, 1978, 1979, 1981, 1986. National Champions: 1980, 1982, 1983, 1987. South American Cup winners: 1981. World Club Champions: 1981.

Originally a rowing club, they added football in 1911: a group of dissatisfied Fluminense players defected to it and thus the birth of the long-standing rivalry between the two clubs came about. Matches between the two clubs invariably attract crowds of 100,000 or more to the Maracana Stadium.

Zico evades a Polish tackle in the 1986 World Cup. At home in Brazil he was Flamengo's brightest star.

Fluminense

Address: Estadio Alvaro Chaves, Rio de Janeiro
Stadium Capacity: 20,000 (top games at Maracana 160,000)
Year Formed: 1902
Colours: Red, green and white striped shirts, white shorts and socks
Honours: League Champions: 1906, 1907 (shared), 1908, 1909, 1911, 1917, 1918, 1919, 1924, 1936, 1937, 1938, 1940, 1941, 1946, 1951, 1959, 1964, 1969, 1971, 1973, 1975, 1976, 1980, 1983, 1984, 1985. National Champions: 1970, 1984.

If Flamengo was known as the 'people's club' then Fluminense has drawn support from the upper classes. There was considerable British influence in the early days and one of the early successes was winning the 16-game Rio title without dropping a point.

Galatasaray

Address: Ali Sami Yen, Istanbul
Stadium Capacity: 35,000
Year Formed: 1905
Colours: Red and yellow halves, red shorts and socks
Honours: League Champions: 1962, 1963, 1969, 1971, 1972, 1973, 1987, 1988. Cup winners: 1963, 1964, 1965, 1966, 1973, 1976, 1982, 1985.

Enjoyed their best domestic season in 1987–88, scoring a club record 86 goals to win the championship. Have competed in Europe regularly but have yet to make an impact.

Gornik Zabrze

Address: Gornik Stadion, Zabrze
Stadium Capacity: 23,000
Year Formed: 1948
Colours: Blue shirts, white shorts and socks
Honours: League Champions: 1957, 1959, 1961, 1963, 1964, 1965, 1966, 1967, 1971, 1972, 1985, 1986, 1987, 1988. Cup winners: 1965, 1968, 1969, 1970, 1971, 1972.

The only Polish club to reach the final of a European competition when they were runners-up to Manchester City in the 1970 European Cup-Winners' Cup, they dominated local football in the 1960s and again in the later 1980s. Formed by the amalgamation of four other clubs and known as the miners' team.

IFK Gothenburg

Address: Ullevi, Gothenburg
Stadium Capacity: 52,000
Year Formed: 1904
Colours: Blue and white striped shirts, blue shorts and socks
Honours: League Champions: 1908, 1910, 1918, 1935, 1942, 1958, 1969, 1982, 1983, 1984, 1987. Cup winners: 1979, 1982, 1983. UEFA Cup winners: 1982, 1987.

In the 1980s they enjoyed a period of success at home and abroad. After winning the UEFA Cup in 1982, they reached the semi-final of the European Cup in 1986 and a year later took their second UEFA Cup. Never out of the top four during the last decade in Sweden.

Grasshoppers

Address: Hardturm Stadion, Zurich
Stadium Capacity: 37,000
Year Formed: 1886
Colours: Blue and white halves, white shorts and socks with blue trim
Honours: League Champions: 1898, 1900, 1901, 1905, 1921, 1927, 1928, 1931, 1937, 1939, 1942, 1943, 1945, 1952, 1956, 1971, 1978, 1982, 1983, 1984, 1990. Cup winners: 1926, 1927, 1932, 1934, 1937, 1938, 1940, 1941, 1942, 1943, 1946, 1952, 1956, 1983, 1988, 1989, 1990.

Remain Switzerland's most successful club but did not win the championship after a hat-trick of titles in the early 1980s until 1990. Reached the semi-final of the UEFA Cup in 1978.

Hajduk Split

Address: Poljud Stadion, Split
Stadium Capacity: 50,000
Year Formed: 1911
Colours: Red and blue striped shirts, blue shorts and socks
Honours: League Champions: 1927, 1929, 1950, 1952, 1955, 1971, 1974, 1975, 1979. Cup winners: 1967, 1972, 1974, 1975, 1976, 1977, 1984, 1987.

Only just avoided relegation in 1987–88 for the first time in their history after dominating the 1970s in particular in both league and cup. Semi-finalists in the European Cup-Winners' Cup in 1973 and the UEFA Cup in 1984.

Hamburg

Address: Volksparkstadion, Hamburg
Stadium Capacity: 61,330
Year Formed: 1887
Colours: White shirts, red trim, red shorts and socks
Honours: League Champions: 1923, 1928, 1960, 1979, 1982, 1983. Cup winners: 1963, 1976, 1987. European Cup winners: 1983. European Cup-Winners' Cup winners: 1977.

Originally known as SC Germania, they absorbed two other clubs in their early years. Had come close to European honours in the 1960s, reaching the final of the European Cup-Winners' Cup in 1968, but had to wait until 1977 before they won it. Also took the European Cup in 1983.

Hamburg's Uwe Seeler and Pele of Brazil, two of the world's most prolific scorers, wave their World Cups.

Honved

Address: Jozsef Bozsik Stadion, Budapest
Stadium Capacity: 30,000
Year Formed: 1949
Colours: All white with red trim
Honours: League Champions: 1950, 1950 (autumn), 1952, 1954, 1955, 1980, 1984, 1985, 1986, 1988, 1989. Cup winners: 1964, 1985, 1989.

Formed as the army club by the Ministry of Sport, they used the Kispest club as a nucleus. They provided the backbone of the Hungarian team which dominated international football in the early 1950s but suffered after the uprising in 1956 before making a comeback in the last decade.

Sandor Kocsis of Honved flourished in the 1950s when Hungarian football was at its peak.

Independiente's captain Enzo Trossero raises the World Cup Championship trophy. It was the club's second such triumph.

Independiente

Address: Estadio Cordero, Avellaneda, Buenos Aires
Stadium Capacity: 68,930
Year Formed: 1905
Colours: Red shirts, blue shorts, red socks
Honours: League Champions: 1922, 1926, 1938, 1939, 1948, 1960, 1963, 1970, 1971, 1983, 1990. National Champions: 1967, 1977, 1978. South American Cup winners: 1964, 1965, 1972, 1973, 1974, 1975, 1984. World Club Champions: 1973, 1984.

They are a multi-sports club who enjoyed some success in the South American Cup in its early years by being one of the first to adopt the Italian *catenaccio* defensive system. This was in sharp contrast to their entertaining, attacking style of earlier times.

Internazionale

Address: Giuseppe Meazza Stadio, San Siro, Milan
Stadium Capacity: 83,107
Year Formed: 1908
Colours: Blue and black striped shirts, black shorts and socks
Honours: League Champions: 1910, 1920, 1930, 1938, 1940, 1953, 1954, 1963, 1965, 1966, 1971, 1980, 1989. Cup winners: 1939, 1978, 1982. European Cup winners: 1964, 1965. World Club Champions: 1964, 1965.

Formed by disgruntled members of AC Milan they adopted a cavalier approach to their football originally but became infamous for the *catenaccio* style of defence in the 1960s under Helenio Herrera. It brought them success at home and abroad.

Helenio Herrera, Inter's 'magician' manager, in June 1965 soon after he had led them to a second European Cup victory.

Juventus

Address: Stadio Delle Alpe, Turin
Stadium Capacity: 71,609
Year Formed: 1897
Colours: Black and white striped shirts, white shorts and socks
Honours: League Champions: 1905, 1926, 1931, 1932, 1933, 1934, 1935, 1950, 1952, 1958, 1960, 1961, 1967, 1972, 1973, 1975, 1977, 1978, 1981, 1982, 1984, 1986. Cup winners: 1938, 1942, 1959, 1960, 1965, 1979, 1983, 1990. European Cup winners: 1985. European Cup-Winners' Cup winners: 1984. UEFA Cup winners: 1977, 1990. Super Cup winners: 1984. World Club Champions: 1985.

Appropriately named Juventus ('youth') by boys under 17, they have been Italy's most popular and successful club, variously nicknamed 'La vecchia signora' ('the old lady'), 'La fidanzata d'Italia' ('the fiancee of Italy') or 'The Zebras' after their striped shirts upon which they are allowed to wear two gold stars, each signifying 10 titles.

Levski-Spartak

Address: Levski-Gerena, Sofia
Stadium Capacity: 60,000
Year Formed: 1914
Colours: All blue

Roberto Baggio scores the most spectacular goal of the 1990 World Cup to show why Juventus value him at £8 million.

Honours: League Champions: 1933, 1937, 1942, 1946, 1947, 1949, 1950, 1953, 1965, 1968, 1970, 1974, 1977, 1979, 1984, 1988. Soviet Army Cup winners: 1946, 1947, 1949, 1950, 1956, 1957, 1959, 1967, 1968, 1970, 1971, 1976, 1977, 1979, 1984, 1987, 1988. Cup winners: 1982, 1984.

The most popular club in Bulgaria, they reverted to their original name in 1989 after four years as Vitosha, following the dissolution of the club in the wake of the infamous Bulgarian Cup final.

Linfield

Address: Windsor Park, Belfast
Stadium Capacity: 30,000
Year Formed: 1886
Colours: Blue shirts, white sleeves, white shorts, blue socks
Honours: League Champions: 1891, 1892, 1893, 1895, 1898, 1902, 1904, 1907, 1908, 1909, 1911, 1914, 1922, 1923, 1930, 1932, 1934, 1935, 1949, 1950, 1954, 1955, 1956, 1959, 1961, 1962, 1966, 1969, 1971, 1975, 1978, 1979, 1980, 1982, 1983, 1984, 1985, 1986, 1987, 1989. Cup winners: 1891, 1892, 1893, 1895, 1898, 1899, 1902, 1904, 1912, 1913, 1915, 1916, 1919, 1922, 1923, 1930, 1931, 1934, 1936, 1939, 1942, 1945, 1946, 1948, 1950, 1953, 1960, 1962, 1963, 1970, 1978, 1980, 1982.

Easily the most successful club in Northern Ireland and particularly effective in the 1980s when they missed out only twice on the championship. Have struggled in the various European competitions without much reward.

Marseille

Address: Stade Velodrome, Marseille
Stadium Capacity: 46,000
Year Formed: 1898
Colours: All white with blue trim
Honours: League Champions: 1937, 1948, 1971, 1972, 1989, 1990. Cup winners: 1924, 1926, 1927, 1935, 1938, 1943, 1969, 1972, 1976, 1989.

Under the presidency of millionaire Bernard Tapie the club managed to buy success on the playing field to achieve a league and cup double in 1989. This was in sharp contrast to the early 1980s when they spent four seasons in the Second Division.

Dreadlocks flying, Ruud Gullit of AC Milan leaps for the ball in the European Cup final of 1989.

AC Milan

Address: Stadio Giuseppe Meazza, San Siro, Milan
Stadium Capacity: 83,107
Year Formed: 1899
Colours: Red and black striped shirts, white shorts and socks
Honours: League Champions: 1901, 1906, 1907, 1951, 1955, 1957, 1959, 1962, 1968, 1979, 1988. Cup winners: 1967, 1972, 1973, 1977. European

Cup winners: 1963, 1969, 1989, 1990. European Cup-Winners' Cup winners: 1968, 1973. Super Cup winners: 1990. World Club Champions: 1969, 1989.

English and Italian businessmen founded the club as the Milan Cricket and Football Club and to this day the English spelling of 'Milan' is retained. Forcibly relegated to the Second Division in 1980 following the bribery scandal, they have resurrected themselves in fine style under the presidency of multi-millionaire Silvio Berlusconi, winning the European Cup two years in succession.

Monaco

Address: Stade Louis II, Monaco
Stadium Capacity: 20,000
Year Formed: 1924
Colours: Red and white diagonally striped shirts, red shorts, white socks
Honours: League Champions: 1961, 1963, 1978, 1982, 1988. Cup winners: 1960, 1963, 1980, 1985.

Enjoyed the patronage of the Monegasque royal family for many years, surviving on small attendances. Did not turn professional until after the Second World War. Won promotion to the First Division in 1953 but were relegated in 1969. The club finished the 1980s as one of the strongest in France.

MTK-VM

Address: MTK Stadion, Budapest
Stadium Capacity: 28,000
Year Formed: 1888
Colours: White shirts, blue trim, white shorts and socks
Honours: League Champions: 1904, 1908, 1914, 1917, 1918, 1919, 1920, 1921, 1922, 1923, 1924, 1925, 1929, 1936, 1937, 1951, 1953, 1958, 1987. Cup winners: 1910, 1911, 1912, 1914, 1923, 1925, 1932, 1952, 1968.

As Magyar Testgyakorlok Kore took over from the British-originated Budapest Gymnastic and Athletic Club. Won all 10 league titles before the professional era began in 1926 and underwent a variety of name changes post-War. Have since added Voros Meteor to their title.

Nacional

Address: Estadio Centenario, Montevideo
Stadium Capacity: 75,000
Year Formed: 1899
Colours: White shirts, red and blue striped collar, blue shorts, white socks
Honours: League Champions: 1902, 1903, 1912, 1915, 1916, 1917, 1919, 1920, 1922, 1923, 1924, 1933, 1934, 1939, 1940, 1941, 1942, 1943, 1946, 1947, 1950, 1952, 1955, 1956, 1957, 1963, 1966, 1969, 1970, 1971, 1972, 1977, 1980, 1982. South American Cup winners: 1971, 1980. World Club Champions: 1971, 1980.

They were the first Uruguayan club formed by locals not foreigners. In 1971 they equalled the number of championships won by their rivals Penarol but are just behind them in overall titles. Have had to sell their best players abroad to survive but have had a reputation for producing replacement talent.

Nandor Hidegkuti, one of MTK's great post-War stars.

Napoli

Address: Stadio San Paolo, Naples
Stadium Capacity: 86,000

Diego Maradona has become the hero of Naples since he arrived in the town in 1984. Here he beats Juventus star De Agostini during a league match in 1988.

Year Formed: 1926
Colours: Light blue shirts, white shorts, light blue socks
Honours: League Champions: 1987, 1990. Cup winners: 1962, 1976, 1987. UEFA Cup winners: 1989.

The well-supported ambitions of the club were never realised until the arrival of Diego Maradona at the cost of £6.9 million. In his third season Napoli achieved a league and cup double and two seasons later won their first European trophy.

IFC Nuremberg

Address: Frankenstadion, Nuremberg
Stadium Capacity: 43,406
Year Formed: 1900
Colours: Red and white shirts, white shorts, red socks
Honours: League Champions: 1920, 1921, 1924, 1925, 1927, 1936, 1948, 1961, 1968. Cup winners: 1935, 1939, 1962.

Dominated German football in the 1920s so much that they were popularly known as 'the club'. Despite suffering relegation on several occasions since the Bundesliga was founded, they have retained their attraction. Reached the European Cup-Winners' Cup semi-final in 1963.

Olympiakos

Address: Karaiskaki, Piraeus
Stadium Capacity: 42,000
Year Formed: 1925
Colours: Red and white striped shirts, white shorts and socks
Honours: League Champions: 1931, 1933, 1934, 1936, 1937, 1938, 1947, 1948, 1951, 1954, 1955, 1956, 1957, 1958, 1959, 1966, 1967, 1973, 1974, 1975, 1980, 1981, 1982, 1983, 1987. Cup winners: 1947, 1951, 1952, 1953, 1954, 1957, 1958, 1959, 1960, 1961, 1962, 1963, 1965, 1968, 1971, 1973, 1975, 1981, 1990.

The leading club in Greece, they reached a crisis point in 1987–88 with changes affecting personnel on and off the field from top to bottom. They made their worst start to any season by failing to win any of the first 11 matches. A wealthy club, they then paid £4.8 million for Lajos Detari a Hungarian striker.

Palmeiras

Address: Parque Antartica, Sao Paulo
Stadium Capacity: 30,000
Year Formed: 1914
Colours: Green shirts, white trim, white shorts and socks
Honours: League Champions: 1920, 1926, 1927, 1932, 1933, 1934, 1936, 1940, 1942, 1944, 1947, 1950, 1959, 1963, 1966, 1972, 1974, 1976. National Champions 1967, 1969, 1972, 1973.

Originally known as Palestra Italia and supported by Italian immigrants. They changed their name in 1942 when Brazil entered the Second World War and all names connected with Axis powers were dropped. Enjoyed considerable success in the 1930s and 1940s.

Panathinaikos

Address: Panathinaikos Stadion, Athens
Stadium Capacity: 25,000
Year Formed: 1908
Colours: Green shirts, white shorts and socks
Honours: League Champions: 1930, 1950, 1953, 1960, 1961, 1962, 1964, 1965, 1969, 1970, 1972, 1977, 1984, 1986, 1990. Cup winners: 1940, 1948, 1955, 1967, 1969, 1977, 1982, 1984, 1986, 1988, 1989.

The oldest surviving club in Greece and the first to reach the final of a European competition when they were runners-up to Ajax in the 1971 European Cup. The rivals of Olympiakos, they are the next most successful club in the country.

Partizan

Address: JNA (Army Stadion), Belgrade
Stadium Capacity: 50,819
Year Formed: 1945
Colours: Black and white striped shirts, white shorts and socks
Honours: League Champions: 1947, 1949, 1961, 1962, 1963, 1965, 1976, 1978, 1983, 1986, 1987. Cup winners: 1947, 1952, 1954, 1957, 1989.

Founded as the Army Club after the War and won the first league and cup double afterwards. Reached the final of the European Cup in 1966 and lost to Real Madrid. Rarely out of contention for domestic honours in recent years.

Penarol

Address: Estadio Centenario, Montevideo
Stadium Capacity: 75,000
Year Formed: 1891
Colours: Black and yellow striped shirts, black shorts and socks
Honours: League Champions: 1900, 1901, 1905, 1907, 1911, 1918, 1921, 1926, 1928, 1929, 1930, 1932, 1935, 1936, 1937, 1938, 1944, 1945, 1949, 1951, 1953, 1954, 1958, 1959, 1960, 1961, 1962, 1964, 1965, 1967, 1968, 1973, 1974, 1975, 1978, 1979, 1981, 1983, 1985, 1986. South American Cup winners: 1960, 1961, 1966, 1982, 1987. World Club Champions: 1961, 1966, 1982.

Penarol's Uruguayan World Cup star Schiaffino (left) was sold to AC Milan in 1954 for a world record fee.

Formed by British railway workers, the club was originally known as the Central Uruguayan Railway Cricket Club. They changed to their present name in 1913 from the district of Montevideo. Uruguay's most successful club and almost uninterrupted in qualifying for the South American Cup. Have also had to sell to stay in business.

Porto

Address: Estadio das Antas, Oporto
Stadium Capacity: 90,000
Year Formed: 1906
Colours: Blue and white striped shirts, blue shorts, white socks
Honours: League Champions: 1935, 1939, 1940, 1956, 1959, 1978, 1979, 1985, 1986, 1988, 1990. Cup winners: 1922, 1925, 1932, 1937, 1956, 1958, 1968, 1977, 1984, 1988. European Cup winners: 1987. Super Cup winners: 1987. World Club Champions: 1987.

Overshadowed by Benfica and Sporting Club, they managed one or two seasons of success before reaching their zenith in 1987 when they achieved a notable treble of international trophies. More than 100 games in the four European competitions.

Ronald Koeman of PSV tussles with Benfica's Rui Aguas during the 1988 European Cup final.

PSV Eindhoven

Address: PSV, Frederiklaan, Eindhoven
Stadium Capacity: 27,000
Year Formed: 1913
Colours: Red shirts, white shorts, red socks
Honours: League Champions: 1929, 1935, 1951, 1963, 1975, 1976, 1978, 1986, 1987, 1988, 1989. Cup winners: 1950, 1974, 1976, 1988, 1989, 1990. European Cup winners: 1988. UEFA Cup winners: 1978.

The electrical concern Philips were behind the formation of the club and their sponsorship continues. Came into their own as a formidable force in the 1980s and have become the best-supported team in the Netherlands. They also equalled HVV's record of 1900–03 by winning four consecutive championships from 1986–89. In 1990 they recruited England manager Bobby Robson.

Racing Club

Address: Estadio Racing Club, Avellaneda, Buenos Aires
Stadium Capacity: 70,100
Year Formed: 1905
Colours: Sky blue and white striped shirts, black shorts and socks
Honours: League Champions: 1913, 1914, 1915, 1916, 1917, 1918, 1919, 1921, 1925, 1949, 1950, 1951, 1958, 1961, 1966. South American Cup winners: 1967. World Club Champions: 1967.

The first Argentine club to win the World Club Championship, they had made their reputation much earlier before the professional era when they were known as 'The Academy'. Achieved a hat-trick of championship successes between 1949 and 1951. Founded originally by locals and French immigrants who were ex-Racing Club de Paris players.

Rapid Vienna

Address: Hanappi Stadium, Vienna
Stadium Capacity: 20,000
Year Formed: 1898
Colours: All white with green trim
Honours: League Champions: 1912, 1913, 1916, 1917, 1919, 1920, 1921, 1923, 1929, 1930, 1935, 1938, 1940, 1941, 1946, 1948, 1951, 1952, 1954, 1956, 1957, 1960, 1964, 1967, 1968, 1982, 1983, 1987, 1988. Cup winners: 1919, 1920, 1927, 1946, 1961, 1968, 1969, 1972, 1976, 1983, 1984, 1985, 1987.

Austria's most successful club, they have had several periods of almost total domination. When Germany annexed the country they even became German champions. Runners-up in the European Cup-Winners' Cup in 1985, they had enjoyed their best years before the major European competitions began.

Real Madrid

Address: Estadio Santiago Bernabeu, Madrid
Stadium Capacity: 90,200
Year Formed: 1902
Colours: White shirts, blue trim, white shorts and socks
Honours: League Champions: 1932, 1933, 1954, 1955, 1957, 1958, 1961, 1962, 1963, 1964, 1965, 1967, 1968, 1969, 1972, 1975, 1976, 1978, 1979, 1980, 1986, 1987, 1988, 1989, 1990. Cup winners: 1905, 1906, 1907, 1908, 1917, 1934, 1936, 1946, 1947, 1962, 1970, 1974, 1975, 1980, 1982, 1989. European Cup winners: 1956, 1957, 1958, 1959, 1960, 1966. UEFA Cup winners: 1985, 1986. World Club Champions: 1960.

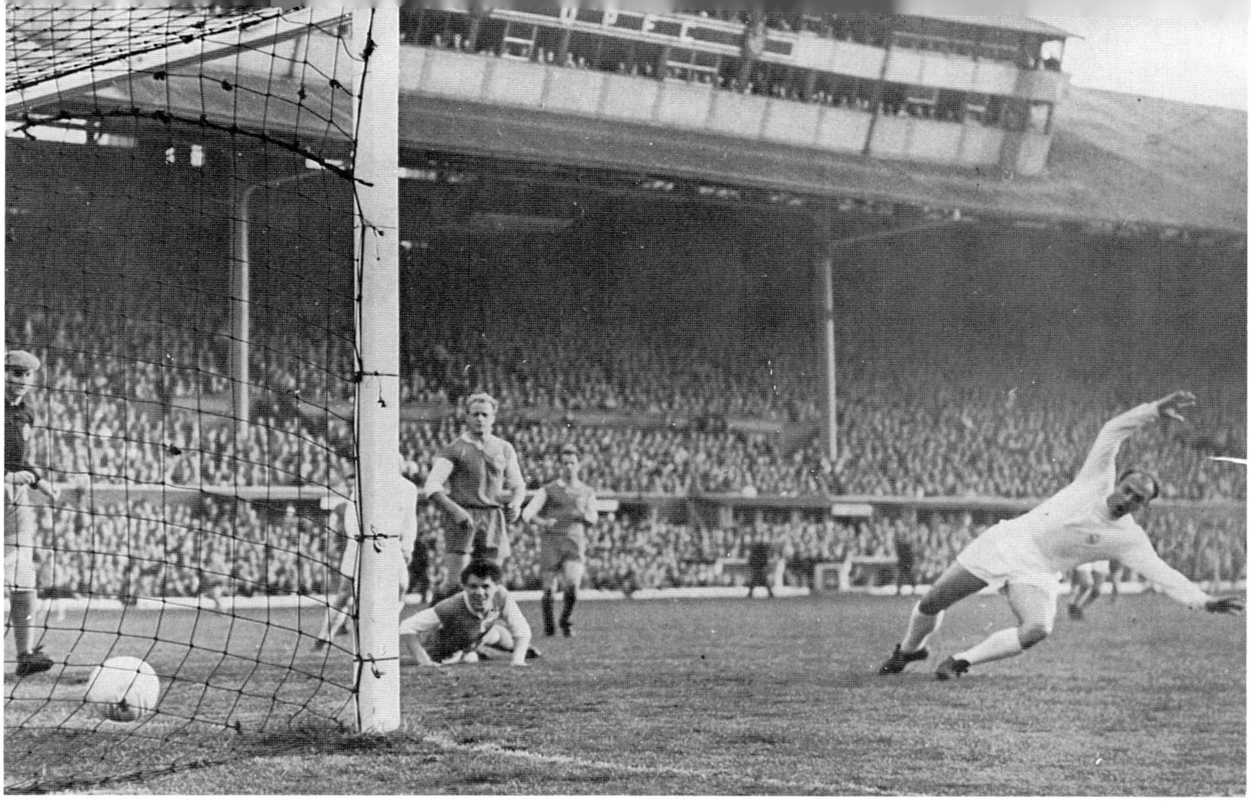

Di Stefano scores the first in the 10-goal thriller that was the 1960 European Cup final. As in the previous four years, Real Madrid emerged victorious.

Largely as a result of winning five European Cup trophies in a row, became the most famous club in the world. Their success and popularity at home had been fostered in the period after Don Santiago Bernabeu became president in 1943. The team reached their peak in the 1960 European Cup final when their talented players displayed individual skill, speed and devastating finishing to beat Eintracht Frankfurt 7–3. But they have not won the major trophy since 1966.

Red Star Belgrade

Address: Crvena Zvezda Stadion, Belgrade
Stadium Capacity: 97,422
Year Formed: 1945
Colours: Red and white striped shirts, red shorts and socks
Honours: League Champions: 1951, 1953, 1956, 1957, 1959, 1960, 1964, 1968, 1969, 1970, 1973, 1977, 1980, 1981, 1984, 1988, 1990. Cup winners: 1948, 1949, 1950, 1958, 1959, 1964, 1968, 1970, 1971, 1982, 1985, 1990.

Founded by Belgrade University students after the War, they are the most successful and popular club in Yugoslavia. Despite regular appearances in Europe, finishing as beaten finalists in the UEFA Cup in 1979 and semi-finalists in the other two European competitions has been the height of their achievements.

River Plate

Address: Estadio Monumental, Buenos Aires
Stadium Capacity: 80,050
Year Formed: 1901
Colours: White shirts, broad red diagonal stripe, black shorts, white socks
Honours: League Champions: 1920, 1932, 1936, 1937, 1941, 1942, 1945, 1947, 1952, 1953, 1955, 1956, 1957, 1975, 1977, 1979, 1980, 1986. National Champions: 1975, 1978, 1981. South American Cup winners: 1986. World Club Champions: 1986.

Argentina's second most popular club, originally formed by English residents. Played in the Uruguayan league as well as at home. Have provided the national team with many outstanding players throughout their history. The most successful team in championship terms.

Roma

Address: Stadio Olimpico, Rome
Stadium Capacity: 85,000
Year Formed: 1927
Colours: Red shirts, yellow trim, red shorts and socks
Honours: League Champions: 1942, 1983. Cup winners: 1964, 1969, 1980, 1981, 1984, 1986. Fairs Cup winners: 1961.

Falcao of Roma leaps over Liverpool's Bruce Grobbelaar in the 1984 European Cup final, but fails to score.

Formed on the amalgamation of three Rome clubs, they have had an inconsistent existence in the Italian league. After an impressive victory in the 1960–61 Fairs Cup, conceded the 1984 European Cup to Liverpool on penalties.

St Etienne

Address: Stade Geoffroy-Guichard, St Etienne
Stadium Capacity: 48,274
Year Formed: 1920
Colours: Green shirts, white shorts, green socks
Honours: League Champions: 1957, 1964, 1967, 1968, 1969, 1970, 1974, 1975, 1976, 1981. Cup winners: 1962, 1968, 1970, 1974, 1975, 1977.

Had some notable domestic successes in the 1970s but fell away during the following decade and were relegated for two seasons before returning to the top flight. Reached the European Cup final in 1976. Between 1957 and 1981 they won 10 championships and six French cups.

Santos

Address: Vila Belmiro, Santos
Stadium Capacity: 30,000
Year Formed: 1912
Colours: All white
Honours: League Champions: 1935, 1955, 1956, 1958, 1960, 1961, 1962, 1964, 1965, 1967, 1968, 1969, 1973 (shared), 1978, 1984. South American Cup winners: 1962, 1963. World Club Champions: 1962, 1963.

Thanks to Pele they dominated Sao Paulo football in the late 1950s and 1960s. Became such an attraction around the world that they regularly played 100 games a year at home and abroad. Founded after British sailors had demonstrated the game in the port of Santos, they celebrated their jubilee year by winning the World Club Championship for the first time.

Sao Paulo

Address: Estadio Morumbi, Sao Paulo
Stadium Capacity: 150,000
Year Formed: 1930
Colours: White shirts, red and black horizontal band, white shorts and socks

St Etienne's Bathenay searches for a way through the Bayern Munich defence in 1976.

Pele, seen here in Sweden in 1966, helped to make Santos one of the world's greatest clubs in the 1960s.

Honours: League Champions: 1931, 1943, 1945, 1946, 1948, 1949, 1953, 1957, 1970, 1971, 1975, 1980, 1981, 1985, 1987, 1989. National champions: 1977, 1986.

Remnants of the Paulistano club which folded in 1929 joined with financially ailing AA das Palmeiras and benefited immediately with the presence of ex-Paulistano goal machine Artur Friedenreich. Later another goalscoring legend, Leonidas da Silva, joined them. First Brazilian club to officially adopt professionalism in 1933.

Shamrock Rovers

Address: Tolka Park, Dublin
Stadium Capacity: 20,000
Year Formed: 1899
Colours: Green and white hooped shirts, white shorts and socks
Honours: League Champions: 1923, 1925, 1927, 1932, 1938, 1939, 1954, 1957, 1959, 1964, 1984, 1985, 1986, 1987. Cup winners: 1925, 1929, 1930, 1931, 1932, 1933, 1936, 1940, 1944, 1945, 1948, 1955, 1956, 1962, 1964, 1965, 1966, 1967, 1968, 1969, 1978, 1985, 1986, 1987.

They have been the overwhelmingly successful club in the Republic of Ireland in league and cup honours. Caused disappointment to many of their supporters when quitting Milltown to share Tolka Park with Home Farm in the late 1980s.

Slavia Prague

Address: Dr Vacka Stadion, Prague
Stadium Capacity: 42,000
Year Formed: 1892
Colours: Red and white halved shirts, white shorts and socks
Honours: League Champions: 1913, 1925, 1929, 1930, 1931, 1933, 1934, 1935, 1937, 1940, 1941, 1942, 1943, 1944, 1947.

Oldest surviving club in Czechoslovakia, they dominated the 1930s and 1940s but have suffered in the more recent past and even had periods in the second division. Sparta's traditional rivals, the two clubs holding complete sway in the professional era between the two World Wars.

Sparta Prague

Address: Letna Stadium, Prague
Stadium Capacity: 35,101
Year Formed: 1893
Colours: Cherry red shirts, white shorts, black socks
Honours: League Champions: 1912, 1919, 1920, 1921, 1922, 1923, 1926, 1927, 1932, 1936, 1938, 1946, 1948, 1952, 1954, 1965, 1967, 1984, 1985, 1987, 1988, 1989, 1990. Cup winners: 1964, 1972, 1976, 1980, 1984, 1988, 1989.

Czechoslovakia's most successful team and one of the most popular. Despite several name changes they are always looked upon as Sparta. Have been the long-standing rivals of Slavia. Began to reassert themselves in the late 1980s as a domestic force.

Spartak Moscow

Address: Lenin Stadion, Moscow
Stadium Capacity: 100,360
Year Formed: 1922
Colours: Red shirts, white hoop, white shorts and socks
Honours: League Champions: 1936 (autumn), 1938, 1939, 1952, 1953, 1956, 1958, 1962, 1969, 1979, 1987, 1990. Cup winners: 1938, 1939, 1946, 1947, 1950, 1958, 1963, 1965, 1971.

The team of the Soviet Producers Co-operative

movement and as such one of the most popular in the country. Enjoyed most success in the late 1950s and early 1960s but have consistently failed to make any impression in Europe.

Sporting Club

Address: Estadio Jose Alvalade, Lisbon
Stadium Capacity: 75,230
Year Formed: 1906
Colours: Green and white hooped shirts, black shorts, green and white socks
Honours: League Champions: 1941, 1944, 1947, 1948, 1949, 1951, 1952, 1953, 1954, 1958, 1962, 1966, 1970, 1974, 1980, 1982. Cup winners: 1923, 1934, 1936, 1938, 1941, 1945, 1946, 1948, 1954, 1963, 1971, 1973, 1974, 1978, 1982. European Cup-Winners' Cup winners: 1964.

The eternal rivals of Benfica, they have been ousted during the last decade having won their last championship title in 1982. Their European highlight occurred in 1964 when, on the way to winning the European Cup-Winners' Cup, they overturned a Manchester United 4–1 first leg lead to win 6–4 on aggregate in the quarter-final.

Standard Liege

Address: Stade de Sclessin, Liege
Stadium Capacity: 30,500
Year Formed: 1898
Colours: Red shirts, white shorts, red socks
Honours: League Champions: 1958, 1961, 1963, 1969, 1970, 1971, 1982, 1983. Cup winners: 1954, 1966, 1967, 1981.

The first Belgian club to make any impact in European football, reaching the semi-finals of the European Cup and the final of the European Cup-Winners' Cup. Flourished when semi-professionalism was introduced in the late 1950s.

Steaua Bucharest

Address: Steaua Stadion, Bucharest
Stadium Capacity: 30,000
Year Formed: 1947
Colours: All red
Honours: League Champions: 1951, 1952, 1953, 1956, 1960, 1961, 1968, 1976, 1978, 1985, 1986, 1987, 1988, 1989. Cup winners: 1949, 1950, 1951, 1952, 1955, 1962, 1966, 1967, 1969, 1970, 1971, 1976, 1979, 1985, 1987, 1988, 1989. European Cup winners: 1986.

Lacatus was just one of Steaua's stars to catch the eye in the 1990 World Cup.

Became the first Rumanian club to win the European Cup in 1986 when they defeated Barcelona on penalties. Overhauled Dinamo's record of championships in the late 1980s and achieved the league and cup double three years in succession. The club of the Rumanian army, they recorded their highest goal aggregate in 1987–88 by scoring 114 goals.

Stuttgart

Address: Neckarstadion, Stuttgart
Stadium Capacity: 67,750

Year Formed: 1893
Colours: White shirts, red hoop, white shorts and socks
Honours: League Champions: 1950, 1952, 1984. Cup winners: 1954, 1958.

Had twice previously reached the semi-final of the UEFA Cup before appearing in the 1989 final only to lose to Napoli. On the domestic front had made their most telling performances in the 1950s.

Torino

Address: Stadio Delle Alpe, Turin
Stadium Capacity: 71,609
Year Formed: 1906
Colours: Dark red shirts, white shorts, dark red socks
Honours: League Champions: 1928, 1943, 1946, 1947, 1948, 1949, 1976. Cup winners: 1936, 1943, 1968, 1971.

Their outstanding period of success was cruelly ended in the Superga air disaster in May 1949. The club's youth team managed to win their last four fixtures against other youth sides to retain the championship. Have never recovered from this tragedy.

Torpedo Moscow

Address: Torpedo Stadion, Moscow
Stadium Capacity: 20,000
Year Formed: 1924
Colours: White shirts, black shorts, white socks
Honours: League Champions: 1960, 1965, 1976 (autumn). Cup winners: 1949, 1952, 1960, 1968, 1972, 1986.

The club of the Likhachev Auto Plant, they played in the Moscow league until winning a place in the newly formed second division and gaining instant promotion to the top division in 1937. Achieved the league and cup double in 1960.

Ujpest Dozsa

Address: Dozsa Stadion, Budapest
Stadium Capacity: 30,000
Year Formed: 1885
Colours: Lilac shirts, white shorts, lilac socks
Honours: League Champions: 1930, 1931, 1933, 1935, 1939, 1945 (spring), 1946, 1947, 1960, 1969, 1970 (spring), 1971, 1972, 1973, 1974, 1975, 1978, 1979, 1990. Cup winners: 1969, 1970, 1971, 1975, 1982, 1983, 1987.

Dominated domestic football in Hungary for half a decade from the late 1960s and also finished runners-up to Newcastle United in the 1969 European Fairs Cup. They were founded as Ujpest, the Dozsa addition coming later to commemorate a war hero. They became the team of the Ministry of the Interior and Police after the Second World War.

Valencia

Address: Estadio Luis Casanova, Valencia
Stadium Capacity: 55,000
Year Formed: 1919
Colours: All white
Honours: League Champions 1942, 1944, 1947, 1971. Cup winners: 1941, 1949, 1954, 1967, 1979. European Cup-Winners' Cup winners: 1980. Fairs Cup winners: 1962, 1963. Super Cup winners: 1980.

Had their best domestic period in the 1940s and most success in Europe in the 1960s when they continued the Spanish domination of the Fairs Cup. Despite a lack of honours in recent years they have maintained a strong challenge in the championship.

Vasco da Gama

Address: Estadio de Sao Januario, Rio de Janeiro
Stadium Capacity: 50,000
Year Formed: 1898
Colours: Black shirts with white diagonal stripe, white shorts and socks
Honours: League Champions: 1923, 1924, 1929, 1934, 1936, 1945, 1947, 1949, 1950, 1952, 1956, 1958, 1970, 1977, 1982, 1987, 1988. National Champions: 1974, 1989.

Late developers compared with the other big Rio clubs, they did not enter the top division until 1923 but won the championship at the first attempt. Provided the nucleus of Brazil's 1950 World Cup squad. Enjoyed backing from Portuguese commercial concerns in the 1940s.

World Cup

The World Cup is football's ultimate test of supremacy. It was first launched in 1930 and has been held every four years since, with the exception of the Second World War years. It is open to all members of FIFA and now regularly attracts two-thirds of the countries affiliated to the world governing body.

However, it began modestly enough, with only 13 entries for the initial tournament held in Montevideo, Uruguay. Interest more than doubled for the 1934 series and, despite a gap of 12 years after the 1938 tournament, maintained a reasonable level of entries until FIFA received applications from 53 countries in 1958.

FIFA's original concept was for a knockout competition, but the low number of participants in 1930 led to an initial stage where the teams split into four groups, with the winners moving into a sudden death semi-final round. There was no provision for third and fourth place between the beaten semi-finalists, but this was subsequently introduced for the 1934 tournament, which was held in Italy. But Uruguay, who had won the competition four years earlier, boycotted the finals because of Europe's lack of interest in their own tournament when only four teams from the old world had made the journey.

Bobby Moore raises the Jules Rimet Trophy after England's 4–2 triumph in 1966.

The increased number of entries meant that a qualifying competition was needed to reduce the numbers down to 16 and the final tournament was played on a strict knockout basis. Italy again underlined the value of staging the competition by emerging as winners. Moreover, they defended their title four years later in France and held on to it.

But with war clouds hovering menacingly over Europe in 1938 there was already one casualty. Austria, who had qualified, found themselves overrun by Germany and had no independent team. Thus only 15 teams competed. Once again it was organised on a sudden death basis.

There was no possibility of staging a World Cup in 1942 because of the Second World War and neither was it feasible to hold one in 1946 so soon after hostilities had ended, but Brazil was chosen as the host nation in 1950. Although sufficient entries had been received, late withdrawals left the finals with only 13 teams. Unfortunately, the decision to use a group system throughout added to the imbalance. Two groups had four teams in each, but one had three and another, ludicrously, just two. The winners then played in a final pool of four teams. So, strictly speaking, there was no actual final match.

To make matters worse for the Brazilian hosts, Uruguay won the deciding match to take the trophy. But FIFA seemed to have learned little for the next World Cup in 1954, held in Switzerland. They retained the group system, but seeded two teams in each who were not required to play against each other. Thus, two teams from each group met in a knockout quarter-final stage, but not before West Germany had been able to field a weakened team against Hungary, gambling on a play-off against Turkey. Hungary beat the Germans 8–3; but in the final, the Germans defeated the Hungarians 3–2!

In 1958 a genuine effort was made to reorganise the entire series on more democratic lines. Again there were four groups of four teams in each and a quarter-final stage which took place after every team had met the other three in its group. Brazil emerged as the winners, the first country to achieve the feat outside their own continent. Sweden, the hosts, reached the final, again to emphasise home advantage. But the Brazilians held on to their crown in 1962 in Chile, where the pattern remained the same.

England hosted the 1966 series and won it by beating West Germany in the final 4–2 after extra time. Although there had been 71 original nominations for entry, the mass withdrawal of the African nations reduced the numbers who actually participated. Despite the increased membership of FIFA, there was a restlessness from many Third World nations who felt their own prospects of reaching the finals were restricted.

Certainly Europe and South America were favoured with final places. In 1966 Europe had nine places plus that of England as hosts, the South Americans three plus Brazil as holders, while the rest of the world had just two.

In 1970 Brazil won their third World Cup in Mexico and kept the Jules Rimet Trophy by beating Italy 4–1 in the final. The trophy was replaced by the FIFA World Cup. Thus, for the 1974 tournament, there was a new trophy and a different formula in the finals. Instead of a quarter-final knockout round, the eight qualifiers – winners and runners-up – from the four groups were split into two further sections of four. The winners of each group met in the final, while the runners-up disputed the match for third and fourth places. But this system could be manipulated by teams who, having ensured sufficient points from their first two matches, could contrive to approach a meaningless third game to suit a place in either of the two final sections.

However, the reason for the change in the pattern of the tournament was simply to increase the total number of matches and, with it, the revenue. Although 99 entries had been received in 1974 and 106 in 1978, the countries not in Europe and South America were still gaining only three places out of the 16 finalists.

Joao Havelange, the Brazilian who became President of FIFA in succession to Sir Stanley Rous, realised the value of obtaining Third World support for his candidature for office by promising them increased representation at the finals.

Home advantage had presented West Germany with the Cup in 1974 and similarly Argentina four years later, but for the 1982 series in Spain, the finals were enlarged to embrace 24 teams and resulted in 108 entries, from the 147 FIFA members, being received. The first stage of the final competition produced six groups of four teams in each. The first two teams in each group went into a second round split into four groups of three. A knockout semi-final stage paired the winners of these last four groups. Italy won their third World Cup in 1982, beating West Germany 3–1 in the final. For the first time at this stage of the competition, penalties were used to settle drawn matches after extra time.

Lothar Matthaus, West Germany's World Cup inspiration in 1990.

In 1986 there was another innovation. Although the initial six groups of four teams were retained as four years earlier, the first two in each, plus the four best third-placed sides overall, moved into a knockout round of 16 teams. This restored the spirit of the original World Cup, designed as a purely sudden death tournament. Argentina achieved their second victory in three competitions by beating West Germany 3–2 in the finals held in Mexico.

Mexico having staged their second World Cup, the venue for 1990 was chosen as Italy, host nation for the second tournament in 1934. In a repetition of the 1986 final, the Germans gained revenge by beating Argentina 1–0 in a poor game. For the 1994 series, the United States of America was the selection.

European Championship

Europe was way behind South America in organising a tournament for its national teams. The man who conceived the idea was Henri Delaunay, Secretary of UEFA and also of the French Football Federation. The success of the European Cup convinced many of UEFA's members that such a competition was a viable proposition. It was to be held every four years.

The first tournament began in 1958 as the European Nations Cup, although not all European countries entered. The four British sides predictably showed no interest, but surprisingly neither did West Germany nor Italy. There were 17 entries and a preliminary round had to be arranged for a knockout series decided on aggregate scores from home and away matches up to the semi-finals. The final was held in 1960. There was a political hiccup in the quarter-finals when Spain refused to play the USSR and withdrew, giving the Soviets a bye into the semi-finals. The last stages of the competition were held in France, the USSR beating Czechoslovakia 3–0 and Yugoslavia overcoming the host nation 5–4. France then lost 2–0 to the Czechs in the game for third place.

Horst Hrubesch celebrates scoring the winner in the 1980 European Championship.

The final in Paris went to extra time before the Soviet Union emerged 2–1 winners over Yugoslavia; but, with France out of the reckoning, the attendance was disappointingly under 20,000.

However, there was increased interest in the second tournament which began in 1962. Twenty-eight countries entered including three of the four UK contingent; Scotland declined. Spain was chosen as the venue for the latter part and the hosts succeeded in reaching the final where, ironically, they met the holders USSR. Spain agreed to play this time and won 2–1 against a defensive-minded Soviet team.

Naturally, the guarantee of only one tie and two games was not popular and it was agreed for the third tournament to overhaul its structure completely. There was also a change of title to the European Football Championship, though the prize was still the Henri Delaunay Cup. Only Iceland of the then members did not enter and the 31 sides were split into seven groups of four teams, the remaining one composed of three. The four British countries were put together and the Home International Championship was used as the means of qualifying. In effect, two consecutive years of this particular domestic competition were utilised.

Neither Spain, the holders, nor Italy, designated as hosts for the final stages, were excused the qualifying section but fortunately for both, they topped their respective groups. England just headed Scotland by a point to reach the quarter-finals, where they beat Spain. In the semi-finals, Italy were fortunate to prevail against the USSR after a goalless draw, which was not decided in the extra period, by the unsatisfactory method of tossing a coin! Doubtless the organisers were relieved. But the disgruntled Soviets then lost 2–0 to England in the match for third place. There was another problem when the final between Italy and Yugoslavia ended 1–1 after extra time. It had been agreed that there would be no further lottery and Italy won the replay 2–0 two days later.

For the 1972 tournament there was an entry of 32 and the finals were staged in Belgium. Once more the Soviets did well to reach the final and the Belgians took third place for themselves. But it was the West Germans who dominated proceedings and ran out excellent 3–0 winners over the Soviets.

Though not the force they had been four years

The hugely gifted Michel Platini of France raises the trophy to the delighted home fans.

earlier, the Germans again made it to the final in 1976. The last four teams battled it out in Yugoslavia whose team, luckily for the organisers, was among that number. In the final itself, Czechoslovakia beat West Germany on penalty kicks after a 2–2 draw.

There was another major change for the 1980 competition. Italy, chosen as the host nation, were excused until the second stage where they joined the seven group-winners in a knockout round. This part of the tournament was also held in Italy, with the eight qualifiers split into two groups of four. The winners of these sections, West Germany and Belgium, met in the final in Rome, the Germans winning 2–1 while the runners-up decided the match for third place. This was also determined by penalty kicks, Czechoslovakia winning the shoot-out, this time 9–8, after a 1–1 draw with Italy.

In the 1984 competition, organised on similar lines with the last eight teams playing in France, the hosts made the most of their free passage to the final stages. Again there was a slight alteration in the proceedings; the first two teams in each group met in the semi-finals. This was easily the most competitive and attractive tournament to date: all four teams in the semi-finals – France, Portugal, Spain and Denmark – displayed pace, skill and imagination. France, improving their already impressive standards, beat Spain 2–0 in the final in Paris, but failed to qualify for the next series, the finals of which were held in West Germany.

Without touching the heights of the 1984 tournament, the 1988 competition produced a winner in the Netherlands whose effective and attractive style brought back memories of the Dutch exploitation of 'total' football in the 1970s.

Arnold Muhren, the elegant Dutch midfielder, crowned his career in the European Championship of 1988.

South American Championship

While FIFA made no immediate move towards organising a World Cup after the formation of their world governing body in 1904, the South Americans were more active in preparing their own competition for national teams. After an attempt by Argentina in 1910 to establish a tournament, it was only from 1916 that one was held on a regular basis.

That same year the four countries taking part – Argentina as hosts, Brazil, Chile and Uruguay – announced the formation of the South American Confederation and this presented the new tournament with the official backing it needed. Initial interest was such that the deciding match between Argentina and Uruguay in Buenos Aires had to be postponed because of overcrowding. It eventually took place the following day and the goalless draw was enough to ensure Uruguay of the title.

The proposal for the annual staging of the Championship was that it be held in one city with the teams meeting each other on a league basis. Teams finishing level on points would play off to determine the winner. Although there was no competition in 1918, it was held each year until 1928.

Paraguay replaced Chile in 1921 but all five nations entered the following year. Argentina became the only regular entry and in 1925 the tournament attracted just three countries and was played on a home and away basis. However, Bolivia made their first appearance in 1926, Peru the following year.

Although there was a tournament in Argentina in 1929, most South American countries were in the throes of introducing professionalism and the competition was not revived until 1935. Six countries entered the next one which was spread over 1936 and 1937. But the event became haphazard again, despite the appearance of Ecuador for the first time in 1939 and Colombia in 1945.

The advent of the Copa Libertadores for club sides in 1960 was a further blow to the South American Championship. The 1967 series, held in Montevideo and won by the hosts Uruguay, was only saved from financial disaster by television rights. But in 1975 a determined effort was made to overhaul the decaying competition. All 10 countries entered, holders Uruguay were given a bye to the semi-finals and the other nine were split into three groups, playing home and away matches. The respective winners joined Uruguay in the semi-finals, again over two legs. Peru emerged as the winners.

Zico of Brazil. His country has rarely taken the competition seriously, but they won it in 1989.

Since then the tournament has been held every four years and the idea of staging it in one country has been revived. The original concept of the Copa America has also given it a wider appeal. Despite this, of the three leading countries in the area – Brazil, Uruguay and Argentina – only the last two have supported it seriously and so they have been the most successful.

African Nations Cup

The African Nations Cup is the third-oldest continental championship for national teams. It began modestly enough in 1957 with just three competitors: Egypt, Sudan and Ethiopia, but has since embraced the entire continent of Africa and has been held almost every two years. However, political upheavals have inevitably caused problems with the number of entries.

For the initial tournament, held in Khartoum, Egypt beat Sudan 2–1 and went on to defeat Ethiopia by four clear goals. Egypt staged the next competition when the same three teams competed. This time each one played two games and, incredibly, Egypt's scores were exactly the same as in the previous championship.

The next series was held in Ethiopia, with the hosts winning in a simple knockout competition when they beat the holders Egypt 4–2 after extra time. In subsequent years, there has been a gradual increase in interest. Ghana won the 1963 version when hosts, the final stages initially being played on a group basis. They kept the Cup in 1965 by defeating hosts Tunisia; but when the competition restarted in 1968 in Ethiopia, they lost in the final to Congo-Kinshasa (now Zaire) in an expanded African Nations Cup.

For the 1990 tournament, the 17th in its history, there were 33 entries. Nine preliminary and 12 first round ties were played on a home and away basis. The six survivors from the second round were joined by the host nation Algeria and the holders Cameroon, both of whom had received exemption until the final stages. From start to finish the tournament was completed in 18 months.

Ghana have been the most successful nation with four wins, adding 1978 and 1982 to their earlier victories. Egypt won their third title in 1986. Altogether nine different countries have been successful in the competition which has managed to overcome the many and varied off-the-field problems that have beset the continent since some of its nations gained independence.

Capacity crowds have been seen in several cities and the competition has shown no sign of diminishing in its attraction. But there have been withdrawals. The 1990 tournament was no exception, with three teams pulling out before the preliminary round and another being disqualified. With no one nation dominating the African Nations Cup for long, there has been an impetus to improve playing standards and the regular opportunity for competitive football has helped towards achieving this aim, as has the success of Cameroon and Egypt in the 1990 World Cup.

Cameroon's Roger Milla controls the ball during the 1988 African Nations Cup final against Nigeria.

Olympic Games

Gold medallists Italy in the notorious 1936 Olympics included a rare, bespectacled player in their side.

Soccer has featured in every Olympic Games since 1908, with the exception of 1932. Undoubtedly the successful 1924 and 1928 competitions convinced FIFA to stage the World Cup in 1930. In modern times the football tournament in the Olympics has attracted more spectators than any other sport.

There was unofficial exhibition football in the 1896 and 1900 Olympics and in 1904, though the sport was still not recognised, the International Olympic Committee awarded a gold medal to Canada. In 1908 the gold was won by Britain, though it was an English team which competed as the other home countries had yet to gain FIFA membership. Britain won it again in 1912 but, by the time the next competition was held in 1920, the vexed question of professionalism was already causing rifts and these differences increased in the next two tournaments.

The four British associations withdrew from FIFA in 1928 over the matter of 'broken time' payments to players and, with the failure of the USA to stage a football tournament in 1932, there was a decline in the Olympics' fortunes. Worse, in 1936, the realisation that Germany was interested in propaganda for its Fascist regime, scarcely did anything to enhance the Olympic ideal. However, Great Britain, though still outside FIFA, did enter!

In the post-War era, interest was rekindled and the Eastern European bloc completely dominated the Olympic tournament after Sweden's gold medal in 1948. Hungary (three times), the USSR (twice), Yugoslavia, Poland, East Germany and Czechoslovakia emphasised the non-amateur success ratio, although any pretence that the Olympics retained its original ideals had vanished.

When FIFA stipulated that no player who had played in the World Cup could appear in the Olympics, it merely convinced competing countries to use the tournament to bring on the best of their younger professionals. France did just that in 1984 when they broke the Eastern bloc monopoly. While the IOC are keen to make the football tournament as open as the rest of the Games, FIFA have no wish to undermine the status of the World Cup and insist that subsequent competitions should be for Under-23 players only.

Other International Competitions

Countries

Before the advent of the World Cup in 1930, there were a number of competitions organised on a regional basis for national teams. South America led the way and since then most regions have had their own tournaments at various intervals and for varying lengths of time.

Argentina and Uruguay were the first to start matches between themselves. Initially, they competed for the Lipton Cup in 1905, followed the next year by the Newton Cup. The first Roca Cup matches involving Argentina and Brazil began in 1914.

However, the previous year had seen the initial Far Eastern Championship, which was organised roughly every four years and survived until 1934, when it was succeeded by the West Asian Games, and restarted as the Asian Games in 1951. In pre-War years China was the dominating force.

Argentina continued their progressive contacts with neighbouring countries with the Rosa Chevalier Boutell Cup in 1923, at a time when the old world was also thinking of competitive football for itself. The Scandinavian Championship for the Nordic Cup was the next to be inaugurated. It was designed to be played every year with each series lasting four years. Each country met the other three each year making 24 matches altogether. Sweden, Denmark, Finland and Norway were the four original entries in 1924.

Europe itself finally emerged in 1927 with the International Cup, an early attempt at a nations cup, though the interested parties were confined to countries in central and eastern Europe. Austria, Czechoslovakia, Hungary, Italy and Switzerland

Cayasso of Costa Rica, one of the most successful nations in the Concacaf Championship.

Beaten finalists in the 1988 Asian Cup, South Korea were one of the few underdogs not to create a major upset in the 1990 World Cup.

competed in the first five tournaments, while Yugoslavia entered the sixth and final one. This was given the title of Dr Gero Cup in memory of the late president of the Austrian Football Association.

The last two tournaments can certainly be said to have encouraged the European governing body to a more broadly-based competition for its member countries. In 1928, the Baltic Cup was launched as a triangular tournament involving Latvia, Estonia and Lithuania and was held annually until 1938, when the Soviet Union annexed the trio as part of a deal with Germany. The Balkan Championship was launched in 1929, played on a league system between Bulgaria, Greece, Rumania and Yugoslavia and revived briefly after the War.

Another newcomer in South America was the Rio Branco Cup in 1931 between Brazil and Uruguay, which, like many others in the area, was held at irregular intervals.

In 1941 the Concacaf Championship started under its original title of the Central American and Caribbean Championship and was held approximately every two years.

The Mediterranean Cup made a brief appearance in 1949 and continued erratically under varying titles in the next few years as other areas attempted to increase their competitive fixture lists. Meanwhile the South Americans added to their calendar.

The Oswaldo Cruz Cup between Brazil and Paraguay began in 1950, the O'Higgins Cup for Brazil and Chile came along in 1955, followed by the Atlantic Cup in 1956. This involved Argentina, Brazil and Uruguay at first and Paraguay joined in for the third tournament in 1975. But the problems in South America were twofold. While the South American Championships were beginning to run into operational problems, the South American Cup was proving very lucrative for clubs who should have supplied players for the national teams.

Yet, while some of the older cups fell by the wayside, others emerged. The Carlos Dittborn Cup began in 1962 between Argentina and Chile, in memory of the late Chilean delegate to FIFA who had personally persuaded the world governing body to stage the 1962 World Cup in his country. The Chaco Cup between Bolivia and Paraguay, the Coronel Bogado Cup for Argentina and Paraguay, the Artigas Cup between Paraguay and Uruguay plus the Pinto Duran Cup involving Uruguay and Chile have all had their moments.

The Asian Cup began in 1956 and has since been held on a four-yearly basis. Other subsequently organised tournaments, such as the Arab Cup and the Gulf Cup have flourished in more recent years, particularly in areas where the opportunities of reaching the latter stages of the World Cup are limited.

Football tournaments are held at such events as the Pan Arabic Games, Mediterranean Games, South East Asian Games and so on, for largely amateur or part-time footballers. But others, like the Pan-American Championships which began in 1952, are used as a springboard for Olympic and World Cup development in South America and Concacaf.

Europe, having established its European Championship, extended its activities to provide an Under-23 competition and this in turn was modified to an Under-21 tournament, when in 1972 it changed its age limit for the 1976–78 series. On a national level, there are youth tournaments in all areas and a World Youth Cup, a World University Championship, and indoor competitions have also become fashionable.

European Cup

The idea of a competition between the leading clubs in various European countries seems so obvious, that in hindsight it is surprising that it did not materialise until 1955. But the credit for the idea of the European Cup belongs solely to Gabriel Hanot, a football writer with the French sports newspaper *L'Equipe*.

Hanot, a former French international who would probably have played more than 12 times for his country but for the First World War, was of pensionable age by the time UEFA, the European governing body, was formed in 1954. But neither they nor FIFA appeared interested in his plans. So Hanot decided to take a more positive approach than merely conducting the discussion in the columns of his newspaper. He invited delegates from 18 countries to attend a meeting in Paris in the spring of 1955. Only three failed to arrive: Scotland's Hibernian sent a telegram of support, while Sparta Prague and Moscow Dynamo pleaded fixture congestion and weather difficulties for their non-acceptance.

The meeting was a total success and plans were drawn up for a tournament to start in the following autumn. FIFA, fearing a threat to their authority, sanctioned the idea with the proviso that clubs entering had to have permission from their national association. UEFA also fell in line and agreed to organise it.

Because of the stipulation that clubs had to obtain permission and other factors, Hanot's original 18 was reduced to 12. Chelsea, the Football League Champions, were forbidden to enter by the misguided insularity which has so often been an English trait. The excuse was 'fixture congestion'. Gwardia Warsaw replaced them, while PSV Eindhoven of the Netherlands and Denmark's Aarhus took over from Holland Sport and KB Copenhagen respectively. But neither the Czechs nor the Soviets took part. Voros Lobogo replaced Honved from Hungary.

Hibernian, who had finished fifth in the Scottish League, did well to reach the semi-finals. All ties until the final were played on a home and away basis with the aggregate of goals deciding the winner. The first final was appropriately held in Paris and won by Real Madrid, who beat the French entry Reims 4–3.

The competition, which had started with a match between Sporting Lisbon and Partizan Belgrade on 4 September 1955 in the Portuguese capital, had immediately proved an enormous success, producing exciting football and financial rewards for the competitors. Its popularity quickly increased and, after the initial tournament, entry was restricted to national league champions, although the country of the holders could enter their league winners as well.

Real Madrid dominated the early years, winning the first five series and reaching a peak in the 1960 final when they defeated Eintracht Frankfurt 7–3 at Hampden Park, Glasgow before a crowd of 135,000. It took another seven years before the Scots were able to applaud victory of their own, away in Lisbon, against Inter-Milan, the Italian club which had come to epitomise the defensive football which had sadly become a by-product of the European

Graeme Souness lifts the European Cup in 1984. It was Liverpool's fourth such success.

Cup. Moreover Celtic achieved their 2–1 win in what was their first season in the competition.

The following year, Manchester United, who had been England's first representatives in 1956–57, albeit against Football League advice, won it in England's first successful attempt. They defeated Benfica of Portugal 4–1 after extra time at Wembley. These two British successes did more in the overall scheme of the competition than merely provide cause for rejoicing in these islands. They broke the monopoly which the Latin countries had enjoyed, as previously only Spanish, Portuguese and Italian teams had triumphed.

Though AC Milan won their second European Cup in 1969, Feyenoord won it for the Netherlands in 1970 and spurred their countrymen from Ajax, whose brand of 'total' football swept aside the negative approach of others, to three successive trophies.

West Germany's Bayern Munich emulated the Dutchmen's feat from 1974 to 1976, before Liverpool stamped their individual style on the European Cup in 1977, one of four trophies to fall to the Anfield club. In fact, English teams did exceptionally well in the years that followed. Nottingham Forest won it in successive years, and Aston Villa achieved another triumph of their own in 1982. Indeed, the Cup did not leave England after 1977 until 1983.

Unfortunately, England's challenge ended in tragedy at the Heysel Stadium in Brussels in 1985 when a group of rioting Liverpool supporters caused the deaths of 39 fans, most of whom were Italian supporters of Juventus. English clubs were banned from European competition as a result.

AC Milan's Marco van Basten takes on the Benfica defence during the 1990 European Cup final.

Although this was the greatest disaster to hit the competition, increased misbehaviour by supporters of various clubs around Europe has brought in its wake the closure of grounds, fines and the suspensions of clubs. But the competition has survived and shows no sign of decreasing in its popularity, although the pressures have grown alarmingly as the necessity to win has overshadowed all other aspects.

European Cup–Winners' Cup

The Dynamo Moscow defender clears the ball, but Rangers emerged 3–2 winners in 1972.

The success of the European Cup prompted a call for the winners of national cup competitions to have their own tournament. But not all Europe's members had regularly competed for cups and the initial years had few entries. However, its own momentum convinced those countries who had been lukewarm about knockout tournaments, to revive their own domestic cups and thus become involved in the Cup-Winners' Cup. It also became possible for the beaten finalists in a national cup to enter, if the winners had already been crowned champions of their league.

Honours have been widespread in this competition: clubs from 11 different countries have won it. Before the ban imposed on them, English clubs had won the Cup-Winners' Cup five times, more than any other country.

Vialli scores for Sampdoria against Anderlecht in the 1990 final to make up for the previous year's disappointment.

Fairs Cup/UEFA Cup

Paul Mariner of Ipswich powers through the AZ 67 Alkmaar defence in the first leg of the 1981 final.

Tough defence from Juventus's Aleinikov in the second leg of the 1990 final enabled them to hold on to their 3–1 first leg lead.

If Gabriel Hanot was the instigator of the European Cup, Ernst Thommen, a Swiss vice-president of FIFA, was the man behind the International Inter-Cities Fairs Cup competition, with its lengthy title and unwieldy time-scale. Its initial tournament was spread over three years.

The formation of UEFA provided the opportunity to put the idea of the competition into practice and, probably because of their involvement in the Fairs Cup, UEFA reacted coolly to the European Cup. Representatives from 10 countries covering 12 cities met in April 1955 to formulate plans. Initially entrants represented cities that held trade fairs and, wherever possible, fixtures were designed to coincide with such events. However, the selection of each city's team was left to the individual country and provided differing interpretations. Barcelona was represented by all but one player from the Barcelona team, the remaining player coming from Espanol, but London selected from all professional clubs in the city.

After the second tournament, which took two years, it was decided to hold it every year with one team representing each city. Although the Fairs Cup had increased in size and popularity, losing its original need to connect it with trade fairs, it needed a complete relaxation of this rule.

In 1971 the Fairs Cup was replaced by the UEFA Cup and this regularly provides for 64 teams; the number of places per country is decided on previous performance and monitored each season. Since entry is restricted to the highest placed teams in each country, it could be said that the UEFA Cup is second in prestige to the European Cup itself.

South American Cup (Copa Libertadores)

This competition for champion clubs in South America was originally contested in 1960 as the Champion Clubs Cup, having been agreed to in principle two years earlier by the South American Football Confederation. Undoubtedly the success of the European Cup influenced the decision to organise a similar tournament.

Promoting a sound idea was one factor, attempting to put it into practice was another far more difficult exercise. To begin with, there was an initial lack of interest from many countries. Then, when it was obvious that there was something of a future for such a competition, club commitments overshadowed the national interests of the South American Championship.

Successful teams invariably discovered that winning the trophy merely brought financial ruin. In its initial years, matches were played in midweek in front of poor crowds, as league and other domestic fixtures took precedence. Only eight teams entered the first series, and even one of these withdrew. Some fielded weakened sides rather than risk injuries for league games.

Penarol of Uruguay became the first winners for two reasons: firstly, they took more interest than any of the other competitors; secondly, they were arguably the best team in it. They needed only a handful of games to achieve their title, as the South American Cup was then based on a knockout system on the home and away aggregate pattern familiar in the European Cup.

Penarol retained their title the following year, but in 1962 a change in the format to a league system of three groups, with the holders given a bye to the semi-final knockout stage, gave the participants more games. Another rule of the competition was that teams from the same country had to face each other before the final; thus Penarol as holders were drawn against Nacional, the Uruguayan champions that season, in the semi-finals.

Having survived this tie Penarol lost in the final to Santos, Pele's club, in a tie which produced enormous problems. Santos won their home leg 2–1 but, in the return, were losing 3–2 shortly after half-time when the Chilean referee, Carlos Robles, was hit on the head by a stone and knocked unconscious. When he recovered, Robles suspended the game but, after discussions lasting 80 minutes, the match was eventually restarted. Santos equalised, but at the time of the goal a flag-waving linesman was struck by another missile from the crowd. The game eventually ended 3–3 but in the subsequent disciplinary hearing, the referee confirmed he had ended the game at 3–2 to Penarol and had merely carried on to avoid further disturbances. A deciding third game gave Santos a 3–0 win.

In 1963, with the holders given a bye to the final, Santos retained the Cup by beating Boca Juniors from Argentina, where interest in the competition was growing considerably. Venezuela's champions entered for the first time in 1964 giving the South American Cup a full complement.

The finals were decided on games won rather than aggregate goals scored and, towards the end of 1965, it was agreed to expand the concept of the tournament still further by including the championship runners-up from each country. This idea had been put forward by Uruguay, for whom either Penarol or Nacional were invariably champions.

Brazil was against the move and withdrew its entry in 1966, by which time the competition's name was changed to the Copa Libertadores. Even so, there were 95 matches played as both semi-final groups were decided on a league basis and only the final survived as one tie. But even this needed three games before Penarol beat Argentina's River Plate.

There then followed the worst period in the Cup's history. Argentina's Estudiantes de la Plata, a small-town club, managed to win the Copa Libertadores three years running, by playing as little football as possible but taking gamesmanship to a frighteningly new dimension. This apart, in 1969 the lengthy competition was causing criticism and Argentina withdrew its entries along with Brazil. So, in 1970, it was streamlined and in succeeding years was modified to produce smaller groups. By 1989 it had five groups of four teams each, a second knockout round involving 16 teams and so on to the final. All told, there were 91 games, including a play-off, which emphasised that the overriding consideration was for as many matches as possible! Indeed, in 1989, there were two South American Cup competitions within one year, in order to accommodate the South American Championship.

African Champion Clubs Cup

The African Champion Clubs Cup was introduced in 1964 at a time when membership of the African Football Confederation was increasing and the Nations Cup was establishing itself. All rounds are based on the European Cup principle of home and away games and aggregate scores, although unlike its European counterpart, the final is held in both competing countries.

Although there was no competition in 1965, it has been held in every season since then. After the initial success achieved by the Cameroon club Oryx de Douala, clubs from the sub-Saharan regions tended to be the more successful until the 1980s when the North African teams began to make their presence felt in a practical way. Even so, clubs from Cameroon have done well overall. Canon Yaounde achieved their first win in 1971 and repeated it in 1978 and 1980. Union Douala were successful in 1979.

Egypt can also claim five wins, with Al Ismaily being successful in 1969, Al Ahly in 1982 and 1987 and Zamalek in 1984 and 1986. North Africa also supplied the 1988 winner for Algeria in Entente Setif who, despite winning their domestic championship to qualify for the competition, had been relegated by the time they won the African Champion Clubs Cup.

Once again the numbers of competing clubs have been depleted by withdrawals as well as by indiscipline on the field and off it. However, the 1989 series attracted 38 entries. In the preliminary round one team was disqualified and another failed to complete the second leg. The first round produced another withdrawal and a second match which was abandoned. Difficulties over travel and financial restrictions have been experienced at regular intervals.

African Cup–Winners' Cup

The twin competition did not emerge until 1975 but has been played on similar lines. Egyptian clubs, and Al Ahly in particular, have been the most successful. Al Ahly won it three years in succession from 1984 to 1986. The two previous years had seen Arab Contractors beginning a five-year domination of the Cup-Winners' Cup by Egypt.

Cameroon again provided the initial winner in Tonnerre Yaounde, and Canon added to their triumphs in the African Champion Clubs Cup by winning it in 1979. Tunisia had their initial victory in 1988 when Club Athletique Bizerte underlined the emergence of North African teams as a parallel with events in the African Cup itself.

Abdel Ghani celebrates as Egypt qualify for the World Cup finals after beating Algeria in 1989.

European Super Cup

Played annually, with several breaks in continuation, the Super Cup involves the European Cup winners and the Cup-Winners' Cup holders in a home and away tie decided on goal aggregate. In 1974 and 1981 the qualified teams could not agree on dates to meet each other and in 1985 the ban imposed on English teams meant that Everton were unable to play Juventus. On two occasions it was agreed to play just one game, simply because it was not possible to find another date to enable the two-legged tie to be completed. Juventus won the first of these in 1984 beating Liverpool 2–0 with home advantage in Turin, and Steaua Bucharest defeated Dynamo Kiev 1–0 in Monaco in 1986.

World Club Championship

This competition began in 1960 and was played on an annual basis between the winners of the European Cup and the South American Cup. In its early years it did not receive official recognition by FIFA, but was organised by UEFA and the South American Confederation. The difference in interpretation of how the game should be played in Europe and Latin America inevitably caused problems and, in its developing era, resulted in several outbreaks of disgraceful behaviour on the field.

Until 1964 the tie was decided on a points basis, rather than by an aggregate of home and away goals, with the decider taking place on the ground of the club drawn at home in the second leg. This gave an unfair advantage to the home team and, even when the rule was changed, the play-off match was still played in the same continent.

From 1968 it was decided to use goal aggregate to determine the winning team, but by this time there had already been a number of incidents. In 1963 Santos became the first team to retain the trophy when they beat AC Milan, but only after a play-off in which a player from each side was sent off.

However, from 1967 to 1970, there were dreadful clashes between Argentine teams and European sides. In 1967 Celtic's goalkeeper Ronnie Simpson was hit by a missile before the game and was unable to play. Then, in the play-off, after provocation by Racing Club players, Celtic had four men sent off to Racing's two. Whereas the Scots were fined by their club, the Argentine players were awarded bonuses.

Estudiantes de la Plata, whose aggressive style had ruined the South American Cup, then turned their attention to European teams. Manchester United's George Best was sent off with an Argentine at Old Trafford in 1968, after Nobby Stiles had been sent off in Buenos Aires for a gesture to a linesman.

AC Milan managed to beat Estudiantes the following year, but only after suffering two nasty injuries, and in 1970 the Dutch side Feyenoord survived after a similar mauling. Their fellow-countrymen from Ajax refused to take part in 1971, but UEFA, instead of supporting this decision, put forward European Cup runners-up Panathinaikos as a replacement. The Greeks lost to Nacional of Uruguay.

Ajax repented in 1972 and overcame Argentina's Independiente by keeping calm throughout the two matches. The following year, by agreement, just one game was played in Rome where Juventus defeated Independiente 1–0. By this time, there were serious doubts whether the two-legged system was likely to remain, but in 1974 Independiente lost over two games to Spain's Atletico Madrid.

The first break in the competition occurred in 1975, when the Argentine team playing in its fourth successive World Club Championship failed to agree dates with Bayern Munich of West Germany. But the two-match pattern was resumed the following year only for Liverpool to decline to meet Boca Juniors in 1978. This time UEFA did not put forward a substitute team.

Any feelings that the fixture should be continued in its current form were dispelled in 1979 when

Paraguay's Olimpia and Malmo of Sweden met each other. In Malmo the attendance was only 4,811, while 35,000 turned up for the return in Asuncion. The competition was only saved by sponsorship from Toyota and the staging of the match in Tokyo, where, with the exception of 1987 in atrocious weather, the game has been a 62,000 sell-out every year.

But European teams, and English ones in particular, have discovered the fixture to be a difficult one, the winners almost inevitably coming from South America with just one or two exceptions. Juventus won on penalties in 1985 against Argentinos Juniors, and Portugal's Porto triumphed in extra time over Penarol two years later. Nottingham Forest and Aston Villa were both disappointed and so too were Liverpool in 1981 and 1984. Even the outstanding AC Milan team of 1989 needed extra time before they finished off Nacional of Colombia, appearing for the first time.

Above: John Wark and Enzo Trossero clash during the 1984 World Club Championship match in Tokyo.

Below: Liverpool's Alan Kennedy beats Independiente's Burruchaga in the air, but the South Americans ended up 1–0 winners.

Other International Competitions

Clubs

At club level the main confederations organise competitions for their leading teams along the lines of the European Champion Clubs Cup. The Asian version began in 1967, the same year as the most well known of these, the Concacaf Champion Clubs Cup. The Asian version ran into problems of conflicting political interests, but has been revived in more recent years. However, the Concacaf tournament has had a slightly more stable history and has been responsible for the development of the Intercontinental Cup, which began as the Inter-American Cup in 1969, played between the winners of the South American Cup and the Concacaf Cup. Again, there was a break in its early years, but it has been successfully revitalised.

The forerunner of the initial European Cup was definitely the Mitropa Cup which began as long ago as 1927. As its name suggests, it has its roots deep in middle Europe and was started by the Austrian Hugo Meisl. It flourished in the 1930s but understandably suffered when the three major European tournaments began after the middle of the 1950s. It also appeared under other titles, including the Zentropa Cup and the Danube Cup, but has amazingly survived in a restricted form until the present. This is due as much to sentiment as to practicality.

However, in western Europe there was little of a serious nature until the Latin Cup began in 1949, which was held on an annual basis until 1957. The four Latin countries – Spain, France, Portugal and Italy – competed, entering one team each. A tournament was held every year in each country in turn, played on a knockout basis. The winning team received four points, the losing finalists three and so on. At the end of four years, the winners were the side with the most points accumulated. But, by the end of the second series, the European Cup had overtaken it.

The mid-1960s also saw the emergence of the Balkan Club Cup, originally for the runners-up of the Balkan countries' leagues, but gradually the number of entries was increased and it was organised along the usual European Cup lines.

In 1970 an Anglo-Italian Cup between teams of the Football League and the Italian league was replaced by a competition for semi-professional teams from the same two countries. A similar idea for amateurs had been used in the Barassi Cup.

Nordahl of Milan and Puskas of Honved lead out their sides during the Mitropa Cup competition of 1955.

Surely one of the most interesting survivors is the International Cup, formerly the Rappan Cup and Intertoto Cup, which began in 1962 and is played during the summer months with invited teams from a variety of European countries plus Israel, and used purely to provide people with the opportunity to fill in their pools coupons during the summer months.

British International Championship

The British Championship was the first international tournament. It began in 1883–84 when the four home countries – England, Scotland, Ireland and Wales – started playing each other on a regular basis every season. Previously, matches between some of them had merely been regarded as friendlies. The first official international of any kind involved England and Scotland on 30 November 1872 at the West of Scotland Cricket Club, Partick, Glasgow. It ended in a goalless draw.

Scotland first met Wales in 1876, England played Wales initially in 1879 and Ireland in 1882 – the same year as Wales also met them for the first time and two years before Ireland's first encounter with Scotland in 1884.

The four countries played each other once in a season, with home games in alternating seasons. Teams level on points at the top of the table shared the title as goal average or goal difference did not count in determining the winner, until the latter system was introduced in 1978–79.

Scotland won three of the initial four tournaments and shared the other with England. But, by the start of the First World War in 1914, England had overtaken the Scots. Wales had won just once in 1906–07 and Ireland had their first triumph in the last season before the abandonment of the competition following the outbreak of hostilities in the First World War.

When the Championship was resumed in 1919–20, Wales were the winners and, in the years up to the beginning of the Second World War, won it on five more occasions. It was their last such success and Ireland had to wait until 1979–80 for their second title. Otherwise the English and the Scots dominated the Championship.

The 1980–81 series was abandoned when both England and Wales declined to play in Northern Ireland because of the political situation. But interest in the entire tournament had been falling off, except for the annual clash between England and the Scots. The 1983–84 competition proved to be the

Kenny Dalglish comes away from Tony Currie during the 1978 Home Internationals. England won the game 1–0.

last as England subsequently refused to play either Northern Ireland or Wales, and Scotland soon followed their action.

Of the 89 tournaments, including the one which was incomplete, England achieved 34 titles outright followed by Scotland with 24, Wales with seven and Northern Ireland with three. Of the shared honours, England had 20, Scotland 17, Wales and Northern Ireland five each.

England and Scotland continued to meet each other annually and a new trophy, the Rous Cup, was introduced in recognition of Sir Stanley Rous's contribution to the game, with one other foreign country invited to complete a three-team tournament at the end of the season.

In all matches involving the four home countries including the Championship, the overall record is as follows:

England v Scotland

Played: 107. England won 43, Scotland 40. Drawn 24.

Goals: England 188, Scotland 168.

Record win: England 9, Scotland 3, 15 April 1961, Wembley.

Best individual performance: Dennis Wilshaw (England) 4 goals, 2 April 1955, Wembley.

Wales v Scotland

Played: 101. Scotland won 60, Wales 18. Drawn 23.

Goals: Scotland 238, Wales 111.

Record win: Scotland 9, Wales 0, 23 March 1878, Old Hampden.

Best individual performance: John Madden (Scotland) 4 goals, 18 March 1883, Wrexham; Willie Paul (Scotland) 4 goals, 22 March 1890, Paisley.

England v Wales

Played: 97. England won 62, Wales 14. Drawn 21.

Goals: England 239, Wales 90.

Record win: Wales 1, England 9, 16 March 1896, Cardiff.

Best individual performance: Steve Bloomer (England) 5 goals, 16 March 1896, Cardiff.

England v Ireland

Played: 96. England won 74, Ireland 6. Drawn 16.

Goals: England 319, Ireland 80.

Bryan Robson beats Northern Ireland's McElhinney during the last ever International Championship match in April 1984.

Record win: Ireland 0, England 13, 18 February 1882, Belfast.

Best individual performance: Willie Hall (England) 5 goals, 16 November 1938, Old Trafford.

Scotland v Ireland

Played: 91. Scotland won 60, Ireland 15. Drawn 16.

Goals: Scotland 253, Ireland 81.

Record win: Scotland 11, Ireland 0, 23 February 1901, Hampden Park.

Best individual performance: Charles Heggie (Scotland) 5 goals, 20 March 1886, Belfast.

Wales v Ireland

Played: 90. Wales won 42, Ireland 27. Drawn 21.

Goals: Wales 181, Ireland 126.

Record win: Wales 11, Ireland 0, 3 March 1888, Wrexham.

Best individual performance: Joe Bambrick (Ireland) 6 goals, 1 February 1930, Belfast.

FA Cup

The Football Association Challenge Cup is the oldest competition in the world. The idea was originally discussed at a meeting in the offices of the *Sportsman* on 20 July 1871 and was approved on 16 October 1871. There were 15 entries for the first competition held that same season, although three of them scratched. Now it attracts in excess of 500 clubs per season.

There is a preliminary round in the early part of September, followed by four qualifying rounds before the first round proper in November. At this stage, the 48 Associate Members of the Football League enter. After the second round in December, the surviving 20 teams are joined by the 44 Full Members of the League from Divisions One and Two. The third round takes place in January. The Cup is played on a strict knockout system and the semi-finals are played on a neutral ground, usually within convenient travelling distance between the respective teams involved. Since 1923, the final has been held at Wembley, usually in May.

The FA Cup had a modest baptism. The first final in 1872 was played between Wanderers and the 7–4 on favourites Royal Engineers at the Kennington Oval, with a crowd of around 2,000 watching. The admission price of one shilling (5p) was thought to be a contributory factor to the low attendance. Wanderers won 1–0, the goal scored by M.P. Betts, an old Harrovian who played under the assumed name of A.H. Chequer because he had once appeared for Harrow Chequers. But there has been subsequent doubt about the authenticity of

Perhaps as many as 200,000 turned up for the first Wembley Cup final in 1923. Not surprisingly, some did not fit on the stands.

his claim to be the scorer. In recent years it was suggested that Thomas Hooman had actually steered the ball between the posts. Certainly, reports of the match were sketchy enough at the time.

However, rather more difficult to understand is how the score in a subsequent final could have been totally confused. It happened in 1877 when Wanderers beat Oxford University 2–1. For many years the score was given as 2–0 and only recent research has unearthed the missing goal, although the Football Association still refuse to include it in their own records.

Since the Challenge Cup was exactly what it claimed to be when first introduced, Wanderers, as winners of the initial tournament, were able to obtain a bye to the final and choose their own venue for it. The Cup itself was worth £20, the money being subscribed from the original 15 entries. But, after Wanderers' second success in 1873, the rule was changed and winners had to participate with other clubs. Still, they managed three consecutive victories from 1876 to 1878 and thus earned the right to keep the Cup but gave it back to the FA on the understanding that it was not to be won outright by any other club.

It cannot be referred to as the English Cup, because Scottish and Irish clubs have appeared in the competition (although neither country is allowed to compete these days); Welsh clubs are still accepted. Indeed, the only occasion that the Cup has gone out of England was when Cardiff City won it in 1927. Queen's Park, the Scottish amateur club, appeared in successive finals in 1884 and 1885, losing on both occasions to Blackburn Rovers. By this time, professionalism was establishing itself and the days of the universities, old boys' teams and the military were over.

The formation of the Football League in 1888 further developed this trend, and to Preston North End went the honour of coupling the first League Championship with the FA Cup in 1889. Only one non-League club has subsequently won the trophy: Tottenham Hotspur were members of the Southern League when they achieved their first win in 1901.

Spurs went on to join the League and emulated Wanderers' feat of winning the Cup five times. Since then they have added two more successes and were not beaten in a final until 1987 when they lost 3–2 to Coventry City. However, their record seven wins is equalled only by Aston Villa and Manchester United, the latter being the only club to win as many as six times at Wembley, where the competition has found a home for more than 60 years.

Clive Allen prepares to shoot in the 1987 final. It was the first time Spurs had lost in an FA Cup final.

Apart from breaks for the First and Second World Wars, the FA Cup has been played for regularly each year. In 1945–46 it was the first major competition to restart after the War and, for one season only, all ties were played on a home and away basis with aggregate scores determining the winner.

From its modest days of minimal spectator interest and small numbers of competitors, the FA Cup has become the most exciting sudden death competition in the world. The clamour for Cup final tickets each year shows no sign of diminishing, particularly since the capacity at Wembley has been gradually reduced by restructuring. The allocation of available places to the competing teams' supporters is an annual headache for the FA.

Although fluctuating attendance figures for League matches have also been reflected in the FA Cup throughout its various rounds over the years, it still manages to attract 2,000,000 spectators each season from its preliminary round to the final.

Football League

Michael Thomas scores for Arsenal to snatch the League title from Liverpool in the last seconds of the season in 1989.

The Football League was formed on 17 April 1888 at the Royal Hotel, Manchester, following a previous meeting a month earlier. Twelve clubs: Accrington, Aston Villa, Blackburn Rovers, Bolton Wanderers, Burnley, Derby County, Everton, Notts County, Preston North End, Stoke, West Bromwich Albion and Wolverhampton Wanderers became founder members. Three other clubs – Sheffield Wednesday, Nottingham Forest and Halliwell – applied for membership, but could not be accepted because of the difficulty of arranging fixtures.

The prime mover behind the idea to formulate a league was a Scot, William McGregor, living in Birmingham and an official of Aston Villa. He corresponded with leading clubs to interest them in regularising fixtures which had been on the increase since professionalism had grown in the preceding years, but were of a haphazard nature.

The first Football League games were played on Saturday, 8 September 1888 and the most successful start was made by Bolton Wanderers, who were three goals ahead against Derby County within six minutes of the kick-off. However, Derby fought back to lead 4–3 at the interval and won 6–3.

Such was the success of the new venture that a Second Division was added in 1892 from the old Football Alliance, a year after the First Division was increased to 14 teams. The top division had itself grown to 16 clubs by 1892 and by 1905 the two divisions had swelled to an overall complement of 40.

Although the League carried on in the first season affected by the First World War, it abandoned the competition at the start of the 1915–16 season and did not resume again until 1919–20. During the War, however, regional competitions were organised. But, with hostilities at an end, further expansion brought the total number of clubs up to 44.

In 1920–21 a Third Division was added, embracing a further 22 clubs and the following season this was split into Southern and Northern Sections, the latter having 20 teams. By 1923 each section comprised 22 clubs.

War again intervened in 1939 when the season was a week old. It meant the abandonment of the official programme, but again regional football was soon organised and carried on throughout the War. The League, which had operated a cup for Third Division clubs in the 1930s, even started a League War Cup to replace the FA Cup which had been postponed during the Second World War.

A full resumption of normal League fare was possible in 1946–47 and in 1950 two clubs were added to each of the regional Third Divisions bringing the total of League members to 92. Of this number only 44 clubs are Full Members, the remainder are Associate Members.

Relegation and promotion for the bottom two clubs and the top two of Divisions One and Two respectively was introduced in 1898–99. Previously, the issues had been decided by a series of Test Matches brought in on the creation of a Second Division. But, on the formation of the regionalised Division Three, only one team came up from each section. This remained until the 1957–58 season, when the 12 lowest-finishing clubs in each of the Southern and Northern Sections formed a new Fourth Division; the top 12 in each, minus the promoted teams but with the relegated sides from Division Two, formed a new Third Division.

By 1958–59 four clubs were relegated and another four promoted between the two new divisions. In 1973 the League accepted three up and three down between the first three divisions.

Throughout the League's history, a varying number of clubs at the bottom of the lowest division have had to seek re-election. However, in 1987 play-offs were introduced in addition to the automatic transfer of promoted and relegated teams between divisions. This has been modified in subsequent seasons. At the same time the bottom club in Division Four was demoted to the GM Vauxhall Conference and replaced by the leading team from that non-League competition.

Goal average was replaced by goal difference for the 1976–77 season, and for the 1981–82 season the old system of two points for a win was replaced by three. Substitutes were first permitted for injured players in the Football League for the 1965–66 season and for any reason in the following term. Two substitutes were allowed in the 1987–88 season.

The League has introduced a number of cup competitions involving both Full Members and Associate Members. The longest surviving is the League Cup, organised in 1960 and subsequently sponsored as the Milk Cup, the Littlewoods Cup and the Rumbelows Cup. The League itself has been sponsored, firstly by Canon in 1983 and then, briefly, by *Today* newspaper before the role was taken over by Barclays Bank in 1987. Liverpool have been the most successful team in the history of the League. Of the 18 Championship titles they have won, 11 have been gained since 1973.

The League's headquarters are situated at Lytham St Annes, Lancashire and were previously sited at nearby Preston.

John Barnes scored 15 goals in his first season at Liverpool helping them on their way to their 17th title in 1987–88.

Football League Cup

The decision to organise a cup competition for all Full and Associate Members of the Football League was taken at the AGM in May 1960. Entry was optional in the early years of the tournament and it was not until the early 1970s that it became compulsory. Even so, 87 clubs took part in the 1960–61 competition and the 112 matches attracted an attendance of 1,204,580, despite widespread criticism from the press, who unfairly compared it with the FA Cup. The number of entries varied from season to season, but gradually the prejudice against it subsided.

In 1971–72, with a full complement of teams, a record aggregate of 2,397,154 spectators was registered for 123 games in the competition. By this time the final had already been switched to a single venue at Wembley which added to the interest and boosted the overall crowd figures. Previously the final had been held on a home and away basis, but in 1967 the final was played at Wembley, which guaranteed a capacity crowd and countrywide interest.

In the early seasons, clubs from all four divisions succeeded in reaching the final, but in recent years it has become more and more difficult for lower division teams to break through. This was evident when entry to the UEFA Cup became possible for the winning team. In the first 23 seasons, 23 different finalists were produced.

Although the competition has been on a strict knockout basis, the first round has always involved home and away matches to allow the Associate Members to have two games at least each season. But, from the 1979–80 season, the home and away structure was extended to take in the second round as well. The semi-final has consistently been played over two legs throughout the history of the competition.

In 1982 the League Cup became the first major tournament in the country to be sponsored when it became the Milk Cup, following a deal with the National Dairy Council that was concluded on 13 March, two weeks before the final. Littlewoods took over the sponsorship for the 1986–87 season for a further four seasons before Rumbelows came in.

Liverpool have been the most successful club in the League Cup winning it four times in succession from 1981 to 1984. In 1990, Nottingham Forest also won the Cup a fourth time. Penalty kicks were first used to decide a League Cup tie in the 1979–80 season.

Although overall attendances have decreased since their peak in the mid-1970s, the competition regularly attracts 1.5 million per season and has established itself as a vital ingredient of the calendar. It is a far cry from its beginnings when the finals had to be postponed until the following season because no suitable dates could be arranged.

Goalscorer Nigel Jemson and Man of the Match Des Walker show off their trophies at the end of the 1990 Littlewoods Cup final.

Other Football League Competitions

The Football League has two cup competitions, one for its Full Members, another for the Associate Members. Both are sponsored, but have had a variety of sponsors and names which has not helped in establishing them in the minds of the public.

However, the first venture in the world of cup football for the League came in the 1930s, with the introduction of the Third Division Cup for the then respective regional sections in the north and south. The FA Cup usually provided the clubs from Division One and Two with lucrative fixtures if they were fortunate enough to make reasonable progress, but the Third Division clubs felt their prospects were limited. So the League gave them their own knockout tournament.

There were two midweek competitions, one for the Northern Section, the other for the Southern. The Third Division Cup began in 1933–34 and was organised annually up to the outbreak of the War in 1939. However, the Southern Section final was not played in its last year. There were undoubted problems in arranging fixtures, bearing in mind that there was no floodlighting facility to ease the congestion in the calendar which required daylight to complete matches. Some games had to be held over until the following season.

It was not a success and, had it not been for the intervention of the War, the League was proposing to reduce entry to the competition to the second and third teams in each section who would compete to reach a North v South final. The idea was not taken up afterwards, but during hostilities the League did institute a successful cup competition of its own to replace the FA Cup which had been shelved for the duration. This League War Cup was the forerunner of the League Cup itself.

In the clamour for still more fixtures, the League toyed with various pre-season and other mid-season tournaments, but none had any lasting success or sustained interest until the Freight Rover Trophy in 1984–85. Playing the final at Wembley provided clubs, who might otherwise have never had the opportunity of appearing there, with the incentive to take it seriously. The Full Members Cup which began in 1985–86 also climaxed in a Wembley final. This was later sponsored as the Simod Cup and then as the Zenith Data Systems Cup which caused much confusion, as did the renaming of the Freight Rover as the Sherpa Van Trophy and then the Leyland Daf Cup.

The League also faced problems with some of its Full Members who seemed uninterested in the provision of a further competition with little prospect of profit, if they were to be quickly eliminated in what was a strictly sudden death tournament. This was not the case in the Associate Members version which operated on a league basis in its early stages. But the financial gain of a Wembley final was not to be lightly dismissed.

Unusually, Steve Bull did not score in the Sherpa Van Trophy final of 1988 against Burnley. Wolves won 2–0.

Scottish Cup

The Scottish Cup was organised following a meeting of clubs to form the Scottish Football Association. There were representatives of seven interested parties at the meeting held at Dewar's Hotel, Glasgow on 13 March 1873: Clydesdale, Dumbreck, Eastern, Granville, Queen's Park, Third Lanark and Vale of Leven. An eighth, Kilmarnock, had sent a letter of support. Queen's Park were the instigators of the gathering, with their secretary Archibald Rae the prime mover. Ironically, this oldest of Scottish clubs, formed in July 1867 by members of the Glasgow YMCA, had already played in the FA Cup.

An international fixture had been played against England and another was due. It was obvious that a body had to be formed to administer the game north of the border and institute a cup competition to rival that operating in England. The member clubs collected £56 for a trophy and 12 medals. Sixteen clubs entered the Scottish Cup, the first ties being played on 23 October 1873. Appropriately enough, Queen's Park became the first winners and retained the trophy in the next two seasons.

Queen's Park repeated their trio of successes after Vale of Leven had emulated their earlier achievement by winning the Cup in 1877 and 1878; in 1879, they were awarded it after a drawn game with Rangers. Their opponents refused to replay, claiming a legitimate goal had been wrongly disallowed. In 1884, Vale of Leven were due to play Queen's Park in the final but asked for a postponement because of injury and illness in their team. The Scottish FA insisted Vale play. Queen's Park turned up without opposition, ran the ball into the vacant goal and were awarded the Cup.

There were two further instances of dispute between finalists, but the worst affair concerned Celtic and Rangers in 1909. The Scottish FA withheld the Cup following a riot at the replay, which ended in a draw, fearing further trouble.

The final was first played at the present Hampden Park ground in 1904 and has been played there every season since 1925, except during the War.

Celtic have been the most successful finalists, winning the Cup 29 times to Rangers' 24. Only one club outside the top division of the Scottish League has succeeded in it, East Fife being members of the old Second Division when they achieved the feat in 1938, beating Kilmarnock 4–2 in a replayed final.

Jock Stein sees the green and white ribbons on the Scottish Cup yet again. In all he won the trophy eight times.

Joe Miller of Celtic, who scored the winner, attacks the Rangers defence during the 1989 final.

Scottish League

The Scottish League was formed in 1890 following a series of meetings between interested clubs who were keen to regularise fixtures. However, there was some opposition from the Scottish Football Association and certain clubs who feared it would lead to the adoption of professionalism. But agreement was reached between 11 clubs: Abercorn, Cambuslang, Celtic, Cowlairs, Dumbarton, Heart of Midlothian, Rangers, Renton, St Mirren, Third Lanark and Vale of Leven.

Of these clubs, Renton had been the most enthusiastic, but found themselves in trouble almost immediately. They had completed only five League games in the 1890–91 season when they were suspended by the Scottish FA for allegedly ignoring the ban on clubs playing St Bernard's, a club in breach of the laws of amateurism. Renton's defence was that they had played Edinburgh Saints, a new team, but the Scottish FA ruled this to be one and the same as St Bernard's. Renton's record was expunged from the competition, but they were able to resume the following season.

In 1893, a Second Division was formed from members of the Alliance League. It was suspended in 1915 because of the First World War, although the First Division carried on throughout hostilities. In 1921 automatic promotion and relegation between the two divisions was brought in. A Third Division was introduced in 1923, but lasted less than three seasons. It was restarted in 1946 when the League was restructured into A, B and C divisions. The latter was reorganised as the Reserve League in 1955 when the first two reverted to being Divisions One and Two.

The biggest shake-up occurred in 1975 when the top 10 clubs of the First Division from the previous season formed a new Premier Division, while the bottom eight together with the top six of Division Two formed Division One. The remainder continued in Division Two.

In recent seasons, moves to head off a breakaway super-league were made with the restructuring of the Premier Division, which increased to 12 clubs in two successive seasons from 1986 to 1988 before reverting to 10. Clubs in the Premier Division play each other four times, those in the lower divisions three times, alternating either an extra home or away fixture each season.

Goal difference replaced goal average in the 1971–72 season and Rangers, with 40 Championships (including one shared), followed by Celtic, with 35, have dominated the competition. Only nine other clubs have won the 19 remaining Championships.

John Greig won the Championship five times in his 16 seasons at Rangers.

Controversial signing Mo Johnston quickly silenced the critics as his goals helped Rangers retain their title in 1989–90.

Scottish League Cup

The success of the wartime Southern League Cup competition convinced the Scottish League that it should be carried on in peacetime. Thus, in 1946, it resumed as the Scottish League Cup, open to members of the League only.

Originally it was arranged on a league basis, with the clubs divided into eight or nine groups, the winners of each group moving into the quarter-finals of a knockout competition. In seasons where nine groups were featured, there was a play-off between two groups to reduce the number to eight.

Although the system guaranteed clubs a definite number of matches, it did not sustain interest, especially as with only one qualifier at most from each group, there were a number of matches which had little or no bearing on the outcome of the group. So, in 1977–78, it was altered to become a straight knockout competition.

Rangers have been the most successful club, winning the Cup on 16 occasions. Celtic have won it nine times, but between 1965 and 1978 they appeared in 14 finals, enjoying five consecutive victories from 1966 to 1970, before losing seven of their last eight. Earlier, Celtic had beaten Rangers 7–1 on 19 October 1957 to record the highest scoring British final.

Only one team from outside the top division has won the League Cup. East Fife beat Falkirk 4–1 after a 1–1 draw in the 1947–48 tournament. Ten different teams have won the trophy. In recent years the tournament has been sponsored. Bell's added their name to it from the 1979–80 season, but from 1984–85 the competition has been sponsored as the Skol Cup.

The Celtic defence holds in this goalmouth scramble from the 1986–87 final, but Rangers went on to win.

Anglo-Scottish Tournaments

Before the advent of extra, chiefly sponsored, cup competitions in the 1970s, there had been only three tournaments involving English and Scottish clubs after the latter had ceased to compete in the FA Cup in 1887.

In 1902 a British League Cup was organised for the benefit of victims of the Ibrox Park disaster. Celtic, Rangers, Everton and Sunderland competed. Celtic won the tournament beating Rangers 3–2 in the final. The trophy itself had been the Glasgow Exhibition Cup which had been won by Rangers but was then donated by them for the new competition.

However, the Glasgow Exhibition Cup was revived in 1938 to coincide with a major exhibition being held in Glasgow. Aberdeen, Celtic, Heart of Midlothian, Rangers, Brentford, Chelsea, Everton and Sunderland all competed. Celtic won again, this time beating Everton 1–0 in the final.

The Coronation Cup of 1953, which marked the crowning of Queen Elizabeth, produced a healthy entry of eight clubs from the two countries: Arsenal, Manchester United, Tottenham Hotspur, Newcastle United, Celtic, Aberdeen, Hibernian and Rangers. Again it was Celtic who triumphed, beating Aberdeen 2–1 in the final.

Irish Football

Eight clubs formed the Irish League in 1890: Clarence, Cliftonville, Distillery, Glentoran, Linfield, Milford, Old Park and Ulster. In 1921, when Ireland split, the southern clubs Shelbourne and Bohemians left the League and, together with other clubs in the south, formed their own Association. The FA of Ireland League was formed the same year. Eight Dublin clubs: Bohemians, Dublin United, Frankfort, Olympia, St James's Gate, Shelbourne, YMCA and W & R Jacobs joined. Athlone Town, the first provincial club, joined in 1922, as did Shamrock Rovers. Fordson of Cork arrived in 1924. A cup competition was inaugurated in 1921.

However, the oldest competition in the whole of Ireland is the Irish Football Association Cup which was instituted in 1880 and competed for by seven teams: Alexander (Limavady), Avoniel, Cliftonville (the oldest club), Distillery, Knock, Old Park and Moyola Park who became the first winners, beating Cliftonville 1–0 in the final.

The Irish Football Association had been launched in 1880, influenced by the findings of J.M. McAlery on a visit to Scotland three years earlier. Visits by Queen's Park and then another Scottish club helped to popularise the game in Ireland. McAlery was made the first honorary secretary. While the League of Ireland has had an interrupted history in both of its main competitions, the First World War caused a break in Northern Ireland and again in the Second World War when the competition was replaced by a regional league, the Irish Cup always carried on.

Non-league St Francis failed to win in the final of the FAI Cup of 1990, as Bray took the trophy for the first time.

Welsh Football

The Welsh Football Association was formed at Wrexham in 1876 and was, for a brief period, known as the Cambrian FA. A cup competition was organised the following year and the first tie was played in October 1877. However, the new authority was short of money and it was more than a year after its formation that a cup and medals were provided for the initial winners of the trophy – Wrexham who had defeated Druids 1–0.

The Welsh League came into being in 1920. Previously Welsh clubs had competed in the Combination. The reserve sides of the Welsh clubs played in the Welsh League.

While winners of the Welsh Cup, which is also open to neighbouring clubs in England, are allowed to compete in the European Cup-Winners' Cup, the Welsh League winners are barred from the European Cup. However, the Welsh authorities are hoping to upgrade their competition to enable Welsh clubs to compete at this level as well.

FIFA

The Federation Internationale de Football Associations (FIFA) was founded in 1904 by representatives from seven European countries: France, Belgium, Denmark, the Netherlands, Spain, Sweden and Switzerland. Membership is now worldwide and embraces 166 different countries. It is the game's controlling body.

That initial gathering on 21 May 1904 had been largely promoted by C.A.W. Hirschman, a Dutch banker, and Robert Guerin, the man behind the formation of the French FA. In the years leading up to that meeting, both men had tried to enlist the support of the English FA but without success, as England, Ireland, Scotland and Wales already had their own 'International Board' and looked upon the Continentals as upstarts. However, over the next few years, they were gradually persuaded to join. England actually agreed in 1905 and the following year D.B. Woolfall, a member of the FA Council, was elected President of FIFA, to underline the esteem in which the English FA was held.

Britain's International Board was still responsible for the Laws of the Game, but in 1913 FIFA was given representation on the Board. However, they were voted out in 1920 when Britain withdrew from FIFA.

In fact, the First World War and its aftermath almost caused the break-up of FIFA. The four British nations, supported by France, Belgium and Luxembourg, decided to boycott Germany and her former allies. But the Scandinavians were adamant that they would play any of the pre-War members, regardless of political attitude. The British isolated themselves, stating they would argue for the expulsion of any country that was prepared to play against any of the Central Powers. There was a real danger that the organisation would either split or disintegrate completely. But the crisis passed when the British left FIFA in 1920.

The British countries rejoined in 1924 but it was a shortlived reunification as, four years later, they quit again over the subject of broken-time payments to amateur players in the Olympics. Moreover, this time they stayed away from FIFA until 1946.

But, meanwhile, FIFA's membership grew appreciably from the seven original countries to 41 by the time of the first World Cup in 1930. Written into the statutes of FIFA had been the important clause to the effect that they alone would have the right to organise a world championship.

It was the success of the football tournaments in the 1924 and 1928 Olympics which finally decided FIFA that a world championship was a viable proposition after all. The four British teams missed out on this important beginning, but FIFA was always keen that they should be involved and maintained links through the International Football Board, to which the four teams had been admitted. When Britain next withdrew from FIFA in 1928, they retained their membership of the International Football Board and this undoubtedly kept relationships on an even level.

By the end of the 1950s the number of member countries was stretching towards the hundred mark. In 1954 the European members had formed the Union of European Football Associations (UEFA) as a subsidiary of FIFA and that same year the Asian Football Confederation was formed. However, these two had been far behind the South Americans, who had formed their own Confederation as long ago as 1916 and were more prepared to act as a branch of FIFA. Further developments have since taken in Africa, North and Central America and the Caribbean as well as Oceania.

Of course, the privileges which the British retain have produced jealousy among other nations. From time to time there have been moves to reduce the four members to just one (Great Britain), since politically there is no division between them. However, it is significant that Great Britain no longer enter the Olympic soccer tournament, fearing that it would merely provide ammunition for those opposed to the individual four who make up the home quartet.

Politics apart, FIFA has developed into a sophisticated organisation which handles every possible aspect of the game's administration. There are standing committees which deal with a variety of matters from the World Cup to finance, referees, players, medicine, technical development, discipline and the press. Every two years a Congress is held to discuss important issues which have arisen and, as well as the World Cup, FIFA is responsible for many other international competitions at all levels including the Olympic Games.

FIFA's Confederations

Asia (AFC) Founded 1954

Members (36): Afghanistan, Bahrain, Bangladesh, Brunei, Burma, China, Hong Kong, India, Indonesia, Iran, Iraq, Japan, Jordan, Kampuchea*, North Korea, South Korea, Kuwait, Laos*, Lebanon, Macao, Malaysia, Maldives, Nepal, Oman, Pakistan, Philippines, Qatar, Saudi Arabia, Singapore, Sri Lanka, Syria, Thailand, United Arab Emirates, Vietnam*, North Yemen, South Yemen.

Independent FIFA member belonging to Zone Asia but not affiliated to AFC: Israel

Africa (CAF) Founded 1957

Members (48): Algeria, Angola, Benin, Botswana, Burkina Faso, Burundi, Cameroon, Cape Verde Islands, Central Africa, Chad, Congo, Egypt, Equatorial Guinea, Ethiopia, Gabon, Gambia, Ghana, Guinea, Guinea-Bissau, Ivory Coast, Kenya, Lesotho, Liberia, Libya, Madagascar, Malawi, Mali, Mauritania, Mauritius, Morocco, Mozambique, Niger, Nigeria, Rwanda, Sao Tome and Principe, Senegal, Seychelles, Sierra Leone, Somalia, Sudan, Swaziland, Tanzania, Togo, Tunisia, Uganda, Zaire, Zambia, Zimbabwe.

Joao Havelange, President of FIFA, promised to help football in the developing countries. In 1990 his hopes were fulfilled.

America – North and Central and Caribbean (CONCACAF) Founded 1961

Members (27): Antigua, Aruba, Bahamas, Barbados, Belize, Bermuda, Canada, Costa Rica, Cuba, Dominican Republic, Grenada, Guatemala, Guyana, Haiti, Honduras, Jamaica, Mexico, Netherlands Antilles, Nicaragua, Panama, Puerto Rico, El Salvador, St Lucia, St Vincent and the Grenadines, Surinam, Trinidad and Tobago, USA.

South America (CONMEBOL) Founded 1916

Members (10): Argentina, Bolivia, Brazil, Chile, Colombia, Ecuador, Paraguay, Peru, Uruguay, Venezuela.

Oceania (OFC) Founded 1966

Members (8): Australia, Chinese Taipei, Fiji, New Zealand, Papua New Guinea, Solomon Islands, Vanuatu, Western Samoa.

Associate Members (8): American Samoa, Cook Islands, Guam, New Caledonia, Niue Island, Northern Marianas, Tahiti, Tonga.

Europe (UEFA) Founded 1954

Members (36): Albania, Austria, Belgium, Bulgaria, Cyprus, Czechoslovakia, Denmark, England, Faroe Islands*, Finland, France, East Germany, West Germany, Greece, Hungary, Iceland, Northern Ireland, Republic of Ireland, Italy, Liechtenstein, Luxembourg, Malta, Netherlands, Norway, Poland, Portugal, Rumania, San Marino, Scotland, Spain, Sweden, Switzerland, Turkey, USSR, Wales, Yugoslavia.

**Member of FIFA not affiliated to particular confederation.*

FIFA's Countries

Afghanistan
Founded: 1933 *Affiliated:* 1948
Clubs: 30 *Players:* 3,300
Colours: All white with red trim

Albania
Founded: 1930 *Affiliated:* 1932
Clubs: 49 *Players:* 3,757
Colours: All red

Algeria
Founded: 1962 *Affiliated:* 1963
Clubs: 780 *Players:* 58,567
Colours: Green shirts, white shorts, red socks
Honours: African Nations Cup winners: 1990

Angola
Founded: 1979 *Affiliated:* 1980
Clubs: 276 *Players:* 4,269
Colours: Red shirts, black shorts, red socks

Antigua
Founded: 1928 *Affiliated:* 1970
Clubs: 60 *Players:* 1,008
Colours: Gold shirts, black shorts and socks

Argentina
Founded: 1893 *Affiliated:* 1912
Clubs: 3,035 *Players:* 306,365
Colours: Blue and white shirts, black shorts, white socks
Honours: World Cup winners: 1978, 1986. South American Championship winners: 1921, 1925, 1927, 1929, 1937, 1941, 1945, 1946, 1947, 1955, 1957, 1959

Aruba
Founded: 1932 *Affiliated:* 1988
Players: 1,500
Colours: Yellow shirts, blue shorts, yellow and blue socks

Australia
Founded: 1961 *Affiliated:* 1963
Clubs: 6,816 *Players:* 433,957
Colours: Gold shirts, green trim, green shorts, white socks, green and gold trim

Austria
Founded: 1904 *Affiliated:* 1905
Clubs: 1,992 *Players:* 253,576
Colours: white shirts, black shorts and socks

Bahamas
Founded: 1967 *Affiliated:* 1968
Clubs: 14 *Players:* 700
Colours: Yellow shirts, black shorts, yellow socks

Bahrain
Founded: 1957 *Affiliated:* 1966
Clubs: 25 *Players:* 2,030
Colours: White shirts, red shorts, red and white socks

Argentina's Mario Kempes, the leading scorer in the 1978 World Cup, heads for goal in the final against the Netherlands.

Jairzinho celebrates Brazil's third goal in the 1970 World Cup final while Facchetti lunges despairingly to stop the ball.

Bangladesh
Founded: 1972 *Affiliated:* 1974
Clubs: 1,265 *Players:* 30,385
Colours: Orange shirts, white shorts, green socks

Barbados
Founded: 1910 *Affiliated:* 1968
Clubs: 92 *Players:* 1,100
Colours: Royal blue shirts, gold trim, gold shorts, royal blue socks, gold trim

Belgium
Founded: 1895 *Affiliated:* 1904
Clubs: 3,362 *Players:* 289,770
Colours: Red shirts with tri-colour trim, red shorts, red socks with tri-colour trim
Honours: Olympic winners: 1920

Belize
Founded: 1980 *Affiliated:* 1986
Colours: Blue shirts, red and white trim, white shorts, blue socks

Benin
Founded: 1962 *Affiliated:* 1962
Clubs: 117 *Players:* 6,700
Colours: All green

Bermuda
Founded: 1928 *Affiliated:* 1962
Clubs: 30 *Players:* 1,947
Colours: Royal blue shirts, white shorts and socks

Bolivia
Founded: 1925 *Affiliated:* 1926
Clubs: 305 *Players:* 15,290
Colours: Green shirts, white trim, white shorts, green trim, green socks
Honours: South American Championship winners: 1963

Botswana
Founded: 1970 *Affiliated:* 1976
Colours: Sky blue shirts, white trim, blue shorts and socks with white and black trim

Brazil
Founded: 1914 *Affiliated:* 1923
Clubs: 12,987 *Players:* 551,358
Colours: Yellow shirts, green trim, blue shorts, white socks, green and yellow trim
Honours: World Cup winners: 1958, 1962, 1970. South American Championship winners: 1919, 1922, 1949, 1989

Brunei
Founded: 1959 *Affiliated:* 1969
Clubs: 22 *Players:* 830
Colours: Gold shirts, black shorts, gold socks

Bulgaria
Founded: 1923 *Affiliated:* 1924
Clubs: 4,328 *Players:* 442,829
Colours: White shirts, green shorts, red socks

Burkina Faso
Founded: 1960 *Affiliated:* 1964
Clubs: 57 *Players:* 4,672
Colours: Red shirts, green shorts, red socks

Burma
Founded: 1947 *Affiliated:* 1947

Cameroon's hero-of-the-moment, Roger Milla, is buried under a pile of ecstatic team-mates after scoring against Colombia during Italia '90.

Clubs: 600 *Players:* 21,000
Colours: Red shirts, white shorts, red socks

Burundi
Founded: 1948 *Affiliated:* 1972
Clubs: 132 *Players:* 3,930
Colours: Red shirts, white shorts, green socks

Cameroon
Founded: 1959 *Affiliated:* 1962
Clubs: 200 *Players:* 9,328
Colours: Green shirts, red shorts, yellow socks
Honours: African Nations Cup winners: 1984, 1988

Canada
Founded: 1912 *Affiliated:* 1912
Clubs: 1,600 *Players:* 224,290
Colours: All red

Cape Verde Islands
Founded: 1982 *Affiliated:* 1986
Colours: All green

Central Africa
Founded: 1937 *Affiliated:* 1963
Clubs: 256 *Players:* 7,200
Colours: Grey-blue shirts, white shorts, red socks, yellow trim

Chad
Founded: 1962 *Affiliated:* 1962–1974; 1988
Colours: Yellow shirts, blue shorts, yellow socks

Chile
Founded: 1895 *Affiliated:* 1912
Clubs: 4,598 *Players:* 609,724
Colours: Red shirts, white trim, blue shorts, white socks

China
Founded: 1924 *Affiliated:* 1931
Clubs: 1,045 *Players:* 2,250,200
Colours: Red shirts, white shorts, red socks

Chinese Taipei
Founded: 1936 *Affiliated:* 1954
Clubs: 53 *Players:* 17,350
Colours: Blue shirts, white shorts, red socks

Colombia
Founded: 1924 *Affiliated:* 1936
Clubs: 3,685 *Players:* 188,050
Colours: Red shirts, tri-colour trim, blue shorts, red socks, tri-colour trim

Congo
Founded: 1962 *Affiliated:* 1962
Clubs: 250 *Players:* 5,940
Colours: All red
Honours: African Nations Cup winners: 1972

Costa Rica
Founded: 1921 *Affiliated:* 1921
Clubs: 431 *Players:* 12,429
Colours: Red shirts, blue shorts, white socks

Cuba
Founded: 1924 *Affiliated:* 1932
Clubs: 70 *Players:* 12,900
Colours: White shirts, red trim, dark blue shorts, white and red socks

Cyprus
Founded: 1934 *Affiliated:* 1948
Clubs: 87 *Players:* 23,000
Colours: Blue shirts, white shorts, blue socks

Czechoslovakia
Founded: 1901 *Affiliated:* 1906
Clubs: 5,972 *Players:* 374,421
Colours: Red shirts, white shorts, blue socks
Honours: European Championship winners: 1976. Olympic winners: 1980

Denmark
Founded: 1889 *Affiliated:* 1904
Clubs: 1,510 *Players:* 323,605
Colours: Red shirts, white shorts, red socks
Honours: Olympic winners (unofficial tournament): 1896

Dominican Republic
Founded: 1953 *Affiliated:* 1958
Clubs: 128 *Players:* 10,706
Colours: Navy blue shirts, white shorts, red socks

Ecuador
Founded: 1925 *Affiliated:* 1926
Clubs: 170 *Players:* 15,700
Colours: Yellow shirts, blue and red trim, blue shorts, red socks

Egypt
Founded: 1921 *Affiliated:* 1923
Clubs: 247 *Players:* 19,735
Colours: Red shirts, white shorts, black socks
Honours: African Nations Cup winners: 1957, 1959, 1986

England
Founded: 1863 *Affiliated:* 1905–1920; 1924–1928; 1946
Clubs: 41,750 *Players:* 1,005,000
Colours: White shirts, royal blue shorts, white socks
Honours: World Cup winners: 1966. Olympic winners: 1900 (unofficial tournament), 1908, 1912

Equatorial Guinea
Founded: *Affiliated:* 1986
Colours: All red

Ethiopia
Founded: 1943 *Affiliated:* 1953
Clubs: 767 *Players:* 20,594
Colours: Green and yellow shirts, yellow and red shorts, red and green socks
Honours: African Nations Cup winners: 1961

Faroe Islands
Founded: 1979 *Affiliated:* 1988
Clubs: 22 *Players:* 3,500
Colours: White shirts, blue shorts, red socks

Fiji
Founded: 1938 *Affiliated:* 1963
Clubs: 140 *Players:* 21,300
Colours: White shirts, black shorts, black socks, white trim

Finland
Founded: 1907 *Affiliated:* 1908
Clubs: 1,140 *Players:* 57,732
Colours: White shirts, blue shorts, white socks

France
Founded: 1919 *Affiliated:* 1904
Clubs: 22,829 *Players:* 1,608,470

Hani Ramzi of Egypt emerged as one of the most complete defenders to play in the 1990 World Cup.

Kocsis of Hungary is dispossessed during a friendly against France in 1956.

Colours: Blue shirts, white shorts, red socks
Honours: European Championship winners: 1984. Olympic winners: 1984

Gabon
Founded: 1962 *Affiliated:* 1963
Clubs: 320 *Players:* 10,000
Colours: Green, yellow and blue shirts, blue and yellow shorts, white socks, tri-colour trim

Gambia
Founded: 1952 *Affiliated:* 1966
Clubs: 30 *Players:* 860
Colours: White shirts, red trim, white shorts, white socks, red trim

East Germany
Founded: 1948 *Affiliated:* 1952
Clubs: 5,771 *Players:* 577,700
Colours: White shirts, blue shorts, white socks
Honours: Olympic winners: 1976

West Germany
Founded: 1900 *Affiliated:* 1904
Clubs: 21,510 *Players:* 4,765,146
Colours: White shirts, black shorts, white socks
Honours: World Cup winners: 1954, 1974, 1990. European Championship winners: 1972, 1980

Ghana
Founded: 1957 *Affiliated:* 1958
Clubs: 347 *Players:* 11,275
Colours: All white

Greece
Founded: 1926 *Affiliated:* 1927
Clubs: 3,678 *Players:* 282,550
Colours: White shirts, blue shorts, white socks

Grenada
Founded: 1924 *Affiliated:* 1976
Clubs: 15 *Players:* 200
Colours: Green and yellow shirts, red shorts, yellow socks

Guatemala
Founded: 1933 *Affiliated:* 1946
Clubs: 1,611 *Players:* 43,516
Colours: White shirts and shorts, white and blue socks

Guinea
Founded: 1959 *Affiliated:* 1961
Clubs: 351 *Players:* 10,000
Colours: Red shirts, yellow shorts, green socks

Guinea-Bissau
Founded: 1974 *Affiliated:* 1986
Colours: All green

Guyana
Founded: 1904 *Affiliated:* 1968
Clubs: 103 *Players:* 1,665
Colours: Green shirts and shorts, yellow socks

Haiti
Founded: 1904 *Affiliated:* 1933
Clubs: 40 *Players:* 4,000

Colours: Black and red shirts, black shorts, black and red socks

Honduras
Founded: 1951 *Affiliated:* 1951
Clubs: 1,050 *Players:* 15,300
Colours: White shirts, blue shorts and socks

Hong Kong
Founded: 1914 *Affiliated:* 1954
Clubs: 69 *Players:* 3,274
Colours: Red shirts, white shorts, red socks

Hungary
Founded: 1901 *Affiliated:* 1906
Clubs: 2,503 *Players:* 129,087
Colours: Red shirts, white shorts, green socks
Honours: Olympic winners: 1952, 1964, 1968

Iceland
Founded: 1929 *Affiliated:* 1947
Clubs: 82 *Players:* 19,400
Colours: Blue shirts, white shorts, blue socks

India
Founded: 1937 *Affiliated:* 1948
Clubs: 2,000 *Players:* 56,000
Colours: White and sky blue striped shirts, white and blue shorts, sky blue socks, white trim

Indonesia
Founded: 1930 *Affiliated:* 1952
Clubs: 2,880 *Players:* 97,000
Colours: Red shirts, white shorts, red and white socks

Iran
Founded: 1920 *Affiliated:* 1945
Clubs: 6,326 *Players:* 306,000
Colours: Green shirts, white shorts, red socks

Iraq
Founded: 1948 *Affiliated:* 1950
Clubs: 155 *Players:* 4,400
Colours: All white

Northern Ireland
Founded: 1880 *Affiliated:* 1911
Clubs: 1,555 *Players:* 24,558
Colours: Green shirts, white shorts, green socks

Republic of Ireland
Founded: 1921 *Affiliated:* 1923
Clubs: 3,503 *Players:* 33,028
Colours: Green shirts, white shorts, green and white socks

Israel
Founded: 1928 *Affiliated:*

Karl-Heinz Rummenigge of West Germany during the 1984 European Championship.

Marco Tardelli slides the ball home for Italy's second in the 1982 World Cup final.

Clubs: 544 *Players:* 30,449
Colours: Blue shirts, white shorts, blue socks

Italy
Founded: 1898 *Affiliated:* 1905
Clubs: 20,117 *Players:* 1,129,667
Colours: Blue shirts, white shorts, blue and white socks
Honours: World Cup winners: 1934, 1938, 1982. European Championship winners: 1968. Olympic winners: 1936

Ivory Coast
Founded: 1960 *Affiliated:* 1960
Clubs: 84 *Players:* 3,655
Colours: Orange shirts, white shorts, green socks

Jamaica
Founded: 1910 *Affiliated:* 1962
Clubs: 266 *Players:* 45,200
Colours: Green shirts, black shorts, gold socks

Japan
Founded: 1921 *Affiliated:* 1929
Clubs: 13,047 *Players:* 358,989
Colours: White shirts, red shorts, white socks

Jordan
Founded: 1949 *Affiliated:* 1958
Clubs: 98 *Players:* 4,305
Colours: All white and red

Kampuchea
Founded: 1933 *Affiliated:* 1953
Clubs: 30 *Players:* 650
Colours: Blue, white and red shirts, white shorts, red socks

Kenya
Founded: 1960 *Affiliated:* 1960
Clubs: 351 *Players:* 8,880
Colours: Red, green and white shirts, red, green and black shorts and socks

North Korea
Founded: 1945 *Affiliated:* 1958
Clubs: 90 *Players:* 3,420
Colours: All white

South Korea
Founded: 1928 *Affiliated:* 1948
Clubs: 476 *Players:* 2,047
Colours: All red

Kuwait
Founded: 1952 *Affiliated:* 1962
Clubs: 14 *Players:* 1,526
Colours: Blue shirts, white shorts, blue socks

Laos
Founded: 1951 *Affiliated:* 1952
Clubs: 76 *Players:* 2,060
Colours: Red shirts, white shorts, blue socks

Lebanon
Founded: 1933 *Affiliated:* 1935
Clubs: 105 *Players:* 8,125
Colours: Red and white shirts, white shorts, red and white socks

Lesotho
Founded: 1932 *Affiliated:* 1964
Clubs: 88 *Players:* 2,076
Colours: Blue, white and green shirts, white shorts, blue and white socks

Liberia
Founded: 1962 *Affiliated:* 1962
Colours: Red shirts, white shorts, red socks

Libya
Founded: 1963 *Affiliated:* 1963
Clubs: 89 *Players:* 2,941
Colours: Green shirts, white shorts, green socks

Liechtenstein
Founded: 1933 *Affiliated: 1974*
Clubs: 7 *Players:* 1,300
Colours: Blue shirts, red shorts, blue socks

Luxembourg
Founded: 1908 *Affiliated:* 1910
Clubs: 199 *Players:* 23,252
Colours: Red shirts, white shorts, blue socks

Macao
Founded: 1939 *Affiliated:* 1976
Clubs: 52 *Players:* 800
Colours: Red and green shirts, red or white shorts and socks

Madagascar
Founded: 1961 *Affiliated:* 1962
Clubs: 775 *Players:* 23,536
Colours: Red shirts, white shorts, green socks

Malawi
Founded: 1966 *Affiliated:* 1967
Clubs: 465 *Players:* 12,500
Colours: All red

Malaysia
Founded: 1933 *Affiliated:* 1956
Clubs: 450 *Players:* 11,250
Colours: All yellow and black

Maldives Republic
Founded: 1982 *Affiliated:* 1986
Colours: Green shirts, white shorts, red socks

Mali
Founded: 1960 *Affiliated:* 1962
Clubs: 128 *Players:* 5,480
Colours: Green shirts, yellow shorts, red socks

Malta
Founded: 1900 *Affiliated:* 1959
Clubs: 242 *Players:* 4,024
Colours: Red shirts, white shorts, red socks

Mauritania
Founded: 1961 *Affiliated:* 1964
Clubs: 59 *Players:* 1,930
Colours: Green and yellow shirts, blue shorts, green socks

Mauritius
Founded: 1952 *Affiliated:* 1962
Clubs: 397 *Players:* 29,375
Colours: Red shirts, white shorts, red socks, white trim

Mexico
Founded: 1927 *Affiliated:* 1929
Clubs: 77 *Players:* 1,402,270
Colours: Green shirts, red and green trim, white shorts, red and green trim, red socks, white trim

Morocco
Founded: 1955 *Affiliated:* 1956
Clubs: 350 *Players:* 19,768
Colours: All red
Honours: African Nations Cup winners: 1976

Mozambique
Founded: 1978 *Affiliated:* 1978
Clubs: 144 *Players:*
Colours: Red shirts, black shorts, black and red socks

Nepal
Founded: 1951 *Affiliated:* 1970
Clubs: 85 *Players:* 2,550
Colours: All red

Netherlands (Holland)
Founded: 1889 *Affiliated:* 1904
Clubs: 7,912 *Players:* 978,324
Colours: Orange shirts, white shorts, orange socks
Honours: European Championship winners: 1988

Netherlands Antilles
Founded: 1921 *Affiliated:* 1932
Clubs: 85 *Players:* 4,500
Colours: White shirts, red and blue trim, white shorts, red, white and blue socks

New Zealand
Founded: 1891 *Affiliated:* 1948
Clubs: 312 *Players:* 52,969
Colours: White shirts, black trim, white shorts and socks

Nicaragua
Founded: 1931 *Affiliated:* 1950
Clubs: 31 *Players:*
Colours: Blue shirts, white trim, blue shorts, blue socks, white trim

Niger
Founded: 1967 *Affiliated:* 1967
Clubs: 64 *Players:* 1,525
Colours: Orange shirts, white shorts, green socks

Nigeria
Founded: 1945 *Affiliated:* 1959
Clubs: 326 *Players:* 80,190
Colours: Green shirts, white trim, white shorts, green socks, white trim
Honours: African Nations Cup winners: 1980

Norway
Founded: 1902 *Affiliated:* 1908
Clubs: 3,449 *Players:* 298,400
Colours: Red shirts, white shorts, blue socks

Oman
Founded: 1978 *Affiliated:* 1980
Clubs: 47 *Players:* 2,340
Colours: Red and white shirts, red shorts and socks

Pakistan
Founded: 1948 *Affiliated:* 1948
Clubs: 882 *Players:* 21,000
Colours: Green shirts, white shorts, green and white socks

Panama
Founded: 1937 *Affiliated:* 1938
Clubs: 65 *Players:* 4,225
Colours: Red and white shirts, blue shorts, red socks

Papua New Guinea
Founded: 1962 *Affiliated:* 1963
Clubs: 350 *Players:* 8,250
Colours: Red shirts, black shorts, red socks

Paraguay
Founded: 1906 *Affiliated:* 1921

The Dutch team of 1988 celebrate their only major honour to date – European Champions.

Hagi of Rumania, one of the most exciting, attacking midfielders in the world.

Clubs: 1,500 *Players:* 140,000
Colours: Red and white shirts, blue shorts and socks
Honours: South American Championship winners: 1953, 1979

Peru
Founded: 1922 *Affiliated:* 1924
Clubs: 10,000 *Players:* 325,650
Colours: All white with red trim
Honours: South American Championship winners: 1939, 1975

Philippines
Founded: 1907 *Affiliated:* 1928
Clubs: 650 *Players:* 45,000
Colours: Blue and red shirts, blue shorts, white socks

Poland
Founded: 1919 *Affiliated:* 1923
Clubs: 5,881 *Players:* 317,442
Colours: White shirts, red shorts, white and red socks
Honours: Olympic winners: 1972

Portugal
Founded: 1914 *Affiliated:* 1926
Clubs: 1,605 *Players:* 55,499
Colours: Red shirts, green shorts, red socks

Puerto Rico
Founded: 1940 *Affiliated:* 1960
Clubs: 175 *Players:* 4,200
Colours: Red and white shirts, blue shorts, blue and white socks

Qatar
Founded: 1960 *Affiliated:* 1970
Clubs: 8 *Players:* 1,380
Colours: White shirts, maroon shorts, white socks

Rumania
Founded: 1908 *Affiliated:* 1930
Clubs: 5,453 *Players:* 179,987
Colours: Yellow shirts, blue shorts, red socks

Rwanda
Founded: 1972 *Affiliated:* 1976
Clubs: 167 *Players:*
Colours: Red, green and yellow shirts, green shorts, red socks

St Lucia
Founded: *Affiliated:* 1988
Clubs: *Players:* 4,000
Colours: Blue and white shirts, black shorts, blue socks

Sao Tome and Principe
Founded: 1975 *Affiliated:* 1986
Colours: All green and yellow

St Vincent and the Grenadines
Founded: *Affiliated:* 1988
Clubs: *Players:* 5,000

El Salvador
Founded: 1935 *Affiliated:* 1938
Clubs: 944 *Players:* 21,294
Colours: All blue

San Marino
Founded: 1931 *Affiliated:* 1988
Clubs: 17 *Players:* 920
Colours: All light blue

Saudi Arabia
Founded: 1959 *Affiliated:* 1959
Clubs: 120 *Players:* 9,600
Colours: All white with green trim

Scotland
Founded: 1873 *Affiliated:* 1910

Clubs: 6,148 Players: 139,000
Colours: Dark blue shirts, white shorts, navy trim, red socks

Senegal
Founded: 1960 *Affiliated:* 1962
Clubs: 75 *Players:* 3,977
Colours: Green shirts, yellow shorts, red socks

Seychelles
Founded: 1979 *Affiliated:* 1986
Colours: Red shirts, white shorts, red socks

Sierra Leone
Founded: 1967 *Affiliated:* 1967
Clubs: 104 *Players:* 8,120
Colours: Green, white and blue shirts, white shorts, blue socks, white trim

Singapore
Founded: 1892 *Affiliated:* 1952
Clubs: 250 *Players:* 8,000
Colours: All white

Solomon Islands
Founded: *Affiliated:* 1988
Clubs: *Players:* 4,000

Somalia
Founded: 1951 *Affiliated:* 1960
Clubs: 46 *Players:* 1,150
Colours: Sky blue shirts, white shorts and socks

Spain's manager Villalonga is chaired off after beating the Soviets 2–1 in the 1964 European Nations Cup.

Spain
Founded: 1913 *Affiliated:* 1913
Clubs: 30,920 *Players:* 343,657
Colours: Red shirts, blue shorts, black socks, yellow trim
Honours: European Championship winners: 1964

Sri Lanka
Founded: 1939 *Affiliated:* 1950
Clubs: 600 *Players:* 18,825
Colours: Maroon and gold shirts, white shorts and socks

Sudan
Founded: 1936 *Affiliated:* 1948
Clubs: 750 *Players:* 42,200
Colours: Green shirts, white shorts, green socks
Honours: African Nations Cup winners: 1970

Surinam
Founded: 1920 *Affiliated:* 1929
Clubs: 168 *Players:* 4,430
Colours: Red, green and white shirts, white or green shorts and socks

Swaziland
Founded: *Affiliated:* 1976
Clubs: 136 *Players:*
Colours: Blue and gold shirts, white shorts, blue and gold socks

Sweden
Founded: 1904 *Affiliated:* 1904
Clubs: 3,400 *Players:* 437,000
Colours: Yellow shirts, blue shorts, yellow socks
Honours: Olympic winners: 1948

Switzerland
Founded: 1895 *Affiliated:* 1904
Clubs: 1,480 *Players:* 182,953
Colours: Red shirts, white shorts, red socks

Syria
Founded: 1936 *Affiliated:* 1937
Clubs: 102 *Players:* 30,600
Colours: All white

Tanzania
Founded: 1930 *Affiliated:* 1964
Clubs: 51 *Players:*
Colours: Yellow shirts, black trim, yellow shorts, yellow and black socks

Thailand
Founded: 1916 *Affiliated:* 1925
Clubs: 168 *Players:* 15,000
Colours: All red

Togo
Founded: 1960 *Affiliated:* 1962
Clubs: 144 *Players:* 4,346
Colours: White shirts, green shorts, red socks, yellow and green trim

Trinidad and Tobago
Founded: 1908 *Affiliated:* 1963
Clubs: 124 *Players:* 5,050
Colours: White shirts, black shorts, red socks

Tunisia
Founded: 1956 *Affiliated:* 1960
Clubs: 215 *Players:* 18,300
Colours: Red shirts, white shorts, red socks

Turkey
Founded: 1923 *Affiliated:* 1923
Clubs: 3,754 *Players:* 87,200
Colours: White shirts and shorts, white and red socks

Uganda
Founded: 1924 *Affiliated:* 1959
Clubs: 400 *Players:* 1,518
Colours: Yellow and black shirts, black and yellow shorts, yellow and red socks

United Arab Emirates
Founded: 1971 *Affiliated:* 1972
Clubs: 23 *Players:* 1,787
Colours: All white

Uruguay
Founded: 1900 *Affiliated:* 1923
Clubs: 1,091 *Players:* 134,310
Colours: Sky blue shirts, white trim, black shorts and socks with sky blue trim
Honours: World Cup winners: 1930, 1950. South American Championship winners: 1916, 1917, 1920, 1923, 1924, 1926, 1935, 1942, 1956, 1959, 1967, 1983, 1987. Olympic winners: 1924, 1928

USA
Founded: 1913 *Affiliated:* 1913
Clubs: 7,000 *Players:* 1,411,500
Colours: White shirts, blue shorts, white socks

USSR
Founded: 1912 *Affiliated:* 1946
Clubs: 50,198 *Players:* 4,800,300
Colours: Red shirts, white shorts, red socks
Honours: European Championship winners: 1960. Olympic winners: 1956, 1988

Vanuatu
Founded: *Affiliated:* 1988

Venezuela
Founded: 1926 *Affiliated:* 1952
Clubs: 1,753 *Players:* 63,175
Colours: Dark red shirts, white shorts, white socks, black trim

Vietnam
Founded: 1962 *Affiliated:* 1964
Clubs: 55 *Players:* 16,000
Colours: Red shirts, white shorts, red socks

Wales
Founded: 1876 *Affiliated:* 1910
Clubs: 1,923 *Players:* 51,578
Colours: All red

Western Samoa
Founded: 1968 *Affiliated:* 1986
Colours: Royal blue shirts, white shorts, royal blue socks, white trim

Yemen AR
Founded: 1962 *Affiliated:* 1980
Clubs: 61 *Players:* 22,000
Colours: All green

Yemen PDR
Founded: 1940 *Affiliated:* 1967
Clubs: 36 *Players:* 1,700
Colours: Light blue shirts, white shorts, light blue and white socks

Yugoslavia
Founded: 1919 *Affiliated:* 1919
Clubs: 7,455 *Players:* 270,229
Colours: Blue shirts, white shorts, red socks

Zaire
Founded: 1919 *Affiliated:* 1962
Clubs: 3,800 *Players:* 64,627
Colours: Green shirts, yellow shorts and socks
Honours: African Nations Cup winners: 1974

Zambia
Founded: 1929 *Affiliated:* 1964
Clubs: 20 *Players:* 4,100
Colours: Green and copper shirts, white, green, black and red shorts, black and red socks with green, red and yellow trim

Zimbabwe
Founded: *Affiliated:* 1965
Colours: Green shirts, gold shorts, green and gold socks

Who's Who of British Football

Ivor Allchurch: An outstandingly artistic inside-forward for Wales, he reached his peak in the 1958 World Cup in Sweden when he compared with the world's best. Most of his career was spent in his native Wales and in the lower divisions, though a spell at Newcastle was less successful. Scored 23 goals in 68 appearances for Wales and shone with Swansea Town and later Cardiff City.

Jimmy Armfield: A consistent right-back who established a club record of 568 League appearances for Blackpool and played 43 times for England. An overlapping defender, he had the instincts of a winger. Had spells in the managerial side of the game before becoming a radio journalist. Was voted the best right-back in the 1962 World Cup.

Alan Ball: Ebullient and resourceful little midfield player who played for England with tireless application in the 1966 World Cup, when he was the youngest squad member at 21. Twice transferred for record fees: Blackpool to Everton for £110,000 in 1966 and Everton to Arsenal for twice that figure five years later. Coached and managed several Football League clubs upon retiring. Won 72 caps.

Gordon Banks and George Best – two players whose careers came to an early end, albeit for different reasons.

Gordon Banks: Discovered by Chesterfield, who have had a tradition of producing fine goalkeepers, he progressed to Leicester City and established himself as England's No.1 before moving to Stoke City in 1967. Courageous and expert at positioning himself, he made his most memorable save in the 1970 World Cup when he diverted a powerful downward header from Pele over the bar. Career was cut short by an eye injury sustained in a 1972 car crash. Won 73 caps.

John Barnes: Finely-built athlete with height and strength, yet has the grace of a ballet dancer. Delightful first touch on the ball and bewildering control and speed. Plays either on the left flank or in the middle. Something of an enigma, he has yet to develop consistency or hit his best form as an international. Groomed by Watford before linking up with Liverpool in 1987. Specialises in wickedly-bending free kicks and long-range drives. He has 58 caps.

Walley Barnes: Came to prominence during the War as a goalscoring inside-foward with Southampton but eventually settled down to become a left-back noted for his anticipation and positional play. Won League honours with Arsenal in 1948 and an FA Cup medal two years later. Was severely injured in the final in 1952 but returned after 12 months out of action and always performed with style. Won 22 Welsh caps.

Cliff Bastin: Was a teenage prodigy and had won most of the game's honours in the 1930s before he was 21. In 1932–33 he scored 33 goals from the left-wing, a record from that position. Discovered by Exeter City, he moved to Arsenal for only £2,000 and went on to score a club record 150 League goals. Was adept at cutting inside defenders and finishing with a devastating shot. Won 21 caps for England.

Jim Baxter: Pencil-slim attacking midfield player who dominated Rangers' play in the mid-1960s. His career suffered after he broke his leg in 1964. Began with Raith Rovers. After less-happy spells at Sunderland and Nottingham Forest he returned to Rangers. Won 34 caps for Scotland and could control games with a stylish and engaging command of the ball.

Peter Beardsley: Had trials with various League clubs before finding his first chance at Carlisle United. Went to Vancouver Whitecaps and was then not retained by Manchester United following a trial period. Finally emerged at Newcastle United and was transferred to Liverpool in 1987. Mercurial little striker with finely-judged control, sharp reactions and a goalscoring hunch at short and long range. He has 45 caps.

George Best: Arguably the best player never to have played in the World Cup finals. A natural talent on the field but unable to live with the pressures of fame off it. Graced many Manchester United and Northern Ireland teams in the late 1960s and early 1970s, revealing speed, shooting ability and an individual close control which took him past opponent after opponent. Played 37 times for Ireland including five games during his spell at Fulham, one of several attempted comebacks of the latter part of his career.

Billy Bingham: Lengthy career as a winger with Glentoran, Sunderland, Luton Town, Everton and Port Vale. He made 56 appearances for Northern Ireland. Quick and tenacious he often gave his most telling performances in international games. Later became a coach and manager as well as controlling the national team. Was a member of the Irish team in the 1958 World Cup.

Danny Blanchflower: A vintage right-half who improved immeasurably with age after unrewarding spells with Glentoran, Aston Villa and Barnsley. Blossomed out with Tottenham Hotspur whom he joined in 1954 from Villa for £30,000 at the age of 28. Never apparenty hurried in his constructive work, he prompted Spurs' attacking moves with invention and masterminded their many successes in the 1960s. Played 56 times for Northern Ireland. His conduct on the pitch was faultless; off the field he was a convincing critic of almost everything.

Steve Bloomer: Was the first prolific goalscorer to be produced in the Football League, scoring 352 goals in a career spent with two unfashionable clubs: Derby County and Middlesbrough. Was a shoot-on-sight inside-forward who cut out the frills, but his scoring record was unmatched for decades. Retired in 1914 to become a coach. Scored 28 goals for England in only 23 internationals.

Liam Brady, who scored the only goal of this 1987 match against Brazil, is more famed for his distribution than for his goals.

Liam Brady: A gifted midfield player with a fine touch from his left foot, he was a master tactician for club and country. Began his senior career with Arsenal but, seeking fresh challenges, moved to Italy where he played variously for Juventus, Sampdoria, Internazionale and Ascoli before returning to West Ham United. Retired at international level with the record of appearances for the Republic of Ireland of 72 caps.

Billy Bremner: Fiery, terrier-like midfield player with combative qualities who became one of Leeds United's most effective weapons in their successes in the 1970s. Converted from a winger into a more involved player in the centre of operations. After 17 years at Elland Road and further spells with Hull City and Doncaster Rovers, entered the managerial ranks with Doncaster, to whom he returned after a spell at Leeds. Won 54 Scottish caps.

Charlie Buchan: Largely regarded as the player who brought about the need for a stopper centre-back, under Herbert Chapman's direction at Arsenal in the 1920s. Cost Sunderland £1,200 when he signed from Leyton in 1911. He joined Arsenal in 1925 for £2,000 plus £100 for each

Sir Matt Busby salutes the Old Trafford faithful following his last game as manager.

goal he scored in the following season. Ironically, he had been on Arsenal's books as an amateur originally, leaving when modest expenses were refused. An inside-forward who used his height to advantage as few had done before him, he had a tactical sense which foxed friend and foe alike. Scored a record 209 League goals for Sunderland alone, but won only six caps for England. Became a journalist and broadcaster.

Frank Buckley: Was one of the first managers to fully develop young talent and use the transfer market effectively. Built his reputation with Wolves in the 1930s producing a stream of 'Buckley Babes'. His teams made use of the long ball and were ceaseless runners. His disciples continued the strain at Molineux for years after his departure. Also managed Notts County, Hull City, Leeds United and Walsall. As a centre-half with Derby County had been capped once by England.

Ron Burgess: Was one of the two influential wing-halves in Tottenham Hotspur's famous 'push and run' style developed in the immediate post-War period, culminating in their Championship title win in 1951. Energetic, he was skilful in both passing and shooting. Won 32 caps for Wales and finished his playing career with Swansea Town.

Sir Matt Busby: Was the most successful and feted club manager in the post-War era, becoming a legendary figure at Manchester United, bravely surviving the Munich air disaster to lead the club to further triumphs. Built three outstanding teams at Old Trafford: the first winning the FA Cup in 1948 and League in 1952, the Busby Babes in the middle 1950s cut down tragically in their youth, and lastly the European Cup success in 1968. His belief in the quality of individual players invariably produced the ultimate in the game: an attractive and effective team. As a player had been a wing-half in the colours of Manchester City and Liverpool and, though he won only one full cap for Scotland, captained his country in several wartime internationals.

George Camsell: Snapped up by Middlesbrough from Durham City, he set a record for goalscoring in a League campaign which lasted just one season, when he scored 59 goals in Division Two during 1926–27. Scored 325 League goals for the club. Centre-forward with good control who would shoot from any angle or distance to achieve his target. Won nine England caps and scored 18 goals.

Johnny Carey: A truly all-round footballer, he was accomplished at full-back, inside-forward, wing-half and even as an emergency goalkeeper. Began with St James's Gate in his native Republic of Ireland before joining Manchester United. Was in his late 20s when the club enjoyed League and Cup successes in the early post-War period. Used the ball cleverly and was an inspirational captain. A gentleman on and off the field, he had varying managerial experience after retiring. Won 29 Republic of Ireland caps and seven for Northern Ireland.

Raich Carter: Another of the players whose career was interrupted by the Second World War, his most productive years internationally coming during this unofficial period of the game's history. An inside-forward with attacking ideas and ease of control, he was well balanced in his movements. His career was spent with Sunderland, Derby County and Hull City, where he was a successful player/manager. Even came out of retirement to play successfully with Cork at 40. Won six caps for England before the War and seven afterwards.

Herbert Chapman: Was without doubt the first outstanding manager to emerge in the game. He masterminded Huddersfield Town to three successive Championships in the 1920s but had left for Arsenal before they had finished the trio. Accomplished the same treble for the Gunners, but died before his work was completed. Undoubtedly made Arsenal the outstanding club in the years before the Second World War. With Charlie Buchan he developed the third back game which changed tactics during the era following the alteration in the offside law in 1925. A firm but fair man he used publicity to telling effect. Yet he was almost lost to the game when manager of Leeds City, who were expelled because of administrative irregularities during the First World War.

John Charles: Became known as the 'gentle giant' in Italian football. His powerful physique made him ideally suited to playing either centre-forward or centre-half, but he rarely used his size as a weapon. Developed by Leeds United, he joined Juventus in 1957 for £65,000 and returned briefly before going back to Roma. Finished his career with Cardiff City and Hereford United. Played 38 times for Wales and would have added to his total but for unavailability in Italy. Scored almost a century of goals in Italian football and was in the Juventus team which beat Real Madrid on their own ground in the European Cup, the Spanish club's first such defeat.

Bobby Charlton shoots for England. He has scored more goals for his country (49) than anyone else.

Raich Carter pours champagne into John Charles' tea cup as Leeds are promoted in 1957. Jack Charlton waits for his.

Bobby Charlton: One of the most popular footballers to be unearthed in the post-War era. He was a survivor of the 1958 Munich air crash and became the epitome of Manchester United's recovery to fame in the succeeding years. Could play either as a striker, in midfield or on the wing and had that rare quality for an English player: flair. Had an explosive shot from long range and there was an expectancy of something imminently exciting whenever he had possession. Ended his career with a brief spell in charge of Preston North End after gaining three records at Old Trafford: most capped player – 106 times for England; most goals in the League – 198; and highest number of League appearances – 606.

Brian Clough: Scored a post-War record 254 League goals for Middlesbrough and Sunderland before injury caused a premature retirement at 27 in 1962. Turned to management and rescued Hartlepools United from virtual extinction before taking over at Derby County. Led them from Division Two to the League Championship, moved on to Brighton and unhappily to Leeds for

44 days before starting an even more rewarding period with Nottingham Forest. From 1975 he embarked on a run of success at home and abroad and in 1990 celebrated 1,000 games as a manager throughout his career. Possessing forthright views, he is a disciple of discipline and his teams rarely cause problems to officials. Critics say that his players are motivated by fear, but he has a loyal following almost unique in modern times. Won two England caps.

Bobby Collins: Diminutive 5ft 4in midfield player, but an effervescent and effective player whose career stretched until he was approaching 40. Began with Celtic before moving into English football with Everton in 1958 and then on to Leeds United where he was a key figure in launching the Yorkshire club out of the Second Division. Finished his career with Bury and Morton. Won 31 caps for Scotland.

Bob Crompton: Became one of the most consistent full-backs in the developing years of professional football. He won 41 caps for England in the years immediately after the turn of the century from 1901–02 to 1913–14. Not tall but strong and one of the first defenders to show an aptitude for tactics. Served Blackburn Rovers as player and later as manager.

Kenny Dalglish: Sharp awareness in the penalty area with the ability to control, make space and shoot in a split-second. Vast tactical experience which he has carried into his successful managerial career with his last club, Liverpool. Began his career with Celtic and is one of the few players to have scored a century of goals in League football on either side of the border. Only Scottish player to achieve as many as 102 caps. Joined the Anfield club for £440,000 in 1977 and became manager in 1985.

William Ralph (Dixie) Dean: Certainly the most effective, and possibly the finest, centre-forward produced in a time when goalscoring spearheads ruled the game. Scored 379 goals in 437 League games between 1924 and 1939, including a record 60 for Everton in 1927–28. Discovered by Tranmere Rovers, he became a legend at Everton before finishing his career with Notts County and a short spell with Sligo Rovers. A marked man, he suffered a number of injuries which restricted his England appearances to 16 games and 18 goals. Made a remarkable recovery from a fractured skull sustained in a 1925 motorcycle accident. Strongly built, he had the ability to score with both feet, had quickness off the mark and above all exceptional heading prowess.

Dixie Dean, Everton's prolific centre-forward, leads his side out in the 1933 Cup semi-final.

Jimmy Dickinson: Thoughtful, unassuming wing-half whose conduct on the field was beyond reproach. Made a club record of 764 League appearances for Portsmouth between 1946 and 1965, missing only 38 games including 17 in one season. Played 48 times for England.

Tommy Docherty: Tough-tackling wing-half with Celtic, Preston North End, Arsenal and Chelsea who became a controversial character when taking up the exacting role of a manager. In a varied career in charge of numerous clubs he also managed Scotland for a spell in 1971, leaving in 1972 to take on the onerous task of leading Manchester United until 1977. Capped by the Scots on 25 occasions.

Peter Doherty: Rated as one of the most accomplished inside-forwards ever produced in Ireland. Tireless, visionary and a reliable marksman, he had a long and successful career with Glentoran, Blackpool, Manchester City, Derby County, Huddersfield Town and Doncaster

Rovers which spanned the Second World War years. His managerial experiences were not quite so successful, but he proved a shrewd mentor in the 1958 World Cup in Sweden when in charge of the Northern Ireland squad. Won 16 caps.

Derek Dougan: Striker who had fine ability on the ball and accuracy in finishing in the air and on the ground. Scored more Football League goals than any other Irishman, serving Portsmouth, Blackburn Rovers, Aston Villa, Peterborough United, Leicester City and Wolverhampton Wanderers. Started with Distillery. Played 43 times for Northern Ireland. Something of a courteous rebel, he became a television pundit and chairman of the Professional Footballers' Association.

Ted Drake: Made history by scoring all Arsenal's goals in their 7-1 win at Aston Villa on 14 December 1935. Helped the Highbury club to three Championships and an FA Cup win after being signed from Southampton. A dynamic leader of the attack whose fearless motivation cost him many injuries and restricted his England career to a mere five caps. As a manager led Chelsea to their 1955 Championship success. Another of the game's gentlemen.

Ted Drake of Arsenal training in December 1935 the week after he had scored seven goals in a match.

Duncan Edwards. Who knows what he would have achieved had he not been struck down at Munich?

Duncan Edwards: From the moment he became the youngest post-War player to turn out for England at 18 years 183 days, his short but highly successful career – cut down by the Munich air disaster – was marked with triumphs at club and national level. One of the Busby Babes, he was strong, well-built and determined. Although his best position was wing-half, he could be equally effective as an inside-forward where his shooting ability was often given full range. He survived the air crash but died shortly afterwards aged just 21. Won 18 caps.

Bobby Evans: For many years was second only to George Young in the number of caps won for Scotland. His 48 internationals came in a 10-year spell when he was rarely absent from the national side. A forceful half-back, he served Celtic from his debut in 1946 until joining Chelsea in 1960. His later career with Newport County, Morton, Third Lanark and Raith Rovers completed two decades in the game.

Tom Finney: In a period when the maximum wage was still imposed on players, he was the ideal one-club man with Preston North End. Could play anywhere in attack but was best-suited to the wing where he tormented defences

Trevor Francis of Birmingham City in April 1971 while still aged just 16.

with his innovation, superb control and finesse. Set two records at Preston for most League appearances (431) and most goals (187); his goalscoring figure is still intact today. Capped 76 times by England, occasionally at centre-forward, and scored 30 goals. His early career coincided with the Second World War, otherwise his official figures would have been even more impressive.

Trevor Francis: Britain's first £1 million player when he joined Nottingham Forest from Birmingham City in February 1979. Fast, penetrating attacker with close control, his game improved when he moved to Italy to join Sampdoria in 1982 and, later, Atalanta. His other clubs were Manchester City, Detroit Express, Glasgow Rangers and Queen's Park Rangers, whom he managed briefly and unsuccessfully from 1988 to 1989 until resuming as a player with Sheffield Wednesday. Won 52 caps.

Neil Franklin: His career was ruined when he tried to better himself in an abortive trip to Colombia in 1950. Up to that time he had played centre-half in all 27 post-War internationals for England. A product of Stoke City just before the War, he was not tall but had exceptional foresight and constructive ability plus superb timing. Suspended for a year by the FA for joining the unaffiliated Colombians, his career petered out with Hull City, Crewe Alexandra and Stockport County. Had a spell as manager at Colchester United.

Hughie Gallacher: Was an enigma; on the field he delighted spectators with speed, skill and shooting ability but had a suspect temperament. Though not tall, his heading for a man of 5ft 5in was remarkable. Off the field he was unable to cope with life and eventually committed suicide at the age of 54. Served Queen of the South, Airdrieonians, Newcastle United, Chelsea, Derby County, Notts County, Grimsby Town and Gateshead, finishing in 1939 with 541 League games and 387 goals. He also scored 22 goals in 20 Scottish internationals. The high spot of his career was the 1926–27 season with Newcastle when he scored a record of 36 goals.

Patsy Gallagher: A light-weight inside-forward who took many knocks but remained a shrewd, well-balanced and constructive player chiefly for Celtic in a 15-year sojourn until 1927 when he

Hughie Gallacher, one of the greatest forwards of all time, in his Newcastle days.

joined Falkirk. Won 15 caps for Northern Ireland and one for the Republic.

Johnny Giles: Started as a winger, but found his career transformed when he moved to inside-forward. Became an outstanding midfield general and ferocious tackler. An influential figure during Leeds United's emergence as the leading team of the early 1970s. Despite his compact size was invariably in the thick of the action. Later in his career was player/manager of West Bromwich Albion, Shamrock Rovers and Vancouver Whitecaps. He also improved the Republic of Ireland's international prospects with his commanding style, winning 60 caps.

Billy Gillespie: For many years was a barometer of his team's success or failure, whether for club or country. Played for Leeds United and Sheffield United and was in the Irish team which beat England for the first time in 1912–13. An inside-forward, he enjoyed a lengthy career despite having a silver plate inserted in one leg after a compound fracture. Scored 12 goals in 25 internationals.

John Goodall: Was one of Preston North End's inside-forwards in their League and Cup triumph in 1889. He played for England 14 times. Born of Scottish parents in London, his brother played for Ireland. Was noted for his close control, while his skilful play more than compensated for his slight frame. Later played for Derby County and was still active in the game in Wales at 49.

Jimmy Greaves: Probably best described as a player with a distinctive flair for goalscoring. Inside the penalty area he had few peers. His acceleration was seemingly effortless, his positioning and anticipation unmatched; he could score with both feet. His record said everything: 357 League goals from 517 games and 44 goals for England in 57 internationals. He was groomed by Chelsea and had a brief flirtation with AC Milan before turning to years of glory with Tottenham Hotspur from 1961. He finished his career with West Ham United. His qualities far outweighed his dislike of training and his over-indulgence in drink. After retiring, he became teetotal and a popular television pundit.

John Greig: Played in a record 496 League games for Rangers, his only senior club, between 1962 and 1978. Was a strong, forceful wing-half who became a tremendous favourite at Ibrox Park.

Jimmy Greaves escapes the attentions of Tommy Smith before it's too late.

Later managed the club. Won 44 caps for Scotland.

Arthur Grimsdell: Often regarded as the complete wing-half, with defensive and attacking qualities equally distributed. Not well-built but quick and tough. He lost some years during the First World War, having joined Tottenham Hotspur in 1912. He remained at Spurs until 1929 when he became player/manager of Clapton Orient. Won six England caps.

Willie Hall: Despite having only a few seasons in the First Division, he made something of an international impact by scoring five goals for England against Northern Ireland in 1938. A compact inside-forward with scheming ability, he had joined Tottenham Hotspur from Notts County in 1932. Had both legs amputated owing to thrombosis. Won 10 caps.

Alan Hansen: Definitive proof that the lack of international appearances is no guide to ability. A slender defender operating in the extra cover role, he has revealed excellent close control and a command of the midfield area when Liverpool have been attacking. Signed from Partick Thistle in 1977. Quiet, unassuming, but always in charge.

He has 26 Scottish caps. Former basketball international.

Eddie Hapgood: Captained Arsenal and England to many successes from left-back where he more than compensated for a lack of height and weight by shrewd use of the ball and timely tackling. Would have added to his 30 caps but for the War years when he was again a regular choice for his country.

Sam Hardy: Rated as one of the most consistently sound performers in goal for England, capped 21 times on both sides of the First World War. Played for Chesterfield, Liverpool, Aston Villa and Nottingham Forest and left his mark wherever he played.

Johnny Haynes: Succeeded in achieving the highest international honours for England despite playing his entire career with 'unfashionable' Fulham. A tactically accomplished inside-forward, he had superb control and vision but was quick to demonstrate his exasperation at the failings of colleagues. Became the first £100-a-week English footballer in 1961. Won 56 caps and captained his country on 22 occasions. Frequently unselfish, despite his own qualities, he could cut through defences with one penetrating pass but remained a consistent goalscorer himself.

Johnny Haynes made 594 League appearances for Fulham between 1952 and 1970.

Harry Hibbs: England had not really solved their goalkeeper problem, following the retirement of Sam Hardy, until he was discovered in 1930. Had safe hands and preferred anticipation to being spectacular. Stayed with Birmingham throughout his career and played 25 times for his country.

Glenn Hoddle: For a tall player he has a stylish, light touch on the ball. He also has the ability to strike long, accurate passes and bend free kicks at will. But he has lacked consistency and some application. His best scoring season for Tottenham Hotspur was in 1979–80 when he had 19 League goals. After 12 seasons as a senior at Spurs he joined Monaco in 1987. He has 53 caps for England.

Jimmy Hogan: Was probably the finest coaching ambassador produced by England. Certainly did much to establish the game in Austria and Hungary after a modest career as a player with various English clubs, including Burnley and Fulham. Favoured the Scottish passing game and was certainly behind the Austrian 'Wunderteam' concept in the 1930s. Had far less recognition when returning to management in this country, but carried on simply for the love of the game.

Joe Hulme: Fast, raiding winger who made five appearances in the FA Cup final between 1927 and 1938 for Arsenal (four times) and Huddersfield (once). Played nine times for England and started his career with York City and Blackburn Rovers. Built up a fine understanding with Alex James at Highbury.

Geoff Hurst: Goes down in history as the player who scored a hat-trick for England in the World Cup final in 1966 on only his eighth international appearance. Started his career as a wing-half but was switched up front at West Ham United by manager Ron Greenwood. Later moved to Stoke City. Scored 24 goals in 49 internationals. Had the ability to hold the ball while support arrived or to take on defences single-handedly.

David Jack: This tall, slightly-built inside-forward was the player who scored the first Wembley Cup final goal for Bolton Wanderers in 1923. He possessed a clever body swerve and was an expert poacher of goals. Began his career with Plymouth Argyle and was signed by Arsenal in 1929 when 30 years old for a record £11,800. Disliked training, preferring to play. Won nine England caps. Went into management after retiring.

Pat Jennings played 1,098 first-class matches in a career stretching well over 20 years.

Alec Jackson: Quick, goalscoring outside-right who emigrated to the USA as a teenager but returned to play for Aberdeen, Huddersfield Town and Chelsea. Was outstanding in Scotland's 1928 'Wembley Wizards' display against England. Had a dispute with Chelsea and left for non-League fare. Won 17 caps for Scotland.

Alex James: He was the focal point of Arsenal's successful counter-attacking play which was instrumental in their domination of the domestic scene in the 1930s. His passing technique was accuracy itself and he was invariably two moves ahead of his colleagues and opponents. Outstanding on the field, outspoken off it; famous for his baggy shorts. Began with Raith Rovers, developed with Preston North End and reached his prime at Highbury. Incredibly, he was capped only eight times by Scotland.

Sandy Jardine: The first Scottish player to make 1,000 senior appearances, a milestone he achieved in 1985. Had developed with Rangers as a utility player before moving to Hearts, where he became manager for a time. Excellent club-man with all-round skill used to best effect in an inventive midfield capacity or in defence. Won 38 caps.

Pat Jennings: Became the most-capped goalkeeper in history with his 119th appearance for Northern Ireland on his 41st birthday during the 1986 World Cup. Discovered by Watford while playing for Newry Town, he progressed to Tottenham Hotspur in 1964 before going to Arsenal and finally back briefly to Spurs. Had large hands, a big heart and was completely cool in command of his area. Had the ability to spread himself, thus reducing the goal target.

Jimmy Johnstone: Under the guiding hand of Celtic manager Jock Stein, this firebrand of a little winger was transformed into a bundle of energy and effectiveness on the right flank for Celtic in the 1960s. On his day could reduce defences to shreds by his intricate dribbling skills and pinpoint crosses. Because of an aversion to flying was restricted to 23 appearances for Scotland.

Cliff Jones: Fleet-footed, versatile winger with the courage and confidence to take on defenders in the penalty area. Born into the famous Welsh footballing family, he was signed by Tottenham from Swansea Town in 1958 and had 10 years at White Hart Lane before finishing his League career with Fulham. Won 59 caps.

Kevin Keegan: Instinctive, inspirational forward with fine balance, low gravity centre and pace laced with craft. Discovered by Scunthorpe United and blossomed with Liverpool before moving to Hamburg where his awareness improved noticeably. Finished his career in England with Southampton and Newcastle United. Won 63 caps. Made a brief appearance as substitute in the 1982 World Cup after injury.

Fred Keenor: Had the unusual experience of helping Wales to win three British International Championships in the 1920s. A versatile half-back with fine leadership qualities, tackling and

Lord Kinnaird, having played in most positions in the game, took up most of the important roles in the FA at various times.

heading prowess. Played for Cardiff City during their halcyon days before ending his career with Crewe Alexandra. Won 32 caps.

Jack Kelsey: Made goalkeeping look easy and had a relaxed approach to the position. Brilliant in the 1958 World Cup for Wales, he was first choice for eight years. Established himself with Arsenal in their Championship-winning 1952–53 season. Won 41 caps.

Lord Alfred Kinnaird: Appeared in a record nine FA Cup finals and was one of the game's earliest pioneers on and off the field. Won three medals with Wanderers and two with Old Etonians. Bearded and a formidable opponent, he played in a variety of positions including goal. Became an FA committee man, treasurer then president. In 1911 the second FA Cup trophy was presented to him to mark his 21 years in the presidential role.

Denis Law: Wiry, fair-haired striker who dominated Manchester United's striking force for a decade from 1962. Had been successfully nurtured by Huddersfield Town before linking up at Old Trafford via Manchester City and Torino. Was not only a supreme goalscorer but a forager with terrier-like persistence. Scored a shoal of goals by fearlessly diving into crowded goalmouths with either foot or head. Quick, clever and rarely caught out by any situation in front of the opponents' goal. Rejoined Manchester City and scored his last goal with a back-heel which sent neighbours United into the Second Division. Scored 30 goals in 55 appearances for Scotland, 236 goals for Manchester United alone in all games and a record 41 in the FA Cup during his career.

Tommy Lawton: Another player who had a huge chunk of his best years cut into by the War years, but was arguably the finest centre-forward of his era. Had a rakish stride, excellent control, could shoot with either foot from any angle or distance. Above all he was a master in the air – hovering like a eagle above the defence before powering in with a header. Was a schoolboy prodigy and a pre-War teenage debutant for Burnley before linking up with Everton as Dean's replacement. After many wartime appearances he joined Chelsea and then Notts County for a record £20,000, before moving to Brentford and then Arsenal where he ended his career at 37. Won 23 peacetime caps, scoring 22 goals. Scored over 250 League goals and as many again during the 1939–45 period.

Francis Lee: Solidly-built little striker with a keen eye for scoring opportunities and the ability to take full advantage of them. Discovered by Bolton Wanderers, he developed with Manchester City from 1967, ending his career with Derby County. Bustling leader whose haul of League goals amounted to 229. Set a record for penalties in 1971–72 with 13 converted in the League alone. Won 27 caps for England.

Billy Liddell: Having joined Liverpool pre-War, he had to wait until just afterwards to win a Championship medal in 1947. Winger with fine pace, strength and finishing alacrity. Also used as a central spearhead with telling effect. Noted for his sportsmanship. Won 28 Scottish caps.

Gary Lineker: Shot to fame in the 1986 World Cup when he finished as top scorer with six goals. Began his career with Leicester City and did not gain full recognition until transferred to Everton. Direct, quick and able to dart into scoring positions in the penalty area, he became an overnight sensation in Mexico. Joined

Gary Lineker scores the first of his three goals in the game against Poland in 1986 to save England's World Cup challenge.

Barcelona where his close control improved dramatically. To Tottenham Hotspur in 1989. He has 58 caps, 35 goals.

Nat Lofthouse: Might be looked upon as the last of the old-fashioned centre-forwards, leading his line with courage, strength and goalscoring power. One-club man with Bolton Wanderers, his early years were restricted by the Second World War, but he still contrived to score 285 goals in 503 League and Cup games in peacetime football from 1946 and 30 in 33 internationals for England. With wartime games his tally was well over 400. Earned the nickname of 'Lion of Vienna' for a typically brilliant and brave solo run and goal against Austria in 1952.

Peter Lorimer: Ferocious-shooting forward whose shot was timed at 90 mph. In one season as a schoolboy scored 176 goals. Set up a Leeds United record 168 League goals, completing the total after short spells in North America and at York City. Was 15 when he made his Leeds debut in 1962. Later in his career moved from a striker on the right into midfield. Won 21 Scottish caps.

Dave Mackay: Wing-half and later more of a central defensive cover. A barrel-chested, lion-hearted and indefatigable player, he was a formidable opponent and a fine colleague, who tackled with the accuracy of a heavyweight scythe. Played for Hearts before joining Tottenham Hotspur in 1959 where he played a leading part in Spurs' successes in the 1960s. Moved to Derby County before becoming a manager with Swindon Town, Nottingham Forest, Derby and Walsall. Coached in Kuwait for some years before returning to lead Doncaster Rovers and Birmingham City. Won 22 Scottish caps.

Billy McCracken: Considered to be the man who was responsible for the 1925 change in the offside law. His timing of a move upfield, when three opponents had to be between an attacker and the opposing goalline at the time the ball was played, caught forwards out on many occasions. However, he had retired in 1923 having won 15 caps for Northern Ireland with Distillery, Newcastle United and Hull City as a fine, thoughtful full-back. Became a manager with Hull, Gateshead, Millwall and Aldershot and carried on scouting into his 90s before his death.

Danny McGrain: Strong-tackling, resourceful full-back who played with remarkable consistency for Celtic, despite waiting several seasons before he broke into the senior side in 1970–71. Recovered from a series of injuries and overcame the handicap of being a diabetic. Finished his lengthy career with a brief spell at Hamilton Academical. Won 62 Scottish caps.

William McGregor: The father of the Football League; prime mover in organising the Football

League in 1888. An Aston Villa man and a Glaswegian, he became the first president of the competition. He retained a deep interest following his retirement and was behind the start of the two major reserve-team competitions, the Central League and the London (later Football) Combination.

Jimmy McGrory: Unique among goalscorers in the British Isles in averaging just over a goal a game in his career. From 1923 to 1937 he produced 410 League goals in 408 matches, chiefly for Celtic and for a season on loan to Clydebank. Short and stocky with broad shoulders and a barrel chest, he was brave, quick off the mark and an expert at converting half-chances. More than a third of his haul came from his heading prowess. Won seven Scottish caps. Had a spell as manager of Kilmarnock and then took charge of Celtic for 20 years.

Jimmy McIlroy: An inside-forward with sound constructive ideas who piloted Burnley to a rare Championship success in 1960. Also instrumental in aiding Northern Ireland's accomplished performances in the 1958 World Cup. Began with Glentoran and later played for Stoke City and Oldham Athletic. Won 55 caps.

Billy McNeill: Commanding centre-half with a dominant personality, he was a long-serving player for Celtic, reaching a peak of achievement when he led the club to their 1967 European Cup success. Also won a record-equalling seven Scottish Cup medals with the club. Later became a manager, chiefly with Manchester City and then Celtic. Won 29 caps.

Bob McPhail: Achieved nine Championship medals with Rangers in the years before the last War. Inside-forward who was skilful and difficult to dispossess, he began with Airdrie and joined the Ibrox club in 1927. Scored 307 League goals and was capped 17 times by Scotland.

Wilf Mannion: Was developing into a first-class inside-forward when the War intervened in 1939. Succeeded in fulfilling his delayed promise when hostilities ended. Played 26 times for England. Scored 100 goals in 357 League games chiefly for Middlesbrough and briefly with Hull City. On the small side, he was a clever distributor with an eye for the goalscoring chance; career spoiled by his clashes with the game's administration.

Sir Stanley Matthews: A unique footballer and the first to be knighted; in his time one of its greatest attractions. Once succinctly described as the 'wizard of dribble'. Mesmerised full-backs with his control and ability to make sufficient space for a pinpoint centre pulled back from the byline, simply by putting his opponent off-balance. Played for Stoke City at the age of 17 and, after a spell at Blackpool, returned and was there at 50, finishing in 1965. Not a prolific goalscorer and in terms of work-rate might have been considered a luxury in modern times, but when in possession was difficult to contain. However, he once scored four goals in a League game and three with his left foot for England against Czechoslovakia in 1937 when he had to move to inside-forward in an emergency. Made 701 peacetime appearances in the League and with his wartime games would have taken his overall total to 1,000 with countless international and representative games. Won a memorable FA Cup final for Blackpool in 1953 and maintained a remarkable standard of fitness into his 70s while still coaching around the world. Won 54 caps.

Stanley Matthews was a magnificent player and, like too few others, has remained a great ambassador for the game.

David Meiklejohn: One of the earliest outstanding centre-halves produced by Rangers. Played a record 492 games for the club in the years between the wars. Fine captain and intelligent player with a command of the defence, he was capped by Scotland on 15 occasions and retired in 1936.

Joe Mercer: At one time held the record of being the only man to have won FA Cup and League Championship medals as a player and then achieved the same success as a manager. Had his career with Everton interrupted by the War, and joined Arsenal after it. A bow-legged wing-half with shrewd, intelligent ideas in midfield, he switched from an attacking stance to a defensive one with ease as the years advanced. Varied managerial career extended from spells with Sheffield United and Aston Villa to triumphs at Manchester City and even a caretaker role with the England team in the mid-1970s. Five England caps but a host of wartime appearances in their colours. Loved the game for its own sake and said he would have played during the War for nothing.

Billy Meredith: Skilful ball-playing winger who became a legend in his own lifetime. Was still playing first-class football at the age of 49. Debut for Manchester City in 1894 and was playing in an FA Cup semi-final in 1924. Played in nearly 1,100 matches, though many were during the First World War and thus not officially recorded. Perfected the art of crossing the ball on the run and passing a split-second before being tackled. Won 48 Welsh caps. Founder member of the Players' Union.

Jackie Milburn: The most popular centre-forward produced on Tyneside by Newcastle United. His career began in the War and blossomed out from 1946 in the immediate post-War years. Long-striding centre-forward who could also play in other attacking positions. Specialised in spectacular goals and his speed left defenders struggling to keep up with him. Made 354 League appearances and scored 177 goals. Won 13 caps.

Bobby Moore: An expert reader of the game with vision and constructive ability, he had the eye for turning defence into attack with precision and accuracy from the centre of defence. Captained England to their World Cup triumph in 1966 and probably played even better four years later in Mexico. Cool and disciplined, he had been groomed by West Ham United and at one time held the club's appearance record. Also made a record 108 appearances for England but since overtaken by Peter Shilton. By any reasonable standard a world-class player. Finished his career with Fulham and dabbled briefly in management before turning to sportswriting.

Stan Mortensen: Had the unusual experience of making his international debut as a wartime substitute for Wales against England for whom he later won 25 caps. Courageous and speedy attacker who survived a wartime air crash to return bravely to the game. Played for Blackpool, Hull City and Southport. Scored a hat-trick for Blackpool in the 1953 FA Cup final.

Alan Morton: Known as the 'Wee Blue Devil' of Rangers, this 5ft 4in left-winger had a range of trickery and skill. He played 495 games for his club and scored 115 goals. Began with Queen's Park and among his 31 caps for Scotland was one from the 1928 victory over England at Wembley immortalised in the 'Wembley Wizards'.

Steve Nicol: Wherever he plays for Liverpool, appears to have few problems in producing a high standard of performance. Nicely balanced player with ease on the ball, he has occupied both flank positions at the back, however in central defence and midfield his attacking instincts have been given free expression. Formerly with Ayr United and signed for Liverpool in 1981. Quick in recovery and to the tackle. He has 23 Scottish caps.

Bob Paisley: Despite reluctantly taking over from Shankly as Liverpool manager, became a legend

Bob Paisley raises the last of his trophies in 1983, having announced his retirement. In all he won 13 in nine seasons.

himself. Had joined the club pre-War from Bishop Auckland and after retiring became one of the important backroom staff at Anfield which provided the stable base for the club's many successes. In terms of trophies won, he developed into the most successful manager in English history in the nine years from 1974 to 1983. A quiet, thoughtful and low-profile successor to the Shankly style, he proved equally effective.

Martin Peters: Was a member of the West Ham United triumvirate of Moore-Hurst-Peters who dominated club and country in 1960s before he moved to Tottenham in 1970. Midfield player who often contributed far more to a game than he appeared to. Invariably ghosted into the right position to finish attacking moves that he began himself with a thoughtful opening-up of defences. Had a spell with Norwich City and ended his career as player/manager of Sheffield United. Won 67 caps.

Sir Alf Ramsey: A solid, stoic full-back in his playing days who had his best years in Tottenham Hotspur's Championship-winning team of 1951 having been signed from Southampton. Rarely wasted the ball when he was in possession. Became manager of Ipswich Town and led them from Third Division obscurity to the First Division Championship, landing the England manager's job as a reward in 1963. Famous as the man who brought the World Cup to England in 1966 and the one who erased wingers from coaching memory for more than a decade, if not forever. Used counter-attacking expertly but eventually became more and more defensive, less adventurous and fell by the wayside. Knighted in January 1967, he later became manager of Birmingham City. Also contrived to earn the respect of his England players in a way appreciated by the loyal but not by many outside the circle. Despite his successes, lacked real confidence. Won 32 caps.

Kevin Ratcliffe: An Everton player from his schooldays, he has become club captain and one of the most consistent central defenders in the British Isles, noted for his speed into tackles and in recovery, and also for his fine heading ability. Has also led Wales for whom he has won 48 caps. Led Everton to their 1985 European Cup-Winners' Cup triumph.

Lawrie Reilly: A noted marksman frequently rescuing his teams with late goals which earned him the nickname of 'Last-minute Reilly'. At only 5ft 7in he was not the tallest of centre-forwards, but proved a handful for defences with his skill, acceleration and finishing ability. Set a goalscoring record for Hibernian with 185 goals and hit 22 in 38 internationals for Scotland between 1949 and 1957. Retired with a knee injury when only 29.

Don Revie: Was responsible for the first significant tactical innovation in the British game since the 1930s when he introduced the Revie Plan, a deep-lying centre-forward, in the 1950s based on the Hungarian principle. Thoughtful, industrious player with Leicester City, Hull City, Manchester City, Sunderland and Leeds United, he eventually became manager of Leeds and transformed them. Despite a fine haul of trophies at home and abroad, United missed out on many others, finishing runners-up in the Championship five times. Despite his totally professional approach to management, which was often an extension of gamesmanship off the field, he often transferred his anxieties to those around him. Became manager of England but had less success and eventually sought more financial rewards in charge of the UAE in 1977. Won six caps.

Bobby Robson: Product of the north-east, he played as an inside-forward and then right-half for Fulham and West Bromwich Albion. Became a manager with Fulham after a spell as player/manager in Vancouver and then took control at Ipswich Town. His success and general conduct enabled him to become England's manager in 1982. Has often appeared to have wilted under the pressures of this exacting role, but has produced teams of discipline, which have been difficult to score against while perhaps lacking the necessary flair and technical skill to succeed at the highest level. However, did well to gain fourth place in the 1990 World Cup. Won 20 caps.

Bryan Robson: Injury-prone midfield player who has courageously fought back from a variety of problems which have included three broken legs during one season at West Bromwich Albion and shoulder injuries at Manchester United. Captain of the Old Trafford club and England, he leads by example. Determined and wholehearted, he has a keen sense of the pattern of play. He can figure in a defensive role or as an attacking player with equal effect. Creative, strong-tackling and ever-ready to accept goalscoring half-chances. Had to undergo a body-building course as a youngster with West Bromwich. He has 87 caps. Signed by United in 1981 for £1.5 million.

Sir Stanley Rous: Combined teaching with refereeing until appointed secretary of the Football Association in 1934 and remained in the post until becoming President of FIFA in 1962. A commanding presence and intellectual giant in footballing matters, he was responsible for the diagonal system of refereeing, the institution of coaching and the wider interpretation of the Laws of the Game. Knighted in 1949 as much for his work during wartime, when he almost single-handedly organised the game, as for his other splendid work for the sport.

Arthur Rowley: Scored a record 434 Football League goals for West Bromwich Albion, Fulham, Leicester City and Shrewsbury Town in the years immediately after the Second World War, ending his career with Shrewsbury as their player/manager in 1965. Might have added to his total but for being something of a late developer. Strongly-built inside-forward with a blistering shot especially from his left, he was a consistent marksman once he established himself.

Arthur Rowley in his Shrewsbury Town days. He scored 152 goals in 236 League games for them between 1958 and 1965.

Ian Rush in action at the start of Liverpool's double-winning season, 1985–86. He is the most deadly striker in the League.

Ian Rush: Caused a sensation when Liverpool paid as much as £300,000 to Chester for him in 1980, but soon proved his worth as a goalscorer. Long-striding leader with good ball control, anticipation and finishing know-how as well as being more of a statuesque target player than many of his contemporaries. Transferred to Juventus in 1987 for £3.2 million but had an unhappy time with illness and injury and returned a year later for £2.8 million. Became Liverpool's second-highest career goalscorer in 1989–90 with nearly 250 goals. He has 44 Welsh caps.

Kenny Sansom: Left-back who holds the Arsenal record for most international appearances, winning 77 of his 86 England caps with them. Consistent, overlapping defender with fine positional sense and control. Began his career with Crystal Palace and later joined Newcastle United and Queen's Park Rangers.

Elisha Scott: Spent most of his career with Liverpool and became Northern Ireland's most illustrious goalkeeper. He had courage, positional sense and sharp anticipation. Once held the Anfield appearance record with 430 League games and finished his career with Belfast Celtic. Won 31 caps. Championship medals in 1922 and 1923, conceding only 63 goals in 81 games in those seasons.

No one has quite matched the affection The Kop held for Bill Shankly, the creator of the modern Liverpool machine.

Len Shackleton: One of the game's most puzzling enigmas; capable of individual brilliance as an inside-forward when the mood took him, but a controversial character who defied the hidebound strictures of the footballing establishment. Discarded as a youth by Arsenal in 1939, he stifled his frustration and annoyance sufficiently to build a fine career with Bradford Park Avenue, Newcastle United and Sunderland. Could almost make the ball talk. Only five England caps, largely because of his scant regard for officialdom. Scored six goals on his debut for Newcastle. Became a journalist.

Bill Shankly: Transformed Liverpool from a modest Second Division club into the finest side in the country and arguably the world from his appointment in 1959 until his retirement in 1974. Had been a grafting wing-half with Carlisle and Preston and a manager with Carlisle, Grimsby, Workington and Huddersfield, winning five Scottish caps. Considered football to be an essential part of life. Straightforward, blunt, a man of the people and devoted to Liverpool, never relaxing his ambition to make them the outstanding team of his era – an ambition which he fulfilled.

Peter Shilton: England's record-holder for international appearances. Muscular goalkeeper and a fitness devotee, his dedication has had its reward. Was a teenage prodigy with Leicester City and moved to Stoke City, Nottingham Forest and Southampton before finishing with Derby County. Authoritative, brave and exceptionally quick at cutting down shooting angles. Also established a record for making more League and Cup appearances plus representative games than any other player, topping 1,200 during the 1988–89 season. He won 125 caps.

Gordon Smith: Technically one of the finest right-wingers produced in Scotland. Had speed, control and was an almost perfect striker of the ball when either passing or shooting. Had the unusual experience of playing in European competitions for three different clubs: Hibernian, Hearts and Dundee. Made his name with Hibs as one of their famous five forwards in the early 1950s. Won 18 caps.

Graeme Souness: Midfield general who came to prominence with Liverpool after arriving from Middlesbrough in 1978. Had been with Tottenham Hotspur but was homesick for the north and did not figure in their League side. Tall, well-built player who had a fearsome reputation as a tackler but was a visionary in constructive play and accurate in distribution. Furthered his career in Italy with Sampdoria before becoming player/manager of Glasgow Rangers and restoring pride of achievement at Ibrox. Won 54 Scottish caps.

Neville Southall: Emerged as a full Welsh international goalkeeper with Everton after many unsettled seasons in Welsh non-League football and unsuccessful trials with several League clubs. Snapped up by Bury from Winsford in 1981, he finally established himself at Goodison Park. Razor-edged reflexes, agility and confidence have earned him wide respect. He has 44 caps.

Jock Stein: Unquestionably the most successful Scottish manager of all time. A student of the game who valued every piece of information in an ambitious career as a coach and manager. As a player he had been a centre-half with Albion Rovers, Llanelli and Celtic, the club with whom he was to have considerable success after retiring. Injury forced a move towards coaching and he learned quickly. Eventually he took over Dunfermline and then Hibernian before returning to Celtic. From 1965 he transformed the club into a domestically dominant outfit and an internationally respected one. Celtic won nine successive League titles, including four doubles and two trebles as Scottish Cup and League Cup honours were taken. In 1967 came the greatest prize – the European Cup, the first British club to win the trophy. Later he assumed control of the Scottish national team where his views were listened to with respect. He died watching Scotland qualify for the 1986 World Cup finals.

Frank Swift: One of the few genuine goalkeeping attractions that the game has produced. Giant of a man who specialised in spectacular one-handed saves. Won an FA Cup-winners' medal in 1934 for Manchester City at 19 and fainted at the end of the game. His best years were swallowed up in the Second World War when he was the outstanding custodian in the country. He won 19 peacetime England caps. Died in the Munich air disaster when on a journalistic assignment.

Peter Shilton would now be completely submerged after bringing hs total to a close at 125 caps. Here, there are a mere 109.

Bert Trautmann: German-born goalkeeper and ex-prisoner-of-war who overcame understandable post-War prejudice to become a firm favourite at Manchester City as a replacement for Swift. Well-built, fearless and spectacular, he will be remembered for bravely playing out the final minutes of the 1956 FA Cup final with a broken neck. Considered his training as a paratrooper helped him to fall and cushion the ball properly.

Chris Waddle: Discovered by Newcastle United while playing for Tow Law Town. Tall, stooping winger with exceptional control and pace. Long-striding and a useful marksman. Transferred from Tottenham Hotspur to Marseille in 1989 for a British record £4.5 million. Able to turn out in any forward position if required. He has 59 caps.

Billy Walker: Spent 15 years from 1919 with Aston Villa as an attacking inside-forward. Scored 214 goals in 478 League appearances and became a successful manager chiefly with Sheffield Wednesday and Nottingham Forest. Good tactician as a player and put this to fine use as a manager. Won 18 England caps.

Bobby Walker: One of the finest exponents of the Scottish close-passing game at the turn of the century. Could play in a variety of forward positions, starring for Hearts in their 1896 Scottish Cup success and League Championship the following year. Fine manipulator of the ball and had great distributive qualities. Won 29 caps.

Tommy Walker: Cool, artistic inside-forward with an eye for goal and for openings for his colleagues. Played for Hearts and Chelsea, his career straddling the Second World War. Became a manager with Hearts and brought the same thoughtful approach to this role, winning two Championships, a Scottish Cup and four League Cups from the 1950s. Won 20 caps for Scotland.

John White: Tragically killed in 1964 in a freak accident when hit by lightning on a golf course, he had masterminded Tottenham Hotspur's 1960–61 League and Cup double-winning team as an inside-forward of rare delicacy and intuition. Began his career in his native Scotland with Alloa and Falkirk. Won 22 caps for Scotland.

Ray Wilkins: Thoughtful, intelligent midfield general who began with Chelsea and moved on to Manchester United for £825,000 in 1979 before going to AC Milan. Short spell with Paris St Germain and then to Glasgow Rangers followed by Queen's Park Rangers. Cool, unruffled approach; fine passing instincts if inclined to be over-cautious at times. Good leader. He won 84 caps.

Ray Wilson: Was an underrated defender in England's 1966 World Cup triumph at left-back, despite coming rather late into international football in his mid-20s. Was renowned for his anticipation and quiet but effective domination of opposing players. Played for Huddersfield Town, Everton, Oldham Athletic and Bradford City and was capped 63 times.

Billy Wright: One of the game's gentlemen and a cultured half-back who began at wing-half and finished in the centre. Joined Wolverhampton Wanderers, his only club, as a groundstaff boy in 1938, turning professional in 1941. Made 105 appearances for England and captained the team on 90 occasions. Retired in 1959 and had a brief spell as Arsenal manager before turning to television sports production.

Billy Wright leads out England in 1959 on the occasion of his 100th cap.

George Young: Dominating centre-half for Rangers and Scotland in the years immediately after the Second World War. Had fine tactical sense and constructive ability. Signed from Kirkintilloch Rob Roy in 1941, he achieved numerous honours at club level and played 53 times for his country.

Who's Who of Overseas Football

Florian Albert: One of the best of Hungary's post-1950s crop of players, he was a clever, technically gifted centre-forward with goalscoring ability on the ground and in the air. Developed with Ferencvaros and later scored 32 goals in 75 appearances for his country, including the 1962 and 1966 World Cup tournaments.

Jose Altafini: Brazilian-born and developed by Palmeiras. Was known as Mazzola and played as such in the 1958 World Cup. Transferred to AC Milan, he later played for Napoli and Juventus under the name of Altafini, to avoid confusion with the Mazzola family in that country. Versatile forward with speed, accuracy and intelligence, he was capped by both Brazil and Italy, eight and six times respectively.

Jose Andrade: Was a member of Uruguay's two Olympic-winning teams in the 1920s and their initial World Cup success in 1930. Fine, athletic right-half who became an early idol in his country. Played for Bella Vista, Nacional, Penarol, Atlanta and Wanderers. Won 31 caps.

Ossie Ardiles: A pocket-sized midfield dynamo who influenced Argentina in their 1978 World Cup success and joined Tottenham Hotspur shortly afterwards. In the wake of the Falklands conflict he was loaned to Paris St Germain before returning. Had started his career with Instituto Cordoba and Huracan and was capped on 42 occasions. Became manager of Swindon Town.

Vladimir Beara: Kept goal like a ballerina, spectacularly graceful but effective for all that style. Yugoslavian international on 60 occasions, he played in the 1950, 1954 and 1958 World Cups. At club level he was developed by Hajduk Split and later starred for Red Star Belgrade before ending his career in West Germany with Alemmania Aachen. Later took up coaching.

Enzo Bearzot: Achieved success by leading Italy to their 1982 World Cup triumph, having taken over as manager five years earlier. Successfully contrived to change the nature of the Italian players from their defence-orientated league system into a more attacking outfit. Also proved

A triumphant Enzo Bearzot is chaired off after winning the World Cup in 1982.

himself to be a fine man-manager. Capped once as a player with Torino.

Franz Beckenbauer: One of the most complete footballers produced in the post-War period and probably West Germany's finest of all time. Spent 12 years as an international, appeared in 103 games for his country and led them to the World Cup success in 1974. Joined Bayern Munich as a boy and was involved in their haul of European honours in the mid-1970s. Developed initially as a midfield player, he later switched to a sweeper's role to even more effect. Considerable capacity for reading the game and dictating the pattern of play, he always appeared to have time – the mark of a first-class performer. Could attack with speed when necessary and had the close control to beat an opponent without difficulty. His distributive qualities were rarely equalled. Continued his career in the USA with New York Cosmos and returned to play for Hamburg. Became West Germany's team manager and took them to runners-up spot in the 1986 World Cup and victory in 1990. Somewhat introverted and criticised for his apparent arrogance. Hence the legend of 'Kaiser Franz'.

Orvar Bergmark: Versatile defender either at right-back or centre-half, he won a record 94 caps for Sweden. Came to the fore with Orebro and, apart from a season with Solna and another two at Roma, he remained loyal to them. Excellent positional play, fine tackling and marking made him an ideal captain. Played in the 1958 World Cup and was manager for the 1970 series.

Twice European Player of the Year, Franz Beckenbauer has won every major honour in the game.

Franz (Bimbo) Binder: Recognised as the first European player to score a thousand goals in first-class football: 1,006 from only 756 games. Had the touch of an expert marksman, simply being in the right place at the right moment. Played for Sturm 19, St Polten and then memorably for Rapid Vienna. Capped 20 times for Austria scoring 16 goals and added nine caps and 10 goals for Germany after the *Anschluss*. Centre-forward or inside-left.

Oleg Blokhin: Dangerous raider on the flanks with an explosive shot. Skilful and deceptively agile and confident. Long-serving player with Dynamo Kiev, he became the first in the Soviet Union to play in as many as 109 international matches. European Footballer of the Year in 1975. Finished his career with the Austrian club Steyr, before finally ending up in Cyprus.

Jozsef Bozsik: One of the new-style right-half backs in Hungary's 4-2-4 formation which altered the face of European football in the 1950s. Famed for his passing skills which frequently carved openings in the opposing defence and for his generalship. Appropriately was a member of the Hungarian National Assembly. Played for Honved and won 100 caps.

Paul Breitner: Industrious and talented defender or midfield player who played for Bayern Munich (two spells), Real Madrid and Eintracht Brunswick. Scored in two World Cup finals, from a penalty in 1974 and in 1982. Tenacious player who could inspire on his day. Won 48 West German caps, scored 11 goals.

Jose Camacho: Tough-tackling but adroit defender who operated either as a full-back or as a defensive midfield marker. One-club man for Real Madrid after being groomed through their nursery team Castilla. Recovered from serious injury and became Spain's most-capped player with 81 appearances. Joined Real in 1975.

Hector Chumpitaz: Compact, well-drilled centre-back who led Peru into the 1970 World Cup. The country's most-capped player with 150 appearances against other nations and representative teams. Lengthy period of service with Universitario Lima.

Paul Breitner's goal in the 1982 World Cup final was not enough to give West Germany victory.

Mario Coluna: Quietly effective and tactically aware midfield player who enjoyed himself at club and country level for Benfica and Portugal respectively in the post-Real Madrid era of the European Cup in the 1960s. Born in Mozambique, he moved from Deportivo Lourenco Marques to Benfica and towards the end of his career to Lyon in France. Won 73 caps.

Johan Cruyff: The Netherlands' most distinguished footballer, but a controversial figure often at odds with officialdom. Played in 48 internationals and scored 33 goals but was disappointed in not collecting a winners' medal in the 1974 World Cup, when he had to be content with a runners-up prize. Began as a youth with Ajax, joined Barcelona for nearly £1 million in 1973, also played in the USA before returning to his home country at Feyenoord and Ajax. Scored 215 League goals in the Netherlands and 47 for Barcelona. Lanky forward with razor-sharp reactions, excellent control and change of pace. He could change the direction of his movement in a split-second. Became a coach and led Ajax and Barcelona to European successes.

Teofilo Cubillas: Made his initial contribution to international football as a bright, promising left-winger for Peru in the 1970 World Cup and matured into a midfield schemer-in-chief with tactical know-how by the 1982 finals. Began with Alianza Lima and had spells in Switzerland with Basle and in the USA with Fort Lauderdale. Won 60 caps.

Zoltan Czibor: Fast, raiding left-winger who was a member of the Hungarian team which dominated the 1950s. Began with Komarom but was groomed by Ferencvaros before joining Honved where his acceleration, change of direction and goalscoring abilities proved crucial to club and country. Later moved to Barcelona. Won 43 caps, scored 17 goals.

Renzo de Vecchi: Unique among footballers, if for no other reason than being known as *Il Figlio di Dio* (the Son of God), but had qualities to match such a grand title. Made his debut for Italy at only 16 in 1910. Skilful full-back with delicate touches, but a firm defender despite his slight frame. Captained the national team on many occasions during his 43 international appearances. Played for Milan and Genoa.

Kazimierz Deyna: Attacking midfield player who became the first Pole to play more than a century of games for his country. Had the misfortune to miss a penalty in the 1978 World Cup on his 100th appearance, but this was one of few disappointments in his lengthy career with Wlokniarz Gdanski, LKS Lodz and Legia Warsaw and then Manchester City from 1978. Ended up in the USA. Won 102 caps, scored 45 goals.

Didi (Waldir Pereira). Almost lost a limb as a youth following a knee injury, but recovered to become an elegant, talented midfield player and the inspiration behind Brazil's 1958 World Cup success when he was nearly 30. Specialised in wickedly swerving free-kicks. Developed a dead ball kick which veered then faded and became known as the *folha seca* (dry leaf). Played for Fluminense and Botafogo before moving to Real Madrid in 1959, where he had an unhappy time because Alfredo Di Stefano wanted no challenger to his authority. Returned to Botafogo a year later and helped Brazil win another World Cup. Won 72 caps.

Alfredo Di Stefano: The strategist; a deep-lying centre-forward who came to prominence with the Real Madrid team which won the European Cup five times in succession from 1956 to 1960. An influential leader, he had stamina, skill and goalscoring ability, though he was rather right-footed. Began in his native Argentina with River Plate and Huracan before moving to Millonarios in Colombia and then went to Spain where he finished his career with Espanol. Seven goals in seven appearances for Argentina, two unofficial games for Colombia and 23 goals in 31 games for Spain. Record 49 European Cup goals and more than 400 for Real Madrid alone. Later coached and managed clubs in Argentina and Spain. Never played in a World Cup final tournament.

Dragan Dzajic: Goalscoring outside-left who established a record of international appearances for Yugoslavia when he overtook Zebec's total of 65 caps in 1972. Quick, alert and with clever footwork, he was also a fine captain. Played chiefly for Red Star Belgrade until finishing his career with Nice and Bastia. Won 85 caps, scored 23 goals.

Having won the 1968 European Championship, Facchetti hoped to make it a double by winning the World Cup in 1970. The Brazilians had other ideas.

Eusebio (da Silva Ferreira): Made his name as an explosive-shooting forward with Benfica and Portugal in the 1960s. Scored 316 goals for his club in 294 league games. Hit 41 goals in 64 appearances for Portugal. Top scorer in the 1966 World Cup finals with nine goals. Fine control at speed but often contained by close marking. Finished his career in the USA, Mexico and finally back in Portugal.

Giacinto Facchetti: Transformed from an ungainly forward into a fine, attacking full-back by Helenio Herrera at Internazionale and became Italy's most-capped full-back with 94 appearances. Also made a club record 476 league appearances. A frequent marksman, he developed a subtle change of pace which caused havoc in opposing defences when he attacked them. Led Italy to victory in the 1968 European Championship.

Elias Figueroa: Central defensive organiser and a fine commanding player who was three times South American Footballer of the Year in the mid-1970s. Wide experience in Uruguay, Brazil, the USA and his native Chile with Colo Colo. Won 50 caps.

Just Fontaine: Goalscoring inside-forward who invariably played as the spearhead of the attack. Joined Nice from USM Casablanca and later moved to Reims but suffered two serious leg injuries at the height of his career and was forced to retire. Scored 30 goals for France in only 21 internationals including a record 13 in the 1958 World Cup. Quick, confident and direct, with good control under pressure, he regularly scored goals with either foot and with his head.

Enzo Francescoli: Attack organiser who was snapped up by Racing Club Paris in 1986 after he had developed in his native Uruguay with Wanderers and with River Plate in Argentina. Transferred to Marseille in 1989. Tall, strong and has splendid control. He has 47 caps.

Artur Friedenreich: In a 26-year career from 1909 to 1935 scored 1,329 goals. Formidable centre-forward with a brave approach to the goalscoring arts. Played in Brazil's first international fixture – against Exeter City in 1914 – and had two teeth knocked out in a tackle. Played for Germania, Ipiranga, Americano, Paulistano, Sao Paulo and

Just Fontaine (right) scores the equalising goal for France against Italy in 1958.

Flamengo. Nine goals in 17 appearances for Brazil.

Garrincha (Manoel Francisco dos Santos): Overcame the handicap of a distorted left leg as a boy to become an exciting right-winger with rapid acceleration. He was comfortable on the ball and expert at crossing accurately. Also had a ferocious shot from dead-ball situations. His nickname was derived from the translation of Little Bird, appropriate for a flying winger. Outstanding in the 1958 and 1962 World Cups, he subsequently suffered a series of injuries and off-the-field problems added to his demise. Played for Pau Grande, Botafogo, Corinthians, Flamengo, Bangu, Portuguesa Santista and Olaria, and was capped 60 times by Brazil.

Francisco Gento: Explosively quick outside-left who dominated the left flank for Real Madrid and Spain in the 1950s and 1960s. Started his career with Nuevo Montana, Astillero and Rayo Cantabria before joining Real Santander. Came to Madrid in 1953. Captained both club and country late in his career. Outstanding in Real's six European Cup successes. Won 43 caps.

Gunnar Gren: Short and slight but with a nimble footballing brain and feet to match. Was a ball-juggling sensation as a youth and developed his skills as an inch-perfect provider of passes. A member of the famous 'Gre-No-Li' trio at AC Milan along with his Swedish colleagues Gunnar Nordahl and Nils Liedholm from 1949. His clubs included Garda, IFK Gothenburg, AC Milan, Fiorentina, Genoa, Orgryte, Gais Gothenburg and Skogens for whom he was still playing at the age of 50. Won 57 caps for Sweden.

Gyula Grosics: Easily Hungary's most accomplished goalkeeper. Was the last line of defence in the 1950s era of outstanding achievement. Played for Dorog, Honved and Tatabanya. Spectacular, occasionally prone to

Hungarian goalkeeper Grosics saves from Mortensen during their famous 6–3 win at Wembley in 1953.

error, but invariably in total command of his penalty area and frequently initiated attacks with ventures outside it. Won 86 caps.

Ruud Gullit: Versatile player with distinctive Rasta dreadlocks, he has moved from sweeper to an attacking midfield role and uses his height, speed and exceptional ball control to devastating effect. His support of other players is above average for a footballer of his ability. Played for Meerboys, DWS Amsterdam, Haarlem and Feyenoord before joining PSV Eindhoven in 1985. Cost AC Milan £5.5 million in 1987. Played a leading role in the Netherlands' success in the 1988 European Championship. He has 46 caps.

Gylmar (dos Santos Neves): Easily Brazil's most accomplished goalkeeper, he made his 100th appearance against England in 1969 at the age of 39. Unhurried and calm, he possessed complete command of his area and was never flustered by the odd mistake he made. Played for Jabaquara, Corinthians and Santos. Conceded only 95 goals for Brazil and was on the losing side on just 14 occasions.

Kurt Hamrin: Another of the excellent crop of Swedish players produced in the immediate post-War period. Ostensibly an outside-right, he was at his most effective when taking the ball past opponents anywhere on the pitch. Small but fast, he played for a variety of clubs including Solna, Juventus, Padova, Fiorentina, AC Milan, Napoli and AIK Stockholm. Won 32 caps, scored 16 goals.

Gerhardt Hanappi: Austria's most-capped international with 93 appearances. Could play in almost any position but best in the right-half berth, although he was capped everywhere except in goal and on the left-wing. Had the ability to make a space for himself and found the best use for the time it gave him. Even when detailed to play left-back to mark Stanley Matthews in 1953 for FIFA, he gave a more than competent display. Played for Wacker and Rapid Vienna.

Sepp Herberger: A shrewd tactician who kept abreast of the latest developments in the game, but always played to the strengths of his team, rather than imposing a style unsuited to them. Had been assistant in pre-War times to Otto Nerz in the German hierarchy and took over as manager in 1936. His greatest achievement was in guiding West Germany to the 1954 World Cup success. An inside-forward in his playing days, he had been capped three times.

Helenio Herrera: Became known as the high priest of *catenaccio*, the blanket defence strategy developed in Italian circles in the 1960s. In the eight years he managed Internazionale they achieved two championships, two European Cups and two World Club Championships. Previously in charge of Barcelona. Born in Argentina, his parents emigrated to North Africa and he became a naturalised Frenchman. Fierce disciplinarian, but successful in his time.

Nandor Hidegkuti: Architect of England's downfall in 1953 when he provided the inspiration from a deep-lying centre-forward role to produce Hungary's sensational 6–3 win at Wembley. Had his career interrupted by the Second World War and was 31 at the time of this milestone victory. Had the ability to unravel weaknesses in the opposition and exploit them with defence-splitting passes. Spent most of his career with MTK Budapest. Scored 39 goals in 68 internationals.

Jairzinho (Jair Ventura Filho): Played a full part in Brazil's 1970 World Cup success, penetrating on the right flank with speed and alacrity. Also managed to score in each of their games in the finals. Fine marksman and able to lead the attack if required. Developed by Botafogo and overcame several injury problems in his career which included a spell in Venezuela. Expert crosses laid on many goals for colleagues. Scored 37 goals for Brazil and won 98 caps.

Paul Janes: An instinctive player with almost perfect distributive qualities, he was switched from right-half to right-back and won 71 caps for Germany from 1932 to 1942. Free kick specialist and penalty taker, he had a lengthy career with Fortuna Dusseldorf.

Robert Jonquet: Possibly France's most gifted centre-back, he won 58 caps and enjoyed considerable success in the 1958 World Cup. His injury in the semi-final cost them dearly. Joined Reims as a youngster and later played for Strasbourg. Commanding player in the air and on the ground and had a stylish approach to his game.

Joseph Jurion: Was almost unique in the modern era for wearing spectacles whenever he played. Despite this apparent hindrance he made 64 appearances for Belgium and captained the team on many occasions during the 1960s. Began as an outside-right but was moved with effect to inside-forward where he was invariably positioned to receive and distribute the ball, which he did with accuracy. Was with Anderlecht for most of his career but later played with Gent and Lokeren.

Sandor Kocsis: Gifted, all-round forward with shot-sure feet and exceptional heading ability. Could make and take scoring chances and his 75 goals for Hungary included seven hat-tricks during the days of Hungarian dominance in the 1950s. Left the country after the uprising in 1956, and had a spell in Switzerland as player-coach with Young Fellows before ending up in Barcelona. Had started with Ferencvaros and later developed with Honved. Won 68 caps.

Raymond Kopa: From Polish extraction, his real name being Kopazewski. Small, but perfectly balanced, he was initially an exciting right-winger but developed into an artistic deep-lying centre-forward who contrived to break down defences with far-sighted distribution. Played for Angers, Reims and Real Madrid, the last two clubs giving him unique European Cup final appearances in the 1950s. Returned to Reims where he renewed his association with his international partner Just Fontaine. Won 45 caps.

Rudi Krol: Dutch defender who began with Ruud-Wit but was groomed by Ajax. Missed one European Cup final with a broken leg but recovered to play in two more. Originally a full-back, he was switched to sweeper with good effect. Later played for Napoli and Cannes. Had height and weight and was adept at breaking up attacks and swiftly putting his team on the offensive with accuracy and style. Won 83 caps. Subsequently became a coach.

Ladislao Kubala: Strongly built, but with the light touch of the artist, he was an accomplished attacking forward. One of a select number of players who have made international appearances for three countries. Born in Hungary, he made his debut for them before moving to Czechoslovakia. Six caps for Hungary and 11 for the Czechs. Defected to the West in 1950 and joined Barcelona. He became a naturalised Spaniard and won 19 caps for them. His first clubs were Ferencvaros, Slovan Bratislava and Vasas and from Barcelona he moved to the coaching ranks but kept his playing credentials. Was with Espanol as a player and coached Zurich, making a European Cup appearance at 39. Played in the USA and returned to coaching, enjoying his most

Kocsis scores the fourth goal in the 1954 England v Hungary re-match. It turned into a 7–1 humiliation for England.

successful spell in charge of the Spanish national team in the early 1970s.

Angel Labruna: An inside-forward with goalscoring instincts and creative flair, he spent an incredible 29 years with River Plate, making his debut at 21 in 1939. Scored nearly 500 goals, including 292 in the league, and late in his long career played for Platense, Green Cross (Chile) and Rampla Juniors (Uruguay). Coached extensively after retiring. Won 37 Argentine caps.

Leonidas (da Silva): Probably the first player to perfect the bicycle kick. He was an 18-year-old when he made his debut for Brazil in 1932. Scored four goals in a World Cup match against Poland in 1938. An agile centre-forward with a lethal finish, he played 23 times for Brazil and had a succession of clubs including Havanesa, Barroso, Sul Americano, Sirio Libanes, Bomsucesso, Nacional (Uruguay), Vasco da Gama, Botafogo, Flamengo and Sao Paulo.

No matter what Maradona's skill may be, in England this is the incident for which he is most remembered.

Nils Liedholm: An inside-forward who joined the Swedish drift into Italian football and remained there to become a leading coach. A fine strategist with exceptional coolness, he had that ease of control which made the game look simple. Served Norrkoping and then AC Milan where he first coached in 1963. Also in charge of Verona, Monza, Varese, Fiorentina, Roma in three spells and Milan twice more. Won 23 caps.

Wlodzimierz Lubanski: Strong, speedy and talented inside-forward with a high scoring rate, he was regarded as Poland's most successful post-War discovery. In 1972 at the Munich Olympics he collected a gold medal in what was his 60th appearance for his country. Played for GKS Gliwice, the Gornik Zabrze nursery team, before graduating to their senior team. Even missed two years with a heart condition before returning to full fitness. Won 80 caps, scored 50 goals.

Sepp Maier: Recovered from an unconvincing start to his international career to become West Germany's most-capped goalkeeper in 1972 when he was a valuable member of their successful European Championship-winning team. Added a World Cup medal two years later. Ungainly in appearance but famed for safe hands and a fearless approach to keeping his charge intact. Played with distinction for Bayern Munich. Won 95 caps.

Diego Maradona: Unquestionably one of the most talented players to have emerged in the last decade. An exceptionally confident attacker, he can beat player after player with consummate ease and blistering pace. Fine close control and lethal from free-kicks with his left foot. Began with Argentinos Juniors and Boca Juniors before moving to Barcelona for £4.2 million and then Napoli in a world record £6.9 million transfer in 1984. Has suffered with injury, illness and the failure to deal with the enormous pressures associated with his talent. Scored 144 league goals in Argentina, 22 in Spain and 59 in his first five seasons with Napoli. He has 79 caps, 29 goals.

Josef Masopust: Was a post-War exponent of Czechoslovakia's pre-War penchant for short-passing a way to goal. A midfield player with left-half inclinations, he had fine control and his dribbling ability frequently put him into scoring positions. Was briefly with his local club Union Teplice before moving to Dukla Prague. Outstanding in the 1962 World Cup in a half-back line of Svatopluk Pluskal and Jan Popluhar. Finished his career with a short spell as a professional in Belgium with Crossing Molenbeek. Won 63 caps.

Sandro Mazzola: Son of the legendary Valentino who was killed in the Superga air disaster in 1949, he had established himself with Internazionale by the time he was 20. Deceptively frail, he was quick, direct and forceful. He proved a fine goalscoring centre-forward and a shrewd, intelligent midfield player when he switched roles. Won 70 caps and scored 22 goals for Italy.

Giuseppe Meazza: One of only two Italian players to play in both the 1934 and 1938 World Cup-winning teams, he was one of the most complete forwards to play for his country. Had faultless technique, acceleration and skill on the ball. Could play best at inside-forward or as leader of the attack. Scored 33 goals in 53 internationals and 267 league goals for Internazionale, AC Milan, Juventus, Varese and Atalanta.

Hugo Meisl: Was the man behind the development of the attractive and effective style of Austrian play in the 1930s known as the 'Wunderteam'. Brought Jimmy Hogan to coach in the country. Strict but caring in his dealings with players. A shrewd tactical awareness made him one of the outstanding managers of any era. His teams played attractively and with success.

Josef Mermans: Strongly-built, forceful centre-forward with a proven record for goalscoring. Had his best years interrupted by the Second World War but made his international debut in 1945. Had made his pre-War debut for Tubantia at the age of 14 in 1936. Joined Anderlecht and hit 37 goals in 1949–50. Won 56 Belgian caps.

Rinus Michels: A modest player at inside-forward in the early 1950s, winning five caps for the Netherlands. His greatest achievements came as a coach, initially with Ajax for whom he won the European Cup in 1971. Moved swiftly to Barcelona where his reputation as a strict disciplinarian but tactically sound manager was fully put to the test. At the age of 60 he guided the Netherlands to the 1988 European Championship title before briefly returning to coach the West German club Bayer Leverkusen.

Gerd Muller was aggressive in the air, despite his lack of inches.

Severino Minelli: Once held the record for the number of appearances by a Swiss international. Played 79 times at right-back and served Kussnacht, Servette and Grasshoppers during a lengthy career. Consistent and dedicated player with a quiet but effective style.

Luis Monti: Had the unusual experience of playing for Argentina in the 1930 World Cup and for Italy in the next, four years later. An uncompromising centre-back, but an accurate distributor of the ball with attacking ideas. He played initially for Boca Juniors and then for Juventus. Won 18 Italian caps.

Gerd Muller: A 5ft 8in, chunky, thick-thighed centre-forward with a low centre of gravity and high rate of scoring: 68 goals in 62 international appearances for West Germany. In all competitive games in the country he amassed 628. Retired from the international game in 1974 after scoring the winning goal in the World Cup. Started with Nordlingen but developed with Bayern Munich, showing fine balance and a keen sense of anticipation in the penalty area. Alf Ramsey reckoned him to be the most dangerous striker among contemporary players. Finished his career in the USA.

Miguel Munoz: Tall, powerful right-half with attacking instincts who was a driving force in the European Cup successes initially achieved by Real Madrid. Began with Logrones and Celta, moving to Real in 1948. Retired to become the club's successful manager for many years and later assumed the arduous task of guiding the national team. Surprisingly won only seven caps.

Jose Nasazzi: Captained Uruguay in the 1924 and 1928 Olympic and 1930 World Cup successes from right-back. Sporting, strong and mobile defender who had a 15-year international career. Played for Nacional and later Bella Vista. Won 59 caps.

Igor Netto: Captained the USSR for nine years as a midfield player. A tall, stylish wing-half he played his entire career with Spartak Moscow. Led the country to its 1956 Olympic triumph. Played 367 league games and won 57 caps.

Gunter Netzer: Tall, Viking-like midfield player who took full advantage of Wolfgang Overath's injury to dictate West Germany's victory in the 1972 European Championship. Had a slightly stooping figure because of a bent backbone. An individualist off the field, he frequently found himself at odds with officialdom. Began with Borussia Moenchengladbach and then moved to Real Madrid. Won 37 caps.

Gunnar Nordahl: Dynamic, bustling but fair centre-forward who succeeded in breaking down defences and records in both Sweden and Italy. Played for Hornefors, Degerfors and Norrkoping in his native country before moving to Italy in 1949, joining AC Milan and then Roma. Returned to Sweden as player/manager of Karlstad. Overall he scored 473 goals in 518 games including 44 in 33 internationals.

Bjorn Nordqvist: Defender of commanding stature and resolute application either at full- or centre-back, he made 115 appearances for Sweden between 1963 and 1978. Began with Hallsberg and developed with Norrkoping before turning professional with PSV Eindhoven in the Netherlands. Back to Sweden with Gothenburg, he then had a spell in the USA with Minnesota Kicks and returned home again with Orgryte.

Ladislav Novak: Right-back who played in three World Cups for Czechoslovakia culminating in the 1962 series when they were runners-up. At one time he held the record of 75 appearances. Though not quick, he had excellent positional sense and timed his tackles to perfection. Served Dukla Prague for many years before moving to Jablonec.

Ernst Ocwirk: Nicknamed 'Clockwork' at Wembley for his finely timed performance in Austria's 2–2 draw with England in 1951. Was the last truly effective attacking centre-half before the days of the sweeper. With excellent control and constructive sense, he appeared to be involved in everything positive on the field. Developed with FK Austria and later played in Italy for Sampdoria. Won 62 caps.

Raimondo Orsi: One of the first Argentines to go to Italy having made his name in the 1928 Olympics. Started his career as an outside-left with Independiente before linking up with Juventus, playing for Italy in the 1934 World Cup. Stylish winger with skill and also a useful marksman. Won 35 Italian caps.

Wolfgang Overath: Masterful midfield player with an educated left foot equally effective at long-range shooting or defence-splitting passing. Chiefly a one-club man with Cologne, for whom he played in well over 400 league games. His international zenith was reached in 1974 during the World Cup success. Won 81 caps.

Daniel Passarella: Inspirational captain of Argentina when they won the 1978 World Cup. Central defender who excelled at tackling and making thoughtful interceptions, he possessed a keen eye for attacking options. Began with Sarmiento and had eight years with River Plate before moving into Italian football with Fiorentina and Internazionale. Won 80 caps.

Pele (Edson Arantes do Nascimento): Probably the most gifted footballer of all time. His range of artistry included amazingly wide peripheral vision, faultless footwork and the complete control which follows from being a naturally gifted ball player. His heading ability was also exceptional and he could bring the best out of his colleagues by his sheer presence. Always on the look-out to achieve the unexpected, he could turn out in any position on the field, including goalkeeper, if required. Began with Bauru and

The incomparable Pele scores in the 1970 World Cup final. A generation on and we still await his equal.

was well coached by pre-War World Cup star Waldemar de Brito, who concentrated on his few weaknesses and allowed his talents full expression. Moved to Santos and made them the most famous club in Latin America. Played in three World Cup-winning teams, 1958, 1962 and 1970. As a youngster was treated unceremoniously by unscrupulous defenders and occasionally retaliated. He was literally kicked out of the 1966 World Cup by Portuguese markers but invariably humiliated his opponents with feints and craft to achieve retribution. Scored a world record 1,363 goals in all matches including 97 in 111 appearances for Brazil. Developed a further career in the USA where he single-handedly popularised the game with New York Cosmos. Since retiring has become the perfect ambassador for the sport.

Pedro Petrone: Was in Uruguay's two 1920s Olympic teams and their 1930 World Cup-winning side. Three times top scorer in the South American Championship, he scored prolifically for Nacional before moving to Italy for one season where he joined Fiorentina, finishing joint top scorer with 25; returned homesick to continue scoring for Nacional. Won 44 caps, scored 37 goals.

Silvio Piola: Tall, dynamic centre-forward who invariably dominated and frustrated defenders. Began with Pro Vercelli and continued his lengthy career with Lazio, Torino, Juventus and Novara, scoring a record 274 goals in the championship. Scored 30 goals in 34 appearances for Italy, including the 1938 World Cup, he would have added to these totals but for the Second World War.

Frantisek Planicka: Goalkeeper of fearsome proportions who was almost a fixture in Czechoslovakian teams in the 1920s and 1930s. At one time held the record for appearances for his country with 74 caps. Played for Slavia Prague in nearly 1,000 games and on average conceded little more than a goal a match.

Michel Platini: Midfield player who had the gift of being able to elude the closest of markers, initiate moves and finish them with skilled understanding and awareness of situations in front of goal. Drifted into scoring positions in a manner which made it difficult to contain him. Expert at dead-ball kicks and penalties. Kept the attack flowing with searching runs and fine distribution. His best moments were achieved when France won the 1984 European

Michel Platini shows he is still capable of the spectacular even in the twilight of his career.

Championship. Played for Nancy, St Etienne and Juventus from 1982 after a £1.2 million transfer. Won 72 caps for France, scoring 41 goals. After retiring, took on the exacting role of French national team manager.

Vittorio Pozzo: Italy's first famous manager, he had been a Manchester United fan in pre-World War One times when he admired their centre-half Charlie Roberts. Modelled his Italian teams on his style. Strict, but shrewd and devoted to the game and his players. Had 20 years in charge of the national team and led them to two World Cup wins in the 1930s. Did his best under the Fascist regime to help the promotion of the national team.

Ferenc Puskas: Had a delightful and deadly left foot but little else to recommend him physically, except for an exceptional footballing brain matched by few others. Of medium height and inclined to be overweight, he was nonetheless a master of sorcery with the ball at his famous left foot. His 83 goals in 84 internationals for Hungary bear testimony to his scoring prowess. He played for Kispest before they became Honved and finished his career spectacularly with Real Madrid, having joined them in 1956 after defecting from Hungary. He also managed to score twice in four internationals for Spain. Scored a career 1,176 goals though many were in non-competitive matches.

Hungary's captain Ferenc Puskas twice scored three or more goals in a European Cup final – a record.

Helmut Rahn: Was the two-goal marksman for West Germany in their 1954 World Cup success and on his day a match-winner from the right-wing. Had a wanderlust career, playing for eight clubs including Rot-Weiss Essen and Cologne where he achieved most success. Could play on either wing and had the confidence to shoot from any angle. Bulky, but surprisingly quick, he often proved a handful for defences. Won 40 caps.

Karl Rappan: An Austrian who made his name as manager of the Swiss national side and by inventing the bolt system of defence, similar to the Italian *catenaccio* defence but with more attacking pretensions. Had four spells at the helm and in his last guided the country to the 1962 World Cup. As a player had served Wacker, FK Austria, Rapid Vienna and Servette. Won four caps.

Ubaldo Antonio Rattin: Notorious as the Argentine player who took eight minutes to leave the pitch when sent off for arguing in the 1966 World Cup against England. A tall, attacking half-back with control and a commanding presence, he was highly popular. Played for Boca Juniors and held a club record of 357 league appearances. Won 37 caps.

Luigi Riva: Possessed a formidable left foot and had speed, height and strength, operating on the left side of the attack. Prolific scorer in league football with 156 goals in the top flight. He also hit 35 goals in 42 appearances for Italy. Began with Legnano and moved to Cagliari. Broke his left leg and his right, but recovered each time.

Roberto Rivelino: Shot to prominence for Brazil in the 1970 World Cup, with viciously-swerving free-kicks and a wide range of tricks on the left-wing. Had a struggle to become a first-class player and needed a strict diet to build up his strength. Groomed by Corinthians, he remained with them for many years before spells with Fluminense and in Saudi Arabia. Made 120 appearances for Brazil.

Gianni Rivera: The golden boy of Italian soccer, he matured at an early age, revealing vision, technical ability and marksmanship. Made his debut in the first division for Alessandria at 15. Moved to AC Milan, playing in 527 league games and scoring 128 goals as a midfield tactician. Won 60 caps, scored 14 goals. Had some managerial success, but was badly shaken when the Milan club was forcibly relegated following the bribery scandal in the early 1980s.

Paolo Rossi: The prodigal son of Italian football who returned from a two-year suspension for his part in the country's bribery scandals to spearhead the World Cup success in 1982. Pacy, skilful and immensely popular, he played variously for Juventus, Como, Vicenza, Perugia and Verona. Scored 20 goals in 46 appearances for Italy.

Karl-Heinz Rummenigge: Tall, skilful, quick attacker with scoring flair and constructive leanings. Able to dictate play from well upfield and possessed excellent positional sense. Formative years with Bayern Munich before joining Internazionale of Milan and ended his career with Servette in Switzerland. Suffered with a series of injuries late in his career but still managed to give memorable performances. Played in the 1982 and 1986 World Cup finals for West Germany. Won 95 caps.

Jose Santamaria: Strong, dependable centre-back who was discovered by Nacional in Uruguay. Achieved 42 caps for his country and was transferred to Real Madrid in 1957, taking part in the Spanish club's later European Cup successes. Added 18 appearances for Spain. Turned to coaching and eventually became national team manager of his new country.

Djalma Santos (Dejalma dos Santos): Had spells in midfield and at centre-back before settling down at right-back. Developed with Portuguesa and was given his first international game by Brazil in 1952. Adept at never allowing himself to be committed by an opponent, preferring to position himself and to wait until the right moment to dispossess the attacker rather than move into a rash tackle. Despite these cautious defensive qualities his attacking features were just as successful. No relation to Nilton Santos, his full-back partner for Brazil. Later played for Palmeiras and Atletico Parana. Won 107 caps.

Juan Schiaffino: Elegant, slenderly built inside-forward with vision, speed, control and finishing ability. Was with Penarol in Montevideo for the early part of his career and masterminded Uruguay's shock win in the 1950 World Cup. Transferred to AC Milan in 1954 for a then world record £72,000 and finished his career with Roma, having settled into Italian football without undue difficulty. Tactically sound, quiet and unassuming. Won 22 Uruguayan caps and four for Italy.

Paolo Rossi returned to the Italian side and became a hero with his six goals in the 1982 World Cup finals.

Angelo Schiavio: One of Bologna's most famous sons. Inside-forward or centre spearhead with a knack of scoring important goals on a regular basis. Hit the winning effort for Italy in the 1934 World Cup. Made 350 league appearances for Bologna and scored 244 goals. Won 21 caps, hitting 15 goals.

Karl-Heinz Schnellinger: Durable, dependable defender with a fine temperament who played in four World Cups for West Germany from 1958 to 1970. Left his home town club of Duren for Cologne and later went to Roma, Mantova and AC Milan. Won 47 caps. Had few peers as a sweeper.

Helmut Schoen, West Germany's highly successful manager, shares a joke with Ron Greenwood.

Helmut Schoen: An inside-forward in his playing days, he was capped by Germany in pre-War times. Succeeded Sepp Herberger as West Germany's team manager in 1964 and enjoyed a run of success which included winning the 1974 World Cup, two years after taking the European Championship title. Preferred to allow players to express themselves on the field with the lightest of direction from the sidelines and had a courteous manner often wrongly regarded as a weakness.

Gaetano Scirea: Extra-cover central defender who invariably appeared to have time to control operations and to launch attacks. Was a member of Italy's successful 1982 World Cup team. Had switched from midfield to become an attractive sweeper. Discovered by Atalanta, he joined Juventus and became one of their most consistent players, making 397 appearances in his league career. Won 74 caps.

Gusztav Sebes: Fine strategist who became Hungary's national coach in the post-War era and was responsible for fashioning the masterful Magyars who dominated the early 1950s. Also produced the 4–2–4 formation which proved outstandingly successful for the team he created. Had played for Vasas Budapest and MTK and was capped once by his country.

Uwe Seeler: Chunky, versatile centre-forward who compensated for his lack of height – he was under 5ft 7in tall. He was an acrobatic striker on and off the ground. Made his international debut in 1954 after the World Cup and completed 72 appearances and scored 43 goals. A one-club man for Hamburg, he scored 760 goals in all games.

Allan Simonsen: Effervescent bundle of energy and expertise in midfield, with an attacking strain which produced many goals for himself and colleagues. Varied career with Vejle in his native Denmark, Borussia Moenchengladbach, Barcelona, Charlton Athletic and back to Vejle. Particularly effective on the right side of the attack. Won 56 caps, scored 21 goals.

Matthias Sindelar: Slender, wispish centre-foward who was aptly known as the 'Man of Paper'. Made his name as leader of Austria's 'Wunderteam' in the 1930s. Difficult to mark, he led the attack unselfishly, making countless openings for his forward colleagues, but was a noted marksman himself. Played for Hertha Vienna, Amateur and FK Austria. Won 43 caps, scored 28 goals. As a Jew, he may have committed suicide in 1939.

Enrique Omar Sivori: A gifted midfield player with a questionable temperament, this Argentine developed with River Plate and came to Italy with Juventus in 1957, forming a devastatingly effective partnership with centre-forward John Charles. Had played 12 times for Argentina and subsequently appeared nine times for Italy, scoring eight goals. Finished his career with Napoli. Top scorer in Italy with 27 goals for Juventus in 1959–60. Coached in Italy and Argentina.

Lennart (Nacka) Skoglund: One of the most attractive wingers produced by Sweden, never happier than when putting defenders off balance with his clever footwork. Another who joined the exodus to Italy, he had played for AIK Stockholm and Solna before joining Internazionale, Sampdoria and Palermo. Returned to Hammarby in 1964. Won 11 caps.

Guillermo Stabile: Was leading scorer for

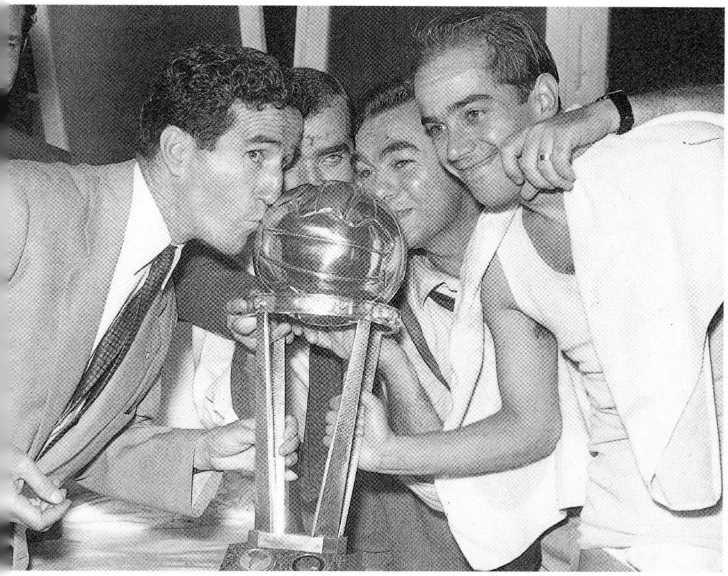

Suarez (right), in his Inter days, celebrates with Herrera after winning the World Club Championship.

Argentina in the 1930 World Cup with eight goals. Began with Huracan then went to Italy playing for Genoa and Napoli, but ended up in France with Red Star Paris and found himself sought by the French as well. Won 31 Argentine caps. Expert at infiltrating opposing defences and finishing adroitly. Became a coach and was in charge of Argentina for 20 years.

Luis Suarez: Was an inside-left and wearer of the famous No.10 shirt in a career of two decades in Spain and Italy. Originally with his home-town club, La Coruna, he later played for Barcelona and Internazionale from 1961. Towards the end of his career as a scheming midfield player he played for Sampdoria. Played 32 games for his country, scoring 13 goals. Coached extensively after retiring and eventually became Spain's manager, guiding them to the 1990 World Cup finals.

Thorbjorn Svenssen: Was the second player in history to make a century of international appearances. First capped in 1947, this lithe but strong centre-back played 104 times for Norway. His club side was Sandefjord and he remained an amateur throughout his career, combining soccer with whaling as a full-time occupation.

Fritz Szepan: A versatile player with considerable technical skill either as a defensive centre-half or inside-forward, he captained Germany in the 1934 World Cup when they defeated the Austrian 'Wunderteam' to take third place. Had a fine relationship with his manager Otto Nerz and served Schalke 04 for many years during their championship successes in the 1930s and early 1940s. Won 34 caps.

Tōstao (Eduardo Goncalves de Andrade): Was an unselfish inspiration as leader of Brazil's attack in the 1970 World Cup, playing despite an operation for a detached retina which prevented him from heading the ball. Scored 33 goals in 55 games for Brazil. His clubs included America (Belo Horizonte), Cruzeiro and Vasco da Gama.

Marius Tresor: Born in Guadeloupe, he became an indomitable figure in the heart of the French defence as a sweeper, showing pace and vision allied to strength. Played for Juventus St Anne, Ajaccio, Marseille and Bordeaux and made over 400 First Division appearances in France. His 65 games for his country included the 1978 and 1982 World Cups.

Marco van Basten: A modern Dutch ball-playing centre-foward of the old school. Probably best remembered for the stunning volley with his right foot at an oblique angle in the 1988 European Championship. Began with Elinkwijk and developed with Ajax before being sold to AC Milan for £1.5 million in 1987. Deceptively lazy style, but noted for his ease of control. Injury-hit in recent years. He has 37 caps, 13 goals.

Gerard (Puck) van Heel: For many years was the Netherlands' most-capped player, making 64 appearances between 1925 and 1953, 29 of them as captain. Would have added to his total but for the War. A left-half of tactical understanding and constructive know-how he was a one-club man for Feyenoord.

Paul van Himst: Reached his peak in the 1972 European Championship when he captained Belgium to third place and won a record-breaking 69th cap. Had joined Anderlecht as a youngster and shot to fame as a teenager for club and country. Powerfully built, he switched from his early centre-forward role to become more of a midfield general and developed his range of fashioning and finishing skills as he matured. Scored 30 goals in 81 appearances for Belgium.

Wilfried van Moer: Energetic, talented midfield player whose career spanned almost 20 years at the top. Played for Beveren, Standard Liege and Antwerp and played more than 50 times for

Belgium. Small but tenacious and a tactical general. Scored 26 international goals. Played in the 1970 and 1982 World Cup finals.

Obdulio Varela: Was the midfield inspiration behind Uruguay's 1950 World Cup success, occupying a wandering position as a centre-half. Played 52 games for his country and assisted Wanderers and Penarol. Fine leader and defensive organiser as well.

Jean Vincent: Outside-left in France's memorable 1958 World Cup team. Could keep possession for long periods while the attack organised itself; he had speed and craft. Could also figure as an inside-forward. Played for Lille and Reims. On retiring coached extensively at home and abroad. Won 45 caps.

Hans-Hubert (Berti) Vogts: Compact, strong-tackling full-back with adventurous tendencies. He joined Borussia Moenchengladbach from his local club VfR Buttgen in 1965. Won a World Cup medal with West Germany in 1974 and his 96 appearances included 38 in succession. Upon retiring he took up coaching and became the national team manager after the 1990 World Cup.

Bernard Vukas: A utility forward with fine control, he played for several Yugoslavian clubs – Concordia, Amater, Hajduk Split – before spells in Italy and Austria with Bologna, Graz AK and Klagenfurt. Among his 59 international appearances, in which he scored 22 goals, were spells on both wings and in the inside-forward position. Remembered for his hat-trick in the Rest of Europe's 4–1 win over Great Britain in 1955.

Fritz Walter: Would probably have become the first German to play 100 times for his country, but for the intervention of the Second World War. Could play either as a centre-forward or deeper at inside-left and captained West Germany in their 1954 World Cup success. Was a one-club man with Kaiserslautern and brought thought and distributive ability to his role as an attacker. Scored 33 goals in 61 international appearances.

Faas Wilkes: Penetrating inside-forward who made an impact from his first game for the Netherlands in 1946 when he scored four goals against Luxembourg. Hit 35 goals in only 38 games and would have added to his total but for playing abroad. Left Xerxes for Internazionale in Milan and then played for Torino, Valencia, Levante, VVV Venlo and Fortuna '54.

Fritz Walter holds the Jules Rimet Trophy while the man himself (left) looks on.

Ernest Willimowski: Goalscoring inside-left famous for his dangerous sorties in the penalty area and his four goals for Poland against Brazil in the 1938 World Cup. Played for Ruch Chorzow until the German invasion when he was given German citizenship and added 13 goals in eight internationals for them. Had played 22 times for Poland.

Lev Yashin: Was probably the best-known and most popular goalkeeper in the post-War era from Eastern Europe. Usually reliable and spectacular, he began with a factory team Tushino before joining Dynamo Moscow as an ice-hockey player! Trained as successor to Tiger Khomich, he graduated to the Soviet Union team playing in Olympics, European Nations Cup and World Cup finals. Won 78 caps and was awarded the Order of Lenin. Had a leg amputated in later years.

Mario Zagalo: Originally a left-winger he became a left-sided midfield player during his career with Brazil. He played in their 1958 and 1962 World Cup-winning teams and was manager during their third triumph in 1970. His club career spanned separate spells with Americo (Rio), Flamengo and Botafogo. After retiring he coached at home and abroad and took the United Arab Emirates to the 1990 World Cup only to be sacked before the finals.

Ricardo Zamora: Established a legendary reputation in Spain during the 1920s and 1930s. In 46 international matches he conceded only 40 goals and was undefeated in 21 games. However, he was beaten seven times by England in 1931. Played for Espanol, Barcelona and Real Madrid where he was feted for his acrobatic style. Later played in France for Nice.

Branko Zebec: Unusually had two outstanding careers in different positions: beginning as an outside-left and continuing as a stopper centre-half. An all-round athletic sprinter and long-jumper, his versatility in the game was impressive. Played for Partizan and Red Star Belgrade, made 65 appearances for Yugoslavia and finished his career in West Germany with Alemannia Aachen. His international debut against Switzerland in 1951 was marked with a hat-trick. Took up coaching at home and abroad with some success.

Zico (Artur Antunes Coimbra): One of the unluckiest players in World Cup terms, but one of its finest. Played for Flamengo, who put him on a body-building course to improve his frail stature. Suffered with injury and loss of confidence in the 1978 World Cup. There was disappointment four years later when the defence failed the Brazilian team and he was carrying another injury in 1986. Still managed to score 66 goals in 88 internationals. Had a couple of seasons in Italy with Udinese before returning to Flamengo. Scored 728 goals in his career. Quick, unselfish midfield-attacker with fine control, precision passing and tireless application.

Dino Zoff: Italy's most-capped player with 112 appearances. A goalkeeper with commanding presence and quick reflexes, he enjoyed a lengthy career culminating with the captaincy of his country in their 1982 World Cup success. Established an international record of being unbeaten in 1,143 minutes of play and 903 minutes in the league. Played for Udinese, Mantova, Napoli and Juventus until he was over 40. Coached the Italian Olympic squad and then Juventus.

Dino Zoff retired at the top, still one of the world's greatest goalkeepers.

Attendances

As far as Football League attendances are concerned, official figures were not issued on a regular basis until after the Second World War, which coincided with the start of the boom period in which more than a million spectators watched a full programme of matches every Saturday. The peak was reached in 1948–49 when a total of 41,271,414 spectators was recorded for the 1,848 games in the four divisions. Since that season crowds have fallen gradually, with one or two exceptions and with a plateau in the 1960s, until a modest but significant rise was achieved four seasons in succession from 1986–87.

The low was reached in 1985–86 when only 16,488,577 watched the 2,028 League games. Interestingly enough, in the year of the League's half-centenary, 1938, figures were officially given as 28,132,933 for 1,848 matches. Only one other season was recorded before the War: in 1906–07, with only two divisions operating, the final aggregate was 10,929,000 and the average crowd was 14,380 – a similar figure to that of 1963–64 when 28,535,022 watched the League programme. The 1937–38 average was 15,225 and in 1989–90 it was 9,550 from a total attendance figure of 19,445,442.

Attendances for the FA Cup have followed a similar pattern to the League, as have those for the League Cup, now known as the Rumbelows Cup.

In Scotland, the revival in crowd figures began earlier than in England and in 1988–89 the Premier Division had an average attendance of 15,708 per game, which represented a rise of 13 per cent on the previous season. The comparable figures for the First Division in the Football League averaged out at 20,552.

The move towards all-seater stadia, which has been accelerated by FIFA's declaration that no World Cup matches for the 1994 tournament can be played in front of standing spectators, will affect many clubs abroad as well as in the Football League. Of the well-known clubs, only the San Siro Stadium in Milan, which is shared by AC Milan and Internazionale, has complete seating. Even the Bernabeu Stadium in Madrid, the home of Real Madrid, seats only a third of its capacity.

UEFA intend to follow the lead given by FIFA so their three major competitions at club level, as well as the European Championship, will eventually be played in all-seater grounds. It seems almost inevitable that all professional tournaments at the highest level will be devoid of standing spectators by the end of the century.

The massed Liverpool fans celebrate another triumph.

Awards

There are numerous awards for players and clubs, the longest standing of which is the Football Writers' Association annual nomination for the Footballer of the Year among Football League players, first awarded in 1947–48.

The French weekly, *France Football*, conducts an annual poll among football writers in various European countries to decide the European Footballer of the Year. Stanley Matthews, who had been the recipient of the first FWA award in 1947–48, became the first player honoured in Europe in 1956. The Dutch player Johan Cruyff became the first to win the European Footballer of the Year trophy on three occasions: 1971, 1973 and 1974. His feat was emulated by Michel Platini of France, who won it three years in succession from 1983 to 1985. *France Football* has also established the Golden Boots Award to the top goalscorer in Europe each year since 1967–68.

In 1974 the Professional Footballers' Association organised a series of annual awards for the Player of the Year, Young Player of the Year and a Merit Award.

In Scotland the Player of the Year award began in 1965, with Billy McNeill as the first winner; and the Scottish PFA began their annual nomination for Player of the Year and Young Player in 1978. Northern Ireland has its own similar events.

Managers have also been recognised. In 1965–66 Bell's Scotch Whisky began an annual award for the Manager of the Year. At the same time they gave monthly awards for each division of the Football League. This sponsored honour was taken over by Barclays Bank in 1988–89. Liverpool managers have dominated the honour: Bill Shankly was Manager of the Year in 1973; Bob Paisley in 1976, 1977, 1979, 1980, 1982 and 1983; Joe Fagan 1984 and Kenny Dalglish 1986, 1988 and 1990.

In addition to their managerial awards, Barclays have introduced a Young Eagle award which has monthly regional winners and also an annual recognition, plus the Barclays Bank service to football award.

South America and Africa have similar awards, organised respectively from 1971 and 1970. The South American poll is organised by the Venezuelan newspaper *El Mundo* and Elias Figueroa of Chile achieved a hat-trick of awards from 1974 to 1976. Zico of Brazil equalled this achievement in 1977, 1981 and 1982.

In 1978 the Italian sports magazine *Guerin Sportivo* organised the first of its annual Bravo awards, for the best young player under the age of 24. Jimmy Case of Liverpool was the initial winner.

David Platt, the PFA Player of the Year in 1990, went on to perform superbly in the World Cup in Italy.

Broadcasting and Television

Radio broadcasts of matches and, more significantly, the televising of games have introduced huge audiences who would otherwise have no live connection with football. The first match to be broadcast on the radio was the First Division game between Arsenal and Sheffield United at Highbury on 22 January 1927. The following week the FA Cup tie between Corinthians and Newcastle United became the second to be relayed.

Subsequently, there were arguments over the advisability of broadcasting commentaries, and both the Football League and Football Association had periods when they banned them, fearful of an effect on attendances at matches. However, the first FA Cup final to be covered on radio was Cardiff City v Arsenal on 23 April 1927 and, though it was relayed the following year, in 1929 no fee could be agreed between the Football Association and the British Broadcasting Corporation. But the BBC managed to provide a live commentary by setting up outside the ground and employing numerous commentators who shuttled between Wembley and the broadcasting point.

Two Italian soldiers watch over a commentator in the 1934 World Cup to ensure he avoids using any cliches.

In 1930, agreement was reached with the FA for the Cup final only and the League refused any coverage of their games. There was some relaxation of the total ban in the late 1930s, while during the War and immediately after it, there were more broadcasts until a further total ban was imposed on League games in 1951.

It did not last and the situation now is almost one of complete freedom for BBC radio and the myriad independent and local stations as well as telephone services to cover matches live. Thus live football is available to a wider listening public than ever before.

As far as television is concerned, there is now an acceptance that live coverage is no longer a threat to attendance at matches, provided that it does not coincide with a full programme of games. But it was fiercely resisted for many years, particularly when attendances were falling almost annually.

Oddly enough, Arsenal probably staged the first match for which any parts were shown either live or in recorded form for television. The live occasion was a practice game at Highbury on Thursday 16 September 1937. At the time the BBC studios and transmitter were at nearby Alexandra Palace. But on 29 August 1936 there had been a televised film taken by the BBC of Arsenal's game with Everton, but the first live transmission had actually come from Germany three months later.

The first FA Cup final at which any part of the game was televised was the 1937 final between Sunderland and Preston North End. After the War, the first BBC televised game was the Barnet v Tooting match on 19 October 1946. The first post-War FA Cup final covered from start to finish was the Charlton Athletic v Burnley game on 26 April 1947. In those days, the Cup final was played when most other Football League clubs were completing normal fixtures. The first FA Cup tie other than the final to be televised was a fifth round tie between Charlton and Blackburn Rovers on 8 February 1947.

By the time that floodlighting had become more acceptable to the footballing authorities, there were numerous friendly matches covered by television, with the ITA also coming into the picture from 1955. In Scotland, the first half of the Clyde v Aberdeen game was screened on 3 September. In 1960 an agreement was made between the Football League and ITA for the screening of a number of matches in

Brian Moore and Ian St John during the first League game to be televised live.

a deal worth £150,000. But, though the Blackpool v Bolton Wanderers match was screened on 10 September 1960 with an evening kick-off, the concept collapsed almost immediately when some of the leading clubs refused to participate.

However, in August 1964 the Football League agreed to allow BBC 2 to screen edited highlights of one League game per week, screened two hours after the match. The first recorded match was Liverpool v Arsenal on 22 August. This broke the previously strong resolve of the footballing authorities and from then on it has been a process of ever increasing coverage.

The current situation favours more live games than recorded highlights, although these are still featured. At present, the IBA has an agreement to show certain Football League and League Cup games, the BBC to broadcast the FA Cup. Satellite and cable television stations are also chasing other competitions.

The televising of football matches not only brings in millions of viewers, it provides millions in revenue. It almost caused the break-up of the Football League in 1988 before an ITV contract for four years worth £44 million was agreed upon. This was followed by the BBC and BSB agreeing a £30 million deal for the FA Cup over five years, as well as some England international games.

The 52 matches of the 1990 World Cup finals in Italy were watched in well over a hundred countries and produced a viewing audience of 31 billion. Televising football has become big business.

John Motson in short sleeves in Mexico – a nice change from the more usual sheepskin coat in rainy Manchester.

Managers and Coaches

Attempting to define the role of either a manager or a coach in modern football is a complicated task. What in Britain is largely considered to be a manager might well be called a coach or even a trainer elsewhere in the world. But, even in these islands, the function of the manager has changed as the game has evolved.

One fact which has not altered is the strength of character required of the individual ideally suited to become a successful manager. That was as true of Herbert Chapman in the years between the Wars as it has been in more recent times with Brian Clough, survivor of more than 1,000 games in charge of five clubs.

Chapman made his name with Huddersfield Town in the early 1920s before moving to Arsenal and earning similar fame at Highbury. Both clubs achieved a hat-trick of League Championships, though Chapman had moved on from Huddersfield before they completed their trio and had died before he could see his fine work at Highbury turn into another trio of titles. But even in Chapman's heyday, a manager was regarded as a secretary–manager at many clubs. His administrative duties far outweighed his attention to matters concerning the team and its playing ability. But in those days players were given every opportunity to express themselves with a natural approach which has certainly been lost in the subsequent decades.

After success at Lincoln, Watford and Aston Villa, Graham Taylor assumed the toughest job in British football – manager of England.

This, of course, ignores the development of the game and the spread of its popularity around the globe. Players from Britain travelled abroad and introduced football wherever they settled. They were the first coaches. Others with a deeper understanding of the game were able to make a living from teaching it. Today, coaching is an industry on a worldwide scale.

Internationally the first 'manager' to stamp his authority was undoubtedly Vittorio Pozzo, the Italian who led his country to victory in the 1934 and 1938 World Cup competitions. Even he had studied the game in England and was able to combine the best features of this version with the Latin style of his native-born players to the best effect.

While coaches were raising standards overseas, the traditional insularity of the British had closed many minds to thoughts of employing managers at top level. The reasoning went that as Britain had developed the game, there was no need for further education. The experience of one man typified the attitude which eventually led us into serious trouble on the field.

Jimmy Hogan was never an outstanding player himself, but he was a dedicated thinker with the knack of teaching others. He was responsible for developing the game in Austria and Hungary, based on the short passing style so beloved by the Scots at the time. He was the brains behind the Austrian 'Wunderteam' of the 1930s. Alas, back home, he was just one of a number of coaches who had established worthy reputations abroad but were snubbed and treated with little respect for their abilities. He did, however, have the last laugh. In his 70th year he was a guest of the Hungarians at

In a notoriously insecure occupation, Brian Clough is the longest serving manager in modern British football.

Wembley when they beat England 6–3 in 1953.

Hogan was not alone. George Raynor masterminded Sweden's efforts in Olympic and World Cup tournaments in the years after the Second World War, but could scarcely find employment on the occasions when he returned home. But the Hungarian massacre had its effect. Gradually it became obvious that the pupils had become the new masters and there was something to be learned from them.

The theory that the best players do not make the best managers has often been borne out. Possessing outstanding talent as a player is no sure way of being able to pass on that expertise to others. But the average player has frequently had to study his own game and that of his colleagues and opponents to compete at the highest level.

Another formula for success has been the dynasty system epitomised at Liverpool in the last three decades. From Bill Shankly, to Bob Paisley, even briefly with Joe Fagan and then Kenny Dalglish, the Merseyside club has developed its own managerial talent.

The Germans did it internationally with Otto Nerz, Sepp Herberger and Helmut Schoen. Against that you have the experience of Brazil, who have had World Cup success but have never achieved it with the same coach. They have relied on the individual brilliance of their players. And this is where the real weakness of coaching lies. It can improve average players, but it cannot produce flair and style. In fact it might even stifle expression. The outstanding teams of any era are simply those with better players than their opponents.

But respect for a manager has brought clubs enormous success. Jock Stein led Celtic to a record nine successive Championships in Scotland. Brian Clough achieved Championships with two different teams, Derby County and Nottingham Forest. A combination of fear and incentive, the stick and the carrot, can often push human beings to surprising achievements, and it applies as much to football as to anything.

Franz Beckenbauer followed in a long line of successful German managers when he won the World Cup in 1990.

Tactics

Tactics have been likened to beauty – they lie in the eye of the beholder. But since it became normal around the 1860s for only 11 players to be used in a team, there have been trends brought about by circumstances which cannot be ignored in the evolution of play. Even in the early years of Queen's Park, they were still using 15 players and the Sheffield Association often preferred 12, while others had reduced the numbers to 11. But there was a predominance of forwards at the expense of defenders, since the object of the game was to score more goals than the opposing side; something which modern critics might consider to have become a lost art.

When England met Scotland for the first official international in 1872, they lined up with a goalkeeper, one back who was known as a threequarter-back, one half-back and eight forwards. The Scots employed a goalkeeper, two backs, two half-backs and six forwards. In practice, everyone except the goalkeeper was disposed to attack.

There was no actual teamwork. Players merely backed up their colleagues if they lost possession or overran the ball. Dribbling the ball became the first tactic and the teams with the better individuals invariably won. Although dribbling has become something which has been discarded in the modern era, the better teams are still composed of the better players.

It was the Scots who developed the art of passing the ball before being tackled, and they generally held the ascendancy over England in international fixtures. So much was this so that the English adopted the same tactics and imported many Scottish players.

Defences had to be strengthened to combat the new system and several teams experimented with three half-backs, though still retaining one full-back. Cambridge University, where the initial rules were drawn up, were one of the first to use a goalkeeper, two full-backs, three halves and five forwards around 1877. Wrexham used the same formula the following year when they beat Druids 1–0 in the Welsh Cup final. However, many other teams still persisted with six forwards and it was not until the middle 1880s that England first tried three half-backs against Scotland, who themselves followed suit in 1887.

It was Preston North End whose successful combination of the Scottish passing game with the stronger midfield area and defence led to their League and Cup double in 1889, when professionalism had been firmly established in England.

While the professionals were progressing, the amateurs looked to the Corinthians for inspiration and found it. They perfected the ability not only to pass the ball, but to draw an opponent and put the ball into space for a colleague to run onto.

The next change which affected team play came many years later from the offside law. From 1867 a player could be offside if fewer than three opponents were nearer their own goalline when the ball was last played. This encouraged defenders to move nearer the halfway line and stoppages for offside became incessant.

It is generally accepted that the man behind the perfection of the offside trap was Bill McCracken, the Newcastle United and Ireland international full-back. But in 1925 the Scottish FA proposed that a player could not be offside if two instead of three opponents were nearer their goalline when the ball was played. The ruling was adopted and the effect on goalscoring was dramatic. In 1924–25 a total of

Alf Ramsey's 'wingless wonders' took the world by storm in 1966 as tactics became more defensive.

Bobby Robson's tactical switches were sometimes forced on him, but in both 1986 and 1990 a better side emerged.

4,700 goals had been scored in the Football League alone; in the first season after the alteration the total rose by a third to 6,373. In order to prevent defences being overrun, the middle of three half-backs was withdrawn to line up with the two full-backs.

At the same time, there was a move to reinforce the midfield area now that one of the halves had virtually become a third full-back, so the two inside-forwards from the five attackers were withdrawn in front of the remaining half-backs. This developed as the 'WM' formation in the 1930s.

The next significant tactical switch was developed by the Hungarians and Brazilians in the 1950s but it should be stressed that variations on the 'WM' formation had been in existence long before this time, although they perfected it. Basically, the centre-forward was withdrawn into midfield, the two inside-forwards pushed up and were supported by wingers. Only one half-back remained, but there were now two central defenders to combat the twin strikers in a 4–2–4 formation.

From here the defensive trend has continued with the wingless 4–3–3 system which Alf Ramsey used successfully for England in the 1966 World Cup, then a 4–4–2 system where midfield areas became saturated. The Italians adopted the sweeper system where a free-back operated behind four defenders.

The two-legged system of European cup games has also influenced tactics and encouraged visiting teams to play defensively. There have been attempts to break away from the defensive stranglehold, notably the Dutch concept of 'total' football in the 1970s – all-out attack and all-out defence.

Disasters

The European Cup final of 1985 turned to horror when 39 died at Heysel.

The worst crowd disaster in the history of British football occurred on 15 April 1989 at Hillsborough, Sheffield, when 94 Liverpool fans were crushed to death and 170 injured following a surge of spectators at the FA Cup semi-final between Liverpool and Nottingham Forest. Another spectator subsequently died as a result of injuries sustained. The supporters were trapped against steel fencing at the front of the Leppings Lane terracing at Sheffield Wednesday's ground at the start of the game.

In 1985 Liverpool had been involved in an entirely different tragedy at the European Cup final against Juventus. On 29 May at the Heysel Stadium in Brussels, 39 died, most of them Italians, and a further 437 were injured after a retaining wall collapsed under pressure from Juventus fans who were being chased by Liverpool followers.

The same year, and less than three weeks earlier, 56 spectators had died and 200 were hurt when fire raged through the wooden stand at Valley Parade, Bradford on 11 May during the game between Bradford City and Lincoln City.

One of the world's worst sporting catastrophes took place on 24 May 1964 in Lima, Peru, at an Olympic qualifying game between Peru and Argentina. Two minutes from the end of the game, Pazos, the Uruguayan referee, disallowed a goal which would have given Peru an equaliser. The crowd erupted and police fired shots into the air. Unfortunately, this produced a stampede for the exits among the 45,000 crowd and resulted in 318 deaths and 500 serious injuries.

Overall, the worst incident occurred on 20 October 1982 at the UEFA Cup match between Spartak Moscow and Haarlem at the Lenin Stadium in Moscow. It was originally thought that 69 people had been killed and 100 injured at the end of the game when spectators had tried to leave hurriedly while others were attempting to surge back following a late Spartak goal. In July 1989 it was reported that 340 Soviet fans had lost their lives, though other accounts give the death toll as 100.

Two other large-scale tragedies involved matches in Buenos Aires, Argentina and Katmandu, Nepal.

In June 1968, 74 died and 150 were hurt when some supporters threw lighted newspaper torches onto rival fans at the River Plate v Boca Juniors match and caused a panic-inspired stampede. There were over 100 deaths and 300 injuries during the Nepal v Bangladesh game in March 1988 when a hailstorm caused spectators to rush for the exits.

There have been other similar disasters in Egypt, Turkey, Mexico, Colombia, Greece, Indonesia and elsewhere.

At the Rangers v Celtic match on 2 January 1971 at Ibrox Park in Glasgow, fans were already leaving the ground down a staircase when Rangers equalised near the end of the game. Many turned back to resume their places only to be swept away by others coming down. It resulted in 66 deaths and 100 injuries. This disaster led to the 1975 Safety of Sports Grounds legislation. Ibrox had previously experienced another tragedy in 1902. On 5 April, part of the West Stand collapsed leaving 25 dead and 500 injured. The match, which had been in progress for about 10 minutes, was resumed after a half-hour delay and finished 1–1, but was subsequently declared unofficial.

On 9 March 1946, there were 33 deaths and more than 400 injuries after barriers collapsed under pressure from a capacity crowd at the FA Cup quarter-final between Bolton Wanderers and Stoke City at Burnden Park. The match went ahead and many thousands in the ground were unaware of what had happened.

Air crashes have accounted for many deaths among players and officials. On 6 February 1958, eight Manchester United players, three officials and eight sports journalists, including Frank Swift the former Manchester City goalkeeper, lost their lives in the Munich disaster. The players were: Geoff Bent, Roger Byrne, Eddie Colman, Duncan Edwards (who died later), Mark Jones, David Pegg, Tommy Taylor and Billy Whelan. Walter Crickmer (secretary), Tom Curry (trainer) and Herbert Whalley (coach) were the other United casualties.

On 14 May 1949, the entire Torino team, including eight internationals, were killed when the aircraft taking them from a game in Lisbon crashed at Superga, near Turin. The toll of 28 included all the club's reserve players, manager, trainer and coach.

The 18-strong squad of the Peruvian club Alianza were killed, as well as eight officials and several youth players, when their plane crashed into the sea off Lima on 9 December 1987. Chile's Green Cross club were involved in a fatal crash which wiped out all on board on 3 April 1961; Bolivia's The Strongest lost their entire squad of 19 players in the Andes on 26 September 1969; and 15 Surinamese players who played for various Dutch clubs lost their lives on 7 June 1989.

In the summer of 1969, two qualifying games for the 1970 World Cup between Honduras and El Salvador were the catalyst to ignite the hostility existing between the two countries. It resulted in a four-day war, although there were no incidents involving the players during these two games or the play-off in Mexico City.

Liverpool fans were again involved in the Hillsborough disaster of 1989, an event which finally changed attitudes to crowd safety.

Fines and Suspensions

Throughout the history of the organised game, clubs and players have had fines and suspensions imposed on them for a variety of misdemeanours. Sanctions have also been taken against various countries by FIFA or the confederations under their control for similar infringements on and off the field.

Chelsea received a Football League record £75,000 fine following serious crowd trouble at the play-off with Middlesbrough on 28 May 1988. Several clubs have had their grounds closed as a result of similar problems. Millwall's ground The Den, for example, was suspended from use for various reasons in 1920, 1934, 1950 and 1978.

There were fines of £50,000 and £20,000 imposed on Norwich City and Arsenal respectively for a free-for-all involving most of the players on both sides at the end of the First Division game between the two teams at Highbury on 4 November 1989.

Enoch West was one of eight players permanently suspended by the Football Association for fixing the result of the Manchester United v Liverpool match on 2 April 1915. A number of these suspensions were lifted after the First World War in recognition of war service, but West's remained until 1945 when he was 62 years old.

Oddly enough, on 3 April 1915, Billy Cook of Oldham Athletic refused to leave the field when ordered off by the referee after 55 minutes of the game with Middlesbrough, who were leading 4–1 at the time. The result of the match was allowed to stand. Cook was suspended for 12 months and Oldham missed winning the League Championship by two points.

Frank Barson, who played for Barnsley, Aston Villa, Manchester United, Watford, Hartlepools, Wigan Borough and Rhyl Athletic, was suspended at least 12 times between 1914–15 and 1930–31, the longest single period being for seven months.

Mark Dennis, playing for Queen's Park Rangers against Tottenham Hotspur on 14 November 1987, was sent off for the 11th time in his career. He had also received 64 cautions in 10 seasons. He was suspended for 53 days, subsequently commuted to eight matches. A year later, he was sent off in a reserve match and fined £1,000. Earlier, Kevin Keegan (Liverpool) and Billy Bremner (Leeds United) had been banned for five weeks (10 matches) after being sent off in the Charity Shield at Wembley in August 1974.

Irregularities over registrations and payments have also cost clubs dearly. Points have been deducted from Football League clubs who have

The police intervene as Arsenal and Norwich players scuffle at the end of their game in November 1989.

Having flung away their shirts, Keegan and Bremner (right) march off the pitch during the 1974 Charity Shield.

fielded unregistered players. Peterborough United were fined £500 and had 19 points deducted for alleged financial irregularities in November 1967. It cost them their place in the Third Division.

Port Vale were fined £4,000 for alleged breaches of regulations concerning payment to players and were expelled from the League at the end of the following season, but they were allowed to seek re-election and were voted back in.

Sunderland were one of the first clubs to have points taken away from their record following the faulty registration of a player. Ted Doig played for them against West Bromwich Albion on 20 September 1890 before the 14 days since his registration had elapsed, as was then required. They were fined £50 and had two points deducted.

Clubs have also been fined for fielding weakened teams, but Exeter City were fined £5,000 for failing to fulfil a Fourth Division fixture at Scunthorpe United on 2 April 1974 because they had nine players suffering from influenza. The game was not played and Scunthorpe were awarded the points.

Clubs who have experienced crowd disorder at European Cup games have been fined and forced to play either on neutral grounds or behind closed doors. Others have been banned for varying periods. After the Heysel Stadium tragedy in Belgium in 1985, Liverpool withdrew from European matches and all English clubs were banned indefinitely. The ban was lifted in 1990, except for Liverpool who had to serve a further term.

FIFA have been strict in dealing with countries who have erred. They suspended Mexico from all competitive games, including the 1990 World Cup, for fielding over-age players in a youth tournament, while Chile were excluded from the 1994 World Cup after an incident in the World Cup game with Brazil on 3 September 1989. The Chilean goalkeeper Roberto Rojas alleged that a fire-cracker thrown from the crowd at the Maracana Stadium in Rio had struck him. He left the field with blood on his face and the rest of the Chilean team walked off. However, it was subsequently revealed that the missile had not hit Rojas. The game was awarded 2–0 to Brazil, Rojas was suspended for life and Chile received their ban.

The Football Association in England has, in recent years, made an increased effort to improve the disciplinary record of clubs by keeping a points system for sendings-off and cautions, imposing fines on those with poor records.

UEFA came down heavily on Hearts for another reason. They increased their fine by £37,000 to £93,000 during 1988–89 after the club had infringed the rules covering the televising of their UEFA Cup quarter-final.

Managers have not escaped punishment. Fines and banishment from the touchline at matches have been frequent in recent years. Jim McLean the Dundee United manager was fined £4,000 and banned for three years from the touchline in April 1988 following a Scottish Cup semi-final incident.

As a result of allegations of bribery and corruption in 1960, extensive investigations later revealed that money had changed hands to fix League matches. In 1963, 10 contemporary and former players, including internationals, were given jail sentences and suspended for varying periods.

In 1990, Swindon Town were relegated from Division One to Division Three following admitted charges of irregular payments to players and officials. They were reinstated in Division Two on appeal to the Football Association. Some officials received fines and suspensions.

Floodlit Football

Floodlights have extended the scope of the game beyond the confines of daylight time and enabled more and more matches to be played during the season. Efforts to instal apparatus were first made in the latter part of last century, but little or no encouragement was received from official sources.

It is generally agreed that the first match by artificial lighting took place at Bramall Lane, Sheffield on 14 October 1878. The participating teams were chosen by the Sheffield Association from local clubs. Electricity was still something of a novelty in the provinces and the game attracted an official attendance of 12,000 with some 7,000 others gaining access without paying. A measure of the interest aroused by the game can be judged from the fact that the 1878 FA Cup final had drawn just 5,000 spectators. The electric power came from two portable engines driving dynamos, one at each end of the ground with the lamps erected on 30-foot high wooden towers.

Another match, in London on 4 November, was less successful and received bad publicity. However, in Manchester on 26 February 1889, flares were used to illuminate a game for the Hyde Colliery Explosion Fund and raised £140. In the late 1920s the idea was revived, but the FA prohibited member clubs from taking part in such games.

The pressures to allow floodlights to be used grew in the early 1950s. Grudging acceptance was given for floodlit friendlies, and in February 1955 the FA decided that, as from 1955–56, replays of FA Cup ties up to and including the second round might be played under lights.

In June 1955, the Football League allowed postponed League games to be played under lights if both clubs were in agreement. Subsequently the floodgates opened for football under artificial lighting and there is no restriction for any competition except that the lights have to be up to a certain standard for play to be allowed.

Without artificial illumination there would have been no implementation of European cup matches, while the growth of international games at national level in the World Cup and other competitions would have been stifled and the game itself restricted in its development. England had already played a fixture under floodlights in the United States when they met the USA in New York on 8 June 1953 before they had the lights switched on for the first time at Wembley for part of the game with Spain on 30 November 1955, as fog had reduced visibility in the second half.

Floodlit matches are now an essential part of a crowded football season.

Injuries and Fatalities

For a body-contact sport, football has a record of comparatively few fatalities and serious injuries, given the extent of the game over the world in more than a century of competitive football.

Sam Wynne was probably the first player to die during a first-class fixture. This Bury full-back collapsed when taking a free kick against Sheffield United at Bramall Lane on 30 April 1927. He died in the dressing room and a post mortem revealed that he had been suffering from pneumonia. The match was abandoned and replayed. Wynne had previously established himself in the records for another reason. Playing for Oldham Athletic against Manchester United on 6 October 1923, he scored two goals for his own side from a free kick and a penalty, but also put through two own goals.

There had already been a number of injuries which subsequently resulted in death. James Dunlop, playing for St Mirren against Abercorn on New Year's Day 1892, fell and cut his knee on a piece of glass. He contracted tetanus and died 10 days later of the infection. A similar tragedy involved Di Jones during a pre-season practice game with Manchester City in August 1902. He sustained a cut on his leg, it turned septic and he died a week later.

William Walker of Leith Athletic died after being accidentally kicked in the stomach during a Division Two game against Vale of Leven on 12 January 1907. During a friendly match with Partick Thistle on Christmas Day 1909, James Main of Hibernian suffered internal injuries and died in hospital four days later.

Bob Benson was heavily engaged on munitions during the First World War and had not played for almost a year when he went to watch Arsenal play Reading on 19 February 1916. Arsenal were a man short and Benson volunteered to play. But, feeling unwell, he left the field and died in the dressing room due to a burst blood vessel.

James Williamson, the Dumbarton goalkeeper, died from his injuries received in a match against Rangers on 12 November 1921 and, two years later on 5 November, Tom Butler a full-back with Port Vale broke his arm against Clapton Orient. Septic poisoning set in and he died six days later.

John Thomson, Celtic's goalkeeper, died seven hours after fracturing his skull in a collision with Sam English of Rangers during a Division One match on 5 September 1931, while Sam Raleigh the Gillingham centre-forward died shortly after suffering concussion in the game with Brighton and Hove Albion on 1 December 1934.

Jim Thorpe, the Sunderland goalkeeper, died a few days after a game against Chelsea on 1 February 1936. His death was due to diabetes, although a coroner's jury found that the illness had been accelerated by the game. Nowadays, diabetes is no hazard. Gary Mabbutt of Tottenham and England is a sufferer but plays without difficulty.

Improved medical knowledge, treatment and surgical skills have wiped away many of the threats to life that injuries produced in the past. However, on 14 February 1953, Derek Dooley, the Sheffield Wednesday centre-forward, fractured a leg in a match against Preston North End. Gangrene quickly set in and the limb had to be amputated.

Ledger Ritson, the Leyton Orient full-back fractured a leg in a game against Northampton Town on 11 September 1948. He recovered but in 1950 it was discovered that a bone had become diseased and the limb was amputated.

Two players were struck by lightning and killed during the Army Cup final replay at Aldershot's Command Ground in April 1948. In another incident, a player died the day after the pitch was struck during an FA Amateur Cup game between Highgate United and Enfield in February 1967. Four others were seriously hurt but recovered. Lightning also killed John White, the Tottenham Hotspur inside-forward, on a London golf course in July 1964.

Injuries which, in earlier times, might have caused the end of a footballer's career have been treated successfully. Denis Smith of Stoke City is believed to be one of the most injured players in history. He retired in 1981 after suffering 12 major and six minor fractures in a 12-year span.

In more recent times, players have used legal methods to seek compensation for injuries suffered at the hands of an opponent. In most instances these have either been dropped or settled out of court, but history was made in April 1988 when Chris Kamara of Swindon Town was fined £1,200 and ordered to pay £250 compensation by magistrates at Shrewsbury after pleading guilty to causing grievous bodily harm to Shrewsbury's Jim Melrose two months earlier. He became the first English professional footballer to be punished in a criminal court for an incident on a football field.

Football Pools

Football pools came into operation in the 1920s and the man behind the idea was a bookmaker called Frederick Jervis. His company launched the first football coupon with eight homes, four aways and a short list of other specially selected games. Prizes were offered for correct solutions. National newspapers were also organising similar competitions with a top prize of £1,000 for forecasting 12 results. It proved so popular that prize money increased until the law stepped in and forbade any newspaper offering rewards for the result of a future event.

But Jervis's Pools carried on and attracted the attention of three wireless telegraphists employed by the Commercial Cable Company in Southern Ireland. All three, Colin Askham, Bill Hughes and John Moores, had been Post Office messenger boys together in Manchester. Moores had been careful with his money, working overtime and running a sports equipment firm on the side. He had saved £1,000, while both Hughes and Askham had £200 each in the bank. They decided to form their own pool, but, not wishing to risk losing their jobs, had to think of a way of remaining anonymous.

Askham had been born Colin Henry Littlewood, but adopted the name of the aunt who had raised him after the death of his parents. Thus Littlewoods Pools were born and began operations in February 1923 from a small office on the top floor at No 38 Church Street, Liverpool. In the first week they sent out 4,000 coupons, distributed outside football grounds in the Manchester area. Just 35 came back and takings amounted to only £4 7s 6d (£4.37$\frac{1}{2}$). A further attempt in Hull, with 10,000 coupons, brought just one return, though it was suspected that the rest had been dumped.

Further disappointments followed. The three organisers were £600 each out of pocket. Moores

Noel Edmonds presents a happy group of pools winners with their cheque – and a bowler hat and umbrella for a rainy day.

offered to buy out his two partners by repaying the £200 they had both lost. They accepted and he recruited his wife, brother Cecil and his sister to help him. Gradually, they paid off the printing bills and improved the business. By 1926 they were receiving 20,000 coupons every week and the weekly turnover was £2,000. They survived a prosecution for alleged contravention of the Ready Money Betting Act on appeal and, by 1932, at the age of 35, John Moores was a millionaire. The rest is history.

But, although the pools prospered and other firms started their own pools, like Vernons, Soccer, Zetters, Empire, Shermans, Copes, Murphys and Strangs, the football authorities were completely opposed to the gambling and betting on their fixtures, which the pools companies profited from without any payment to them.

To stop the pools companies, the Football League hierarchy astounded the football world by resorting to the sensational move of scrapping sets of their original scheduled fixtures and substituting others, which were kept so secret that the League did not even notify the clubs until it was too late for the pools companies to print the new matches on their coupons. Clubs were informed by telephone on Thursday afternoons where and against whom they were to play two days later. The wholesale upheaval this caused officials and players had to be witnessed to be believed.

The operation was put into effect in the spring of 1936. Clubs were guaranteed their home fixture, as originally planned, but the identity of their opponents was kept quiet until two days before the match. The new arrangement began on 7 March. For example, Arsenal were due to play Brentford, but Huddersfield actually played at Highbury. Brentford went to Leeds United instead of Wolves, who were switched to Blackburn. And so it went on throughout the four divisions of the League.

For three weeks this system operated, but the scheme failed as the pools managed to issue makeshift coupons. In fact, it caused untold problems for the League who then had to sort out the mess they had made for themselves by rearranging fixtures. Swansea Town, for instance, had to play a Division Two match at Plymouth on Good Friday, 10 April and another, a day later, at Newcastle. That remains the longest distance in the League's history ever travelled by a team in fulfilling two fixtures within 24 hours.

Fortunately, an agreement was reached between the two parties and the pools firms paid the League

A pools coupon marked with eight lucky crosses that brought a York woman £266,981 in 1980.

an annual fee, increased from time to time, for the use of the fixtures. In 1959 the Football League won a test case for copyright of their fixture list. The pools companies agreed to pay for their use.

Even the Second World War did not prevent betting on pools. After a short break, while wartime regional football was organised, the government agreed to restart the pools. The firms amalgamated as the Unity Pool, with the coupons printed in newspapers to save newsprint, in what was a complete turnround from the original ruling against them. But it took another court ruling in 1945 to once again ban the publication of coupons in newspapers.

One pools firm, Strangs of Edinburgh, had not joined Unity Pool and introduced the first treble chance selection. But, when Unity was disbanded in 1946, the major companies reverted to their own identity and took up the treble chance idea for themselves.

Pay and Transfers

Once professionalism was legalised in England in 1885, payments to players varied and it was not until 1901 that a maximum wage rule was imposed at £4 a week. Subsequent increases brought the upper level to £20 in 1958. In 1947, a minimum wage was agreed for the first time, but the most significant change came about with the abolition of the maximum in 1961. It is generally considered that Johnny Haynes of Fulham was the first player in England to be paid as much as £100 a week. By the late 1980s, it was not uncommon for leading First Division players to be paid as much as £100,000 a year and wage bills for clubs could easily top £1 million.

By the same token, transfer fees for players have escalated. There were similar attempts to restrict them, but these met with much less success than the wage controls. The reason for this was simple: the clubs benefited from a no-restriction system of buying and selling players. In 1899, the Football Association suggested to the Football League that there should be a transfer limit of £10. Nothing came of this but in 1908 a larger figure of £350 was imposed, but it lasted only four months. The first four-figure transfer came when Middlesbrough paid £1,000 to Sunderland for Alf Common in February 1905. The present record for domestic football stands at £2.3 million for Gary Pallister's move from, ironically, Middlesbrough to Manchester United in September 1989.

Manchester United's £2.3 million signing Gary Pallister emerged as one of the most solid defenders in England in 1990.

Alf Common was the first £1,000 transfer in 1905. It was money well spent as he saved Middlesbrough from relegation.

Chris Waddle in action against Rumania in May 1985 winning his second cap. In 1989 he became the most expensive British player ever when Marseille paid £4.5 million for his services.

In 1922, the Football League decided that all transfer fees should be treated as private and confidential. The figures published in the press were usually estimated and often the two clubs involved might provide differing figures on the same transfer.

The George Eastham case in 1963 resulted in a declaration being made which said that the system of retaining a player after the expiration of his contract was not binding in law. However, this was overcome by the insertion of an option clause in the player's contract. The next move came in 1978 when the Football League agreed to freedom of contract for players. However, the player's registration remains with the club for whom he last played, until such time as he signs for another.

Worldwide transfer fees have also risen sharply in recent years, but again the amounts quoted are frequently estimated. Diego Maradona's transfer from Barcelona to Napoli in 1984 was originally put at £6.9 million, but over the years this has been scaled down to a lower figure. Roberto Baggio's transfer from Fiorentina to Juventus has been estimated at almost £8 million, making him the world's most expensive player. The World Cup sent prices even higher for those who performed well.

Referees and Linesmen

Referees were not mentioned in the Football Association Laws until 1881; previously umpires had controlled matches. But, in the formative years of the game in the early part of the 19th century, matches were often played without even one umpire. The conduct of the players produced sufficient self-control. But the development of organised football, and with it the keenness of competition, required a single authority on the field to administer the Laws.

Umpires had invariably been supplied by each team. They were first mentioned in the Laws in 1874 by which time the FA Cup competition was already in its third year. Referees certainly became more common because in 1878 there was the first recorded use of a referee's whistle.

In 1891 umpires were finally abolished and replaced by referees and linesmen. The Football League had been in operation for three years and in 1888 had fixed the fee for a referee at 10s 6d per match ($52\frac{1}{2}$p). In 1989 the match fees had risen to £100 for a referee and £50 for a linesman.

The establishment of the referee meant that he was the sole authority on the field of play with no official appeal against his decision. His function is to enforce the Laws and decide any disputed point, keep a complete record of the game, retain powers of discretion over infringements of the Laws and generally control the operation of a match. The function of the linesman is to indicate when the ball has gone out of play, or if a player is offside and assist the referee in his duties of administering the Laws of the Game.

There have been a number of occasions when interested parties have put forward the idea of two referees. It was first seriously suggested in 1935 at the AGM of the Football League but was rejected by

George Courtney, one of the most respected referees in Britain and the world.

31 votes to 18. However, it was tried out in an international between England and The Rest at West Bromwich on 27 March 1935, as well as at a match between the Football League XI and West Bromwich Albion on 8 May. A further attempt to put the idea into practice failed at the League's AGM in 1937, but in the light of increasing problems of discipline on the field in modern times, it shows no sign of being put to rest forever.

In 1950 another important step was taken when the International Board decided that referees for international matches should be drawn from neutral countries rather than those involved in the specific game in question. In friendlies it is often agreed between the opposing teams for a local official to take charge.

Sponsorship

The obvious advantages of sponsorship are often seen only as giving short-term financial assistance. This applies to the sponsoring of either clubs or competitions. Usually, the longer the association with a sponsor, the more successful and satisfactory it is. For example, the Rothmans Football Yearbook has been published annually since 1970.

One of the earliest competitions to be sponsored for Football League clubs was the Watney Cup, sponsored by the brewery of the same name. It was a pre-season tournament organised among teams which had scored most goals in the four divisions. The introduction of the penalty shoot-out was one of its lasting innovations.

At the same time, there was another competition in existence involving teams from England and Scotland, sponsored as the Texaco Cup during the 1970–71 season. The fuel crisis in the mid-1970s saw the withdrawal of this financial injection, although the competition carried on as the Anglo-Scottish Cup for one season.

Scotland's equivalent of the Watney Cup was the Drybrough Cup and it survived longer, but only after a break of four years in the mid-1970s, having started operations in 1971.

The Football League had already engaged in sponsorship with the National Dairy Council turning the League Cup into the Milk Cup, when Canon (UK) Ltd clinched a £3 million deal to put their name on the Football League itself for three years from 1983. It was then the biggest sponsorship of its kind in the sporting world.

At the same time, shirt advertising was agreed for televised soccer in exchange for 10 live matches on the screen for the 1983–84 season. This proved a significant breakthrough and led to clubs gaining a variety of sponsors.

Canon might well have continued their sponsorship but for the events at the Heysel Stadium in 1985. However, they were succeeded briefly by the *Today* newspaper. Unfortunately, the media in general seemed not unnaturally averse to giving a rival organisation such publicity and the sponsorship was withdrawn in 1987 to be replaced by Barclays Bank. Their initial three-year deal included a clause that gave them an option to withdraw after a year if there was an increase in hooliganism among fans. The sponsorship was worth £4.55 million.

Arsenal v Spurs in the League? Or is it Holsten v JVC in the Barclays League?

Scotland, too, has enjoyed similar support for the Scottish League, first through Fine Fare and then B & Q, while Bell's and latterly Skol have sponsored the Scottish League Cup. More recently, Tennents gave their name to the Scottish FA Cup.

World Cup Finals

URUGUAY 1930

Pool 1
France 4, Mexico 1. Argentina 1, France 0. Chile 3, Mexico 0. Chile 1, France 0. Argentina 6, Mexico 3. Argentina 3, Chile 1.

	P	*W*	*D*	*L*	*F*	*A*	*Pts*
Argentina	3	3	0	0	10	4	6
Chile	3	2	0	1	5	3	4
France	3	1	0	2	4	3	2
Mexico	3	0	0	3	4	13	0

Pool 2
Yugoslavia 2, Brazil 1. Yugoslavia 4, Bolivia 0. Brazil 4, Bolivia 0.

	P	*W*	*D*	*L*	*F*	*A*	*Pts*
Yugoslavia	2	2	0	0	6	1	4
Brazil	2	1	0	1	5	2	2
Bolivia	2	0	0	2	0	8	0

Pool 3
Rumania 3, Peru 1. Uruguay 1, Peru 0. Uruguay 4, Rumania 0.

	P	*W*	*D*	*L*	*F*	*A*	*Pts*
Uruguay	2	2	0	0	5	0	4
Rumania	2	1	0	1	3	5	2
Peru	2	0	0	2	1	4	0

Pool 4
United States 3, Belgium 0. United States 3, Paraguay 0. Paraguay 1, Belgium 0.

	P	*W*	*D*	*L*	*F*	*A*	*Pts*
United States	2	2	0	0	6	0	4
Paraguay	2	1	0	1	1	3	2
Belgium	2	0	0	2	0	4	0

Semi-finals
Argentina 6, United States 1. Uruguay 6, Yugoslavia 1.

Final (Montevideo, 30 July 1930, att. 90,000): Uruguay (1) 4, Argentina (2) 2.
Uruguay: Ballesteros, Nasazzi, Mascheroni, Andrade, Fernandez, Gestido, Dorado, Scarone, Castro, Cea, Iriarte. *Scorers:* Dorado, Cea, Iriarte, Castro.
Argentina: Botasso, Della Tore, Paternoster,

The Uruguay team which won the first World Cup in 1930.

A poster from the World Cup of 1934. For the second time, the home side was victorious.

Evaristo J., Monti, Suarez, Peucelle, Varallo, Stabile, Ferreira, Evaristo M. *Scorers:* Peucelle, Stabile.
Leading scorer: Stabile (Argentina) 8.

ITALY 1934

First Round
Italy 7, United States 1. Czechoslovakia 2, Rumania 1. Germany 5, Belgium 2. Austria 3, France 2. Spain 3, Brazil 1. Switzerland 3, Netherlands 2. Sweden 3, Argentina 2. Hungary 4, Egypt 2.
Second Round
Germany 2, Sweden 1. Austria 2, Hungary 1. Italy 1, Spain 1. Italy 1, Spain 0 (replay). Czechoslovakia 3, Switzerland 2.
Semi-finals
Czechoslovakia 3, Germany 1 (in Rome). Italy 1, Austria 0 (in Milan).
Third Place Play-off
Germany 3, Austria 2 (in Naples).
Final (Rome, 10 June 1934, att. 50,000): Italy (0) (1) 2, Czechoslovakia (0) (1) 1 (aet).
Italy: Combi, Monzeglio, Allemandi, Ferraris IV, Monti, Bertolini, Guaita, Meazza, Schiavio, Ferrari, Orsi. *Scorers:* Orsi, Schiavio.
Czechoslovakia: Planicka, Zenisek, Ctyroky, Kostalek, Cambal, Krcil, Junek, Svoboda, Sobotka, Nejedly, Puc. *Scorer:* Puc.
Leading scorers: Schiavio (Italy), Nejedly (Czechoslovakia), Conen (Germany) 4 each.

FRANCE 1938

First Round
Switzerland 1, Germany 1. Switzerland 4, Germany 2 (replay). Cuba 3, Rumania 3. Cuba 2, Rumania 1 (replay). Hungary 6, Dutch East Indies 0. France 3, Belgium 1. Czechoslovakia 3, Netherlands 0. Brazil 6, Poland 5. Italy 2, Norway 1.
Second Round
Sweden 8, Cuba 0. Hungary 2, Switzerland 0. Italy 3, France 1. Brazil 1, Czechoslovakia 1. Brazil 2, Czechoslovakia 1 (replay).
Semi-finals
Italy 2, Brazil 1 (in Marseilles). Hungary 5, Sweden 1 (in Paris).
Third Place Play-off
Brazil 4, Sweden 2 (in Bordeaux).
Final (Paris, 19 June 1938, att. 45,000): Italy (3) 4, Hungary (1) 2.
Italy: Olivieri, Foni, Rava, Serantoni, Andreolo, Locatelli, Biavati, Meazza, Piola, Ferrari, Colaussi. *Scorers:* Colaussi 2, Piola 2.
Hungary: Szabo, Polgar, Biro, Szalay, Szucs, Lazar, Sas, Vincze, Sarosi, Szengeller, Titkos. *Scorers:* Titkos, Sarosi.
Leading scorer: Leonidas (Brazil) 8.

Action from the final of the 1938 competition in which Italy retained their title.

BRAZIL 1950

Pool 1

Brazil 4, Mexico 0. Yugoslavia 3, Switzerland 0. Yugoslavia 4, Mexico 1. Brazil 2, Switzerland 2. Brazil 2, Yugoslavia 0. Switzerland 2, Mexico 1.

	P	*W*	*D*	*L*	*F*	*A*	*Pts*
Brazil	3	2	1	0	8	2	5
Yugoslavia	3	2	0	1	7	3	4
Switzerland	3	1	1	1	4	6	3
Mexico	3	0	0	3	2	10	0

Pool 2

Spain 3, United States 1. England 2, Chile 0. United States 1, England 0. Spain 2, Chile 0. Spain 1, England 0. Chile 5, United States 2.

	P	*W*	*D*	*L*	*F*	*A*	*Pts*
Spain	3	3	0	0	6	1	6
England	3	1	0	2	2	2	2
Chile	3	1	0	2	5	6	2
United States	3	1	0	2	4	8	2

Pool 3

Sweden 3, Italy 2. Sweden 2, Paraguay 2. Italy 2, Paraguay 0.

	P	*W*	*D*	*L*	*F*	*A*	*Pts*
Sweden	2	1	1	0	5	4	3
Italy	2	1	0	1	4	3	2
Paraguay	2	0	1	1	2	4	1

Pool 4

Uruguay 8, Bolivia 0.

Morlock slides home Germany's first goal in the 1954 final, reversing their defeat by Hungary in the first round.

Final Pool (Replaced knockout system)

Uruguay 2, Spain 2. Brazil 7, Sweden 1. Uruguay 3, Sweden 2. Brazil 6, Spain 1. Sweden 3, Spain 1.

The last game in the final pool (below) also happened, by chance, to be the decider.

Uruguay (0) 2, Brazil (0) 1 (Rio de Janeiro, 16 July 1950, att. 199,850)

Uruguay: Maspoli, Matthias Gonzalez, Tejera, Gambetta, Varela, Andrade, Ghiggia, Perez, Miguez, Schiaffino, Moran. *Scorers:* Schiaffino, Ghiggia.

Brazil: Barbosa, Augusto, Juvenal, Bauer, Danilo, Bigode, Friaca, Zizinho, Ademir, Jair, Chico. *Scorer:* Friaca.

	P	*W*	*D*	*L*	*F*	*A*	*Pts*
Uruguay	3	2	1	0	7	5	5
Brazil	3	2	0	1	14	4	4
Sweden	3	1	0	2	6	11	2
Spain	3	0	1	2	4	11	1

Leading scorer: Ademir (Brazil) 7.

SWITZERLAND 1954

Group 1

Yugoslavia 1, France 0. Brazil 5, Mexico 0. France 3, Mexico 2. Brazil 1, Yugoslavia 1.

	P	*W*	*D*	*L*	*F*	*A*	*Pts*
Brazil	2	1	1	0	6	1	3
Yugoslavia	2	1	1	0	2	1	3
France	2	1	0	1	3	3	2
Mexico	2	0	0	2	2	8	0

Group 2

Hungary 9, Korea 0. West Germany 4, Turkey 1. Hungary 8, West Germany 3. Turkey 7, Korea 0.

	P	*W*	*D*	*L*	*F*	*A*	*Pts*
Hungary	2	2	0	0	17	3	4
West Germany	2	1	0	1	7	9	2
Turkey	2	1	0	1	8	4	2
Korea	2	0	0	2	0	16	0

Play-off: West Germany 7, Turkey 2.

Group 3

Austria 1, Scotland 0. Uruguay 2, Czechoslovakia 0. Austria 5, Czechoslovakia 0. Uruguay 7, Scotland 0.

	P	*W*	*D*	*L*	*F*	*A*	*Pts*
Uruguay	2	2	0	0	9	0	4
Austria	2	2	0	0	6	0	4
Czechoslovakia	2	0	0	2	0	7	0
Scotland	2	0	0	2	0	8	0

Group 4
England 4, Belgium 4. England 2, Switzerland 0. Switzerland 2, Italy 1. Italy 4, Belgium 1.

	P	W	D	L	F	A	Pts
England	2	1	1	0	6	4	3
Italy	2	1	0	1	5	3	2
Switzerland	2	1	0	1	2	3	2
Belgium	2	0	1	1	5	8	1

Play-off: Switzerland 4, Italy 1.

Quarter-finals
West Germany 2, Yugoslavia 0. Hungary 4, Brazil 2. Austria 7, Switzerland 5. Uruguay 4, England 2.

Semi-finals
West Germany 6, Austria 1 (in Basle). Hungary 4, Uruguay 2 (in Lausanne).

Third Place Play-off
Austria 3, Uruguay 1 (in Zurich).

Final (Berne, 4 July 1954, att. 60,000): West Germany (2) 3, Hungary (2) 2.
West Germany: Turek, Posipal, Kohlmeyer, Eckel, Liebrich, Mai, Rahn, Morlock, Walter O., Walter F., Schaefer. *Scorers:* Morlock, Rahn 2.
Hungary: Grosics, Buzansky, Lantos, Bozsik, Lorant, Zakarias, Czibor, Kocsis, Hidegkuti, Puskas, Toth J. *Scorers:* Puskas, Czibor.
Leading scorer: Kocsis (Hungary) 11.

SWEDEN 1958

Group 1
West Germany 3, Argentina 1. Northern Ireland 1, Czechoslovakia 0. West Germany 2, Czechoslovakia 2. Argentina 3, Northern Ireland 1. West Germany 2, Northern Ireland 2. Czechoslovakia 6, Argentina 1.

	P	W	D	L	F	A	Pts
West Germany	3	1	2	0	7	5	4
Czechoslovakia	3	1	1	1	8	4	3
Northern Ireland	3	1	1	1	4	5	3
Argentina	3	1	0	2	5	10	2

Play-off: Northern Ireland 2, Czechoslovakia 1.

Group 2
France 7, Paraguay 3. Yugoslavia 1, Scotland 1. Yugoslavia 3, France 2. Paraguay 3, Scotland 2. France 2, Scotland 1. Yugoslavia 3, Paraguay 3.

	P	W	D	L	F	A	Pts
France	3	2	0	1	11	7	4
Yugoslavia	3	1	2	0	7	6	4
Paraguay	3	1	1	1	9	12	3
Scotland	3	0	1	2	4	6	1

The Swedish goalkeeper Svensson clears from Pele in the 1958 final, but Pele scored twice in Brazil's 5–2 triumph.

Group 3
Sweden 3, Mexico 0. Hungary 1, Wales 1. Wales 1, Mexico 1. Sweden 2, Hungary 1. Sweden 0, Wales 0. Hungary 4, Mexico 0.

	P	W	D	L	F	A	Pts
Sweden	3	2	1	0	5	1	5
Hungary	3	1	1	1	6	3	3
Wales	3	0	3	0	2	2	3
Mexico	3	0	1	2	1	8	1

Play-off: Wales 2, Hungary 1.

Group 4
England 2, USSR 2. Brazil 3, Austria 0. England 0, Brazil 0. USSR 2, Austria 0. Brazil 2, USSR 0. England 2, Austria 2.

	P	W	D	L	F	A	Pts
Brazil	3	2	1	0	5	0	5
England	3	0	3	0	4	4	3
USSR	3	1	1	1	4	4	3
Austria	3	0	1	2	2	7	1

Play-off: USSR 1, England 0

Quarter-finals
France 4, Northern Ireland 0. West Germany 1, Yugoslavia 0. Sweden 2, USSR 0. Brazil 1, Wales 0.

Semi-finals
Brazil 5, France 2 (in Stockholm). Sweden 3, West Germany 1 (in Gothenburg).
Third Place Play-off
France 6, West Germany 3 (in Gothenburg).
Final (Stockholm, 29 June 1958, att. 49,737):
Brazil (2) 5, Sweden (1) 2.
Brazil: Gilmar, Santos D., Santos N., Zito, Bellini, Orlando, Garrincha, Didi, Vava, Pele, Zagalo.
Scorers: Vava 2, Pele 2, Zagalo.
Sweden: Svensson, Bergmark, Axbom, Boerjesson, Gustavsson, Parling, Hamrin, Gren, Simonsson, Liedholm, Skoglund. *Scorers:* Liedholm, Simonsson.
Leading scorer: Fontaine (France) 13.

CHILE 1962

Group 1
Uruguay 2, Colombia 1. USSR 2, Yugoslavia 0. Yugoslavia 3, Uruguay 1. USSR 4, Colombia 4. USSR 2, Uruguay 1. Yugoslavia 5, Colombia 0.

	P	*W*	*D*	*L*	*F*	*A*	*Pts*
USSR	3	2	1	0	8	5	5
Yugoslavia	3	2	0	1	8	3	4
Uruguay	3	1	0	2	4	6	2
Colombia	3	0	1	2	5	11	1

Group 2
Chile 3, Switzerland 1. West Germany 0, Italy 0. Chile 2, Italy 0. West Germany 2, Switzerland 1. West Germany 2, Chile 0. Italy 3, Switzerland 0.

	P	*W*	*D*	*L*	*F*	*A*	*Pts*
West Germany	3	2	1	0	4	1	5
Chile	3	2	0	1	5	3	4
Italy	3	1	1	1	3	2	3
Switzerland	3	0	0	3	2	8	0

Group 3
Brazil 2, Mexico 0. Czechoslovakia 1, Spain 0. Brazil 0, Czechoslovakia 0. Spain 1, Mexico 0. Brazil 2, Spain 1. Mexico 3, Czechoslovakia 1.

	P	*W*	*D*	*L*	*F*	*A*	*Pts*
Brazil	3	2	1	0	4	1	5
Czechoslovakia	3	1	1	1	2	3	3
Mexico	3	1	0	2	3	4	2
Spain	3	1	0	2	2	3	2

Group 4
Argentina 1, Bulgaria 0. Hungary 2, England 1. England 3, Argentina 1. Hungary 6, Bulgaria 1. Argentina 0, Hungary 0. England 0, Bulgaria 0.

	P	*W*	*D*	*L*	*F*	*A*	*Pts*
Hungary	3	2	1	0	8	2	5
England	3	1	1	1	4	3	3
Argentina	3	1	1	1	2	3	3
Bulgaria	3	0	1	2	1	7	1

Quarter-finals
Yugoslavia 1, West Germany 0. Brazil 3, England 1. Chile 2, USSR 1. Czechoslovakia 1, Hungary 0.
Semi-finals
Brazil 4, Chile 2 (in Santiago). Czechoslovakia 3, Yugoslavia 1 (in Vina del Mar).
Third Place Play-off
Chile 1, Yugoslavia 0 (in Santiago).
Final (Santiago, 17 June 1962, att. 68,679):
Brazil (1) 3, Czechoslovakia (1) 1.
Brazil: Gilmar, Santos, D., Mauro, Zozimo, Santos N., Zito, Didi, Garrincha, Vava, Amarildo, Zagalo. *Scorers:* Amarildo, Zito, Vava.
Czechoslovakia: Schroiff, Tichy, Novak, Pluskal, Popluhar, Masopust, Pospichal, Scherer, Kvasniak, Kadraba, Jelinek. *Scorer:* Masopust.
Leading scorer: Jerkovic (Yugoslavia) 5.

ENGLAND 1966

Group 1
England 0, Uruguay 0. France 1, Mexico 1. Uruguay 2, France 1. England 2, Mexico 0. Uruguay 0, Mexico 0. England 2, France 0.

	P	*W*	*D*	*L*	*F*	*A*	*Pts*
England	3	2	1	0	4	0	5
Uruguay	3	1	2	0	2	1	4
Mexico	3	0	2	1	1	3	2
France	3	0	1	2	2	5	1

Group 2
West Germany 5, Switzerland 0. Argentina 2, Spain 1. Spain 2, Switzerland 1. Argentina 0, West Germany 0. Argentina 2, Switzerland 0. West Germany 2, Spain 1.

	P	*W*	*D*	*L*	*F*	*A*	*Pts*
West Germany	3	2	1	0	7	1	5
Argentina	3	2	1	0	4	1	5
Spain	3	1	0	2	4	5	2
Switzerland	3	0	0	3	1	9	0

Group 3
Brazil 2, Bulgaria 0. Portugal 3, Hungary 1. Hungary 3, Brazil 1. Portugal 3, Bulgaria 0. Portugal 3, Brazil 1. Hungary 3, Bulgaria 1.

Held's shot is blocked by Fulham's George Cohen in the 1966 final.

	P	*W*	*D*	*L*	*F*	*A*	*Pts*
Portugal	3	3	0	0	9	2	6
Hungary	3	2	0	1	7	5	4
Brazil	3	1	0	2	4	6	2
Bulgaria	3	0	0	3	1	8	0

Group 4
USSR 3, North Korea 0. Italy 2, Chile 0. Chile 1, North Korea 1. USSR 1, Italy 0. North Korea 1, Italy 0. USSR 2, Chile 1.

	P	*W*	*D*	*L*	*F*	*A*	*Pts*
USSR	3	3	0	0	6	1	6
North Korea	3	1	1	1	2	4	3
Italy	3	1	0	2	2	2	2
Chile	3	0	1	2	2	5	1

Quarter-finals
England 1, Argentina 0. West Germany 4, Uruguay 0. Portugal 5, North Korea 3. USSR 2, Hungary 1.
Semi-finals
West Germany 2, USSR 1 (at Goodison Park). England 2, Portugal 1 (at Wembley).
Third Place Play-off
Portugal 2, USSR 1 (at Wembley).
Final (Wembley, 30 July 1966, att. 93,802):
England (1) (2) 4, West Germany (1) (2) 2 (aet).
England: Banks, Cohen, Wilson, Stiles, Charlton J., Moore, Ball, Hurst, Hunt, Charlton R., Peters.
Scorers: Hurst 3, Peters.
West Germany: Tilkowski, Hottges, Schulz, Weber, Schnellinger, Haller, Beckenbauer, Overath, Seeler, Held, Emmerich. *Scorers:* Haller, Weber.
Leading scorer: Eusebio (Portugal) 9.

Did it cross the line? Roger Hunt thinks so as England score a third goal in extra time. Hurst settled the matter with the last kick of the game and England were World Champions.

MEXICO 1970

Group A
Mexico 0, USSR 0. Belgium 3, El Salvador 0. USSR 4, Belgium 1. Mexico 4, El Salvador 0. USSR 2, El Salvador 0. Belgium 0, Mexico 1.

	P	*W*	*D*	*L*	*F*	*A*	*Pts*
USSR	3	2	1	0	6	1	5
Mexico	3	2	1	0	5	0	5
Belgium	3	1	0	2	4	5	2
El Salvador	3	0	0	3	0	9	0

Group B
Uruguay 2, Israel 0. Italy 1, Sweden 0. Uruguay 0, Italy 0. Israel 1, Sweden 1. Sweden 1, Uruguay 0. Israel 0, Italy 0.

	P	*W*	*D*	*L*	*F*	*A*	*Pts*
Italy	3	1	2	0	1	0	4
Uruguay	3	1	1	1	2	1	3
Sweden	3	1	1	1	2	2	3
Israel	3	0	2	1	1	3	2

Group C
England 1, Rumania 0. Brazil 4, Czechoslovakia 1. Rumania 2, Czechoslovakia 1. Brazil 1, England 0. Brazil 3, Rumania 2. England 1, Czechoslovakia 0.

	P	*W*	*D*	*L*	*F*	*A*	*Pts*
Brazil	3	3	0	0	8	3	6
England	3	2	0	1	2	1	4
Rumania	3	1	0	2	4	5	2
Czechoslovakia	3	0	0	3	2	7	0

Group D
Peru 3, Bulgaria 2. West Germany 2, Morocco 1. Peru 3, Morocco 0. West Germany 5, Bulgaria 2. West Germany 3, Peru 1. Bulgaria 1, Morocco 1.

	P	*W*	*D*	*L*	*F*	*A*	*Pts*
West Germany	3	3	0	0	10	4	6
Peru	3	2	0	1	7	5	4
Bulgaria	3	0	1	2	5	9	1
Morocco	3	0	1	2	2	6	1

Quarter-finals
Uruguay 1, USSR 0. Italy 4, Mexico 1. Brazil 4, Peru 2. West Germany 3, England 2.
Semi-finals
Italy 4, West Germany 3 (in Mexico City). Brazil 3, Uruguay 1 (in Guadalajara).

Carlos Alberto, surrounded by delighted fans, hoists the Jules Rimet Trophy which Brazil won outright in 1970.

Third Place Play-off
West Germany 1, Uruguay 0 (in Mexico City).
Final (Mexico City, 21 June 1970, att. 107,412):
Brazil (1) 4, Italy (1) 1.
Brazil: Felix, Carlos Alberto, Brito, Piazza, Everaldo, Gerson, Clodoaldo, Jairzinho, Pele, Tostao, Rivelino. *Scorers:* Pele, Gerson, Jairzinho, Carlos Alberto.
Italy: Albertosi, Burgnich, Cera, Rosato, Facchetti, Bertini (Juliano), Riva, Domenghini, Mazzola, De Sisti, Boninsegna (Rivera). *Scorer:* Boninsegna.
Leading scorer: Muller (West Germany) 10.

WEST GERMANY 1974

Group 1
West Germany 1, Chile 0. East Germany 2, Australia 0. West Germany 3, Australia 0. East Germany 1, Chile 1. East Germany 1, West Germany 0. Chile 0, Australia 0.

Franz Beckenbauer was the inspiration of the victorious German side of 1974.

	P	*W*	*D*	*L*	*F*	*A*	*Pts*
East Germany	3	2	1	0	4	1	5
West Germany	3	2	0	1	4	1	4
Chile	3	0	2	1	1	2	2
Australia	3	0	1	2	0	5	1

Group 2
Brazil 0, Yugoslavia 0. Scotland 2, Zaire 0. Brazil 0, Scotland 0. Yugoslavia 9, Zaire 0. Scotland 1, Yugoslavia 1. Brazil 3, Zaire 0.

	P	*W*	*D*	*L*	*F*	*A*	*Pts*
Yugoslavia	3	1	2	0	10	1	4
Brazil	3	1	2	0	3	0	4
Scotland	3	1	2	0	3	1	4
Zaire	3	0	0	3	0	14	0

Group 3
Netherlands 2, Uruguay 0. Sweden 0, Bulgaria 0. Netherlands 0, Sweden 0. Bulgaria 1, Uruguay 1. Netherlands 4, Bulgaria 1. Sweden 3, Uruguay 0.

	P	*W*	*D*	*L*	*F*	*A*	*Pts*
Netherlands	3	2	1	0	6	1	5
Sweden	3	1	2	0	3	0	4
Bulgaria	3	0	2	1	2	5	2
Uruguay	3	0	1	2	1	6	1

Group 4
Italy 3, Haiti 1. Poland 3, Argentina 2. Argentina 1, Italy 1. Poland 7, Haiti 0. Argentina 4, Haiti 1. Poland 2, Italy 1.

	P	*W*	*D*	*L*	*F*	*A*	*Pts*
Poland	3	3	0	0	12	3	6
Argentina	3	1	1	1	7	5	3
Italy	3	1	1	1	5	4	3
Haiti	3	0	0	3	2	14	0

Group A
Brazil 1, East Germany 0. Netherlands 4, Argentina 0. Netherlands 2, East Germany 0. Brazil 2, Argentina 1. Netherlands 2, Brazil 0. Argentina 1, East Germany 1.

	P	*W*	*D*	*L*	*F*	*A*	*Pts*
Netherlands	3	3	0	0	8	0	6
Brazil	3	2	0	1	3	3	4
East Germany	3	0	1	2	1	4	1
Argentina	3	0	1	2	2	7	1

Group B
Poland 1, Sweden 0. West Germany 2, Yugoslavia 0. Poland 2, Yugoslavia 1. West Germany 4, Sweden 2. Sweden 2, Yugoslavia 1. West Germany 1, Poland 0.

Johan Cruyff was unable to help the Dutch to victory in the 1974 final. His side conceded only one goal to get there.

	P	*W*	*D*	*L*	*F*	*A*	*Pts*
West Germany	3	3	0	0	7	2	6
Poland	3	2	0	1	3	2	4
Sweden	3	1	0	2	4	6	2
Yugoslavia	3	0	0	3	2	6	0

Third Place Play-off
Poland 1, Brazil 0 (in Munich).
Final (Munich, 7 July 1974, att. 77,833): West Germany (2) 2, Netherlands (1) 1.
West Germany: Maier, Vogts, Schwarzenbeck, Beckenbauer, Breitner, Bonhof, Hoeness, Overath, Grabowski, Muller, Holzenbein. *Scorers:* Breitner (pen), Muller.
Netherlands: Jongbloed, Suurbier, Rijsbergen (De Jong), Haan, Krol, Jansen, Van Hanegem, Neeskens, Rep, Cruyff, Rensenbrink (Van der Kerkhof R.) *Scorer:* Neeskens (pen).
Leading scorer: Lato (Poland) 7.

ARGENTINA 1978

Group 1
Italy 2, France 1. Argentina 2, Hungary 1. Italy 3, Hungary 1. Argentina 2, France 1. France 3, Hungary 1. Italy 1, Argentina 0.

	P	*W*	*D*	*L*	*F*	*A*	*Pts*
Italy	3	3	0	0	6	2	6
Argentina	3	2	0	1	4	3	4
France	3	1	0	2	5	5	2
Hungary	3	0	0	3	3	8	0

Group 2
West Germany 0, Poland 0. Tunisia 3, Mexico 1. Poland 1, Tunisia 0. West Germany 6, Mexico 0. Poland 3, Mexico 1. West Germany 0, Tunisia 0.

	P	*W*	*D*	*L*	*F*	*A*	*Pts*
Poland	3	2	1	0	4	1	5
West Germany	3	1	2	0	6	0	4
Tunisia	3	1	1	1	3	2	3
Mexico	3	0	0	3	2	12	0

Group 3
Austria 2, Spain 1. Brazil 1, Sweden 1. Austria 1, Sweden 0. Brazil 0, Spain 0. Spain 1, Sweden 0. Brazil 1, Austria 0.

	P	*W*	*D*	*L*	*F*	*A*	*Pts*
Austria	3	2	0	1	3	2	4
Brazil	3	1	2	0	2	1	4
Spain	3	1	1	1	2	2	3
Sweden	3	0	1	2	1	3	1

Joe Jordan of Scotland leaps to challenge Dutch keeper Jongbloed in his side's greatest performance of 1978.

Ardiles and Neeskens battle for the ball in the 1978 final. Argentina won 3–1 on home territory.

Group 4
Peru 3, Scotland 1. Netherlands 3, Iran 0. Scotland 1, Iran 1. Netherlands 0, Peru 0. Peru 4, Iran 1. Scotland 3, Netherlands 2.

	P	*W*	*D*	*L*	*F*	*A*	*Pts*
Peru	3	2	1	0	7	2	5
Netherlands	3	1	1	1	5	3	3
Scotland	3	1	1	1	5	6	3
Iran	3	0	1	2	2	8	1

Group A
West Germany 0, Italy 0. Netherlands 5, Austria 1. Italy 1, Austria 0. Netherlands 2, West Germany 2. Netherlands 2, Italy 1. Austria 3, West Germany 2.

	P	*W*	*D*	*L*	*F*	*A*	*Pts*
Netherlands	3	2	1	0	9	4	5
Italy	3	1	1	1	2	2	3
West Germany	3	0	2	1	4	5	2
Austria	3	1	0	2	4	8	2

Group B
Brazil 3, Peru 0. Argentina 2, Poland 0. Poland 1, Peru 0. Argentina 0, Brazil 0. Brazil 3, Poland 1. Argentina 6, Peru 0.

	P	*W*	*D*	*L*	*F*	*A*	*Pts*
Argentina	3	2	1	0	8	0	5
Brazil	3	2	1	0	6	1	5
Poland	3	1	0	2	2	5	2
Peru	3	0	0	3	0	10	0

Third Place Play-off
Brazil 2, Italy 1 (in Buenos Aires).
Final (Buenos Aires, 25 June 1978, att. 77,000): Argentina (1) (1) 3, Netherlands (0) (1) 1 (aet).
Argentina: Fillol, Passarella, Olquin, Galvan L., Tarantini, Ardiles (Larrosa), Gallego, Ortiz (Houseman), Bertoni, Luque, Kempes. *Scorers:* Kempes 2, Bertoni.
Netherlands: Jongbloed, Krol, Poortvliet, Brandts, Jansen (Suurbier), Haan, Neeskens, Van der Kerkhof W., Rep (Nanninga), Van der Kerkhof R., Rensenbrink. *Scorer:* Nanninga.
Leading scorer: Kempes (Argentina) 6.

SPAIN 1982

Group 1
Italy 0, Poland 0. Peru 0, Cameroon 0. Italy 1,

Bryan Robson's flying header against France in 1982 was his and England's second goal.

Peru 1, Poland 0, Cameroon 0. Poland 5, Peru 1. Italy 1, Cameroon 1.

	P	W	D	L	F	A	Pts
Poland	3	1	2	0	5	1	4
Italy	3	0	3	0	2	2	3
Cameroon	3	0	3	0	1	1	3
Peru	3	0	2	1	2	6	2

Group 2
Algeria 2, West Germany 1. Austria 1, Chile 0. West Germany 4, Chile 1. Austria 2, Algeria 0. Algeria 3, Chile 2. West Germany 1, Austria 0.

	P	W	D	L	F	A	Pts
West Germany	3	2	0	1	6	3	4
Austria	3	2	0	1	3	1	4
Algeria	3	2	0	1	5	5	4
Chile	3	0	0	3	3	8	0

Group 3
Belgium 1, Argentina 0. Hungary 10, El Salvador 1. Argentina 4, Hungary 1. Belgium 1, El Salvador 0. Belgium 1, Hungary 1. Argentina 2, El Salvador 0.

	P	W	D	L	F	A	Pts
Belgium	3	2	1	0	3	1	5
Argentina	3	2	0	1	6	2	4
Hungary	3	1	1	1	12	6	3
El Salvador	3	0	0	3	1	13	0

Group 4
England 3, France 1. Czechoslovakia 1, Kuwait 1. England 2, Czechoslovakia 0. France 4, Kuwait 1. France 1, Czechoslovakia 1. England 1, Kuwait 0.

	P	W	D	L	F	A	Pts
England	3	3	0	0	6	1	6
France	3	1	1	1	6	5	3
Czechoslovakia	3	0	2	1	2	4	2
Kuwait	3	0	1	2	2	6	1

Group 5
Spain 1, Honduras 1. Northern Ireland 0, Yugoslavia 0. Spain 2, Yugoslavia 1. Honduras 1, Northern Ireland 1. Yugoslavia 1, Honduras 0. Northern Ireland 1, Spain 0.

	P	W	D	L	F	A	Pts
Northern Ireland	3	1	2	0	2	1	4
Spain	3	1	1	1	3	3	3
Yugoslavia	3	1	1	1	2	2	3
Honduras	3	0	2	1	2	3	2

Group 6
Brazil 2, USSR 1. Scotland 5, New Zealand 2. Brazil 4, Scotland 1. USSR 3, New Zealand 0. Scotland 2, USSR 2. Brazil 4, New Zealand 0.

	P	W	D	L	F	A	Pts
Brazil	3	3	0	0	10	2	6
USSR	3	1	1	1	6	4	3
Scotland	3	1	1	1	8	8	3
New Zealand	3	0	0	3	2	12	0

Group A
Poland 3, Belgium 0. USSR 1, Belgium 0. Poland 0, USSR 0.

	P	W	D	L	F	A	Pts
Poland	2	1	1	0	3	0	3
USSR	2	1	1	0	1	0	3
Belgium	2	0	0	2	0	4	0

Group B
West Germany 0, England 0. West Germany 2, Spain 1. Spain 0, England 0.

	P	W	D	L	F	A	Pts
West Germany	2	1	1	0	2	1	3
England	2	0	2	0	0	0	2
Spain	2	0	1	1	1	2	1

Group C
Italy 2, Argentina 1. Brazil 3, Argentina 1. Italy 3, Brazil 2.

	P	W	D	L	F	A	Pts
Italy	2	2	0	0	5	3	4
Brazil	2	1	0	1	5	4	2
Argentina	2	0	0	2	2	5	0

Group D
France 1, Austria 0. Northern Ireland 2, Austria 2. France 4, Northern Ireland 1.

	P	W	D	L	F	A	Pts
France	2	2	0	0	5	1	4
Austria	2	0	1	1	2	3	1
Northern Ireland	2	0	1	1	3	6	1

Semi-finals
Italy 2, Poland 0 (in Barcelona). West Germany 3, France 3 (in Seville) (*West Germany won 5–4 on penalties*).

Third Place Play-off
Poland 3, France 2 (in Alicante).

Final (Madrid, 11 July 1982, att. 90,089): Italy (0) 3, West Germany (0) 1.
Italy: Zoff, Bergomi, Cabrini, Collovati, Scirea, Gentile, Oriali, Tardelli, Conti, Graziani (Altobelli) (Causio), Rossi. *Scorers:* Rossi, Tardelli, Altobelli.
West Germany: Schumacher, Kaltz, Forster K-H., Stielike, Forster B., Breitner, Dremmler (Hrubesch), Littbarski, Briegel, Rummenigge (Muller), Fischer. *Scorer:* Breitner.
Leading scorer: Rossi (Italy) 6.

MEXICO 1986

Group A
Bulgaria 1, Italy 1. Argentina 3, South Korea 1. Italy 1, Argentina 1. South Korea 1, Bulgaria 1. Argentina 2, Bulgaria 0. South Korea 2, Italy 3.

	P	W	D	L	F	A	Pts
Argentina	3	2	1	0	6	2	5
Italy	3	1	2	0	5	4	4
Bulgaria	3	0	2	1	2	4	2
South Korea	3	0	1	2	4	7	1

Group B
Belgium 1, Mexico 2. Paraguay 1, Iraq 0. Mexico 1,

Briegel flattens Conti and Italy have a penalty in the 1982 final.

Argentina's Pumpido saves brilliantly at the post from a German shot.

Paraguay 1. Iraq 1, Belgium 2. Paraguay 2, Belgium 2. Iraq 0, Mexico 1.

	P	W	D	L	F	A	Pts
Mexico	3	2	1	0	4	2	5
Paraguay	3	1	2	0	4	3	4
Belgium	3	1	1	1	5	5	3
Iraq	3	0	0	3	1	4	0

Group C
USSR 6, Hungary 0. Canada 0, France 1. France 1, USSR 1. Hungary 2, Canada 0. Hungary 0, France 3. USSR 2, Canada 0.

	P	W	D	L	F	A	Pts
USSR	3	2	1	0	9	1	5
France	3	2	1	0	5	1	5
Hungary	3	1	0	2	2	9	2
Canada	3	0	0	3	0	5	0

Group D
Spain 0, Brazil 1. Algeria 1, Northern Ireland 1. Northern Ireland 1, Spain 2. Brazil 1, Algeria 0. Algeria 0, Spain 3. Northern Ireland 0, Brazil 3.

	P	W	D	L	F	A	Pts
Brazil	3	3	0	0	5	0	6
Spain	3	2	0	1	5	2	4
Northern Ireland	3	0	1	2	2	6	1
Algeria	3	0	1	2	1	5	1

Group E
Uruguay 1, West Germany 1. Scotland 0, Denmark 1. Denmark 6, Uruguay 1. West Germany 2, Scotland 1. Scotland 0, Uruguay 0. Denmark 2, West Germany 0.

	P	W	D	L	F	A	Pts
Denmark	3	3	0	0	9	1	6
West Germany	3	1	1	1	3	4	3
Uruguay	3	0	2	1	2	7	2
Scotland	3	0	1	2	1	3	1

Group F
Morocco 0, Poland 0. Portugal 1, England 0. England 0, Morocco 0. Poland 1, Portugal 0. England 3, Poland 0. Portugal 1, Morocco 3.

	P	W	D	L	F	A	Pts
Morocco	3	1	2	0	3	1	4
England	3	1	1	1	3	1	3
Poland	3	1	1	1	1	3	3
Portugal	3	1	0	2	2	4	2

Second Round
Mexico 2, Bulgaria 0. USSR 3, Belgium 4 (*aet, 90 mins 2–2*). Brazil 4, Poland 0. Argentina 1, Uruguay 0. France 2, Italy 0. Morocco 0, West Germany 1. England 3, Paraguay 0. Denmark 1, Spain 5.

Quarter-finals
Brazil 1, France 1 (*aet, 90 mins 1–1, France won 4–3 on penalties*). West Germany 0, Mexico 0 (*aet, West Germany won 4–1 on penalties*). Argentina 2, England 1. Spain 1, Belgium 1 (*aet, 90 mins 1–1, Belgium won 5–4 on penalties*).

Semi-finals
Argentina 2, Belgium 0 (in Mexico City). France 0, West Germany 2 (in Guadalajara).

Third Place Play-off
France 4, Belgium 2 (in Cuauhtemoc, Puebla).

Final (Mexico City, 29 June 1986, att. 114,580): Argentina (1) 3, West Germany (0) 2.
Argentina: Pumpido, Cuciuffo, Olarticoechea, Ruggeri, Brown, Giusti, Burruchaga (Trobbiani), Batista, Valdano, Maradona, Enrique. *Scorers:* Brown, Valdano, Burruchaga.
West Germany: Schumacher, Berthold, Briegel,

Jakobs, Forster K-H., Eder, Brehme, Matthaus, Allofs (Voller), Magath (Hoeness), Rummenigge.
Scorers: Rummenigge, Voller.
Leading scorer: Lineker (England) 6.

ITALY 1990

Group A

Italy 1, Austria 0. USA 1, Czechoslovakia 5.
Italy 1, USA 0. Austria 0, Czechoslovakia 1.
Austria 2, USA 1. Italy 2, Czechoslovakia 0.

	P	W	D	L	F	A	Pts
Italy	3	3	0	0	4	0	6
Czechoslovakia	3	2	0	1	6	3	4
Austria	3	1	0	2	2	3	2
USA	3	0	0	3	2	8	0

Group B

Argentina 0, Cameroon 1. USSR 0, Rumania 2.

'Toto' Schillaci of Italy was the unexpected star of Italia '90 and one of the few to set the competition alight.

Paul Gascoigne and Klaus Augenthaler clash in the midfield during the thrilling semi-final.

Argentina 2, USSR 0. Cameroon 2, Rumania 1.
Argentina 1, Rumania 1. Cameroon 0, USSR 4.

	P	W	D	L	F	A	Pts
Cameroon	3	2	0	1	3	5	4
Rumania	3	1	1	1	4	3	3
Argentina	3	1	1	1	3	2	3
USSR	3	1	0	2	4	4	2

Group C

Brazil 2, Sweden 1. Scotland 0, Costa Rica 1.
Brazil 1, Costa Rica 0. Sweden 1, Scotland 2.
Brazil 1, Scotland 0. Sweden 1, Costa Rica 2.

	P	W	D	L	F	A	Pts
Brazil	3	3	0	0	4	1	6
Costa Rica	3	2	0	1	3	2	4
Scotland	3	1	0	2	2	3	2
Sweden	3	0	0	3	3	6	0

Group D

UAE 0, Colombia 2. West Germany 4, Yugoslavia 1. Yugoslavia 1, Colombia 0. West Germany 5, UAE 1. West Germany 1, Colombia 1. Yugoslavia 4, UAE 1.

	P	W	D	L	F	A	Pts
West Germany	3	2	1	0	10	3	5
Yugoslavia	3	2	0	1	6	5	4
Colombia	3	1	1	1	3	2	3
UAE	3	0	0	3	2	11	0

Andreas Brehme scores from the penalty spot as the Germans beat an undistinguished Argentina in the 1990 final.

Group E
Belgium 2, South Korea 0. Uruguay 0, Spain 0. Belgium 3, Uruguay 1. South Korea 1, Spain 3. Belgium 1, Spain 2. South Korea 0, Uruguay 1.

	P	*W*	*D*	*L*	*F*	*A*	*Pts*
Spain	3	2	1	0	5	2	5
Belgium	3	2	0	1	6	3	4
Uruguay	3	1	1	1	2	3	3
South Korea	3	0	0	3	1	6	0

Group F
England 1, Republic of Ireland 1. Netherlands 1, Egypt 1. England 0, Netherlands 0. Republic of Ireland 0, Egypt 0. England 1, Egypt 0. Republic of Ireland 1, Netherlands 1.

	P	*W*	*D*	*L*	*F*	*A*	*Pts*
England	3	1	2	0	2	1	4
Republic of Ireland	3	0	3	0	2	2	3
Netherlands	3	0	3	0	2	2	3
Egypt	3	0	2	1	1	2	2

Second Round
Cameroon 2, Colombia 1 (*aet, 90 mins 0–0*). Czechoslovakia 4, Costa Rica 1. Brazil 0, Argentina 1. West Germany 2, Netherlands 1. Italy 2, Uruguay 0. Republic of Ireland 0, Rumania 0 (*aet, Republic of Ireland won 5–4 on penalties*). England 1, Belgium 0 (*aet, 90 mins 0–0*). Spain 1, Yugoslavia 2 (*aet, 90 mins 1–1*).
Quarter-finals
Italy 1, Republic of Ireland 0. Yugoslavia 0, Argentina 0 (*aet, Argentina won 3–2 on penalties*). Cameroon 2, England 3 (*aet, 90 mins 2–2*). Czechoslovakia 0, West Germany 1.
Semi-finals
Argentina 1, Italy 1 (in Naples) (*aet, 90 mins 1–1, Argentina won 4–3 on penalties*). West Germany 1, England 1 (in Turin) (*aet, 90 mins 1–1, West Germany won 4–3 on penalties*).
Third Place Play-off
Italy 2, England 1 (in Bari)
Final (Rome, 8 July 1990, att. 73,603):
West Germany (0) 1, Argentina (0) 0.
West Germany: Illgner, Brehme, Kohler, Augenthaler, Buchwald, Berthold (Reuter), Littbarski, Hassler, Matthaus, Voller, Klinsmann.
Scorer: Brehme (pen).
Argentina: Goycochea, Lorenzo, Serrizuela, Sensini, Ruggeri (Monzon), Simon, Basualdo, Burruchaga (Calderon), Maradona, Troglio, Dezotti (*Monzon and Dezotti sent off*).
Leading scorer: Schillaci (Italy) 6.

European Championship Finals

(formerly European Nations' Cup)

FRANCE 1960

Semi-finals
Yugoslavia 5, France 4 (in Paris). USSR 3, Czechoslovakia 0 (in Marseilles).
Third Place Play-off
Czechoslovakia 2, France 0 (in Marseilles).
Final (Paris, 10 July 1960, att. 17,996):
USSR (0) (1) 2, Yugoslavia (1) (1) 1 (aet).
USSR: Yashin, Tchekeli, Kroutikov, Voinov, Maslenkin, Netto, Metreveli, Ivanov, Ponedelnik, Bubukin, Meshki. *Scorers:* Metreveli, Ponedelnik.
Yugoslavia: Vidinic, Durkovic, Jusufi, Zanetic, Miladinovic, Perusic, Sekularac, Jerkovic, Galic, Matus, Kostic. *Scorer:* Netto og.

SPAIN 1964

Semi-finals
USSR 3, Denmark 0 (in Barcelona). Spain 2, Hungary 1 (in Madrid).
Third Place Play-off
Hungary 3, Denmark 1 (aet, in Barcelona).
Final (Madrid, 21 June 1964, att. 120,000):
Spain (1) 2, USSR (1) 1.
Spain: Iribar, Rivilla, Calleja, Fuste, Olivella, Zoco, Amancio, Pereda, Marcellino, Suarez, Lapetra. *Scorers:* Pereda, Marcellino.
USSR: Yashin, Chustikov, Mudrik, Voronin, Shesternjev, Anitchkin, Chislenko, Ivanov, Ponedelnik, Kornaev, Khusainov. *Scorer:* Khusainov.

ITALY 1968

Semi-finals
Yugoslavia 1, England 0 (in Florence). Italy 0, USSR 0 (in Naples) (*Italy won toss*).
Third Place Play-off
England 2, USSR 0 (in Rome).
Final (Rome, 8 June 1968, att. 75,000): Italy (0) (1) 1, Yugoslavia (1) (1) 1 (aet).
Italy: Zoff, Burgnich, Facchetti, Ferrini, Guarneri, Castano, Domenghini, Juliano, Anastasi, Lodetti, Prati. *Scorer:* Domenghini.
Yugoslavia: Pantelic, Fazlagic, Damjanovic, Pavlovic, Paunovic, Holcer, Petkovic, Acimovic, Musemic, Trivic, Dzajic. *Scorer:* Dzajic.
Replay (Rome, 10 June 1968, att. 60,000): Italy (2) 2, Yugoslavia (0) 0.
Italy: Zoff, Burgnich, Facchetti, Rosato, Guarneri, Salvadore, Domenghini, Mazzola, Anastasi, De Sisti, Riva. *Scorers:* Riva, Anastasi.
Yugoslavia: Pantelic, Fazlagic, Damjanovic, Pavlovic, Paunovic, Holcer, Hosic, Acimovic, Musemic, Trivic, Dzajic.

Yashin of the USSR clears from Kostic of Yugoslavia in the final of 1960.

Jean Tigana slots the ball between approaching Spanish defenders.

BELGIUM 1972

Semi-finals
USSR 1, Hungary 0 (in Brussels). West Germany 2, Belgium 1 (in Antwerp).
Third Place Play-off
Belgium 2, Hungary 1 (in Liege).
Final (Brussels, 18 June 1972, att. 43,437):
West Germany (1) 3, USSR (0) 0.
West Germany: Maier, Hottges, Schwarzenbeck, Beckenbauer, Breitner, Hoeness, Wimmer, Netzer, Heynckes, Muller, Kremers. *Scorers:* Muller 2, Wimmer.
USSR: Rudakov, Dzodzuashvili, Khurtislava, Kaplichny, Istomin, Troshkin, Kolotov, Baidachni, Konkov (Dolmatov), Banishevski (Kozinkievits), Onishenko.

YUGOSLAVIA 1976

Semi-finals
Czechoslovakia 3, Netherlands 1 (aet, in Zagreb). West Germany 4, Yugoslavia 2 (aet, in Belgrade).
Third Place Play-off
Netherlands 3, Yugoslavia 2 (aet, in Zagreb).
Final (Belgrade, 20 June 1976, att. 45,000):
Czechoslovakia (2) (2) 2, West Germany (1) (2) 2 (*aet, Czechoslovakia won 5–3 on penalties*).
Czechoslovakia: Viktor, Dobias (Vesely F.), Pivarnik, Ondrus, Capkovic, Gogh, Moder, Panenka, Svehlic (Jurkemik), Masny, Nehoda. *Scorers:* Svehlic, Dobias.
West Germany: Maier, Vogts, Beckenbauer, Schwarzenbeck, Dietz, Bonhof, Wimmer (Flohe), Muller D., Beer (Bongartz), Hoeness, Holzenbein. *Scorers:* Muller, Holzenbein.

ITALY 1980

Group 1
West Germany 1, Czechoslovakia 0. Greece 0, Netherlands 1. West Germany 3, Netherlands 2. Czechoslovakia 3, Greece 1. Czechoslovakia 1, Netherlands 1. West Germany 0, Greece 0.

	P	*W*	*D*	*L*	*F*	*A*	*Pts*
West Germany	3	2	1	0	4	2	5
Czechoslovakia	3	1	1	1	4	3	3
Netherlands	3	1	1	1	4	4	3
Greece	3	0	1	2	1	4	1

Group 2
Belgium 1, England 1. Spain 0, Italy 0. Spain 1, Belgium 2. Italy 1, England 0. England 2, Spain 1. Italy 0, Belgium 0

	P	*W*	*D*	*L*	*F*	*A*	*Pts*
Belgium	3	1	2	0	3	2	4
Italy	3	1	2	0	1	0	4
England	3	1	1	1	3	3	3
Spain	3	0	1	2	2	4	1

Third Place Play-off
Italy 1, Czechoslovakia 1 (aet, in Naples) (*Czechoslovakia won 9–8 on penalties*).
Final (Rome, 22 June 1980, att. 47,864):
West Germany (1) 2, Belgium (0) 1.
West Germany: Schumacher, Briegel, Forster K-H., Dietz, Schuster, Rummenigge, Hrubesch, Muller, Aloffs, Stielike, Kaltz. *Scorer:* Hrubesch 2.
Belgium: Pfaff, Gerets, Millecamps, Meeuws, Renquin, Cools, Van der Eycken, Van Moer, Mommens, Van der Elst, Ceulemans. *Scorer:* Van der Eycken.

FRANCE 1984

Group 1
France 1, Denmark 0. Belgium 2, Yugoslavia 0.
France 5, Belgium 0. Denmark 5, Yugoslavia 0.
France 3, Yugoslavia 2. Denmark 3, Belgium 2.

	P	*W*	*D*	*L*	*F*	*A*	*Pts*
France	3	3	0	0	9	2	6
Denmark	3	2	0	1	8	3	4
Belgium	3	1	0	2	4	8	2
Yugoslavia	3	0	0	3	2	10	0

Group 2
West Germany 0, Portugal 0. Spain 1, Rumania 1.
Spain 1, Portugal 1. West Germany 2, Rumania 1.
West Germany 0, Spain 1. Portugal 1, Rumania 0.

	P	*W*	*D*	*L*	*F*	*A*	*Pts*
Spain	3	1	2	0	3	2	4
Portugal	3	1	2	0	2	1	4
West Germany	3	1	1	1	2	2	3
Rumania	3	0	1	2	2	4	1

Semi-finals
France 3, Portugal 2 (aet, in Marseilles). Denmark 1, Spain 1 (aet, in Lyon) (*Spain won 5–4 on penalties*).
Final (Paris, 27 June 1984, att. 80,000): France (0) 2, Spain (0) 0.
France: Bats, Battiston (Amoros), Le Roux, Bossis, Domergue, Giresse, Platini, Tigana, Fernandez, Lacombe (Genghini), Bellone. *Scorers:* Platini, Bellone.
Spain: Arconada, Urquiaga, Salva (Roberto), Gallego, Camacho, Francisco, Julio Alberto (Sarabia), Senor, Victor, Carrasco, Santillana.

WEST GERMANY 1988

Group 1
West Germany 1, Italy 1. Spain 3, Denmark 2.
West Germany 2, Denmark 0. Italy 1, Spain 0.
West Germany 2, Spain 0. Italy 2, Denmark 0.

	P	*W*	*D*	*L*	*F*	*A*	*Pts*
West Germany	3	2	1	0	5	1	5
Italy	3	2	1	0	4	1	5
Spain	3	1	0	2	3	5	2
Denmark	3	0	0	3	2	7	0

Group 2
England 0, Republic of Ireland 1. Netherlands 0, USSR 1. Netherlands 3, England 1. Republic of Ireland 1, USSR 1. England 1, USSR 3. Netherlands 1, Republic of Ireland 0.

	P	*W*	*D*	*L*	*F*	*A*	*Pts*
USSR	3	2	1	0	5	2	5
Netherlands	3	2	0	1	4	2	4
Republic of Ireland	3	1	1	1	2	2	3
England	3	0	0	3	2	7	0

Semi-finals
West Germany 1, Netherlands 2 (in Hamburg).
USSR 2, Italy 0 (in Stuttgart).
Final (Munich, 25 June 1988, att. 72,308):
Netherlands (1) 2, USSR (0) 0.
Netherlands: Van Breukelen, Van Aerle, Van Tiggelen, Wouters, Koeman R., Rijkaard, Vanenburg, Gullit, Van Basten, Muhren, Koeman E. *Scorers:* Gullit, Van Basten.
USSR: Dassayev, Khidiatulin, Aleinikov, Mikhailichenko, Litovchenko, Demianenko, Belanov, Gotsmanov (Baltacha), Protasov (Pasulko), Zavarov, Rats.

Mikhailichenko chases after the ball in the 1988 final. It was the USSR's fourth appearance at this stage.

European Cup Finals

1955–56	Real Madrid 4, Stade de Reims 3
1956–57	Real Madrid 2, Fiorentina 0
1957–58	Real Madrid 3, AC Milan 2 (aet)
1958–59	Real Madrid 2, Stade de Reims 0
1959–60	Real Madrid 7, Eintracht Frankfurt 3
1960–61	Benfica 3, Barcelona 2
1961–62	Benfica 5, Real Madrid 3
1962–63	AC Milan 2, Benfica 1
1963–64	Inter-Milan 3, Real Madrid 1
1964–65	Inter-Milan 1, Benfica 0
1965–66	Real Madrid 2, Partizan Belgrade 1
1966–67	Celtic 2, Inter-Milan 1
1967–68	Manchester United 4, Benfica 1 (aet)
1968–69	AC Milan 4, Ajax Amsterdam 1
1969–70	Feyenoord 2, Celtic 1 (aet)
1970–71	Ajax Amsterdam 2, Panathinaikos 0
1971–72	Ajax Amsterdam 2, Inter-Milan 0
1972–73	Ajax Amsterdam 1, Juventus 0
1973–74	Bayern Munich 1, Atletico Madrid 1
Replay	Bayern Munich 4, Atletico Madrid 0

PSV players dive on top of Van Breukelen after he has saved the decisive penalty in the 1988 final.

Celtic goalkeeper Simpson leaps for a cross. He kept a clean sheet and the European Cup came to Britain for the first time.

1974–75	Bayern Munich 2, Leeds United 0
1975–76	Bayern Munich 1, St Etienne 0
1976–77	Liverpool 3, Borussia Moenchengladbach 1
1977–78	Liverpool 1, FC Brugge 0
1978–79	Nottingham Forest 1, Malmo 0
1979–80	Nottingham Forest 1, SV Hamburg 0
1980–81	Liverpool 1, Real Madrid 0
1981–82	Aston Villa 1, Bayern Munich 0
1982–83	SV Hamburg 1, Juventus 0
1983–84	Liverpool 1, AS Roma 1 (aet) *Liverpool won 4–2 on penalties.*
1984–85	Juventus 1, Liverpool 0
1985–86	Steaua Bucharest 0, Barcelona 0 (aet) *Steaua Bucharest won 2–0 on penalties.*
1986–87	FC Porto 2, Bayern Munich 1
1987–88	PSV Eindhoven 0, Benfica 0 (aet) *PSV Eindhoven won 6–5 on penalties.*
1988–89	AC Milan 4, Steaua Bucharest 0
1989–90	AC Milan 1, Benfica 0

European Cup-Winners' Cup Finals

1960–61 Rangers 0, Fiorentina 2
2nd Leg Fiorentina 2, Rangers 1
1961–62 Atletico Madrid 1, Fiorentina 1 (aet)
Replay Atletico Madrid 3, Fiorentina 0
1962–63 Tottenham Hotspur 5, Atletico Madrid 1
1963–64 Sporting Lisbon 3, MTK Budapest 3 (aet)
Replay Sporting Lisbon 1, MTK Budapest 0
1964–65 West Ham United 2, Munich 1860 0
1965–66 Borussia Dortmund 2, Liverpool 1 (aet)
1966–67 Bayern Munich 1, Rangers 0 (aet)
1967–68 AC Milan 2, SV Hamburg 0
1968–69 Slovan Bratislava 3, Barcelona 2
1969–70 Manchester City 2, Gornik Zabrze 1
1970–71 Chelsea 1, Real Madrid 1 (aet)
Replay Chelsea 2, Real Madrid 1
1971–72 Rangers 3, Dynamo Moscow 2
1972–73 AC Milan 1, Leeds United 0
1973–74 FC Magdeburg 2, AC Milan 0
1974–75 Dynamo Kiev 3, Ferencvaros 0
1975–76 RSC Anderlecht 4, West Ham United 2
1976–77 SV Hamburg 2, RSC Anderlecht 0

Goalscorer Kevin Sheedy attacks for Everton in the 1985 final against Rapid Vienna.

Anderlecht's Marc Degryse contests the ball with Sampdoria's Luca Pellegrini in 1990.

1977–78 RSC Anderlecht 4, Austria Vienna 0
1978–79 Barcelona 4, Fortuna Dusseldorf 3 (aet)
1979–80 Valencia 0, Arsenal 0 (aet)
Valencia won 5–4 on penalties.
1980–81 Dynamo Tbilisi 2, Carl Zeiss Jena 1
1981–82 Barcelona 2, Standard Liege 1
1982–83 Aberdeen 2, Real Madrid 1
1983–84 Juventus 2, FC Porto 1
1984–85 Everton 3, Rapid Vienna 1
1985–86 Dynamo Kiev 3, Atletico Madrid 0
1986–87 Ajax Amsterdam 1, Lokomotiv Leipzig 0
1987–88 Mechelen 1, Ajax Amsterdam 0
1988–89 Barcelona 2, Sampdoria 0
1989–90 Sampdoria 2, RSC Anderlecht 0 (aet)

UEFA Cup Finals

(Fairs Cup until 1971)

1955–58	London 2, Barcelona 2
2nd Leg	Barcelona 6, London 0
1958–60	Birmingham City 0, Barcelona 0
2nd Leg	Barcelona 4, Birmingham City 1
1960–61	Birmingham City 2, AS Roma 2
2nd Leg	AS Roma 2, Birmingham City 0
1961–62	Valencia 6, Barcelona 2
2nd Leg	Barcelona 1, Valencia 1
1962–63	Dynamo Zagreb 1, Valencia 2
2nd Leg	Valencia 2, Dynamo Zagreb 0
1963–64	Real Zaragoza 2, Valencia 1
1964–65	Ferencvaros 1, Juventus 0
1965–66	Barcelona 0, Real Zaragoza 1
2nd Leg	Real Zaragoza 2, Barcelona 4 (aet)
1966–67	Dynamo Zagreb 2, Leeds United 0
2nd Leg	Leeds United 0, Dynamo Zagreb 0
1967–68	Leeds United 1, Ferencvaros 0
2nd Leg	Ferencvaros 0, Leeds United 0
1968–69	Newcastle United 3, Ujpest Dozsa 0
2nd Leg	Ujpest Dozsa 2, Newcastle United 3
1969–70	RSC Anderlecht 3, Arsenal 1
2nd Leg	Arsenal 3, RSC Anderlecht 0
1970–71	Juventus 2, Leeds United 2
2nd Leg	Leeds United 1, Juventus 1 *Leeds United won on away goals rule.*
1971–72	Wolverhampton Wanderers 1, Tottenham Hotspur 2
2nd Leg	Tottenham Hotspur 1, Wolverhampton Wanderers 1
1972–73	Liverpool 3, Borussia Moenchengladbach 0
2nd Leg	Borussia Moenchengladbach 2, Liverpool 0
1973–74	Tottenham Hotspur 2, Feyenoord 2
2nd Leg	Feyenoord 2, Tottenham Hotspur 0
1974–75	Borussia Moenchengladbach 0, Twente Enschede 0
2nd Leg	Twente Enschede 1, Borussia Moenchengladbach 5
1975–76	Liverpool 3, FC Brugge 2
2nd Leg	FC Brugge 1, Liverpool 1
1976–77	Juventus 1, Athletic Bilbao 0
2nd Leg	Athletic Bilbao 2, Juventus 1 *Juventus won on away goals rule.*
1977–78	Bastia 0, PSV Eindhoven 0
2nd Leg	PSV Eindhoven 3, Bastia 0
1978–79	Red Star Belgrade 1, Borussia Moenchengladbach 1
2nd Leg	Borussia Moenchengladbach 1, Red Star Belgrade 0
1979–80	Borussia Moenchengladbach 3, Eintracht Frankfurt 2
2nd Leg	Eintracht Frankfurt 1, Borussia Moenchengladbach 0 *Eintracht Frankfurt won on away goals rule.*
1980–81	Ipswich Town 3, AZ 67 Alkmaar 0
2nd Leg	AZ 67 Alkmaar 4, Ipswich Town 2
1981–82	IFK Gothenburg 1, SV Hamburg 0
2nd Leg	SV Hamburg 0, IFK Gothenburg 3
1982–83	RSC Anderlecht 1, Benfica 0
2nd Leg	Benfica 1, RSC Anderlecht 1
1983–84	RSC Anderlecht 1, Tottenham Hotspur 1
2nd Leg	Tottenham Hotspur 1, RSC Anderlecht 1 (aet) *Tottenham Hotspur won 4–3 on penalties.*
1984–85	Videoton 0, Real Madrid 3
2nd Leg	Real Madrid 0, Videoton 1
1985–86	Real Madrid 5, Cologne 1
2nd Leg	Cologne 2, Real Madrid 0
1986–87	IFK Gothenburg 1, Dundee United 0
2nd Leg	Dundee United 1, IFK Gothenburg 1
1987–88	Espanol 3, Bayer Leverkusen 0
2nd Leg	Bayer Leverkusen 3, Espanol 0 (aet) *Bayer Leverkusen won 3–2 on penalties.*
1988–89	Napoli 2, Stuttgart 1
2nd Leg	Stuttgart 3, Napoli 3
1989–90	Juventus 3, Fiorentina 1
2nd Leg	Fiorentina 0, Juventus 0

FA Cup Finals

1871–72 The Wanderers 1, Royal Engineers 0
1872–73 The Wanderers 2, Oxford University 0
1873–74 Oxford University 2, Royal Engineers 0
1874–75 Royal Engineers 1, Old Etonians 1 (aet)
Replay Royal Engineers 2, Old Etonians 0
1875–76 The Wanderers 1, Old Etonians 1 (aet)
Replay The Wanderers 3, Old Etonians 0
1876–77 The Wanderers 2, Oxford University 1 (aet)
1877–78 The Wanderers 3, Royal Engineers 1
1878–79 Old Etonians 1, Clapham Rovers 0
1879–80 Clapham Rovers 1, Oxford University 0
1880–81 Old Carthusians 3, Old Etonians 0
1881–82 Old Etonians 1, Blackburn Rovers 0
1882–83 Blackburn Olympic 2, Old Etonians 1 (aet)
1883–84 Blackburn Rovers 2, Queen's Park 1
1884–85 Blackburn Rovers 2, Queen's Park 0
1885–86 Blackburn Rovers 0, West Bromwich Albion 0
Replay Blackburn Rovers 2, West Bromwich Albion 0
1886–87 Aston Villa 2, West Bromwich Albion 0
1887–88 West Bromwich Albion 2, Preston North End 1
1888–89 Preston North End 3, Wolverhampton Wanderers 0
1889–90 Blackburn Rovers 6, The Wednesday 1
1890–91 Blackburn Rovers 3, Notts County 1
1891–92 West Bromwich Albion 3, Aston Villa 0
1892–93 Wolverhampton Wanderers 1, Everton 0
1893–94 Notts County 4, Bolton Wanderers 1
1894–95 Aston Villa 1, West Bromwich Albion 0
1895–96 The Wednesday 2, Wolverhampton Wanderers 1

Charlie Roberts, captain of Manchester United's first Cup-winning side, in 1909.

1896–97 Aston Villa 3, Everton 2
1897–98 Nottingham Forest 3, Derby County 1
1898–99 Sheffield United 4, Derby County 1
1899–1900 Bury 4, Southampton 0
1900–01 Tottenham Hotspur 2, Sheffield United 2
Replay Tottenham Hotspur 3, Sheffield United 1
1901–02 Sheffield United 1, Southampton 1
Replay Sheffield United 2, Southampton 1
1902–03 Bury 6, Derby County 0
1903–04 Manchester City 1, Bolton Wanderers 0
1904–05 Aston Villa 2, Newcastle United 0
1905–06 Everton 1, Newcastle United 0
1906–07 The Wednesday 2, Everton 1
1907–08 Wolverhampton Wanderers 3, Newcastle United 1
1908–09 Manchester United 1, Bristol City 0
1909–10 Newcastle United 1, Barnsley 1
Replay Newcastle United 2, Barnsley 0
1910–11 Bradford City 0, Newcastle United 0
Replay Bradford City 1, Newcastle United 0
1911–12 Barnsley 0, West Bromwich Albion 0
Replay Barnsley 1, West Bromwich Albion 0 (aet)
1912–13 Aston Villa 1, Sunderland 0
1913–14 Burnley 1, Liverpool 0
1914–15 Sheffield United 3, Chelsea 0
1919–20 Aston Villa 1, Huddersfield Town 0 (aet)
1920–21 Tottenham Hotspur 1, Wolverhampton Wanderers 0
1921–22 Huddersfield Town 1, Preston North End 0
1922–23 Bolton Wanderers 2, West Ham United 0
1923–24 Newcastle United 2, Aston Villa 0
1924–25 Sheffield United 1, Cardiff City 0
1925–26 Bolton Wanderers 1, Manchester City 0
1926–27 Cardiff City 1, Arsenal 0
1927–28 Blackburn Rovers 3, Huddersfield Town 1
1928–29 Bolton Wanderers 2, Portsmouth 0
1929–30 Arsenal 2, Huddersfield Town 0
1930–31 West Bromwich Albion 2, Birmingham 1
1931–32 Newcastle United 2, Arsenal 1
1932–33 Everton 3, Manchester City 0
1933–34 Manchester City 2, Portsmouth 1
1934–35 Sheffield Wednesday 4, West Bromwich Albion 2
1935–36 Arsenal 1, Sheffield United 0
1936–37 Sunderland 3, Preston North End 1
1937–38 Preston North End 1, Huddersfield Town 0 (aet)
1938–39 Portsmouth 4, Wolverhampton Wanderers 1

Jackie Milburn's header in 1955 was the quickest goal in any FA Cup final.

Dave Beasant saves a penalty in the 1988 final to bring about one of the greatest upsets in Cup history.

1945–46	Derby County 4, Charlton Athletic 1 (aet)
1946–47	Charlton Athletic 1, Burnley 0 (aet)
1947–48	Manchester United 4, Blackpool 2
1948–49	Wolverhampton Wanderers 3, Leicester City 1
1949–50	Arsenal 2, Liverpool 0
1950–51	Newcastle United 2, Blackpool 0
1951–52	Newcastle United 1, Arsenal 0
1952–53	Blackpool 4, Bolton Wanderers 3
1953–54	West Bromwich Albion 3, Preston North End 2
1954–55	Newcastle United 3, Manchester City 1
1955–56	Manchester City 3, Birmingham City 1
1956–57	Aston Villa 2, Manchester United 1
1957–58	Bolton Wanderers 2, Manchester United 0
1958–59	Nottingham Forest 2, Luton Town 1
1959–60	Wolverhampton Wanderers 3, Blackburn Rovers 0
1960–61	Tottenham Hotspur 2, Leicester City 0
1961–62	Tottenham Hotspur 3, Burnley 1
1962–63	Manchester United 3, Leicester City 1
1963–64	West Ham United 3, Preston North End 2
1964–65	Liverpool 2, Leeds United 1 (aet)
1965–66	Everton 3, Sheffield Wednesday 2
1966–67	Tottenham Hotspur 2, Chelsea 1
1967–68	West Bromwich Albion 1, Everton 0 (aet)
1968–69	Manchester City 1, Leicester City 0
1969–70	Chelsea 2, Leeds United 2 (aet)
Replay	Chelsea 2, Leeds United 1 (aet)
1970–71	Arsenal 2, Liverpool 1 (aet)
1971–72	Leeds United 1, Arsenal 0
1972–73	Sunderland 1, Leeds United 0
1973–74	Liverpool 3, Newcastle United 0
1974–75	West Ham United 2, Fulham 0
1975–76	Southampton 1, Manchester United 0
1976–77	Manchester United 2, Liverpool 1
1977–78	Ipswich Town 1, Arsenal 0
1978–79	Arsenal 3, Manchester United 2
1979–80	West Ham United 1, Arsenal 0
1980–81	Tottenham Hotspur 1, Manchester City 1 (aet)
Replay	Tottenham Hotspur 3, Manchester City 2
1981–82	Tottenham Hotspur 1, Queen's Park Rangers 1 (aet)
Replay	Tottenham Hotspur 1, Queen's Park Rangers 0
1982–83	Manchester United 2, Brighton & Hove Albion 2 (aet)
Replay	Manchester United 4, Brighton & Hove Albion 0
1983–84	Everton 2, Watford 0
1984–85	Manchester United 1, Everton 0 (aet)
1985–86	Liverpool 3, Everton 1
1986–87	Coventry City 3, Tottenham Hotspur 2 (aet)
1987–88	Wimbledon 1, Liverpool 0
1988–89	Liverpool 3, Everton 2 (aet)
1989–90	Manchester United 3, Crystal Palace 3 (aet)
Replay	Manchester United 1, Crystal Palace 0

Football League Champions

Season	Max Pts	Champions	Pts
1888–89	44	Preston NE	40
1889–90	44	Preston NE	33
1890–91	44	Everton	29
1891–92	52	Sunderland	42
1892–93	60	Sunderland	48
1893–94	60	Aston Villa	44
1894–95	60	Sunderland	47
1895–96	60	Aston Villa	45
1896–97	60	Aston Villa	47
1897–98	60	Sheffield U	42
1898–99	68	Aston Villa	45
1899–1900	68	Aston Villa	50
1900–01	68	Liverpool	45
1901–02	68	Sunderland	44
1902–03	68	The Wednesday	42
1903–04	68	The Wednesday	47
1904–05	68	Newcastle U	48
1905–06	76	Liverpool	51
1906–07	76	Newcastle U	51
1907–08	76	Manchester U	52
1908–09	76	Newcastle U	53
1909–10	76	Aston Villa	53
1910–11	76	Manchester U	52
1911–12	76	Blackburn R	49
1912–13	76	Sunderland	54
1913–14	76	Blackburn R	51
1914–15	76	Everton	46
1919–20	84	WBA	60
1920–21	84	Burnley	59
1921–22	84	Liverpool	57
1922–23	84	Liverpool	60
1923–24	84	Huddersfield T*	57
1924–25	84	Huddersfield T	58
1925–26	84	Huddersfield T	57
1926–27	84	Newcastle U	56
1927–28	84	Everton	53
1928–29	84	Sheffield W	52
1929–30	84	Sheffield W	60
1930–31	84	Arsenal	66
1931–32	84	Everton	56
1932–33	84	Arsenal	58
1933–34	84	Arsenal	59
1934–35	84	Arsenal	58
1935–36	84	Sunderland	56
1936–37	84	Manchester C	57
1937–38	84	Arsenal	52

Allan Clarke in action in 1973–74. That season Leeds started with a record 29 consecutive undefeated matches.

FOOTBALL LEAGUE CHAMPIONS

Phil Neal of Liverpool in May 1980. Afterwards, he collected the fourth of his record eight League medals.

1938–39	84	Everton	59
1946–47	84	Liverpool	57
1947–48	84	Arsenal	59
1948–49	84	Portsmouth	58
1949–50	84	Portsmouth*	53
1950–51	84	Tottenham H	60
1951–52	84	Manchester U	57
1952–53	84	Arsenal*	54
1953–54	84	Wolverhampton W	57
1954–55	84	Chelsea	52
1955–56	84	Manchester U	60
1956–57	84	Manchester U	64
1957–58	84	Wolverhampton W	64
1958–59	84	Wolverhampton W	61
1959–60	84	Burnley	55
1960–61	84	Tottenham H	66
1961–62	84	Ipswich T	56
1962–63	84	Everton	61
1963–64	84	Liverpool	57
1964–65	84	Manchester U*	61
1965–66	84	Liverpool	61
1966–67	84	Manchester U	60
1967–68	84	Manchester C	58
1968–69	84	Leeds U	67
1969–70	84	Everton	66
1970–71	84	Arsenal	65
1971–72	84	Derby Co	58
1972–73	84	Liverpool	60
1973–74	84	Leeds U	62
1974–75	84	Derby Co	53
1975–76	84	Liverpool	60
1976–77	84	Liverpool	57
1977–78	84	Nottingham F	64
1978–79	84	Liverpool	68
1979–80	84	Liverpool	60
1980–81	84	Aston Villa	60
1981–82	126	Liverpool	87
1982–83	126	Liverpool	82
1983–84	126	Liverpool	80
1984–85	126	Everton	90
1985–86	126	Liverpool	88
1986–87	126	Everton	86
1987–88	120	Liverpool	90
1988–89	114	Arsenal*	76
1989–90	114	Liverpool	79

**Won on goal average/difference*

League Cup Finals

Played as two legs until 1966

1960–61 Rotherham United 2, Aston Villa 0
2nd Leg Aston Villa 3, Rotherham United 0 (aet)
1961–62 Rochdale 0, Norwich City 3
2nd Leg Norwich City 1, Rochdale 0
1962–63 Birmingham City 3, Aston Villa 1
2nd Leg Aston Villa 0, Birmingham City 0
1963–64 Stoke City 1, Leicester City 1
2nd Leg Leicester City 3, Stoke City 2
1964–65 Chelsea 3, Leicester City 2
2nd Leg Leicester City 0, Chelsea 0
1965–66 West Ham United 2, West Bromwich Albion 1
2nd Leg West Bromwich Albion 4, West Ham United 1
1966–67 Queen's Park Rangers 3, West Bromwich Albion 2
1967–68 Leeds United 1, Arsenal 0
1968–69 Swindon Town 3, Arsenal 1 (aet)
1969–70 Manchester City 2, West Bromwich Albion 1 (aet)
1970–71 Tottenham Hotspur 2, Aston Villa 0

Norman Whiteside goes past Alan Hansen in the 1983 final. Liverpool won the Cup for the third year in succession.

Ray Houghton on the ball for Oxford in 1986. He scored in his side's surprise 3–0 victory over QPR.

1971–72 Stoke City 2, Chelsea 1
1972–73 Tottenham Hotspur 1, Norwich City 0
1973–74 Wolverhampton Wanderers 2, Manchester City 1
1974–75 Aston Villa 1, Norwich City 0
1975–76 Manchester City 2, Newcastle United 1
1976–77 Aston Villa 0, Everton 0
Replay Aston Villa 1, Everton 1 (aet)
Replay Aston Villa 3, Everton 2 (aet)
1977–78 Nottingham Forest 0, Liverpool 0 (aet)
Replay Nottingham Forest 1, Liverpool 0
1978–79 Nottingham Forest 3, Southampton 2
1979–80 Wolverhampton Wanderers 1, Nottingham Forest 0
1980–81 Liverpool 1, West Ham United 1 (aet)
Replay Liverpool 2, West Ham United 1
1981–82 Liverpool 3, Tottenham Hotspur 1 (aet)
1982–83 Liverpool 2, Manchester United 1 (aet)
1983–84 Liverpool 0, Everton 0 (aet)
Replay Liverpool 1, Everton 0
1984–85 Norwich City 1, Sunderland 0
1985–86 Oxford United 3, Queen's Park Rangers 0
1986–87 Arsenal 2, Liverpool 1
1987–88 Luton Town 3, Arsenal 2
1988–89 Nottingham Forest 3, Luton Town 1
1989–90 Nottingham Forest 1, Oldham Athletic 0

Scottish Cup Finals

1873–74	Queen's Park 2, Clydesdale 0
1874–75	Queen's Park 3, Renton 0
1875–76	Queen's Park 1, Third Lanark Rifle Volunteers 1
Replay	Queen's Park 2, Third Lanark Rifle Volunteers 0
1876–77	Vale of Leven 1, Rangers 1
Replay	Vale of Leven 1, Rangers 1
Replay	Vale of Leven 3, Rangers 2
1877–78	Vale of Leven 1, Third Lanark Rifle Volunteers 0
1878–79	Vale of Leven 1, Rangers 1
	Vale of Leven were awarded the Cup when Rangers failed to turn up for the replay.
1879–80	Queen's Park 3, Thornliebank 0
1880–81	Queen's Park 2, Dumbarton 1
	Dumbarton objected to one of the goals, and a replay was ordered by the SFA.
Replay	Queen's Park 3, Dumbarton 1
1881–82	Queen's Park 2, Dumbarton 2
Replay	Queen's Park 4, Dumbarton 1
1882–83	Dumbarton 2, Vale of Leven 2
Replay	Dumbarton 2, Vale of Leven 1
1883–84	*Vale of Leven failed to turn up, and so the Cup was awarded to Queen's Park.*
1884–85	Renton 0, Vale of Leven 0
Replay	Renton 3, Vale of Leven 1
1885–86	Queen's Park 3, Renton 1
1886–87	Hibernian 2, Dumbarton 1
1887–88	Renton 6, Cambuslang 1
1888–89	Third Lanark 3, Celtic 0
	The SFA agreed to a replay when it was discovered, after the match, that because of the snowbound pitch, both teams had agreed in advance to treat the game as a friendly.
Replay	Third Lanark 2, Celtic 1
1889–90	Queen's Park 1, Vale of Leven 1
Replay	Queen's Park 2, Vale of Leven 1
1890–91	Heart of Midlothian 1, Dumbarton 0
1891–92	Celtic 1, Queen's Park 0
	Because of crowd encroachment, the SFA ordered a replay.
Replay	Celtic 5, Queen's Park 1
1892–93	Queen's Park 0, Celtic 1
	Because the pitch was frozen, the SFA ordered a replay.
Replay	Queen's Park 2, Celtic 1
1893–94	Rangers 3, Celtic 1
1894–95	St Bernard's 2, Renton 1
1895–96	Heart of Midlothian 3, Hibernian 1
1896–97	Rangers 5, Dumbarton 1
1897–98	Rangers 2, Kilmarnock 0
1898–99	Celtic 2, Rangers 0
1899–1900	Celtic 4, Queen's Park 3
1900–01	Heart of Midlothian 4, Celtic 3
1901–02	Hibernian 1, Celtic 0
1902–03	Rangers 1, Heart of Midlothian 1
Replay	Rangers 0, Heart of Midlothian 0
Replay	Rangers 2, Heart of Midlothian 0
1903–04	Celtic 3, Rangers 2
1904–05	Third Lanark 0, Rangers 0
Replay	Third Lanark 3, Rangers 1
1905–06	Heart of Midlothian 1, Third Lanark 0
1906–07	Celtic 3, Heart of Midlothian 0
1907–08	Celtic 5, St Mirren 1
1908–09	Celtic 2, Rangers 2
Replay	Celtic 1, Rangers 1
	The SFA withheld the Cup following a riot by spectators who were angered at the decision not to play extra time.
1909–10	Dundee 2, Clyde 2
Replay	Dundee 0, Clyde 0 (aet)
Replay	Dundee 2, Clyde 1
1910–11	Celtic 0, Hamilton Academical 0
Replay	Celtic 2, Hamilton Academical 0
1911–12	Celtic 2, Clyde 0
1912–13	Falkirk 2, Raith Rovers 0
1913–14	Celtic 0, Hibernian 0
Replay	Celtic 4, Hibernian 1
1919–20	Kilmarnock 3, Albion Rovers 2
1920–21	Partick Thistle 1, Rangers 0
1921–22	Morton 1, Rangers 0
1922–23	Celtic 1, Hibernian 0
1923–24	Airdrieonians 2, Hibernian 0
1924–25	Celtic 2, Dundee 1
1925–26	St Mirren 2, Celtic 0
1926–27	Celtic 3, East Fife 1
1927–28	Rangers 4, Celtic 0
1928–29	Kilmarnock 2, Rangers 0
1929–30	Rangers 0, Partick Thistle 0
Replay	Rangers 2, Partick Thistle 1
1930–31	Celtic 2, Motherwell 2

Billy McNeill of Celtic leaps clear of the Dundee United players in the 1974 final.

Replay	Celtic 4, Motherwell 2
1931–32	Rangers 1, Kilmarnock 1
Replay	Rangers 3, Kilmarnock 0
1932–33	Celtic 1, Motherwell 0
1933–34	Rangers 5, St Mirren 0
1934–35	Rangers 2, Hamilton Academical 1
1935–36	Rangers 1, Third Lanark 0
1936–37	Celtic 2, Aberdeen 1
1937–38	East Fife 1, Kilmarnock 1
Replay	East Fife 4, Kilmarnock 2 (aet)
1938–39	Clyde 4, Motherwell 0
1946–47	Aberdeen 2, Hibernian 1
1947–48	Rangers 1, Morton 1 (aet)
Replay	Rangers 1, Morton 0 (aet)
1948–49	Rangers 4, Clyde 1
1949–50	Rangers 3, East Fife 0
1950–51	Celtic 1, Motherwell 0
1951–52	Motherwell 4, Dundee 0
1952–53	Rangers 1, Aberdeen 1
Replay	Rangers 1, Aberdeen 0
1953–54	Celtic 2, Aberdeen 1
1954–55	Clyde 1, Celtic 1
Replay	Clyde 1, Celtic 0
1955–56	Heart of Midlothian 3, Celtic 1
1956–57	Falkirk 1, Kilmarnock 1
Replay	Falkirk 2, Kilmarnock 1 (aet)
1957–58	Clyde 1, Hibernian 0
1958–59	St Mirren 3, Aberdeen 1
1959–60	Rangers 2, Kilmarnock 0
1960–61	Dunfermline Athletic 0, Celtic 0
Replay	Dunfermline Athletic 2, Celtic 0
1961–62	Rangers 2, St Mirren 0
1962–63	Rangers 1, Celtic 1
Replay	Rangers 3, Celtic 0
1963–64	Rangers 3, Dundee 1
1964–65	Celtic 3, Dunfermline Athletic 2
1965–66	Rangers 0, Celtic 0
Replay	Rangers 1, Celtic 0
1966–67	Celtic 2, Aberdeen 0
1967–68	Dunfermline Athletic 3, Heart of Midlothian 1
1968–69	Celtic 4, Rangers 0
1969–70	Aberdeen 3, Celtic 1
1970–71	Celtic 1, Rangers 1
Replay	Celtic 2, Rangers 1
1971–72	Celtic 6, Hibernian 1
1972–73	Rangers 3, Celtic 2
1973–74	Celtic 3, Dundee United 0
1974–75	Celtic 3, Airdrieonians 1
1975–76	Rangers 3, Heart of Midlothian 1

St Mirren's Ian Ferguson beats Malpas of Dundee United in 1987 to help his club towards their first major trophy in almost 30 years.

1976–77	Celtic 1, Rangers 0
1977–78	Rangers 2, Aberdeen 1
1978–79	Rangers 0, Hibernian 0
Replay	Rangers 0, Hibernian 0 (aet)
Replay	Rangers 3, Hibernian 2 (aet)
1979–80	Celtic 1, Rangers 0 (aet)
1980–81	Rangers 0, Dundee United 0 (aet)
Replay	Rangers 4, Dundee United 1
1981–82	Aberdeen 4, Rangers 1 (aet)
1982–83	Aberdeen 1, Rangers 0 (aet)
1983–84	Aberdeen 2, Celtic 1 (aet)
1984–85	Celtic 2, Dundee United 1
1985–86	Aberdeen 3, Heart of Midlothian 0
1986–87	St Mirren 1, Dundee United 0 (aet)
1987–88	Celtic 2, Dundee United 1
1988–89	Celtic 1, Rangers 0
1989–90	Aberdeen 0, Celtic 0 (aet)
	Aberdeen won 9–8 on penalties.

Chris Morris holds off Ally McCoist of Rangers in 1989 as Celtic win the Cup for the 27th time.

Scottish League Champions

Season	Max Pts	Champions	Pts
1890–91†	36	Dumbarton	29
		Rangers	29
1891–92	44	Dumbarton	37
1892–93	36	Celtic	29
1893–94	36	Celtic	29
1894–95	36	Hearts	31
1895–96	36	Celtic	30
1896–97	36	Hearts	28
1897–98	36	Celtic	33
1898–99	36	Rangers	36
1899–1900	36	Rangers	32
1900–01	40	Rangers	35
1901–02	36	Rangers	28
1902–03	44	Hibernian	37
1903–04	52	Third Lanark	43
1904–05	52	Celtic††	41
1905–06	60	Celtic	49
1906–07	68	Celtic	55
1907–08	68	Celtic	55
1908–09	68	Celtic	51
1909–10	68	Celtic	54
1910–11	68	Rangers	52
1911–12	68	Rangers	51
1912–13	68	Rangers	53
1913–14	76	Celtic	65
1914–15	76	Celtic	65
1915–16	76	Celtic	67
1916–17	76	Celtic	64
1917–18	68	Rangers	56
1918–19	68	Celtic	58
1919–20	84	Rangers	71
1920–21	84	Rangers	76
1921–22	84	Celtic	67
1922–23	76	Rangers	55
1923–24	76	Rangers	59
1924–25	76	Rangers	60
1925–26	76	Celtic	58
1926–27	76	Rangers	56
1927–28	76	Rangers	60
1928–29	76	Rangers	67
1929–30	76	Rangers	60
1930–31	76	Rangers	60
1931–32	76	Motherwell	66
1932–33	76	Rangers	62
1933–34	76	Rangers	66
1934–35	76	Rangers	55
1935–36	76	Celtic	66
1936–37	76	Rangers	61
1937–38	76	Celtic	61
1938–39	76	Rangers	59
1946–47	60	Rangers	46
1947–48	60	Hibernian	48
1948–49	60	Rangers	46
1949–50	60	Rangers	50
1950–51	60	Hibernian	48
1951–52	60	Hibernian	45
1952–53	60	Rangers*	43
1953–54	60	Celtic	43
1954–55	60	Aberdeen	49
1955–56	68	Rangers	52
1956–57	68	Rangers	55
1957–58	68	Hearts	62
1958–59	68	Rangers	50
1959–60	68	Hearts	54

Gordon Strachan of Aberdeen was a crucial member of the side that broke the Glasgow monopoly in the early 1980s.

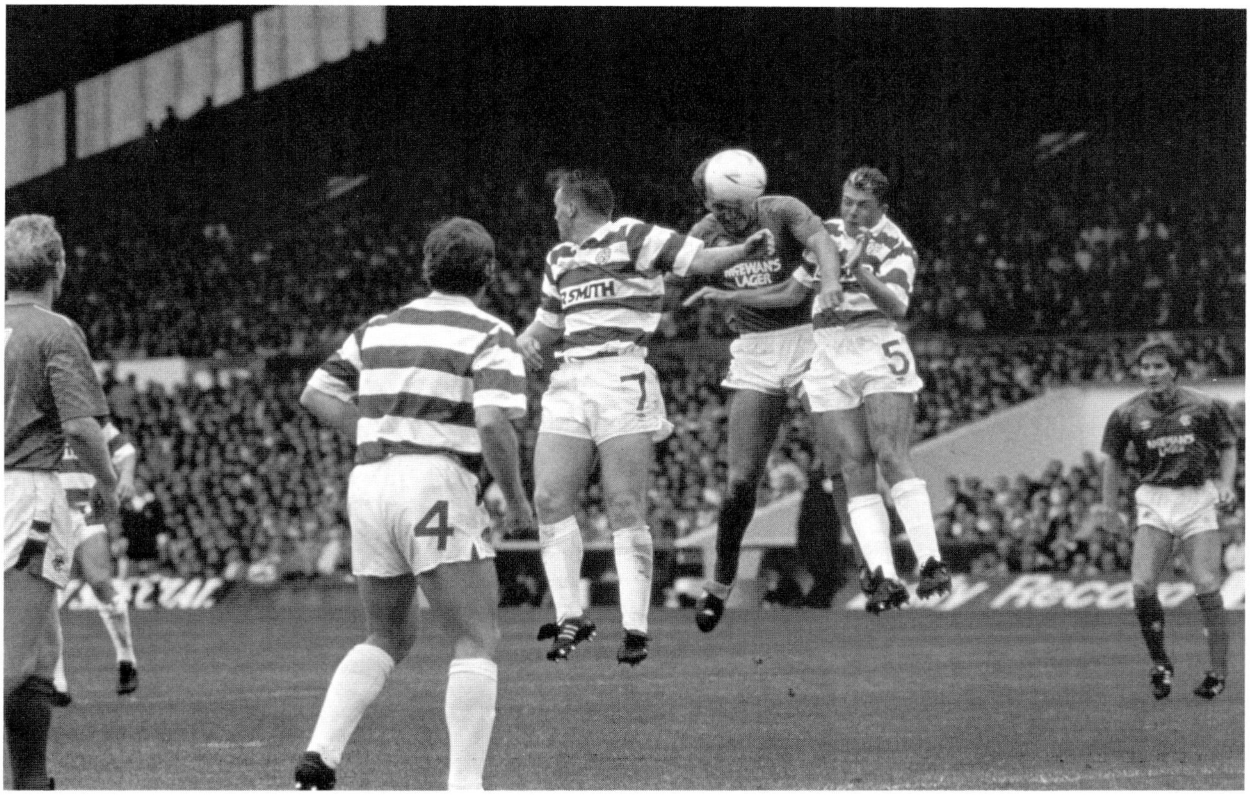

Terry Butcher of Rangers clears the Celtic defence to score in August 1989. Rangers went on to be Champions.

1960–61	68	Rangers	51
1961–62	68	Dundee	54
1962–63	68	Rangers	57
1963–64	68	Rangers	55
1964–65	68	Kilmarnock*	50
1965–66	68	Celtic	57
1966–67	68	Celtic	58
1967–68	68	Celtic	63
1968–69	68	Celtic	54
1969–70	68	Celtic	57
1970–71	68	Celtic	56
1971–72	68	Celtic	60
1972–73	68	Celtic	57
1973–74	68	Celtic	53
1974–75	68	Rangers	56
1975–76	72	Rangers	54
1976–77	72	Celtic	55
1977–78	72	Rangers	55
1978–79	72	Celtic	48
1979–80	72	Aberdeen	48
1980–81	72	Celtic	56
1981–82	72	Celtic	55
1982–83	72	Dundee U	56
1983–84	72	Aberdeen	57
1984–85	72	Aberdeen	59
1985–86	72	Celtic*	50
1986–87	88	Rangers	69
1987–88	88	Celtic	72
1988–89	72	Rangers	56
1989–90	72	Rangers	51

**Won on goal average/difference.*
†Championship shared after 2–2 draw in the play-off.
††Won on a play-off.
Note: From 1975–76 Premier Division.

Scottish League Cup Finals

1946–47	Rangers 4, Aberdeen 0
1947–48	East Fife 0, Falkirk 0
Replay	East Fife 4, Falkirk 1
1948–49	Rangers 2, Raith Rovers 0
1949–50	East Fife 3, Dunfermline Athletic 0
1950–51	Motherwell 3, Hibernian 0
1951–52	Dundee 3, Rangers 2
1952–53	Dundee 2, Kilmarnock 0
1953–54	East Fife 3, Partick Thistle 2
1954–55	Heart of Midlothian 4, Motherwell 2
1955–56	Aberdeen 2, St Mirren 1
1956–57	Celtic 0, Partick Thistle 0 (aet)
Replay	Celtic 3, Partick Thistle 0
1957–58	Celtic 7, Rangers 1
1958–59	Heart of Midlothian 5, Partick Thistle 1
1959–60	Heart of Midlothian 2, Third Lanark 1
1960–61	Rangers 2, Kilmarnock 0
1961–62	Rangers 1, Heart of Midlothian 1
Replay	Rangers 3, Heart of Midlothian 1
1962–63	Heart of Midlothian 1, Kilmarnock 0
1963–64	Rangers 5, Morton 0
1964–65	Rangers 2, Celtic 1
1965–66	Celtic 2, Rangers 1
1966–67	Celtic 1, Rangers 0
1967–68	Celtic 5, Dundee 3
1968–69	Celtic 6, Hibernian 2
1969–70	Celtic 1, St Johnstone 0
1970–71	Rangers 1, Celtic 0
1971–72	Partick Thistle 4, Celtic 1
1972–73	Hibernian 2, Celtic 1
1973–74	Dundee 1, Celtic 0
1974–75	Celtic 6, Hibernian 3
1975–76	Rangers 1, Celtic 0
1976–77	Aberdeen 2, Celtic 1 (aet)
1977–78	Rangers 2, Celtic 1 (aet)
1978–79	Rangers 2, Aberdeen 1
1979–80	Dundee United 0, Aberdeen 0 (aet)
Replay	Dundee United 3, Aberdeen 0
1980–81	Dundee United 3, Dundee 0
1981–82	Rangers 2, Dundee United 1
1982–83	Celtic 2, Rangers 1
1983–84	Rangers 3, Celtic 2 (aet)
1984–85	Rangers 1, Dundee United 0
1985–86	Aberdeen 3, Hibernian 0
1986–87	Rangers 2, Celtic 1
1987–88	Rangers 3, Aberdeen 3 (aet)
	Rangers won 5–3 on penalties.
1988–89	Rangers 3, Aberdeen 2
1989–90	Aberdeen 2, Rangers 1 (aet)

Aberdeen finally beat Rangers in 1989–90, the third successive final between the two sides in the competition.

Index

INDEX

INDEX

INDEX

Picture credits

The publishers would like to thank the following for permission to reproduce copyright material:

Allsport: 53, 59, 62, 69

Associated Press: 50, 141, 187

Associated Sports Photography: 24, 25, 81, 110, 135, 182

Colorsport: 14, 16, 23, 28, 29, 30, 32, 36, 39, 42, 51, 68, 76, 90, 95, 97, 98 top, 99 top, 104, 109, 112, 116, 117, 118, 119, 121 right, 122, 123, 124, 125, 128, 131, 134, 136, 143, 157 left, 158, 160, 161, 162, 163, 168, 180, 181, 194, 195, 198 right, 200, 201 bottom, 204

The Hulton Picture Company: 9, 10, 11, 52, 67, 83 top, 92, 114, 120, 121 left, 139, 140, 166, 167, 172, 173 bottom, 174, 175, 177, 190 left

MTI Hungary: 60 left, 63

Popperfoto: 65, 105, 138, 149, 150, 178

Press Association: 108

S & G Press Agency Ltd: 146

Sportsfile, Dublin: 101

Topham Picture Library: 61 top, 89

All other pictures from Bob Thomas Sports Photography.

Jacket pictures

Front: Argentine fans (Bob Thomas Sports Photography)
Ruud Gullit (Colorsport)
Diego Maradona (Allsport)
Paul Gascoigne (Bob Thomas Sports Photography)

Back: Pele (Bob Thomas Sports Photography)

Acknowledgements

A–Z of World Soccer; FIFA News; Guerin Sportivo; The Hamlyn A–Z of British Football Records; Annuario del Calcio Mondiale; Peter Dunk; Mavis Suckling.

GOTHIC

THE DARK HEART OF FILM

EDITED BY JAMES BELL

FOREWORD BY SIR CHRISTOPHER FRAYLING

BFI
21 Stephen Street
London W1T 1LN

www.bfi.org.uk

First published 2013

ISBN 978-1-84457-682-1

A CIP catalogue record for this book is available from the British Library

Typeset in Caecilia and Benton Sans
Designed by chrisbrawndesign.com
Printed in England by Colt Press

Front Cover:
Klaus Kinski and Isabelle Adjani in 'Nosferatu the Vampyre' (1979)

Back Cover:
Deborah Kerr in 'The Innocents' (1961)

Inside Front Cover:
Melissa Stribling and Christopher Lee in 'Dracula' (1958)

Inside Back Cover:
Lon Chaney in 'The Phantom of the Opera' (1925)

This page:
Daniel Radcliffe in 'The Woman in Black' (2012)

CONTENTS

FOREWORD

BY SIR CHRISTOPHER FRAYLING

It is said that all photographs – by turning a moment into a memory – are like spirit photographs; by extension, all motion pictures become ghost stories, especially in retrospect. Late night Hollywood movies on television have a cast of dead people, something that was inconceivable before the 20th century. No wonder then, that only with the advent of cinema did 'the Gothic' come into its own. Before that, as a literary form it was waiting in the wings: not quite respectable, reviled by the Victorian academic establishment, best read late at night when the critical faculties were half asleep. 'Gothic film', the possibilities of which were spotted very early in the medium's history, propelled a long-marginalised and sometimes subversive form of literature from the past into the wider cultural bloodstream, and in the process turned it into myth. In an extended special effect which has lasted over a century, the literature of horror has both stayed in the world of literature and left it altogether to enter popular mythology and what one critic has called "the geography of inexperience". The Gothic has remained centre stage, especially since the 1920s, at the dark heart of film. Today, if a five-year old can chew it, Frankenstein's creature, the vampire Count, the mad scientist, the haunted house and the skeleton in the cupboard will appear on the wrapper.

The poet Coleridge famously reckoned that the literature of horror was "English in is origins, English in its materials and English by re-adoption". He was writing about the first phase of the Gothic novel, from Horace Walpole to Ann Radcliffe. A little later, the aristocratic villain – mad, bad and dangerous to know – whose family tree extended from Milton's Satan (who had all the best tunes) through to Lord Byron, was so indelibly associated with grand tourists that over in Ireland Charles Robert Maturin included in his novel *Melmoth the Wanderer* an old Spanish crone screaming "No English–Mother of God protect us–Avaunt Satan!", which suggests that Byron wannabes wandering around Europe in Regency times had a similar reputation on the continent as today's shaven-headed football supporters waving the flag of St George. The other staple of the 'classic' Gothic novel – the much-put-upon heroine – emerged from the literary tradition founded on Samuel Richardson's 'Clarissa'. Coleridge argued that the predilection for "desire with loathing strangely mix'd" was English rather than German: rural folktales from the oral tradition were not, he wrote, the same thing as Gothic novels. Equally, French fairy stories belonged to a different tradition, one of courtly manners. More recent critics have sometimes argued that our national talent for horror has something to do with repression and an inability to deal with sexual – and sometimes political – themes in a straightforward way: there's metaphor in our madness. Hence the fact that we are so good – the envy of the world – at diplomacy, advertising and telling nasty stories. Salvador Dali, when asked why the Surrealist movement hadn't caught on more widely in England – after giving an understandably inaudible lecture about his paranoid-critical method in London in summer 1936, dressed in a metal diving suit which had almost asphyxiated

(Opposite)
Bela Lugosi's Count lurks in the shadows in Tod Browning's 'Dracula' (1931).

him – is said to have replied that the English were unconscious surrealists from the moment they got up in the morning: they did not need an art movement to license their taste for the bizarre and the eccentric. What the Surrealists called "the castle question" seemed to come naturally to the English.

Actually, it was to transpire that Coleridge should have written "British" rather than "English". Where the three great foundation texts of the Gothic in film are concerned, Mary Shelley linked *Frankenstein* with fond memories of childhood visits to Scotland (and Victor Frankenstein aborts his female creature in the Orkneys); Robert Louis Stevenson was born and raised in Edinburgh (and *Strange Case of Dr Jekyll and Mr Hyde* originally had more to do with the New and Old towns of that city than with its ostensible location in the West End of London – or, according to Hollywood, the East End); Bram Stoker was an Anglo-Irishman from suburban Dublin who spent most of his twenties working as a junior civil servant at the gingerbread court of the Viceroy in Dublin Castle and whose first published work was a turgid tome of 248 pages entitled *The Duties of Clerks of Petty Sessions in Ireland* – which had more to do with being strangled by red tape than being bitten by vampires and vampiresses in the land beyond the forest. *Dracula* belongs, in part, to a form of pre-1916 Protestant Irish Gothic – in dialogue with Maturin and J. Sheridan LeFanu – complete with crumbling big houses, eccentric aristocrats who stay up all night, ancestry, guilt and the occult. The blend of Celtic myth and English storytelling would seem to have produced the most heady brew of metaphor, folktale, adventure, suggestion and sadism – a brew which was and is second to none at creating unease, and making readers question what they usually take for granted. In short, it is now accepted that the great horror stories of the Gothic represent one of the most significant contributions by British (and Irish) writers to the art of the 20th and 21st centuries, and THE most significant contribution to popular culture. The basic elements of the Gothic imaginative universe have become as immortal as Milton's Satan and disciples, and as the daughters of the Medusa. It is astonishing how resilient the old stories have proved to be. Despite the best efforts of the arts establishment – at least until recently – they just won't lie down. Charles Dickens wisely wrote of ghosts in 'A Christmas Tree' (1850) that "it is worthy of remark that they are reducible to a very few general types and classes; for, ghosts walk in a beaten track". The same could most certainly be said of Gothic film. Some critics reckon, as writer Geoffrey O'Brien has noted, that these "types and classes" are "crucial to a genre that seems to define itself by constantly recapitulating everything it has been… To watch many horror movies is in some sense to watch the same movie over and over: they are drawn to their past in the same way that their characters are compelled to go back to the ancestral crypt… The rest is ornament and variations on a theme, a matter of more masks or bigger masks or more convincingly detailed masks…".

This super-movie has survived many variations through the 20th century and beyond: silent Grand Guignols of the early 1920s followed by German Expressionism and its camp Hollywood counterpart in the early 1930s; the drive-in triple features of the 1950s; the rise of Hammer Films, when British cinema at last discovered sex and the gore was presented for the first time in seaside postcard colours; the Italian pop surrealism of the 1960s; the psycho killers and seriously dysfunctional families of the 1970s and 1980s; the shift from margin to mainstream in the 1990s, taking over from the Western as the backbone of an industry; the renaissance of the living dead. Above all, perhaps, the transition from pre-World War II horror (where normal society was where the heroes and heroines lived) to post-1970s horror (where the horror has become a form of liberation, and normality itself has become strange). Today there are audiences schooled in the halls of Hogwarts and following the *Twilight* path to romance. If it has become difficult for mere mortals to say "I love you" with a straight face, then good-looking vampires are there to say it for you.

This BFI Compendium – the second, after *39 Steps to the Genius of Hitchcock* – traces the story of the more masks and bigger masks and more detailed masks, exploring many of the sinister roots and branches of Gothic film along the way. Starting with 'Monstrous', the beast at the window and the beast within, moving on to 'The Dark Arts' of the occult, cursing and bad science, and then to 'Haunted' houses and possessed people of various descriptions, the book concludes with 'Love is a Devil', where homage to satanic majesties can lead to all manner of delightful transgressions. In the course of this Grand Tour of the Gothic, we learn many things: that vampires – no longer aristocrats – can now have a psychology and a beautiful body, that the gender balance among monsters is at last being redressed, that the British have had a decisive influence on horror films as well as books, and that Grand Guignol films started a lot earlier than many of us supposed; we learn about waking nightmares as well as the more conventional kinds, about Italian, Eastern European and Japanese horrors, about the curious ability of the horror film to seem old-fashioned and transgressive both at the same time; and about how saintly Gothic architecture managed to seem malign; finally, we discover how the frustrated love that dare not speak its name sometimes finds space to shout its name in Gothic film, and how the traditional put-upon heroine is now turning the tables. Curator Martin Myrone, in a stimulating essay on the visual art of horror, refers to the Gothic as a notoriously "trans-medial, genre-defying, migrating and polluting phenomenon". Children's stories at one end of the spectrum and postmodern slasher movies at the other. One central theme of *Gothic – The Dark Heart of Film* is how the core elements of the Gothic have changed and mutated over time – but somehow they have endured as well.

The BFI, through promethean editor James Bell, ably assisted by his contributors, has created a monster of a book. It's alive!

PART I
MONSTROUS

MONSTROUS

VAMPIRES

BY ANNE BILLSON

"What if I'm not the hero? What if I'm the bad guy?" asks Edward Cullen, the brooding vampire boyfriend in *Twilight*, the film version of Stephenie Meyer's bestselling supernatural romance. Edward needn't have worried. As Bella describes him in *Breaking Dawn*, the final book in Meyer's tetralogy, he has "the most beautiful soul, more beautiful than his brilliant mind or his incomparable face or his glorious body."

Soul? Since when have these onetime eternally damned bloodsucking entities been in possession of souls, let alone glorious bodies? Robert Pattinson, who in the *Twilight* films looks like a statue of Adonis covered in talcum powder, is a creature very different from those played by Max Schreck and Bela Lugosi in the earliest vampire films. And beautiful souls are not the only thing vampires have acquired in the 90 years since Graf Orlok rose from his coffin. Thanks to the *Twilight Saga*, they are now at the centre of one of the top ten highest grossing film franchises of all time. No longer confined to a horror subgenre, the undead have emerged from the shadows to become teen idols, lifestyle models and children's entertainers. Once upon a time, drawing attention to their presence so flagrantly would have put them at risk from stake-wielding Van Helsings, holy men brandishing crucifixes or villagers waving blazing torches. But nowadays they're more likely to find themselves buried beneath a scrum of squealing fans.

"The vampire feeds on the very stuff of wish-fulfilment and dreams, which is at the essence of the cinematic experience," wrote David Pirie in *The Vampire Cinema* (Hamlyn, 1977). Vampires were a part of folklore and popular literature long before the cinema was invented, but it was film that showed us what they looked like. Two vampire stories in particular provided the blueprint – Bram Stoker's *Dracula* and J. Sheridan Le Fanu's *Carmilla* – but the image of the vampire has changed radically over the past century. Films don't feed on our blood, like vampires, but on our dreams, siphoning them off and serving them back to us in refracted forms. Traditionally, the vampire casts no reflection, but instead it reflects *us*; each generation sees in the vampire what it fears or desires, or fears *and* desires, for they are often the same thing.

Films, like vampires, thrive on darkness. To see a filmed image you have to shut out the sunlight and cast your surroundings into night, so it's fitting that cinema's first major addition to the vampire playbook should be the creature's vulnerability to daylight, to set alongside the absence of reflection and aversion to running water. Like the image on a screen when the curtains are drawn back to let light into a darkened room, Graf Orlok fades into nothingness at the end of F.W. Murnau's 1922 film *Nosferatu, eine Symphonie des Grauens*. Light became as important as stakes and holy water in the vampire-hunter's arsenal.

It's thanks to cinema that Dracula, and by extension the vampire, has been elevated to an instantly recognisable visual cliché on a par with Sherlock Holmes or James Bond. Though Murnau's

(Previous page)
Max Schreck as Graf Orlok in F.W. Murnau's 'Nosferatu' (1922).

(Opposite)
Klaus Kinski and Isabelle Adjani in Werner Herzog's 'Nosferatu the Vampyre' (1979).

Nosferatu was an unofficial adaptation of *Dracula* (Stoker's estate almost succeeded in having all prints of it destroyed), it owes its visual style more to German artist and occultist Albin Grau, the film's producer and art director, than to Stoker's descriptions. Schreck's portrayal of the vampire (like Klaus Kinski's in Werner Herzog's dreamlike 1979 remake *Nosferatu the Vampyre*) is as a hideous walking cadaver, more ratlike than batlike, with bald head, long fingernails and pointy teeth, whereas in the novel Jonathan Harker describes "a tall old man, clean shaven save for a long white moustache" while Mina Harker later describes him as "a tall, thin man, with a beaky nose and black moustache and pointed beard..." Nevertheless, the cinema invariably depicts Dracula and other vampires as clean-shaven; the several exceptions include John Carradine, who wrote in his introduction to *House of Dracula (The Original Shooting Script)*, published in 1993: "To date, I have the distinction of being the only actor who looked the part as visualized by Bram Stoker in 1897," as well as Christopher Lee in Jesús Franco's *El Conde Dracula* (*Nachts, Wenn Dracula Erwacht*, 1970), and Gary Oldman in Francis Ford Coppola's *Bram Stoker's Dracula* (1992).

But it was clean-shaven Bela Lugosi in Tod Browning's *Dracula* (1931) who established the image of the vampire in the public consciousness. Henceforth, the Dracula kit would consist of white tie formalwear and a cape that can be extended by the arms to somewhat resemble the wings of a giant bat. It's Lugosi's Dracula who is referenced in vampire spoofs like *Abbott and Costello Meet Frankenstein* (1948), *Mother Riley Meets the Vampire* (1952) (both of which starred Lugosi himself) or *The Munsters*, in children's entertainment like *Sesame Street* or the cartoon series *Count Duckula*, or in products such as the breakfast cereal Count Chocula.

But there was still one essential element missing from the Lugosi vampire – fangs. In Stoker's *Dracula*, Harker remarks on Count Dracula's "peculiarly sharp white teeth" which "protruded over the lips". But Graf Orlok's pointy ratlike teeth in *Nosferatu* would be the last time for several decades that the vampire's preternatural dental work would be visible. Thanks to Karl Freund's Expressionist cinematography, more emphasis was placed on Lugosi's piercing gaze than on his teeth, which are only barely glimpsed, or are concealed behind a cape in what would become one of Dracula's signature poses. The first films to make an explicit feature out of fangs

(Above)
Unlike the elegant onscreen Draculas to come, Max Schreck's vampire in 'Nosferatu' (1922) is closer to a hideous cadaver.

(Opposite, top)
Christopher Lee bares his fangs in Hammer's 'Scars of Dracula' (1970).

(Opposite, bottom)
One of the original production sketches by Albin Grau, the producer and art director of 'Nosferatu' (1922).

were Mexican director Fernando Méndez's *El vampiro* (1957) and its sequel *El ataúd del vampiro* (1958), starring Germán Robles as the dashing Count Karol de Lavud. Sandra Harrison also sported prominent fangs in the AIP teen-horror *Blood of Dracula* (1957), a follow-up to the same year's *I Was a Teenage Werewolf* and *I Was a Teenage Frankenstein*, whose sweater-girl garb was an exception to the more usual flowing robes of fangless *femme fatales* like Gloria Holden in *Dracula's Daughter* (1936) or Annette Stroyberg in *Blood and Roses* (1960). Harrison was also ahead of her time in that her character underwent extreme facial transformation, something that wouldn't happen to other vampires for another three decades.

Christopher Lee's fangs made only brief but effective appearances in *Dracula* (1958), but they became increasingly prominent in the sequels of the 1960s and 1970s, though the act of biting into the victim's neck was still obscured by cloak or camera angle. Once Hammer discovered fangs, that frisson-generating moment when the vampire's lips first curl back to reveal its true nature, with or without an accompanying feral hiss, became one of the most popular conventions of vampire cinema.

Hammer also added colour to the vampire's black and white dress code – specifically red, as in red trickles of blood, red contact lenses and the scarlet lining of the Count's cloak. But beyond making vampires sexier, the new wave of vampires spearheaded by Hammer didn't challenge the characterisation of the vampire as European nobility. Three of the most notorious real-life historical models for Dracula were Vlad III, Prince of Wallachia, the Countess Elizabeth Báthory and Baron Gilles de Rais, and the idea of a decadent aristocracy living off the blood of its social inferiors has passed down not just to Count Dracula and his relatives, but to *El Vampiro*'s Count de Lavud, Count von Krolock in *Dance of the Vampires* (1967), Count Yorga, Blacula

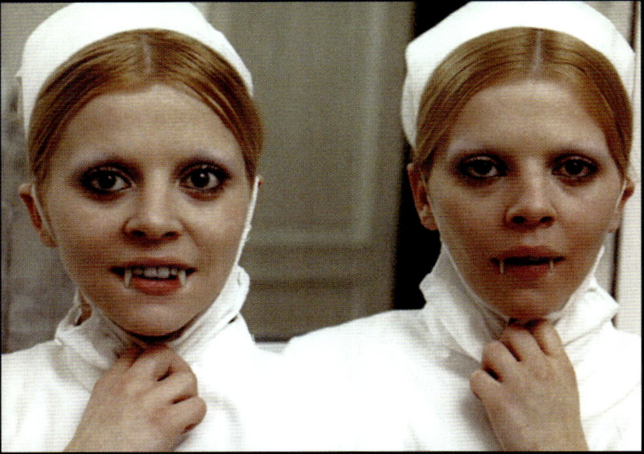

Jean Rollin's 'Lips of Blood' (1975)

Though Joseph Sheridan Le Fanu's 1872 novella *Carmilla* predates Bram Stoker's *Dracula*, its notion of a passive-aggressive girlish vampire hasn't often been imitated; most adaptations play up the lesbian eroticism and make its monster – memorably, Annette Vadim in her husband Roger's *Blood and Roses* (*Et mourir de plaisir*, 1960), Ingrid Pitt in *The Vampire Lovers* (1970) and Alexandra Bastedo in *The Blood Spattered Bride* (*La novia ensangrientada*, 1972) – a sexy, bloodthirsty wildcat rather than a manipulative, sickly kitten.

In the silent era, female vampires proliferated – but only metaphorically, thanks to the Kipling poem 'A Fool There Was', which took a Polidori-esque approach by depicting a seductress as a metaphorical vampire. Theda Bara made her name and career playing 'the Vampire' in the 1915 film of the same name, and the character type took off. The many films of the 1910s and 20s that use 'vampire' in the title refer to a species of goth gold-digger who's out for money rather than blood. So much so that in *Dracula's Daughter* (1936), when the hero announces that he's out hunting vampires, his butler deadpans, "I thought one did that with chequebooks, sir."

The first true female vampire in cinema is Edna Tichenor as the kohl-eyed Bat Girl in Tod Browning's now-lost *London After Midnight* (1927), though she turns out to be fake. In 1931, Bela Lugosi's Dracula has three silent wives and turns feeble Lucy into a wraith. All four are left undead at the end of the film by an oversight, though *Dracula's Daughter* picks up with Gloria Holden as the Count's melancholy, bisexual heiress. Carl Dreyer's *Vampyr* (1932) features an old female vampire who has had few imitators, while Browning's *Mark of the Vampire* (1935), a remake of *London After Midnight*, casts Carol Borland as Luna: her flowing white robes, long black hair and pale face – and feral hiss – prefigure many a Hammer hoyden or Morticia Addams joke.

When Hammer revived Gothic horror with added plunging necklines, they brought on a parade of buxom fanged starlets. Valerie Gaunt as Christopher Lee's unnamed companion in *Dracula* (1958) coins the type, but others (Andrée Melly, Isobel Black, Isla Blair) feature in follow-ups like *The Brides of Dracula* (1960) and *The Kiss of the Vampire* (1963). In all of these, vampire women are minions to Dracula types, brutally disposed of by prurient authoritarians – Barbara Shelley is gang-staked by monks in *Dracula Prince of Darkness* (1966). Even when Pitt's Carmilla is given a lead role, she's less formidable than continental vampire women like Barbara Steele's Asa in Mario Bava's *Black Sunday* (1960), the African-seeming Jacqueline Sieger in Jean Rollin's *Le Viol du vampire* (1968) or Delphine Seyrig's Dietrich-look Elisabeth Bathory in Harry Kümel's *Daughters of Darkness* (1971).

Sometimes inspired by the historical Báthory, who was accused of bathing in virgins' blood, female vampires proliferated in the 1970s, often independent of any Dracula-style 'masters': Celeste Yarnall as *The Velvet Vampire* (1971), Mariclare Costello as the suicide bride of *Let's Scare Jessica to Death* (1971), Lesley Gilb as den mother in *Lemora: A Child's Tale of the Supernatural* (1973), Marianne Morris and Anulka in *Vampyres* (1974), Marilyn Chambers as a science-created mutant in *Rabid* (1978), Catherine Deneuve's icy club queen in *The Hunger* (1983).

These in turn spun off even showier characters, like Nai Bonet as disco queen *Nocturna* (1979), and made room for stunt castings like Grace Jones (*Vamp*, 1985), Sylvia Kristel (*Dracula's Widow*, 1988) and Anne Parillaud (*Innocent Blood*, 1992).

Female vampires are ideological warring grounds in artier efforts like Abel Ferrara's *The Addiction* (1995) and Michael Almereyda's *Nadja* (1994), but also ideally suit X-rated fantasies like *Out for Blood* and *Trampire* (both 1990). In both areas of activity, plots tend to involve a female vampire created or mentored by a dominant male whom they reject in order to find their own identity, and this indicates a shift in the genre. Stories about how vampires relate to humans give way to stories about how vampires relate among themselves: Anne Rice's Lestat has to contend with his eternal-child 'daughter' (Kirsten Dunst in *Interview with the Vampire*, 1994) and the mother he turned into a night stalker (Lena Olin in *Queen of the Damned*, 2002). Even the *Twilight* films follow this arc, with Bella (Kristen Stewart), in the end, not just a girl who falls in love with a vampire but a girl who becomes a vampire.

Neil Jordan's *Byzantium* (2013) postulates enmity between female and male vampires; the mother-and-daughter team are on the run from aristocratic users who don't want them in the boys' club.

(Top)
'Dracula' (1931). Bela Lugosi's Count defined the image of the vampire for the public.

(Above)
Hammer's 'Dracula' (1958) brought a new sexiness to the onscreen vampire.

(an African prince) and the various incarnations of Carmilla, from Roger Vadim's *Blood and Roses* to Hammer's Karnstein trilogy and the Countess Báthory in *Daughters of Darkness* (1971).

As befitting their social status, vampires invariably lived in castles or mansions set apart from – and often located geographically higher than – the common hordes of villagers or peasants forming the bulk of their food supply. Even today, there's a tendency to look upon the vampire as a superior kind of monster – sexier than the zombie, more cunning than Frankenstein's monster, less hapless than the Wolf Man, better dressed than the Mummy. When the undead are drawn from the ranks of the proletariat, they're zombies, faceless shambolic masses, whereas vampires are seen not just as powerful, intelligent, charismatic individuals but – as the years have gone by – more sympathetic, perhaps as a result of an erosion in rigid moral standards as once dictated by organised religion, as well as the burgeoning appeal of the rebel outsider, the rise of the conflicted anti-hero and the enshrinement of the wishes of the individual over the needs of society.

The biggest shifts in the way vampires are perceived have been prompted by television. In 1967, the American daytime TV quasi-Gothic soap *Dark Shadows* introduced a vampire into its line-up of characters; Barnabas Collins attracted a loyal following and gradually turned from a sinister villain into the show's lovelorn protagonist. That same year, 1967, Anne Rice began to write the short story that would presently be expanded into *Interview with the Vampire* (1976), in which the vampires are not villains but romantic neo-hippy anti-heroes who dress in black velvet and antique lace and seemingly prefer discussing their feelings and philosophies to biting necks – another step towards rehabilitation and redemption. By the time Collins was played by Johnny Depp in Tim Burton's

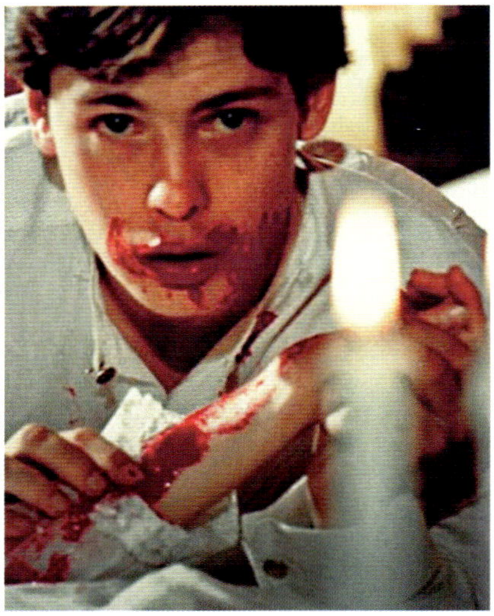

(Above)
John Amplas as the eponymous 'vampire' in George A. Romero's pioneering 'Martin' (1977), who uses razor-blades instead of fangs.

(Above, right)
Lina Leandersson as Eli in Tomas Alfredson's 'Let the Right One In' (2008), which is set in a modern-day housing estate on the outskirts of Stockholm.

big screen version of *Dark Shadows* (2012), there was never any question the vampire was anything but a hero, albeit one who had to struggle constantly against the dark side of his nature.

But a fashion makeover was urgently required; in the 1960s and 1970s traditional vampire garb, which could have passed for posh formalwear in 1930s Hollywood, started looking like a Halloween costume. ("How would you like to go around looking like a head waiter for 700 years?" complains George Hamilton as Count Dracula in the spoof *Love at First Bite*, 1979). Even Count Yorga and Blacula, at large in modern California, subscribed to the Dracula dress-code. Sartorially stuck in the past, male vampires became a joke; send-ups proliferated, and the creature's failure to adapt to the modern world led to a scarcity of serious vampire movies in the late 1970s, their place in the horror pantheon giving way to more up-to-the-minute bogeymen such as psychopaths, zombies and aliens.

Female vampires, meanwhile, were still subscribing to variations on the Carmilla look, the floaty chiffon style merging with the hippy-chick fashions of the late 1960s and echoed by other female vampires such as the pointedly named Diane LeFanu in *The Velvet Vampire* (1971) and Jean Rollin's erotic vampires in films such as *Le Viol du vampire* (1968) and *La vampire nue* (1969). Most *soignée* of them all, Countess Bathory in *Daughters of Darkness* (1971) is visibly a creature born of the movies – a Dietrichesque diva from Hollywood's golden age, platinum blonde hair tightly coiffed, impeccably made up (vulgar fangs would have ruined the perfection of her lipstick) and swanning around in chiffon, ostrich feathers or sequins. But it was still fancy dress.

It was George A. Romero who gave vampires the first truly modern makeover, doing for them what he had already done for zombies in *Night of the Living Dead* (1968) – giving them social relevance in the modern world. Romero's *Martin* (1977) is set in a suburb of Pittsburgh (the director's favourite stamping-ground) where the industrial decay and moral confusion of the economically depressed 1970s couldn't be more different from Universal's studio sets or Hammer's leafy Bray. Martin, misunderstood teenager, works as a delivery boy and uses razor-blades instead of fangs to tap his victims' veins, but he's also depicted sympathetically, as much a victim of his circumstances as the lonely housewives on whom he preys.

Martin's youth marks him out as a missing link between Dracula and the vampires in later teen-orientated vampire films – in the throes of a desperate identity crisis, he even kits himself out in a Dracula cloak and fangs – but the lifestyle he leads is grim. Romero's film passed almost unnoticed and didn't start a trend, though social realist vampires operating in the modern world as what would shortly be known as serial killers would later reappear in Kathryn Bigelow's vampire western *Near Dark* (1987), and, later still, in Tomas Alfredson's *Let the Right One In* (2008), set in a working-class housing estate near Stockholm. These films address the downside of living for aeons, and the harsh practicalities of having continually to seek blood for

(Top)
Kathryn Bigelow's vampire western 'Near Dark' (1987).

(Above)
The vampire (Kiefer Sutherland) as misunderstood teenager in 1987's 'The Lost Boys'.

sustenance, concerns rarely addressed in more fanciful vampire yarns. It's not all swanky clothes, neck-biting and superpowers; the lives these vampires lead are the lives of society's outcasts – miserable, shabby and rootless.

Meanwhile, the revolution in practical special effects that led to a resurgence of werewolf movies in the early 1980s (spearheaded by the innovative transformation effects in *An American Werewolf in London* and *The Howling*) was slow to spread to vampire movies, but once it did the way vampires looked changed yet again. Red contact lenses and fangs were no longer enough; when not trying to pass for human, vampires metamorphosed into elaborate and visibly monstrous variations on Graf von Orlok, with exaggerated fangs and fingernails, pointed ears, bad skin and blazing eyes. And the damage these new movie vampires could inflict on their victims at last became explicit. No more strategically placed cloaks – in *Vamp* (1986) you could actually see exotic dancer-cum-vampire Katrina (Grace Jones) tearing into her victim's neck.

The rise of the post-punk Goth subculture coincided with the publication of *The Vampire Lestat* in 1985, the first of Anne Rice's sequels to *Interview with the Vampire*, and fans eagerly embraced the trappings of vampirism as an alternative lifestyle choice. Encouraged by Rice's introspective first-person narratives, a new wave of vampire-lovers viewed the creatures as misunderstood, often conflicted, but glamorous, rebellious and brave – perfect role models for alienated teenagers. At the same time, the tagline of *The Lost Boys* (1987): 'Sleep all day. Party all night. Never grow old. Never die. It's fun to be a vampire', implied that teenagers were already halfway to leading the life of the living dead, and signalled that vampire movies were no longer being aimed at adults.

Cinema was slow to catch up with this radical rethinking of the vampire's

(Above)
Kirsten Dunst, Brad Pitt and Tom Cruise in the film adaptation of Anne Rice's 'Interview with the Vampire' (1994).

image, despite a sprinkling of jokey teen-themed vampire films like *Fright Night* (1985), Goth-friendly one-offs such as *The Hunger* (1983) in which chic bloodsuckers stalked New York's nightclubs to a soundtrack of 'Bela Lugosi's Dead' by Bauhaus, and the long delayed film of *Interview with the Vampire* (1994) in which the vampire Louis pays tribute to cinema itself as "...a mechanical wonder [that] allowed me to see the sun rise for the first time in two hundred years...". And once again it was television that prodded the creatures definitively out of their subgenre ghetto and into mainstream culture when Joss Whedon, unhappy with the film made from his original screenplay of *Buffy the Vampire Slayer* (1992), turned the concept into a seven-season TV phenomenon which ran from 1997 to 2003. It wasn't so much the blonde cheerleader's vampire-slaying that made her so influential as her intimate relationships with two of the vampires, which flew in the face of accepted wisdom by suggesting that bloodsuckers could be good boyfriend material.

It was a short step from the vampires of Anne Rice's novels and *Buffy*, which depicted them as romantic anti-heroes with hopes, fears and histories, albeit still capable of evil, to *Twilight*, Stephenie Meyers's bestselling Young Adult tetralogy (filmed in five parts from 2008 to 2012) in which the leading vampire character is a paragon of self-denial, almost as passive as the narrator-heroine; both characters are cyphers whose lack of strong personality allows young audiences to project themselves and their emo-fantasies into the roles, conveniently ignoring the fact that Edward Cullen is actually Bella Swan's senior by some 80 years, making their relationship the vampire equivalent of a paedophile posing as a teen in an internet chatroom.

Whatever its flaws, *The Twilight Saga* has as much right to be a part of the continuing story of vampire cinema as any other film. Predictably, with its "vegetarian" vampires who glitter in the sunlight, it has attracted derision – often, ironically, from genre fans who grew up with *Blade* (1998) and *Underworld* (2003) and their sequels, in which the vampires wear tight leather trousers, do martial arts, or loll around wanly like New Romantic refugees, all a long way from Schreck and Lugosi.

But the useful thing about vampires, and the reason they're so durable in zeitgeist terms, is that they have always offered a multiplicity of metaphors. You name it, vampires can symbolise it – from capitalism, class and religion, to addictions (both physical and emotional), disease and death, sexuality or abstinence, from the quest for eternal youth and the processes of ageing to Eleanor in *Byzantium* (2013), who by limiting her victims to the acquiescent old and infirm provides them with a sort of assisted suicide service. Vampires have reinvented themselves time and again to appear in new guises and appeal to new generations and changing social attitudes. No longer confined to the horror subgenre, they can nowadays be found in romantic comedies (Amy Heckerling's *Vamps*), action films (*Stakeland*), special effects extravaganzas (*Van Helsing*), science fiction (*Daybreakers*), pornography (*Vampire Sex Diaries*), westerns (*John Carpenter's Vampires*), Tex-Mex genre hybrids (*From Dusk Till Dawn*), musicals (*Suck*), anime (*Vampire Hunter D*), martial arts (*Blood the Last Vampire*, expanded from the anime of the same name), mock-docs (Vincent Lannoo's *Vampires*), art movies (Claire Denis's *Trouble Every Day*), feminist *Lebensfreude* (*Wir sind die Nacht*) and family films (*Hotel Transylvania*). There's a vampire for every taste, and then some.

This is also why there's no need to worry about vampires being defanged by *Twilight* or any other swoony fang-fiction fare. Vampires were around before cinema existed, and will no doubt be around long after cinema as we know it has been replaced by hitherto unimaginable technology, whether or not it involves a way of telling stories by casting shadows. But the shadows will always be there, in one way or another, because they're a part of us. There's a lot of life in the undead yet.

TV Vampires

By Stacey Abbott

A boy, Mark Petrie, wakes in the middle of the night to find the figure of his best friend Danny Glick, recently deceased, emerging from white mist and floating outside his bedroom window. With pale skin, hollow eyes, and protruding fangs, Danny scratches at the glass, begging to be invited in: "Open the window. Open the window Mark. Please, let me in. It's OK Mark; I'm your friend".

This sequence from Tobe Hooper's 1979 television adaptation of Stephen King's *Salem's Lot* encapsulates those Gothic elements that make the vampire both frightening and difficult to resist. First, vampires appear as our friends. They promise intimacy, but instead bring pain, death and damnation. Danny Glick's scratches at the window also highlight the importance of thresholds to the vampire – creatures that must be invited into our homes. One of the most unsettling features of the vampire is that their victims are complicit in their fate – they've chosen to let them in. Thresholds are a key component of the Gothic, a genre that haunts the liminal space between life and death. The sound of Danny's fingernails on the glass is an uncanny reminder of the thin barrier that separates us and them, life and death.

The TV screen itself mirrors the glass barrier of the window. Television is another threshold through which we choose to invite the vampire into our homes, and we do so from as early as childhood. Long before seeing a film adaptation of *Dracula* or reading Bram Stoker's novel, children learn to recognise the Count through TV series such as *Count Duckula* (1988-1993), *Mona the Vampire* (1999-2003) and *Young Dracula* (2006-) – not to mention Count von Count in *Sesame Street* (1969-). The trend continues through teen programmes such as *Buffy the Vampire Slayer* (1997-2003) and *Vampire Diaries* (2009), where vampirism becomes a metaphor for teen angst, physical change and sexuality. Then in more grown-up fare like *Angel* (1999-2004), *Being Human* (2008-2013), *The Lair* (2007-2009) and *True Blood* (2008), the vampires deal with adult issues surrounding morality, redemption, sexual identity, and addiction.

'Salem's Lot' (1979)

The vampire has been a regular feature on TV since the 1960s, which saw the launch of *The Munsters* (1964-66) and *The Addams Family* (1964-66) – supernatural-family sitcoms that featured vampiric matriarchs Lily Munster and Morticia Addams, both of whom possess the vampire's smouldering sexuality alongside a mother's nurturing qualities. In 1968, the British anthology series *Mystery and Imagination* (1966-1970) saw Dracula played by Denholm Elliott, who brings out a startling independence in the women he vampirises. British television returned to *Dracula* with Philip Saville's celebrated BBC adaptation, *Count Dracula* (1977), which starred Louis Jourdan as a Machiavellian monster, calm and calculating in his corruption of Britain. At a time when cinematic versions of *Dracula* were becoming increasingly anachronistic alongside modern horror films, Dracula on TV remained sinister and frightening.

In 1967, the American Gothic soap opera *Dark Shadows* introduced a vampire, Barnabas Collins, to improve its flagging ratings. The original plan was to feature him for a few weeks before putting a stake through his heart, but the producers were met by an unexpected phenomenon: Barnabas Collins began to get fan mail. Fans saw a tragic quality in the character and the writers responded by emphasising an element of self-loathing that fuelled his desire for a cure to his vampiric curse. The reluctant vampire was born.

It's been argued that the appearance of vampires on television has domesticated them, causing them to lose their monstrous identity: the vampires in the aforementioned children's series are either vegetarians or channel their obsessive behaviour into their love of counting; Lily Munster and Morticia Addams use their vampiric appearance to highlight sexuality over monstrosity. Serial vampire dramas, beginning with *Dark Shadows* but continuing through *Forever Knight* (1989-1996), *Angel*, *Being Human*, *The Vampire Diaries* (2009-) and *True Blood* (2008-), have furthered the development of the sympathetic vampire, a figure who seeks to deny its vampire identify and live a human-like life.

However this argument ignores a key, uniquely televisual aspect: seriality. Reluctance may make our attraction to these characters more comfortable, but the suspense of each series is built around the potential that the vampire will give in to its blood lust – which each does, at some point. Their inevitable weakening makes their crimes all the more disturbing. Angel threatens and murders Buffy's friends in *Buffy the Vampire Slayer*, Stefan Salvatore reveals a tendency to rip off the heads of his victims in *The Vampire Diaries*, and Mitchell, in a fit of revenge and sexual fervour, slaughters all the passengers in a train carriage in *Being Human*. These are not the actions of a domesticated monster, but those of a creature that has been restrained for too long. Their fall from grace is not a sign of their failure to be human, more that they are all too human and susceptible to the human weaknesses – jealousy, greed, revenge – which fuel their monstrosity.

Vampires have not been defanged by television; on the contrary, inviting them to cross the threshold into our homes has only implicated us deeper in their emotionally complicated and morally ambiguous world.

Count von Count in 'Sesame Street'

Costuming Vampires

By Catherine Spooner

Costume is not mere window-dressing in Gothic film but intrinsic to its effect. Masks, veils and disguises are ubiquitous from the earliest days of the Gothic novel, and significant less for what they hide than for the act of hiding itself. Fear inheres in the concealing gesture, from David Lynch's repeated motif of red drapes to the masked figure that dogs the revellers in *The Masque of the Red Death* (1964). Elsewhere, the theatricality of the Gothic results in a preoccupation with dress-up and performativity, with the terrors and delights of constructing a self through clothes.

Nowhere is costume more prominent than in the vampire film. Screen vampires are clothes horses: they exude glamour. Vampire films demonstrate an acute awareness that vampirism is a performance: one that requires adherence to certain sartorial codes. Even where these codes are broken, as in the scruffy child vampire Eli from Tomas Alfredson's *Let the Right One In* (2008), the effect is created through the viewer's understanding that the film is working against convention.

Male vampires are often dandies. The dandy and the modern vampire both emerged at roughly the same time, in Regency Britain. John Polidori's *The Vampyre* of 1819, which fictionalised his employer Lord Byron in the role of lady-killer Lord Ruthven, set a template of vampire-as-dandy that has never been fully shaken off. Dandies are not necessarily flamboyant, but rather combine a careful management of their personal appearance with superior wit and taste. On film, the characteristic male vampire wears a version

Female Vampires

Musidora as Irma Vep (*Louis Feuillade, 'Les Vampires,' 1915*) The vampires of Feuillade's serial are not supernatural creatures but a subversive criminal organisation. Nevertheless the mysterious and seductive Irma Vep, played by Musidora, proved influential on vampire costuming, her close-fitting black catsuit suggesting a sinuous, fetishistic sex appeal.

Ingrid Pitt as Carmilla Karnstein (*Roy Ward Baker, 'The Vampire Lovers,' 1970, costumes by Brian Cox*) In Hammer Films' Karnstein cycle, a trilogy inspired by J. Sheridan Le Fanu's *Carmilla* (1872), the association with the white empire line dress is sealed as Ingrid Pitt and Yutte Stensgaard (*Lust For a Vampire*, 1971) appear in garments that recall not the period of the source text but rather that of the 'original' Gothic.

Delphine Seyrig as Elizabeth Báthory (*Harry Kümel, 'Daughters of Darkness,' 1971, costumes by Bernard Perris*) Delphine Seyrig sports a series of high glamour costumes designed by Bernard Perris in *Daughters of Darkness*, most notably a reptilian silver sequinned gown that offers a new take on the fetishistic theme of dress-as-skin.

Sadie Frost as Lucy Westenra (*'Bram Stoker's Dracula,' 1992, costumes by Eiko Ishioka*) Ishioka's Oscar-winning costumes for *Bram Stoker's Dracula* offered a new inflection of perennial themes by introducing Japanese and Oriental influences. Sadie Frost's Lucy is clothed in a new spin on the classic white dress: a spectacular bridal gown with a vast ruff like that of a frilled lizard.

of the 19th-century black suit, the costume immortalised by Bela Lugosi in *Dracula* (1931). From Tony Scott's *The Hunger* (1983) onwards, in which the opening sequence shows Goth band Bauhaus singing 'Bela Lugosi's Dead' in a nightclub, the black suit is often given a subcultural styling, purveying Romantic angst and outsider cool. The Gothic dandy rises again in the form of the contemporary Goth.

Female vampires are ineluctably associated with the white empire line dress, the décolleté style that held sway during the phase of the Gothic novel's greatest popularity at the turn of the 18th century. The first female vampire in English literature, Geraldine from Samuel Taylor Coleridge's narrative poem 'Christabel' (1800/1816), arrives out of the forest "Dressed in a silken robe of white", implicitly recalling the insubstantial fashions of the day. Female vampires in 19th-century fiction continue to wear white, often nightgowns or shrouds. The white gown becomes a substitute for skin, the inevitable splash of red blood marking the crossing of boundaries between the inside and outside of the body, predator and victim, purity and danger. Elsewhere, following Musidora's iconic performance as Irma Vep in Louis Feuillade's *Les Vampires* (1915), the fetishistic appeal of closely-fitting fabric, leather or plastic again simulates skin while simultaneously closing off access to the vampire's body, making her paradoxically tactile yet untouchable. Far from stale convention, each new reiteration of vampire costume speaks to and about its predecessors, adding new layers in the construction of vampire identity.

Male Vampires

Bela Lugosi as Dracula
(*Tod Browning, 'Dracula', 1931, costumes by Ed Ware and Vera West*) Bela Lugosi's iconic performance set the template for 20th-century male vampire style. The costume bears the traces of its theatrical origins (in Hamilton Deane's stage adaptation of *Dracula*) in its high collar, which was used to assist the vampire's disappearance on stage.

James Marsters as Spike (*'Buffy the Vampire Slayer', costumes by Cynthia Bergstrom*) Spike's trench coat is an over-determined garment, reworking the cape while carrying connotations of the Blaxploitation era and the Punk and Goth subcultures. It is ambiguously gendered, with military origins but feminised by its long skirts – evoking the vampire's propensity to challenge boundaries and borders.

David Bowie as John Blaylock
(*Tony Scott, 'The Hunger', 1983, costumes by Milena Canonero*) *The Hunger* crystallised the association between vampires and Goth subculture with David Bowie and Catherine Deneuve seeking out victims in a Goth nightclub. Vampire performativity is suggested by Bowie later removing his black wig.

Johnny Depp as Barnabas Collins (*Tim Burton, 'Dark Shadows', 2012, costumes by Colleen Atwood*) Colleen Atwood's Oscar-nominated costumes for Johnny Depp's Barnabas Collins (seen above with Michelle Pfeiffer as Elizabeth Collins Stoddard) play on both the early 1970s revival of dandy styles and the culture clash comedy enabled by the costume anachronism.

The British Influence

By Barry Forshaw

(Above) British actors Colin Clive, Elsa Lanchester, Boris Karloff and Ernest Thesiger in James Whale's 'Bride of Frankenstein' (1935).

Hammer Film Productions always promoted a certain notion of Britishness in its colourful output. Whatever Mitteleuropean country a film might be set in, such actors as Peter Cushing and Christopher Lee continued to declaim with their customarily crisp Oxford accents. But Hammer's folding in of a version of Albion along with its blood-drenched pleasures was only part of a lengthy process of the domestic export of Britishness into Gothic cinema across the world. Britain has provided an enduring backbone of talent both in front of and behind the camera, from literary sources both monstrous and romantic (*Dracula*, *Jane Eyre*, *Frankenstein*, *Wuthering Heights*, *Uncle Silas*...) to Gothic heroines such as Joan Fontaine and Barbara Steele, and Byronic leading men from James Mason to Robert Pattinson.

There may have been few British horror films before Hammer's breakthrough in the late 1950s, but the British influence was nonetheless crucial throughout the first wave of horror cinema with Universal Studios' output of the 1930s. Tod Browning's *Dracula* (1931) has Bram Stoker's novel as its source, but if it today looks rather stage-bound in places, that is because the more immediate influence was Stoker's fellow Irishman Hamilton Deane's 1924 stage version – the first adaptation to be authorised by Stoker's widow. Deane's play toured England before going to Broadway in 1927, for a production that starred Bela Lugosi as the Count and Edward Van Sloan as Van Helsing. Both actors reprised their roles for Browning's seminal film.

But if the influence of British theatre was somewhat masked in the case of *Dracula*, the next film in the Universal horror cycle brought the British contribution to the fore. The groundbreaking *Frankenstein* (1931) by British director James Whale shaped Gothic cinema for years to come. Whale also made use of a weighty cadre of British acting talent, which unmistakably informs the character of his work: Colin Clive as Dr Frankenstein, Boris Karloff as the creature in *Frankenstein*; Elsa Lanchester as both Mary Shelley and the memorable female monster in the sequel *Bride of Frankenstein* (1935); Ernest Thesiger contributing his theatrical characterisations in *Bride of Frankenstein* and *The Old Dark House* (1932); Charles Laughton in *The Old Dark House*; Claude Rains in *The Invisible Man* (1933)... This was a British revolution exported to the world – just as Hammer was to undertake two decades later.

James Whale's arrival in America was part of the assiduous cherry-picking by Hollywood of many European talents, and Whale would realise his most thoroughly individual work on US shores. Whale's *Frankenstein* also has a distinctly British black humour; the opening scene, with its concatenation of grotesquery (grave-robbing, scarred hunchback, a body on a gibbet, Frankenstein skulking behind gravestones), is infused with a deliciously macabre wit.

Accomplished though *Frankenstein* was, Whale's magnum opus was to be the sequel, *Bride of Frankenstein* (1935). The film's British sensibility is immediately apparent from the prologue, which depicts Mary Shelley, Percy Shelley and Lord Byron at their famous gathering at Lake Geneva in 1816. Elsa Lanchester's incarnation of the bride is one of horror cinema's key icons; her bandage-wrapped body, gruesomely stitched neck and electric hairstyle renders the actress (as shot from a variety of startling angles by the director) both attractive and repellent.

Whale refined his approach through such films as *The Old Dark House* and his blackly comic version of H.G. Wells's *The Invisible Man*. The latter film is proof that few English directors adopted such an ambiguous attitude to their own country: the curious English village setting of the film contrasts piquantly with the increasingly psychopathic behaviour of Claude Rains's Griffin, the eponymous invisible man. The film allows Whale to confront the English class system; Griffin's attempts to better his social standing (there is a repeated emphasis on his poor upbringing) have led him to be an 'invisible man' in a variety of ways.

The aesthetic influence of German Expressionism may have been as important as Britishness of the James Whale variety to American Gothic horror cinema of the 1930s and 40s, but at RKO Val Lewton still made use of British acting talent, casting Boris Karloff in *Isle of the Dead*, *The Body Snatcher* (both 1945) and *Bedlam* (1946). British texts such as *Jane Eyre*, *Rebecca* and *Wuthering Heights* also provided the bedrock of the cycle of Gothic melodramas made in Hollywood in the 1940s.

However the key change came in the late 1950s with Hammer's worldwide success. Directors such as Terence Fisher utilised saturated colour, impressive production design and vaunting imagination to create a new landscape of the Gothic, one enthusiastically taken up by the likes of American independents like Roger Corman. Whatever country these Hammer films were set in, they remained ineluctably British, populated by impeccable English actors such as Lee and Cushing, along with such alumni of the Royal Shakespeare Company as Richard Pasco and Charles Gray. With the success abroad of the Hammer *Dracula* and *Frankenstein* adaptations, the company even felt confident enough to abandon one commercial imperative that had been key from the 1940s onwards: the importing of an American star in order to sell the films in the American market. Christopher Lee, radiating sexuality in crimson-lined cape, could, it seemed, sell a film quite as effectively.

The exporting of British Gothic was not a one-way street. In Italy, directors such as Mario Bava and Riccardo Freda produced distinctive, strikingly staged simulacra of British Gothic. Italian filmmakers realised that they had to overcome a certain prejudice: that of Italian audiences, sniffy towards the native product. This resulted in a series of unlikely Anglo-Saxon-sounding pseudonyms, such as 'John Old' for Bava and 'Robert Hampton' for Freda. The latter was to produce one of the most curious hybrids in the field, the dark study of necrophilia *The Horrible Secret of Dr Hichcock* (1962), which opens in foggy London in 1885, had a British leading man in Robert Flemyng, and also starred the woman who was to become the most iconic figure in Italian horror, Rank Organisation starlet turned queen of the Italian Gothic film, Barbara Steele, whose big eyes had already been immortalised in Bava's *Black Sunday* (1960).

Italy was not alone in re-exporting British-inspired horror; the Spanish/Italian production *The Living Dead at the Manchester Morgue* (1974), shot on location in Manchester and the Peak District, was one of the most inventive films in the burgeoning zombie genre, while the Spanish connection could also be noted in Narciso Ibáñez Serrador's *La residencia* (*The House that Screamed*, 1969), which stars British actor John Moulder-Brown, as well as the same director's *Who Can Kill a Child* (1976), which features British actress Prunella Ransome. Similar British masquerades are to be found in the films of the 'king' of Spanish horror, actor, writer and director Paul Naschy (such as the truly bizarre Jack the Ripper film *Seven Murders for Scotland Yard*, 1974), and the equally eccentric Spaniard Jess Franco's *Jack the Ripper* (1976), made in West Germany and featuring Klaus Kinski.

The British presence in international Gothic cinema remains a key ingredient to this day; the success of Daniel Radcliffe and Robert Pattinson demonstrating that British actors remain the ideal brooding Gothic lead. Moreover, the revival of Hammer with *The Woman in Black* suggests that the studio that had so much to do with infusing a British sensibility into international Gothic cinema is right back at the bleeding heart of things.

(Top)
The witch Asa (Barbara Steele) has a spiked mask applied in 'Black Sunday' (1960).

(Above)
James Whale (right) and cinematographer John J. Mescall peruse a model of Frankenstein's monster on the set of 'Bride of Frankenstein'.

MONSTROUS

THE TORMENTED

BY JONATHAN RIGBY

A black screen, resounding to the shrill brass and percussion of a conspicuously atonal overture. A pause, then a wolf howl goes up and a pair of feral eyes surge out of the darkness. Frowning down over them is a strangely ridged Neanderthal brow, without eyebrows. The eyes themselves, bloodshot, are flickering watchfully from side to side. As the opening credits unfold, we notice a globular tear depending from one of those scary-looking eyes. It quietly drops. And several more have fallen, from both eyes, before the credits are over.

So begins Terence Fisher's 1961 film *The Curse of the Werewolf*, an early Hammer horror that was comprehensively savaged by the British Board of Film Censors. Luckily, the credits sequence contained no projectile Kensington Gore – or provocative fusions of sex and horror – to arouse the censors' ire. As a result, its startling image of hate-filled lupine eyes pumping out unhappy tears comes down to us as an unusually poetic expression of a motif deeply rooted in the Gothic imagination.

Simply put, by no means all monsters are the kind of inhuman propagators of unrepentant evil exemplified by Bram Stoker's *Dracula*. With the man-made creature of Mary Shelley's *Frankenstein* as their exemplar, there are others for whom monstrousness is a curse and a torment. They retain sufficient humanity to see their lot as a sadistic joke of Fate. They suffer under a compulsion to commit evil yet hate every minute of it. And they offer a teasingly ambiguous response to the question that lies at the heart of so much Gothic fiction – how far can a person degenerate and remain human?

Why, *these* unfortunate creatures can degenerate into wolves, or be artificially 'generated' from charnel-house left-overs, or devolve into poisonous plant life after contact with 'something' in Outer Space… Yet, somehow, they still hold the proverbial mirror up to nature. For all the hideousness of their appearance and the blood-bolted horror of their deeds, the torment they undergo inspires sympathy; sometimes even empathy. Though rarely fulfilling Aristotle's concept of the tragic hero as exalted in rank, they're perfectly positioned to bring on catharsis via the Aristotelian formula of pity and terror.

Our complicated response to these creatures (mingling fascination with repulsion, horror with a barely comprehended fellow feeling) arises from the very human impulse to reject the freakish or physically unlike. Through the misunderstood monsters of literature and film, we're given an opportunity to redeem these ignoble, pre-programmed feelings – an opportunity, in fact, to *assimilate* the 'other', the 'outsider' – on the principle that in these monsters we see a nightmare reflection of ourselves.

This doubling effect was evident as far back as the Anglo-Saxon epic *Beowulf*, in which the hero's climactic battle with his hideous opposite Grendel is so imprecisely recounted that it's difficult to work out who is doing what to whom. In Shakespeare's *The Tempest*, the high-minded Prospero admits a twisted kinship with the 'demi-devil' Caliban in the words "this thing of darkness I / Acknowledge mine." And in

(Opposite)
Boris Karloff in Jack Pierce's iconic Monster make-up for 'Bride of Frankenstein' (1935).

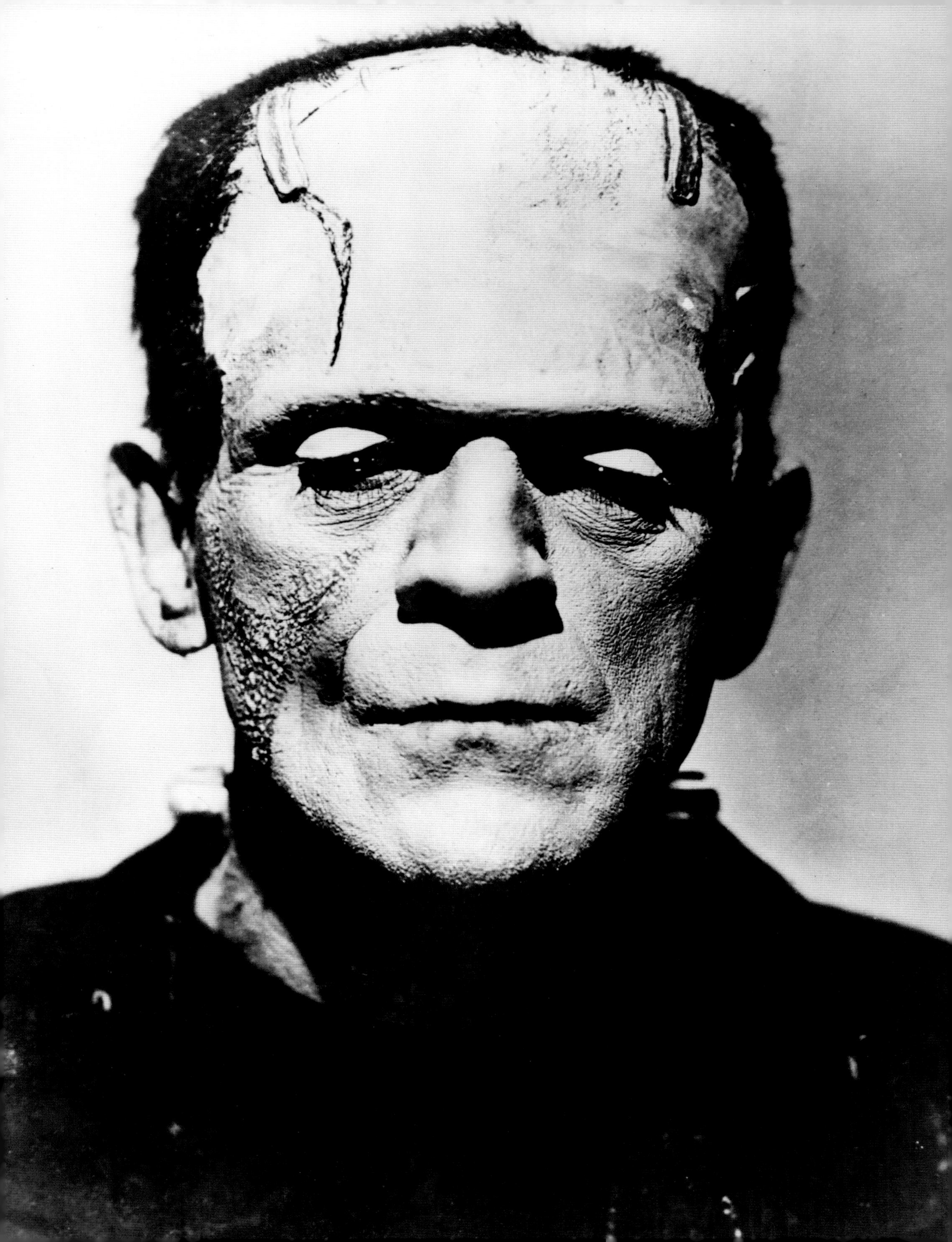

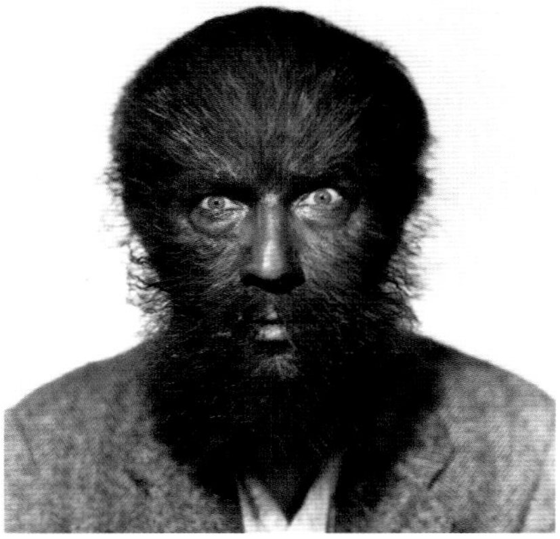

(Above)
Bela Lugosi in a test make-up for the Sayer of the Law in 'Island of Lost Souls' (1932).

(Opposite)
Christopher Lee offered a radically new interpretation of 'The Creature' in 'The Curse of Frankenstein' (1957).

(Below)
The 'Man' (Hugh Armstrong) laments over the deceased 'Woman' (June Turner) in 'Death Line' (1972).

Frankenstein, it's the monster who tries to instil the same concept in its capricious maker's head: "You, my creator, detest and spurn me, thy creature, to whom thou art bound by ties only dissoluble by the annihilation of one of us."

Conspicuously eloquent in Mary Shelley's book, the monster has been robbed of speech in most film adaptations, leaving the eloquence to the mimetic gifts, or otherwise, of the actors playing him. In James Whale's *Frankenstein* (1931), Boris Karloff's monster is a million miles from the braindead psychopathic brute envisaged in the film's planning stages. Instead, he moves from puzzled yearning when first encountering sunlight, to inarticulate fury when tormented by the jealous hunchback Fritz, childlike excitement during his brief lakeside idyll with the doomed Maria and finally shrieking hysteria when trapped in a blazing windmill. Reviewing Karloff's performance, one contemporary critic came up with a nutshell statement of the whole monster conundrum: "he arouses," opined *Motion Picture* magazine, "morbid sympathy as well as loathing." In its own way, this is worthy of standing beside the Coleridge formulation – "desire with loathing strangely mix'd" – that's regularly invoked to explain the heartless allure of vampires.

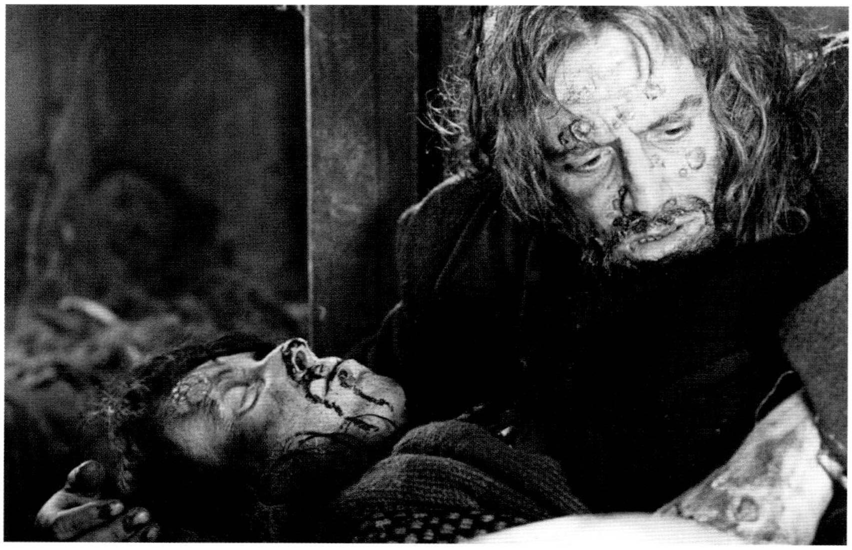

Fitted with a genuinely gruesome mix-and-match make-up rather than the Deco dead look sported by Karloff, Christopher Lee's interpretation in Fisher's *The Curse of Frankenstein* (1957) inspires less empathy but arguably touches a more disturbing chord. For he presents Frankenstein's creation as a brain-damaged child, the dislocated brain struggling to co-ordinate the component parts of an unfamiliar body. Profound pity is our horrified response, all the more so when the poor thing is shot down, then summarily resurrected with no noticeable improvement in his prospects.

Frankenstein monsters may come and Frankenstein monsters may go, but perhaps the most interesting re-interpretation remains Jack Smight's sprawling TV movie *Frankenstein: The True Story* (1973). Developing a hint provided by Fisher's 1958 film *The Revenge of Frankenstein*, this one makes Michael Sarrazin's monster a beautiful young man. But only at first; he deteriorates rapidly. In this way Smight's film exploits a disquiet related to but distinct from the 'born monstrosity' horror of most adaptations. Instead we have the horror of disease, bodily decay and gradual dissolution, things that will be encountered by each one of us at some time or other.

This theme reached an affecting apotheosis in David Cronenberg's *The Fly* (1986), in which the scientist (Jeff Goldblum) becomes the monster, quite literally falls to pieces before our eyes, morphs into a fly-human hybrid and is climactically blown to smithereens by his traumatised girlfriend. The fear of ageing and physical collapse also provided a subtext for the weirdly affirmative metamorphosis of Jesús Gris (Federico Lupi) in Guillermo del Toro's splendid *Cronos* (1993).

As hi-tech as Cronenberg made it look, the species splicing of *The Fly* was

prefigured in H.G. Wells's 1896 novel *The Island of Doctor Moreau*, which in turn echoed both *Frankenstein* and *The Tempest*. When the book became *Island of Lost Souls* in Hollywood's halcyon horror year of 1932, nobody was better pleased with the British censor's decision to ban Erle C. Kenton's film than Wells himself. Yet Wells's governing themes – the evils of imperialism, irresponsible science and social conditioning – came through strongly in the finished product.

Balancing Charles Laughton's smooth-chopped Moreau (a kind of techno-Prospero lording it over a whole island of misshapen Calibans), Bela Lugosi's fur-faced Sayer of the Law reverently intones "Not to spill blood. That is the Law. Are we not men?" in the dismal shanty town to which he and his fellow Beast Men have been confined. His final repudiation of Moreau is one of horror cinema's most overwhelmingly cathartic moments, Lugosi's trademark cadences carrying with them a massive freight of tortured emotion. Direct to camera, he wails, "You made us in the House of Pain! You made us – *things!* Not men! Not beasts! Part men, part beasts! *Things!*" The Beast Men's subsequent evisceration of Moreau on his own operating table remains as potent an image of social uprising as Depression-era Hollywood produced. Why? Because the film has persuaded us to identify with the inhuman yet human Beast Men far more than the human yet inhuman Moreau.

Forty years later, another classic image of the downtrodden and dispossessed was presented in Gary Sherman's *Death Line*. Society's rejects are located this time, not on a South Seas island, but in the subterranean depths of Russell Square tube station. The Man, so called, is the last of a long 'line', his ancestors having been rendered troglodytes – and cannibals, to boot – by an 1892 cave-in. Now he tends to the tiered ranks of his deceased forebears and sobs in profound distress over the corpse of his pregnant wife. The film draws an inescapable parallel between the Man's unfeigned emotion and the atrophied posturing of the various civil servants, MI5 men, coppers and trendies above ground.

Brilliantly played by Hugh Armstrong, the Man presents as stiff a challenge to audience sympathies as horror cinema provides. For some, the horrendous degradation in which he lives (initially revealed in a justly famous seven-minute tracking shot), together with his unlovely appearance (a decomposed Fagin, riven with septicaemic plague), preclude their engagement with his plight. For others, however, his three-word vocabulary ("Mind the doors!") isn't just a blackly humorous masterstroke. It also underlines his claim to be cinema's most horribly pathetic misunderstood monster of all.

The prototype for all such monsters was furnished by Robert Wiene's *The Cabinet of Dr Caligari* (*Das Cabinet des Dr Caligari*). Starting production 12 months after the conclusion of World War I, the dispossessed here were the millions of young men who had been slaughtered in the trenches, all of them distilled into the gaunt, black-clad figure of Cesare, a youthful somnambulist sent out on missions of murder by the crazed demagogue Caligari. "Awaken for a moment from your dark night," says Caligari – and the look of unfathomable horror in Conrad Veidt's black-edged eyes as he finally forces them open reminds us how often filmmakers have used eyes (proverbially, the windows to the soul) to let us know that monsters aren't the soulless destroyers they seem. Similarly, Cesare's upraised butcher knife – stilled at sight of the sleeping girl he's been assigned to kill – was to set in motion any number of monsters whose hearts are softened by beauty.

A fusion of these motifs – the monster's limpid gaze and his unconditional surrender to beauty – provides the emotional fulcrum of Fisher's *The Mummy* (1959). Here, Christopher Lee's Kharis communicates a 4000-year-old sense of love and loss entirely through his expressive eyes and body language. Kharis's head works almost coyly as he reaches for the reincarnation of his former princess, finally lolling down in spaniel-eyed desolation when the woman fails to recognise him. Again, the monster's vibrant emotional life is juxtaposed with the frozen, life-denying attitudes of his Victorian pursuers.

In scenes like these, then, eyes are used to underline the apparent paradox of the monster's continued humanity. Eyes are crucial, also, to the resurrected pianist in the Michael Curtiz thriller *The Walking Dead* (1936), in which Karloff once again took a character conceived as brutish and added, not just pathos this time, but a spiritual dimension. Here is a revenant who, in killing off the mobsters who framed him into the electric chair, does so merely by looking at them. But what a look. Glistening with both implacable hatred and compassionate tears, it may have influenced the credits sequence of *The Curse of the Werewolf* described above. It's also echoed in Stuart Heisler's *The Monster and the Girl*,

(Above)
Reissue artwork for the Michael Curtiz chiller 'The Walking Dead' (1936).

Myths survive as long as hey speak to something undamental in the human psyche. On the evidence of extant narratives, from *Gilgamesh* to *True Blood*, the news is that not only has the idea of physical transformation – from human into (sometimes monstrous) animal – been speaking to us in this way for millennia, but that it might well be enjoying its greatest resonance in the 21st century.

Vampires, of course, take as axiomatic their place at the top of the aberration hierarchy. But while their presence in the collective imagination is venerable (entities who survive by feeding on the blood of the living are an ancient and international staple, with root sources ranging from Babylonian tales to Hebrew demonology and Greek myth) the coherent, dapper and highly seductive version the world has come to know and love doesn't go back much further than the 18th century. Before that vampiric activities were as often attributed to spirits or demons, or, courtesy of Christianity's omnivorous appropriation, to the Devil Himself. These earlier forms are non-human or incorporeal agents, *sui generis* parasites, without, strictly, any metamorphic element at all.

For shape-shifting proper – and with a tradition easily as old and widespread as their manicured and chauffeur-driven nemeses – it's werewolves. Or *lycanthropos* (Greece). Or *loup-garou* (France). Or *hombre lobo* (Spain). Or *weerwolf* (Netherlands). The person who becomes, via curse, infection, or lunar influence, a ravenous wolf, or – equally ravenous – a human-lupine hybrid.

What's the appeal? Vampires, for all their dolorous longevity, are consoled by aesthetic refinement and irresistible good looks, as well as allowing us to indulge our fantasies [illegible] without the drag of piling up moral Brownie points for a ticket into Heaven. But why has something as down-and-dirty as lycanthropy – the hair, the teeth, the claws, the snout – stood the test of time? How, exactly, does this idea speak to us?

Like most myths it has variant forms. Some versions allow for voluntary transformation, regardless of what the moon is doing. Some werewolves, like Lon Chaney's Larry Talbot in *The Wolf Man* (1941) and David Naughton's David Kessler in *An American Werewolf in London* (1981) retain no memory of their bestial binges, but have to piece the nauseous truth together from circumstantial evidence after the fact. For others, like Henry Hull's Dr Glendon in *Werewolf of London* (1935) and Katharine Isabelle's Ginger in *Ginger Snaps* (2000), the continuity of their identity is never in doubt: they know what they've done. The only question is how they choose to act on the knowledge. The corollary of this is that to watch werewolf movies chronologically (the earliest known is a silent black-and-white, *The Werewolf*, made in 1913, now lost) is to watch the gradual shift from reflex rectitude – in the early narratives the monster is always at odds with his or her condition, always looking for a cure – to moral ambiguity:

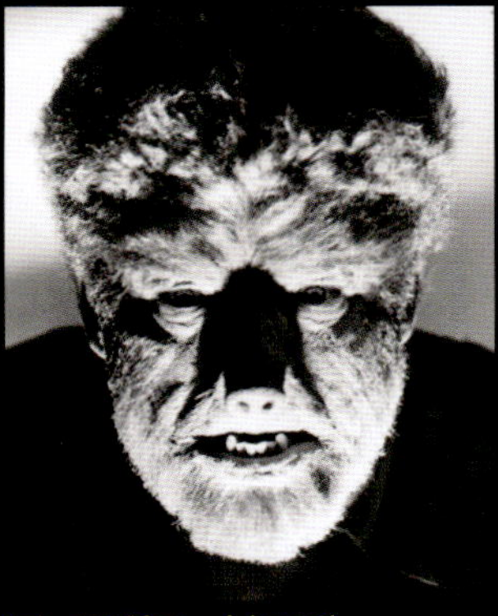

'The Wolf Man' (1941)

David Naughton in 'An American Werewolf in London' (1981)

for protagonists in the later stories there's no denying that while it's a bad lookout for the mauled or murdered victims, it feels pretty good to the werewolf at the time.

'At the time' is key. Vampires, once they become vampires, are vampires, exclusively, forever. All their human credentials are void and any claim on our kinship pointless. For werewolves, the situation is more ticklish. They're only werewolves when they're werewolves. Species divorce never gets its decree absolute. They don't leave their humanity behind. They just get a like-it-or-not vacation from it once a month. It's this binary nature that gives the myth its psychic clout. The werewolf's condition is the human condition, wildly inflated, terrifyingly enlarged: a creature capable of love, empathy, humour, imagination, reason and moral sense – all the pretty functions, in fact – but compromised (tragically or farcically) by the thudding insistence of the plainer ones: hunger, aggression, libido. The Curse dramatises the woeful gap between the way we'd like to be and the way we all too often are. It exploits our duality in the baldest possible way, reminding us that for all [illegible] the evolutionary umbilical remains uncut: the wild animal sleeps only ever lightly, and sometimes comes spectacularly wide awake.

The potential for myth-as-sexual-warning-fable is obviou – and has been repeatedly realised, from the folk tale of 'Little Red Riding Hood' to the playful ambivalence of Neil Jordan's *The Company of Wolves* (1984). The very word 'wolf' has become a synonym for a predatory charmer. But the cautionary tales only work because they concede the power of the charm. Our feelings about the animal aspect of ourselves are deliciously mixed: we're afraid of it, yes, but we're thrilled by it, too.

There are exceptions – notably the comedy *Teen Wolf* (1985) and the tongue-in-chee *Wolf* (1994) – but traditionally werewolf movies end with the creature dead. Granted the superficial moral architecture demands it, but we're always a bit sorry to see the hairy devils go. We know how good it feels to let the animal out once in a while, and that, in the end, is why the myth of lycanthropy has lasted: it manifests our fear of the beast within – and our desire [illegible]

a noir-ish 1941 potboiler that picked up the Curtiz film's gangland setting but transplanted the framed man's brain into (what else?) a gorilla. Luckily, Hollywood's 'go to' ape-suit guy, Charles Gemora, had the most phosphorescently lachrymose eyes in the genre.

Similarly, in *The Quatermass Xperiment* (1955) director Val Guest makes much of Richard Wordsworth's profoundly anguished eyes. Wordsworth's infected astronaut succumbs to a creeping metamorphosis prefiguring the fear of ageing and death exploited in *The Fly* and other 1980s body-horrors; not for nothing is he confined to a hospital bed for much of the action. Even when he's fully transformed into an octopoid monstrosity roosting in the upper reaches of Westminster Abbey, a recognisably human shriek echoes out through the stained glass when 'it' is climactically electrocuted.

Some monsters have *only* their eyes to identify them, as indicated by the title of Georges Franju's 1959 classic *Eyes Without a Face* (*Les Yeux sans visage*). Edith Scob's porcelain Christiane, horribly disfigured in a car accident, drifts doll-like round a massive provincial château in a featureless latex mask, provoking terror as well as pity when she briefly takes it off. Again, Scob's mournful eyes are used to point up the purity of soul that negates her robotic appearance; her driven father and female guardian – obsessive, mechanised, inhuman – are the *real* robots. Yet they have faces.

Like *The Walking Dead*, *The Monster and the Girl* and *The Quatermass Xperiment*, *Les Yeux sans visage* trades on the 'misunderstood monster' motif without recourse to the 'unrequited love' angle typified by *The Mummy*, whether in Karl Freund's 1932 version or Fisher's entirely different 1959 film. Thwarted romance, bringing with it the juxtaposition of beauty and ugliness, has been a rewarding theme for filmmakers since the silent era.

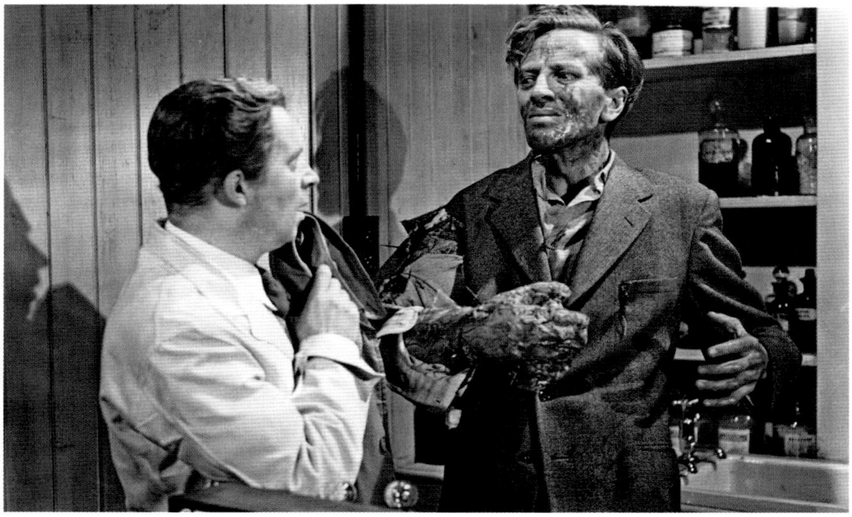

Wallace Worsley's *The Hunchback of Notre Dame* (1923) presented Lon Chaney as the gargoyle Quasimodo, responding gratefully to the tenderness of Patsy Ruth Miller's Esmeralda. Not wishing to repeat the trick, Chaney subsequently turned *The Phantom of the Opera* (1925) into a featureless psychopath with no extracurricular interest in his pupil, Christine. Future adaptations would 'correct' this apparent oversight, though neither Hunchback nor Phantom would quite retain their status as archetypal figures, eventually devolving to the level of Disney cartoon (Hunchback) and saccharine musical (Phantom). Not so the mighty *King Kong*, 50-foot protagonist of the 1933 RKO classic, whose interest in Fay Wray anthropomorphised the unrequited love motif. Stirring ancient memories of man's origin among the apes, Kong provides viewers with the most deep-rooted identification figure of all, though this frisson is presumably lost on creationists.

Passing the buck, Kong's venal nemesis claims that "Beauty killed the Beast" in the film's final moments, identifying this modern myth as an outgrowth of a much older one. Though destined, like the Hunchback, to be Disneyfied in the 1990s, the folkloric Beauty and the Beast survives in the leonine form of Jean Marais in Cocteau's magical *La Belle et la Bête* (1946), making daily marriage proposals to Josette Day's luminous Belle and finally expiring of a broken heart. The kiss that has a

transformative effect on 'Beast' could also be used for pulpier, more perverse ends. In Chano Urueta's *El monstruo resucitado* (1953), the neurotic and atrociously disfigured Dr Ling (José María Linares-Rivas) resides, like Marais' Beast, in a meticulously art-directed castle. Having been profoundly affected by the kiss bestowed on him by a female reporter (Miroslava Stern), he goes berserk on discovering her true agenda, hatching a plot to surgically 'uglify' all beautiful people – starting with her.

Of course, misunderstood monsters would become rather tedious if there weren't an equal number of unrepentant ones to counterbalance them. Just two years after creating the first prototype in *Caligari*, German filmmakers provided the template for the second in the alien implacability of F.W. Murnau's *Nosferatu*. Failing to understand this important distinction, subsequent adaptors of *Dracula* have sought to soften even the King Vampire, looking enviously at *The Mummy*'s 'reincarnated love' plot and simply bolting it on. First attempted in Robert Kelljan's *Blacula* (1972) and Dan Curtis's TV movie *Dracula* the following year, this method failed resoundingly in Francis Coppola's bloated 1992 epic *Bram Stoker's Dracula*.

(Above)
Angharad Rees as the tragic Edwardian murderess of Hammer's 'Hands of the Ripper' (1971).

(Opposite, above)
Mutating astronaut Richard Wordsworth and horrified pharmacist Toke Townley in 'The Quatermass Xperiment' (1955).

(Opposite, below)
Edith Scob as the latex-masked Christiane in 'Eyes Without a Face' (1959).

(Below)
Sissy Spacek returns home after a baptism of blood in 'Carrie' (1976).

Though her father stubbornly resists the humanisation process, it worked well enough for *Dracula's Daughter* (1936); in her despair, Gloria Holden's Countess Zaleska even sought help from a psychiatrist. So too did Simone Simon's unhappy Irena in Jacques Tourneur's *Cat People* (1942). Here again, female monsters are divided between the remorseless man-made vamp incarnated by Brigitte Helm in Henrik Galeen's *Alraune* (1927) and the tragically conflicted variety established by Holden and Simon. Among the latter are plague carrier Marilyn Chambers in Cronenberg's *Rabid* (1977), vampire Anne Parillaud in John Landis's *Innocent Blood* (1992) and disturbed veterinary assistant Angela Bettis in Lucky McKee's *May* (2002), plus two others who visited psychiatrists – serial killer Angharad Rees in Peter Sasdy's *Hands of the Ripper* (1971) and werewolf Amanda Ooms in Ben Bolt's TV mini-series *Wilderness* (1996).

Pre-eminent in this category, Sissy Spacek in Brian De Palma's *Carrie* (1976) not only engages all the viewer's sympathy but also exactly embodies the monster's words from *Frankenstein*: "I was benevolent and good; misery made me a fiend."

With a shift in 21st-century Gothic towards monsters as heroes, even role models, the equivocal messages given out by the traditional misunderstood monster have lost some currency. And, in out-and-out horror, new priorities among producers and audiences have also made the archetype less prevalent than it once was. For the slicker and more brutal horror cinema becomes, the more thoroughly is 'pity' expunged from the ancient equation of pity and terror.

In Alfred Hitchcock's *Psycho* (1960), for example, Norman Bates makes a deeply disturbing appeal to our emotions, his mother fixation leading us, in Kenneth Tynan's words, "straight to the heart of a mystery as horrendous as anything in *Oedipus*." Nor was

(Above)
Howard Sherman as the bewildered 'Bub' in 'Day of the Dead' (1985).

(Above, right)
Anthony Perkins in 'the Hamlet of horror roles' in 'Psycho' (1960).

Norman's interpreter, Anthony Perkins, being unduly self-aggrandising when he referred to Norman as "the Hamlet of horror roles." Yet the slasher mode eventually sparked off by *Psycho* would feature the kind of faceless 'force of evil' killers exemplified by Michael Myers in John Carpenter's *Halloween* (1978). That the slasher mechanism is dependent on this kind of unknowable figure became abundantly clear when a *Halloween* remake in 2007 tried to establish a misanthropic (and entirely unconvincing) back-story for Michael.

The millennial craze for zombie films, still ongoing, provides a faint echo of the fears of ageing and corruption familiar from *The Fly* and *Cronos*, but the effect is subordinate to the undead's usefulness as an ever-multiplying metaphor for dehumanisation. A zombie with a personality may be an oxymoron, but interesting undercurrents are set to work on the rare occasions when the undead are given touches of remembered humanity. Whether dimly recalling how to use a disposable razor or donning headphones and responding clumsily to music, Howard Sherman's sublime 'Bub' in George Romero's *Day of the Dead* (1985) induces an "aw, isn't he cute?" response – complicated, of course, by the awareness that he could still rip out our entrails at a moment's notice. Echoing this confused response are isolated 21st-century curios like *Fido* (2006), *Colin* (2008) and *Harold's Going Stiff* (2011).

These are exceptions, however. More typical is Christopher Smith's 2004 film *Creep*, an unofficial *Death Line* makeover in which the overwhelmingly emotional 'Man' becomes an unattached and barely human troglodyte called Craig, making zero appeal to viewer empathy. Similarly, 21st-century takes on Mary Shelley have thrown up creatures that either induce bored indifference (the so-called 'Universal Xenograft' of Jed Mercurio's 2007 TV *Frankenstein*) or weird fascination (the wing-sprouting hermaphrodite of Vincenzo Natali's 2009 film *Splice*). But not identification or involvement.

As a result, it's rare now to share that queasy feeling of kinship expressed by Prospero on contemplating Caliban. Which is a shame, for the best and most subversive monsters are the ones who engage our half-nauseated emotions, the ones who make us feel pity as well as terror… Those things of darkness, as Prospero put it, that we must acknowledge ours.

The Gothic Anthology Film

By Mark Gatiss

From *Unheimliche Geschichten* in 1919 to *Trick 'r Treat* 90 years later, portmanteau films have been enduringly popular. Here's a special favourite...

Alone amongst the often ramshackle delights of the Amicus portmanteau movies, Kevin Connor's *From Beyond the Grave* (1973) exudes a dark, queasy, very British atmosphere all of its own.

This is almost certainly down to its choice of source material. Rather than using EC comics as its inspiration (as do its more famous stablemates, *Tales from the Crypt* (1972) and *The Vault of Horror*, 1973), *From Beyond the Grave* revels in the curious stories of R. Chetwynd-Hayes. The previous use of predominantly American sources (including Robert Bloch for *The House that Dripped Blood* (1971), *Torture Garden* (1967) and *Asylum*, 1972) always felt like an uneasy alliance. The stories have a mid-Atlantic feel that, with notable exceptions, simply don't translate to a rainy Shepperton backlot.

No, Chetwynd-Hayes has the right stuff and *From Beyond the Grave* is essentially the result of that happy parlour game beloved of portmanteau horror fans – a film made up of the best stories from all the others.

Traditionally, the portmanteau links its stories together with a fairly flimsy framing device, from the granddaddy of them all in *Dead of Night*'s psychiatrist to Dr Schreck's tarot readings in *Dr. Terror's House of Horrors* (1965). Interestingly, almost all of them cut back from the tale itself to the victim's rather bemused reaction. *From Beyond the Grave*, though, simply gets on with the next story, its victims despatched with somewhat Draconian methods given the nature of their petty crimes. It can certainly be argued that the framing device – Temptations Ltd, a seedy junk shop presided over by a gaunt, cloth-capped Peter Cushing, and a burglar's frustrated attempts to rob the premises – is nothing to write home about. But what elevates it is Cushing's beautiful, mischievous performance, complete with sly Northern accent.

Our first customer is the great David Warner, who defrauds Cushing out of a rare mirror ("I know my antiques!") only to find, after somehow 'activating' it via a seance, that the mottled old thing contains an evil spirit demanding blood sacrifices. ("Feed me more blood!") The ensuing story is extraordinarily grim, sending Warner spiralling downwards on a Ripper-like course of ghastly murders.

The second story can justly claim to be one of the strangest and most unsettling things ever to grace a British horror film. Seedy Ian Bannen takes refuge from his miserable home life by trying to impress ex-serviceman and match-seller Donald Pleasence. To boost his Desert Rat credentials he steals a medal from Temptations Ltd (Cushing: "Naughty. Shouldn't have done that") and is drawn into a ghoulish affair with Pleasence's otherworldly daughter. The sordid, Pinter-esque feel of these sequences is genuinely unnerving, creating a nightmarishly bleak vision of suburbia, full of well-shot, unsettling details like a pair of lace-gloved hands gently snipping hair from the back of Diana Dors's head as she sits on a crowded bus.

Next comes the obligatory 'light relief' story – a staple of the portmanteau as far back as *Dead of Night*'s golfing episode. This being Amicus's finest hour, though, the story is a genuine delight and not the one that, as so often, lets the side down.

Pompous Ian Carmichael (a light comedian of genius) offers less than he should for an antique snuff box (Cushing: "I hope you enjoy snuffing it")

Peter Cushing in 'From Beyond the Grave' (1973)

but ends up with a decidedly un-blithe spirit digging into his shoulder. Just as in the Coward play, the unwilling Carmichael eventually begs an eccentric medium (Margaret Leighton) to help exorcise the creature. When the possessed Nyree Dawn Porter smashes down the front door bellowing "Life! Life!" it is a beguilingly creepy moment.

The final story is essentially a replay of the first (and both are deeply in hock to the 'Haunted Mirror' segment of *Dead of Night*), with Ian Ogilvy tempted to swindle Cushing over a massive, grotesquely carved door that, rather unimaginatively, he wants to put over his stationery cupboard. What he doesn't know is that the door is bathed in human blood and is the key to a time-travelling charm by which Restoration alchemist Jack Watson has gained eternal life. When Ogilvy first passes through the door into the charmed 'Blue Room' beyond, the film achieves a rare, eerie beauty. The sun seems to be shining outside this cobwebby room that somehow exists outside of time, and when we hear the sound of Watson's approaching footsteps we feel genuine alarm.

With the rather perfunctory burglar sub-plot resolved we have a lovely, polished, well-directed, genuinely eerie portmanteau with a top-notch cast and a wonderful sense of 'rightness' about it.

A few years ago, I got to know David Warner and couldn't wait to ask him about his work on the film. "I've never seen it," he shrugged apologetically. "Is it any good?" Well, yes it is. It's still the kind of horror film I'm happiest watching, and in *From Beyond the Grave* Amicus finally got it dead right.

The Gothic and Comedy

By Reece Shearsmith

(Above)
Billy Cornelius and Kenneth Williams in 'Carry On Screaming!' (1966), which seamlessly weaves the Carry On team's familiar bawdy comedy into a horror story.

The link between Gothic horror and comedy is a surprisingly close one, even before any attempt at injecting comedy into the horror has been made. Something so overblown and grand as the Gothic is ripe to be undercut with a comedic touch, and sometimes the most po-faced of horror films can become increasingly hysterical quite unintentionally.

This isn't to say that the deliberate marrying of these two genres is by any means easy. In fact 'comedy horror' is a delicate balance that often falls one way or the other, leaving the experience of watching either too frightening and not funny enough, or vice versa. But when it's done right, the release that the comedy allows only serves to heighten our viewing pleasure and unnerve us all the more.

Great moments of Gothic horror that wilfully ooze a sense of glee can create a hugely satisfying experience, despite the uncomfortable nature of the ride. If we are lulled by moments of levity, the Gothic gravitas hits home with a greater power. In life we laugh a lot (hopefully!) but in film and television, moments where people laugh – or seem at least to laugh genuinely – are often lacking, and it's always a surprise and delight to see it happen. Everything is brought closer to home; suddenly we are vulnerable to the darker elements because we recognise ourselves in the world onscreen.

One of the strangest and most unsettling elements in the Gothic tale of murder and madness *The House in Nightmare Park* (1973) is the very presence of Frankie Howerd. He shouldn't be there, and yet it is Howerd's very 'ordinariness' in an extraordinary situation that lends the film a sense of dread, as well as letting us know, tonally, that we are not to take the horror too seriously. This sense of conflict – or rather the expectation of it – reinforces the comedy and heightens the peculiar. It is often the very exercise of putting humour (or at least the threat of it!) into a tale otherwise darkly told that creates that most delicious of pleasures – the Gothic or horror comedy.

Douglas Hickox's *Theatre of Blood* (1973) is a sublime example of this. Gothically overblown (with its plot about a series of grisly Shakespeare-inspired murders) and with a sense of nasty fun, it produces a perfect marriage of genuinely gut-wrenching gore and moments of quite hysterical comedy. Vincent Price is perfectly cast as the, shall we say, 'misunderstood' Shakespearean actor Edward Lionheart, exacting his murderous revenge on a group of mean-spirited critics. Price's own acknowledgement of his status as a horror icon is utilised here to great effect, precisely because he approaches Lionheart and the eight Shakespearean roles we see him play with deadly seriousness. Price doesn't play Lionheart as a bad actor – quite the opposite: it is the critics themselves who are the real grotesques here. Lionheart's proud refusal to perform in anything but Shakespeare has us rooting for him as he leads them to their increasingly inventive deaths. Lionheart himself applauds his own 'performances' at the end of the film, letting the audience in on the biggest joke of all: that in teaching the critics a lesson he has also given them the greatest performances of his career. The only caveat is that the performances also happened to be the last thing that any of them saw.

The Carry On team made an admirable stab (no pun intended) when they entered *Carry On Screaming!* into the canon of Gothic comedy in 1966. The film seamlessly weaves their own brand of lewd, bawdy comedy into a story that mixes *Frankenstein*, *House of Wax* and the *Jekyll and Hyde* stories quite brilliantly. The scenes featuring Oddbod and his strange offspring Oddbod Junior are eerily effective – especially the 'creation' of the latter by Jon Pertwee, playing the eccentric Dr Fettle. The sight of these lumpen monsters roaming mist-laden forests looking for defenceless maidens to abduct is particularly disturbing, not to mention the chilling fate of Dan Dann the lavatory man!

The Old Dark House (1932) took a genre that was then relatively new, and yet James Whale's film was already brilliantly subverting it, casting 'horror' stars that audiences didn't expect to see playing the darkness for laughs. The vital ingredient for a successful horror comedy is having actors – and indeed writers and directors – that know how to pull off the Gothic 'for real', otherwise the whole enterprise risks falling into a shambolic self-parody that doesn't work on any level. These films (naming no names, but it doesn't take long to think of some examples) suffer since there seems to be no love or duty of care towards the genre they think they are aping, and therefore they become a hollow, artless experience.

In my own work with *The League of Gentlemen* and latterly *Psychoville*, the rule was always the same: when you are doing the horror stuff, you take it seriously. That way, the comedy remains a release from scenes that don't let you off the hook with a nod or a wink. The Gothic mixed with the mundane was always a key ingredient for us to explore.

I would suggest that the more successful of the films that embrace and intertwine the Gothic and the blackly humorous all work because in doing so they display a world which is in fact more recognisably real than something wholly 'comic' or something wholly 'Gothic'. There can be very human laughs in the midst of the darkest of situations. In fact, there probably always should be.

(Above) Edward Lionheart (Vincent Price) serves up a poodle pie to Meredith Merridew (Robert Morley) in 'Theatre of Blood' (1973).

(Left) Frankie Howerd in 'The House in Nightmare Park' (1973).

(Bottom, left) Steve Pemberton as Tubbs and Reece Shearsmith as Edward, with Michael Sheen in 'The League of Gentlemen's Apocalypse' (2005).

MONSTROUS

THE LIVING DEAD

BY ROGER LUCKHURST

The photograph, the writer Roland Barthes once observed, is premised on a complete contradiction. It captures the living instant, the here and now, and magically makes what is momentary live forever. Yet the same shutter also freezes and fixes the moment, taking it out of time, making every image deathly and every portrait a *memento mori*. The delight at what is captured and preserved by the black box of the camera is haunted by the monument to loss that every photograph becomes.

Cinema only reinforces the sense that the magical animation of the moving image has death coiled within it. Maxim Gorky famously described his evening with the Lumière brothers' show in 1896 as 'the Kingdom of Shadows' that revealed 'not life but its shadow, not motion but its soundless spectre.' Some of the first trick ghosts on film were made by the music hall mentalist and pioneer Brighton film-maker George Smith at the turn of the century. An ancient Egyptian mummy was first magically reanimated by special effects in Walter Booth's 1901 film, *The Haunted Curiosity Shop*. Rudyard Kipling's ghost story, 'Mrs Bathurst' (1904), is a very early suggestion that the new-fangled technology of celluloid will profoundly disturb the boundary between what is living and dead.

In attempting to answer the question 'What is Cinema?' critic André Bazin mused that it perhaps revealed 'a fundamental psychical human need to reverse the finality of death.' One of the most magical moments in the history of cinema is in the final scenes of Carl Dreyer's austere film about faith, *Ordet* (1955). Inger has died in childbirth; her corpse is laid out in an open coffin and the family gathers around her. The camera takes so long over its compassionate gaze at the dead woman that, eventually, in a tiny but utterly sublime moment, her hand begins to move, her eyes flicker open, and she is welcomed back to life. Plot-wise, it is an affirmation of faith. But this is also an expression of the near supernatural animating power of the cinematic gaze, too.

Movies can reanimate the dead with the simplest of devices to disadjust time: the flashback and the voice-over. This is what allows the impossibility of a dead man to narrate Billy Wilder's *Sunset Blvd.* (1950) or overlapping flashbacks to bring Charles Foster Kane back from death. The time-scrambled editing of *Point Blank* (1967) or *Don't Look Now* (1973) means that the viewer is left unsure at first at what points the protagonist is living or dead.

For every art-house contemplation of this essence of cinema, there are a thousand horror films that joyously and messily transgress this boundary of life and death in gory and uncomplicated ways. Even Dreyer's Inger is shadowed by the hallucinatory images of the lively corpses of the undead staring out of coffin windows in Dreyer's much earlier *Vampyr* (1932). The emotional reaction sought in horror generally has a simpler, more visceral aim: to shock. These moments also have their place in cinema history, famous instants when what we had thought was dead proves to be still alive. The corpse rises slowly from the bath in

(Opposite)
George A. Romero's 'Night of the Living Dead' (1968) reflected the revolutionary disorder of its time.

(Top)
The shocking moment when the 'corpse' of Michel Delassalle (Paul Meurisse) rises from the bathtub in Henri-Georges Clouzot's 'Les Diaboliques' (1955).

(Above)
Allan Gray (Julian West) staring out of his own coffin in Carl Dreyer's 'Vampyr' (1932).

Les Diaboliques (1955). Carrie's hand shoots out of the grave in Brian De Palma's cheap but effective shock edit. Michael's body sits back up deep in the murky background behind Laurie in *Halloween* (1978). And it happens in reverse: there is the genius of pulling on the shoulder of the chatty, interfering, dominating Mrs Bates under that basement lightbulb, only to wheel round the screaming skull of a woman long dead, mummified in her death agonies. Hitchcock had to invent strict rules of spectatorship for *Psycho*, all to preserve that inaugural moment of shock. Feeble echoes, confusing the dead with the living, still pulse forty years later as the central narrative trick of *The Sixth Sense* (1999) or *The Others* (2001).

This slippage of category from living to dead or animate to inanimate – and vice versa, of course – is at the heart of what Sigmund Freud called 'the Uncanny'. In a very odd essay, full of broken-off speculations and unfinished trains of thought, Freud tried to pin down this elusive emotion, hard to define because it is all about that queasy, shivery feeling when things slip their definitions. Nearly all of Freud's examples were either borrowed from Gothic fiction or have since become standard horror film tropes.

Dolls and automata are uncanny because they are inert objects that either mimic life too well or become malevolently animate and defy human agency. Chess-playing automata imitated human reason in the Enlightenment to the amazement of all the courts of Europe (even if some of these automata were fake machines hiding human operators). By the late 1960s, HAL wins all his chess games and then silently eliminates his human crew in *2001: A Space Odyssey* (1968) and the robots start to return fire in *Westworld* (1973), an implacable Yul Brynner marching on without a human face. After the gently unnerving segment of Ealing's portmanteau film *Dead of Night* (1945) by Cavalcanti, where the archetypal ventriloquist's dummy takes over its master, our dolls have got steadily nastier. Uncanny mimicry was redoubled when the press began speculating in 1993 that the child murderers of the toddler James Bulger had imitated scenes from *Child's Play 3* (1991), featuring the murderous doll, Chucky. Who or what was the inert imitative mechanism in this baleful chain of influence?

Doubles are uncanny too, Freud argued. We double or multiply ourselves as a way of hanging on to life; but this other self goes rogue, turns nasty, comes back at us as a persecutor, a harbinger of death. This is the plot of Poe's 'William Wilson' or Stevenson's *Strange Case of Dr Jekyll and Mr Hyde*. It appears early in cinema again, in *The Student of Prague* (1913), where Balduin is tormented by his own mirror reflection, a work at the centre of the first psychological study of the 'doppelgänger' by Otto Rank. Twins are ominous portents in many cultures: Kubrick's uncanny sisters in *The Shining* (1980), tempting Danny to an eternal playground, are descendants of the murderous twin in Robert Mulligan's *The Other* (1972) or the merciless band of identical blond moppets from *Village of the Damned* (1960), announcing the inevitable supersession of the human race. The deathly double lies behind every version of the Jekyll and Hyde story, the bright promise of virile renewal turning into monstrous desire, uncontainable violence and self-murder. To project unspeakable desires too hard onto the outside is to see their deathly return as a menace to the living: the lesson of Jack Clayton's *The Innocents* (1961), a brilliant take on the psychical ghosts of *The Turn of the Screw*.

But the most uncanny thing, of course, is the corpse that continues to move. This is the main business of the Gothic tradition and horror film. The extraordinary persistence of figures of the undead, from the very origins of cinema to the present day, suggests that these creatures continue to perform crucial cultural work. Transgressors, they mark out the limits proper to human life. But they are constantly renewed and transformed as condensations of anxiety because this is a boundary that has become weirdly unstable at the hands of modern science and medicine. This is the zone of uncertainty in which the Gothic plies its trade.

(Above)
Mervyn Johns is attacked by the ventriloquist's dummy in 'Dead of Night' (1945).

Although ghosts and golems stalk early cinema, James Whale's *Frankenstein* (1931) transposes to Hollywood one of the foundational myths of Gothic modernity, the narrative of how science has moved inexorably towards unravelling the secrets of the very generation of life. Mary Shelley composed the novel in 1818 out of the circuit of radical materialists and artisan-scientists who witnessed electrical tests on the twitching limbs of dead frogs and executed criminals in makeshift demonstrations in London. These groups argued for a purely biological origin rather than trusting to faith in a divine spark of life. This was an atheistic belief that led to the suppression of many medical texts during a period of political unrest. In 1931, it was still the case that Colin Clive's unhinged delivery of Henry Frankenstein's celebration of his animation of the corpse had to be censored. We get his delirious repetition of "IT'S ALIVE!" but not every print has restored his awkward following line: "In the name of God? Now I know what it feels like to be God."

Where Shelley's book is very uninterested in Doctor Frankenstein's technique of re-animation, Whale's *Frankenstein* begins a cinematic obsession with the technologies for reanimating corpses. The camera roves amongst bubbling flasks, surgical instruments and the electrical sparks of Van der Graaf generators. Doctor Frankenstein's mad progenitors continue to mess around in the laboratory with dead things. A title like *The Return of the Living Dead* (1985) is the dark promise of a horror cinema that will always come back. There is a line of biomedical horror that will lead past *Coma* (1978) and end up in the abject Gothic bodies of TV series like the *X-Files* or *Fringe*, where paranormal science entirely rubs out any boundary between self and other, human and alien, life and death.

The Enlightenment was meant to banish ignorance and superstition, but the lively dead of the Gothic rudely mock this claim, stalking every advance of science. The modern vampire first became a subject of attention in 1732 when the sophisticated metropolitan *London Journal* reported on the case of Arnold Paul. Paul's body had been dug up thirty days after his death, after repeated sightings of his wandering body around his village, and was discovered not only without signs of decomposition but bloated with fresh blood. He was staked through the heart – a traditional way of pinning a wandering soul back in the corpse – and the body then burnt by a frenzied group of peasants. This took place on the very edges of Europe, the far-flung terrain of the Hungarian borders of the Habsburg Empire. More cases were soon reported from Romania.

Paul's story was presented in Vienna and London as a case of ridiculous folk superstition, more evidence of the need for Enlightened education. A radical sceptic like Voltaire was much amused by these credulous stories. And yet these tales were enthusiastically collected, anthologised and circulated, suggesting that they held a more complicated allure. Indeed, the vampire has moved steadily from the margins of Europe and set up at the heart of the modern city. This is exactly the trajectory of Count Dracula in Bram Stoker's novel, from his ancestral castle on the blurry edges of Christian Europe and the Ottoman East to the North of England, then the Eastern boundary of London, and finally, most terrifyingly, to a house on Piccadilly but a short walk from Buckingham Palace

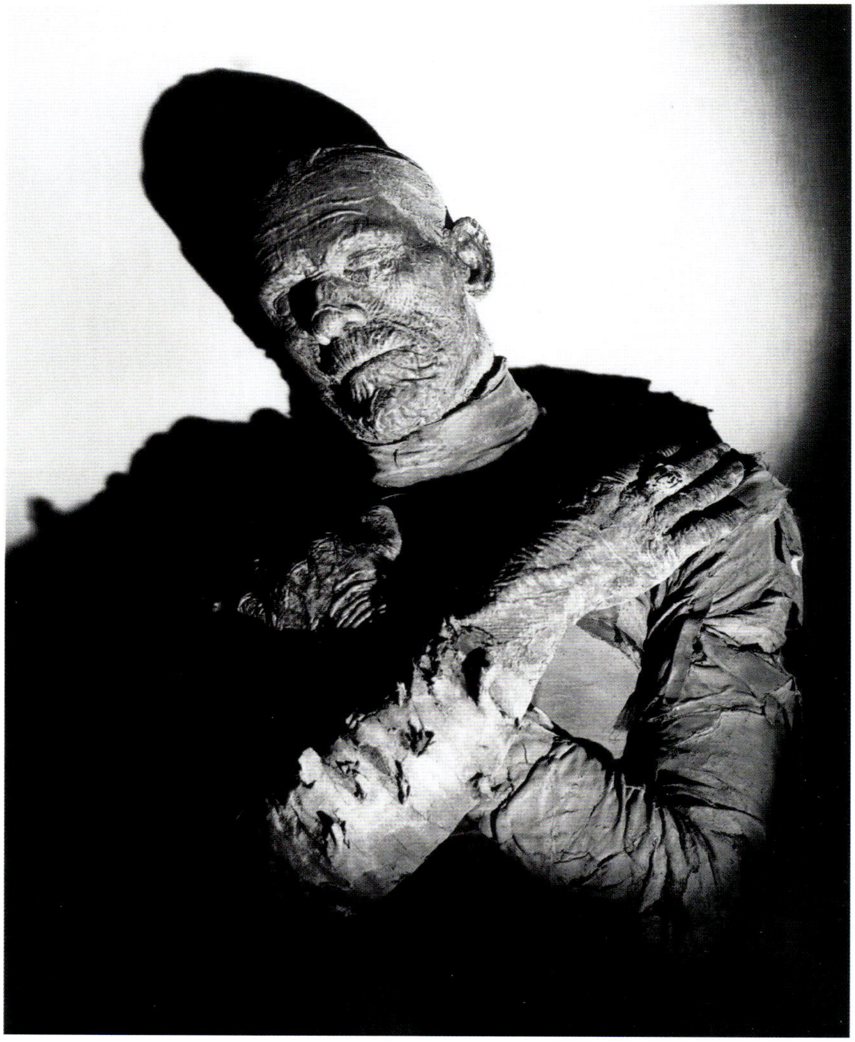

and the symbolic centre of Empire.

Vampire film has similarly moved from the spectral landscapes of *Nosferatu* (1922) or the Greece of Mark Robson's haunting *Isle of the Dead* (1945) and has left behind Hammer's hokey castles and revolting peasants to enter the modern urban realm. There are brilliant vampiric portraits of rust-belt inner-city decay in *Martin* (1976), night-time New York in *The Addiction* (1995), or the sprawl of Los Angeles in *The Lost Boys* (1987) and its hellmouth suburbs in *Buffy the Vampire Slayer* (1997-2003). The vampire has always been able to morph between ancient and modern, sacred and secular versions. For every undead vampire demon visiting from hell, there are ambiguous creatures with blood disorders that hesitate in the margins between science and superstition, the maybe-vampires of *Martin* (1977), *Near Dark* (1987) or *Midnight Son* (2011).

The ancient undead mummy shuffles less certainly towards the modern world, yet our obsessive retelling of mummy curse stories also belongs to recent times. Ancient Egyptians had much more sophisticated beliefs than the crude narratives of vengeful violence repeated in the cycles of mummy cinema. These superstitions appear in the Western Gothic only in the wake of the imperial occupation of Egypt in the late 19th century. Universal's classic *The Mummy* (1932) was scripted by John Balderston, who as a journalist in the 1920s had been in the Valley of the Kings to report on the final unveiling of Tutankhamun's face from beneath his death mask in 1925. Boris Karloff's Imhotep is the bad conscience of the West's scramble for ancient loot amongst the august tombs of the dead. Hammer made their version of *The Mummy* in 1959, just three years after the catastrophe of Suez had made Egypt the graveyard of British imperial hopes.

Uncanny artefacts come to life throughout cinema, from Auguste and Louis Lumière's dancing skeleton (*Le*

(Opposite, top)
The Ancient Egyptian priest Imhotep (Boris Karloff) awakens from centuries of slumber in Universal's classic 'The Mummy' (1932).

(Opposite, bottom)
Hammer's version of 'The Mummy' was made just three years after the Suez crisis.

(Above)
The zombies in Val Lewton's 'I Walked with a Zombie' (1943) are Caribbean slaves cast into a dreamworld between life and death by a voodoo magician.

(Right)
Victor Halperin's 'White Zombie' (1932) played on American fears about the primitive magic supposedly used in its colony Haiti.

Squelette joyeux, 1895) to the menacing statue of an Assyrian demon behind Regan's possession in *The Exorcist* (1973) to the comical shenanigans after hours in the Smithsonian in *Night at the Museum* (2006). Some museum objects refuse to be curated, instead remaining lively and disturbing: the premise of many a Gothic short story.

But it is the zombie that is no doubt the most dominant living dead creature of our apocalyptic times. The aristocratic lone vampire or mummy has been replaced by the anonymous hordes of zombies, a multitude of baying, hungry corpses. They insistently overrun every last stand of the human survivors, and horror cinema replays this scenario over and over again, as if in search of a less apocalyptic ending. Zombies were once a small band of mournful Caribbean slaves, cast, as in Val Lewton's *I Walked with a Zombie* (1943), into a dreamworld between life and death by a voodoo magician. Melodrama came from the threat of an inversion of power: primitive magic can snare the American visitor to Haiti, turning the coloniser into the undead servant of the colonised. This is the worry at the base of Victor Halperin's *White Zombie* (1932), made whilst American forces were attempting to suppress native superstitions in Haiti, but only a year before America abandoned its occuptation of the island. The lone shuffling zombie begins to multiply in Hammer's *The Plague of the Zombies* (1966), the undead workers this time Cornish tin-miners reviving a moribund industry. The film is a bizarre rendition of Marx's theory that the owners of the means of production will suck the living labour from workers, alienating them even unto (un)death.

But the film credited with turning zombies into the multitude of the consumer masses is George A. Romero's *Night of the Living Dead* (1968). Although the characters never use the term zombies, and Romero was adapting Richard Matheson's vampire novel, *I Am Legend,* Romero's cult hit has spread like a contagion through global cinema (in 2013, the first Bollywood zombie musical, *Goa Goa Gone,* finally appeared).

For many, it is no coincidence that *Night of the Living Dead* appeared in 1968, a year of revolutionary disorder and dissent around the world. The racial politics of *Night* is explicit and explosive: a black hero is lynched by a redneck posse and the outbreak is seemingly contained by state-sanctioned mass extermination. What has been less noticed is that 1968 was also the year that an Ad Hoc Committee of the Harvard Medical School came together and radically redefined the definition of brain death. The Harvard medics eventually decided to exclude EEG tests to determine brain death, because it transpired that the brain activity of these bodies could prove disturbingly lively. There has been controversy over precisely where to define brain death as opposed to the more definitive cardiopulmonary definition of death ever since. A tiny percentage of those in persistent vegetative states do wake up and recover cognitive functions: we are fascinated by these stories. No wonder you have to shoot zombies through the head. After 1968, the biomedical boundary between the living and the dead has become strangely unclear. The continuing success of the zombie apocalypse film again proves how Gothic cinema is a cultural register of how unnerved we remain when the boundaries of the human are put under pressure by scientific and technological advance. Catastrophe is the order of the day, whether zombies are a biomedical disaster – from *The Crazies* (1973) to *28 Days Later* (2002) – or simply register fears of the collapse of the public sphere, from the critical edge of *Pontypool* (2008) to the vacuous rehearsal of the apocalypse plot in *Zombieland* (2009). We live in anxious times: we can expect the undead to live on in this spectral half-life for a long time to come.

(Above)
The dancing skeleton in Auguste and Louis Lumière's 'Le Squelette joyeux' (1895).

(Below)
Cornish tin-miners rise from the grave in Hammer's 'The Plague of the Zombies' (1966).

(Bottom)
Zombies are the result of a biomedical disaster in Danny Boyle's '28 Days Later' (2002).

Gore and the Gothic

By James Blackford

Scenes of graphic gore can rank among the most thrilling, artistically creative and downright terrifying moments in horror cinema. Think of a zombie tearing into flesh in *Dawn of the Dead* (1978), a drill-bit being driven slowly into a forehead in *City of the Living Dead* (1980) or an eyeball being pierced by a spike of wood in *Zombie Flesh Eaters* (1979). Such scenes are staples of the so-called 'gore film', a strain of horror cinema that has usually been seen as occupying the opposite end of the genre's spectrum to the more refined terrors of the Gothic. Gore has been cast as a low-brow thrill, privileging visceral reactions of revulsion and disgust over the Gothic's more psychological terrors. Gore in horror is seen somewhat like sex in pornography, fulfilling a sensational function for horror cinema's equivalent of the dirty mac brigade, out looking for titillation.

However, the relationship between gore and the Gothic is far more complex than this simplistic distinction suggests. Far from being opposites, the two great traditions of horror have in fact overlapped throughout their history, going back past the Grand Guignol theatre to paintings by such artists as Goya or Blake.

Central to the appeal of such silent masterpieces as *The Hunchback of Notre Dame* (1923) and *The Phantom of the Opera* (1925) was the horrific make-up worn (and self-applied) by Lon Chaney, which made vividly real the deformations suggested in Victor Hugo and Gaston Leroux's novels. In early sound cinema, films such as James Whale's *Frankenstein* (1931) again offered audiences representations of physical deformation. The success of Hammer Film Productions in the late 1950s also saw explicitly gory Gothic films reach wide audiences.

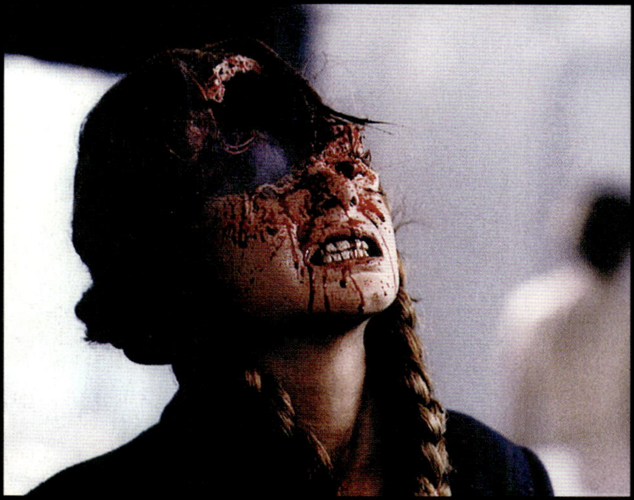

Lucio Fulci's 'The Beyond' (1981)

Terence Fisher's *The Curse of Frankenstein* (1957) boasted several grisly laboratory scenes and lingered on the grotesque detail of Baron Frankenstein (Peter Cushing) closely examining an eyeball with a magnifying glass – a scene that proved too shocking for its time and was cut by the US censor.

Notwithstanding Herschell Gordon Lewis's efforts in the US, in the 1960s it was the cinema of mainland Europe that would up the ante in terms of gore. George Franju's poetic *Eyes Without a Face* (1960), about a surgeon's twisted attempts to restore his disfigured daughter's face, features a prolonged skin-grafting sequence that was unprecedented in feature-filmmaking at the time. The film inspired other filmmakers to make ever-gorier 'surgical horrors', such as Spanish exploitation-auteur Jess Franco's *The Awful Dr. Orlof* (1962) and *Faceless* (1988), the latter a fully-fledged gore-fest.

Mario Bava's *Black Sunday* (1960) was on the one hand a celebration of the Gothic aesthetic pioneered by Universal in the 1930s, but Bava added several strikingly modern sequences of gory violence. The opening scene sees a mask with long nails protruding on the inside hammered violently onto the witch Asa's face, all shown in a horrific close-up which goes beyond anything Hammer had then dared to show. Bava's film spawned a wave of Italian Gothic horror films that accentuated sex and sadomasochism, and Bava himself would make increasingly graphic and perverse films in both the Gothic and *giallo* genres throughout the 1960s and 70s.

However, the real turning point for gore cinema came with George A. Romero's *Night of the Living Dead* (1968), which updated the Gothic mainstays of zombies and old dark houses for troubled, modern times. Before Romero, zombies had been rather impotent, somnambulist slaves. Romero re-invented them as everyday people turned rabid flesh-eaters. The film was a landmark shift in terms of graphic splatter: blood and guts are strewn across the screen in *Night of the Living Dead* (and its five sequels), and henceforth the zombie would be synonymous with graphic gore.

Romero had made gore central to the Gothic, but it was two Italians who would go on to make horror cinema's purest expressions of the Gothic-gore aesthetic. With *Suspiria* (1976) and *Inferno (1980)*, Dario Argento relocated the gory, misogynistic setpieces of his earlier *gialli* into hallucinatory, supernatural horror films that drew heavily on the Gothic tropes of witches and nightmarish spaces.

Argento was a pioneer, but it was his compatriot Lucio Fulci who would perfect the art of the Gothic gore film. In *Zombie Flesh Eaters* (1979), Fulci merged the extreme splatter found in Romero's films with the doctors, voodoo, and exotic Caribbean locales found in earlier Hollywood Gothic films such as *I Walked With a Zombie* (1943) and *Voodoo Island* (1957). Here the gore reaches unconscionably over-the-top heights, as eyes are impaled on spikes of wood and throats are ripped out; but Fulci films the violence lovingly, inviting aesthetic appreciation as well as provoking visceral revulsion. Fulci took the use of gore to new artistic heights, making it his artistic signature and using it expressionistically. It's an approach that runs unchecked in his delirious Gothic revival films *City of the Living Dead* and *The Beyond* (1981), the skeletal narratives of which see the gates of hell (in Dunwich and Louisiana respectively) opened to spew forth hordes of lumbering zombies.

In these films Fulci deliberately uses many classic archetypes of the Gothic – old dark houses, ornate furnishings, plumes of fog – to create surreal nightmare realms where the fragmented narratives become mere vehicles for sequences of show-stopping gore. The films elevate Gothic imagery and aestheticised gore above all else. Several distinctive gore films by other Italian directors like Michele Soavi have followed in his wake, but Fulci's remains as pure a Gothic-gore cinema as has yet been realised.

Theatres of War

By Matthew Sweet

On Valentine's night in 1927, Count Dracula materialised in a back street off the Strand. Curiously, he did it in the form of Raymond Huntley – that sour, patrician actor who played judges, headmasters and chief constables in half a century of British films. In the confines of the Little Theatre, Huntley came and went in a flash of magnesium, caused a picture to crash from the wall, and exhorted his Renfield to swallow a mouse - played by a clockwork model named Billie. Most of the critics came out sniggering. The audience, however, responded differently. "Night after night," asserted the *Daily Express*, "women and men faint as horror is piled on horror on the stage." The publicity-canny management hired a nurse to attend each performance and administer first aid to the overcome. The medicine was brandy. Uptake was enthusiastic.

The production – adapted and led by the actor-manager Hamilton Deane – was hardly radical: it had been flapping around the provinces for years. Its arrival in London, however, caused powerful forces to stir. It proved that the appetites and anxieties that had motivated Gothic fiction since the late 18th century could still resonate in an audience of the metropolitan 20th. It suggested that 1920s London contained an enormous number of girls who were as hungry for "Horrid Mysteries" as the heroine of Jane Austen's *Northanger Abbey* (1817) – and that the majority of them were actually boys. "The curious thing," reflected the London diarist of the *Derby Evening Telegraph*, "is that mostly it is the male members of the audience, and not at all the ladies, who find themselves overcome by the grip of the vampire drama's uncanny thrill. When I asked why this should be, my friend replied that many of our men nowadays are either military-unfits or shell-shocks." The trauma of war had turned Britain into a nation of vampire-lovers.

Tradition drew Dracula to the Little Theatre. In 1920, under the management of José Levy and the artistic stewardship of Sybil Thorndike and Lewis Casson, it had become the British home of Grand Guignol – the proprietary name for a form of theatrical ultraviolence pioneered in a similarly compact Parisian venue. On the stage of the Little Theatre, Thorndike was poisoned, strangled, entombed in plaster and had her eyes gouged out with knitting needles. The form had its enemies: the playwright St John Ervine declared that Guignol appealed only to "overfed voluptuaries and creepy-crawly people with flabby insides" – but he was silenced when the Little Theatre management commissioned him to make his own contribution to the genre, *Progress* (1922), in which a scientist, aiming to make war "more expeditious", invents a gas-bomb capable of exterminating the populations of whole cities. Ervine, who hated cinema almost as much as he had once professed to dislike Guignol, became the first Little Theatre playwright to see their horrors transposed to the screen. During the run of *Progress*, the cameras of the Gaumont cinemagazine *Around the Town* came to observe Sybil Thorndike using a carving knife to consign the inventor – and his discovery – to oblivion.

When film historians have looked back on Gothic horror before Universal, they have sometimes betrayed their frustration that a cinema of poetry and electricity and the supernatural did not spring, fully formed, onto the screen in the first decade of the 20th century. Guignol was a form of neurotic realism. It shared the Gothic's preoccupation with the asylum and the laboratory, but it was not concerned with the sublime. As horror plots often prove, however, family history is inescapable. James Whale – father of *Frankenstein*, wedding planner to *Bride of Frankenstein* – trod the boards of the Little Theatre in a Guignol play about a scientist who electrifies a severed head in order to elicit a plea to a charge of murder. The actor-playwright HF Maltby crafted shocks for the Little Theatre before Tod Slaughter employed him to revive an even older Gothic stage tradition for shockers such as *The Crimes of Stephen Hawke* (1936) and *Sweeney Todd* (1936). Tod Browning's 1931 *Dracula* may now read like an exotic film-poem, but its shocks are as much material as supernatural. Madmen eating flies; blood transfusions; the cruel irony of a servant who kills her mistress with an act of kindness: these elements were Bram Stoker's children, but they were perfectly at home at the Little Theatre

A self-conscious cinema of Grand Guignol emerged in the early 1920s, in the form of five series of one and two-reelers made by Fred Paul. "No connection with the Little Theatre, London" insisted the posters – a legal caveat that told audiences to anticipate something that was almost exactly the same. *The Nurse* was based on an original story, but the publicity images – depicting a hospital patient charging towards an open window – recalled a notorious defenestration scene in José Levy's 1921 production of Lucien Descaves's play *Seven Blind Men*. Paul gave the game away by telling the *Kinematograph Weekly* that he hoped to capitalise upon the popularity of "the fare that forms the menu at the Little Theatre."

A handful of these films survives: rich and riveting little dramas about fear, pain, violence and moral cruelty in Britain after the Great War. ("Life as it really is," asserted Fred Paul, "its sordidness and cruelty.") In *A Game for Two*, a forger's fiancée cons her way into a lawyer's grand suburban home and discovers that she is the fall girl in her lover's latest scheme. In *The Last Appeal*, an unwitting judge sentences his illegitimate son to death. (A note begging for clemency comes too late: he gazes, ashen-faced, at the unforgiving clock.) In *The Jest*, a boarding-house joker plays a vicious trick on a fellow lodger, dragging up as his long-lost wife. The prank backfires: the old man takes a knife to the figure he believes is his treacherous spouse. His grinning face fills the final shot - "Revenged at last!" screams the intertitle. "My wife .... I've killed her."

Fred Paul's Guignol series receives a glancing reference in Denis Gifford's *Pictorial History of Horror Movies* – that absinthe-green Bible in which many of us first learned of Caligari, Nosferatu, Lugosi and Karloff – but in most accounts their presence is ghostly, marginal. In Gothic stories, troublesome relations tend to be locked in attics. The stage tradition that populated 1930s Hollywood with vampires and scientists deserves its share of light and air. If it were to come downstairs and take its place in the drawing-room, it might have a story to tell us: one about a theatre of shell-shock that crossed the Atlantic and found itself caught in the gaze of Karl Freund, refugee from UFA; one about a Christmas Day game in No Man's Land that only ended when Abbott and Costello met Frankenstein.

In January 1931, an interview appeared in *Motion Picture Classic* magazine that purported to offer Bela Lugosi's thoughts on the appeal of filmed horror. "During the War," he asserted, "women fought, manoeuvred, bribed and schemed to get to the front-line trenches. In their hearts, in their conscious minds, they believed that they were striving for that place in order to perform deeds of duty and mercy to their fellow-men. But mixed in with this high motive was the ghoulish compulsion to see men torn and bloody and in agony, the horrible fascination of horror, the need to look upon the suffering, which is a part of their destiny." A few weeks later, just two days before Valentine's night 1931, four years after Raymond Huntley fluttered his cloak across the stage of the Little Theatre, Lugosi's Dracula manifested in cinemas across America – speaking lines from Hamilton Deane's adaptation. Reports of fainting and screaming, of brandy and smelling-salts, sped through the American press.

(Above)
Tod Slaughter, who became famous for his over the top performances on stage and in films such as 'Sweeney Todd' (1936).

(Opposite)
The original publicity poster for Fred Paul's 'The Nurse' (1921).

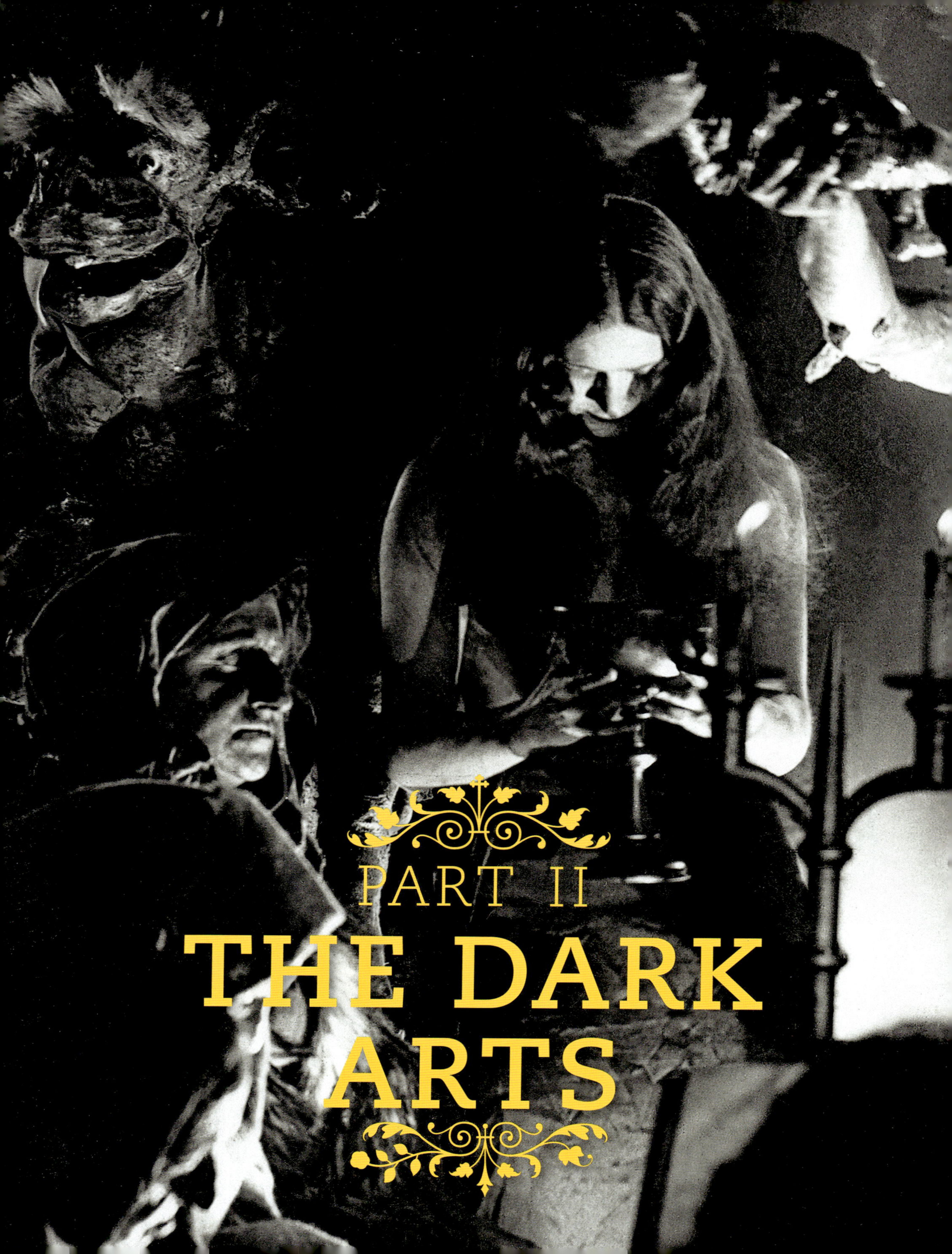

PART II
THE DARK ARTS

THE DARK ARTS

BLACK MAGIC

BY RICHARD T. KELLY

If a Gothic tale should embrace diabolism and/or witchcraft then the famous conventions of the style will enjoy a notable enhancement. Where, for instance, the setting of the story is some forbidding castle or high ancestral pile, the usual hidden doors and passages will probably lead to rooms that host occult gatherings and rituals – the solemn Black Mass, the orgiastic sabbath. Or where secrets essential to the plot exist in writing, these are likely to lie within a lavishly bound *grimoire* containing oaths for the invocation (and, with luck, the extirpation) of evil.

Evil is the key to what we might call the Gothic occult in cinema. Undoubtedly one leaves behind the scenic-romantic Gothic of Ann Radcliffe's famous novels – or, say, the Victorian Gothic mystery of Guy Ritchie's *Sherlock Holmes* (2009) – wherein seemingly supernatural occurrences are exposed as the cunning works of Man. Instead, the viewer must reckon with evil as a metaphysical force in the world – evil done for evil's sake, so that more evil may follow. This age-old enemy is just as integral to the Gothic growing-pains fight against 'dark magic' of the *Harry Potter* movies as it is to more gory Gothic-shaded horrors like the *Silent Hill* franchise or Sam Raimi's frenzied tales of demonic possession (all of which might just as easily be called *The Evil Dead*).

As such, the Gothic occult tends to benefit from a strong villain – if not Satan himself then some unusually gifted apostle. The hero must in turn exude goodness or, at least, innocence, so that a sound moral norm is established, the better to be attacked. But goodness can be assailed by temptation just as thoroughly as terror. We would kid ourselves not to grant that notions of 'evil' can stir up fascination as well as moral horror within the human breast.

A film-historical case in point is Benjamin Christensen's *Häxan* (1922), which sets out as an illustrated tract, an ostensibly solemn effort to expose medieval consternation about witches as hysterical expressions of all too human flaws and prejudices. Yet for all its cinematic accomplishment *Häxan* was rated morally dubious and pursued by censorship: this, perhaps, because Christensen was 'of the devil's party', as Blake wrote of Milton – and knowingly so, at least in a showman's sense. The outlandish confession of diabolism extracted by torture from aged weaver Maria (Maren Pedersen) seals *Häxan*'s critique of clerical hypocrisy; but in Christensen's visualising of her ravings the picture really comes alive, generating a fabulously rich image-repertoire of diabolical revelry. Christensen himself played Satan and, very evidently, loved it.

If Christensen's motives were not entirely pure, there was an apparent moral urgency in those filmmakers of the silent era who addressed the demonic through the myth of Faust – the pact with the Devil so that forbidden knowledge, power and pleasures come the covenanter's way, at the price of his soul. Faustian tales work as low comedy too, but in Gothic dress they are always tragedies, concerned with the guileful means by which Satan, the Deceiver, engineers one man's damnation so as to

(Previous page)
Benjamin Christensen's 'Häxan' (1922).

(Opposite)
Mocata (Charles Gray) poised to sacrifice Tanith (Nike Arrighi) in 'The Devil Rides Out' (1968).

multiply the sum of misery in the world.

The Student of Prague (1913), scripted by the shady German poet-novelist Hanns Heinz Ewers (with generous thefts from Poe and Hoffman), is rich in Gothic reverberations. Balduin (Paul Wegener), young and penniless, seeking the means to romance a countess, pacts with a capering sorcerer named Scapinelli – not the very devil, but impishly black of garb and pointy of beard. In return for a shower of gold Scapinelli confiscates Balduin's reflection in the mirror: the student laughs it away, rashly, for in the Gothic occult what the glass shows us is a 'double', a menacing second self. Sure enough, not long after Balduin's *doppelgänger* has stepped through the mirror he is dogging Balduin's steps, committing infamous acts in his name, hounding him to his grave.

The Student of Prague was remade with a few more bells and whistles in 1926, the same year that F. W. Murnau entered the field formidably with his UFA 'super-production' of *Faust*. Its scenario gestured to Goethe: Faust (Gösta Ekman) is a venerable scholar-scientist driven to despair when he cannot save his town from plague. But the plague has been sent by Emil Jannings's Mephistopheles, enveloping the town inside his monstrous wings (one of the picture's many blackly ravishing tableaux.) Mephistopheles then entices Faust to renounce God and save the townsfolk by sorcery. The pact is a trap: Satan intends to use the ensnared as an instrument of greater evil, namely the seduction and abandonment of radiant peasant girl Gretchen (Camilla Horn).

Still, in a supremely affecting denouement Murnau does fashion a means for Faust to redeem himself. Siegfried Kracauer thought Murnau 'thoroughly vulgarised' the metaphysics of *Faust*; and it's not a major thesis on the problem of evil. It is, though, a stirringly romantic, visually stupendous benchmark in cinema. No director has conjured a more malefic mood within

the frame than Murnau – 'impregnating everything, down to the cloth of a garment, with diabolism', as Lotte Eisner put it. Arguably the only flaw in the design is Emil Jannings, who pitches his leering mischief to the back row of the theatre.

In fairness to Jannings it's a big ask for any actor to incarnate the Devil. Some form of Satanic surrogacy can actually summon up a greater sense of malevolence. *The Omen* (1976) imagines the Antichrist as a whey-faced five-year-old boy inveigled into close proximity with earthly powers. *The Exorcist* (1973) sees a Babylonian demon inhabit the 12-year-old daughter of a divorcée actress in Washington D.C. Neither of these hit movies was especially 'Gothic', though each has its moments – *The Exorcist*'s iconic image of the priest standing in silhouette before the fog-wreathed facade of a Georgetown house that seems to exhale evil; or the mission of *The Omen*'s ill-fated heroes to a ruined Italian cemetery, guarded by hounds, where they disinter the bones of a jackal. But both pictures exude the drear, depressed feel of the mid-1970s, and deserve credit for playing Satan with such dramatic conviction in our secular age.

The early Gothic novel in English was usually more comfortable setting devilment in a bygone century and a more 'backward' place: priest-ridden southern Europe, for example. Matthew Lewis's *The Monk* (1796), racy as hell and hotly consumed in its day by 'scandalised' readers, is such a book. Its protagonist Ambrosio, a Capuchin friar in Madrid at the time of the Inquisition, is outwardly pious but inwardly seething with a lust that will lead him to perdition. Interestingly, Dominik Moll's elegant 2011 film extracts the lubricity of Lewis's novel by having Ambrosio (Vincent Cassel) entrapped by Satan, in the monastic rose garden he tends like a private Eden. There, he's bitten by a centipede and, in a venom-induced delirium, seduced by the Devil's handmaiden. His blood thus provoked and poisoned, Ambrosio proceeds to damn himself and several others. This is not the take on *The Monk* imagined by Luis Buñuel, who was drawn to the novel more for its debunking of clerical hypocrisy.

However, the massive influence of *The Exorcist* led to an outbreak of horror films about crazed girls frothing and shrieking curses at priests, the action often transplanted (in Gothic style) to convents chock-full of repressed nuns seeking intercourse with someone or something. Mexican cinema was particularly inspired, the best of its productions in this vein Juan López Moctezuma's *Alucarda* (1978), derived from Le Fanu's *Carmilla*, Stoker's *Dracula* and Sade's *Justine*, and full of startling, artful images.

The titular anti-heroine (Tina Romero) is a raven-haired orphan in a convent where carnality in all forms is reviled (and from a pulpit before an altar of agonised flesh, a host of life-size crucified figures). Alucarda seizes on a new initiate, Justine (Susana Kamini) with unnerving fervour, introducing her playmate to a nearby forest, a Pan-like gypsy, and an eerie crypt

(Opposite, top)
Director Benjamin Christensen himself played Satan in the remarkable 'Häxan' (1922).

(Opposite, bottom)
Balduin (Conrad Veidt) makes his fateful pact with the sorcerer Scapinelli (Werner Krauss) in 'The Student of Prague' (1926).

(Below)
Emil Jannings's Mephistopheles envelops the town in his wings in F.W. Murnau's 'Faust' (1926).

where an opened casket seems to possess the girls with demonic vitality sufficient to raze their convent to the ground.

Alucarda and the film that bears her name appear to extol an earthy, lusty worship of life, as opposed to the self-mortifying death-cult of Christ. But she and Moctezuma can't have it both ways. We have seen the girls debauched by something – someone – evil: one whom the priest identifies as 'the seducer, the enemy of virtue, the perpetual persecutor of innocence.'

Another key Satanic surrogate is the sorcerer, who would have made little impact on film had he remained the pre-Enlightenment warlock in robe and pointed hat. He had to be magicked into the 20th century. And whatever view one has of the scurrilous English occultist Aleister Crowley (1875-1947), cinema's account of black magic would hardly be conceivable had it not the self-embroidered legend of 'The Beast' to draw upon.

Edgar G. Ulmer had certainly read of Crowley's infamy while preparing *The Black Cat* (1934), and it rubbed off in his rendering of Hjalmar Poelzig (Boris Karloff), a treasonous Hungarian war criminal, clad in black silk with a sharp widow's peak, looking and sounding like death partially warmed. Poelzig has expunged any guilt over the war, having pledged himself to Satan. His mansion offers the film's great twist on a Gothic trope, for it is no dank stone edifice but a Bauhaus construction of chrome and glass with Art Deco fittings. Below stairs, though, is a hall where Karloff leads fellow Satanists in a modernist Black Mass: a deranged, campy occasion, unlikely to have impressed 'The Beast' in point of rigour.

Dennis Wheatley, the staunchly conservative English adventure writer, actually met Crowley, and formed a sceptical opinion, but was sufficiently diverted to fictionalise him in *The Devil Rides Out* (1934), filmed by Hammer in 1968. Mocata (Charles Gray) is the high-level 'adept' ('ipsissimus') in a magical fraternity patterned on Crowley's own, fought by aristocratic occult expert the Duc de Richleau (Christopher Lee). Gray seems at first rather a stock villain, burly in purple robes as he presides over a terribly tame *sabbat*. But gradually he reveals a command of the dark arts, blithely hypnotising one of Richleau's allies from the depths of an armchair, then sending forth an assortment of fiends – from a very large-bodied spider to a horsebound Angel of Death – to attack Richleau and his cohorts while they seek protection inside a runic chalk circle.

Perhaps the screen's most persuasive

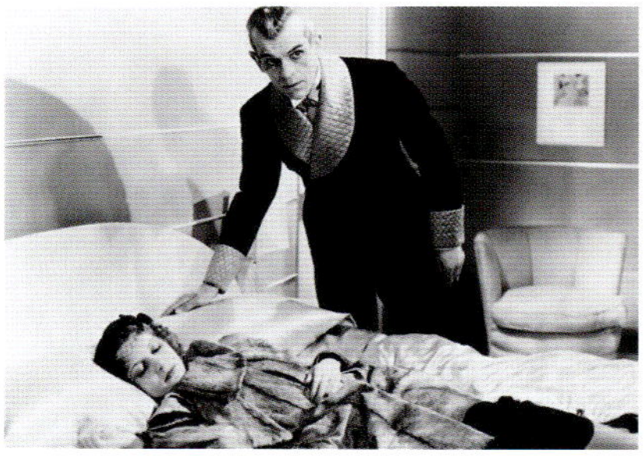

(Top)
'The Devil Rides Out' (1968), Hammer's most memorable flirtation with the dark arts.

(Above left)
Hjalmar Poelzig (Boris Karloff) with Joan Alison (Jacqueline Wells) in an incongruous Art Deco setting in 'The Black Cat' (1934).

(Above right)
Prospero (Vincent Price) tries to lure Francesca (Jane Asher) into Satanism in 'The Masque of the Red Death' (1964).

(Opposite)
'Night of the Demon' (1957), a high point of 1950s occult horror.

Crowley proxy, though, is spell-caster, cult leader and children's magician Dr Julian Karswell (Niall MacGinnis) in Jacques Tourneur's *Night of the Demon* (1957), inspired by M.R. James's story 'Casting the Runes'. When Karswell's cult is threatened with exposure by tough-minded psychologist John Holden (Dana Andrews), he accepts the vendetta and, barely raising his voice, summons varied faceless and elemental forces to drive Holden off his country estate. Tourneur and MacGinnis succeed in making demonic power feel commonplace and tangible, even in daylight. Yet the film's most unsettling achievement is its sense that Karswell, despite his portly swagger, is barely less wary than his victims of the forces he unleashes and yet cannot command. "I do what I do out of fear also", he confides to his mother. "It's part of the price."

Some cinematic Satanists show no fear of damnation: they just burn with a desire to turn the world upside down, invert the Cross and its values. They're insistent, too, about the inherent superiority of their worldview – notably Vincent Price's medieval Prince Prospero in *The Masque of the Red Death* (1964), the most admired of Roger Corman's Edgar Allan Poe movies. Prospero vaunts Satan as a god not of hate but 'reality and truth'. "If a god of love and life ever did exist", he tells pious peasant Francesca (Jane Asher), "he is long since dead. Someone – some*thing* – rules in his place." And Prospero professes ease with this new dispensation. But the reality is that plague is rife in the countryside around his castle: Satan does not rule over Death, and Prospero's wealth won't save him. The Satanist, like his Master, is routinely guilty of the pride that comes before a fall.

Successful Satanism must proceed with greater guile, not crowing before the game is won. Secretive covens do better than charismatic leaders in this regard. *The Seventh Victim* (1943), one of those RKO releases for which producer Val Lewton is routinely credited as *auteur*,

(Above)
The iconic Pinhead in director Clive Barker's gory twist on the infernal pact, 'Hellraiser' (1987).

(Below, top)
The Coven of Manhattan Satanists meets in producer Val Lewton's 'The Seventh Victim' (1943).

(Below, bottom)
New York is again home to Satanism in Roman Polanski's 'Rosemary's Baby' (1968).

is admired for the sombre, literate mood it builds on a B-movie budget. But its coven appears rather a shabby bunch, professing faith in 'Satanic majesty and power' yet exhibiting no gift for invoking it. A creepier kind of New York cabal emerges in Roman Polanski's film of Ira Levin's *Rosemary's Baby* (1968).

A plaintive stock figure in Gothic fiction is the innocent heroine of tremulous temperament, put in peril by marriage to a saturnine anti-hero. Such a girl is Rosemary Woodhouse (Mia Farrow), who feels her relationship with actor husband Guy (John Cassavetes) deteriorate after their move into a Manhattan apartment building (its exterior the high neo-Gothic gables of New York's famous Dakota) populated by eccentric old folk. Of Rosemary's creeping fear that a coven has chosen her to bear Satan's spawn, Polanski has always insisted that she is just suffering an especially nervous pregnancy – her plight "a chain of only superficially sinister coincidences." You could see it that way – up to a point. Readers of Gothic romance did usually want their heroine to be delivered from evil. But sensation-seeking filmgoers sometimes wish otherwise.

We come to a difficult admission: that the Gothic occult may indulge a certain phantasy – perverse, masochistic – of succumbing to wickedness, suffusing oneself with sin. Take Hazel Court as Juliana, Prospero's mistress in *The Masque of the Red Death*. Before a dark altar she brands her breast and offers up her soul: "Lord Satan, demon lover of all those who wish to live in your eternal night... send me a demon so I may know him, to be your wife." What she is sent are nightmarish apparitions and bloody death; yet Prospero tells his guests to rejoice ("She's just married a friend of mine.").

The base allure of the dark, whatever its costs, shines too from Mario Bava's *Black Sunday* (1960), thanks to Bava's luscious monochrome picture-making but mainly to the singular presence of Barbara Steele in the dual role of innocent Katia and vampiric witch Asa. It's not exactly that we cheer Asa on, yet the energies of the piece are with Steele's darker half: her vicious glee in hailing Satan and "a beautiful life of evil and hate", her extraordinary looks as if crafted on a slab by some cosmetically-minded Frankenstein.

The double, the bodily remains restored by blood, the passionate kiss between abomination and supplicant – all of these Bava's film shares with Clive Barker's *Hellraiser* (1987), a gory twist on the infernal pact that earnestly endeavours to propose pleasures of a sadomasochistic sort in the torments of the netherworld. The movie's main Gothic treats are the cruel leather-fetish wardrobes of the Cenobite demons and the gilded puzzle box – or 'lament configuration' – by which they are called into our world; and, as their leader relishes in the sequel *Hellbound* (1988), "It is not hands that summon us. It is desire."

If there's one director whose flair and tastes feel closest to the spirit of the Gothic occult, it could be Dario Argento, protégé and inheritor of Mario Bava. Above all in the films known as his 'Three Mothers Trilogy', Argento seems possessed – or liberated – by a love of Gothic leitmotifs and their visual possibilities.

The founding myth of his trilogy, expounded in the breathless intro to the second film *Inferno* (1980), is a book written by an architect-alchemist who built residences around the world for a sorority of three ancient witches. Mater Suspiriorum (Mother of Sighs) lives in Freiburg and is the villainess of *Suspiria* (1977). Mater Tenebrarum (Mother of Shadows) may be found in New York, and lurks behind *Inferno*. Mater Lachrymarum, a resident of Rome, belatedly moves centre-stage in *Mother of Tears* (2007).

Suspiria opens by night at Munich airport with the arrival of American Suzy

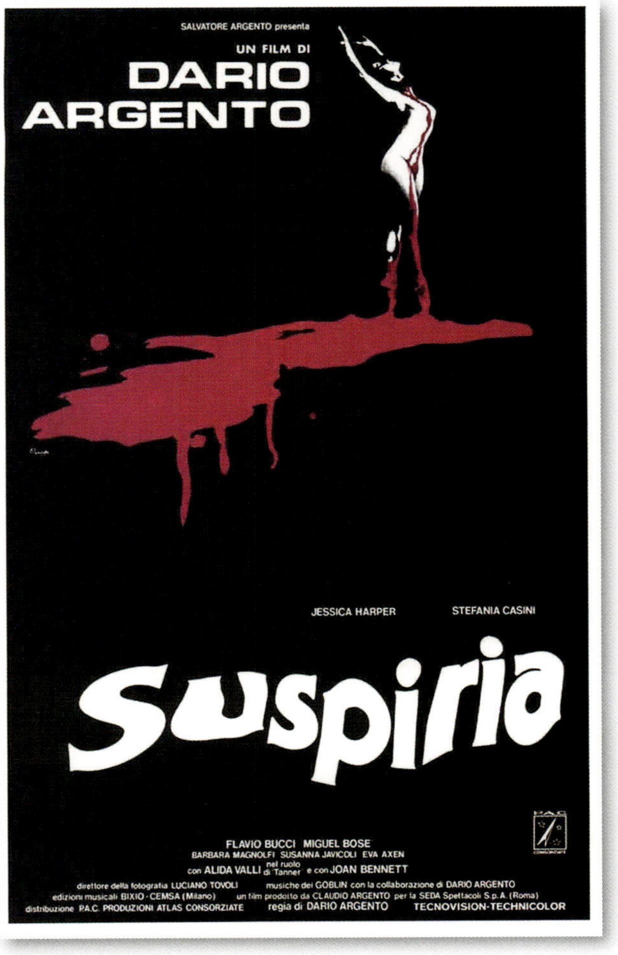

(Above)
The Italian poster for 'Suspiria' (1977), the first film in Dario Argento's 'Three Mothers Trilogy'.

(Below, left)
Jessica Harper as American ballet student Suzy Bannion in 'Suspiria'.

(Below, right)
Mark (Leigh McCloskey) confronts Mater Tenebrarum (Veronica Lazar) in Argento's 'Inferno' (1980). The mirror trick shot was designed by Mario Bava, who was an uncredited special effects advisor on the film.

Bannion (Jessica Harper). But the moment she passes warily beyond the hissing doors of the terminal into inky night and lashing rain Suzy is in a Gothic world, as surely as Snow White stumbling through the forest. Her journey by taxi to the ballet school where she is enrolled, scored like an electronic Black Mass, is one of cinema's eeriest rides, up there with Murnau's *Nosferatu* and Victor Sjöström's *The Phantom Carriage* (1921). The school's secret resides, of course, in the cellar: it is the lair of the Mother of Sighs, its staff a coven of witches, and Suzy must find a way to burn them all down.

Inferno takes us to Manhattan and thickens the Gothic brew. This time the Mother's cellar is an ornate drawing room submerged in water, guarded by rotting cadavers. Dramatis personae include a melancholic countess and a crippled dealer in antiquarian books. The questing hero (Leigh McCloskey) is a cipher, but we're less interested in his fate than in the final revelation of Mater Tenebrarum (through a mirror's surface, no less).

Inferno's choppy storytelling might be taken for Argento having no more concern for structure than he has for eliciting characterful performances. On the other hand, you could see it as an ingenious analogue to the Gothic novel's famous penchant for 'discontinuous narrative'. In fact, you could take the Three Mothers Trilogy *in toto* as wicked fun – were it not for Argento's other great love, the killing of female characters in ghastly, convoluted ways that puncture the mood of witchy maleficence.

But then you can't have everything, as Herr Doktor Faust was made to realise. In the daylight of reasoned analysis, the cinema of the Gothic occult recoils from too much scrutiny. Suffice to say it's an entertainment that allows us to mull in relative comfort over the forms that evil may take; also, perhaps, the measure of moral fitness in ourselves.

Mario Bava and the Italian Gothic

By Tim Lucas

The Italian Gothic cinema took shape one fateful evening when director Riccardo Freda, a former art critic, accepted an invitation from Mario Bava – then moonlighting on his camera crew for the arena sequences of *Spartaco* (1954) – to accompany him home to see the lifesize figures sculpted in wax by his father. The ban on horror films had been lifted in post-Mussolini Italy and one of the first to be imported was *House of Wax* (1953) which, along with the statues, catalysed their pact to make the first Italian horror film of the sound era. Rome was known for its sun, wine, women and song, but it wasn't lost on Freda and Bava, as they toiled by day filming gladiators in the arena, that Rome was also where the notion of death as entertainment was born.

Freda was always willing to take a gamble, but horror was never his passion. However, Bava was described by colleagues as the most frightened man they ever met; he had superstitions about owls and the colour purple, and made a habit of nervously checking his home for hiding intruders each night before retiring. A former painter, Bava understood the psychological values of light and shadow, as well as colour, and his unique sensibilities would evolve a new visual vocabulary for Gothic cinema. In a sense, he nudged it forwards and backwards, forwards to new strains of morbidity and backwards to Gothic architecture's roots in the Romanesque. Bava was also a compulsive reader and had read not only the classic texts of horror and dark fantasy but the genre's contemporary specialists. His favorite writer was H.P. Lovecraft.

The first Freda/Bava collaboration, *I vampiri* (1957), slightly predates the Gothic revival spearheaded by Hammer's *The Curse of Frankenstein* (also 1957). It's a modern-day story that turns Gothic whenever its crusading reporter hero (Dario Michaelis) enters the castle of the Duchess du Grand. The aged, black- veiled Duchess resides there with her chic granddaughter, Gisèle du Grand, played by Freda's wife and muse, Gianna Maria Canale – because, in fact, they are one and the same. The Duchess is a female vampire on her second lifetime, kept alive by transfusions from abducted showgirls, and she pines for Michaelis because he resembles his late father, a lost love whose portrait she has enshrined. The Duchess pays tribute to the Evil Queen in *Snow White and the Seven Dwarfs* (1937), one of the few frightening films permitted to play in Italy in preceding years, and her archetype echoes throughout Italian horror, notably in Dario Argento's *Suspiria* (1977).

Two ideas from *I vampiri* – romantic obsession with ancestral portraits and a secret fireplace passage connecting living quarters to a family crypt – were cards that Bava would replay in his smash directorial debut, *Black Sunday* (*La maschera del demonio*, 1960). By then, Hammer Films had carried the Gothic horror genre into the colour era under the aegis of director Terence Fisher, who favoured a style of staid order disrupted by a few well-chosen feral outbursts, filmed with a distinctly locked-down camera. Bava not only invested his lighting and sets with macabre personality, but his cinematography was more mobile and expressive, cutting or zooming in, free to follow characters into the dark or spin 360° circles around them. At the same time, he accentuated the dreamlike quality of his dark fairy tale by shooting in black-and-white, moving back to the Old World ambience of Universal while floridly advancing beyond what Hammer were doing, even in the departments of gore and sadism.

Bava's masterpiece was influential, not least of all his casting of British actress Barbara Steele, a large-eyed sphinx of a brunette who subsequently played the muse to other directors of the Italian Gothic cinema: Riccardo Freda (*L'orribile segreto del Dott. Hichcock*, 1962; *Lo spettro*, 1963); Antonio Margheriti (*Danza macabra*, 1964; *I lunghi capelli della morte*, 1965); Massimo Pupillo (*5 tombe per un medium*, 1965); Mario Caiano (*Amanti d'oltretomba*, 1965); Camillo Mastrocinque (*Un angelo per Satana*, 1965). Such was the self-loathing at the heart of Italian Gothic cinema that all of these aforementioned directors worked under English pseudonyms, with Freda (that is, "Robert Hampton") going so far as to emulate Hitchcock's thrillers (*Hichcock* is a kind of *Vertigo*) and the colourful Edgar Allan Poe films of California-based Roger Corman.

Bava's directorial career covered all the bases, but he returned to the Gothic – always in colour, subsequently – with *The Whip and the Body* (*La frusta e il corpo*, 1963), a passionate love story, starring Christopher Lee, of sadomasochism beyond the grave produced by the *Hichcock* people to emulate Fisher rather than Corman, resulting in a pronounced visual debt to painters like Thomas Gainsborough. Bava's ghost story *Kill, Baby... Kill!* (*Operazione paura*, 1966) brought the curtain down on the golden age of Italian fantasy, begun with *I vampiri*. Filmed in the rustic mountain village of Calcata, it's Bava's most *Italian* Italian Gothic and counterbalances a tale of the spectral revenge of a child with a love story between a doctor (Giacomo Rossi-Stuart) and his young assistant (Erika Blanc). After several years spent infusing contemporary stories with Pop Art stylistics, Bava returned to the Gothic with 1972's *Baron Blood*, in which a 17th-century Austrian sadist (Joseph Cotten) is resurrected by people restoring his castle for the tourist trade. Bava's next film was *Lisa and the Devil* (1973), which starred Elke Sommer as a tourist lost in Toledo, Spain, who is disoriented to the point of finding herself ensconced in a *Marienbad*-like villa with various lost souls damned to eternal replays of their darkest deeds. A rare example of the horror genre playing host to an art film, *Lisa* is a fascinating tour of love and death whose influences range from Dostoevsky to Lovecraft and du Maurier, passionately scored with Paul Mauriat's interpretation of Rodrigo's 'Concierto de Aranjuez'. It also bears a curious resemblance to an earlier Italian Gothic, Antonio Margheriti's UK-set *The Unnaturals* (*Contronatura*, 1969) – which, like his earlier *Danza macabra*, finds the living and the dead indistinguishable from one another, the past and present coexisting in a manner very true to Rome.

(Opposite) The American poster for Mario Bava's masterful debut, 'Black Sunday' (1960).

(Above) Boris Karloff in Bava's anthology film 'Black Sabbath' (1963).

(Left, top) Bava returned to the Gothic with 1972's 'Baron Blood'.

(Left, bottom) Elke Sommer, Telly Savalas and Alida Valli in 'Lisa and the Devil' (1973).

THE DARK ARTS

MAD SCIENCE

BY MARK KERMODE & SIR CHRISTOPHER FRAYLING

It's Alive!" A brief glimpse at the history of horror movies tells us that, for the first century of Gothic cinema, few things were scarier than science. Moving into the cultural space previously occupied by alchemists, sorcerers and necromancers, mad scientists swiftly became the default bogeymen of the moving image, their practices unfathomable, their crimes mythical: eating fruit from the forbidden tree of knowledge; making Faustian pacts in the name of science; playing God with their attempts to control and create life; stealing Promethean fire from the heavens – all with terrible consequences.

Through movies as diverse as *Doctor X, Island of Lost Souls, The Hands of Orlac, Eyes Without a Face, The Awful Doctor Orlof, Re-Animator, The Fly, The Human Centipede (First Sequence) et al*, Gothic cinema has revelled in the portrayal of science as a black art, with scientists constantly tearing at the locks of Pandora's Box, learning too late that it is indeed possible to know too much.

Through the motif of mad science, horror films have explored the contemporary anxieties of the day, whether it be genetic engineering, nuclear destruction, poisonous irradiation, plastic surgery, artificial life, or automated death. At the root of all this madness are a handful of key tales which underwrite the recurrent obsessions of the genre, most notably Robert Louis Stevenson's *Strange Case of Dr Jekyll and Mr Hyde* and Mary Shelley's *Frankenstein*, popular novels which jointly gave birth to a rich seam of terrifying cinema. Both deal explicitly with the horrors of scientific experimentation, and both have been adapted and re-adapted for the screen on a regular basis from the dawn of cinema to the present day.

It is significant (and ironic) that cinema itself was born of science, a mysterious innovation whose inception was connected both to the cult of the inventor which flourished in the late 19th century, and to the mystique of the fairground sideshow, for decades the domain of the conjuror, the hypnotist, and the medium. Long before film became the most popular art form of the day, magicians were producing phantasms out of thin air using techniques which prefigured the strange alchemy of nitrate film. George Méliès himself was a conjuror by profession whose fondness for science led him to become a pioneer of the new medium of moving images. No surprise then that from the outset cinema was fascinated both by science and magic, the two most frequently being brought together in the spectre of the mad scientist who meddles with the laws of nature, with hellish results.

In 1908, a production of *Dr Jekyll and Mr Hyde* directed by Otis Turner became the first of many celluloid adaptations of Stevenson's novel (a reported five separate versions were in the can by 1910). Crucially, while Stevenson's 1886 source text remained fairly circumspect in its descriptions of Hyde's wild rampages, the movies amplified the homicidal element to this tale of the repressed unleashed by mad science. Conflating the novel's narrative with the growing legend of Jack the Ripper, Gothic cinema reconfigured Dr

(Opposite)
Peter Cushing as Baron Frankenstein in Terence Fisher's 'The Curse of Frankenstein' (1957).

The EDISON
KINETOGRAM
VOL. 1 LONDON, APRIL 15, 1910 No. 1
SCENE FROM
FRANKENSTEIN
FILM No. 6604
EDISON FILMS TO BE RELEASED
FROM MAY 11 TO 18 INCLUSIVE

(Above, left)
Augustus Phillips as Frankenstein, in his laboratory in J. Searle Dawley's 1910 adaptation of Mary Shelley's novel.

(Below)
Fredric March as Dr. Henry Jekyll in Rouben Mamoulian's 1931 film of Robert Louis Stevenson's novel.

(Above, right)
J. Searle Dawley's film featured on the cover of the first UK edition of the 'Edison Kinetograph' in 1910. The image shows Charles Ogle as the Monster.

(Opposite)
'The Cabinet of Dr. Caligari' (1920). Dr. Caligari (Werner Krauss, left, with Conrad Veidt, right) laid the template for the mad scientist in cinema.

Jekyll's misadventures as an increasingly outré spectacle which ramped up the derangement of its central divided soul. Whereas the novella's anti-hero had beaten to death the MP Sir Danvers Carew, later screen incarnations of Mr Hyde were up to their elbows in blood, the (sexually motivated) lust to kill becoming a recurrent factor of Jekyll's cinematic experiments. In 1931, Rouben Mamoulian's classic adaptation was marketed under the tagline 'Put yourself in *her* place! The dreaded night when her lover became a MADMAN!' By the early 1970s, the screen archetype of the murderous Mr Hyde had become so entrenched that Hammer were

able to knowingly deconstruct it in *Dr Jekyll & Sister Hyde* (1971), in which the lonely scientist's experiments give birth to a female alter-ego – a gender shift representing the divide between ego and id – with posters promising 'SHOCK! After SHOCK!' as 'the sexual transformation of a man into a woman will actually take place before your very eyes!'

By contrast, the attempt to create life *without* women is equated with the unnatural art of science in *Frankenstein*, another archetype which recurs throughout the history of horror movies. In 1910, the Edison company made the first screen version of *Frankenstein*, a silent short directed by J. Searle Dawley of which only a single print now survives. What's significant about this earliest incarnation of one of Gothic cinema's most enduring tales is its evocation of the scientist's laboratory – an assortment of bubbling cauldrons and magic powders presided over by the good doctor with much superstitious hand waving and incantatory carrying-on (a nod to the exotic roots of alchemy). Whereas Shelley's source had all but glossed over the actual creation of her monster, this innovative screen version revels in the strange wizardry of Frankenstein's scientific art, using a classic piece of celluloid trickery – a skeleton set on fire and filmed *backwards* – to create the illusion of the human form being conjured from a bubbling cauldron. Thus were the special effects of cinema and the ooga-booga of science forever wedded in the cinematic imagination.

While *Frankenstein* prepared the way, it was Robert Wiene's *The Cabinet of Dr Caligari* (1920) that laid the template of the mad scientist which would be repeated and imitated for generations to come. Bringing together the disparate strands of Gothic cinema, the figure of Dr Caligari masqueraded as a sideshow magician controlling a somnambulist in whose unnatural deeds one can detect elements of both Frankenstein's monster and of Dracula's vampirism. (When

'Gothic' (1986)

'Bride of Frankenstein' (1935)

A crack of lightning. Fear and electricity. Heady visions. It has assumed something like the status of a creation myth – the idea that Gothic horror was born at the Villa Diodati, the Swiss home of Lord Byron, during one feverish night of storytelling and who-knows-what in the month of June, 1816.

The facts are clear enough, Byron's houseguests indisputable: his physician-companion Dr Polidori, Shelley, Mary Godwin and her half-sister Claire Clairmont. What could scarcely have been imagined, even by the greatest poets of their age, is that two of the tales conceived that night would endure and propagate immeasurably, becoming staples of popular culture for 200 years. Polidori's *The Vampyre* (the direct progenitor of *Dracula*) and Mary's *Frankenstein*.

An old dark house on a stormy night, with even more stormy emotions within – this was a drama that cried out to be written, and it became my first produced screenplay, *Gothic* (1986), directed by Ken Russell, starring Natasha Richardson and Gabriel Byrne. I was frankly astonished that it hadn't been told before.

Yes, *Bride of Frankenstein* (1935) gave a witty, if unconvincing, vignette of Regency japes, but not the full story of the vivid characters, and certainly conveyed nothing of the heated and malevolent passions circulating that summer. I wanted blood and thunder, sin, blasphemy, and death. Not forgetting bad dreams. If it was about the birth of horror it had to, surely, be a horror film itself? The characters had to be Gothic archetypes through and through (…Dark Lord, Fatal Woman, Corrupt Monk…), albeit that they were based on real people.

My 'Byron' on the page wasn't Dennis Price or Richard Chamberlain (or Ken's first choice, Bob Geldof) but Peter Wyngarde: he sneered in virtually every stage direction. He also enters the film in exactly the way the haughty, aristocratic Christopher Lee enters *Dracula* (1958): gliding down a staircase to greet his guests, a deliberate signal that this is a Hammer film, in all but name. A touch singularly lost on most critics, who, misdirected by the presence of Julian Sands as Shelley, perhaps expected a Merchant-Ivory biopic about the great Romantic poets.

The clue was in the title. *Gothic* was also intended to be like the play *Marat/Sade* – we are the audience looking through the bars of the asylum at the mad people, the hallucinating, the terrified, the deluded: those who thought they were God. The original script was bookended by scenes with Mary Shelley on her deathbed, as unreliable narrator. But Ken wasn't interested in Mary Shelley's fantasies, he was interested in Ken Russell's. In many ways, though, the proceedings are augmented by his irreverence: unfettered, subversive, someone who, if nothing else, understood creativity as an act of conjuration.

On the other hand Mary, pre-Freud, understood the essence of horror – the desire and the repression of the desire. She wrote that she wished her child could be 'warmed by the fire' and made alive again, yet the creature she brought back from the dead in fiction became an angel of wrath and murderous vengeance. So, notwithstanding James Whale's teaser with Elsa Lanchester, her alter-ego isn't the 'Bride' but Frankenstein himself; creator of life from dead matter.

Mary Shelley's brilliance is that she combined the external world of galvanism and scientific advancement with her internal anxiety, resulting in a work of mythic resonance. Likewise Polidori using the raw material of his relationship with Byron, a vampiric combination of longing for power and sadomasochistic dread.

There have been other versions of the events at Diodati since ours. *Haunted Summer* (1988), another blend of 'mind games, drugs and sex', starred Alex Winter as Polidori. Released the same year, Gonzalo Suárez's *Rowing with the Wind* (*Remando al viento*), became famous for bringing together Hugh Grant and Elizabeth Hurley (as Byron and Claire respectively). If Lord Byron were alive today, would he have had *his* phone hacked? (Almost certainly yes.)

But what does Diodati really mean? Literally? Apparently the root Deodatus translates as "given by God" or "presented by God".

The real thing "given by God" at Diodati was the creative gift. Granted to two poet-geniuses, it enabled God's creation, Man, to turn against Him. Atheists challenging His ultimate power, defying His authority with acts of sin and heresy. With electricity they could raise the dead. With the drinking of blood they could achieve immortality. With the imagination, anything was possible.

Monsters were raised in 1816, and they could not be put back in the ground. Thank God.

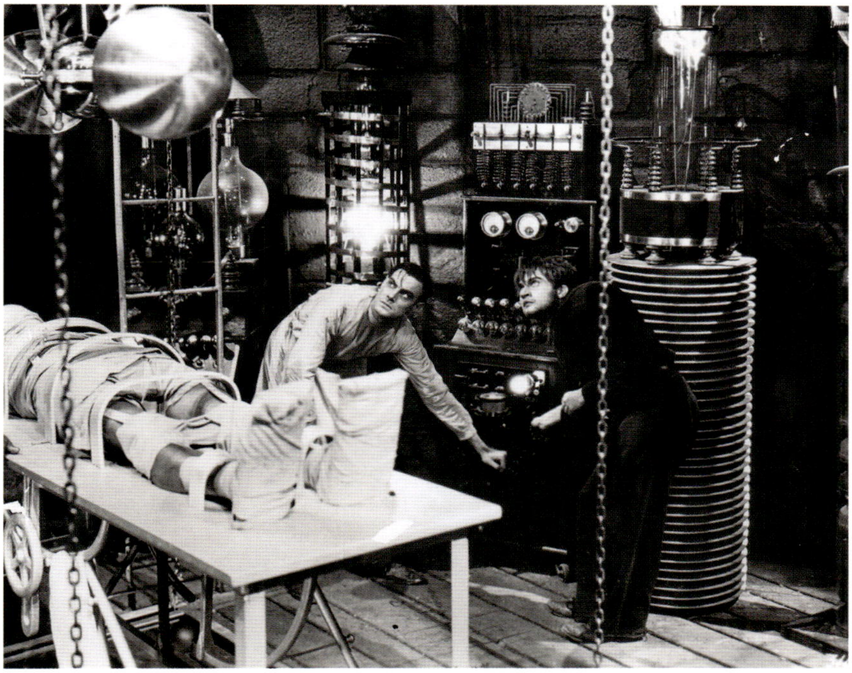

screen adaptation of *Frankenstein,* the innovations of which effectively superseded the source material in the popular imagination. Today, when one thinks of Frankenstein's monster, it is the image of a lumbering Boris Karloff with artificially squared brow and ugly electrodes through his neck which leaps to mind (the pacemaker was invented by Dr Jean Rosenbaum after watching Whale's movie and wondering whether it was actually possible to control the human heart with electricity). Yet the creature of Shelley's source text had a monstrous beauty; indeed, his primary imperfection was a deadness behind his 'watery' eyes which seemed to indicate an absence of soul – the one element which Frankenstein, for all his scientific brilliance, could not conjure from used body parts. In fact, the creature of Shelley's source bears more resemblance to the alien 'technicians' of Ridley Scott's *Prometheus* (huge, muscular, beautiful yet empty-eyed) than it does to Whale, Karloff and make-up artist Jack Pierce's epochal creation. (One can indeed read *Prometheus* as a latter-day incarnation of the *Frankenstein* myth in which the aliens are the mad scientists and *we* are the results of their monstrous experiments.)

(Above)
Colin Clive (left), seen here with Dwight Frye (right), portrays the doctor in 'Frankenstein' (1931) as a manic Old Etonian.

(Below)
Kenneth Branagh's doctor in his 'Mary Shelley's Frankenstein' (1994) is closer to the figure described in Shelley's novel.

King Kong carried Fay Wray across the rooftops of New York a decade later, he was merely mimicking an infamous kidnapping sequence from *Caligari,* which cast a long Expressionist shadow over Gothic cinema.) By the time Fritz Lang came to make *Metropolis* in 1926, advances in special effects photography had provided the toolbox to create the definitive laboratory scene, replete with arcs of electricity whizzing across the screen, tinted fluids in bubbling retorts, and tiny neon lights inserted into test tubes to make chemicals glow with an unearthly light. In the middle of all this ungodly invention is the figure of Rotwang – the archetypal mad-haired inventor whose artificial hand tied him back to the traditions of witches and sorcerers whose inner corruption was signalled by outer disfigurement; and forward to the generation of cinematic Dr Strangeloves who followed in his wake.

More than 20 years after The Edison Company first breathed screen life into Mary Shelley's novel in 1910, James Whale's 1931 movie became the defining

As with Rudolf Klein-Rogge's Rotwang, Colin Clive's Frankenstein looks less like a young, handsome, optimistic research student (as Shelley portrayed him), than a manic Old Etonian, creeping around his laboratory screeching "It's alive!", prefiguring the popular image of Frankenstein as having spent maddening years of practising his art, rather than one who has stumbled all-too enthusiastically upon his first youthful experiment. By the time Peter Cushing was playing Frankenstein in the Hammer movies, the idea of the doctor being anything *but* old had become all but inconceivable. (Cushing also played a grandfatherly Doctor Who in two feature films from the 1960s which depicted the eponymous hero – the ultimate mad

scientist? – not as a Time Lord but as an eccentric grandfather.) No wonder audiences responded with such hostility to the buff figure of Kenneth Branagh striding around his laboratory with his shirt open in the critically maligned flop *Mary Shelley's Frankenstein* (1994) – an underrated return to the roots of the character which alienated viewers by going against the conventions of mad science which cinema (rather than Shelley) had set in stone.

Just as adaptations of Frankenstein have been a constant of 20th-century horror, so Gothic chillers have exhibited a long-standing (and clearly related) fascination with genetic engineering and organ transplants, the latter of which became the subject of frenzied research during and immediately after World War I. In 1924, Robert Wiene gave Conrad Veidt's pianist the deceptively deadly fingers of a murderer in *The Hands of Orlac*, an adaptation of Maurice Renard's novel which would be remade as *Mad Love* in 1935 with Peter Lorre and Colin Clive – the most celebrated of many subsequent remakes and reinterpretations. In 1932, Charles Laughton's Dr Moreau dreamed of crossbreeding humans and animals in *Island of Lost Souls*, which was long refused a BBFC certificate on the grounds that it was 'against nature' – a telling reaction to a classic tale of 'mad science'. The censors were similarly alarmed by Georges Franju's *Eyes Without a Face*

(Left, top)
Mad surgeon Dr Gogol (Peter Lorre) shows off his steel gauntlets in 'Mad Love' (1935).

(left, middle)
A transplant operation in Robert Wiene's original 'Hands of Orlac' (1924) apparently gives Conrad Veidt's pianist the hands of a murderer.

(left, bottom)
Charles Laughton's Dr. Moreau is attacked by the Beast-Men he created in 'Island of Lost Souls' (1932).

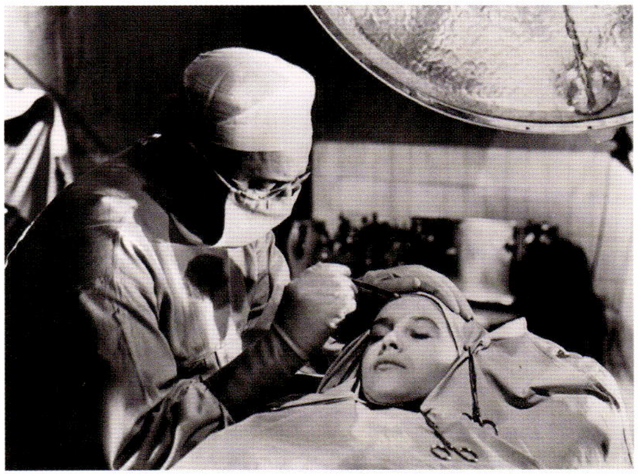

(Above)
The French poster for Georges Franju's hauntingly poetic classic 'Eyes Without a Face' (1959).

(Left)
One of the shockingly graphic face transplant scenes in 'Eyes Without a Face'.

(1959), a hauntingly poetic nightmare containing extraordinary scenes of facial transplants which would be echoed in movies as diverse as Jess Franco's *The Awful Doctor Orlof* (aka *The Demon Doctor*, 1962), John Woo's *Face/Off* (1997), and most recently Pedro Almodóvar's *The Skin I Live In* (2011), a very modern horror whose anti-hero bears the recognisably tragic taint of Dr Frankenstein.

If the first half of the 20th century saw the figure of the mad scientist being established as cinematic archetype, the post-war period marked a notable shift in the source of screen anxieties. In the wake of the atomic bomb, the role of the scientist as 'the destroyer of worlds' (the phrase from Hindu scripture famously quoted by Robert Oppenheimer) became less a fiction than a harsh reality. Unsurprisingly, Gothic cinema responded in spades; from the fire breathing lizard of *Godzilla* (*Gojira*, 1954) to the giant ants of *Them!* (1954), the writhing octopus of *It Came from Beneath the Sea* (1955), and the rampaging spider of *Tarantula* (1955), the effects of nuclear experimentation were manifested in the creation of giant beasts – often domestic, always terrifying. Yet even as the results of 'mad science' were everywhere evident on screen, scientists themselves seemed to become something of a lesser evil, their threat eclipsed by the newly emergent monster of the faceless corporation or government.

Just as post-war movies such as *The Dam Busters* (1955) had promoted the idea of the benevolent boffin (a word first coined during WWII) spending his days smoking pipes and scrawling on blackboards for the good of the war effort, so Gothic cinema began to lose faith in the inherent scariness of the scientist *per se*. Arguably the most popular mad scientist of the 1960s was Jerry Lewis as *The Nutty Professor* (1963), a comic creation whose goofiness chimed with the Gothic pastiche of *The Munsters* or *The Addams Family*, a formula revisited at the end of the 20th century by Eddie

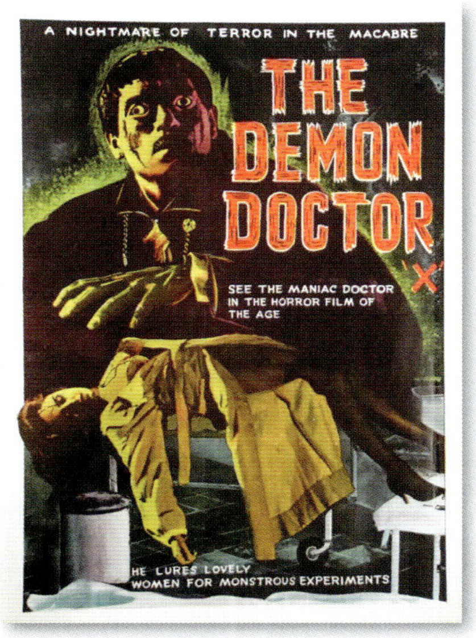

(Above)
The British poster for Jess Franco's 1962 shocker inspired by 'Eyes Without a Face', often known by its US title, 'The Awful Dr. Orlof'.

(Below)
Jeff Goldblum slowly becomes Brundlefly in David Cronenberg's reimagining of 'The Fly' (1986).

Murphy to popular (if not critical) acclaim. In the 1970s, Udo Kier was the campest Frankenstein in town in Paul Morrissey's gaudily satirical *Flesh for Frankenstein* (1973); in the 1980s, Steve Martin and David Warner vied for the biggest laughs in *The Man With Two Brains* (1983); there's even a strong thread of humour in the otherwise repulsive *The Human Centipede (First Sequence)* (2010) whose sadistic scientist plays more like a sick joke than a genuine figure of fear.

As individual scientists lost their edge in the fabric of nightmares, so the spectre of faceless cartels and corporations who owned and misused their work began to grip the Gothic imagination. Today, it appears that we are more worried about systems managers than scientists, a shift which can be traced back to the tensions of the Cold War when public fears were focused more upon the people threatening to use atomic weapons than those who invented them. In the 1993 blockbuster *Jurassic Park* (a horror movie posing as family adventure, recently revived in 3D), Jeff Goldblum's Dr Ian Malcolm famously berates the creators of the dinosaur emporium by claiming that "you didn't earn the knowledge for yourselves, so you don't take any responsibility for it. You stood on the shoulders of geniuses to accomplish something as fast as you could ... [but] your scientists were so preoccupied with whether or not they *could* that they didn't stop to think if they *should*".

Goldblum himself had previously played the other side of that coin in David Cronenberg's *The Fly* (1986), a remake of the 1958 shocker in which David Hedison had portrayed a scientist who accidentally spliced himself with an insect during a fairly benign teleportation experiment. Significantly Goldblum's Seth Brundle tells Geena Davis's heroine that he is not really a scientist at all, but more of a "systems management man. I farm bits and pieces out to guys who are much more brilliant that I am ... there's a lot of stuff in there I don't even understand."

From the figure of the mad doctor working alone in his laboratory to the 'systems manager' collating (and misusing) the efforts of others, Brundle perfectly encapsulates the recurrent themes of Gothic cinema's ongoing obsession with mad science: like Frankenstein, he creates unnatural life; like Dr Jekyll, his experiments release his dark side; like Prometheus, he steals fire from the heavens, only to get his fingers burned. And, in the modern world, his experiments are backed by Bartok Science industries who "leave me alone because they know they'll end up owning it. Whatever it is ..."

The anxieties about science may change – chemistry in the 1920s (after the poison gas of WWI), medicine in the 1930s, nuclear physics in the 1950s (after Hiroshima) – and genetic engineering since – but they are always there, and the iconography for expressing them has proved surprisingly resilient. The real creation myth for today is no longer Adam and Eve – whatever creationists may say – it is Frankenstein, the human being engineered by a scientist in a laboratory. Thanks to countless Gothic movies.

The Avant Garde Gothic

By William Fowler

The most notorious of Gothic and occult enthused filmmakers – not only in the experimental arena but possibly in all cinema – is surely Kenneth Anger. "I have always considered movies evil; the day that cinema was invented was a black day for mankind", he once said. Anger's beautifully shot 16mm films explore alternative states of consciousness, often using esoteric imagery and carefully chosen pop music. In *Invocation of My Demon Brother* (1969), Anger is seen performing a full-blown, ceremonial ritual designed to draw out and amplify the shadow aspect to his personality. In *Rabbit's Moon* (1950), the jovial interplay between a wide-eyed Pierrot clown and a teasing Harlequin unfolds in a moonlit wood, before concluding with the Pierrot's death. It was, according to the American occultist, shot on flammable nitrate stock left over from *Orphée* (1950), Jean Cocteau's stylish reworking of the myth of Orpheus and his descent into the underworld.

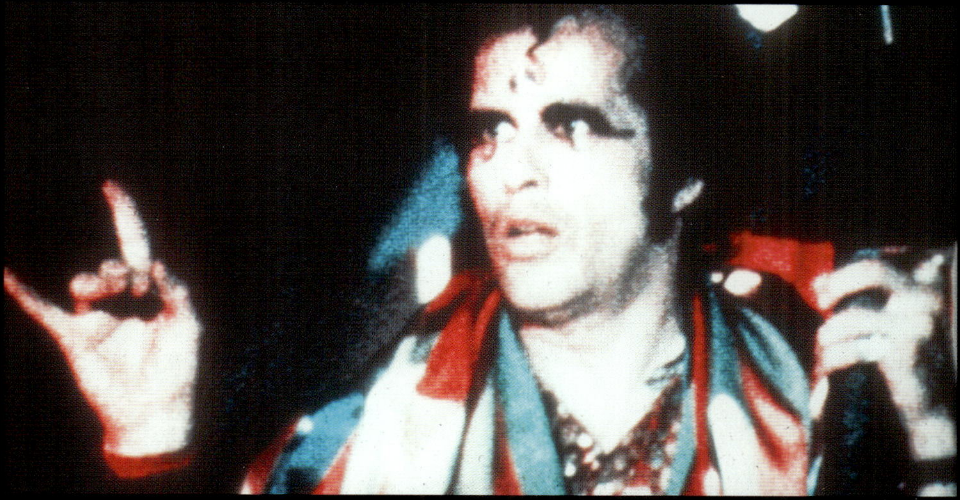

Kenneth Anger in his own 'Invocation of My Demon Brother' (1969)

Anger's films have historically been framed in the 'mythopoetic' tradition, a defiantly non-realist mode that explored trance states and desire. The mother of the movement was voodoo enthusiast Maya Deren, who appeared in and made (with Czech filmmaker Alexander Hammid) the spooky *Meshes of the Afternoon* (1943). In it, Deren chases a tall, dark, gown-covered figure and then wakes in a nightmarish house where she encounters an unknown male and later her own double. The dreamlike story continues in a looping fashion; she goes through – and sees herself going through – the same actions, again and again, almost like a self-aware zombie. The film has had an enormous influence on David Lynch.

Artist Stephen Dwoskin, who relocated to London from New York in 1964, frequently evoked the dream space of the 'old dark house' in his work. *Central Bazaar* (1976) sees a group of semi-naked men and women explore thoughts and fantasies in a contained space decorated with candles, and at one point to the sound of thunder (dubbed over the action). His later, confrontational, sexualised videos *Nightshots* (2007), *The Sun and the Moon* (2008) and *Dreamhouse* (2009) also unfold in this same semi-metaphysical, mythic location – as do several pieces by Ben Rivers, such as *Old Dark House* (2003) and *House* (2005/2007), which see torchlights being shone on or inside ruined and decayed domestic structures, as if some unknown person were trying to root out trauma. Rivers, who is in many ways the modern Gothic filmmaker *par excellence*, has travelled far and wide searching out lost places and people, going to the very outskirts of society and even abandoned islands (*Slow Action*, 2010). He also hand-processes his films, introducing scratches and dust, making them appear like ready-made, found objects.

In the 1960s, avant garde filmmakers frequently strove to undermine notions of authority and encourage distinctly personal responses in the viewer, often by looking in the shadows or exploring fragmentation. Antony Balch's *Towers Open Fire* (1963) and *The Cut-Ups* (1966) both incorporate footage of William Burroughs performing the groundbreaking, Dada-esque Cut-Up technique, folding and slicing through fragments of text and recombining them in new forms, releasing new meanings – or, if you will, 'spirits' – buried and hiding from the conscious mind. *The Cut-Ups* flashes these images at the brain at an astonishing rate, using repetition to de-programme the viewer and open up the 'third eye'.

When it comes to metaphysics – the space of the mind – Paul Sharits, Stan Brakhage and Derek Jarman moved even further out from figurative, narrative filmmaking, sometimes focusing almost exclusively on the mesmerising qualities of pure light and/or flash frames so as to bypass conscious thought. Tensions around perception and the corporeal body were also explored in expanded, performative cinema works by Malcolm Le Grice and Lis Rhodes in the 1970s, as they have been in single screen pieces by Emily Wardill and Ed Atkins since 2005.

Dark shadows and gloomy atmospheres may not be something that you immediately associate with the refined, intellectual rigour of the avant garde, but the two worlds have clearly overlapped. So too have their audiences – both enjoying a certain outsider status. The aforementioned Antony Balch, who was both a cinema manager and a filmmaker, understood this and frequently screened raucous, sinister movies such as *The Corpse Grinders* (1971), *Don't Deliver Us From Evil* (1971) or his very own *Secrets of Sex* (1970) (narrated by an Egyptian mummy) alongside the experimental works that he had made with William Burroughs (*Towers Open Fire* even featured a still of Bela Lugosi – Balch, like artist-filmmaker Jeff Keen, was a serious fan of the otherworldly Hungarian). An interest in the avant garde does not preclude an enthusiastic, wide ranging taste in cinema – or a sense of humour. Kenneth Anger's *Invocation of My Demon Brother* concludes with a sign held up by a wizened, zombie dwarf. The message? 'ZAP. YOU'RE PREGNANT. THAT'S WITCHCRAFT.'

Central and Eastern European Gothic

By Michael Brooke

Although many classic Gothic tales memorably utilised central and eastern European locations, the region itself has produced disappointingly little homegrown Gothic cinema. The commercial imperatives underpinning the generic specialisms of AIP and Hammer had no equivalent behind the Iron Curtain, and the fact that many of the films mentioned below ran into official trouble (some were banned outright) demonstrates that Gothic material was still considered dangerously subversive over two centuries after the publication of Horace Walpole's *The Castle of Otranto*.

In a *Doppelgänger*-esque coincidence, Czechoslovakia's most consistently 'Gothic' filmmakers were born on the same day. The Slovak Juraj Herz is best known for the strikingly Expressionist *The Cremator* (*Spalovac mrtvol*, 1968) in which an insane crematorium director believes that he is not so much incinerating corpses as liberating their souls. Resembling a Gainsborough melodrama soaked in potent hallucinogens, *Morgiana* (1972) casts the same actress (Iva Janžurová) as two warring sisters, often observing them from a cat's perspective. Other Herz films, including the psychological drama *Oil Lamps* (*Petrolejové lampy*, 1970), fairytales *Beauty and the Beast* (*Panna a netvor*, 1978) and *The Ninth Heart* (*Deváté srdce*, 1978) and the horror film *The Ferat Vampire* (*Upír z Feratu*, 1981) display a similar sensibility.

As for Herz's Czech 'twin' Jan Švankmajer, *The Ossuary* (*Kostnice*, 1970) turns a famous 19th-century 'bone chapel' into a riotously potent celebration of death's aesthetic potential. *The Castle of Otranto* (*Otrantsky zámek*, 1977) satirises the fakery behind Walpole's novel by fusing a mockumentary about the castle's alleged Bohemian origins with animated sequences drawn from the text. *The Fall of the House of Usher* (*Zánik domu Usheru*, 1981) visits Edgar Allan Poe's mansion after its inhabitants' departure, their traumas physically embedded in its brickwork and the surrounding mud. The relentlessly claustrophobic *The Pendulum, the Pit and Hope* (*Kyvadlo, jáma a nadeje*, 1983) fuses Poe's short story with Villiers de l'Isle-Adam's 'A Torture by Hope' to convey elaborately mechanised horrors from the helpless victim's perspective. Two Poe stories also inspired the feature-length *Lunacy* (*Šílení*, 2005), as did the writings and persona of the Marquis de Sade.

Besides Jirí Barta's animated *The Pied Piper* (*Krysar*, 1986) and Jirí Svoboda's 'Gothic noir' *The Damned House of Hajn* (*Prokletí domu Hajnu*, 1988), the best known Czech Gothic film is Jaromil Jireš's *Valerie and her Week of Wonders* (*Valerie a týden divu*, 1970). This turns the onset of menarche into an elaborate fantasy crammed with pristine white bedrooms, cobwebbed crypts, and the regular morphing of formerly reassuring authority figures into monsters, notably a vampiric creature straight from *Nosferatu*.

In Poland, Wojciech Has's *The Saragossa Manuscript* (*Rekopis znaleziony w Saragossie*, 1965) was adapted from Jan Potocki's labyrinthine 1815 novel in which tales by multiple tellers bewilderingly but seductively intertwine around each other. Later Has films like *The Hourglass Sanatorium* (*Sanatorium pod Klepsydra*, 1973) were inspired by actual historical epochs, but their landscapes are as likely to be populated by dream figures and elaborate automata as flesh-and-blood creations.

Other Polish specialists in the phantasmagorical, Walerian Borowczyk, Roman Polanski and Andrzej Zuławski, relocated abroad to evade the fetters of Communist censorship. However, one of Zuławski's Polish features, *The Devil* (*Diabeł*, 1972) shows an 18th-century political prisoner rescued and manipulated by a black-clad figure of potentially diabolical origin. Poland's second big-screen horror film, it was preceded by Janusz Majewski's *Lokis* (*Lokis - Rekopis profesora Wittembacha*, 1970), an adaptation of Prosper Mérimée's vaguely lycanthropic 1869 novella in which a scholar turns up a grisly family legend with all-too current repercussions. Borowczyk turned the same source into the much more graphically sexualised *The Beast* (*La Bête*, 1975), and his later *The Blood of Dr Jekyll* (1981) interspersed Jekyll's theories about 'transcendental medicine' with Hyde's assaults on his victims, their age and gender irrelevant when it comes to sating his monstrous lusts.

Further eastwards, Gothic pickings are slimmer. Although there were Hungarian and Romanian versions of Arnold Ridley's perennial *The Ghost Train* (*Kísértetek vonata* and *Trenul fantoma*, both 1933), and *Vlad Tepes* (1979), a Romanian fim about one of Dracula's real-life progenitors, it seems that Transylvania was first used as a horror-film location as recently as 1991 (the US-made *Subspecies* series), while the first local vampire film, Faye Jackson's British co-production *Strigoi* (2009), eschewed the genre's traditional Gothic trappings in favour of a present-day update of specifically Romanian folklore. Serbia has maintained a small-scale horror tradition since Đorde Kadijevic's *The Moth* (*Leptirica*, 1973), the most distinctively Gothic example being Kadijevic's *A Holy Place* (*Sveto mesto*, 1990), which gave Nikolai Gogol's 1835 story 'The Viy' an erotic and indeed incestuous spin.

'The Viy' was also adapted by Gogol's compatriots, including the Soviet Union's only true horror film, *Viy, or Spirit of Evil* (1967). Directed by Konstantin Yershov and Georgi Kropachyov, it takes a splendidly Hammer-esque approach to the tale of a young seminarist who is required to spend three nights in a crypt with a female corpse who proves anything but inanimate.

(Opposite)
Two soldiers (Igor Przegrodzki and Gustaw Lutkiewicz) peruse the titular 'The Saragossa Manuscript' (1965)

(Left)
Viktoria (Iva Janžurová) lures Otylie (Nina Divíšková) to her doom in Juraj Herz's delirious melodrama 'Morgiana' (1972).

(Below)
13-year-old Jaroslava Schallerová in the title role of 'Valerie and her Week of Wonders' (1970).

THE DARK ARTS

WAKING NIGHTMARES

BY RAMSEY CAMPBELL

Confusion, nightmares and mental disintegration. Madness, psychosis and a sense of creeping dread. Such themes lurk throughout the Gothic. Their presence had been implicit before Edgar Allan Poe – the story of *Frankenstein* had, after all, come to Mary Shelley in a dream – but Poe brought it to the fore. The modern horror story starts with him. His example echoes through the 19th-century literary Gothic and beyond. The cinema has found Poe to be a uniquely rich source – he is by far the most adapted of all Gothic writers.

Poe created a number of classical forms for the Gothic field. 'The Tell-Tale Heart' establishes the unreliable narrator, who could be telling us a ghost story but may be unwittingly displaying his derangement – whose heart can the narrator hear if not his own? The tale also depicts how a perception of ugliness can grow obsessive and ultimately psychotic, but so can beauty: in 'Berenice' it's the narrator's obsession with his victim's finest feature that leads to mutilation and horror. 'The Fall of the House of Usher' takes the atmospheric scene-setting of the original 18th-century Gothic novels and conflates it with the psychological – conjuring a nightmarish sense that both marks the characters in the tale and is summoned in the mind of the reader. The incestuous obsession of hypersensitive Roderick Usher is so passionate that his mental collapse (aggravated, we may note, by hearing his unreliable friend read the *Mad Trist* aloud) undermines the foundations of his mansion (which, like the brain it embodies, is already fractured). The poem contained in 'Ligeia' sums up these tales and the genre Poe engendered in two lines: "And much of Madness and more of Sin / And Horror the soul of the plot."

In Ireland, J. Sheridan Le Fanu distilled the modern ghost story from the Gothic novel. Le Fanu's 1872 story 'Green Tea' deals more deliberately than Poe with mental collapse, observing it soberly rather than conveying it directly. This clinical view of the process belongs to Dr Martin Hesselius, the Swedenborgian psychologist who introduces and comments on the case of a clergyman who is driven to suicide by the apparition of a malevolent monkey. Hesselius rounds off the tale with an explanation that the reader may well find inadequate – we can certainly see the demon as the clergyman's repressed self. In France, Guy de Maupassant took the narration of madness deeper into nightmare and grotesque comedy; the antic furniture of his 1890 story 'Qui sait?' is both hilarious and unsettling, the one because of the other.

As for the Gothic cinema of derangement, it too begins with Poe. It's hardly surprising that the medium was so ready to communicate the extremes of mental experience – after all, film may be said to project our shared unconscious on the screen. It's also surely crucial that it unites drama with music and an edited version of reality to communicate a total experience. We may wonder how Wagner might have used it, and more to our present point, it's ideally suited to communicating a Gothic sense of madness.

(Opposite)
Jack Nance in David Lynch's 'Eraserhead' (1977).

One of many examples from early cinema is Maurice Tourneur's *Le système du docteur Goudron et du professeur Plume (1913)*, which adapts a one-act Grand Guignol play based on Poe's 'The System of Doctor Tarr and Professor Fether', a satirical piece meant to address a contemporary controversy about the treatment of the mentally ill. In all these versions the lunatics have taken over the asylum, and the central issue is how distinguishable or otherwise they are from the supposedly sane. Not just the instability of sanity but its untrustworthiness is at the core of much horror.

The following year D. W. Griffith took on Poe in *The Avenging Conscience*, primarily a version of 'The Tell-Tale Heart', in which visions beset the protagonist and drive him to murder his uncle before walling up the corpse, having borrowed the idea from 'The Black Cat' (literally, since the whole thing proves to be his nightmare brought on by reading Poe). The narrative structure – a series of tableaux – underlines the melodramatic aspects of Poe. The late John Brunner accused Poe's madmen of "phony grandiloquence", but that's often an aspect of madness, as is melodrama, indeed monodrama.

The ideas of German Expressionism proved to be an ideal visual correlative for the distorted inner monologues of Poe. Paul Wegener's *The Student of Prague* (1913) was inspired by Poe's story 'William Wilson', in which the protagonist's double might be said to represent his insanity. Robert Wiene's *The Cabinet of Dr Caligari* (1920) introduces the deranged landscape to Gothic cinema, and is also the first film to seek (in the scene of the somnambulist's awakening and elsewhere) to be as frightening as possible. The Expressionistic distortions of the settings are retrospectively defined as the visions of an inmate of an asylum, a resolution suggested by the director who was originally to make the film, Fritz Lang – whose work often deals with a Gothic sense of mental disintegration. In *The Testament of Dr Mabuse* (1933), the criminal madman's influence possesses the director of the asylum, whose delirium seems to permeate the hallucinatory landscape of the climactic car chase. When Ray Milland ventures out of the asylum in *The Ministry of Fear* (1944), the world proves to be as unhinged as any paranoid delusion.

(Above)
Fredric March's Oscar-winning dual title role as 'Dr Jekyll and Mr Hyde' (1931).

The silent cinema's bids to depict derangement reach their apotheosis in Japanese director Kinugasa Teinosuke's *A Page of Madness* (1926). The central theme – a husband takes the job of caretaker at an asylum in the hope of rescuing his incarcerated wife – is almost immediately overwhelmed by the film's visual style, which unleashes the techniques of Expressionist film and of the avant garde. The film doesn't even offer intertitles as a narrative anchor, instead conveying as directly as possible the experience of mental disintegration. In Japan showings were accompanied by a live narrator, but his absence only adds to the directness of the film.

Le Fanu's story 'Green Tea' had let loose the Id in monstrous form, and Robert Louis Stevenson's *Dr Jekyll and Mr Hyde* gives it another physical manifestation, in a moral variant of the werewolf legend and a favourite text for the cinema to elaborate. In 1920 alone three films based on Stevenson's novel were released, including one (*The Head of Janus*, sadly lost) by F.W. Murnau. Rouben Mamoulian's 1931 version remains the most frightening, not just in making us watch our own transformation through the doctor's eyes, but in Hyde's naked relish of his sadism. Victor Fleming's 1941 version rediscovers the dark depths Fritz Lang's *Fury* found in Spencer Tracy – they were seldom admitted again. Jean Renoir's *Experiment in Evil* (*Le Testament du docteur Cordelier*, 1959) lets the Hyde figure tempt us with his balletic grace and seductive impishness before he goes too far. Hammer Films had two striking ideas on the theme: Terence Fisher's *The Two Faces of Dr Jekyll* (1960), where Hyde is a handsome fellow on the surface – the man his alter ego might wish to be – and Roy Ward Baker's *Dr Jekyll & Sister Hyde* (1971), a Jungian reading of the situation, where the doctor's anima takes over.

In the 1920s H.P. Lovecraft built on Poe and other models in his endeavour to perfect the weird tale. One of Lovecraft's fundamental assumptions was that the human mind would be unable to cope with the alien – supernatural or

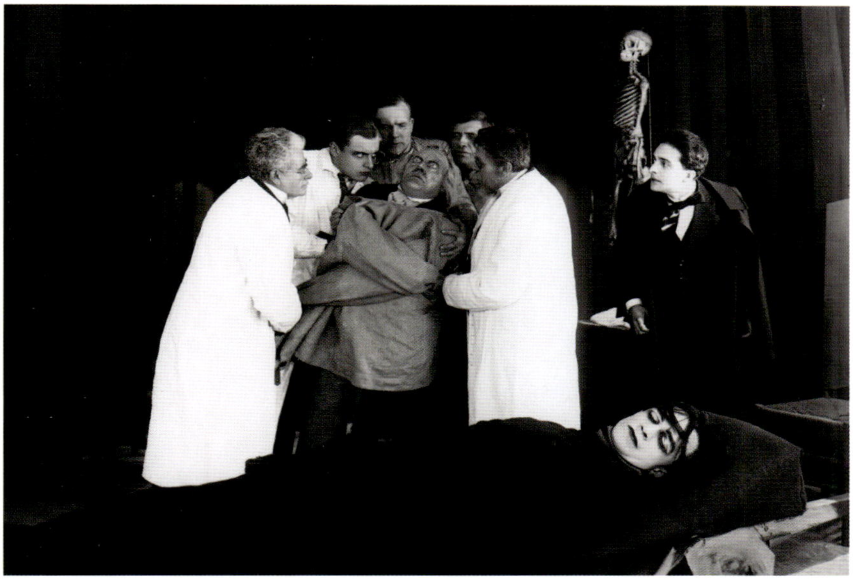

(Above)
Cesare the somnambulist (Conrad Veidt), seemingly oblivious to the commotion around the straightjacketed Dr Caligari (Werner Krauss) in 'The Cabinet of Dr Caligari' (1920).

(Below)
The asylum in Kinugasa Teinosuke's groundbreaking 'A Page of Madness' (1926).

otherwise. This may be acknowledged in science fiction films like *Communion* (1989) and *Fire in the Sky* (1993), but surprisingly seldom in the horror film. Bramwell Fletcher's hysterical response to the resurrection in *The Mummy* (1932) ("he went for a little walk") is a striking exception; even though incarcerated in an asylum in the 1959 Hammer version, his equivalent (Felix Aylmer) hardly seems insane.

Scientists may suffer temporary lunacy as a result of hubris; in James Whale's 1931 *Frankenstein*, actor Colin Clive's Dr Frankenstein certainly appears to when his creature comes alive ("It's alive! It's alive!"). Later practitioners are more prone to madness, either as a result of their research (Claude Rains's invisible man in James Whale's 1933 version of H. G. Wells's story, for instance) or as the reason they conduct their experiments. The ultimate example is Dr Heiter in *The Human Centipede (First Sequence)* (2010), who creates his monstrous handiwork just because he can.

One film that may espouse Lovecraft's principle is Carl Dreyer's *Vampyr* (1932), where the protagonist Allan Gray appears entranced by the uncanniest landscape in all cinema. Most of the action takes place in dazzling sunlight, which only emphasises the omnipresence of the supernatural. Is this the territory of a waking dream, where our shadows are free to roam, or magic realism? Or might the ferry summoned at the outset by a figure with a scythe but left unused until the protagonists board it in the final scene suggest an eerier interpretation? *Vampyr*'s closest cinematic relative might be Alain Resnais's *Last Year in Marienbad* (1961), where the central characters' relationship to and responsibility for the fractured narrative are just as indefinable.

To return to Poe, it's worth noting how productive of short films his tales became. Jules Dassin's *The Tell-Tale Heart* (1941) shows how film noir derives from dark Expressionism, while the deranged animation of the 1953 UPA short based on the same story belies narrator James Mason's pretence of sanity. Edward Abraham's 1962 BFI production *The Pit* conveys much of the intensity of Poe's torture story with lighting and sound but no dialogue, and Alexandre Astruc's 1964 film gains power from its austere faithfulness to the tale. By contrast, *Toby Dammit* (Fellini's segment of the 1968 Poe anthology *Histoires Extraordinaires*) expresses the dark comedy of Poe's tale in its visual frenzy.

Psycho (1960) discovers the wit that madness can command – the wordplay of derangement. "Mother isn't quite herself today" and other lines from Robert Bloch's novel are enshrined in the film, which – along with *Frenzy* (1972) – epitomises Alfred Hitchcock's fascination with charming maniacs. Both book and film bring on a psychiatrist to provide an explanation that doesn't sum up all we've seen, much in the manner of Hesselius.

British writers explored extreme mental states too. Paul Ableman's *I Hear Voices* is narrated by a schizophrenic who may never leave his bed. Whether or not the events are distortions of his memories, they're unnervingly eloquent and often disconcertingly hilarious, though at times the prose is overwhelmed by incoherence. Thomas Hinde's *The Day the Call Came* is a black comedy of paranoia narrated by the man who's waiting for the coded call. Here and in *The Investigator* Hinde conveys how the deranged can pass as sane, not only to themselves. The deceptive clarity of the narration has its cinematic equivalent in Luis Buñuel's examinations of mental disintegration, *The Criminal Life of Archibaldo de la Cruz* (1955) and *El* (1953) in particular. While Buñuel never abandoned Surrealism, and delighted in undermining our trust in narrative – at what point does Tristana's dream begin, for instance? – the disruption of the matter-of-fact tone of *El* by hallucinations in the church conveys the character's experience with disconcerting directness.

(Above)
A thicket of clutching hands emerges through the walls in Polanski's 'Repulsion' (1965).

(Below, top)
Max von Sydow in Ingmar Bergman's chilling 'Hour of the Wolf' (1968).

(Below, bottom)
Harriet Andersson as the schizophrenic subject of Bergman's 'Through a Glass Darkly' (1961).

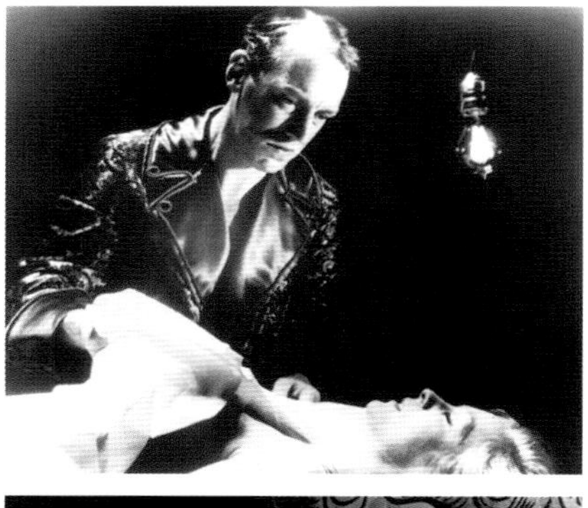

The literal portrayal of hallucination pervades Polanski's *Repulsion* (1965). Like the transformed wallpaper in *The Tenant* (1976), another of the director's Gothic studies of mental collapse, it appears to derive from his experience with LSD (which terrified him, as it did J. G. Ballard, who declared that it was akin to schizophrenia). Polanski's most subtly paranoid film is *Rosemary's Baby* (1968), where – as in Ira Levin's novel – the long first section of the narrative seems so innocent that the audience is driven to look for conspiracies long before the protagonist is aware of them.

Flamboyant depictions of psychological collapse are central to much of Stanley Kubrick's work. Paul Mazursky's mad scene in *Fear and Desire* (1953) prefigures Jack Nicholson's in *The Shining* (1980) – which is closer to Poe than the novel in announcing madness from the outset. Like Peter Sellers in *Dr Strangelove* (1964), Nicholson captures the deranged comedy of madness, which sees its vastest version in the cybernetic death of HAL 9000. Perhaps scenes like these are where Kubrick risks losing his famous creative control, and his superego lets the unconscious off the leash.

Ingmar Bergman might not seem central to a discussion of Gothic nightmares, but when the attic door swings open in *Through a Glass Darkly* (1961), we may share (if only for an irrational moment) the schizophrenic daughter's fear of the spider god. It's significant too that in *The Magician* (1958) an encounter with the apparently supernatural drives the victim mad. Mental alienation is in fact central to Bergman's work, and finds its most sustained expression in the Fårö trilogy. It splinters the narrative of *Persona* (1966) into a delirium of possibilities, and leads to the bleak coda of *Shame* (1968), but more to our point here, it brings the director's Gothic tendencies to the surface in *Hour of the Wolf* (1968).

This film is both an autobiographical metaphor (Max von Sydow plays an artist who is destroyed by his demons – by his inability to contain or express them) and a tribute to the horror film, with visual references including Hitchcock's *The Birds* (1963) and Lugosi's Dracula. The "Hour of the Wolf" is, von Sydow's character tells us, "the time between night and dawn, just before the light comes… when demons had a heightened power and vitality, the hour when most people died and most children were born, and when nightmares came to one".

Still, the director most concerned to convey the outer limits of mental experience is David Lynch. Lynch frequently abandons all notions of conventional narrative and every reassurance of realism to convey a sensation of nightmarish Gothic and mental disarray firmly in the Poe lineage. For instance, if the lady behind the radiator in *Eraserhead* (1977) is some form of hallucination, what is the film proposing as diegetic reality? It may be possible to grasp *Lost Highway* (1997) and *Mulholland Dr.* (2001) as depicting a specific psychological state, where in each case the second section of the film is a florid attempt by the protagonist to deny everything that happened in the first, but *Inland Empire* (2006) shatters in so many directions that it's impossible to identify the narrative centre or even to be sure which of the scattered personalities (if any) is experiencing the whole. Given Lynch's frequent recourse to elements of noir, Jim Thompson comes to mind. His preoccupation with abnormal psychology is exemplified in *The Killer Inside Me* but reaches its extreme in *Savage Night*, which ends as both a parody of Gothic narration and either a ghost story or a living nightmare, however living is defined in the context. Indeed, some of Thompson's work – the unfilmable cannibalistic epilogue of *The Getaway*, for instance – takes us right back to Poe.

Poe's suggestion that doctors and

(Above)
Now totally crazed, Jack Torrance (Jack Nicholson) stalks his son through the snow-shrouded maze in 'The Shining' (1980).

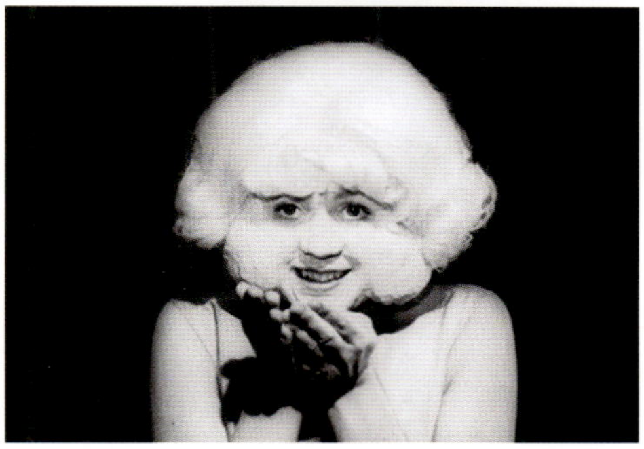

(Right)
The 'Lady in the Radiator' (Laurel Near) in David Lynch's 'Eraserhead' (1977).

(Bottom)
The 'Mystery Man' (Robert Blake) in Lynch's 'Lost Highway' (1997).

(Above, top)
Boris Karloff as the head physician in 'Bedlam' (1946).

(Above, middle)
Leonardo DiCaprio as the mentally insecure protagonist of Martin Scorsese's 'Shutter Island' (2010).

(Below)
Natalie Portman's schizophrenic ballerina in Darren Aronofsky's 'Black Swan' (2010).

other carers for the mentally ill are less distinguishable from their charges than they should be is virtually a convention of the genre. The lascivious attendant is a generic staple – in *Terminator 2* (1991) he's a plot device – though the theme is treated with poignant ambiguity in Robert Rossen's broodingly Gothic *Lilith* (1964), where Warren Beatty's therapist falls for the otherness of Jean Seberg's inmate. In the Val Lewton production *Bedlam* (1946) Boris Karloff's sadistic head physician actually meets a fate out of Poe (specifically, 'The Cask of Amontillado'). To what extent is the psychiatrist's medieval attitude to Michael Myers in *Halloween* (1978) responsible for his patient's state? In *Hellbound* (Tony Randel's 1988 sequel to Clive Barker's *Hellraiser*) the head psychiatrist compels a patient to mutilate himself as an occult sacrifice. This film and others demonstrate how stylised, in fact conventionalised, portrayals of asylums in the genre have become – increasingly so as the real institutions have closed down (though in Georges Franju's 1959 *La Tête contre les murs* the place is as clinical as Franju's style, and no less frightening because of it). Indeed, in *Shutter Island* (2010), Scorsese's intention was to recall Val Lewton films (though not specifically *Bedlam*). By the time we reach Reece Shearsmith and Steve Pemberton's *Psychoville* (BBC, 2009-2011), the asylum is the stuff of macabre comedy, or horror disguised as comedy (and like its predecessor *The League of Gentlemen*, sometimes only just disguised).

The serial killer has become the favourite contemporary psychotic, and Hannibal Lecter unites him with the unreliable psychiatrist in an iconic figure. Lecter may be seen as Dracula for our time, and just as fantastic a monster. Like Stoker's Count, he's arguably more cultured and intelligent than his adversaries, and as the novels and films pile up it seems that – like the vampire – Lecter may offer some transcendent experience to some of the people who encounter him, at least Clarice Starling. As in quite a few spinoffs from Stoker's novel, the later Lecter tales strive to humanise him. In real life, serial killers are likely to be inadequate but so convinced of their own significance that they commit their atrocities to persuade the world of it. Still, we aren't talking realism but fantasy. The Gothic – the horror story – tells its own kind of truth.

By now insanity has become a matter for narrative play. Even the explosion of narrative in order to depict a mental state has migrated to popular cinema in films such as *Identity* (2003) and *The Ward* (2010). Does Lars Von Trier's *Melancholia* (2011) chronicle the psychological effects of a threatened Armageddon, or is the threat a projection of the protagonist's psyche? *Babycall* (2011) appears to be a study of paranoid schizophrenia but ultimately lurches in quite another direction (rather as the cult 1971 American Gothic horror *Let's Scare Jessica to Death* confounds the generic expectations set up by the title and proves to be a ghost story after all). Darren Aronofsky's *Black Swan* (2010) would be entirely at home among the most flamboyant films of Bava and Argento, those masters of Technicolor Gothic. As Natalie Portman's ballerina succumbs to schizophrenia under the pressures of her art and her home life, her visions – her inner self projected onto other characters, her body transforming in the fashion of a fairy tale – overtake the narrative. The broken mirror that figures in the finale is the perfect symbol of the shattered reflection with which she peoples her world.

Do we need to seek an explanation for the popularity of the theme? Perhaps there's some truth in that old saw about creativity and madness. After all, storytelling can unleash the unconscious – nakedly so with the likes of Lynch – and what are films if not dreams writ large? Don't call me delusional for suggesting that the theme may recur as long as we have the cinema.

In Silent Film No One Can Hear You Scream...

By Bryony Dixon

Cinema was the defining medium of the Gothic in the 20th century. Novels, stories, paintings, poems and plays had borne its themes since the 18th century, and its loose definition and sensational appeal made it peculiarly adaptable for film. Early filmmakers exploited all of the Gothic's delicious devices: spooky castles, spectral brides, tombs and skeletons. The Gothic offered a number of settings familiar to early film audiences from existing media: the medieval, populated with devils and sorcerers; ancient Egypt with its mummies and curses; and the exotic East with its sophisticated pleasures and refined tortures.

Later, a subtler strategy emerged in which filmmakers would tease the audience by showing them as little as possible and allowing the imagination to supply the horror, as in Hitchcock's Ripper tale, *The Lodger* (1927). The most successful, to our 21st century sensibilities anyway, were the films that tried to disorient you, to capture the essence of Gothic – a fear of the return to a past filled with death, superstition, cruelty, madness and grotesque creatures.

Germany and the aesthetic of *Mitteleuropa* were bound to dominate the transition of Gothic literary tradition into film, but it was given added impetus by a specific outburst of cinematic creativity in post-war Berlin based on Expressionism – a literary, artistic and theatrical form that translated into a cycle of self-conscious films in which deliberately unrealistic sets heighten the uncanny nature of the viewing experience.

Tapping directly into the world of childhood fairytales but heaping on the very present horrors of wartime injury and mental trauma, the German Expressionist film proved how powerful cinema could be at rendering the Gothic for a mass audience – not to mention spawning the first horror franchise, Paul Wegener's *Golem* series. The classics produced in this era still work for contemporary audiences because of something disturbing in silent film itself – the slight distancing effect of the removal of one of the senses, emotionally heightened by music, allows the imagination full rein. The distorted angles in *The Cabinet of Dr Caligari* (1920), the confronting of one's mirror image, so unsettling in *The Student of Prague* (1913), or the use of changing speed in Murnau's *Nosferatu* (1922) – as when the carriage that greets Jonathan Harker speeds off at an unnatural pace, or in Max Schreck's scuttling, spider-like movements – are as disturbing now as then.

Gothic memes weave through early French, Italian, Scandinavian and American films; from the diabolical fantasies of Méliès and Pathé Frères in France in the 1890s to the Italian adaptations of the *Inferno* and *Cabiria*. There was even an Italian silent version of *Jane Eyre* in 1915. Elements of the Gothic crept into Gaumont serials such as *Fantômas* in the 1910s, and supernatural creatures are found in the sagas of Scandinavian filmmakers of the 1920s, notably Benjamin Christensen's *Häxan* (1922). Poe was enthusiastically taken up by many early filmmakers, among them DW Griffith, who reworked 'The Tell-Tale Heart' for his *The Avenging Conscience* (1914). Mary Shelley's *Frankenstein* was first adapted in 1910 by director J. Searle Dawley for Edison. Most tantalising of all the American silent Gothic films is Tod Browning's *London After Midnight* (1927), starring Lon Chaney. The film is now sadly lost – the last known print was destroyed in a fire in the MGM vaults in 1967.

But what of Britain,

'The Mistletoe Bough' (1904)

originator of so much literary and stage Gothic? Where were the films of its great classics, *Dracula*, *Frankenstein*, *The Monk*, *The Mysteries of Udolpho*, *The Castle of Otranto*, *Jane Eyre*? Was it a distaste for fantasy? A reaction against the tendency in foreign cinemas? Was it simply unfashionable in the face of 1920s modernism? Were British producers afraid of being thought to be pandering to sensationalist tastes?

The truth is probably a combination of all of these things. There were some films that we should classify as Gothic made in Britain in the early days of cinema, but most of them just don't survive. We have very early comedies playing with Gothic tropes, such as *The Haunted Curiosity Shop* (1901), *Wanted, a Mummy* (1910) and early Christmas ghost stories like *The Mistletoe Bough* (1904). But among those which haven't survived are *The Basilisk* (1912), various versions of *Maria Marten or the Murder in the Red Barn*, *The Duality of Man* (1910), *Dr Trimball's Secret* (1913), *The Fakir's Spell* (1914), *Wraith of the Tomb* (1915), *The Monkey's Paw* (1915), *She* (1916) and *The Beetle* (1919), a tale about an ancient Egyptian princess bent on revenge. Later productions we do have include sensation-specialist Fred Paul's macabre tales in the Grand Guignol series (1921), classic ghost stories filmed in their original locations in *Haunted Houses and Castles of Great Britain* (1926) and Oriental serials such as *The Mystery of Dr Fu Manchu* (1924) and *Dr Sin Fang* (1928). Other producers made cheap and cheerful adaptations of Gothic classics such as British & Colonial's *Gems of Literature* series, which included another *Mistletoe Bough* (1923) and *The Bells* (1922), which was remade in the US four years later starring Lionel Barrymore and Boris Karloff. More borderline Gothic offerings were *The Hound of the Baskervilles* (1921), *The Man without Desire* (1923), *She* (1925), an incomplete *Monkey's Paw* (1923) and the spoof films *What Next?* (1928), *The Ghost Train* (1927) and *Prelude* (1927), an odd one-off version of Poe's 'The Premature Burial' intended to be accompanied by Rachmaninoff's unnerving 'Prelude in C Sharp Minor'.

The last silent Gothic film made in the UK was Walter Summers's *Chamber of Horrors* (1929), about a murderer who goes insane during a night in Madame Tussauds. Unfortunately it is also now lost, as is the first British horror of the sound era, *Black Waters* (1929), an 'old dark house' story set on a boat, filmed in the US by Herbert Wilcox just as the taste for Gothic was about to swing back into fashion.

Gothic Art's Cinematic Legacies

By Martin Myrone

The relationship between the canon of Gothic literature of the 'classic' phase (c.1760-1830) and the visual imagery of the same date is far from simple: the relationship of this early Gothic art and writing to modern cinema no more so. Now often understood as, by definition, a trans-medial, genre-defying, migratory and polluting phenomenon, we should not expect that homologies between Gothic productions in different media and eras need be predictable, explicit or orderly.

Early Gothic publications did sometimes carry engraved illustrations, although these images tended to be of a conventional character and rarely reflected the formal extravagance and moral ambiguity which might be found in the accompanying texts. Amateur artists often also produced their own watercolour renditions of subjects from favourite Gothic novels and poems, generally also in a conventional pictorial style that barely registered the more extreme themes of their literary sources.

More rarely, professional artists produced works of a more ambitious character directly referencing Gothic literary sources, but there are only a handful of oil paintings or large finished watercolours which literally illustrate modern Gothic texts.

Nonetheless, there are parallels and resonances between Gothic literature of the 'classic' phase and precisely contemporary visual art, and between these and modern cinema. The exploration of supernatural and horrific themes, the focus on ruins and mysterious landscapes, and the particular motifs of hermits, banditti and monks were characteristics of visual art in the last third of the 18th century, prompted perhaps by the popularity of Gothic writings but also by the more general vogue for the Sublime as an aesthetic category encompassing the overwhelming and mysterious, and by more material influences such as public art exhibitions and an expanding art market, which encouraged artists to take more commercial routes and emphasise visual effects over moral or literary content.

As with Gothic literature, these developments were centred on Britain, where the commercialisation of culture was most advanced.

At the head of this phenomenon was the Swiss-born Henry Fuseli, whose famous declaration that "One of the most unexplored regions of art are dreams" encapsulated a willingness to engage with obscure or repressed emotional territory. His subjects were generally drawn from classical literature, Shakespeare, Milton and the modern poets: Gothic literature was too tainted by association with a feminised, 'low' readership. If Fuseli was grandly addressing the poetic imagination, we can also interpret him as pursuing sensational themes and images for commercial purposes – and to proto-cinematic effect.

Fuseli had his peers, followers and imitators who

The Nightmare

Since it was first exhibited at London's Royal Academy of Arts in 1782, Henry Fuseli's painting *The Nightmare* has stood as an icon of Gothic horror. Both the original version (Detroit Institute of Arts) and a later version on an upright format (Goethe-Museum, Frankfurt) have been reproduced, pastiched, parodied and reworked innumerable times.

It was knowingly re-staged in Ken Russell's *Gothic* and evoked in publicity materials for the film. The motif of the young woman in partial undress pinned down by a dwarfish or monstrous tormentor, her arm hanging limply, can be detected in numerous other scenes from across the history of cinema, in films from Carl Dreyer's *Vampyr* to Jean Cocteau's *La Belle et la Bête*.

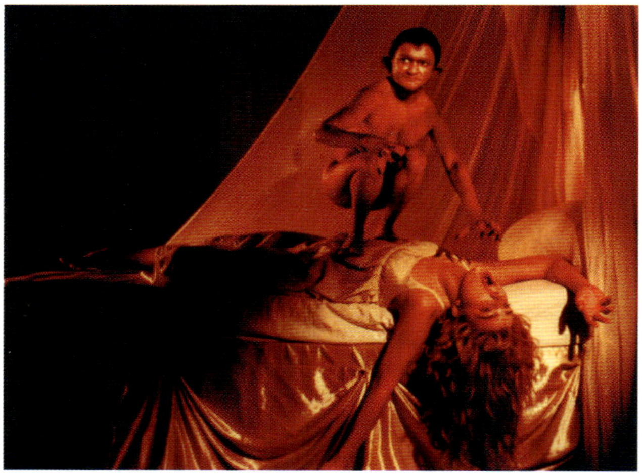

The poster image for Ken Russell's 'Gothic' (1987)

'Vampyr' (1932)

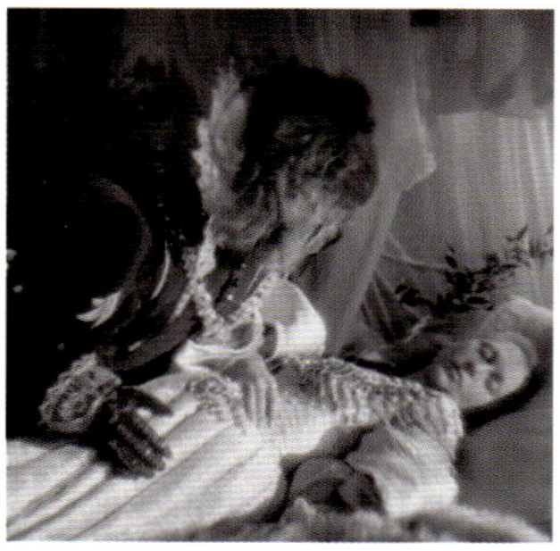

'La Belle et la Bête' (1946)

carried a 'Fuselian' engagement with supernaturalism and horror through to the early 19th century, while these themes became prevalent in the stridently satirical caricature images which proliferated at the same moment, notably with the work of James Gillray. Elsewhere in Europe, the Venetian draughtsman Giovanni Battista Piranesi produced critically acclaimed and widely collected etched scenes of terrific architectural fantasy which paralleled the literary investigation of uncanny spaces. With his etched series produced in the midst of revolution and war in his native Spain, Francisco de Goya's stark images of supernatural weirdness, violence and horror at the limits of the visible and the imaginable register his knowledge of Gillray's Gothic grotesquery.

The work of Fuseli and similar artists of the weird and horrible fell into disrepute in the Victorian era. Just as the more confrontational tendencies within Gothic literature were subsumed within the supernatural tale and ghost story, the fantastic elements of late 18th-century Gothic art were translated into fairy painting, and the supernatural and horrible generally eschewed in literary subject painting.

The more direct legacy lies, though, in the endurance of forms of popular visual culture and spectacular display. Ghosts, skeletons, burning cities, ruins, terrific storms and mountain landscapes proliferated in the iconography of the new technology-based side-shows and visual entertainments including the magic lantern, Philip James de Loutherboug's mechanical moving-landscape show the Eidophusikon (1781) and from the 1790s the Phantasmagoria, populist theatre and pantomime.

While high-minded literary criticism of the early 19th-century turned decisively against the visual, the vitality of such populist visual forms endured through the 19th century – to the point of connecting directly with the emergence of cinema.

The reappearance in cinema of motifs and effects first apparent in the Gothic art of the late 18th century should then be unsurprising. Occasionally, most decisively and extensively with the case of Fuseli's *The Nightmare*, the allusion is direct and knowing. But this image – together with Goya's prints and Piranesi's architectural fantasies – has also entered a common design sourcebook via the innumerable reproductions and reworkings over history.

The images and motifs of the Gothic underpin modern horror cinema, reappearing in historicised guise (notably with Roger Corman and Mario Bava's films), in a more or less knowing fashion, or resurfacing through parodic, ironic or revisionist workings. More importantly still, the testing out of boundaries (between high art and low, good taste and bad, moral certainty and nihilism) which animated the visual art of the Gothic both anticipated and helped shape the uneasy status of horror cinema.

Nightmare interiors
Piranesi's *Carceri* etchings of fantastic interiors provided a template for visionary architecture through the 19th and 20th centuries, and can be seen directly echoed in the set design of the Universal horrors of the 1930s, such as James Whale's *Frankenstein*.

'Frankenstein' (1931)

Ruins and ominous mansions
An anxious preoccupation with the past was embodied in visual form by ruined abbeys and castles, as in De Loutherbourg's *Philosopher in a Moonlit Churchyard*, and is still a motif of Gothic cinema.

Manderley in Hitchcock's 'Rebecca' (1940)

Roger Corman's 'House of Usher' (1960)

Violation
The sexual violence so often suggested in Gothic literature and art was made explicit in Goya's nihilistic *Caprichos* print series (1797-99), ranging in tone from the satirical to the nihilistic.

Wallace Worsley's 'The Hunchback of Notre Dame' (1923)

Body horror

While body-horror has a place in the array of early Gothic literature, it is much rarer in the visual arts. The cannibal horror and perverted fairytale atmosphere of horror cinema such as *The Texas Chain Saw Massacre* (1974) were, though, trailed by James Gillray's 1792 satire on the French revolution, *Un petit souper, à la Parisienne*.

'The Texas Chain Saw Massacre' (1974)

The Monstrous

Perhaps second only to Fuseli's *The Nightmare* as a visual icon of the Gothic, William Blake's *The Ghost of a Flea* (c1819-20) set a model for monstrous hybridity: nominally human, but with lizardly skin and bull-neck, grossly muscular and primal.

'Frankenstein and the Monster from Hell' (1973)

'Nosferatu' (1922)

PART III

HAUNTED

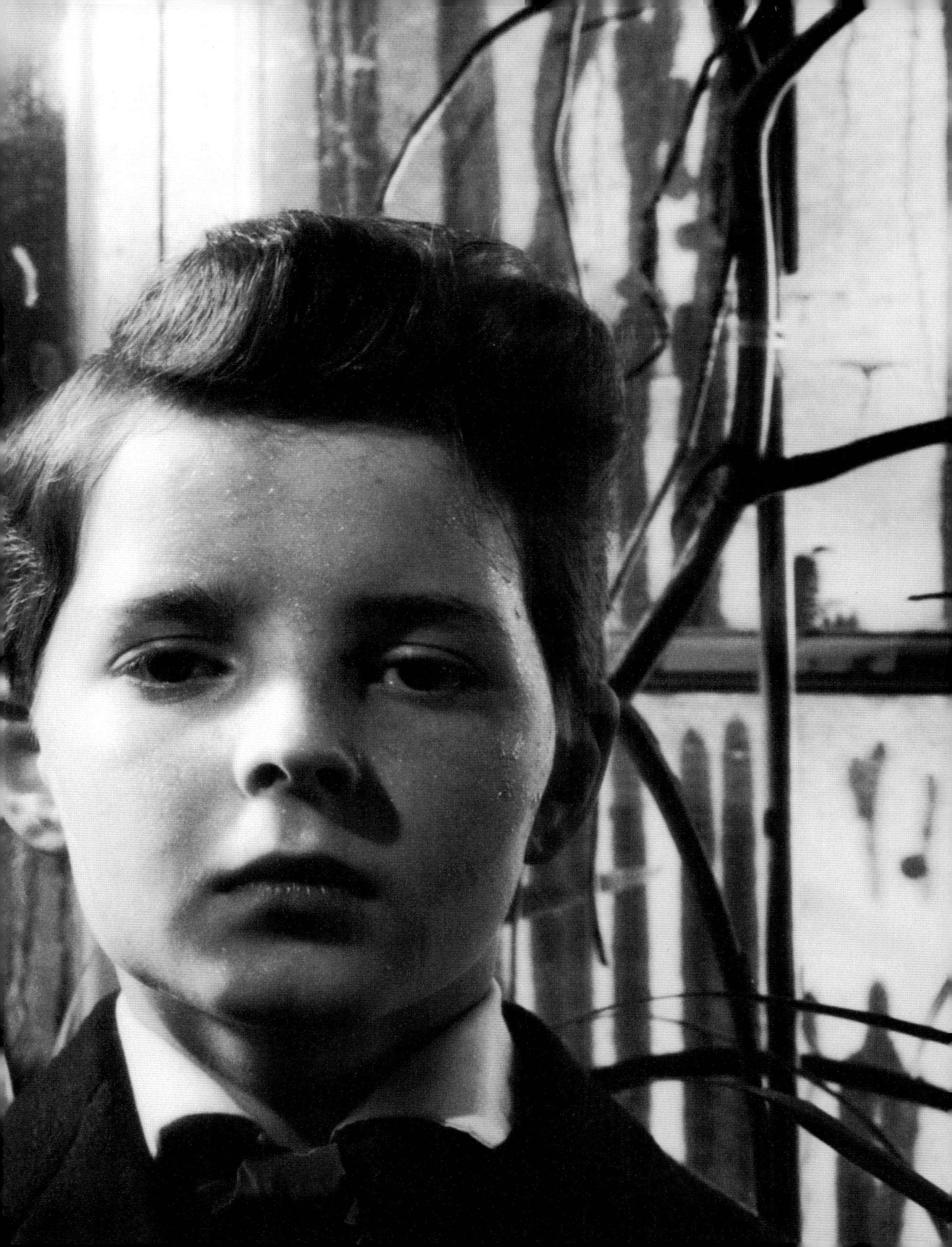

HAUNTED

SPECTRES OF THE PAST

BY ROGER CLARKE

"I am Madame la Morgue – Mrs Deadhouse! I will present you my friends Monsieur Cadavre and Monsieur Squelette".
Madame de la Rougierre to her young charge Maud, *Uncle Silas*, J. Sheridan Le Fanu, 1865.

The decay of historic institutions. The hypocrisy of religious and authority figures. The theatre of murder. Dominik Moll's version of the 18th-century Gothic novel *The Monk* (2011), concerning a leading, inspirational figure who conceals a career of sexual predation, has resonance, now perhaps more than ever. Hiding in plain sight is a Gothic meme that never goes away.

But it would be foolish to overplay the self-refreshing relevance of Gothic: that it is rather old-fashioned is much of its appeal. The Edwardian terrors of M.R. James have stalked BBC Christmas TV schedules for many decades – with their unquiet tombs, haunted libraries, secret diaries and occultic infarctions. Two of the best, Lawrence Gordon Clark's *A Warning to the Curious* (1972) and Jonathan Miller's *Whistle and I'll Come to You* (1968), take place in the sandy, isolated beaches of James's childhood in East Anglia. Charles Dickens gave us Scrooge but he also gave us *The Signalman* (1976) with Denholm Elliott, another ghost story produced by the BBC.

In 2002, FilmFour delivered an excellent 12-minute version of Robert Aickman's short story *The Cicerones*, with Mark Gatiss playing a Jamesian-style scholarly single man approached by a procession of ambiguous boy 'cicerones' in a cathedral, one of whom arrives at noon – which was, until the 19th century, as traditional a time as midnight for ghosts to appear. Written and directed by Gatiss's fellow *League of Gentlemen* alumnus Jeremy Dyson, it recalls J. Sheridan Le Fanu's *Schalken the Painter* (filmed by the BBC in 1979) and M.R. James's predatory *Lost Hearts* (also filmed by the BBC, in 1973), which story, by the way, was James's least favourite of his own 'entertainments', an early effort that troubled him for artistic and perhaps personal reasons. Gatiss has been in the vanguard of modern ghost-Gothic on TV, also with his *Crooked House* (2008) mini-series, where the very fabric of a house embodies a curse.

Attacks on the living

There are two Gothic archetypes who have stalked the screen since the earliest flickering days of movie projection. One is a clouding of the mind, embodied by 'The Woman in Black'. The other is the 'King of Terrors', essentially the grim reaper, once used to describe an onstage Broadway skeleton ghost in 1860s New York. They both embody an attack by the corrupt on the living.

Over the centuries the notion of what ghosts actually *are* has changed a number of times. In the medieval era they were often tied in to religious instruction, or performed as an animated corpse, as detailed in Andrew Joynes's book *Medieval Ghost Stories* (2001). In Jacobean times ghosts were tricks played by the devil, a notion still alive in many Hollywood films today. Ghosts traditionally strayed into the waking world from Purgatory, which

(Previous page) The ghost of Quint (Peter Wyngarde) appears behind Miles (Martin Stephens) in Jack Clayton's 'The Innocents' (1961).

(Opposite) Claire Bloom (left) and Julie Harris (right) in Robert Wise's 'The Haunting' (1963).

(Above)
The animated skeleton appears in many early films, such as Georges Méliès's 'Le manoir du diable' ('The Haunted Castle', 1896).

(Below)
The figure of Death, with scythe, collects the souls of the dead in Victor Sjöström's 'The Phantom Carriage' (1921).

did not exist in Protestant theology. You can recognise this type of belief-system in films such as *Paranormal Activity* (wrongly named, since it technically describes supernatural activity, and paranormal means events that will someday be explained by science). It is a puritan hangover from the 17th century, the 'Jamestown Effect' if you like.

Since the 1960s our notion of ghosts has changed again. A recent survey showed that people now believe ghosts are a 'feeling' in a house – ghosts have become an emotion field. This is the domain of the Woman in Black, the shadow-trap.

The Kingdom of Shadows

"Last night I was in the Kingdom of Shadows," wrote Maxim Gorky in early July 1896. The travelling Lumière programme, a short-film portmanteau illuminating a new and exciting form of entertainment, had finally reached Russia. Gorky, dressed customarily in his black peasant's smock, happened to see it at the Nizhny-Novgorod fair. It was the ghostliness that disturbed him, as if he had been watching a bad dream while fully and painfully awake. He described one film in particular: "Curses and ghosts, the evil spirits that have cast entire cities into eternal sleep… three men seated at a table, playing cards. Their faces are tense, their hands move swiftly… It seems as if these people have died and their shadows have been condemned to play cards in silence unto eternity," he observed, with a shudder.

The innate ghostliness of film was pre-empted by several key Victorian inventions. From 1855 commercial companies such as the London Stereoscopic Company in Cheapside produced double-exposed ghost pictures to prove the 'folly' of ghost belief. Theatre has always found ghosts to be crowd-pleasers. From 1863 a theatrical invention (a primitive form of holographic projection) known as 'Pepper's Ghost' became hugely successful in theatres all over England and the US. As with the slides in earlier magic lantern shows, including one witnessed by Samuel Pepys in 1666, agitated skeletons were a favourite theme. A show at Wallack's Theatre on Broadway in 1863 was a sensation: the 'King of Terrors', as the skeleton was known, was accompanied by the theatrical music device known as 'sneak music'. The pre-cinema history of such performances goes back a long way: in 1797, for instance, Étienne-Gaspard Robert set up a show in a former Capuchin convent near Place Vendôme, which involved the dollied approach of a grinning skeleton.

The Lumière show seen by Gorky in the summer of 1896 had reached London a few months earlier, where it more or less coincided with the arrival of the X-Ray as a public curiosity – often in art and/or technology shows similar to those that were screening the new Lumière technology. The paying public, without any safety concerns or protection at all, allowed themselves to be X-rayed for fun – even the Prime Minister Lord Salisbury popped in to have his hand skiagraphed (as the technology was then known). It's curious now to realise that X-Ray and film were, for a few brief months in 1896, rival forms of entertainment.

By the time of Swedish director Victor Sjöström's silent masterpiece *The Phantom Carriage* (1921), Death was presented as a sadder figure than the 'King of Terrors'. With his scythe and carriage, here Death's lot is as a refuse collector; the dead he picks up are thrown into his phantom carriage like sides of beef. But in the early years of cinema all was busy, childish fairground effect. Nonetheless, projected on noisy early cameras, there was always the unspoken threat that the film itself would kill you (there was at least one major cinema fire in Paris that left much of the audience as charred remains).

The animated Gothic skeleton ambled and clacked very well into this potentially deadly new technology, and soon there were films by Georges Méliès (*Le manoir du Diable*, 1896; *The Vanishing Lady*, 1896; *Le palais des mille et une nuits, 1905*) and the Lumière brothers (*Le Squelette joyeux*, 1895) in which the skeleton has a pivotal role. There's a death's-head phantom too in *Uncle Josh in a Spooky Hotel* (Edwin S. Porter, 1900) – an early incarnation of the comedy Gothic that still arises in Hollywood every now and again, such as Tim Burton's *Beetlejuice* (*The Ghost Train* and *The Ghost of St Michaels*, both 1941, the latter starring a schoolboy Charles Hawtrey, are further British examples). Comedy Gothic is also there in early Spanish cinema such as Segundo de Chomón's *Haunted House* from 1908, which includes apports (objects paranormally appear and disappear), sheeted phantoms and self-preparing meals as good as anything designed by Jan Švankmajer.

Many of these early films made hay with the acephalous, popping heads on and off like a bonnet, for the headless ghost in particular has always had a place in British cultural history since the ghost of Anne Boleyn stalked a number

(Above)
An exhibition of 'Pepper's Ghost' in a British theatre, circa 1865. This optical effect using mirrors was invented by Henry Dircks and developed by John Henry Pepper.

(Below)
A haunting scene in the Dickens adaptation 'The Signalman' (1976), one of the BBC's celebrated 'Ghost Stories for Christmas'.

Tellers of Tales

By Lisa Kerrigan

"Once upon a time…". The age-old storyteller's refrain immediately sets the scene for a fantastical tale, transporting the listener to the world of the imagination. A story well told can cast an engrossing spell merely through the manner in which words are imparted – the intimacy created between the teller and the listener adding to the unsettling effect of the story.

In the classic works of Gothic fiction, authors frequently made use of an epistolary form to make the reader a confidante or a witness – whether in the personal and direct mode of address found in *Jane Eyre*, or in the diary entries that make up Bram Stoker's *Dracula*. It is surely no coincidence that Mary Shelley's inspiration for *Frankenstein* arose from a session of reading ghost stories at Villa Diodati, and that acts of storytelling are so central to that narrative, as both Victor and the creature take turns to relate their tales. Anne Rice's *Interview with the Vampire* is just that, a life story told to a willing listener. Beyond the page, Dickens and Wilkie Collins embarked on reading tours where the public could enjoy tales told directly by the authors with the shared thrill of being part of an audience. And of course, M.R. James's ghost stories began life by being performed to gatherings of friends and students in his Cambridge rooms at Christmastime.

Being highly atmospheric and effective but with a minimum of technical requirements, ghost story readings were a natural candidate for the schedules in the early days of broadcasting in Britain. Valentine Dyall's well loved role as the BBC's storyteller 'The Man in Black' saw him introduce creepy tales and literary adaptations on the Home Service and the Light Programme in the 1940s.

'A Strange Experience with Algernon Blackwood' (1949)

Another popular figure on radio, and later in television, was the prolific author of weird tales Algernon Blackwood. Inspired by his extensive travels and interest in the extraordinary things to be found in nature, Blackwood's stories – such as 'The Willows' and 'The Wendigo' – are filled with wonder and the uncanny, and he brought a touch of the supernatural to the birth of television when he appeared in the BBC's inaugural high-definition broadcast from Alexandra Palace on 2 November 1936.

When television resumed after the war, Blackwood caused a sensation with his rendition of a ghost story on Halloween night 1947, and thereafter regularly featured in a series called *Saturday Night Story*. Blackwood related his stories as personal experiences, with acquaintances suffering ghostly encounters or inexplicable misadventures. Using nothing more than his voice and an air of worldly erudition, these direct-to-camera tales brought Blackwood's haunting visage into living rooms, where families would gather round in much the same way as M.R. James's friends did or as people still do around a campfire. So popular was Blackwood's to-camera storytelling that it made the leap to the big screen in a series of short films made in 1949. These six shorts promised 'A Strange Experience with Algernon Blackwood' and featured the author telling tales such as 'Lock Your Door' in a living room set which arguably lacked the intimacy of his television readings.

Following Blackwood's death in 1951, his work was resurrected for television a decade later by Associated-Rediffusion. In the series *Tales of Mystery*, John Laurie played Blackwood and introduced adaptations of a selection of his stories. This evolution of the storyteller into a host is characteristic of the development of ghost stories on television, where to-camera readings have been eclipsed by dramatisations, and narrators have become narrative participants.

Nevertheless, old-fashioned ghost story readings do occasionally return to haunt our screens, as in the series *Late Night Story* (BBC, 1978), which saw Tom Baker telling frightening tales on the theme of childhood (some concocted by Nigel Kneale) or *Classic Ghost Stories* (BBC, 1986) with Robert Powell reading tales from M.R. James. In 2001 BBC Choice presented *The Fear*, in which actors including David Harewood and Samantha Morton read tales from Poe and Arthur Conan Doyle, among others. This series was unusual in including women in its onscreen storytellers, hitherto largely a male preserve. The BBC also revived its 'Ghost Stories for Christmas' strand in 2000, casting Christopher Lee as 'the Antiquary' (clearly inspired by M.R. James) in a recreation of James's candlelit entertainments.

On radio, storytelling still thrives in tandem with dramatisation, perhaps because a voice whispering to the ear still has the capacity to thrill, and the unseen is still the most infinitely chilling special effect. 'The Man in Black' has also endured, from *Appointment with Fear* to his most recent incarnation: Mark Gatiss, who took up the role in 2009.

The personal touch of a good storyteller still has the power to remind us of the original childhood thrill of being caught up in the imagined, frightening world of the ghost story, whether it was in being told a bedtime story, reading a novel late at night, sitting among the audience in a darkened cinema or in our own family living room in front of the television.

(Above)
The archetypal figure of the headless horseman, as seen in Tim Burton's 'Sleepy Hollow' (1999).

of palaces and stately homes and the odd music-hall number with her "head tucked underneath her arm" (Stanley Holloway, 1934). Made in 1895, Alfred Clark's *The Execution of Mary Queen of Scots* includes what may well be the first ever film special effect: the severed head (so associated with the French revolution and that other Gothic mainstay, the mob). The great folkloric ghosts of the 18th century – beside phantom monks and nuns – were headless riders and coach-drivers, often with headless horses. The Anglophile American writer Washington Irving knew that well enough when he wrote the story that eventually became Tim Burton's *Sleepy Hollow* (1999).

Women in Black

In Britain, ghost belief is inextricably tied up with the suppression of Roman Catholicism in the 16th century. For years, to express belief in ghosts was to identify yourself as a Roman Catholic, and thus available for state sanction. A succession of Parliamentary acts began the process of legalising Roman Catholicism after 1778 in Great Britain, triggering riots and the full flush of the Gothic novel. Suddenly dungeons, wicked priests, demented convents and pacts with the devil all reappear. One figure in particular is of interest – the nun.

A phantom nun first appears in England in an account published in 731, as the ghost abbess who visits the deathbed of a nun named Tortgith. Tortgith negotiates with the dead abbess as to the time of her own demise – she is a religious visitant, it is true, but also the death-bringer. So the first British ghost we have recorded is in an Essex girl in a nunnery.

We first find the nun resurgent in *The Monk* (1796) by Byron's snaggle-toothed friend Matthew Lewis, when we get a description of this paranormal creature, the 'Bloody Nun'. She is vengeance, she is disease, she is the handmaiden to Satan. Soon after, the nun became a default ghost whenever people looked for them. She flits folklorically through the lanes of Regency Brighton, or the gardens of Borley Rectory, the most haunted house in England, as early as 1843. We also find the 'black nun' of Threadneedle Street by the Bank of England from around 1840.

By the time of Georgian England, this sinister creature is not just dressed in black, but her habit enshrouds a foreign malignancy – specifically, a foreign woman who is often French or Spanish. Her witch-like ascendancy can be dated rather precisely to the trial and the eventual public execution of Mrs Maria Manning in 1849, who went to the gallows sheathed in black satin and wearing black gloves – a fashion detail that both horrified and excited Thomas Hardy and Charles Dickens. Manning was a haughty French-speaking lady's maid from Switzerland, and appears, or rather a version of her appears, as Hortense in *Bleak House* (1853) and as the governess in J. Sheridan Le Fanu's *Uncle Silas* (1864), which was filmed in 1947 with Greek stage actress Katina Paxinou playing the governess.

Who was this terrifying murderess with her satin sheen as glossy as a raven's wing, her face doubly obscured by a black

(Above, left)
Pauline Moran, terrifying as the Woman in Black in the 1989 TV adaptation of Susan Hill's novel.

(Above, right)
Mrs Danvers (Judith Anderson) in 'Rebecca' (1940) seems to be in communion with the dead mistress of the house.

(Left)
Costume Designer Sophia Harris's original sketch for the ghostly Miss Jessel in 'The Innocents' (1961).

(Above, centre)
Greek actress Katina Paxinou as the sinister governess in the 1947 adaptation of 'Uncle Silas'.

(Opposite)
Haley Joel Osment in 'The Sixth Sense' (1999). Children are often the conduits for ghostly forces.

(Below)
The ghost of Miss Jessel (Clytie Jessop) rises from the reeds in 'The Innocents'.

lace veil and a black blindfold? Maria Manning had murdered her lover and buried him in the kitchen, preparing the grave two weeks in advance. As many as 50,000 people turned out as she stepped up the gallows on Horsemonger Lane, including Dickens himself.

Twenty years passed. Clearly, Manning was still a topic of conversation amongst ordinary people. Word got out that her ghost had been seen appearing at a window at Bermondsey. Before long, 400 people were gathering outside the empty house every evening. There was substantial police intervention. It seems plausible to suggest that, since she was causing riots two decades after her death, the notion of a deadly murderess, a foreigner, a woman in black capable of returning from the grave, had become deeply embedded in the English psyche.

Up until then, English ghosts had always been white-garbed: for centuries, the ghost was traditionally clothed in its shroud or winding sheet. The subject of clothes on ghosts was a serious theological problem – if they were indeed souls of the dead then they would probably be naked.

Sometimes The Woman in Black idea doesn't even have to be a ghost. Sometimes she has just the suggestion of the deathly, such as Mrs Danvers in *Rebecca* (1940) who seems to be in communion with the dead mistress of the house. Sometimes she can be like the unstable abbess in the film *The Devils* (1971). It's no coincidence that Margaret Hamilton, who played the wicked witch in *The Wizard of Oz* (1939), plays the sinister broom-wielding housekeeper in *13 Ghosts* (1960), the aw-shucks fairground spookerama which incidentally includes a headless circus lion tamer and a flaming skeleton.

We find her, more piteous than evil, in *The Lady's Maid's Bell*, featured in the Granada series *Shades of Darkness* (1983-1986), adapted from an Edith Wharton short story. In recent years

The Woman in Black, at least the version originally written in novel form by Susan Hill in 1983, has become a huge hit on the West End stage, as well as proving the substance for two different film adaptations. The first is the TV movie made in 1989, written by Nigel Kneale, with Pauline Moran as the child-stalking wraith. The second *The Woman in Black* (2012) stars Daniel Radcliffe as the solicitor sent to sort out the estate at Eel Marsh House. While rummaging through the papers and detritus of the old manor house, and staying much later in the afternoon than he should do, he incurs the very unwelcome interest of the vengeful spectre who in this version (adapted by Jane Goldman) has morphed into a full-scale child-killing ogre, as opposed to an angry, wronged mother trying to get her son back from her sister. With its Essex/Kent marshes and Jacobean house, this is very much the haunted realm of Miss Havisham in *Great Expectations* (1946).

The idea of protecting children against ghosts is a late Victorian one, datable to an apparently true tale of the haunting of Hinton Ampner published in the *Gentleman's Magazine* in 1871. It is almost certainly the source story for Henry James's *The Turn of the Screw* and we see it in two standout film versions, Jack Clayton's *The Innocents* (1961) and Alejandro Amenábar's *The Others* (2001). It is interesting that the latter is filmed and written by a Spanish director; ruined boys in Spanish ghost-Gothic also appear in films such as Juan Antonio Bayona's *The Orphanage* (2007) and Guillermo del Toro's *The Devil's Backbone* (2001).

There isn't much of a folkloric tradition of ghostly children in the UK, compared to, say, Poland, but the idea of the ghostly imperilment of children provides compelling drama – childhood as a conduit for, and of interest to, dangerous magical forces. Both *The Woman in Black* (2012) and *Mama* (2013) (produced by Guillermo del Toro) concern themselves with the safety of children, who do not grasp the threat. It's the same with *The Sixth Sense* (1999), *Paranormal Activity* (2007) and *Poltergeist* (1982). Children not realising that ghosts are a moral danger is powerful stuff. It's not always remembered, but *The Exorcist* (1973) house was already haunted before the demon turned up – by one 'Captain Howdy'. There doesn't seem to be a trace of the Rex Harrisons (*The Ghost and Mrs Muir*, 1947) about this captain, however.

(Above)
The 'fox spirit' or 'Huli jing' in Siu-Tung Ching's 'A Chinese Ghost Story' (1987).

(Below)
Gene Tierney in 'The Ghost and Mrs Muir' (1947).

Some child ghosts have malign intent: in *Ju-on: The Grudge* (2002), for instance, the boy ghost Toshio is simply a young male version of his mother the Woman in Black, observing, and waiting to strike, like a spider.

The first time we see the dead governess in *The Innocents* and the ghost in *The Woman in Black* they seem to be creatures of the marshes and the lake. This is her natural home. These beings emerge from wells, water-tanks, cisterns, baths, lakes, vaults and graves. She's the witch from the water – seen in *Ghost Story* (1981), *What Lies Beneath* (2000) and most recently in *Mama*. She's the old lady in the bath in room 237 in *The Shining* (1980). In Asian cinema we find her in *Dark Waters* (2002) and *Ringu* (1998), though M.R. James had at least two ghost stories with entities that live down wells (and another that involves a transposable curse, and a further story that involves a malign presence peering through a curtain of hair).

The 'woman in black' is related to the 'fox spirit' or *Huli jing* that has stalked Japanese and Chinese culture immemorially, but who in those cultures is more aligned to fairy blindness and enchantments, as in Mizoguchi's *Ugetsu monogatari (1953)* and Siu-Tung Ching's *A Chinese Ghost Story* (1987).

Are these things demons? Spirits? Whether ghosts are the formerly living or are instead 'elemental', never-human *simulacra* is a debate familiar to Shakespeare, or at least, Shakespearean scholars in the case of Hamlet's ghost, who was in fact a popular subject for early films – one was made by Cecil Hepworth in 1913, making use of a castle set built at Lulworth Cove. *Hamlet* also set the scene for the idea of the haunted building beside the crashing sea; clifftop female hauntings are also to be found in *The Uninvited* (1944), *The Lady in White* (1988) and (role reversed) *The Ghost and Mrs Muir*.

These days, towers and Gothic battlements don't have quite the suggestive power that they did to, say, Jane Austen, but the idea of Gothic confinement still does. We have a haunted submarine in *Below* (2002) – perhaps based on the legend of the haunted WWI submarine, the U65 – and imprisonment in a haunted house in Robert Wise's *The Haunting* (1963), which was fairly old-fashioned even for its time. All haunted bedroom tales in the UK date from Walter Scott's 1829 story 'The Tapestried Chamber'. He introduced the neat trick of solving the exposition problem built into every ghostly tale by identifying the ghost from a family portrait. In this day and age however, when hotels advertise their haunted rooms rather than sealing them up, as in *1408* (2007), and when the house at Amityville (featured in the 1979 *The Amityville Horror* and a further nine films since) has had to change its famous windows to dissuade sightseers, anyone who came up with a venue that would guarantee a haunting every time would make a great deal of money.

I'll leave you with a detail from that father of the English language ghost story, J. Sheridan Le Fanu, taken from 'An Account of Some Strange Disturbances in Aungier Street', published in 1853. A ghost manifests in a bedroom. It is night. "A picture suddenly flew up to the window, where it remained fixed, as if by an electrical attraction, and my discipline of horror then commenced, to last perhaps for hours. The picture thus mysteriously glued to the window-panes, was the portrait of an old man, in a crimson flowered silk dressing-gown, the folds of which I could now describe, with a countenance embodying a strange mixture of intellect, sensuality, and power, but withal sinister and full of malignant omen." The moving picture? Cinema is all there in that moment, in the Gothic haunted room, and the animated face of the dead looking down with no love lost for the living.

A Message from the Other Side

By Simon McCallum

"I shall not commit the fashionable stupidity of regarding everything I cannot explain as a fraud." – Carl Jung

If photography and the moving image were the defining inventions of the Victorian age, Spiritualism was its religion. The movement had been gathering pace since the 1840s, when the Fox sisters of New York claimed to have made contact with the spirit world, sparking an international sensation. The birth of cinema in the 1890s coincided with Spiritualism's zenith in the United States and Europe, where it enjoyed immense popularity among the burgeoning middle classes, women, and social reformers. The bereaved flocked to it in the wake of the American Civil War and later the Great War, which fuelled a revival into the 1920s.

Formal organisations such as the Spiritualist Church were founded, partly in response to the activities of fraudulent spirit mediums and 'trance lecturers'. Such showmanship fascinated early filmmakers, who were often well accustomed to presenting the wonders of the cinematograph among the mêlée of travelling fairs at the turn of the new century.

In Britain, the séance and its paraphernalia – spirit cabinets, automatic writing, table turning – exerted huge public fascination. The evangelism of 'true believers' galvanised the search for scientific proof of life after death, with the formation in London of the Ghost Club in 1862 and the Society for Psychical Research (SPR) in 1882. For the flourishing popular press, exposing crooked 'psychics' became something of a blood sport.

In 1906, British cinema pioneer R.W. Paul tapped into this trend with *The Medium Exposed? Or, A Modern Spiritualistic Séance*. Preserved in the BFI National Archive, this ingenious six-minute saga sees a gathering of affluent suburban Spiritualists expose a charlatan mid-séance. While his accomplice escapes, the 'medium' is manhandled into a trunk, thrown down a hill and pelted with eggs.

The character of the fraudulent medium, and the association of Spiritualism with crime and deceit, crops up in a number of British films. Maurice Elvey's *At the Villa Rose* (1920) is a murder mystery set on the French Riviera. Enhanced with eerie colour tinting, the film deploys the (by then familiar) tropes of the séance to cover up the murder of a rich widow and an attempted jewellery theft. In Bryan Forbes's *Séance on a Wet Afternoon* (1964), Kim Stanley plays a committed, albeit unstable, medium. Haunted by the death of her newborn son, she stages a kidnapping in a misguided attempt to gain recognition for her psychic abilities.

A young man gets involved with a group of Spiritualists following the death of his girlfriend in John Harlow's *Spellbound* (1941), and is driven out of his mind when her spirit manifests at a séance. While not an outright condemnation, the film warns of the dangers of "new thought"; old-fashioned prayer saves the day. It was based on Robert Hugh Benson's 1909 novel *The Necromancers*, written after Benson was ordained as a Roman Catholic priest (the Catholic Church had a deep aversion to Spiritualism). Anticipating controversy, the British Board of Film Censors banned *Spellbound*, until it was endorsed with an introduction by prominent Spiritualist Hannen Swaffer, in which he welcomes the opportunity for debate and refutes any suggestion that Spiritualists are prone to madness.

Television has offered a platform for working mediums. The subject of *Things Unseen: Ena Twigg - Medium* (1971) first encountered what she called her "misty people" at the age of seven, and here demonstrates her clairvoyant abilities. *The Reunion* (1995) features clairaudient medium Mavis Pittilla and her local Spiritualist Church congregation. Yet the age-old suspicion lingers. The *Second City Firsts* play *The Medium* (1973) centres on a group of women who invite a supposed seer to a party to give readings - with unsettling results.

In the 21st century, TV mediums including Derek Acorah, best known for hit paranormal investigation show *Most Haunted* (2002-10), and Sally Morgan (aka 'Psychic Sally') have become embroiled in scandal. Comedy series *High Spirits with Shirley Ghostman* (2005) lampoons such 'celebrity psychics': Marc Wootton's acid-tongued phoney medium communes with everyone from Colonel Sanders to Princess Diana, ably assisted by canine 'spirit guide' Sheba. *Derren Brown: Séance* (2004) saw the popular mentalist reveal the tricks of Victorian fraudsters, culminating in a live séance in which the TV audience was invited to participate.

A chilling landmark in British television, *Ghostwatch* (1992) purported to be a live Halloween broadcast from a North London house haunted by a malevolent spirit nicknamed 'Pipes'. It was in fact a scripted, pre-recorded drama. At its extraordinary finale, the investigation triggers a "massive séance", with psychic energies unleashed into the studio – and the homes of the viewing public. Many felt duped, and the resulting press furore, which recalled Orson Welles's 1938 *War of the Worlds* radio broadcast and saw the programme suppressed for a decade, is well documented.

Writer Stephen Volk drew on the Enfield Poltergeist case, investigated by the SPR's Maurice Grosse in the late 1970s. Grosse was unhappy with *Ghostwatch*'s veiled references to Enfield, which he revisited in video diary form for *Ghostbuster - The Real Thing* (1996), but its impact on a generation of British filmmakers was significant. Anticipating the likes of *Most Haunted*, it also influenced international horror cinema – not least the *Paranormal Activity* franchise.

On-screen investigators may now bring science to bear on the spirit world, but they owe a debt to those Victorian showmen and women who harnessed Spiritualism to thrill audiences… and perhaps to reassure us that there is indeed an 'Other Side'.

'The Medium Exposed? Or, A Modern Spiritualistic Séance' (1906)

Japanese Gothic

By Jasper Sharp

The Land of the Rising Sun is also the land of long shadows: the shadows of Japan's self-imposed 300-year period of isolation throughout the Tokugawa era, culminating with the country opening up to the rest of the world with the dawn of the Meiji period (literally 'Enlightened Rule') in 1868; the tenebrous literary worlds conjured up within the twilight zone between a newly-introduced wave of genre fiction from abroad and an indigenous vernacular culture by writers such as Izumi Kyoka (1873-1939) and Edogawa Rampo (1894-1965), whose *nom-de-plume* derived from the phonetic approximation in Japanese of Edgar Allan Poe; the shadows burnt into the ravaged cityscapes of Hiroshima and Nagasaki by the radioactive flash that brought an abrupt end to the dark days of war; the inky darkness stretching beyond the glaring neon and video screens confining a generation left dispossessed after the collapse of the Bubble Economy in the mid-1990s.

Japan's own forays into the Gothic are often obscured by the shadows of foreign influence. When mapped onto its own cultural contours, the shapes formed prove alien, unsettling and unique. However, ghostly tales of the type first unleashed on the West by that great interpreter of Japanese culture, Lafcadio Hearn, in the 1904 compendium *Kwaidan: Stories and Studies of Strange Things*, formed a part of Japanese literary and oral traditions at least as far back as the beginning of the medieval Heian period in the eighth century, the roots of many traceable back

(Above) Nakata Hideo's 'Ringu' (1998), which spearheaded the 'J-Horror Boom'.

(Left) Mizoguchi Kenji's 1953 masterpiece 'Ugetsu Monogatari'.

(Opposite) Kobayashi Masaki drew from stories collected by Lafcadio Hearn for his 1964 film 'Kwaidan'.

to Chinese sources. Hearn's fables were later rendered onscreen with chilling efficacy by Kobayashi Masaki in *Kwaidan*, which claimed the Jury Special Prize at Cannes in 1965, although Japanese critics claimed that the film too obviously pandered to foreign tastes for the exotic.

The country had its own *kaidan-banashi* ('ghost story-telling') traditions to draw upon, fuelled by Buddhist narratives of karmic retribution infused with Shintoist beliefs of ancestral worship and an animistic world in which gods, or rather spirits, dwell in everything. Numerous films have been made based on works such as *The Ghost of Yotsuya* (*Tokaido Yotsuya kaidan*), a Kabuki play written by Tsuruya Nanboku IV (1755–1839) in 1825, or Sanyutei Encho's *The Ghost of Kasane Swamp* (*Shinkei Kasanegafuchi*) and *Tales of the Peony Lantern* (*Kaidan botan doro*), ancient folktales adapted by the author in the late 19th century, either for the stage or to be rendered as solo oral performances enhanced with sound and lighting effects.

The cinema screen proved the perfect modern medium through which such staples of these stories as the *onryo* (vengeful ghost) or *kaibyo* (ghostly cats that can adopt the form of a beautiful woman) could manifest themselves, like dark murmurings from a forgotten feudal past. Following early exponents of the *fantastique* such as Méliès, local filmmakers like Makino Shozo quickly learned that through a judicious use of edits, or by merely stopping and starting the camera, 'ghosts' could be made to appear and vanish onscreen as if by magic, resulting in such titles as *Broken Dishes at the Haunted Mansion* (*Bancho sarayashiki*, 1914) and *Taro of Ban: Tasuke Isshin Exterminates Ghosts* (*Banno Taro: Isshin Tasuke yokai taiji*, 1914).

We know too that the German proto-horrors *The Student of Prague* (1913) and *The Golem* (1915) were released in Japan. The author Tanizaki Junichiro wrote enthusiastically about such films, claiming that "moving pictures are dreams made more vivid than ordinary dreams." The flickering patterns of light and dark conjured up overseas had a huge bearing on his output. He later wrote the script for *The Lust of the White Serpent* (*Jasei no in*, 1921), directed by a recent returnee from Hollywood, Thomas Kurihara, and adapted from a ghostly tale of love from beyond the grave by the Tokugawa-era poet, Ueda Akinari.

Ueda's tale later achieved more widescreen recognition when it was filmed by Mizoguchi Kenji as *Ugetsu* (*Ugetsu monogatari*, 1953), which is often mistakenly held up as the beginning of Japan's filmic fascination with the supernatural. It is worth noting that Mizoguchi himself had drawn upon the fantastical works of E.T.A. Hoffman for his 1923 film *Blood and Spirit* (*Chi to rei*), and his *Passion of a Woman Teacher* (*Kyoren no onna shisho*, 1926), based on Encho's *Ghost of Kasane Swamp*, had even played in Europe. Sadly, most of these prewar titles remain just that – mere titles, the prints long since lost, as do such intriguing-sounding Hollywood derivatives as Kumaga Soya's *King Kong Appears in Edo* (*Edo ni arawareta Kingu Kongu*, 1938). However, rare surviving works such as Ushihara Kiyohiko's *The Ghost Cat and the Mysterious Shamisen* (*Kaibyo nazo no shamisen*, 1938) demonstrate a haunting, expressionistic verve equal to, if not surpassing, that of American or European Gothic horrors of the era.

By the time of Tanizaki's requiem to traditional aesthetics, the 1933 essay 'In Praise of Shadows', the relative cultural liberalism of the Taisho period (1912-1926) was long past its zenith as it yielded to the early Showa era, the "period of enlightened peace" that proved anything but. Horror was banned from Japanese screens during the war years, only for the genre to explode like pent-up forces from a repressed id during the 1950s. Production during this time rested largely in the hands of the Daiei and Shintoho studios, with Nakagawa Nobuo at the latter often credited as the first director to formulate the genre along Western lines. Nakagawa's films, including the seminal version of *Ghost of Yotsuya* (1959) and his stunning invocation of Buddhist hell, *Jigoku* (1960), routinely drew on the more gruesome aspects of the nation's exuberant traditions, thus mirroring rather than echoing the popular appeal of Terence Fisher's sensual reinterpretations of the Frankenstein and Dracula stories for Hammer during the same period. Marked out by their chilling atmospheres and an emphatic, almost Kabuki-esque flourish to their thrills, they defined the Japanese horror film of the era. Meanwhile, while the more populist side of the genre remained largely unheralded outside of Japan, Shindo Kaneto's political allegories of *Onibaba* (1964) and his take on the *kaibyo* ghost cat sub-genre, *Kuroneko* (*Yabu no naka no kuroneko*, 1968) played the international art-house circuit to critical acclaim.

After several decades of relative neglect, Japanese horror cinema resurfaced dramatically at the turn of millennium with what has been termed the 'J-Horror Boom', spearheaded internationally with the success of Nakata Hideo's *Ringu* (1998), and followed by such films as Nakata's *Dark Water* (*Honogurai mizu no soko kara*, 2002) and Shimizu Takashi's *Ju-on* (2002). Despite its contemporary setting, paranoid evocation of technology as a source of fear and explicit evocation of Western influences like *The Haunting* (1963), *Poltergeist* (1982) and *Videodrome* (1983), *Ringu*'s spare visual approach and measured pacing hark back to the Japanese ghost tales of yore, transplanting its maleficent *onryo* spectre, clad in traditional funereal garb and with face obscured by lank locks of jet black hair, into a 21st century context, proving beyond question that it is impossible to keep a good ghost down.

HAUNTED

THE OLD DARK HOUSE

BY KIM NEWMAN

The Old Dark House (1932), James Whale's film based on J.B. Priestley's novel *Benighted* (1928), announces itself with a title which stands in for an entire sub-genre of horror. The old dark house was the focus of the Gothic imagination well before the invention of the cinema. The genre is crowded with old dark houses – buildings which are more than architecture, inhabited by desperate characters, full of secret passageways and bricked-up rooms, haunted by spectres and guilts. Portraits of evil ancestors hang on the walls (eyeholes cut away), suits of ancient armour (some containing skeletons) are cobwebbed, bloodstains refuse to vanish and the configuration of corridors and staircases and rooms changes from moment to moment.

Old dark houses squat atop Carpathian mountains or moulder deep in Louisiana swamps, sit quietly in American suburbs or fester on British council estates. They are hard to find on the map but impossible to avoid in a storm. These spots – which Stephen King called the Bad Places – are everywhere. The best inhabitants can hope for is a last-reel conflagration, with the stones falling into a tarn or the grounds sewn with salt. The worst is that the house is still standing come the morning, and another night is only a sunset away.

Consider: the castles of Otranto and Udolpho, the Houses of the Seven Gables and the Seven Corpses, the Villa Diodati and Strawberry Hill, Northanger and Nightmare Abbeys, Elsinore in *Hamlet* and Dunsinane in *Macbeth*, Castle Dracula and the House of Usher, Thornfield Hall in *Jane Eyre* and Cold Comfort Farm, Borley Rectory and 10 Rillington Place, Manderley in *Rebecca* and Xanadu in *Citizen Kane*, the Chateau d'Yf in *The Count of Monte Cristo* and the Baltimore State Hospital for the Criminally Insane in *The Silence of the Lambs*, the laboratory out-buildings of Dr Frankenstein and Dr Jekyll, Norma Desmond's place on Sunset Blvd and the tract home of the Hudson Sisters in *What Ever Happened to Baby Jane?*, Hill House and Hell House, the Bates Motel in *Psycho* and the Old Franklin Place in *The Texas Chain Saw Massacre*, the Overlook Hotel in *The Shining* and the Freiburg Tanzakademie in *Suspiria*, the Myers House in *Halloween* and the Marsten House in *Salem's Lot*, the Dakota in *Rosemary's Baby* and Stephen King's Rose Red, the McNeil residence in *The Exorcist* and the Lutz home in *The Amityville Horror*, the House in Nightmare Park and the Last House on the Left, the mansions of Cruella de Vil and Montgomery Burns, the Houses by the Cemetery and at the Edge of the Park, the House with the Laughing Windows and the House on Haunted Hill, Rooms 237 and 1408, SPECTRE's volcano lair and Gordon Gekko's glass-and-steel penthouse, Slytherin in *Harry Potter* and Mount Doom in *The Lord of the Rings*.

"Don't big empty houses scare you?" Bob Hope is asked in *The Cat and the Canary* (1939); "not me," he replies, "I used to be in vaudeville." Old dark houses can be the Paris Opera which is home to the Phantom or the shuttered theatres of *The Last Warning* (1929), *Tread Softly* (1952) and *The Flesh and Blood Show* (1972). Old dark houses can even be lighthouses, railway stations, ghost trains, prisons, insane asylums, hospitals, motorcars,

(Opposite)
The house overlooking the Bates Motel, one of Gothic cinema's definitive old dark houses, in Alfred Hitchcock's 'Psycho' (1960).

(Above)
Charles Wilder (Douglass Montgomery) waits for the unsuspecting Joyce Norman (Paulette Goddard) in the 1939 remake of 'The Cat and the Canary'.

(Below)
The Lutz home, seen here in 'Amityville II: The Possession' (1982).

(Bottom)
The gates to Xanadu, Charles Foster Kane's monument to himself in 'Citizen Kane' (1941).

the wrecked SS Elizabeth Dane in *The Fog* (1980) or the space-faring Nostromo in *Alien* (1979). Department stores after hours where the dummies come to life, wax museums where corpses are dressed up in the dioramas, hedge mazes that are home to frozen corpses, playrooms where the toys move after the children have gone to bed...

A House isn't just a home – the House of Usher, for instance, refers to a family as well as a structure, a corrupt dynasty which must fall. Priestley's Femms and some of their visitors encapsulate the ills of the country, knocked about by the First World War, and doomed to decay and obsolescence. The House of Usher is also America in crisis, incestuous and oversensitive and teetering on a tarn, and the ailing author's body, as in the song 'This Old House'.

Whale strips Priestley's text of all but the trace elements of a political theme and plays up the eccentric, theatrical elements of his archetypal melodrama. A violent thunderstorm forces lost travellers – mired in a border country somewhere between England and Wales, shot in sunny California – to take refuge in the eponymous house, which is home to a mad harridan (Eva Moore), a twitchy coward (Ernest Thesiger), a hulking brute butler (Boris Karloff), a dying patriarch played by a woman (Elspeth Dudgeon) and a soft-spoken pyromaniac (Brember Wills) who has yet to burn the place down.

The film sets the capstone on a strain of cinema which had flourished for a decade, drawn from the Broadway mystery-comedy plays of the 1920s (such as *The Cat and the Canary*, *The Bat*, *The Gorilla*, *Seven Keys to Baldpate*, *The Ghost Breaker*) which had been successes as silent films and were all remade swiftly as talkies to add howling winds, creaking doors, cutting remarks and screams in the night (Roland West made *The Bat* as a silent in 1926 and remade it under the self-explanatory title of *The Bat Whispers* in 1930).

Always happy to borrow respectfully from the back catalogue, Whale recreates one of the strongest images from Paul Leni's *The Cat and the Canary* (1927): a corridor lined with draughty windows which make white curtains billow inward like ghostly shrouds. Whale must have been aware of Leni's ghost on the Universal lot. Leni made *Waxworks* (*Das Wachsfigurenkabinett*, 1923) in Germany before being imported to Universal as the prestige director of *The Cat and the Canary* and *The Man Who Laughs* (1928). He died prematurely of blood poisoning in 1929, not long after finishing *The Last Warning* – if he'd lived, he would have had his pick of Universal's spooky early talkie projects. Effectively, Leni's death made way for Whale to nab *Frankenstein* (1931) and have a Hollywood career. Similarly, the 1930 demise of silent bogeyman Lon Chaney created a vacancy that Bela Lugosi and Boris Karloff would fill, lending their accents to talking terror.

Whale's *Old Dark House*, as much farce as horror, casts its shadows over many later essays in the form, beginning with T. Hayes Hunter's British-made *The Ghoul* (1933), from the novel by Frank King, which poaches Thesiger and Karloff and discovers an Egyptian tomb on the estate of a mad archaeologist who refuses to lie dead.

The 1939 Bob Hope remake of *The Cat and the Canary* kicked off a whole cycle of Old Dark House pictures – including such comedy-spookers as *The Ghost Breakers* (1940), *The Black Cat* (1941), *Whistling in the Dark* (1941) and *One Body Too Many* (1944) – which would persist in such nostalgic skits as *The Rocky Horror Picture Show* (1975), *Murder By Death* (1976), *Clue* aka *Cluedo* (1985) and *Dark and Stormy Night* (2009). These are films defined by their sets – endlessly recycled, down to distinctive Iron Maiden and skeleton props – and supporting actors: Bela Lugosi as a red herring butler, Gale Sondergaard as the sinister housekeeper, George

(Above)
Appropriately spooky poster artwork for James Whale's 'The Old Dark House' (1932).

Zucco as a conniving lawyer, Willie Best as a terrified minion, Milton Parsons as a cadaverous undertaker, Lionel Atwill as a pompous host. Even such exercises in dementia as the indescribable *Sh! The Octopus* (1937) and the madcap *Murder, He Says* (1945) rely on these familiar, comforting shivers, as wisecracking comedians poke fun at the conventions of an earlier decade's thrillers (from authors like Mary Roberts Rinehart or Edgar Wallace) though it's a moot point as to whether they were ever taken seriously even in their heyday. P.G. Wodehouse was prone to taking pot-shots at Agatha Christie's country house murders and Ben Travers's seminal stage comedy *Thark* (filmed in 1932) is also an old dark house mystery. When Vincent Price shows Peter Lorre the family crypt in *The Raven* (1963), Lorre looks at the cobwebs and deadpans (in an improvised line) "Gee, hard place to keep clean, huh?"

There has always been a joke lurking in the gloom. Why on Earth would anyone stay at Cold Comfort Farm if they had a choice? Or is the whole thing a put-on, like the elaborate practical joke melodramas staged in multiple versions of *Seven Keys to Baldpate* (where a publisher provides a far-fetched plot to distract a pretentious author) or James Whale's underappreciated biopic footnote *The Great Garrick* (1937).

The masterstroke of *The Old Dark House*, which was scripted by Benn Levy, with additional dialogue by R.C. Sherriff, is that it is about nothing but shadows. Most old dark house films have MacGuffins – wills read at midnight, diamonds concealed in the chandelier, dynamite in the basement, grasping heirs disguised as madmen, smugglers' caves under the cellars, a mad wife in the attic – but *The Old Dark House* has no such plot motor; even its last-reel maniac is a kind of innocent. When the sun comes up and the rain stops, things go on much as before, and little is resolved: a few casualties, but no conflagration, no true heiress, no justice… When William Castle and Hammer Films clumsily remade *The Old Dark House* in 1963, they included a surprise killer knocking off the family one by one in the hope of securing a hidden fortune – and even brought in the bomb from *The Ghoul* to blow the culprit up at the end.

Hitchcock summed up the MacGuffin as something the characters are vitally concerned with, but the audience isn't really interested in. By not including anything of moment in his film, Whale builds comic and horror set-pieces around absurdly trivial things like the meagre fare on offer at the Femm dinner table ("Have a potato") or timid Thesiger's seemingly irrational and elaborate terror at the prospect of going upstairs in his own house. By stripping out any plot mechanics and even Priestley's authorial intent, Whale forces the viewer to invest this Old Dark House with meaning. The Femm house is out of time and space, in a muddy, rainy, no man's land that hints that this might after all be about the War (Sherriff scripted Whale's first stage and film success, the trenches drama *Journey's End*) and the puppet play enacted there makes the audience stand-in visitors reassess their own priorities and commitments.

In a more sinister manner, old dark houses are also black mirrors. "All that we are is coming out in this Keep," the 'good' Wehrmacht officer (Jurgen Prochnow) tells the Nazi (Gabriel Byrne) in Michael Mann's WWII horror, *The Keep* (1983). "You have scooped the many diseased psyches out of the German gutter… You have infected millions with your twisted fantasies. What are you meeting in the granite corridors of this Keep? Yourself?"

The novelist Jonathan Coe took up Priestley's project in *What a Carve Up!* (1985), a book which engages with the obscure 1961 film of the same name, a comedy remake of *The Ghoul* starring Sid James and Kenneth Connor. In Coe's book the inhabitants of an old dark house represent the various evils of Great Britain in the Thatcher years, and the house is again a building, a family and a nation, all crumbling and corrupt and doomed.

The readings of Stanley Kubrick's Stephen King-derived *The Shining* (1980) advanced in the documentary *Room 237* (2012) also unpick political significance in what seems to be primarily a personal tale, set in a hotel which is a cosmic morass of spiritual evil, though the story boils down to a single family clawing at each other. Four presidents stayed at the Overlook, the manager tells Jack Torrance (Jack Nicholson) while giving him the tour, not mentioning that two of them were Harding and Nixon, while massacres – the Donner Party's descent to cannibalism, the Native American trail of tears, Mafia slayings, the Holocaust and whatever happened to the woman in Room 237 - are evoked by near-subliminal details.

The modernist palace of Satanist architect Hjalmar Poelzig (Boris Karloff) in Edgar G. Ulmer's *The Black Cat* (1934) is a New Light House, but built on the corpse-filled rubble of the fort Poelzig betrayed to the enemy during the War. The sacrilege attracts a figure of nemesis in Vitus Werdegast (Bela Lugosi), an old

(Above)
Satanist architect Hjalmar Poelzig (Boris Karloff) descends the stairs of his modernist house in Edgar G. Ulmer's 'The Black Cat' (1934).

(Below)
Jack Torrance (Jack Nicholson) surrounded by the opulent architecture of the Overlook Hotel in 'The Shining' (1980).

comrade just out of prison and intent on peeling back the mask of respectability the perverse villain has put up by stripping him of his skin. The anecdote is given added bite by the rumour (which Ulmer must have been aware of) that Lugosi felt Karloff had usurped his career by starring in *Frankenstein* and becoming a bigger horror star than he.

Old dark houses are, of course, traps. "The spider, spinning his web for the unwary fly," Count Dracula (Lugosi) comments in Tod Browning's *Dracula* (1931) as he shows a visitor around his unclean castle, which is home to all manner of unTransylvanian vermin, from the three shrouded brides who decorate the tombs to giant insects and a shuffling armadillo.

In classical Gothic narratives, old dark houses (usually castles or palaces) are prisons for heiress heroines who are to be pressed into marriage to a dastard. The epitome of this plot, ever so slightly satirically, is J. Sheridan Le Fanu's splendid *Uncle Silas* (1864), filmed notably in 1947 by Charles Frank and starring Jean Simmons and Derrick De Marney. Spiced up with incest and near-cannibalism, this sort of confinement-narrative enjoyed a late 20th-century resurgence in the sado-slush books of V.C. Andrews (*Flowers in the Attic*, 1979, etc).

A variant on the villain's castle is the unholy convent, where heroines are mistreated to soften them up for forced marriage (this features in Matthew Lewis's *The Monk* (1796), Eugene Sue's *The Wandering Jew* (1844), and many others). Castle Dracula is a prison for the feminised hero Jonathan Harker – a key incident, with the letter for help thrown from the window and into the wrong hands, comes from Le Fanu and would recur often (eg: in *Fanatic*, 1964).

Modern incarnations of the

(Top)
The house is a prison for Jean Simmons's Caroline Ruthyen in 'Uncle Silas' (1947), the epitome of the confinement-narrative in which an heiress is pressed into marriage to a dastard.

(Above)
The old dark house as a black mirror in Michael Mann's World War II horror 'The Keep' (1983)

confinement narrative include asylums used to confine the sane but inconvenient or, in another derivation from Poe, run by malignant sadists who are more insane than the inmates (a compendium of evil asylum themes is advanced in the second season of the TV series *American Horror Story*). It is also the model for the rape-factory brothel of *The Seasoning House* (2012), which is purportedly set in the Balkans in the 1990s but draws on narrative conventions that would have seemed antiquated when Mrs Radcliffe or M.G. Lewis were in their heyday.

In the era of torture porn, restraint and confinement in dungeons and cellars – the torture chambers of the *Hostel* films or the Heath Robinson death trap basements of the *Saw* films – have become as commonplace as they were in the era of abducted heiresses and dastardly noblemen. Paul Sheldon (James Caan) in *Misery* (1990) is a writer of Gothic historical fiction about a put-upon heiress who suffers mightily – of course, he becomes a trussed-up, tortured, mutilated, doped spectre of himself, forced to recycle played-out conventions for his biggest fan, who won't let the genre die even if she doesn't mind the author passing away.

Visitors who are forced to take shelter in old dark houses by a storm or a bet (or the terms of a billionaire's will) are often lured to their deaths, suffering in the torture pits or stifled in the four-poster bed or stabbed in the shower. But these places are also inescapable for the original inhabitants; Shirley Jackson's title *We Have Always Lived in the Castle* is suggestive, as is Norman Bates's self-diagnosis that we all have our personal traps and learn to live in them.

There's an infernal dimension to the goings-on in most old dark houses, as in Jackson's Hill House in *The Haunting* (1963), a house which is waiting to be haunted by the protagonist, or even the Paris house where Céline and Julie find a melodrama played out over and over, with variations, in Jacques Rivette's *Céline and Julie Go Boating* (1974).

(Above)
Hill House in Robert Wise's 'The Haunting' (1963) seems to have been waiting to be haunted by Eleanor Lance (Julie Harris).

(Below)
Gothic novelist Paul Sheldon (James Caan) is imprisoned in the home of his 'biggest fan', the psychopathic Annie Wilkes (Kathy Bates), in 'Misery' (1990).

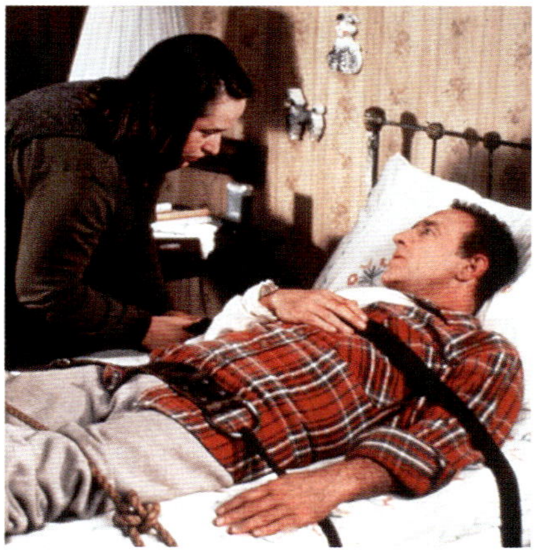

Like Kafka's castle – beyond mists and perhaps phantasmal – or Borges's infinite library, old dark houses can become universes unto themselves. The title of Mark Z. Danielewski's novel *House of Leaves* (2000), in which a house (and the narrative) unfolds and opens up vastly, refers not to leaves like a tree's but leaves like a table's. An often-repeated line is "I shall never leave this house", which always turns out to be true. Bram Stoker, in his original draft of *Dracula*, had the vampire's castle spontaneously fall down when he was staked, as if only the monster's force of will kept it standing.

In Roger Corman's run of 1960s films derived from Edgar Allan Poe, the ending of the House of Usher was ritually restaged, with the same stock footage of a burning slat roof falling in, as characters played by Vincent Price go up in flames along with their residences, strangled by buried-alive or back-from-the-dead female relations, passing from the world in a blaze of destruction that presaged the 'burn, baby, burn' ethos of the counterculture by doing away with the corrupt old regime.

And yet, no matter how many times the ceiling falls in flames, the old dark house still stands. Horace Walpole wasn't being entirely serious in *The Castle of Otranto* (1764) and the ridiculous elements of old dark house Gothic were in evidence well before Jane Austen set out to deconstruct the form in *Northanger Abbey* (written 1798-99). The light leading men and flapper heroines of *The Cat and the Canary* and *Seven Keys to Baldpate* kept the patter going amidst hooded masterfiends and secret passageways in the 1920s, and Whale saw that black humour could complement as well as leaven the chills.

Electric light and a coat of paint, some throw-rugs and scatter-cushions… they won't change anything, for the old dark house is more than a melodramatic convenience, it is a Gothic necessity.

The Original Gothics

By David Punter

The early days of cinema are steeped in Gothic. Film, with its sudden projection of characters and events into the 'real world', was from the beginning associated with ghosts and phantoms. But there also quickly arose a repertoire of the 'filmable Gothic', which revolved around three literary texts – Mary Shelley's *Frankenstein*, Bram Stoker's *Dracula*, and Robert Louis Stevenson's *Strange Case of Dr Jekyll and Mr Hyde* – and various of Edgar Allan Poe's short stories.

But this filmic history of the Gothic does not conform to the literary one. In literary terms, it could fairly be said that there are five masterworks of the 'original Gothic', spanning the years from the 1760s to the 1820s: Horace Walpole's *The Castle of Otranto*; Ann Radcliffe's *The Mysteries of Udolpho* and *The Italian*; Matthew Lewis's *The Monk*; and C.R. Maturin's *Melmoth the Wanderer*. Yet these works have never been satisfactorily translated into film. In the case of Radcliffe, no significant attempt has ever been made on her virtue (unlike that of her heroines), and the same is true of Maturin. Lewis's case is more interesting, and here there have been various ventures, beginning with the Luis Buñuel and Jean-Claude Carrière-scripted *Le moine* in 1972, but these have amounted to very little. *The Castle of Otranto* has suffered from a similar deficit; the only significant attempt has been Jan Švankmajer's 17-minute short (1977), which, although intriguing in itself, arguably does scant justice to a book widely regarded as the origin of all things Gothic.

Jan Švankmajer's 'Castle of Otranto' (1977)

Why should this be? I think the first answer lies in language. *Frankenstein*, although almost always regarded as a Gothic novel – for some critics *the* quintessential Gothic novel – is in many respects not Gothic at all. That is to say, it is written, for the most part, in a down-to-earth style which is startlingly modern. *Dracula* is 'modern' in an even more remarkable way; despite its core of the supernatural, the actual recounting employs a huge variety of technologies which were modern at the close of the 19th century: telecommunications, diaries, ships' logs and so forth. *Jekyll and Hyde*, again, has a core of modernity: the writing is rarely affected or pompous, and we follow events, as readers, with a minimum of distancing from what is taking place. Poe's stories, though in many respects archaic, are nevertheless short, pungent, eminently visual.

The case of the 'original Gothics' is different; the very substance of their appeal is a kind of inflated rhetoric. Gothic, we need to remember, was the midwife of Victorian stage melodrama: can these particular melodramas be properly filmed? It depends to a large extent on being overwhelmed by the sheer presence of the characters, the mustachio-twirling villain, the fainting heroine – matters which lose their immediacy in a more distanced medium.

The second issue is related: leaving Walpole aside, the other four key texts are driven by a deep anxiety about religious excess, specifically in the form of Roman Catholicism. For Shelley, Stoker, Stevenson, this is not the heart of the matter; but for Radcliffe, Lewis, Maturin, it is, and their versions of fear are difficult either to replicate in a secular society or to find suitable equivalents for without totally transposing their belief structures.

The third is length, or better, capaciousness. It is impossible to generalise, because *Dracula* is a long novel, *The Castle of Otranto* a short one; nevertheless, when approaching any of Radcliffe's works or Maturin's, we are confronted with a set of huge, rambling textual structures which suited audiences 200 years ago – all of these books were best-sellers – but now suits us no more than do Tennyson's longer poems. Any text can be abbreviated, but shorn of the swelling, operatic language, what is left?

Dominik Moll's 'The Monk' (2011)

The monster; the vampire; the double; the revenant. It is on these four examples of the uncanny that the interest of film has fallen. By contrast, Walpole's jokey tricks with giant helmets and the problems of heredity, Radcliffe's ghosts and skeletons which often turn out to be nothing of the kind; Maturin's endless depictions of the wanderer and the pact with the devil – these seem diffuse themes without a central visual core to which film can attend. It is not that we are unconcerned with the past, but the original Gothics seem like 'the past dealing with the past', which is one stage too removed. More importantly, they *cannot be updated*; their rhetoric, their language, their vocabulary of emotion and gesture are too embedded in their own time which means that their *action* would wither and die (perhaps as in the dying breaths of Dracula) if we were to try to tear them from their roots.

The mystery remains *The Monk*, for it shares this difficulty of rhetoric, but at the same time deals tersely with crime, transgression, persecution, diabolism, rape, murder. Could it be that with Lewis the problem is the opposite? That his themes are too close to home? New attempts at adapting it for the screen were made by Francisco Lara Polop in 1990 and Dominik Moll in 2011, and perhaps the definitive version will arrive soon.

The Architecture of Gothic Cinema

By Claire Smith

The earliest Gothic spaces appeared in the 12th century in the area around Paris. They were infatuated with height, light and volume, defined by the soaring architecture of Saint-Denis Abbey and Notre Dame de Paris. As Gothic style wandered about Europe in the centuries that followed like the quintessential Gothic hero – from Transylvania to Britain – it took in a range of influences. As late as the 1550s, architects were fusing a detailed study of the natural world with an expressive visual vocabulary and the externalisation of emotion; an attention to form and decoration; detailed window tracery; pointed arches; rib vaults and buttresses; botanical motifs; and elegant, curved figures.

The 19th century Gothic architecture revival – which became one of the most popular styles among the rich of the time – reanimated these motifs through the introduction of spectacle and sensation, injecting contemporary fantasy into ruined remains. The forerunner in Britain was the romantic theatricality of Horace Walpole's Strawberry Hill house in Twickenham (which he purchased in 1747, and spent over £20,000 remodelling before his death in 1797) , and it reached its most visible in the towering grandeur of the Palace of Westminster, designed by Sir Charles Barry in 1835.

With the advent of cinema, art directors were quick to follow suit in resurrecting past tropes and traits, fusing the wonders of revivalism with the expressive elegance of medievalism. These necromancers of Gothic cinema paid homage to the strange exoticism of the past as a place, and the ruinous landscape of the present. But through vigorous reworking, they transmuted architectural elements from the benign into the malign. They borrowed from the stylistic leaps made by German Expressionism, eliding emotion and design, and taking into account every element of the set to present chilling, ominous spaces. Structures were stylised, shadows lengthened, and motifs exaggerated, transforming the past into a place to be feared. Investing formal design elements with a heightened symbolism, cinema's Gothic architecture became a revenant of a past age; an uncompromising reminder of the ravages of time.

Nosferatu (*F.W. Murnau, 1922*)
Murnau chose a Romanesque castle for the setting of his masterpiece, punctuating eastern European ruins with specific Gothic motifs. In this scene, art director Albin Grau creates a pointed arch akin to a coffin, recasting a motif usually associated with the soaring height of cathedrals as one of oppression and containment. The stylised set includes many Expressionist techniques, particularly chiaroscuro to suggest both architectural spaces and states of mind.

Dracula (*Tod Browning, 1931*)
Perhaps the definition of a Gothic cinematic space, *Dracula* was widely emulated. Ruined architecture, heavy drapes, exaggerated cobwebs and plenty of spaces for horrors to hide in (corridors, galleries and staircases), quickly became a shorthand for the domestic abode of terror. Taking the winding, echoing stone staircases described in Bram Stoker's *Dracula*, set designers John Hoffman, Charles D. Hall and Hermann Rosse forewent realism in pursuit of the impossible, imagined spaces of the novel, creating a precarious, skeletal link to the subterranean crypt. Lit from below, the exposed edges created an ominous, jaw-like shadow on the supporting wall.

The Phantom of the Opera (*Rupert Julian, 1925*)
Setting the benchmark for Universal's Gothic aesthetic, Rupert Julian's film brought together art director E.E. Sheeley, assistant art director Sidney Ullman, consulting artist Ben Carré, and technical director A.A. Hall to realise an intricate vision of Paris. The great Opéra de Paris is thought to have followed Charles Garnier's original plans, lending an air of realism to the performative and social spaces of the film. The refuge in the basement offers a descent into fantasy and into the fears of the subconscious. Architectural forms are made strange, and many of the spaces that would become archetypal to the cinematic Gothic – the prison, the tomb, the crypt – stem from this film's reworking of formal Gothic elements. Everything is slightly out of scale, out of kilter, offering plenty of opportunities for distorted and nightmarish shadows. The designers also had to placard several blocks of a typical 19th-century Parisian street with medieval facades. These street fronts set the visual tone for Universal's subsequent series of horror movies.

The Ghoul (*T. Hayes Hunter, 1933*)
Much like Universal's *The Mummy* of the previous year, *The Ghoul* capitalised on the lingering interest in the excavation of Tutankhamun's tomb by Howard Carter in the early 1920s, and the tales of rebirths, reanimation and cursed beings that had woven their way into the cultural imagination. The house takes on an active role, with a foreboding personality that threatens to overshadow its inhabitants. The design is typical of art director Alfred Junge's immaculate style; a fusion of historical, Germanic-inspired references and contemporary visual flourishes, against which cinematographer Günther Krampf could carefully choreograph his dance of light and shadow.

HAUNTED

CHILDREN OF THE NIGHT

BY GUILLERMO DEL TORO

Through the years, I've become convinced that early horror fiction emanated from fairytales and folklore. They share many a narrative characteristic and a flair for the grotesque. Oftentimes the central figure in these tales is that of a child. The early Gothic tales also require an innocent or 'pure' protagonist at their centre in order to function. Sometimes that protagonist is a damsel in distress, sometimes it's a noble young man and sometimes it's a child figure.

Take for example J. Sheridan Le Fanu's *Uncle Silas*; the protagonist, Maud Ruthyn, is a very young girl who threads both characteristics and has to survive a complex and perverse adventure. Often in Gothic tales a pre-pubescent female child will undergo a rite of passage from childhood to puberty by confronting dark portents. A virginal figure goes through a journey that includes the discovery of a new, dark dimension of life. The loss of one or both parents, the journey to a dark edifice and the unveiling of a secret history is common to both fairy tales and Gothic ones. Most of these youthful characters emerge, almost inevitably, into a stage of existential, disappointing adulthood of some kind or other.

A sophisticated exercise in perception like Henry James's *The Turn of the Screw* makes the children figures of great ambiguity: either vessels of terror or victims lost in a vast, dark world. And in James's work, the 'purity' of the damsel is revealed to be as much a hindrance as a sign of virtue.

There's an ongoing debate about whether Henry James was actually endorsing the ghosts in the tale to be real or not. Some people, like Truman Capote, who co-wrote Jack Clayton's masterful 1961 adaptation *The Innocents*, believe that he endorsed the idea, while others, namely the critic Edmund Wilson, in his 1934 essay 'The Ambiguities of Henry James', very definitely believe he did not – that he wanted it to be all a Freudian construction in the head of the governess. The haunting is desire and the haunted edifice is the mind.

Desire and sexuality will always be latent in most fairytales and horror tales – particularly in Victorian examples and, in later years, in M.R. James's ghostly tales. Rather revealingly, James tended to focus his revulsion on slender, wrinkled, wet and hairy dark objects of horror.

M.R. James also uses children or child-like figures in some of his tales – sometimes as victims or witnesses, as in 'The Wailing Well' and 'A School Story' or 'Martin's Close', and sometimes as figures of great unease, as in 'Lost Hearts', one of the many James stories filmed by Lawrence Gordon Clark for the BBC's *Ghost Stories for Christmas* series in the 1970s.

The function of the child as receptor and witness of the supernatural is most definitely bound to the function such a character fulfils in fairytale narratives. The child provides both the avatar and the vicarious gaze for the audience to behold the supernatural. The state of grace of these characters allows the manifestations of the uncanny.

Once again, these are ideas inherited from fairytales, where those who are 'pure of heart' have a propensity to see a world

(Opposite)
Sally Anne Bruce as Pearl, with Robert Mitchum as the Big Bad Wolf, Preacher Harry Powell, in Charles Laughton's 'The Night of the Hunter' (1955).

(Top)
Rachel Cooper (Lillian Gish) is a Mother Goose-like protector of children in 'The Night of the Hunter'.

(Above)
Christopher Davis and Michelle Foster as the ghostly orphans in 'Lost Hearts' (1973).

hidden to all other mortals – a reality that is invisible and inaccessible to adults. This precept is imprinted into the Gothic tale by its heritage; by a lineage that runs directly from fairytale narratives. In both narratives, the child can transit, quite literally, between worlds – can see the two sides of the looking glass.

Children thus become ambassadors of hidden worlds to the adult audience. Notably in the case of Charles Laughton's masterful Southern Gothic film *The Night of the Hunter* (1955), the child figures and the fairytale flavour of the film allow for the atmosphere to become magical while rooted in harsh realism. John and Pearl, the brother and sister who take flight from Robert Mitchum's murderous preacher Harry Powell, could easily have stepped out of a Grimm or a Nordic fairytale, whose tone Laughton very deliberately evokes.

Laughton does just enough tweaking of the atmosphere to take it into a new, fantastic realm; images like Shelley Winters's hair floating in the water, after she has been killed by Mitchum and hidden at the bottom of the river, are absolutely breathtaking and beautiful. Or there's the Mother Goose-like presence of Lillian Gish – guarding the children, shotgun in hand, against the Big Bad Wolf, Robert Mitchum, as he sings the eerie hymn 'Leaning on the Everlasting Arms' while sitting on a stump outside her house in the dark night. It's Gish who utters the defining line "It is a hard world for little things", but also tells us that "the wind blows and the rain it is cold, yet they abide… they abide and they endure".

The end of innocence

The rite of passage in Gothic tales often requires the ambulation into a labyrinth of sorts, either the dark woods or a haunted edifice, or both. Much like adolescence, it is necessary for the child to get lost in order to emerge into the world, fully formed.

In films such as *Lemora: A Child's Tale*

of the Supernatural (1973) or *Valerie and Her Week of Wonders* (1970), as in a Hans Christian Andersen story (for example, 'The Snow Queen'), the elasticity of the girl's age varies depending on the function needed to propel the story, and she can go from childhood to early adolescence in the most pliable ways.

It is, however, very telling that most of these tales spring, more often than not, from the male mind. It is important to note that whenever a female writer has tackled them, these tales typically become intelligent, complex and empowering – as they do in Angela Carter's stories certainly, notably so in 'The Company of Wolves'. In Carter's tale, filmed by Neil Jordan in 1984, there is an acknowledgement of the complexity and the potency of the female psyche, rather than a reduction to a role-playing figure.

Reflecting on these films and books was instrumental for me in making *Pan's Labyrinth* (2006) and *The Devil's Backbone* (2001), because the role of Mitchum, in terms of his functionality, is to represent an absolute: the Man in Black and the corruption of an accepted institution. But the Man in Black is also a figure of great fear in classic fairytales, or the tales of E.T.A. Hoffmann, such as 'The Sandman'. The battle in the Gothic and fairytales is waged over the grey area of spirituality by characters that represent pure black and pure white. This doesn't mean that in more sophisticated retellings you can't contaminate these colours, but effectively their function needs to remain delineatory: black and white, good and evil.

The Devil's Backbone was also an homage to one of the premier purveyors of magic in the horror genre: Mario Bava. Bava elevates everything he touches by producing profoundly affecting 'eye protein', not 'eye candy'. Every decision he makes in terms of colour, saturation, composition or lighting feeds into the story, making the tonal range extend and allowing for the magic elements to

(Above)
Martin Stephens as Miles, and Deborah Kerr as Miss Giddens, in Jack Clayton's 'The Innocents' (1961).

(Below)
Sarah Patterson in 'The Company of Wolves' (1984), adapted from Angela Carter's story. The film acknowledges the complexity of the young female psyche.

(Above)
Mario Bava's 'Kill, Baby… Kill!' (1966) was a key influence on del Toro's own 'The Devil's Backbone' (2001).

(Opposite, left)
Mia Farrow as the grieving mother tormented by the ghost of a child in 'Full Circle' (1977).

(Opposite, top right)
The ghost of the murdered boy appears at the window in 'The Devil's Backbone'.

(Opposite, bottom right)
Ivana Baquero as Ofelia in del Toro's 'Pan's Labyrinth' (2006).

exist on screen. Think for example of *Kill, Baby… Kill!* (1966) – an emblematic film that has influenced the image of the ghost child more than probably any other. But Bava understands that the ghost is a delicate creature, an endangered one in this logical world, so he elevates the visuals in his film to create an image-based 'terrarium' – a habitat that allows the manifestation to exist. In almost all of world literature and cinema you will find a ghost child figure, both because there is an essential need to pervert the function of an innocent figure into a haunting one, and because the association of opposites – youth and death – is so unnerving, so unnatural to us. The more innocent and painful the ghost is, the more unsettling it is.

Bava in *Kill, Baby… Kill!* also smartly crafts a link between the child and the social fabric that surrounds the apparition. The ghost represents some form of collective guilt that is beckoned into haunting the town by the guilt of all its inhabitants. The idea of the ghost as a social representation was very important to me in crafting my own tale in *The Devil's Backbone*.

There is a displacement of horror when you ascribe that function to a figure that is fragile – think of the typical device of the sobbing ghost. Fraught emotions and images of fragility allow us to recognise ourselves in these horrifying figures. They have feelings and emotions and therefore they are intelligent; they exist beyond the illusion, the mirage, the shimmer of a figure. These dead things have a will.

Now and then we find intelligent exercises that exploit the inherent role-playing that comes between and adult and a child. Think of the novel *Julia* by Peter Straub, or Richard Loncraine's excellent film adaptation *Full Circle* (1977) that starred Mia Farrow as the mother grieving the death of her child. The story attributes not only malevolence but *intelligent* malevolence to the ghost of a

child. This is a carefully laid narrative that allows us to get trapped in the web of emotions Julia feels. Straub created one of the most powerful ghost stories ever not only because of his big twist ending but because he creates a sophisticated, emotional fabric in which to display the concept of good and evil in a completely modern way. As the ghostly character is revealed to be malevolent, we witness how impossible it is for Julia to quench her maternal instinct – the hardwired need in her as a mother to embrace and protect. There is a sense of almost magnetic attraction between the victim and the predator in haunted tales; it's rare and beautiful. The same is also true of the house and victim of Shirley Jackson's *The Haunting of Hill House*, in which the house seems determined to possess a character that has an unfathomable need to be possessed, to belong to someone or something.

Equally rooted in our social norms is the idea of the ghost child as a victim of a crime – there is hardly a more heinous crime than the murder of a child. You can examine a tale as typical and beautiful as 'Lost Hearts' by M.R. James, which has a secret murder in the past of the central antagonist, M.R. Abney, a man who seems, to the outside world, befuddled, eccentric and benign. But as Abney reveals himself to be predatory, the story acquires an unsettling resonance and gives it an oblique sense of abuse and perversion.

This notion can link something as thoroughbred as 'Lost Hearts' to something as sophisticated as *The Turn of the Screw*, because the abuse or the child's exposure to an adult compulsion is always more effective when it is oblique rather than frank and exploitative.

The complex social fabric that links us as adults to children is instrumental in our understanding of the world. To see or think of an evil child is out of the realm of our social structure – it shatters our very foundation. The perversion of our firmly held notions of innocence and evil when we are confronted with the 'evil child' figure is the same as happens with any other harmless character or object in horror tales, for example a doll or a clown. Part of the feeling of the uncanny comes from the displacement of the function of evil into something that is essentially inoffensive and benign, and which we welcome in our daily lives.

That is a very interesting aspect of *The Omen* (1976) a story that is dependent on a sort of Gothic trapping: the idea of the ambassador in a foreign country (think of early Gothic novels that all depended on exotic locales in Italy or Spain), and a shameful secret, hidden from plain

(Above)
Harvey Stephens as Damien in 'The Omen' (1976).

(Above, right)
The murderous child Rhoda (Patty McCormack) with her mother Christine (Nancy Kelly) in Mervyn LeRoy's 'The Bad Seed' (1956).

view – in this instance, the death of the ambassador's child. The crime and supplanting of the baby by members of an occult sect is then mixed, with unusual potency, with Judeo-Christian mythology. Lee Remick functions somewhat as the innocent character in the whole disturbing affair. But *The Omen* is not quite a Gothic tale even if there are some of the surface trappings.

To most adults, the notion of duality in childhood is terrifying. Our society seems to equate innocence with ignorance, and the fact that a child can be sophisticated is, by itself, a scary fact. The fact that a child can plan a murder like in Mervyn LeRoy's *The Bad Seed* (1956), or can enact an murderous insurgence like in Narcisco Ibáñez Serrador's *Who Can Kill a Child?* (1976), is almost akin to having supernatural powers like in *The Omen*. The very idea that a child can be the vessel of something foul and malignant like in *The Exorcist* (1973) or *Rosemary's Baby* (1968) produces in all of us a sense of inadequacy and loss. These seemingly different plot devices actually come from the same root – the recognition of something alien to the identity adults normally ascribe to a child, be it intelligence, be it malevolence or possession. The supplanting of one function for another is the essence of all horror – the recognition of something that is there in the eyes of a child but that shouldn't be there. It operates at a very basic level of fear.

There is the occasional story that combines the hardcore fairytale with a hardcore Gothic, like Ray Bradbury's novel *Something Wicked This Way Comes*. Sadly Jack Clayton's original cut of his 1983 adaptation was tampered with by the studio, but even in its tampered form it retains some of the basic flavour of Bradbury's tale. And in Jonathan Pryce we again encounter a new version of the Man in Black – taking over the Robert Mitchum role, as it were.

Something Wicked This Way Comes, Kill, Baby… Kill!, Who Can Kill a Child?, The Devil's Backbone… all involve the collective, and invoke the idea that evil can permeate or be permeated by an entire social group. It's not just one person and one crime; it's almost the corruption of an entire town or a system. Again, if you go back to fairy tales, it is the town that calls the Pied Piper of Hamelin, but it is the children that pay the price.

oizarre, alternate universes, naunted houses and shadowy gardens, family tragedy and ocal legend, misunderstood nonsters and supernatural eenagers... such are the things hat make up the children's Gothic on British television. Children's television has ong been a rich area for the exploration of the fantastic, and one of the few spaces to allow programme makers the formal experimentation needed to represent the ghosts, ghouls and monsters of the Gothic.

Gothic programmes lodge n our memories of childhood viewing, but often as not much more than haunting snapshots: depending on your age, you might recall such moments as the march of the 'Uglie Wuglies' (terrifying scarecrows brought to life) in the BBC's adaptation of E Nesbit's *The Enchanted Castle* (BBC1, 1979), or Tolly (Alec Christie) chanting "Green Noah, demon tree, evil ingers can't catch me!" in *The Children of Green Knowe* (BBC1, 1986), or perhaps the hooded mob of children in *Moondial* (BBC1, 1989), images of Roland (Philip DaCosta) trapped in a bizarre world accessed via the ift shaft in his family's tower block in *King of the Castle* (HTV, 1977), or the groaning of the stones in *Children of the Stones* (HTV, 1977).

There are at least five distinct traditions of children's Gothic television. Firstly, beginning with a cycle of original serial drama produced for ITV in the 1970s, there are dramas set n contemporary locales, but often involving some kind of time travel or other dislocation n space and time. In such dramas, a realist setting and the casting of 'ordinary kids' serves to suggest that fear and terror lurk just around the corner for the young. Many of these programmes were created by a core creative team at HTV, including *The Georgian House* (1976), *The Clifton House Mystery* (1978), *Children of the Stones* and *King of the Castle*, but also *The Owl Service* (Granada, 1969) and *Century Falls* (BBC1, 1993).

Secondly, and relating in particular to a cycle of Gothic costume dramas for children produced by the BBC in the late 1970s and 80s such as *The Secret Garden* (BBC1, 1975), *The Enchanted Castle, The Children of Green Knowe* and *Moondial*, are the literary adaptations in which narratives take place in a distant past, and at heritage locations such as stately homes and ornamental gardens. In both of these cycles, houses and their hidden spaces are central, we see plucky children exploring secret rooms, hidden gardens and parallel buildings in order to solve mysteries or bring hidden injustices to light. These two forms were also brought together in the third cycle of Gothic children's television: the anthology dramas made by Thames television, such as *Shadows* (1975-78) and *Dramarama Spooky* (1983).

Away from drama, a fourth cycle of children's programming is the children's Gothic adventure game show. The first of these, *Knightmare* (Anglia, 1987-94), saw Gothic spaces and characters employed to frame a series of puzzles or physical trials faced by a 'dungeoneer' and a team watching and guiding him or her onscreen, under the direction of the Treguard of Dunshelm (played by Hugo Myatt). Inspired by ZX Spectrum adventure games *Atic Atac* and *Dragontorc*, *Knightmare* placed the child viewer in the middle of a Gothic nightmare. The format was more recently revisited in *Trapped!* (CBBC, 2007-2009) and *Trapped Ever After* (CBBC, 2010), which featured a group of 'Unfortunates' (the child participants) trapped in 'The Tower' and controlled by the evil 'Voice'.

A recent cycle of children's Gothic television has figured the child protagonist as the possessor of supernatural powers – as the 'troubled monster' rather than (or perhaps as well as) an entrapped but courageous victim. In the era of *Twilight* (2008) and *The Vampire Diaries* (CBS, 2009-), we get *Wolfblood* (CBBC, 2012) in which Maddy (Aimee Kelly) struggles to come to terms with her secret other life as a werewolf, and *Young Dracula* (CBBC, 2006-2008), featuring Gerran Howell as Vladimir Dracula, a young vampire who would much rather be normal, much to his family's disgust.

Childhood is an unsettling time of transition, and throughout it the family home should be the key site of security and stability. Given the focus on houses and families in children's Gothic television, the specific fears at play here all point to the separation anxiety of being removed from home and family. At the root of such a fear is a fear of isolation – a growing awareness that the world is full of potentially dangerous strangers. In short, a fear of growing up.

Gillian Hills in 'The Owl Service' (1969)

Russell Hunter in 'Shadows' (1975-78)

Children and the Gothic

By Charlie Higson

It's hard to believe that James Whale's *Frankenstein* was considered almost too frightening for audiences to watch when it was released in 1931, and several scenes, including the sequence where the monster drowns the little girl, were censored. Anyone can buy the DVD on Amazon now, and it's a PG. Tim Burton's *Frankenweenie* (2012) has reimagined the concept as a kids' animation and *Hotel Transylvania* (2012), also aimed squarely at children, cheerfully throws together the great Universal movie monsters and adds more modern fiends like zombies into the mix. We've come a long way since George A. Romero invented the cannibal flesh-eating zombie with *Night of the Living Dead* in 1968. Nobody watching that film on its first release would have dreamt that not much more than 40 years later kids would be happily settling down to watch *ParaNorman* (2012), a full-on zombie apocalypse animation film.

There is no denying that kids have an appetite for horror, and that we are far less sensitive about exposing them to scary movies than we used to be. The *Harry Potter* films are at least as frightening as those produced by Hammer when I was growing up. But why are kids so obsessed with death and gore and horror?

I recently visited my local school where a group of 13-year-olds were reading out some of the stories they'd written for a creative writing course. I was fully expecting the slightly worthy efforts that usually come out of these courses; instead there was an alarming onslaught of violence, nastiness, depravity and murder. As someone who has made a living out of writing children's books full of violence, nastiness, depravity and murder I could hardly complain, but it was still a shock. Afterwards I talked to one of the girls who had read out a particularly horrific story, and she explained to me, with great relish, "What you've got to understand, Mr Higson, is that *kids love death*."

Why is that? And is it anything new? Certainly, since the 1950s, most horror films have been aimed at and enjoyed by teenagers, and horror fiction has always been a useful entry-level genre for youngsters to graduate from children's books to adult ones.

One reason for this is that while teenagers are obsessed with death and violence, they are too young to really understand the consequences. For them it's just gross-out entertainment, and certainly my own appetite for horror films greatly diminished when I had children. Maybe this is why so many teenagers go on killing sprees in American schools. They don't really have any idea of the pain they are bringing into the world (this is also one reason why child soldiers are so sought after in Africa). For the first time in their lives, though, the distraught survivors of these massacres are learning all too quickly what death really means – and they are too young to deal with it. This is why horror films are important for adolescents – they deal, on a fantasy level, with many serious issues that they are starting to become aware of, and may be finding hard to confront. Not only the growing awareness of their own mortality, but also disease, ageing, and the fear we all have of our own bodies – what's inside them, what might come out of them, and how they can go wrong. *Carrie* (1976), with its notorious 'first period' scene, perfectly encapsulates the relationship between teenage anxieties and horror. Perhaps, instead of sex education for teenagers we should just make them watch the early body-horror films of David Cronenberg – *Shivers* (1974), *Rabid* (1977) and *The Brood* (1979), which show both the miseries our bodies can inflict on us, and the joys.

Gore and an obsession with our bodies is only one

strand of horror, though; the other is fear. Many people more learned than me have written papers on why we love to be scared, but the bottom line is: it's a blast. The unique power and attraction of fear can perhaps best be illustrated by another personal anecdote. I once took my boys to one of those 'attractions' where you're chased around some gloomy cellars by actors dressed as zombies. Before they went in they were very blasé. They'd been brought up on a diet of horror films and were laughing at the cheesiness of the whole set up. When they came out at the other end some 20 minutes later, however, it was as if they'd been pumped full of drugs. They were hyperactive, overstimulated and gibbering incessantly. It was the most intense experience they'd ever had. I thought this must be how solders might feel after a fire-fight. *Alive*. They had *survived*. It was *thrilling*, and how often do we get the chance to be properly thrilled? Fear is one of the most powerful of human emotions, and one that we have to learn to recognise, understand and control. The 'safe' scares of a rollercoaster, or a bungee jump, or a horror film, not only give us a massive kick and leave us feeling buzzing and elated (and slightly sick...) but they help to prepare us for dealing with genuine fears in our real lives.

We love to be thrilled/scared from an early age. All parents play that game where you pretend to be a big scary monster and chase your toddlers around the house until they scream themselves sick. Testing yourself all the time – am I going too far? Am I being *too* scary? Should I hold back a bit? Should I try harder? Are they getting bored? Will they wet themselves? Horror filmmakers (and authors) play the same game with their viewers/readers.

Being chased, having nightmares, daring yourself to watch your first scary movie, this is all part of growing up, of entering the adult world. In my day this was a very explicit rite of passage – sneaking into your first X certificate film (later changed to the less glamorous 18 certificate). For me it was Nicolas Roeg's *Don't Look Now* (1973), still my favourite horror film and actually a very grown-up one, not really aimed at teenagers. Most societies have some kind of coming-of-age ritual, and perhaps this is the closest we in the west have to such a concept: are you big enough to watch a *really* scary movie?

We are all of us scared of different things, though, and with children it seems to be things that they can relate to that press their buttons. I was doing a signing session for one of my horror books once when a tiny girl came up to me and when I asked her if she'd ever watched anything really frightening she nodded; I asked her what it was, expecting the usual *Harry Potter* or *Doctor Who*, and she replied "*Saw.*" "Didn't that really freak you out?" I asked. "Yes," she replied. "It's got a really scary clown in it." She hadn't been bothered by all the dismemberments and mutilations, but a man in a clown mask...

Similarly, growing up in a very male household my own boys would happily watch *Jaws* or *Alien* from an early (for 'early', read 'far too young') age, but one of them was so terrified of Mrs Trunchbull, the teacher in *Matilda* (1990), that he couldn't watch it. His brother couldn't watch *Poltergeist* (1982), because it was too real for him. Set, as it is, in a normal family home, and featuring a clown doll. And they had

(Opposite) Daniel Radcliffe as the boy wizard in 'Harry Potter and the Prisoner of Azkaban' (2004).

(Above) Johnny Depp in the title role of 'Edward Scissorhands' (1994).

(Below) The wicked Queen in Disney's 'Snow White and the Seven Dwarfs' (1937).

all three been terrified of Disney's *Snow White and the Seven Dwarfs* (1937), which has two key scary sequences: the transformation of the beautiful queen into the wicked witch (a very stark and powerful portrayal of the ravages of the ageing process), and the scene in the forest where the trees turn into monsters and menace the abandoned girl.

On the whole, though, Disney films tend to belong to the hokey, folksy, cosy, Addams Family, Halloween pumpkin genre of horror films – the spawn of Washington Irving, all moss-strewn branches, creaky old Norman Bates style houses and harmless ghosts and ghouls, typified by the Haunted Mansion ride at Disneyland. It's fun, it's spooky, it has supernatural elements, but it's not actually frightening, and it certainly isn't gory.

The director who has really capitalised on the genre of the Teenage Gothic is Tim Burton. Goth, as a teenage movement, grew out of post punk music in the early 1980s, typified by gloomy, doom-laden music and black clothing, black make-up and long black hair. Basically, black – lots of black, none more black. Probably the first and most influential portrayal of the morbid, black-encased, moody, introspective, misunderstood teenage Goth outsider in cinema was Lydia Deetz, played by Winona Ryder in *Beetlejuice* (1988) and reincarnated as Mavis in *Hotel Transylvania*. Burton went on to become the patron saint of cinematic Goth. Like Disney's Haunted House ride, Burton doesn't set out to scare us – he is presenting Goth as a lifestyle choice. We are on the side of monsters and against the torch-carrying villagers. His sympathies lie with the outsiders: with teenage Goths, vampires, zombies, a boy with scissors for hands – the awkward monsters that teenagers believe themselves to be. It's an accessible Goth aesthetic that he has honed over 30 years, from *Beetlejuice* through *Batman*, *Edward Scissorhands*, *Sleepy Hollow*, *Corpse Bride*, *Sweeney Todd*, *Alice in Wonderland*, *Dark Shadows*, *Frankenweenie*. A string of morbid, black fairytales that won't give anyone nightmares, have made huge amounts of money, and whose influence can be seen in all of the recent animation films I've mentioned, as well as family films like *The Addams Family* (1990) and *Coraline* (2009).

Most families have a proto-Goth of some sort – "Oh, he/she's the weird one, into skulls and vampires and the living dead, I don't know where he/she gets it from" – and for them horror films aren't there to scare, but to reassure.

HAUNTED LANDSCAPES

BY JAMES BELL

The landscapes of the Gothic are many and various, from the romantic Italian scenery in Ann Radcliffe's *The Mysteries of Udolpho* to the looming peaks of the Carpathian mountains which hide Graf Orlok's castle in *Nosferatu* (1922); from the moonlit graveyard of a *Mitteleuropean* village in Hammer's *The Brides of Dracula* (1960) to the urban gloom of Gotham City; from Yorkshire's windswept moors to the fairytale-like Deep South in *The Night of the Hunter* (1955); from the outwardly quaint Summerisle in *The Wicker Man* (1973) to the unfathomable depths of space through which the spaceship Nostromo drifts in *Alien* (1979); from the Norfolk and Suffolk coastlines of an M.R. James story to the small-town America of *Blue Velvet* (1986), where grotesquerie and terror lie just beneath the placid surface...

The specifics of the landscapes may change, but they all share an expressive power to convey the frightening and the repressed. These haunted landscapes are the canvases on which a Gothic story plays out; but they are also places that themselves seem possessed of the very terrors that lie at the heart of the age. The Italian landscapes described in Ann Radcliffe's novels were also the settings chosen by her contemporaries Horace Walpole and Matthew Lewis, reflecting the fears many Britons had at the time of a resurgent Catholicism following the gradual dismantling of anti-Catholic laws and the horrors of the French Revolution.

Geographical accuracy is of little significance to the Gothic; what is important is the landscape's expressive potential. Bram Stoker had never visited the Transylvania he wrote about in *Dracula*; had he done so he would have found fewer foreboding peaks and rather more pastoral fields. But Transylvania then (as now) was an unknown other, a faraway land onto which author and reader alike could project any terrors he or she wished to.

Cinema too has seen little need to depict such landscapes accurately – Black Park near Hammer's Bray Studios, for instance, famously stood in for Transylvanian forests on many occasions. Indeed, the cinema has made a virtue of artificiality in creating its onscreen landscapes. The studio-based creations of the Universal horrors of the 1930s helped to define the archetypal Gothic landscape – a heightened amalgam of an imagined version of a *Mitteleuropean* village, mist-shrouded forests, graveyards dramatically lit by lightning, foggy city streets and gloomy crypts.

The cumbersome cameras and technical limitations of early cinema restricted what landscapes could be seen onscreen, which may be one reason why domestic ghost stories and Edgar Allan Poe were the favoured source texts for the silents. Poe's tales mostly take place in what we might call the landscape of the mind, an interior world that cinema has proven especially adept at depicting.

What is clear is that cinema and television have enabled such haunted landscapes to be visualised as never before, drawing from descriptions found in the original Gothic literature and examples from fine art and expanding on them to create vivid, immersive worlds full of dread and fear.

(Opposite)
The church cemetery in the opening scenes of David Lean's 'Great Expectations' (1946).

Nightmare Worlds *('Vampyr', Carl Dreyer, 1932)*
Dreyer drew from fine art for inspiration when creating *Vampyr*'s uncanny landscape, whose eerie atmosphere has never been equalled – though Herzog's *Nosferatu* (1979) and many of David Lynch's films suggest its influence. It was shot on real locations near Paris; Dreyer's assistant Eliene Tayar recalled that he asked her to find "a factory in ruins, a chopped-up phantom worthy of the imagination of Edgar Allan Poe." Like Poe, in *Vampyr* we are in a landscape of the mind, one with its own logic. We're rarely sure of where we are, the camera floating unmoored around a nightmarish world of dancing shadows and sinister ferrymen.

Blasted Heaths *('Wuthering Heights', Andrea Arnold, 2011)*
"My love for Heathcliff resembles the eternal rocks beneath: a source of little visible delight, but necessary" says Cathy in Emily Brontë's novel. Much has been written about the symbolism of the barren moors in 19th-century Gothic novels like *Wuthering Heights* and *Jane Eyre* – the rugged landscape expressing the raw emotions of the characters – and they have been well-used by filmmakers. William Wyler's 1939 film doesn't quite capture their feel – filmed, as it was, in the San Fernando Valley – and a more authentic use of the real locations was made by Andrea Arnold in her grimly downbeat 2011 adaptation.

Super-productions *('Faust', F.W. Murnau, 1926)*
Murnau's film is an early example of how the growing sophistication of special effects allowed filmmakers to present ever more spectacular and immersive Gothic landscapes. *Faust* was a costly super-production mounted at Babelsburg's Ufa studios, whose art design by Robert Herlth and Walter Röhrig displays the influence of the great German theatre director Max Reinhardt. As he had for *Nosferatu* (1922), Murnau looked to Romantic painters like Caspar David Friedrich for inspiration in creating stunning, atmospheric landscapes like the one above.

New Lands *('Picnic at Hanging Rock', Peter Weir, 1975)*
In her book *Fantastic Metamorphoses, Other Worlds*, Marina Warner writes of the 'Imperial Gothic' – how European interest in the supernatural shifted with a growing interest in the spirit beliefs of colonised peoples. Peter Weir's film (about a group of Australian schoolgirls who disappear on a rock sacred to local Aboriginals) captures the anxious mystery these uncharted landscapes must have held for their settlers – the sense that they harboured ancient ghosts, angered at the newcomers whose towns sat precariously at the edge of the unfathomable interior.

Stylised Naturalism *(Sleepy Hollow', Tim Burton, 1999)*
The exaggerated, unreal landscapes in Tim Burton's 'postmodern Gothic' films are knowing homages to the classic Gothic cinema of the past. The twisted trees and mist-shrouded forests of *Sleepy Hollow* accentuate artificiality, making no attempt to disguise the fact that they are creations designed by production designer Rick Heinrichs, and built on stages at England's Leavesden studios. Heinrichs has described his approach as "stylised naturalism," and his creations evoke the studio-created Gothic landscapes in films by James Whale, Roger Corman, Mario Bava and Terence Fisher.

Expressionism *('The Cabinet of Dr. Caligari', Robert Wiene, 1919)*
In her book *The Haunted Screen*, Lotte Eisner explains that in Weimar-era cinema, more importance was given to art direction than perhaps any other other aspect. Designers Hermann Warm, Walter Röhrig and Walter Reimann immediately recognised the potential *Caligari* held to be told in an Expressionist way, and created the deliberately distorted perspectives, bisecting angles and painted shadows that form the film's landscapes, which at once suggest the twisting back-alleys of a medieval town, express the fractured psyche of Cesare, the somnambulist, and provoke anxiety and terror in the mind of the viewer.

Haunted Shores *('The Uninvited', Lewis Allen, 1944)*
"They call them the haunted shores – these stretches of Devonshire and Cornwall and Ireland which rear up against the westward ocean. Mists gather here, and sea fog, and eerie stories..." Ray Milland's voiceover at the start of Lewis Allen's film captures why coastlines are an evocative landscape for the Gothic, being at the mercy of the forces of nature and with a long history of transitory visitors from distant lands. Seafront towns have also been effectively used in vampire films, such as Ostend in *Daughters of Darkness* (1971), and Hastings in *Byzantium* (2013).

The Ripper's London *('The Lodger', John Brahm, 1944)*
Shrouded in pea-souper fog, and ill-lit by flickering gas lamps, the labyrinthine East End streets of Jack the Ripper's London are immediately suggestive of unseen danger. Hitchcock adapted Marie Belloc Lowndes's novel *The Lodger* in 1927, but the heavy mood of dread was even better captured in John Brahm's 1944 film – despite being shot in a studio the other side of the Atlantic. Victorian London has become an archetypal landscape in Gothic cinema, used in films from David Lynch's *The Elephant Man* (1980) to Italian Riccardo Freda's *The Horrible Dr. Hichcock* (1962).

Urban Gothic *('The Crow', Alex Proyas, 1994, above)*
Cityscapes were central to such noirs as *The Seventh Victim* (1943), and found new expression from the 1980s in graphic novels by Alan Moore and Frank Miller. *The Crow* borrows such stylings to portray a city of eternal night, blighted by crime and drenched in rain and neon. A similarly hellish vision marks David Fincher's *Se7en* (1995) and the Gotham City of Christopher Nolan's *The Dark Knight* trilogy, while China Miéville has also explored the Gothic potential of the urban environment in his novels.

Ghost Towns *('28 Days Later...', Danny Boyle, 2002, below)*
The depopulated London in Danny Boyle's film updates the barren landscape, turning the modern metropolis into a ghost town. It prompts us to imagine the post-human fate of cities, and finds real-life echoes in photographs of failing cities such as Detroit. The sequel, *28 Weeks Later* (2007), makes use of the London Underground, an evocative setting also used in *Quatermass and the Pit* (1967), *Death Line* (1972), *Creep* (2004) and, in a memorable scene, *An American Werewolf in London* (1981).

Southern Gothic

By Michael Atkinson

Rarely if ever has a regional genre of fiction basked in the heat of its own seediness as wantonly as Southern Gothic. It's a subgenre contingent on exploiting an entire subculture's historical penchant for vice and self-destruction, and as such it's always exuded as much bad-boy allure as cheesy perversity. Perpetually on the edge of melodramatic pulp, even when coming armed with Nobels and Pulitzers, Southern Gothic has danced on the South's graves because it's fun to do so, not due to any high sense of moral purpose; it's a lowdown paradigm fixated on sin and scandal. Leave it to the Deep South to give rise to a truly modern brand of Gothic – supernaturalia and mythology being hardly necessary when you have the hothouse reality of the American subtropics.

In literary terms, Southern Gothic was more or less popularly defined between the wars and into the middle century through the writing of Flannery O'Connor, Eudora Welty, William Faulkner, Carson McCullers, Doris Betts, Tennessee Williams, Katherine Anne Porter, and many other, lesser lights, and the form's ingredients were both simple and seductive: sexual violence and dysfunction, deranged religious repression, the dry rot of faux aristocracy, festering family secrets, bastardhood, incest, lynch-ready racial tension, and all-American self-reliant gun lust, all of it brewed and fermented in a humid landscape exponentially less lawful, educated and civilised than the rest of the nation. How truthful the portrait has been remains an open question.

Clearly, the legacy of the South's 19th and early 20th centuries was fertile territory for writers, thanks to the lingering moral horror of slavery and the generations of vainglorious affluence it produced. Since, in a social sphere where the American Civil War is *still* remembered bitterly as an unjust decimation of a romantic way of life, the South has stood as an underdeveloped battleground between soul-killing poverty and old money so old the coins are worn smooth.

Hollywood took its time to read the soiled bedsheets – at first, the South got swathed in the reactionary sanctimony of D.W. Griffith. But soon Southern Gothic was discovered, perhaps first in the pages of Faulkner – *The Story of Temple Drake* (1933), adapted from *Sanctuary*, was radically sanitised but still racy enough to help precipitate the Hays Code, and therein put an end to the 'pre-Code' era of licentious cinema. Censorship or not, Southern Gothic as a subgenre was destined to be an irresistible showbiz gambit, filthy with illicit sex, violence, picturesque decaying mansions, heavy mystery plotting, outrageous accents and characters so broadly drawn any actor worth his salt can embarrass himself enough in five minutes to last an entire career. Lillian Hellman's filmed plays *The Little Foxes* (1941) and *Another Part of the Forest* (1948) stepped into the muck early, as did Jean Renoir, rather earnestly, with *Swamp Water* (1941), and Frank Borzage with *Moonrise* (1948). Charles Laughton's ur-Gothic one-off masterpiece*The Night of the Hunter* (1955) had little impact to speak of on its first release. But it was the theatrical corpus of Tennessee Williams that supplied an ongoing and seminal wellspring to the movies, from the 1950 version of *The Glass Menagerie* onward, essentially defining the subgenre's tone of sweaty anxiety and drawling psychopathy. Thanks to him, Southern Gothic became in the postwar era a bonafide industry formula, often adapted from sordid bestsellers but just as often spawned as original exploitation: *Bayou* (a.k.a. *Poor White Trash*) (1957), *God's Little Acre* (1958), *The Long, Hot Summer* (1958), *The Sound and the Fury* (1959), *Suddenly, Last Summer* (1959), *Sanctuary* (1961), *All Fall Down* (1962), *Cape Fear* (1962), *Toys in the Attic* (1963), Herschell G. Lewis's gorefest *2000 Maniacs* (1964), *Hush… Hush, Sweet Charlotte* (1964), Otto Preminger's lavishly silly *Hurry Sundown* (1967), *Reflections in a Golden Eye* (1967), *The Heart Is a Lonely Hunter* (1968), and so on.

Quickly, though, and probably due to both Williams's ubiquity and the Nixon/'Nam era's new sexual frankness, Southern Gothic became by the 1970s rather quaint, and a familiar template for camp and psychotronic excess. Serious purveyors of the genre, even if they were dipping into the spacious Williams oeuvre, found themselves lost in an antique world. Everyone else winked. Once you get to the maniacal bad taste of Richard Fleischer's *Mandingo* (1975), Southern Gothic became what it had always wanted to be, even in Faulkner's hands: an ironic debauch, a safely lurid place to wallow in clichés of decadence, sadism and the generic bad behaviour that makes pulp stories cook. Ensuing usages of the terrain have ranged from pretentious (Alan Parker's *Angel Heart*, 1987) to cosy-cute (1991's *Fried Green Tomatoes at the Whistle Stop Café* became a hit by being all Southern-fried chick lit, but mixed in murder and cannibalism).

Despite the quick passage into kitsch, Southern Gothic persists as a viable treasure chest. The New Wave era offered standout variants like Don Siegel's *The Beguiled* (1971) and John Huston's magisterial adaptation of O'Connor, *Wise Blood* (1979), just as more recently we've seen the landscape explored anew, with a withering focus on genuine poverty, in David Gordon Green's *George Washington* (2000) and *Undertow* (2004), Lance Hammer's *Ballast* (2008), and Debra Granik's *Winter's Bone* (2010), the Ozarks setting of which merely demonstrates how well the Southern Gothic dynamic can travel in America. Quentin Tarantino's *Django Unchained* (2012), with its psychosis-oozing Candyland plantation, may have returned to the old-fashioned tropes and pushed them into pure self-parody, but today's Southern Gothic is a matter of grim New World Order backwoods realism, and no less Gothic for that.

Kirk Douglas and Jane Wyman in 'The Glass Menagerie (1950)

British Folk Gothic

By Rob Young

During World War II, when city dwellers were imperilled by the threat of aerial bombing, newsreel footage of the English countryside acted as a balm to the nation. In propaganda films of the age, and most famously in the documentaries of Humphrey Jennings such as *A Diary for Timothy* (1945), Home Counties fields, leafy lanes and rambling inns offered an image of something worth fighting to preserve. In Powell and Pressburger's *A Canterbury Tale* (1944), montage techniques cast the spell of time travel into the mix: a hawk turns into a Hurricane; knights transform into modern-day soldiers. The Kentish fields were haunted by the spirits of Chaucerian pilgrims, and were symbolic of an utter, timeless sense of peace. Another film from the same year, Basil Dearden's *The Halfway House*, featured a Welsh inn as a timeslip portal. Each of these suggested that in the remote, unwatched corners of the landscape, strange and secret forces were quietly preserved.

Colour brought something extra to the notion of the English pastoral. Hammer's 1959 version of *The Hound of the Baskervilles*, directed by Terence Fisher, was largely studio bound, but the bleakness of Dartmoor and the ivy-strangled dilapidation of the abbey were conveyed in misty, faded tones that felt authentically English. Fisher's colour palette helped to define a modern cinematic notion of the British Gothic. Directed by John Gilling, Hammer's *The Plague of the Zombies* (1966) is one of the studio's finest movies and one directly tied to the condition of England, with its undead tin-mine labourers a hideous inverse of the kind of cheerful labourer seen in industrial films such as those produced by the National Coal Board. *The Plague of the Zombies* also followed 1963's Tony Richardson smash *Tom Jones* by including vivid, rumbustious footage of a fox hunt, this time with a human, female quarry. In this it echoed another Powell and Pressburger creation, 1950's *Gone to Earth*, probably the duo's finest evocation of a rural England, caught part-way between Merrie and maudlin. Roger Corman's *Tomb of Ligeia* (1964) and Terence Fisher's *The Devil Rides Out* (1968) also abandoned the lavish interiors of their earlier films, and took place instead among muddy trackways and sombre woodlands, ruined abbeys and looming country mansions. Period and historical films had mostly been either black and white extensions of the theatre stage, or rendered in oversaturated Ladybird-book hues. But in colour, the hazy, damp light and earthy palette of the English countryside began to give British Gothic films their own distinct visual signature.

These scattered examples fed into the brief flowering of the micro-genre known as 'folk horror'. It only really boils down to a small handful of pictures made in the late 1960s and early 1970s, beginning with Michael Reeves's *Witchfinder General* (1968), continuing via Piers Haggard's *Blood on Satan's Claw* (1970) and culminating in *The Wicker Man* (1973). These are films which departed from the generic horror tropes of the previous two decades, filmed in outdoor locations under natural light, and steeped in real or imagined superstitions, pagan rituals and forms of communal hysteria. Cults –sexually liberal, renegade alternative communes – are often pitted against the forces of authority, reflecting an age of growing mistrust about the developing countercultural youthquake of hippiedom and pop culture.

Witchfinder General is notable for its choice of locations – centred on the medieval village of Lavenham in Suffolk, where real witch hangings of the sort depicted in the film took place three centuries earlier. Here the East Anglian light and 'big sky' play a central part in setting the atmosphere, and its recreation of period flavour could shortly be seen in costume dramas such as *Alfred the Great* (1969) and *Cromwell* (1970). In keeping with its earthy realism, there is no actual magic depicted in *Witchfinder General* – it deals with the effects of fear and paranoia on a small rural community, and the disruption caused by the Matthew Hopkins character (played chillingly cruel and straight by Vincent Price).

Blood on Satan's Claw begins with a tranquil agrarian scene – a ploughman tilling the Buckinghamshire soil. We are again deep within 17th-century England. Like *Quatermass and the Pit* and many other British horror and sci-fi movies, it turns on something being dug up or dislodged from its resting place – a piece of the past literally resurfacing after a lengthy interment, to cause havoc in the present day. Here it's a revolting skull which the ploughman's blade upturns, with one undecomposed eye and still half-covered with flesh and fur. This demonic survival, the rest of the film implies, is responsible for the surge of erotic cults and human sacrifice that is sweeping the tranquil village. Haggard's cinematographer Dick Bush emphasised the community's ties to the earth by placing the camera very low in many shots, occasionally even in a hole so that the lens tip barely protruded out of the soil.

Bush's previous credits included Peter Watkins's *Culloden* (1964), and Jonathan Miller's eerie BBC films *Alice In Wonderland* (1966) and *Whistle And I'll Come To You* (1968). The latter, the first of a series of M.R. James ghost stories that have become the epitome of uncanny television, also hinges on an unwholesome relic being pulled out of the ground – this time, an ancient bone flute from a Templar burial site on the Suffolk coast. Here and in *A Warning to the Curious* (Lawrence Gordon Clark, 1972), the East Anglian coastline is bleak and forlorn, a vast blank canvas for the projections and hauntings of its mentally snowblind protagonists.

Over the opening credits of *The Wicker Man*, Sgt Howie flies his seaplane over ghastly jagged mountainous islands, more like something in Borneo than Scotland. Emphasising his remoteness from the security of the mainland, these fabulous peaks recall the perilous journeys of fairytale heroes. Summerisle itself, though composed from dozens of different locations around Scotland, is a consummately conceived alternative world – a testbed British fiefdom repatriated to paganism. The strangeness of its mise-en-scène is partly due to being filmed in autumn while set in spring, so there is a curious disconnect between the bright spring light we expect, and the faded sunset glow. The scene looks colder than it's supposed to be, which adds to the general sense of chill and unease as the events unfold and Howie is drawn into a web of deceit among the islanders.

'Folk horror' trickled rapidly down into television, and proved itself especially sympathetic to children's programming. In a seam that runs roughly from *The Owl Service* (ITV, 1969) to *Children of the Stones* (HTV, 1977), astro-archaeology and megalithic sites exerted forces on communities or individuals stranded in remote, cut-off locations. These were eerie and disturbing fictions in which modern-day children encountered atavistic forces and buried racial memories. The backdrop to *The Owl Service* was the colossal mountain of Cader Idris, locally known as King Arthur's Seat. *Children of the Stones* made use of the stone circle at Avebury in Wiltshire, a rough-hewn henge whose stones were filmed in handheld close-up, imbuing them with a disturbing sentience (intensified by Sidney Sager's chilling, dissonant choral music). Shot during the long summer drought of 1976, the land has a parched, desolate quality appropriate to the way the autonomous life of the villagers is being sucked out by the local landowner.

At the same time, adult television drama was exhibiting many similar traits, where the isolation from the city, and from means of communication, feed into the tension and narrative drive. The BBC *Play for Today* series threw up a good few of these, including *Robin Redbreast* (1969), in which an urbane single woman leaves London and unwittingly becomes a breeder for a sacrificial cult operating in a rural hamlet. *Murrain* (1975), Nigel Kneale's contribution to ATV's *Against the Crowd* series, uncovers a suspected witch being persecuted in a distant farming community, while in *Baby* (1976), an episode from Kneale's *Beasts* anthology, the land itself exerts a cursed, barren effect upon those who live in it. All three programmes take place around damp, crumbling cottages in relentlessly grey weather, and use sound especially effectively – *Baby* in particular derives much of its claustrophobic horror through the repetitive tape loops of cawing crows and mysterious shuffling noises from adjacent rooms.

The British Gothic landscape was less prevalent during the 1980s and 90s: the Merchant Ivory films, Granada's 1981 *Brideshead Revisited* adaptation, and the mass of popular Austen/Brontë/Dickens costume dramas depicted the countryside in more tasteful, picturesque terms, without a hint of magic. More recently, though, a renewed appreciation of the 'hauntological' properties of the earlier films has stirred up memories which can been felt in Patrick Keiller's psychogeographical surveys, Andrew Kötting's *This Filthy Earth* (2001), the films of Ben Wheatley (*Kill List*, *Sightseers* and *A Field in England*), or Mark Gatiss's homage to the BBC Ghost Stories, *Crooked House* (2008). Though very different stylistically, all these take place in British Gothic territory: a landscape encrusted with mysteries and dark secrets.

(Opposite)
The unforgettable finale of 'The Wicker Man' (1973).

(Below)
Jo Gilkes (Jane Wymark) with her horrifying discovery in Nigel Kneale's 'Baby' (1976).

PART IV
LOVE IS A DEVIL

LOVE IS A DEVIL

PRINCES OF DARKNESS

BY DAVID PIRIE

"Who could resist his power? His tongue had dangers and toils to recount — could speak of himself as of an individual having no sympathy with any being on the crowded earth, save with her to whom he addressed himself."
***The Vampyre*, John Polidori, 1819**

The first I ever heard of the major Gothic themes was when I was four and my mother described the stories of *Frankenstein* and *Dracula*. I can still remember the sheer impact of that moment. The Gothic strain in literature and film was always grounded in its villains, and these twin myths must be among the most potent that we have, comprising the two opposite poles of the horror monster: Mary Shelley's tormented freakish victim – sympathetic despite monstrous acts – and, in stark contrast, Bram Stoker's hypnotic and charming Prince of Darkness figure, often (though not always) supernatural and driven by a will to do diabolical evil.

The Prince of Darkness has often been identified with vampirism or cannibalism but, in its essential form, the character personifies the power of evil and fear, and may be neither cannibal nor vampire nor male. In any of its many incarnations (which might include Dracula, Hannibal Lecter, Fu Manchu, Colonel Kurtz, Freddy Krueger – or female equivalents like the fictionalised Countess Báthory or the evil queen in Disney's version of *Snow White*) the character begs the whole question of evil itself: what is it? Does it truly exist?

Most of us can easily find models for Shelley's tormented outsider. We have all seen someone bullied. We may well have been bullied ourselves. A fierce but wounded animal offers the same traits. But the creator of a Prince of Darkness has no such security. None of us has ever met one. It is a philosophical and religious question whether they exist at all.

Even mass murderers tend to be disappointing as fictional models, too often exhibiting what Hannah Arendt famously called "the banality of evil". "The sad truth," she wrote in her 1978 book *The Life of the Mind*, "is that most evil is done by people who never make up their minds to be good or evil."

This conclusion is enormously challenging to the creator of a Prince of Darkness. If the worst mass murderers in history pale into feebleness beside their actions, then where is any possible model for a character like Dracula, whom Stoker explicitly wanted to personify evil? He needs to be recognisably human and yet embody something beyond human as well. He needs to intrigue and charm while he also repels.

No surprise then that when Bram Stoker achieved his creation he seems to have had little interest in the murderers of his day. One exception might be Jack the Ripper, but even here we are essentially dealing with a phantom, for the Ripper's legendary status arose from the mystery surrounding him as much as the crimes. If the Ripper had been identified, the uncanny aura of his murders would surely have vanished.

It seems then that the Princes of Darkness cannot emerge directly from life – they were (and still are) a fusion

(Previous page)
Anton Walbrook as the scheming husband in Thorold Dickinson's 'Gaslight' (1940)

(Opposite)
"Good evening, Clarice." Anthony Hopkins as Hannibal Lecter in 'The Silence of the Lambs' (1991).

of dream, desire and dread, of myth and urban legend, an amalgam of the supernatural, the forbidden and the real.

Inevitably, the first inspiration for any character designed to represent ultimate evil was (as Stoker admitted) the Christian devil Satan and his associated demonology. The evil witch-queen too seems rooted in a notion of witches serving and communing with demons or the devil. Satanic associations are easy to find in the villains and 'fatal men' of Gothic literature, burning or blazing eyes being a common one.

But Satan is hardly an easy character to portray and can very quickly become comical, the stuff of nursery rhymes and dressing up (a danger just as likely to befall Dracula). And so writers looked to real historical figures who appeared to embody some of his attributes. Easily the most important of these would prove to be Lord Byron.

By the early 19th century Byron had become the tabloid-style sensation of the literary world, provoking scandal and adulation in equal measure. Women were said to faint at his feet. Grossly exaggerated accounts of his activities circulated widely, in themselves building on horrific tales of other predatory aristocrats of the past like Gilles de Rais, who was tried for the mass slaughter of children in the 15th century. In 1816 Byron's mistress Lady Caroline Lamb published *Glenarvon*, a novel in which Byron is portrayed as the fatal nobleman Ruthven Glenarvon, who preyed on his mistresses and is finally claimed by the devil. This was a useful start, but the crucial text is John Polidori's *The Vampyre*.

In 1816 John Polidori, a young and somewhat naïve physician educated in Edinburgh, had been taken up, like some literary groupie, by the famous and fêted Byron. The young doctor travelled with the poet almost as a superior kind of servant; he was more than once publicly humiliated by Byron and in the end was brutally dropped. But Polidori was present at the all-important gathering with the Shelleys at the Villa Diodati on Lake Geneva in 1816.

Perhaps because he had been cruelly treated, Polidori got his own back writing a novella that he prefaced with all sorts of disclaimers, but which was in its own way a kiss-and-tell. *The Vampyre* is a fantasy autobiography in which a young man called Aubrey (obviously Polidori himself) is taken up by the fascinating nobleman Lord Ruthven (Byron). Ruthven has a "dead grey eye" that fascinates but also can sparkle "with more fire than that of the cat whilst dallying with the half-dead mouse". Aubrey gradually begins to realise that Ruthven is a wicked demon who spreads evil as far as he can, giving money to beggars who follow vice and depriving those who might do good. The nobleman, in fact, has a determination that any woman (or man) with virtue should be tempted and degraded into self-destruction. By the end of the story Ruthven is revealed to be a vampire, so forging the crucial connection that formed the fictional Prince of Darkness: a link between the devil and a real living human, Byron.

For a time it was assumed that Byron had written the book himself as a kind of confession. This enabled its readers to suspend disbelief and indulge in all their fantasies that the notorious rake and reputed atheist Lord Byron was a living human devil. Within its short pages is the paradigm for so much that came later: the sweet, unassuming hero taken up by the charismatic, sexually omnivorous nobleman; the hero's dawning realisation that he alone knows Ruthven's true nature; the desperate attempt to stem the tide of evil.

Dracula followed some 80 years after *The Vampyre*. Stoker took Polidori's story much further, adding real suspense, making the sexuality live on the page and underpinning it with a fabulously constructed pre-science fiction fable in which the whole of the repressed Victorian world would be invaded by an alien demon. Polidori was the catalyst; Stoker provided the masterpiece. The stage was set for the onscreen Prince of Darkness with the coming of cinema at the dawn of the 20th century.

In film the Prince of Darkness would offer great opportunities but also terrible pitfalls. To make such a character real and frightening on screen, as opposed to just a manifestation of menace, is extraordinarily challenging. To go further and make a Prince of Darkness truly convincing and even recognisable – despite all the alien qualities involved – so that an actor can play it and understand the motivation is, I would argue, an epic achievement. So epic that the best examples are rare, as opposed to the camp waxworks that all too easily stand in for it.

For the Prince's attributes of power and sexuality may be appealing but how quickly, when pushed to a limit (especially a supernatural limit), they become monotonous, incredible, one-dimensional and dull. Where is the light and shade, the subtlety, the affecting detail?

Many have assumed that the answer lies in giving the Prince a heart. In some strains of the Gothic, this can work wonders. Heathcliff in *Wuthering Heights* partakes of the Byronic, and has aspects of the damned and the demonic lover, but finally (though he may frighten occasionally) he is not a symbol of fear but a psychological study of emotional deprivation, grand passion and revenge. Heathcliff is the true precursor of the teen-rebel heroes of the 1950s (as played by James Dean and Marlon Brando) who are too sympathetic to be Princes. The same is true of Edward Cullen in the *Twilight* books and films: for all his vampire associations Edward is the offspring of Heathcliff not Dracula.

Even so, many attempts have been made to humanise Dracula in this way and they have usually failed. Stoker offered a hint of a lost love but the hint was enough: a lovelorn Dracula quickly loses all menace. Instead, and much more effectively, Stoker stressed the character's duality: his charm, his courtesy and his grasp of Victorian mores are matched by his animal cruelty. He can move from the study of Victorian railway timetables to descending his castle wall for prey, crawling face down.

The best cinematic examples of the character will employ this duality and also move the plot with real rapidity. If you hesitate, allowing too much introspection on the one hand or too much theatricality on the other, the Prince of Darkness quickly crumples into the pantomime villain, which is its lowest form.

F.W. Murnau's *Nosferatu* (1922) used some of the novel's plot but Universal's 1931 *Dracula* is the first fully-fledged adaptation of Stoker's novel, and the first popular Prince of Darkness movie. The film would break new ground and enter history but it also sacrificed all the subtleties Stoker had sweated to instil into his creation. Lugosi's Dracula announces his glowering brutishness

(Above)
Robert Pattinson as Edward Cullen, a modern-day Heathcliff in 'The Twilight Saga Breaking Dawn Part 1' (2011).

(Opposite)
Christopher Lee in 'Dracula Prince of Darkness' (1965). Lee's portrayal returned the Count to the seductive figure described by Bram Stoker.

(Below)
Lord Byron, as painted by Richard Westall. Byron was the tabloid sensation of the 19th century, and the enduring model for many a Prince of Darkness.

from the first time he opens his mouth. He is distinctive yet utterly one-dimensional. The sexual element is heavy-handed and superficial. Unlike Karloff, who had all the range of a modern actor, Lugosi was frozen in a striking bravura posture, the living tableau of a silent stage actor trapped in modern sound movies. The film was a huge success but, though some disagree with me, I continue to argue that as an influence on the emergent horror film – struggling for freedom from stage melodrama – this performance was not merely bad but a setback.

Lugosi's portrayal ensured that the least interesting aspect of the character – grotesque, ghoulish, foreign – would be how it was portrayed and perceived for decades, until in 1958 Christopher Lee and Hammer (specifically director Terence Fisher and producer Anthony Hinds) returned the Count to something much closer to what Stoker had intended: sexy, charismatic, savage yet anglophile. Hammer had to fight a lengthy and knife-edge battle with the UK censor to do this, especially over one scene where the Count approaches Mina in an explicitly sexual way. As the correspondence shows, Hinds ducked and weaved with the BBFC's John Trevelyan while his examiners seethed in the background, aching to ban the film outright. "Uncouth, uneducated, disgusting and vulgar," wrote Hammer's implacable opponent, examiner Audrey Field.

Hinds pleaded he had misunderstood their instruction, that he would face crippling costs and Trevelyan eventually gave in, though, he wrote scoldingly, "we consider… the sex element is still too prevalent".

But the game was won and the result was a breakthrough. Much of the sexuality was returned to the character and the Prince would now have a new lease of life, with Christopher Lee proving one of the great screen actors in such roles. He would be a Prince again as Dr Fu Manchu in *The Face of Fu Manchu* (1965), which, like the Sax Rohmer books on which it was based, employed a hotchpotch of mystical (and marginally racist) ideas and props to create an effectively oriental Prince of Darkness.

Stevenson's Mr Hyde, the evil alter ego of Jekyll, emerged, like Stoker's Dracula, partly from a writer's nightmare. But we will never know Stevenson's original Hyde since the initial manuscript was burned by his horrified wife and the version of the novel we have is effectively censored by its own author. In film, Hyde is usually too brutish to qualify as a Prince but there are exceptions and *The Two Faces of Dr Jekyll* (1960) is perhaps the most vivid. Paul Massie's bearded scientist is transformed into the demonic and dapper Jekyll, who – like Polidori's Ruthven more than Stoker's Count – revels only in diabolical evil and cruelty.

By the 1960s it was becoming easier for filmmakers to portray the character in more varied guises. For example, Roman Castevet – beautifully played by Sidney Blackmer in Roman Polanski's *Rosemary's Baby* (1968) – is the head of a Manhattan Satanic coven, and makes, on any showing, a chillingly impressive urban Prince. Castevet is committedly cruel, very mysterious and conveys an insidiously false kindness. In one scene, he even harks back to Charles Maturin's classic 1820 Gothic novel *Melmoth the Wanderer* when he seems to hint that he has travelled to every city in the world, including (in answer to a challenge) Fairbanks, Alaska.

The Prince of Darkness is usually a handsome, formidable figure but it is not essential. Freddy Krueger in *A Nightmare on Elm Street* (1984) has the appearance of an ogre, but his energy, demonic cruelty and humour, as well as his supernatural aspiration ("I am God"), entitles him to be a member of this club.

Even so we had to wait a long time for a real successor to Dracula and it finally came with Hannibal Lecter, who combines a professional intelligence and charm with pure savagery, and a fiendish delight in the consequences of his own evil. Brilliantly and painstakingly created in the books by Thomas Harris (and later incarnated to perfection by Anthony Hopkins in *The Silence of the Lambs*, 1991), here was a cultural breakthrough not unlike Stoker's.

Harris and the writers and directors who have adapted his creation for the screen saw that to make a monster as large as this convincing, and vividly celebrate this cultivated man's savagery, they had to orchestrate their props with infinite care. Hannibal's signature became a hideous restraining mask

(Top)
The worldly Roman Castevet (Sidney Blackmer, centre) in Roman Polanski's 'Rosemary's Baby' (1968).

(Above)
Freddy Krueger (Robert Englund) in 'A Nightmare on Elm Street' (1984) has the appearance of an ogre, but the cruelty and humour of a Prince of Darkness.

(Opposite)
Heath Ledger's Joker in 'The Dark Knight' (2008) is a new Prince of Darkness for our times.

to stop his bite, and many other kinds of restraint, each one reinforcing our impression of his power. These medieval bonds are brilliantly counterpointed by his civilised wit.

There is no question that Stoker's Dracula inspired Harris. Many people have tried a modern Dracula with little success, leaving the Count merely a stranded anachronism; Harris's genius cracked the equation. In addition to so much else he imagined a kind of modern, non-supernatural sequel to *Dracula* where the Count is not staked but caged.

Hannibal stands out clearly from the hundreds of serial-killer villains who populate books, films and TV programmes, illustrating just how hard it is to create an original version of the Prince. Intriguingly, about the same length of around 80 years separates the first appearance of Hannibal from *Dracula* as separated *Dracula* from *The Vampyre*. Can we then expect another breakthrough circa 2060? If so, it will surely depend on the anxieties of the time: *Dracula* reflected Victorian sexual repression; Hannibal has many similarities yet also seems to represent a late 20th-century fear of rampant individualism, a figure outside society who can devour it. Serial killers may admire him but they too are outsiders – Hannibal has no wish to start a clan or 'family' like Dracula did.

Another more recent Prince suggests a further theme; the Joker (Heath Ledger) in Christopher Nolan's *The Dark Knight* (2008) adds a fear of terrorism into the mix. In the Batman comics and earlier films, the Joker was a criminal with a penchant for funny clothes and practical jokes, but in *The Dark Knight* he becomes a scarred, anarchist enigma, intent only on destruction and chaos. It is true that he offers macabre details about his origin and his scars, but they are entirely contradictory so certainly to a degree fabricated. When temporarily incarcerated he is without fingerprints, the police find no match for his DNA,

(Above)
As played by David Morrissey, the one-eyed Governor in 'The Walking Dead' is a complex new Prince of Darkness figure.

his clothes are without labels, and there are only lint and knives in his pockets.

In this way Ledger's Joker seems partly to be based on the John Doe character so memorably played by Kevin Spacey in David Fincher's *Se7en* (1995), who was equally anonymous. But Spacey's character was more clearly an obsessive with an Old Testament agenda; the Joker, as he says repeatedly, has no rules and wants only to see things burn. "I am," he says, "an agent of chaos… the thing about chaos is it's fair."

The statement is purposefully contradictory (how could chaos be fair?) but the Joker is a mass of contradictions that tap directly into our own fears – our incomprehension of people who would blow up things just to kill other people. The Joker may lack subtlety, but he clearly exploits even more contemporary anxieties than Hannibal.

Another possibly more complex Prince of Darkness has recently appeared in the TV series *The Walking Dead*, developed by Frank Darabont. Based on the comic books by Robert Kirkman and Charlie Adlard, *The Walking Dead* puts an epic spin on the zombie genre, adding themes that have never before been explored. In 2012 the show introduced a complex new character called The Governor, who runs a small community, offering protection from the zombies. The Governor is enigmatic but his roots would seem to lie in the almost forgotten horror villain General Zaroff, a big-game hunter who grew bored and decided to hunt human prey. Zaroff's first appearance was in Richard Connell's 1924 short story 'The Most Dangerous Game', followed by the film *The Hounds of Zaroff* in 1932.

The original Zaroff had some of the hallmarks of a Prince of Darkness, but did not quite qualify. He was finally just a bored Russian aesthete with sadistic tendencies. But the one-eyed Governor (brilliantly played by David Morrissey) takes the character to another level. Superficially caring and clever, he is initially revered by his community but secretly keeps the heads of living zombies on his wall, rejoicing in their eternal suffering. Also – unlike Zaroff, who had a strong moral code – the Governor pretends to a morality he clearly despises, and privately delights in torture and murder, revelling in slaughter for its own sake and lying repeatedly to all those who trust him.

The Governor also manages to dupe people with his sexual charm and apparent kindness. It would seem finally that the Governor is driven by a purely demonic intent to make those around him suffer, and to betray and deceive to a degree that recalls nobody so much as Polidori's Ruthven. Yet his mysterious charm and occasional mood changes continue to beguile and tantalise. The Governor may be a minor Prince figure compared to a Hannibal Lecter or a Dracula, but he is a fascinating creation nonetheless; and he cements my view that, though these characters are agonisingly hard to bring to life, the fictional Prince of Darkness continues to have a unique place in testing our understanding of what it means to be human.

The Gothic Slasher

By Nick Pinkerton

The casualties steadily mount as a psychopath whittles down the cast one by one, leaving only a lone survivor, almost always female, to stagger away dazed and speckled in arterial spray.

The tropes that define the slasher (or 'bodycount') movie aren't hard to define, but the question of the subgenre's ancestry is not so easy. The usual tack is to begin the story with one of the watershed hits — say *The Texas Chain Saw Massacre* (1974) or *Halloween* (1978). Even when histories of the slasher cast back further, they don't usually go beyond a malevolent pair of films released within a few months of one another in 1960: Michael Powell's *Peeping Tom* and Alfred Hitchcock's *Psycho*. From these sprang innumerable imitators, beginning with cash-in tagalongs like William Castle's *Homicidal* (1961) or Francis Ford Coppola's *Dementia 13* (1963) and leading to the boom period lasting, roughly, from the late 1970s to the mid-80s, the era of *My Bloody Valentine* and *Maniac* and *Prom Night* and a dozen movies whose titles warned us *Don't...* do this and that — films that, in the main, borrowed their famous predecessors' familiar, contemporary settings, as well as their unstoppable, maniacal killing machines.

It should firstly be remembered that the slasher is not the exclusive property of the English-speaking world—there are the Italian *gialli*, including seminal titles like Mario Bava's *Blood and Black Lace* (1964) and Dario Argento's *The Bird with the Crystal Plumage* (1970), as well as the West German *Krimi* of the 1960s, outrageously plotted films based on the works of Edgar Wallace, set in a 'Britain' of the pop imagination. Moreover, the slasher has a progenitorship that predates *Psycho*. Looking at the backlot set of Alfred Hitchcock's film, one sees a telltale sign of the modern slasher's legacy in Gothic horror, often thought to be its diametric opposite. On a rise behind the clean, modern Bates Motel sits the Bates home, a looming, lonely Victorian heap, a brooding relic redolent of novels beginning on black and storm-toss'd nights, of passages hidden behind bookcases, secret panels, fog-shrouded cemeteries, and devolved madmen on the prowl.

In the 1927 silent *The Cat and the Canary*, stylishly directed for Universal by German émigré Paul Leni, most of these hoary clichés are on hand. Yet *The Cat and the Canary* also anticipates things to come: early on in the film, which concerns a dramatis personae stalked by a malevolent entity, you see an instance of the villain-POV shot — the shot used to such bravura effect at the opening of *Halloween* and famously soundtracked by the "*Ki ki ki, ma ma ma*" of *Friday the 13th* (1980). (The killer-POV also appears in vital proto-slashers like Charles B. Pierce's 1976 *The Town that Dreaded Sundown* and Bob Clark's 1974 *Black Christmas*.)

Matching the anxious visuals of German Expressionism to a narrative in which an assembled group is terrorised by a lurking menace, *The Cat and the Canary* is considered one of the essential works of the 'old dark house' genre, the apotheosis of which is none other than, yes, Universal's *The Old Dark House* (1932). With their slowly-dwindling casts of victims, often gathered at a single, isolated location — think Agatha Christie's proto-bodycount *And Then There Were None* — the 'old dark house' movies were an ancestor of the more brutal slasher, just as surely as jump blues preceded rock 'n' roll.

While the slasher equivalents of Elvis, *Peeping Tom* and *Psycho*, are rightly better remembered for creating the subgenre's template, they

Laird Cregar in John Brahm's 'The Lodger' (1944)

were beaten to the screen by *Jack the Ripper* (1959), shot at Shepperton Studios, written by Hammer stalwart Jimmy Sangster, and dramatising the story of perhaps the world's most famous psychopath. It wasn't the first film to address the subject: German-born director John Brahm had previously played with the Ripper murders in *The Lodger* (1944), itself a loose remake of *The Lodger* (1927), the first certifiably Hitchcockian film by a young Hitchcock, not long returned from an apprenticeship in Germany. All of which only goes to show that the ancestry of the seemingly quintessentially American slasher is a combination of German Expressionism, English pulp sensationalism, and Gothic horror.

We may even view the Ripper as the prototype of the slasher villain — certainly his doctor's bag is as much trademark as Jason's hockey mask — and so can draw a line straight from Whitechapel to Camp Silver Lake, from the penny dreadful to the video nasty. While the bodycount movie may remain among the most spat-upon of subgenres, it cannot be denied its own grand tradition.

The Kings of Horror

By Vic Pratt

The story of cinema is often told in terms of great directors, yet in the history of Gothic films – particularly in the halcyon days of Hollywood horror – audiences hungry for dark thrills were lured into their seats predominantly by the charismatic players who starred in them: a select band of now-legendary gentlemen whose names became synonymous with the genre.

But to become irrevocably steeped in the Gothic – to be crowned a King of Horror – could be as much a curse as a blessing. Aspirations towards supposedly more serious acting work, outside of the confines of a critically derided genre, were often thwarted by the harsh truth that producers and audiences would not accept them any other way. "Who wants to see me do *Hamlet?"* asked the great Peter Cushing, after finding fame through his work at Hammer. "Very few. But millions want to see me as Frankenstein, so that's the one I do." Cushing accepted his fate philosophically. For others, though, uneasy sat the crown.

The silent era's King of Horror was surely American actor Lon Chaney (1883-1930). Always fascinating to watch, pain, sadness and sometimes cruelty lurked in Chaney's eyes. He seemed to have a dark desire to share the anguish of the doomed souls he portrayed – a masochistic willingness to undertake excruciating agonies to make his performances real. Portraying a legless criminal in *The Penalty* (1920) he hid his strapped-back legs in a leather harness and painfully walked on his knees. Ideally cast as a tormented, sometimes monstrous outsider, he was superb as *The Phantom of the Opera* (1925). Inevitably, uncomfortable make-up finished off the Phantom's hideous visage: Chaney thrust a painful device up his nose to achieve a distinctive flare of the nostrils.

Cinemagoers loved Chaney's grotesquerie. A catchphrase was coined: "Don't step on it – it may be Lon Chaney!" But he didn't need to hide behind horrific make-up; *The Unknown* (1927) saw him barefaced as a villainous knife thrower, who has his arms amputated in an attempt to win the love of a girl revolted by a man's embrace. The painfully achieved amputation gimmick fascinates the eye, but it is Chaney's masterful performance as the maddened lover which lingers in the heart.

As the sound era began, heirs apparent to Chaney's crown were two Europeans: Englishman Boris Karloff (1887-1969) and Hungarian Bela Lugosi (1882-1956). Both would find screen immortality through one key portrayal for Universal Pictures in the 1930s: for Boris, Frankenstein's monster; for Bela, Count Dracula. But their careers would take very different paths.

Dracula (1931) saw Lugosi reprise the role he'd made famous on stage, and a legend was born. But his mannered, theatrical style – combining overwrought gesture with slow, sometimes guttural articulation of his lines – divided opinion. Was he a great actor, or, as Karloff tactfully suggested, a "great technician"? Certainly, Lugosi needed a director who could accommodate his peculiar style. Given adequate space to perform by Victor Halperin in the splendidly eerie *White Zombie* (1932), shortly after *Dracula,* Lugosi was magnificent. Other directors were not so prepared to indulge Lugosi's idiosyncrasies. Proud Lugosi ended up battling for low-budget roles he would once have considered beneath his dignity, and only played Dracula onscreen once more, in *Abbott and*

Costello meet Frankenstein (1948). Lugosi was not always happy with how the Count had defined his career, but he donned the famous cape again in his last film, Ed Wood's notorious *Plan 9 from Outer Space* (1957), and when he died, he was buried in it – to be precise, he was buried in one of them, for Lugosi had a selection in his wardrobe.

Karloff was always proud of his portrayal of the monster in *Frankenstein* (1931). "My dear old monster, I owe everything to him," he attested, "he's my best friend." Karloff portrayed Frankenstein's creation as a childlike innocent, with the inarticulate anguish of a toddler. The tender performance aptly demonstrated Karloff's skill as an actor, whether in iconic make-up or not. Playing *The Mummy* (1933), he escaped his funereal wrappings too quickly, but was no less charismatic in a fez. Karloff had a looming gravitas that could not be ignored, whether he played a monster, or, as would become more common, a scientist meddling with ungodly forces.

Karloff, too, appeared in his fair share of substandard material over the years. But whereas Lugosi concluded his career with Ed Wood, suffering such indignities as wrestling a rubber octopus stolen from Republic Studios in *Bride of the Monster* (1954), Karloff's reputation was cemented with two latter-day career highlights. Both drew upon the audience's familiarity with his screen persona. Michael Reeves's *The Sorcerers* (1967) saw Karloff's archetypal mad scientist ingeniously relocated to grimy 1960s London; Peter Bogdanovich's *Targets* (1967) saw Karloff virtually playing himself as Byron Orlok, horror star of a bygone era, and accidental target of a dysfunctional young sniper at a drive-in cinema, while one of Orlok/Karloff's own films plays.

About the time of Lugosi's demise, velvet-voiced American Vincent Price (1911-1993) was emerging as a contender for the horror crown. Prominent thanks to a flamboyant portrayal of a mad, hideously scarred revenger in *House of Wax* (1953), Price didn't take his grisly work as seriously as his predecessors. His gleeful villainy, though wonderfully entertaining, was often self-consciously theatrical. "I must confess that it's hard for me not to break up with laughter when we're doing some of these pictures," he confessed. He was perhaps a little disappointed to give up the serious dramas he'd played in previously. But, like Karloff, Price understood the value of typecasting. He was perfectly cast in Roger Corman's flamboyant adaptations of Poe, including *House of Usher* (1960) and *Pit and the Pendulum* (1961). A master of tongue-in-cheek humour, Price was highly adept at spoofing the horror genre, but there lingered the sense that here was an actor who, if kept under directorial control, could be genuinely frightening. Occasionally this was proven. Michael Reeves forced Price to play it straight as 17th-century inquisitor Matthew Hopkins in *Witchfinder General* (1968). Forbidden to ham it up, Price gave perhaps his most chilling performance.

If Price felt slightly miffed by his association with horror, British-born Peter Cushing (1913-1994) did not. He took his work very seriously indeed, as his carefully annotated scripts attest. Together with fellow Englishman Christopher Lee (1922-), he was at the forefront of a glorious Gothic revival in 1950s British cinema that shocked the censors. Thrilled by Universal *Frankenstein* films as a boy, Cushing eagerly embraced the opportunity to portray the Baron in Hammer's *The Curse of Frankenstein* (1957), with Lee as the monster. Cushing's intense but dignified performance helped restore gravitas to the Frankenstein tale, worn away thanks to Universal's exploitation of the monster in preceding decades. Its success paved the way for exceptional re-workings of *Dracula* (1958), with Cushing as Van Helsing and Lee as the Count, and *The Mummy* (1959), with Cushing as enfeebled archaeologist Banning, and Lee as the superhuman, reanimated Egyptian priest Kharis. Both climaxed with titanic struggles between these stern adversaries and signalled the beginning of successful series.

Tall, dark, aristocratic and menacing, Lee was a perfect foil for the impeccably upstanding Cushing; together they were an unbeatable combination. Both men were integral to Hammer's revival of the Gothic. Like their predecessors, they had the power to make the unreal plausible, and the supernatural seem real. Lee, inextricably linked with the Count, grew unhappy with the distance that grew between Stoker's original Dracula and Hammer's revisionist take as the series progressed. By the time of *Dracula A.D. 1972* (1972) – a modern-day reworking which saw the Count's vampiric acolytes trendily clad in skinny-fit black rollnecks and sunglasses – Lee was eager to escape the role. He did this the following year, donning a kilt as aristocratic Pagan Lord Summerisle in *The Wicker Man* (1973).

As modern attempts to reinvigorate the formula reflected, the old Gothic was being challenged by more contemporary horrors – Hitchcock's *Psycho* (1960) had demonstrated that vampires, monsters and mad scientists were old hat. Admittedly, Norman Bates had the requisite Gothic mansion, but – superficially, at least – he looked like an upstanding All-American boy.

The Kings of Horror were of another time, another world. The flamboyant, charismatic outsider was no longer scary – more tangible terrors lurked at the heart of society. The villain of *Targets* was a motiveless, nondescript youth gone crazy with a rifle, shooting between swigs of cola – faceless, indistinct. "Is this what we were afraid of?", Karloff/Orlok queries, as he confronts the boy in the final reel. Yet it was. Karloff's strange charisma was no longer threatening. He and the other Kings of Horror seemed like noble reminders of a lost era of innocence.

(Opposite, top) Peter Cushing, Vincent Price and Christopher Lee starred together in 'House of the Long Shadows' (1983).

(Opposite, bottom) Lon Chaney as 'The Phantom of the Opera' (1925).

(Below) Boris Karloff and Bela Lugosi in 'The Raven' (1935).

LOVE IS A DEVIL

DAUGHTERS OF DARKNESS

BY VICTORIA NELSON

In the final decades of the last century, while waitresses were busy turning into waiters and poetesses into poets, a dramatic metamorphosis was taking place in the movies: a sizeable number of formerly passive horror and fantasy heroines ducked into a phone booth, shed their corsets and leaped out as kick-ass superheroes. In real life as on the silver screen this upgrade proved superficial at best, but there's no denying the dramatic look of the transformation from, say, Marguerite Gance as the buried-alive wife in Jean Epstein's *The Fall of the House of Usher* (1928) to Kristen Stewart as Bella, *Twilight*'s powerful immortal who also happens to be a vampire. In a relatively short span of time, the perennial swooning damsel in distress had turned into a millennial female jock.

To track this shift properly, we need to look back at the original literary Gothic. In the classic Gothic novel as imagined by its early practitioners Horace Walpole, Ann Radcliffe and Matthew Lewis, a young woman (who is never the protagonist unless her story is written by a woman) finds herself embedded in a Russian dolls' nest of confining structures – societal, familial, personal, even architectural, for typically she is also trapped in a mansion, castle, abbey or nunnery which harbours terrible secrets. A daughter and a virgin, not a wife or mother, this vulnerable young woman falls into the clutches of an older male villain, a father or father figure who wields power in all these spheres. By story's end the tyrant is defeated or killed through the agency of others and the charged Gothic edifice that once imprisoned the young woman blows up or burns down; sometimes she herself is the collateral damage.

For a good two hundred years thereafter, these stock Gothic characters and situations carried on largely unchanged in print, on stage, and finally in the movies. Think Frances Dade as Lucy in Tod Browning's *Dracula* (1931), Joan Fontaine as the meek second Mrs. de Winter in Alfred Hitchcock's *Rebecca* (1940), Julie Harris as Eleanor, the neurotic spinster of Robert Wise's *The Haunting* (1963). All are young women who might or might not be rescued, might or might not live to see another day.

The character traditionally labelled the Gothic heroine, however, was rarely a true heroine in the sense of being the story's protagonist; in classic Gothic stories written by male writers (a tradition the critic Ellen Moers has dubbed the Male Gothic, though Mary Shelley also belongs to it), most serve as minor or ensemble characters. Within a single story they are frequently doubled as the young woman who lives and the young woman who dies. In Bram Stoker's *Dracula* and most of its film iterations, Mina Harker is saved; Lucy Westenra dies – and becomes a vampire. Despite Stoker's own bias against the 'New Woman' of his day, it is Lucy, the more traditional and virtuous of the two, who is sacrificed and her less conventional alter ego Mina who survives. A century later, it would be an axiom of 'slasher' teen horror films (*Prom Night*, *Friday the 13th*, etc.) that the chaste girl survives while the sexually adventurous girl falls prey to the serial killer.

(Opposite)
Kristin Stewart as Bella, with Mackenzie Foy as her daughter Renesmee in 'The Twilight Saga: Breaking Dawn – Part II' (2012).

In contrast to the Male Gothic, the early women Gothic writers made their heroines the protagonist, and in this Female Gothic tradition the heroine always survives. The Gothic heroine as leading character became even more firmly established in the women's romance, a later offshoot of Female Gothic whose template was definitively set by the Brontë sisters in the mid-19th century. Featuring far less gore and sexual mayhem than the original Gothic, this subgenre focused squarely on the heroine and gave her a radically different love interest – the dangerous man who was formerly the villain. In *Jane Eyre* the Byronic Edward Rochester becomes the main character's love and ultimately her husband; his dark essence is tamed and harnessed in the service of domesticity (or not: consider Heathcliff in *Wuthering Heights*). The task of the heroine in the Gothic romance novel is to transform the *homme fatale*'s darkness into light, a convention that would assume great importance in the Gothic vampire romance novels and films of the early 21st century, which fashion their female heroes out of the young woman who dies.

For the other roots of this new female hero, we must look to the dark side. Wicked women were in short supply in the original Anglo-American Gothic of the Protestant tradition, whose monsters and villains remained mostly male straight through the mid-20th century. There were always a few, of course: in film versions minor characters such as Dracula's brides, Elsa Lanchester as the Bride in James Whale's *Bride of Frankenstein* (1935), Mrs Danvers and the unseen dead wife in *Rebecca* (Rochester's mad wife Bertha transformed into an evil offstage flapper).

But after the mid-20th century female villains and malevolent female apparitions began creeping onto western cinema screens in greater numbers. Hammer supplied endless female vampire variations on the Dracula story (*The Brides of Dracula*, *Countess Dracula*) and by the early 1970s the so-called Karnstein trilogy (*The Vampire Lovers*, *Lust for a Vampirel*, *The Twins of Evil*) inspired by J. Sheridan LeFanu's *Carmilla*.

Catholic southern Europe contributed its share of terrifying supernatural female antagonists, such as Asa the witch in Mario Bava's *Black Sunday* (1960). So did Asia: the trickle of ghostly Japanese films reaching the West starting with *Kwaidan* and *Onibaba* (both 1964) had turned into a flood by century's end with the J-Horror and K-Horror booms, inspiring a host of Hollywood remakes. Many of the female spooks in these pan-Asian films are spirits returned from the dead seeking vengeance for wrongs perpetrated against them in life (a typical figure in the centuries-old Asian ghost story tradition). In life, however, these ghost antagonists were in fact true Gothic heroines, innocents who were abandoned or murdered by a man within an extreme patriarchal structure. Nakata Hideo's *Ringu* (1998) pits the vengeful female spirit of a murdered child against the hapless reporter Reiko and her son. In *Ju-On* (*The Grudge*, 2002), the haunting of a house by a murdered woman and her son results in many deaths and the spirit's possession of the main female character, Rika.

The *femme fatales* of most of the Hammer Gothic films, in contrast, are sexually experienced supernatural seductresses who start out bad and stay that way. Gradually, however, their evil qualities begin to bleed (as it were) into the Hammer 'cursed heroines' of the same period, not-quite-protagonists who start out as virtuous objects of male desire before transforming into malevolent creatures who must be destroyed along with the human woman they've possessed. Unlike Male Gothic figures like Dr Jekyll who are the authors of their own horrific change, these female characters are unconscious vessels of a curse or malevolent supernatural force; they shapeshift from damsel in distress to *femme fatale* in the same story,

(Above)
Marguerite Gance in Jean Epstein's 'The Fall of the House of Usher' (1928).

(Below)
Joan Fontaine, the classic Gothic heroine in white, in Hitchcock's 'Rebecca' (1940).

blurring the boundaries of role. In Terence Fisher's *The Gorgon* (1964), for example, the doctor's assistant Carla (Barbara Shelley) is possessed by the snake-headed Greek spirit (Prudence Hyman), who is dispatched (along with poor Carla) by beheading after she has turned a number of Carla's male admirers into stone.

Modern horror stories draw on ancient, often unacknowledged folk beliefs. The notion that women are more vulnerable to supernatural penetration than men was a doctrine of medieval Catholicism that remains a fixture of popular culture to this day. (Until very recently, can you think of a single instance of demonic possession requiring a Hollywood priest's services that involves a man writhing on the floor and not a woman?) Likewise, the beautiful woman who turns into a monster is the 'loathly lady' of medieval ballads, a fairy or other supernatural creature who combines the qualities of hag and maiden, old and young, beautiful and hideous, in the same body.

When the loathly lady is split into two characters, such as Asa and her innocent descendant Katia in *Black Sunday*, their identity is reinforced by casting the same actress in both roles. Crone and virgin also comprise a classic doubled character: Think Valerie and her grandmother in Jaromil Jireš's *Valerie and Her Week of Wonders* (1970). Other directors, memorably David Lynch with *Mulholland Dr.* (2001) but also Robert Aldrich with *What Ever Happened to Baby Jane?* (1962) and Darren Aronofsky with *Black Swan* (2010), found further intriguing ways to merge and double Gothic heroines and villainesses, youth and age, beauty and monstrosity.

A handful of Anglo-American Gothic films of the mid-20th century treated the heroine turned evil antagonist in more psychologically nuanced ways. Like its literary source, Henry James's *The Turn of the Screw*, Jack Clayton's *The Innocents* (1961) balances delicately the

(Above)
Barbara Steele as the wicked witch Asa in Mario Bava's 'Black Sunday' (1960), her face perforated by the spikes of the mask she has been forced to wear.

(Right)
The vengeful mother, wearing a demon mask in Shindo Kaneto's 'Onibaba' (1964).

possibility of real ghosts against the workings of an overactive imagination while leaving the distinct impression, as the highstrung young governess's voluminous Victorian gowns morph ominously from white to black, that she has hounded her young charge Miles to death with her own projected fantasies.

Robert Wise's *The Haunting* (1963) similarly psychologises Shirley Jackson's *The Haunting of Hill House*. Eleanor, a submissive young woman who has sacrificed her life serving an invalid mother, has been the victim of a poltergeist experience in her childhood. Unlike James's governess, she is attracted to the disturbing phenomena of the Gothic mansion she is brought to by an enterprising psychic researcher. Through a series of visual cues – Eleanor is constantly seeing her own reflection in the house's mirrors and polished floorboards – along with her voiceover that seems to survive death, Wise suggests that Eleanor is either projecting her own secret rage on, or simply merging with, the house's darkness.

The repressed Gothic heroine turned vengeful Fury finds her ultimate expression in Brian De Palma's *Carrie* (1976), based on the novel by Stephen King. In De Palma's film there is no ambiguity about the fact that Carrie's powers are supernatural, as she transforms from sympathetic victim into a killer who wreaks hormonal vengeance on the guilty and innocent alike. The haunted Gothic mansion is a high school auditorium, and it blows up right on schedule, just like the Castle of Otranto two centuries earlier. The striking difference in outcome is that the agent of destruction this time is not divine intervention but rather the Gothic heroine's own expertly channelled rage.

Some more recent Gothic films present the female victim turned revenant in new and interesting ways: Claire, protagonist of Neil Jordan's *In Dreams* (1999), sacrifices her life to become, by story's end, the ghostly nemesis stalking the serial killer who has murdered her daughter and her husband. In Matthieu Kassovitz's *Gothika* (2003) the psychiatrist Miranda is possessed by the ghost of a 14-year-old girl who forces her to murder her own husband. The husband, it turns out, is the one who tortured and killed the girl; once he and his accomplice are dead, the ghost vanishes.

In her 1992 study *Men, Women and Chainsaws: Gender in the Modern Horror Film*, Carol Clover identified a new kind of Gothic heroine in the 'slasher' subgenre: the Final Girl (that is, the last targeted female victim left alive, with whom the young male audience of these films identifies). In the ongoing migration of the villain's traits into the heroine, she ultimately takes on the attributes of her would-be killer. The Final Girl of the original *The Texas Chain Saw Massacre* (1974) is saved by a man; by 1986, in its first sequel, the heroine (who bears the decidedly masculine name 'Stretch') not only slays Chop-Top, the last of Leatherface's family, all by herself, but even apes Leatherface's crazed chainsaw-wielding moves from the first movie.

The Gothic gained a second brand-new pop culture heroine in the 1980s: the busty, martial arts-proficient warrior babe of Japanese anime narratives. This Gothic character merged rather incongruously with US feminist sensibilities to produce the antithesis of the helpless, swooning heroine: glamorous street fighters like Alice, the fearless zombie slayer of the *Resident Evil* series (2002–), or leather-coated, semi-automatic rifle-toting Selene of the *Underworld* series (2003–), a vampire protagonist whose star-crossed fate is to love a werewolf.

The true exemplar of this new Gothic female hero is Buffy, the eponymous star of Joss Whedon's *Buffy the Vampire Slayer*, which began life as a 1992 movie, then became a long-running television series. Buffy cemented the image of the fighting, female Gothic hero in the Hollywood mainstream. Smart, self-confident and beautiful without being an anime-style fantasy pinup, Buffy is a wholesome cheerleader who uses her martial arts prowess to vanquish vampires. True to form, before long Buffy also finds herself consorting with the enemy when she experiences the classic Gothic Romance heroine's love affair with a dangerous *homme fatale*, in this case the reformed vampire Angel. Because of an inconvenient gypsy curse, Angel reverts to his essential nature the instant they consummate their love and so Buffy loses him. Later she has sex, but no romance, with the unreconstructed vampire Spike.

Once human women and vampire men start mating, thesis and antithesis turn into a synthesis that makes the good girls and the bad guys very hard to tell apart. Beauty now runs with the beast. The modern Gothic is rife with examples in which the heroine meets the monster, mates with the monster, and finally becomes a monster herself – but often a monster with redeeming qualities.

The *Alien* series was foundational in creating this arc for the new Gothic female protagonist, which reached its peak by the end of the century. Tough, androgynous Ripley combats the creature action hero-style in Ridley Scott's *Alien* (1979). Ripley's female antagonist, the Alien Queen, makes her first appearance in James Cameron's *Aliens* (1986), in which Ripley also becomes the motherly protector to the orphaned Newt. In David Fincher's *Alien³* (1992), Ripley takes her own first step from hero to Gothic creature when she finds she's been implanted with the Alien Queen's egg and tries to kill herself by leaping into a vat of molten lead. By Jean Pierre Jeunet's *Alien: Resurrection* (1997) Ripley is brought back to life as a dead-eyed clone carrying the Aliens' DNA yet still choosing good over evil by saving the android Call and sacrificing the Alien Queen's newborn – the first offspring of what is now Ripley's own hybrid species.

Like the videogame babes, Ripley

(Opposite, left)
Joan Crawford and Bette Davis as the Hudson sisters in 'What Ever Happened to Baby Jane?' (1962).

(Opposite, right)
Marilyn Burns as the prototypical 'Final Girl', saved from Leatherface at the end of 'The Texas Chain Saw Massacre' (1974).

(Above)
Sarah Michelle Gellar as Buffy, the true exemplar of the new Gothic warrior-heroine.

(Left)
The Gothic heroine as action hero: Sigourney Weaver as Ripley in 'Alien' (1979).

(Above)
FBI Agent Clarice Starling (Jodie Foster) in 'The Silence of the Lambs' (1991) epitomises the new Gothic heroine as female detective.

(Below)
Kate Beckinsale as the leather-clad vampire Selene in 'Underworld' (2003).

belongs to the Male Gothic tradition. But the Female Gothic was undergoing its own sea change, inserting female leads in professions formerly the purview of the male Gothic hero. The young investigator Clarice in Jonathan Demme's *The Silence of the Lambs* (1991) epitomises the new Gothic heroine as female detective. As for scientists, Rappaccini's daughter – the quintessential old Gothic heroine, victim of her mad scientist father's experiments in Nathaniel Hawthorne's story of the same name – has wound up as Rappaccini herself, a trend that began with the prescient *The Man Who Changed His Mind* (1936). The calculating gleam in surgeon Claire Wyatt's eye as she abandons her principles to reverse the body swap her mad scientist boss has made with her fiancé marks this smart, self-confident young female scientist as the forerunner of what would be a Gothic staple by the end of the century: the lab-coated female, sometimes a control freak (*The Deep Blue Sea*, 1999), sometimes a sidekick (*Jurassic Park*, 1993), but always a babe.

The gradual merging of Male and Female Gothic strands produced, by century's end, a recognisable new female hero. Having absorbed both the fighting prowess of the male hero on one hand and the morally ambiguous nature of her usually supernatural antagonists on the other, she was now monster and action hero rolled into one. As part of the post-millennial mainstreaming of supernaturalism, male and female vampire 'good guys' are now as common as their evil counterparts; in such television series as *True Blood* and *The Vampire Diaries* they are integrated into ordinary human life as disenfranchised minorities.

Bella, the female protagonist of the film series based on Stephenie Meyer's *Twilight* novels, seems at first to be a traditional Gothic heroine. A teenage human cast in the modest mould of Jane Eyre, she is possessed by a burning desire to become equals with her good-guy vampire lover Edward Cullen (he and his coven abstain from drinking human blood), but this time in the only way she knows how – by turning into a vampire herself. Becoming the monster is not the same for Bella as it was for Ripley, however. Transcending both death and the killer instincts of the vampire, Bella surpasses all the Cullens; she's an immortal with an infallible memory who can fly through the air, kill and eat a mountain lion, and discern the tiniest particles of the universe with her naked eye. Where Lucy Westenra in *Dracula* was a virtuous maiden in life and a bloodthirsty vampire in death, Bella in death becomes a virtuous demigoddess who uses her exalted status for good rather than evil – and, in a small bow to matriarchy, Bella's daughter Renesmee, the human-vampire hybrid, promises to surpass even her mother. We have travelled a long way here, from Lucy and the Alien Queen alike.

Of course Gothic cinema and fiction still has its share of victim heroines. Having gained the empowering elements of the female villain while shedding her karmic bad vibes, however, the contemporary female Gothic hero is mostly about supernaturalising, demonstering, and mythmaking. Justine, the latest of Lars Von Trier's suffering Gothic heroines, takes on the powers of witch and seer in the face of planetary destruction in *Melancholia* (2011). Ofelia, the child hero of Guillermo del Toro's *Pan's Labyrinth* (2006), enacts a mythic journey from life to death to immortality not unlike Bella's in *Twilight*. But Ofelia performs no action-hero stunts when she transitions to the other side; in a story that blends reality and fantasy as deftly as James's *The Turn of the Screw*, after death this human girl ends up the good Princess Moanna, influencing events above ground from her golden uterine underworld.

The Gothic female hero as a goddess ruling our world? Stay tuned.

Queer Gothic

By Brian Robinson

"[The somnambulist] can be compelled to perform acts which, in a waking state, would be abhorrent to him..."
The Cabinet of Dr. Caligari, 1920.

Horror films have always rejoiced in subversion, perversion, decadence and daring, and so their attraction for gay audiences is perhaps no surprise, offering as they do examples of forbidden desires with which that audience can identify.

For Oscar Wilde homosexual desire was famously "the love that dare not speak its name", but through the Gothic, writers and filmmmakers have found a way to let loose repressed desire. The queer is inscribed in the DNA of Gothic fiction: many of its writers – such as Horace Walpole, William Beckford, Mary Shelley and Bram Stoker – were rumoured to be gay or bisexual, and whether it's Dracula, Frankenstein or Dorian Gray, the legion of anti-heroes they created all speak of forbidden love and *otherness*. These shadowy figures are single men with an androgynous quality – collectors with an interest in arcane knowledge, a passion for dramatic clothing, a fondness for make-up, redolent with the whiff of sulphur or the heady scents of Oriental perfumes.

A Rebours (Against Nature) is a key text in this strain of the Queer Gothic. J.K. Huysmans's 1884 novel concerns an exquisitely decadent dilettante with an over-refined sense of aesthetics, and was an influence on Wilde's *The Picture of Dorian Gray*. Similar is the Comte de Lautréamont's long 1869 poem *Les Chants de Maldoror*, with its devilish delight in horrors.

A defining moment of the Queer Gothic is the famous gathering at Villa Diodati in 1816. Percy Bysshe Shelley and his wife Mary Shelley were both rumoured to be bisexual and intimates of the bisexual and famously promiscuous Byron. The fourth famous guest, John Polidori, may or may not have been homosexual, but he was certainly close to Byron, whose character inspired *The Vampyre*, Polidori's story of an aristocratic, sexually rapacious vampire.

Hurd Hatfield in 'The Picture of Dorian Gray' (1945)

Polidori's tale was a key influence on Bram Stoker when writing *Dracula*, a novel whose invitation to queer readings hardly needs spelling out – the Freudian simplicity of a man who wants to penetrate another with his teeth in order to feed his unnatural hunger for blood speaks of the horror the merest suggestion of buggery brought to many Victorian heterosexuals, and of the horror of a blood-born contagion (inspired perhaps by Stoker's own reported syphilis).

These novelists set the template, but it was on film that the tropes of the Queer Gothic would find their full flowering. As with the literary Gothic, not only have many onscreen characters in Gothic cinema lent themselves to a queer reading, but the actors and directors who have played or presented them were often gay themselves – including two of the most influential, F.W. Murnau and James Whale.

Gay directors of Gothic cinema have typically brought a queer subtext to their films, which when partnered with gay actors becomes undeniable – and hugely enjoyable. Albert Lewin's *The Picture of Dorian Gray* (1945) is enriched when one learns that Hurd Hatfield, who plays Dorian, was himself a sophisticated gay man who relished his role. Hatfield's tone of voice and less than wholly masculine demeanour amounts to a rare portrait of the queer at a time when any overt portrayal would be blocked by censors.

James Whale's *Bride of Frankenstein* (1935) is another glorious example, with its arch acting by Colin Clive and Ernest Thesiger as the camp scientists, and Elsa Lanchester unforgettable as the Bride in a role in which she almost seems to be a drag queen. Consider too how the creature recoils in horror when he sees himself in Whale's original film, and is hounded by a mob of villagers determined to root out the 'monster' in their community.

This ability of Gothic cinema to convey the socially unacceptable is brilliantly conjured-up in the performances of Vincent Price in Roger Corman's Poe adaptations. Price is an ingratiatingly feline personality, suavely elegant and devastatingly manipulative, but rendered in such an over-ripe, thespian manner as to convey his own (rumoured) bisexuality to those able to read the signs.

Like Judith Anderson's Mrs. Danvers in Alfred Hitchcock's *Rebecca* (1940), Gloria Holden's Countess Marya Zeleska in *Dracula's Daughter* (1936) conveys barely subtextual lesbianism. The film was an early entrant in the subgenre of the lesbian vampire film, which reached its height in the cycle of exploitation films of the late 1960s and early 70s.

As the social changes of the 1960s took hold, the ambiguous performance of homosexuality gave way to the overt and obvious. The genie was out of the bottle: Roman Polanski struck out with an unambiguously gay vampire in *Dance of the Vampires* (1967); films such as Paul Morrissey's *Flesh for Frankenstein* (1973) displayed a new sexual explicitness; and *The Rocky Horror Picture Show* (1975) revelled in its outrageous campery. It would take another generation before things calmed down into something more subtly powerful like *Interview with the Vampire* (1994), in which Tom Cruise and Brad Pitt's characters smoulder for each other on the screen.

Queer vampires may now be allowed out of the shadows, but if anything they seem less terrifying than those ambiguous figures of earlier times, when queer desire fought to find expression – and found a natural home in the dark heart of the Gothic.

Scream Queens and Vampire Lovers

By Josephine Botting

Chaney, Cushing, Karloff, Lee, Lugosi, Price... While the roster of male horror stars is long and distinguished, you'd be hard pressed to name many women who have built a career out of the genre.

Yet without the fairer sex, where would horror films be? Seeing a burly bloke clutched in the hairy hand of a gigantic ape or attacked in the shower by a knife-wielding hag just wouldn't have the same effect. From early on, producers exploited the link between horror and sex, making it almost an integral part of the genre. And once the new sexual freedom of the 1960s took off, it led to the downfall of many a young woman who strayed into the path of the psychopaths and evil spirits waiting to hold them to account for their crimes against morality.

Categorised as 'Scream Queens', actresses in the early days of horror almost exclusively played victims. Fay Wray was the first – one obituary designating her scream "the most famous since Edvard Munch's". When offered the part of Ann Darrow in *King Kong* (1933), she was promised a tall dark leading man and was disappointed not to find Cary Grant waiting on set. But her (dyed) blonde hair and expression of wide-eyed terror made Wray the perfect beauty to the giant ape's beast. No stranger to horror, she'd already appeared in *Doctor X* (1932), *The Vampire Bat* (1933) and *Mystery of the Wax Museum* (1933), but the image of her petite frame, scantily clad and clinging onto the ape's huge fingers, was to define her career for years to come.

Into the 1940s, British actress Evelyn Ankers inherited Wray's crown, starring in *The Wolf Man* (1941), *The Ghost of Frankenstein* (1942) and *The Mad Ghoul* (1943). Naturally blonde and more robust than Wray, she wasn't afraid to penetrate the mist-laden woods to save Lon Chaney Jr from the murderous wolf on the prowl, unaware that her beau is that wolf. Yet Ankers could belt out a piercing scream or throw a faint with the best of them: her vocal power earned her the nickname 'Queen of the Screamers'.

The 1940s also saw actresses play the occasional female monster, harking back to Elsa Lanchester's stand-out portrayal as the Monster's Mate in *Bride of Frankenstein* (1935). French actress Simone Simon brought an exotic otherness to Jacques Tourneur's *Cat People* (1942), while in the UK Siobhan McKenna took a similar role in Lance Comfort's *Daughter of Darkness* (1947), murdering men who arouse her lust.

The 1960s saw two Barbaras – Shelley and Steele – take their places in the horror hall of fame. Both were given major breaks by the Italian film industry, going on to gain a reputation through their work in genre cinema.

Barbara Steele became the doyenne of Euro horror and a genre star of impressive pedigree, working for directors Mario Bava, Roger Corman, Michael Reeves and David Cronenberg. Beautiful and unblemished, yet with the timeless look of an ancient soul, Steele could switch from alluring to evil with a mere furrowing of the brow; no one could be chained up in a cellar and whipped quite so decorously, nor seek revenge so mercilessly. The film which best demonstrates her versatility is Bava's *Black Sunday* (1960), in which she undergoes a transformation on camera from the beautiful Katja to Asa, the witch brought to life after two centuries in a tomb.

After working in Italy, Barbara Shelley made her genre debut in *Cat Girl* (1957); the film's director, Alfred Shaughnessy, later wrote, "By using her, I fear we condemned a very beautiful and talented actress to a long career in horror films." Indeed, Shelley went on to appear in a host of horror titles including *Blood of the Vampire* (1958), *The Shadow of the Cat* (1961) and *Dracula Prince of Darkness* (1966). Her down-to-earth warmth and intelligence shone through even as she dealt with unearthly children, mad monks and, in one of her best performances, insectoid aliens in *Quatermass and the Pit* (1967). Far from being 'condemned', Shelley was granted cult immortality by her horror roles, particularly for Hammer, the company that promoted many luscious ladies to prominence, among them Veronica Carlson, Madeline Smith and Caroline Munro.

As the decade wore on, Hammer continued to up the sex quotient in their films and actress Ingrid Pitt was perfectly placed to provide it. Although she appeared in only four horror films, through astute self-publicity she built a career as ambassador for the genre. Her performances as a lesbian vampire (in *The Vampire Lovers*, 1970) and Countess Báthory (in *Countess Dracula*, 1970) are striking in their sensuality; in *The Wicker Man* (1973) she is surely the sexiest librarian ever seen on screen. Pitt's Eastern European origins lent her persona a rare exoticism, something also possessed by a very different Hammer star, Jamaican-born Martine Beswick. A former Bond girl, her short horror filmography belies her ideal looks for the genre – dark-haired, olive-skinned and beautiful in a strong-jawed, almost mannish way, she was perfectly cast against Ralph Bates in gender-swap horror *Doctor Jekyll & Sister Hyde* (1971).

While Hammer were spicing up the genre with beautiful women, there was an older generation of stars who turned to horror for a new lease of life. The sub-genre dubbed 'harridan-Gothick' has its roots in Gloria Swanson's almost vampiric presence in *Sunset Blvd* (1950) and peaked with Bette Davis's thoroughly repellent performance in *What Ever Happened to Baby Jane?* (1962) and Joan Crawford's axe murderer in William Castle's *Strait-Jacket* (1964).

Several Hollywood stars came to Britain to further their career renaissance, with Davis murdering children in *The Nanny* (1965) and bullying her family in *The Anniversary* (1968) while Tallulah Bankhead imprisoned Stefanie Powers in *Fanatic* (1965). Joan Crawford's horror career began in 1927 with circus horror *The Unknown*, in which she plays the glamorous assistant to Lon Chaney's armless knife-thrower; 40 years later she was back under the big top in *Berserk* (1967), now promoted to ringmistress. Also in Britain, Sheila Keith proved herself a uniquely chilling presence in such transgressive shockers as *Frightmare* (1974) and *House of Mortal Sin* (1975).

Although the slasher movies of the 1980s appeared to punish women for their sexual indiscretions, the fairer sex began to fight back and a new breed of horror actresses came to the fore. In *Halloween* (1978), Jamie Lee Curtis defeats the masked killer, representing a generation of women turning the tables and coincidentally avenging her mother Janet Leigh's infamous demise at the hands of Norman Bates in *Psycho* 18 years earlier. Via Sigourney Weaver's combative Ripley in *Alien* (1979), by the 1990s the hunted became the hunter as Sarah Michelle Gellar rose to fame as TV's *Buffy the Vampire Slayer* (1997-2003). Far from the helpless swooning required in horror's earlier days, these actresses had to be lean and mean as they tooled up to do battle with the supernatural.

Into the 21st century, the *Twilight* series has restored romance to the Gothic – with star Kristen Stewart willing to sacrifice her soul to be with the one she loves, for eternity. Her performance is deliberately restrained, offering a blank canvas onto which teenage girls can project their own romantic fantasies. Stewart's screen persona is less dynamic than the horror stars that went before and gone are the days when a woman's last resort was to fill her lungs for an ear-piercing scream...

(Opposite, top) Ingrid Pitt and Madeline Smith in 'The Vampire Lovers' (1970).

(Opposite, bottom) Fay Wray, the original scream queen, in a publicity still for 'King Kong' (1933).

(Above, left) Evelyn Ankers with Lon Chaney Jr. as the tormented Larry Talbot, aka 'The Wolf Man' (1941).

(Above, right) Barbara Shelley in 'Dracula Prince of Darkness' (1966).

LOVE IS A DEVIL

TAINTED LOVE

BY HELEN OYEYEMI

H*ere he goes again...* Bluebeard tears meat off a sizeable bone and chews mechanically. He casts a glance or two in his wife's direction, but his mind is on the task ahead. There's blood to be shed, probably the wife's, in such hectic quantities that the eye won't accept it as real and will instead perceive its almost decorative quality. The blood will lie on the floor and invite comparison to a thick coat of varnish. Like varnish, the depth of the colour is proportionate to the number of layers applied. Layer upon layer upon layer... Not being a man for divorce or desertion, Bluebeard has ended all his marriages with murder. He tells these women, he tells them quite clearly that he has a secret that must not be disturbed, and the very next thing they do is seek the secret out.

George Méliès's *Bluebeard* (1901) is a satisfyingly weird introduction to the part cinema plays in reworking and illuminating basic elements of the Bluebeard narrative. The old tale features a woman who, having been wooed and won by a charismatic, powerful man (sometimes a magician, sometimes an artistocrat, depending on the tradition consulted) uncovers evidence of her husband's murderous nature. Traditionally this revelation centres around the discovery of the corpses of the man's several previous wives, as in Perrault's 17th-century retelling of the tale, which doubles as a somewhat arch warning to women against succumbing to what the gender discourse of the time posited as an inborn excess of curiosity. But over time, and in the hands of various storytellers, key motifs of the story – the secret room, the key that unlocks horrific knowledge – have been developed in order to reflect with increasing sophistication the risks that we take when we marry. The 19th-century Gothic romance, typified by the events recounted in Charlotte and Emily Brontë's *Jane Eyre* and *Wuthering Heights*, found a natural affinity with the sheer darkness of the Bluebeard narrative – for the characters of the so-called Female Gothic, romance is inseparable from the violence of the emotions it evokes. Centuries later, writers as diverse as Daphne du Maurier (*Rebecca*), Angela Carter (*The Bloody Chamber*), Kurt Vonnegut (*Bluebeard*), John Franklin Bardin (*Devil Take the Blue-tail Fly*) and Margaret Atwood (*Bluebeard's Egg*) continue to rework and respond to the Gothic conception of secrets as both foundation and fuel of passion.

Méliès's *Bluebeard* is similarly organised around Bluebeard's secret. Time is short in his retelling of this tale, so the imperative to communicate with energy is even greater. The pace is madcap; Bluebeard's gestures simultaneously forbid and instruct his new bride to open the door that guards his secret. No sooner has Bluebeard left home than a spindly-limbed, man-sized imp jumps out of the pages of a book and further insists that the forbidden door be opened. The poor wife exists in a story that insists on one more death, just one more.

By the time of Catherine Breillat's *Bluebeard* (2009) it's plain to see that Bluebeard has begun to have serious doubts about whether or not serial killing is really for him. We hear emotion in

(Opposite)
Bella Mallen (Diana Wynyard), is tormented by her husband Paul (Anton Walbrook) in Thorold Dickinson's 'Gaslight' (1940).

his voice and see yet more in his eyes as he asks his wife for the proof that she's disobeyed his command and is therefore fit for execution. "Madam, don't think me mischievous," he says, "but you must return the keys I gave you. We're both bound by that rule." He's anxious and sorrowful; this isn't weakness, but advance mourning. It's a disconcertingly attractive snapshot of masculinity that's also glimpsed in many other films about women whose husbands mean to do away with them.

Cinematic romance has always been a risky business for the characters involved. Every imaginable vulnerability associated with falling in love reveals itself at the whim of genre, from the mishaps and misunderstandings around every corner of a screwball comedy to the cold deceptions that run through the veins of *film noir*. After Méliès's version, prominent film retellings of the tale approached Bluebeard as a ladykiller strictly in the tongue-in-cheek sense – as in the 1923 Gloria Swanson comedy *Bluebeard's Eighth Wife*, and Ernst Lubitsch's film of the same title in 1938, starring Claudette Colbert and Gary Cooper; both of these Bluebeards are guilty of serial heartbreak, but nothing more.

But that changed by the 1940s, the Golden Age of the Gothic Hollywood Romance. It was in 1940 that Alfred Hitchcock's adaptation of Daphne du Maurier's *Rebecca* slid into the popular imagination like a sheet of black ice, inspiring other films that share its thematic and stylistic preoccupations.

Several of the finest, tautest dramas of the 1940s feature homes that offer no shelter, the horrifying inscrutability of the love object and long, long shadows cast by the past. While the psychological melodramas of this era don't exactly represent a re-evaluation of gender relations, at the very least they hint at the distances between the home front and the battlefield, all these women bound to men whose secrets can't find their way into words. Hitchcock himself found ways to refract his Bluebeard retelling, maximising psychoanalytic elements of the tale in *Spellbound* (1945), and amplifying the danger of self-disclosure in *Suspicion* (1941) and *Notorious* (1946).

The alarming questions that Hollywood films of the era were asking about love and marriage also found their way into the seminal film of the American avant garde cinema, Alexander Hammid and Maya Deren's *Meshes of the Afternoon* (1943), in which a man and woman repeatedly pursue each other through the rooms of a house, up and down staircases, the woman falling in and out of the windows and through the doorways, collaborating with multiple manifestations of herself to reveal (or bury?) some secret locked up in the visual language of domestic drama – a key, a bread knife, a flower.

A year later, in Jacques Tourneur's *Experiment Perilous*, daisies will be used by Nick Bedereaux (Paul Lukas) to skilfully insinuate that his wife Alicia (Hedy Lamarr) is a danger to her own child, and it will be a floral arrangement that alerts Celia Lamphere (Joan Bennett) to the plans her husband Mark (Michael Redgrave) has in mind for her in *The Secret Beyond The Door*, though Fritz Lang won't make that film until 1947. In the meantime the character played by Deren appears fascinated by a figure that wears dark robes. Its face is an oval of reflective glass, and this figure draws close to her, but never close enough to touch. While *Meshes of the Afternoon* can be interpreted in a variety of ways (many of them having nothing to do with marriage at all) the film seems to me to probe the notion that the intentions and character of the person one consents to live with are more elusive than is strictly rational.

'Till death do us part' – that's where the danger is. Our attention lingers on the figure of the wife killer, just as the wife killer is drawn to his final wife, the woman who will survive her marriage to him. From the first there is a strange dynamic; Bluebeard and his wife can't live together. I mean this both in the sense of domestic compromise and in a more literal sense – the man constitutes a threat to his wife, and if she's his true match, she constitutes an equal threat to him. That's the only equilibrium that there can ever be for these two. The gesture with which the gentleman widower Stephen Lowry in Arthur Lubin's 1955 film *Footsteps in the Fog* takes his housekeeper Lily Watkins by the neck is a capitulation of sorts; she's consciously provoked him into making a claim on her.

What kind of woman wants to marry such a man? "Bluebeard is very ugly, but very rich," one of the two child narrators of Breillat's *Bluebeard* explains to the other. "You have to be poor to love him." This can be understood literally, insofar as the betrothal stories we've been told have until relatively recently approached the union as a financial contract as well as a social one. Issues of money and social class distort the sympathy between Jane Eyre and Mr Rochester – memorably played by Joan Fontaine and Orson Welles in director Robert Stevenson's 1943 adaptation, and in innumerable versions for both cinema and TV since, the most recent being Cary Fukunaga's 2011 adaptation, with Mia Wasikowska and Michael Fassbender – and in *Experiment Perilous*, Joseph L. Mankiewicz's *Dragonwyck* (1946) and *Footsteps in the Fog* it's impossible for our working class heroines to resist the lures of status and elegance.

But in all three of these films, the wife-killer's seductive wealth (and his bride's corresponding poverty) isn't strictly material. What these men are rich in is experience. In *Gaslight*, both the 1940 British version by Thorold Dickinson, starring Anton Walbrook and Diana Wynyard, and George Cukor's 1944 Hollywood remake starring Ingrid Bergman and Charles Boyer, and in

(Opposite)
The hanging corpses of Bluebeard's previous brides are revealed in a ghastly tableau from Georges Méliès's 'Bluebeard' (1901).

(Top)
Orson Welles as a brooding Rochester opposite Joan Fontaine's 'Jane Eyre' (1943).

(Above)
Bluebeard (Dominique Thomas, right) and his potential spouse Marie-Catherine (Lola Creton) in Catherine Breillat's 'Bluebeard' (2009).

Peter Godfrey's *The Two Mrs Carrolls* (1947), where money isn't an overt consideration, the husbands are well-travelled, somewhat weathered, and exhibit a greater assurance of what is real and possible than that available to your average love-struck young woman.

Very near the beginning of *The Two Mrs Carrolls*, painter Geoffrey Carroll (Humphrey Bogart) reminds his bride-to-be Sally Morton (Barbara Stanwyck) of the work he's been prevented from doing since meeting her, and Sally makes him promise that their love story is really true before laughingly submitting to Geoffrey's pragmatism.

Dragonwyck's Miranda Wells (Gene Tierney) falls in love with Nicholas Van Ryn (Vincent Price) as they waltz around the ballroom of his mansion, surrounded by disapproving onlookers who whisper about her because they consider a farmer's daughter to be very far from Van Ryn's equal. Van Ryn has just assured Miranda that as long as they're together the opinions of others are insignificant, and the couple whirl across the dancefloor, smiling into each other's eyes, heads held high. Miranda and Van Ryn are central and essential to this image – the only real man and woman in the room, the staring party guests having smudged into the lush periphery, just as Van Ryn commanded. And we begin to see how the intense focus that two people turn upon each other dissolves their perception of the world external to their relationship.

Who can say whether or not this fascination is love? It seems more likely to be the mutual watchfulness of two people who are subconsciously aware that they could well be the death of each other. Either way, it's the past that keeps them from enjoying this private universe. Bluebeard's wealth of experience ultimately separates him from his wife; he knows things she can't know, and these concealments come to prey on both their minds.

(Opposite)
The shadow play performance of the Bluebeard tale in Jane Campion's 'The Piano' (1993).

(Left)
Gene Tierney as Miranda Wells and Vincent Price as Nicholas Van Ryn in 'Dragonwyck' (1946).

(Bottom)
The poster for 'Footsteps in the Fog' (1955) highlights the film's most dramatic moment.

In Thorold Dickinson's *Gaslight*, this kind of relationship becomes like Deren and Hammid's simultaneously and yet separately inhabited house in *Meshes of the Afternoon;* the instability of such an atmosphere means that the more assured inhabitant can most effectively wield his power to dictate meaning. By manipulating events and insisting on a certain interpretation of them, Bella Mallen's husband is able to divide her from herself and persuade her that she's insane (and therefore lacks the competence to administrate her own property). The man would have his wife believe that she falls into trances and steals things for no reason; he'd have her believe that the memory of each of her small and senseless thefts evaporates the moment they're committed. After weeks and months of incidents she denies responsibility for until shown 'proof', Bella is on the point of surrender. Seated in the audience of a public concert, Paul Mallen quite easily causes Bella to cry out with bewilderment simply by reaching into her handbag and showing her the pocket watch he's been looking for all day.

Paul Mallen's sinister machinations are echoed in *Experiment Perilous*, in technique, if not in motive. These particular Bluebeards seem undefeatable by any innate resource that their tormented wives might possess, and rescue comes from knights in shining armour whose formidable deductive powers enable them to decode the dual realities of an unhappy marriage.

More modern re-imaginings of Bluebeard tend, interestingly, to defend or vindicate the secret-keeper. Michael Powell's *Herzog Blaubarts Burg* (1964) is based on Béla Bartók's 1911 opera *Bluebeard's Castle*, a drama of trust versus jealousy that highlights the dynamic between the newlyweds as that of a man acquiescing to what is ultimately his wife's death wish. The same opera was adapted for the BBC in 1988 as *Duke Bluebeard's Wife*, the set design and director Leslie Megahey's camera pushing the gloomy Gothic atmosphere to the hilt. And Jane Campion's *The Piano* (1993) demonstrates the power of mystery through Ada (Holly Hunter), a mute heroine whose wilful silence drives others to force speech, or at least acknowledgement, from her. This film, in which a key proves to be both a husband and a wife's undoing, just as in the original Bluebeard tale (even though in Campion's film it's not a door key but the piano key upon which Ada inscribes her love for George, the character played by Harvey Keitel), has been argued by Maria Tatar in her book *Secrets Beyond the Door: 'Bluebeard' in Folklore, Fiction and Film* to be a feminist reworking of the narrative. The roles are reversed so that it's the wife Ada's secret that destroys the union, but the original tale quietly but effectively makes itself felt within the film when a Bluebeard shadow play is performed, and prompts the watching Maori audience to storm the stage, believing the murders to be real.

While the films I mention half-answer the question of what brings Bluebeard and his wife together, only Dickinson's *Gaslight* shows us something of what it takes to survive him. I'm thinking of the scene where Bella puts Paul Mallen's fantasy to an end simply by entering into his own logic. He has treated her as a madwoman for most of their marriage, and at his hour of urgent need she pleads his indulgence one more time: the request he makes is too sane for her to understand.

In most of his forms Bluebeard does what he can to maintain control, whether that applies to land, as reflected in Van Ryn's obsession with producing a male heir to Dragonwyck, or whether he uses his cunning in the pursuit of variety, as Geoffrey Carroll does, only desiring a wife for as long as she inspires his art. At his very worst, Bluebeard makes a mere puppet of his female victim – in Edgar G. Ulmer's *Bluebeard* (1944) this is a literal danger for the women pursued by the story's villain; he creates a puppet in each woman's likeness before he kills her. Perhaps it's the realisation of the extent of the wife-killer's control that leads his final wife to take it from him. Lack has enabled her before; she married him to take a share of his knowledge and his self-possession, but he doesn't share. So it could be that the key to surviving Bluebeard is the same as Breillat's key to loving him: you have to be poor to do it.

La Belle et la Bête

By Marina Warner

Monster bridegrooms threaten the heroine in fairytales that take place among polar ice floes, in roiling deserts, isolated villages, and gloomy mist-wreathed forests; the beast can come in a fantasy shape – as a dragon or serpent or rhinoceros or yellow dwarf, or, as A.S. Byatt translates one such beast in a tale by Mme D'Aulnoy, as 'the great green worm'. They can also assume a more ordinary animal appearance – a ram, or a frog. The frog, though hardly very frightening, is repulsive to the princess in the Grimm Brothers' story when she finds him sitting on her pillow, and she hurls him against the wall – whereupon the enchantment is undone, and he turns into a beautiful young prince. As for other kinds of beasts, bears are probably the most popular animal – alongside wolves (though when the bridegroom takes the form of a wolf, the story is taking a different turn, into Gothic horror rather than fairytale).

When Jean Cocteau made his film of *La Belle et la Bête* in 1946, he imagined a beast who has no rival for hideous fascination among fairytale beasts before or since: Jean Marais's growling, slowed, incantatory delivery, his sweeping, elaborately princely magnificence of apparel, his thick pelt curling out exuberantly from his lace collar and fine linen as he springs and lopes, and, above all, his staring pale eyes in the great leonine and brindled mask of his face with the two sharp incisors defining his mouth, has never been matched for erotic power. He captures a perfect and irresistible synthesis of repulsiveness and attractiveness, which evokes a genuine frisson of desire in me every time I see it; Cocteau's realisation of a dream about the power of love, as personified by Belle, exercises its seduction again and again over me, even while my common sense, my reason, and a long habit of scepticism about romance tell me I must resist.

Jean Marais' Beast hovers behind many different enchanted monsters and retellings. Disney's *Beauty and the Beast* (1992), one of the company's greatest successes, pays open tribute to Cocteau; so does Angela Carter in her virtuoso fairytale retellings, in *The Bloody Chamber* (1979); especially in 'The Tiger's Bride'. She was responding, as so many viewers have done, to Cocteau's specifically cinematic brilliance, for he wasn't content to create sumptuous pictures and stage tableaux. He never forgets that film is movement, and so his Beast is all aquiver with life: who can ever forget how he seems to catch fire when Belle rejects him and how his whole body smokes and his claws and pelt smoulder after he's made a kill, while he visibly grieves at these signs of his own monstrosity?

I don't remember when I first came across the fairytale

of Beauty and the Beast in the version that Jean Cocteau adapted. I could have been told it or read it in any number of places; in any case it was in my bloodstream, as it still is in any child who loves books and especially books of myths and fairy stories. I know I found many different variations on this ancient and worldwide story in the 'coloured' Fairy Books which Andrew Lang compiled (Rose, Green, Olive, Red etc.). 'Beauty and the Beast' was included in the first of the series, *The Blue Fairy Book* of 1889, citing the source as Mme de Villeneuve's *La Belle et la Bête* (1740), but in fact following the much shorter retelling of Villeneuve's compatriot Mme de Beaumont, which had appeared 16 years later.

Aristocratic Frenchwomen like Mme D'Aulnoy, Mme de Murat, and Villeneuve created a vogue for fairytales in their salons in the late 17th and early 18th centuries in Paris. They were reinventing the form as a vehicle to attack conventions of their day, especially those concerning their condition as women: they polished their feline wit and poetic fancy to expose tyrannical fathers and husbands and to argue for greater independence for women over education and money. Above all they sought the right to choose and have lovers, as well as mix with men on other terms – in friendship, or for intellectual stimulus.

Mme de Villeneuve is the first fairytale writer to take the traditional figure of a monster bridegroom and set her Beauty and the Beast in a worldly setting of aristocratic wealth, sophistication, and corruption resembling her own contemporaries' circumstances – her fairies are thinly disguised courtiers and social operators of the time. The Beast's mother is an Amazonian queen who leaves him in the care of his godmother while she rides out at the head of her armies to defend her lands from attack. When he grows up, this godmother looks on him with sudden interest, and propositions him. When he rejects her advances, she turns him into a monster who, like Cocteau's in the film, can only express himself like a brute. In this story, the question he puts to Beauty every night is no euphemism. He simply asks her to go to bed with him; but through her goodness, grace and kindness, she sees through this shocking lack of decorum and he is restored to his true self and the wicked godmother unmasked and punished.

Mme Jeanne-Marie Leprince de Beaumont was a French governess working in England, and she refashioned Villeneuve's fairytale for a French and English miscellany she put together in 1756-57 for her pupils: *Le Magasin des enfants/The Misses' Magazine*. She throws the emphasis on Belle's sincerity and tenderness and the importance

(Opposite) Beauty (Josette Day) and her magnificent Beast (Jean Marais) in Jean Cocteau's 'La Belle et la Bête' (1946).

(Above) The original poster design for Jean Cocteau's film.

of recognising someone's inner being; it's a simple parable about female goodness rewarded, with Beauty another Cinderella who gets her prince. Unlike many of her contemporaries who attack the arranged marriages of the time, Mme de Beaumont deliberately set out to soothe the fears of elite young women about the economic unions that have been planned for them. When the Beast nearly dies, Beauty's tears splash down on him and revive him – the scene reverberates with Christian redemption – he is baptised by love. (Angela Carter remarked crossly that Beaumont was one of the writers of fairytale who set out "to house-train the id.") It is true that Beaumont also rewrote, for example, the novel *Pamela* by Samuel Richardson because she admired it and wanted her girls to read it, but felt it was too racy for their eyes and ears.

Whereas Beaumont's writings are mostly rather insipid, pious stuff and have been deservedly left unread, her version of Beauty and the Beast was destined to become one of the most famous fairytales ever published, and has inspired an unaccountable number of films, cartoons, television series, modern spin offs, fictions for adults and children; it's taken on the character of an archetypal, founding myth. This form of the redemption tale is now a staple modern romantic fantasy.

Both Villeneuve and Beaumont depend on different earlier romances; in particular they draw on the ancient fairytale that inaugurates the Beauty and the Beast tradition in western literature, 'The Tale of Cupid and Psyche' from Apuleius's 2nd-century metaphysical novel, *The Metamorphosis of Lucius, or the Golden Ass*. In that classical text, a disreputable old woman tells a young bride who has been abducted by bandits "a story to make her feel a little better". All kinds of elements flow from this ancient romance into the fairytale and then straight into Cocteau's film: when Psyche is carried off by the west wind to meet her unknown lover, invisible servants in the enchanted castle dress and feed and entertain her; her sisters become jealous of her riches and conspire against her, telling her that her unseen lover is a monster who will devour her. At the end, this mysterious stranger is revealed to be none other than the god of Love. Cocteau, helped by the designer-artist Christian Bérard, re-imagined several of these motifs for the cinema with startling original effects: the living candelabra moving and pointing the way and their eyes eerily following the action from their position fixed to the wall.

Cocteau touches in many magical effects of his own, some invented, some borrowed from the fairytale repertory, from the story of Sleeping Beauty (the creeper-wreathed Beast's castle and Belle's bedroom wound with flowers are modeled on Gustave Doré's illustrations to Charles Perrault). When Belle weeps by her father's bedside and her tears fall as diamonds, the magical effect comes from another Perrault story, called 'Les Fées' ('The Fairies') and known in English as 'Diamonds and Toads'. Cocteau's script also adds a strong plot line to Beaumont's story, involving Belle's brother, Ludovic, and his equally feckless friend, Avenant, who wants to marry Belle. Jean Marais also plays Avenant, and so when the Beast comes back smiling and beautiful as Prince Charming, Belle notices something familiar about him. Has the Beast taken on his appearance because she admitted to him that she was fond of Avenant? Or does Cocteau want to suggest that a ne'er-do-well like Avenant can also be transformed by love?

Jean Cocteau invokes the persona of the storyteller, and of Mme de Beaumont herself, when he writes the credits like a schoolteacher on a blackboard. In the diary he kept during the making of the film, Cocteau comments that he was trying to give the film the feeling of a 'recitation'. He was making a fairytale for grownups, without fairies but with wonders, living statues, magic horses, and, of course, the enchanted beast, and he tells us in voice over at the beginning that he wants his erotic wonder tale to compel the kind of belief that children's imaginations experience instinctively. So the film unfolds to a perfectly poised slow tempo in surreal settings that gain intensity from the fabulous decor and costumes, the glittering lighting and the many moments of magic effects. The candle-lit shadow-play deepens the Gothic atmosphere of the Beast's castle, harking back to early Expressionist classics of the genre. Masterminded by the cinematographer Henri Alékan, with the help of magnesium flares and red powder and endless arc lamps and reflectors, his virtuoso use of chiaroscuro brings out the lustre of Belle's silks and chiffons, her pearls and diamonds, and her crystal mirrors and tableware; her rich dresses, goosedown coverlet and sheeny bedclothes as well as her simple coifs and fluttering laundry turn the flesh and blood beauty of Josette Day into a dream of feminine allure, a fairytale Madonna. The film is a classic of fantasy filmmaking – and directors have paid direct homage to Cocteau's original techniques: in Jacques Demy's *Peau-d'Ane* (*Donkeyskin*, 1970), Jean Marais returns as another kind of Beast, the incestuous king. In many ways, however, the film's influence has not been deep enough and much more could still be learned from it.

The Beauty and the Beast cycle of fairytales spins off into numerous different tales, but the true heart of the tale always leads to the restoration of the Beast to human form, on our recognition through the power of Belle's love of his inner human qualities as well as his beauty. This differs from most metamorphoses in myths, which cannot be reversed: Daphne for example will remain a laurel tree for ever; Actaeon dies as in his condemned form as a stag. Fairytales hold out hope – not only for restoration but for the possibility of change as well. When the Beast becomes a man he is not altogether the same person; he has been through a double metamorphosis – Jean Marais' prince is even more beautiful and certainly less feckless and violent than his double, Avenant. Cocteau's classic film of fine-spun aesthetic erotics changed a way of looking at fairytales. He took a nursery standard and made a ravishing and endlessly satisfying allegory about truth and illusion, sincerity and hypocrisy, with image sequences that swim through mirrors and flames, as the characters hope to discover truth in love.

(Opposite, top) The Beast (Jean Marais) carries Beauty (Josette Day) through a room full of haunted candelabra.

(Opposite, bottom) Jean Marais, Josette Day, Jean Cocteau and Michel Auclair on set.

(Below) Beauty (Josette Day) and the Beast (Jean Marais) in the gardens of the Beast's castle.

Family Gothic

By Geoffrey O'Brien

Family Gothic is not a precisely definable genre or subgenre. It is more like the only genre: the fundamental underlying premise of imaginative work, if we take it to encompass, for instance, the *Oresteia*, *Hamlet*, *King Lear*, the Grimm fairy tales, the Ring Cycle, and significant chunks of the Hebrew Bible. (To that should of course be added a good deal of the historical record from the most ancient dynasties onward.) In Europe and America, the 19th century saw its great blossoming in fiction (*Wuthering Heights*, *Jane Eyre*, *The House of the Seven Gables*, *Bleak House*) and drama (everyone from Sardou to Ibsen). Through adaptation it made its way inevitably to the cinema, infiltrating other genres from Western to horror film. To find it in pure form is rare, but its strands are everywhere.

Hard to say where the Gothic splits off from the mere ordinary resentments, conflicts, and frustrated longings within families. The Gothic has generally required some fairly overt transgression — parricide or incest or patriarchal curse or infant buried in the backyard — to distinguish itself. But after the cultural moment when Freud or some comic book version of Freud began to permeate all melodramatic representations of the relations of parents, children, and siblings, even the smallest domestic transactions became fraught with ominous portents. At the same time the notion of 'family' broadened to encompass every variety of surrogate: platoon, school class, office staff, theatrical troupe, convent, coven, cult, libertine ménage, criminal band. Nothing but families, then, and therefore nothing but the ever-present possibility of Family Gothic.

The early silents kept things simpler. They liked to depict generically happy families — if only as a prelude to unfolding the sufferings in store for them — and the deviation of any family from that norm could generally be attributed to the fault or failing of a single individual: a father who drank or gambled or contracted syphilis before marriage, a mother who strayed from fidelity, a child improperly reared and therefore wide open to the seductions of evil. The title could nearly always be 'The Buried Crime' or 'The Fatal Secret'. The central drama was often the punishment of the errant wife, as in Carmine Gallone's *Il Fior di Male* (1915), in which Lyda Borelli is finally knifed to death, unknowingly, by the illegitimate son she abandoned in her youth.

In America, at least, the harshness of such resolutions would be softened in the 1920s and 30s as unwed mothers at least sometimes found their way to atonement and a second chance. Europe, with its deep aristocratic structures, was always in any event the heartland of Family Gothic. The social and financial catastrophes that befell in Hollywood's pre-Code era were sometimes fatal but more often could be gotten around by deft improvisation, confirming the American preference for what William Dean Howells called "a tragedy with a happy ending." The true Gothic retreats from daily life into the oneiric sacrificial rituals memorialised in horror films like *The Mummy* (1932), *Black Moon* and *The Black Cat* (both 1934).

The 1940s — more specifically the war years and their immediate aftermath — would be, in America and to some extent in England, the heyday of Family Gothic in full regalia. Literary adaptations abounded, whether of Charlotte Brontë (*Jane Eyre*, 1943), Wilkie Collins (*The Woman in White*, 1948), or J. Sheridan Le Fanu (that ultimate family nightmare *Uncle Silas*, 1947). Screens were awash in period costuming (*Hangover Square*, 1945; *All This and Heaven Too*, 1940) as if under the spell of some ancestral curse. Orson Welles had a lot to do with it. If *Citizen Kane* (1941) and *The Magnificent Ambersons* (1942) were not in a precise sense Gothic, they cast Gothic shadows on scenes of family life, and with their evocation of time and memory suggested the infinite persistence of childhood suffering. In American melodramas of the 40s, family becomes the place where bad memories are laid down for all time, preferably with a Franz Waxman or Miklos Rozsa score to orchestrate the strange marriage of trauma and formal elegance.

The *Gaslight* theme of the murderous spouse (*Sleep My Love*, 1948; *Ivy*, 1947) and the *Jane Eyre* theme of the governess or nurse drawn into a family maze (*I Walked with a Zombie*, 1943; *Dragonwyck*, 1946) are joined by self-consciously Freudianised variations on the motifs of the devouring mother (*Now, Voyager*, 1942), the mad twin (*The Dark Mirror*, 1946), the dangerously father-fixated daughter (*Leave Her to Heaven*, 1945), the unjustly disinherited heir bent on revenge (*Son of Fury*, 1942), the spoiled psychotic brother (*Shadow of a Doubt*, 1943; *Secret Beyond the Door*, 1947; *Experiment Perilous*, 1944; *House by the River*, 1950), the evil conspiratorial clan (*My Name Is Julia Ross*, 1945, *Dark Waters*, 1944), and — a theme to be endlessly revisited in coming decades — the murderous child (*The Strange Love of Martha Ivers*, 1946). Westerns are taken over by recurring nightmares and family blood feuds: *Pursued*, 1947; *Ramrod*, 1947; *The Furies*, 1950).

The English in the same period had the benefit of a sharper sense of aristocratic privilege and abuse, culminating in a film like Anthony Asquith's *Fanny by Gaslight* (1944), in which Phyllis Calvert is orphaned not once but twice through the malevolent waywardness of James Mason's Lord Manderstoke. The Miss Havisham scenes in David Lean's *Great Expectations* (1946) were perhaps the most widely internalised image of Family Gothic that any film of the period realised; and the domestic spaces charted in Carol Reed's *The Fallen Idol* (1948) succeeded in suggesting something inherently Gothic about the condition of being a child. In France, at the same moment, Jean Cocteau and Jean-Pierre Melville were revealing a different kind of childhood Gothic in *Les enfants terribles* (1950); the private world shared by its mutually obsessed siblings was the matrix for many more such.

In the 1950s the Gothic cedes ground to sociology. Mobsters and juvenile delinquents muscle in on family curses and haunted portraits. Ghosts are replaced by scientifically plausible mutants. Rock 'n' roll (at least for the moment) is anti-Gothic. Psychotherapy, which had assumed Gothic trappings in Alfred Hitchcock's *Spellbound* (1945) and Fritz Lang's *Secret Beyond the Door*, now takes on an air of clinical matter-of-factness. There's nothing dreamlike about the murderous little girl in Mervyn LeRoy's *The Bad Seed* (1956): she's just a grotesque tabloid case history. The family melodrama becomes the Sirkian soap opera, with the incestuous conflicts of *Written on the Wind* (1956) raging not in shadowy vaults but in wide open Technicolor spaces. It is in fact the age of the dynastic drama, from *East of Eden* to *The Man from Laramie* (both 1955), as father-son conflicts erupt into open warfare. The raging father of *Bigger Than Life* (1956), turning the suburban dream home into brightly-coloured nightmare, is not mad but merely on the wrong medication. Two notable exceptions to the general trend: Otto Preminger's *Angel Face* (1952), haunted by the very precision with which Preminger charts the familial hot-house in which Jean Simmons's malevolence opens like a flower, and — it goes without saying — *The Night of the Hunter* (1955), the ultimate American Gothic, making itself thoroughly at home in the murkiest swamps and darkest basements.

For what followed, it would be simplest to say: then came *Psycho* (1960). The Fatal Secret of the old melodramas had come back with a bloody vengeance. Childhood was now the very cradle of horror. This was Gothic for an age without extended families — the sinister aunts and uncles, stepfathers and stepmothers of earlier melodrama now tended to erode into the primal dealings of parents and their offspring. Evil was transmitted by cruelty to children, or through cruelty witnessed by children: the indelible abusive spectacle or secret torture recreating itself in baroquely elaborate crimes and mutilations. *What Ever Happened to Baby Jane?* (1962), *Paranoiac* (1963), *Bunny Lake is Missing* (1965), an endless succession of Italian *gialli* — the same elements mingled again and again to produce variants on the same ritual, with or without some sort of happy ending. Flamboyant gore edged toward camp as aging divas took their last bows in fright-wigs. Horror and the parody of horror came close to merging, even as the perception of history itself was caught up in the general air of grotesquerie, so that, in Luchino Visconti's *The Damned* (1969), Nazi Germany became merely one more staging ground for Family Gothic. One might also mention Richard Fleischer's *Mandingo* (1975), the point where American family melodrama finally acknowledged its historical roots in the culture of slavery.

It becomes increasingly difficult to separate out the Gothic strain — the strain specifically European in its origin — from the more general evolution of horror in the decades that followed. The mutations were rapid and occurred globally. Stanley Kubrick in *The Shining* (1980) gave the nuclear family all the room it needed to fall prey to its own demons — no cramped old dark house this, or *Bigger Than Life*-style suburban two-bedroom, but an interior scaled to the vastness of the wilderness surrounding it. David Cronenberg might be singled out as shifting Family Gothic to the molecular level in *The Brood* (1979) and elsewhere. What begins to go missing is the very notion of family as something firmly settled. Cronenberg's *A History of Violence* (2005) hinges on a sense of drift and disconnection; nobody knows where anyone comes from any more.

The ancient lineages that were the stuff of family melodrama persisted for a time in Claude Chabrol's meticulous analyses of the French elite and its domestic arrangements, and, most profoundly, in the work of Luis Buñuel. Films like *Viridiana* (1961) and *Tristana* (1970) don't have to try to be Gothic — they exude, as if it were the most natural thing in the world, a sense of the poisons that can flourish in the heart of families, and in the societies that those families help weld together. In Buñuel this is not a matter of retrospection but of direct experience: the past is very much alive in its malevolence.

As an envoi, there is the film that offers the most intricate and mesmerising of farewells to all those complications of family, all the narratives of abandonment and revenge spiralling down mirrored halls of memory: Raúl Ruiz's *Mysteries of Lisbon* (2010). It is not like reading a 19th-century novel; it is like being a 19th-century novel.

(Opposite)
Agnes Moorehead and Tim Holt confront each other in Orson Welles's 'The Magnificent Ambersons' (1942).

(Below)
The Torrance family (Shelley Duvall, Danny Lloyd, Jack Nicholson) discuss the cannibalistic Donner Party incident en route to the Overlook Hotel in 'The Shining' (1980).

CONTRIBUTORS

Stacey Abbott is Reader in Film and Television Studies at the University of Roehampton. Her recent publications include *TV Horror: Investigating the Dark Side of the Small Screen* (I.B. Tauris, 2013), and *Supernatural: TV Goes to Hell* (ECW Press, 2011).

Michael Atkinson is a regular contributor to *Sight & Sound*, and author of *Ghosts in the Machine: Speculations on the Dark Heart of Pop Cinema*.

James Bell is Features Editor at *Sight & Sound* and editor of the BFI Compendium *39 Steps to the Genius of Hitchcock*.

Anne Billson is a film critic, novelist and photographer with a degree in Graphic Design. Her books include *Suckers*, a vampire novel, and monographs on *The Thing* (BFI Modern Classics) and *Let the Right One In* (Devil's Advocates, Auteur Publishing).

James Blackford is a DVD and Blu-ray producer at the BFI.

Josephine Botting is a curator of fiction film at the BFI National Archive, and is currently writing a PhD thesis on British film director Adrian Brunel.

Michael Brooke is a freelance writer and film historian specialising in British and central-eastern European cinema.

Ramsey Campbell's horror fiction has spanned half a century. His novels include *The Grin of the Dark* and *The Kind Folk*. His non-fiction, including essays on film, is collected as *Ramsey Campbell, Probably*. He reviews films for *Video Watchdog*.

Roger Clarke is the author of *A Natural History of Ghosts: 500 Years of Hunting for Proof (2012)* and *Story of the Scene* (2009).

Bryony Dixon is curator of silent film at the BFI National Archive. She specialises in British silent cinema, and is the author of the BFI screenguide *100 Silent Films*.

Glen Duncan's novels include *Talulla Rising*, *The Last Werewolf* and *By Blood We Live*.

Barry Forshaw is the author of *British Gothic Cinema*.

William Fowler is curator of Artists' Moving Image at the BFI National Archive.

Sir Christopher Frayling is a British educationalist and writer. His books include *Vampyres: Lord Byron to Count Dracula* (1978, revised 1992), *Nightmare: The Birth of Horror* (1996), *Mad, Bad and Dangerous?: The Scientist and the Cinema* (2005) and, most recently, a Film Classics monograph on *The Innocents* (BFI/Palgrave MacMillan).

Mark Gatiss is an actor, screenwriter and novelist. As well as co-creating both *The League of Gentlemen* and *Sherlock*, he has written several scripts for *Doctor Who*.

Charlie Higson is an English actor, comedian and author. His many novels include *The Enemy* and *The Dead*.

Richard T. Kelly is the author of the novels *Crusaders* (2008) and *The Possessions of Doctor Forrest* (2011). He has written several studies of film-makers: *Alan Clarke* (1998), *The Name of this Book is Dogme 95* (2000), and the authorised biography *Sean Penn: His Life & Times* (2004).

Mark Kermode is a contributing editor to *Sight & Sound*, and the author of *It's Only a Movie*, *The Good, the Bad and the Multiplex*, and the forthcoming *Hatchet Job*.

Lisa Kerrigan is a curator of television at the BFI National Archive.

Tim Lucas is the author of *Mario Bava: All the Colors of the Dark*, and is the editor of *Video Watchdog*.

Roger Luckhurst is professor of modern and contemporary literature at Birkbeck College, University of London. His publications include *The Mummy's Curse: The True History of a Dark Fantasy* and a Film Classics monograph on *The Shining* (BFI/Palgrave MacMillan).

Simon McCallum is a curator at the BFI National Archive and programmes the BFI's network of Mediatheques around the UK.

Martin Myrone is Lead Curator, pre-1800 British Art at Tate Britain. He was curator of *Gothic Nightmares: Fuseli, Blake and the Romantic Imagination* (Tate Britain, 2006).

Victoria Nelson is the author of *Gothicka* and *The Secret Life of Puppets*.

Kim Newman's fiction includes *The Hound of the D'Urbervilles* and the *Anno Dracula* novels; his non-fiction includes *Nightmare Movies* and BFI Classics *Cat People* and *Doctor Who*. He writes for *Sight & Sound* and *Empire*. His official web-site is www.johnnyalucard.com

Geoffrey O'Brien is Editor in Chief of the Library of America. His recent works include *Early Autumn*,

The Fall of the House of Walworth and *Stolen Glimpses, Captive Shadows: Writing on Film 2002–2012*.

Helen Oyeyemi is the author of the novels *The Icarus Girl* (2005) *The Opposite House* (2007), *White is for Witching* (2009) and *Mr Fox* (2011). She was included on the 2013 Granta Best Of Young British Novelists list.

Nick Pinkerton is a freelance journalist and film programmer. He has written about films for *Sight & Sound*, *ArtForum*, *The Village Voice*, *Moving Image Source* and *Reverseshot.com*.

David Pirie is a screenwriter, novelist and former *Time Out* film editor. The recently updated *A Heritage of Horror* was the first ever study of UK horror films. His most recent screen credit is *Murderland* with Robbie Coltrane.

Vic Pratt is a curator of fiction film at the BFI National Archive. He co-founded and co-programmes *The Flipside*.

David Punter is Professor of English at the University of Bristol. His many books include *William Blake: Selected Poetry and Prose* (1988) and *The Gothic* (Blackwell, 2003).

Jonathan Rigby is the author of several books, among them *English Gothic: A Century of Horror Cinema* (2000), *American Gothic: Sixty Years of Horror Cinema* (2007) and *Studies in Terror: Landmarks of Horror Cinema* (2011).

Brian Robinson is Communications Manager, Archive and Heritage at the BFI, and Senior Programmer of the London Lesbian and Gay Film Festival.

Jasper Sharp is a writer and curator specialising in Japanese cinema, whose publications include *Midnight Eye Guide to New Japanese Film* (2004, with Tom Mes), *Behind the Pink Curtain* (2008) and *The Historical Dictionary of Japanese Cinema* (2010).

Reece Shearsmith is an actor, writer and comedian. He co-created, wrote and starred in *The League of Gentlemen* and *Psychoville*.

Claire Smith is curator of posters and designs at the BFI.

Catherine Spooner is a Senior Lecturer in English Literature at Lancaster University. Her books include *Fashioning Gothic Bodies* (2004), *Contemporary Gothic* (2006), *The Routledge Companion to Gothic* (2007, co-edited with Emma McEvoy) and *Post-Millennial Gothic: Comedy, Romance and the Rise of Happy Gothic* (forthcoming in 2014).

Matthew Sweet is a writer and broadcaster. His books include *Shepperton Babylon: The Lost Worlds of British Cinema*.

Guillermo del Toro is the director of, among others, *Pan's Labyrinth*, *The Devil's Backbone*, *Hellboy*, *Cronos* and *Pacific Rim*.

Stephen Volk has written many screenplays for film and television, including *Gothic* (1986), *Ghostwatch* (1992), *Afterlife* (2005-6) and *The Awakening* (2011).

Marina Warner is Professor of Literature, Film and Theatre Studies at the University of Essex. Her books include *From the Beast to the Blonde (1994)*, *No Go the Bogeyman* (1998) and *Stranger Magic: Charmed States & the Arabian Nights* (2012).

Helen Wheatley is Associate Professor in Television & Film Studies at the University of Warwick. Her publications include *Gothic Television* (Manchester University Press, 2006).

Rob Young is the author of *Electric Eden: Unearthing Britain's Visionary Music*, and Editor-at-Large of *The Wire* magazine.

PICTURE CREDITS

All images courtesy of BFI National Archive/Special Collections, except: p20 (bottom left), p21 (top right), p33, p53, p118 (bottom right), p120 (top), p142 (bottom left) courtesy of the Ronald Grant Archive; p28, p32 (top left), p49, p55, p99, p153 courtesy of the Kobal Collection; p123 courtesy of Network Distributing; p56, p57, p110 courtesy of Arrow Films; p87 (top left) courtesy of Getty Images; cover image and p11 © Cat's Collection/Corbis; p79 Piranesi's 'Carceri', p80 Goya's 'Caprichos', p81 Gillray's 'Un petit souper, à la Parisienne' © Trustees of the British Museum; p80 De Lutherbourg's 'Philosopher in a Moonlit Courtyard' © Yale Center for British Art, Paul Mellon Collection; p78 Fuseli's 'The Nightmare' © Detroit Institute of the Arts, courtesy of The Art Archive, Kobal Collection; p81 Blake's 'The Ghost of a Flea' © Tate, London 2013.

ACKNOWLEDGEMENTS

Thank you to all of the writers. Special thanks for their advice and assistance to Laura Adams, Nigel Arthur, James Blackford, Michael Brooke, David Edgar, Christopher Frayling, Jane Giles, Ronnie Hackston, Nick James, David Jenkins, Roger Luckhurst, Kim Newman, Francesco Simeoni, Claire Smith, Isabel Stevens, Tom Webb, Rob Winter and Nick Wrigley. Particular thanks to Jonathan Rigby for his tireless and invaluable advice and careful reading. Further thanks to Lisa Kerrigan for her encouragement, to Christopher Brawn, this book's designer, and to Rhidian Davis and Vic Pratt, the 'dark hearts' of the BFI's Gothic project.

TIMELINE OF THE GOTHIC

1667
John Milton's *Paradise Lost* is first published

1764
Horace Walpole's *The Castle of Otranto* is published

1782
Henry Fuseli exhibits the first version of his painting *The Nightmare*

1796
Matthew Lewis publishes *The Monk: A Romance*

1816
Lord Byron, Percy Shelley, Mary Shelley and John Polidori spend the summer at Villa Diodati on Lake Geneva

1818
Mary Shelley's *Frankenstein; or, The Modern Prometheus* is first published

1845
Edgar Allan Poe publishes his poem 'The Raven'

1886
Robert Louis Stevenson's *Strange Case of Dr Jekyll and Mr Hyde* is first published

1897
Bram Stoker publishes *Dracula*

1904
M.R. James's first collection of ghost stories is published as *Ghost Stories of an Antiquary*

1910
The first film adaptation of *Frankenstein* is made in America by the Edison Company

1920
Robert Wiene's *The Cabinet of Dr. Caligari* is released.

1922
Max Schreck plays Graf Orlok in F.W. Murnau's seminal *Nosferatu*

1924
Hamilton Deane's production of *Dracula* opens on the British stage

1925
Lon Chaney stars in *The Phantom of the Opera*

1931
Tod Browning makes *Dracula*, starring Bela Lugosi, for Universal Studios. James Whale's *Frankenstein* follows

1932
Carl Dreyer's *Vampyr* is released. Boris Karloff stars in Karl Freund's *The Mummy* and James Whale's *The Old Dark House*

1935
James Whale's *Bride of Frankenstein* is released

1940
Alfred Hitchcock's *Rebecca* and Thorold Dickinson's *Gaslight* are both released

1942
Val Lewton produces *Cat People*, directed by Jacques Tourneur, the first of his horror pictures for RKO

1945
Ealing Studios release the influential portmanteau film *Dead of Night*

1946
Jean Cocteau's *La Belle et la Bête* is released

1957
Terence Fisher's *The Curse of Frankenstein* and Jacques Tourneur's *Night of the Demon* are both released

1958
Peter Cushing and Christopher Lee star in Terence Fisher's *Dracula*

1959
Georges Franju makes the influential *Eyes Without a Face*

1960
Hitchcock's *Psycho* is released. Mario Bava makes *Black Sunday*. Roger Corman makes *House of Usher*

1961
Deborah Kerr stars as Miss Giddens in Jack Clayton's *The Innocents*

1962
Bette Davis and Joan Crawford star in Robert Aldrich's *What Ever Happened to Baby Jane?*

1963
Robert Wise's *The Haunting* is released

1968
George A. Romero's *Night of the Living Dead* and Roman Polanski's *Rosemary's Baby* are both released

1971
The M.R. James adaptation *The Stalls of Barchester* becomes the first in the BBC's annual 'Ghost Story for Christmas' series

1973
The Wicker Man is released. *The Exorcist* becomes the first horror film to be nominated for the Best Picture Oscar

1976
Dario Argento's *Suspiria* is released

1979
Werner Herzog's *Nosferatu the Vampyre* is released

1980
Stanley Kubrick's *The Shining* is released

1981
John Landis makes *An American Werewolf in London*

1991
Anthony Hopkins and Jodie Foster star in *The Silence of the Lambs*

1997
The first season of *Buffy the Vampire Slayer* is broadcast

1998
Nakata Hideo's *Ring* is released, sparking the 'J-Horror ' boom

2006
Guillermo del Toro's *Pan's Labyrinth* is released

2008
The film adaptation of Stephenie Meyer's *Twilight* is released. Thomas Alfredson's *Let the Right One In* is released

2012
Daniel Radcliffe stars in the Hammer Films production of Susan Hill's *The Woman in Black*